MATLAB 6 for Engineers

Books are to be returned on or before
the last date below.

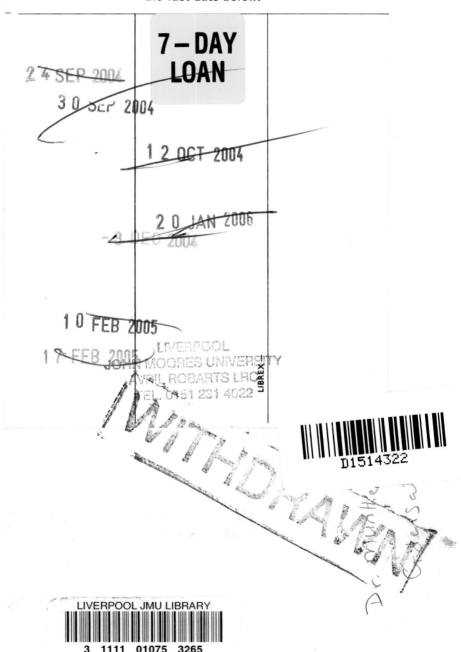

**7 – DAY
LOAN**

2 4 SEP 2004

3 0 SEP 2004

1 2 OCT 2004

2 0 JAN 2005

-3 DEC 2004

1 0 FEB 2005

1 7 FEB 2005

LIVERPOOL
JOHN MOORES UNIVERSITY
AVRIL ROBARTS LRC
TEL. 0151 231 4022

LIBREX

D1514322

LIVERPOOL JMU LIBRARY

3 1111 01075 3265

To the memory of our parents who are no longer with us:
Rosie, Lilli and Jean

MATLAB 6 for
Engineers

Adrian Biran
Moshe Breiner

An imprint of **Pearson Education**

Harlow, England · London · New York · Reading, Massachusetts · San Francisco
Toronto · Don Mills, Ontario · Sydney · Tokyo · Singapore · Hong Kong · Seoul
Taipei · Cape Town · Madrid · Mexico City · Amsterdam · Munich · Paris · Milan

LIVERPOOL
JOHN MOORES UNIVERSITY
AVRIL ROBARTS LRC
TEL. 0151 231 4022

Pearson Education Limited
Edinburgh Gate
Harlow
Essex CM20 2JE

and Associated Companies throughout the world

Visit us on the World Wide Web at:
www.pearsoneduc.com

First published 1995
Second edition 1999
Third edition 2002

© Pearson Education Limited 1995, 1999, 2002

The rights of Adrian Biran and Moshe Breiner to be identified as authors of this work have been asserted by them in accordance with the Copyright, Designs and Patents Act 1988.

All rights reserved. No part of this publication may be reproduced, stored in a retrieval system, or transmitted in any form or by any means, electronic, mechanical, photocopying, recording or otherwise, without prior written permission of the publisher or a licence permitting restricted copying in the United Kingdom issued by the Copyright Licensing Agency Ltd, 90 Tottenham Court Road, London W1P 0LP.

The programs in this book have been included for their instructional value. They have been tested with care but are not guaranteed for any particular purpose. The publisher does not offer any warranties or representations nor does it accept any liabilities with respect to the programs.

Many of the designations used by the manufacturers and sellers to distinguish their products are claimed as trademarks. Pearson Education has made every attempt to supply trademark information about manufacturers and their products mentioned in this book. A list of the trademark designations and their owners appears below.

ISBN 0 130 33631 9

British Library Cataloguing-in-Publication Data
A catalogue record for this book is available from the British Library

Library of Congress Cataloging-in-Publication Data

Biran, Adrian.
  MATLAB 6 for engineers / Adrian Biran, Moshe Breiner.
    p. cm.
  Includes bibliographical references and index.
  ISBN 0-13-033631-9 (pbk.)
    1. MATLAB.   2. Numerical analysis–Data processing.   3. Engineering mathematics–Data processing.
I. Breiner, Moshe.   II. Title.

QA297 .B522 2002
620′.001′51–dc21   2002075410

Trademark notice

DEC and VAX are trademarks of Digital Equipment Corporation. KEDIT is a trademark of Mansfield Software Group Incorporated. TEX is a trademark of American Mathematical Society. Simulink and Spline Toolbox are registered trademarks of The MathWorks Incorporated. SUN is a trademark of Sun Microsystems Incorporated. Microsoft Windows, Excel, Word and Paint are trademarks of Microsoft Corporation. UNIX is a registered trademark of The Open Group. Linux is a registered trademark of Linus Torvalds. Lotus 1-2-3 is a registered trademark of Lotus Development Corporation.

10 9 8 7 6 5 4 3 2 1
06 05 04 03 02

Typeset by 68 in 10/12pt Times
Printed in Great Britain by Henry Ling Ltd., at the Dorset Press, Dorchester, Dorset

Contents

Preface to *MATLAB 6 for Engineers*

Why a third edition?

The third edition of our book is meant to include some of the powerful improvements introduced in MATLAB 6. Additionally, we are aware that with this release the software grew to such an extent that the danger appears of not being able to see the forest because of the trees. Often, MATLAB 6 provides several possibilities of performing the same task and the beginner may get lost when faced with such a wide choice. Therefore, we think that an important task of the book is to guide the reader through the MATLAB 6 forest and choose a sufficient set of commands and functions that enable the completion of most engineering tasks.

The help facilities of MATLAB 6 contain excellent reference material. As the reader can easily access that help, we feel no necessity to compete in that direction, but leave our book as a tutorial, as it was conceived from the beginning. We also continue our policy of introducing new notions in small portions dispersed throughout the book.

We assume that the reader is familiar with the most elementary features of the operating system installed on the computer. Thus, for instance, a PC user should have some familiarity with Windows or Linux. The examples in this book run mainly under the Windows operating system.

What is new in this edition

New features included in this book are the MATLAB desktop, the editor/debugger, the basic fitting interface, elements of handle graphics, exchanging data with spreadsheets, and function handles. In trying to keep up with the development of the software and current trends in technology, we have added a few examples. Thus, the logistic map inserted in Chapter 7 allowed us to introduce the notions of bifurcation, period doubling and chaos. In Chapter 5 we give an example of a Bézier curve. At the end of the book we append a completely new chapter, Chapter 18. There we detail better the data types structures and cell arrays introduced in earlier chapters, and present functions that convert from one data type to another. In the same chapter we introduce graphical user interfaces, GUIs, giving two examples, and very briefly touch on the subject of object-oriented programming in MATLAB. We have also added new exercises. The publisher has provided a website for additional examples and exercises; the address is www.booksites.net/biran.

A message to the reader

Following many years of MATLAB experience and discussions with students and teachers, we have one important message to convey to the reader. The user-friendly facilities of MATLAB do not eliminate the need to know mathematics. We have heard teachers saying that they would not allow students to use the package before they know linear algebra. They fear that students could say, 'If it is so easy to invert a matrix, **A**, by simply writing inv(A), why should the student learn a tedious manual procedure?' We are aware, indeed, of students who pay no attention when the teacher states a definition or a theorem. Who needs this, they think, when we have software today that solves all problems? The truth is that, without knowing elementary algebra and calculus, one can obtain MATLAB results without being able to check their validity and meaning. We give in our book examples of incorrect polynomial roots calculated by the function roots (see Exercise 6.19), and show that the backslash operator always yields a result when applied to a system of linear equations. Only a user who knows some linear algebra can decide if that result is the general solution, a particular solution, a solution in the least-squares sense, or simply no solution (see Section 6.4). The help facilities of MATLAB briefly state the limitations of the roots function and of the backslash operator without detailing the consequences. In our book we explain the above problems and we provide a minimum of theoretical background to help the reader.

Acknowledgements

As with most books of this type, we would not have been able to do our job without help. Therefore, it is our pleasure to thank Mrs Naomi Fernandes of The Mathworks, and Mr Baruch Pekelman, the Manager of Omikron Delta and Mathworks agent in Israel, for keeping us up to date with the developments of the software and kindly answering our questions. Mrs Irina Abramovici and Mrs Rachel Birman, consultants at the Taub Computer Center, Technion – Israel Institute of Technology, gave us essential advice on the use of LATEX, GSview and other software. It was a privilege to work with the Pearson Education editorial team led by Ms Karen Sutherland and Ms Alex Seabrook, and comprising Ms Pauline Gilette, Ms Bridget Allen and Ms Karen McLaren.

Preface to *MATLAB 5 for Engineers*

This second edition of the book *MATLAB for Engineers* is adapted to version 5 of MATLAB. The new features of MATLAB 5 include powerful program-development tools, new data types and structures, more graphic and visualization features, additional mathematical functions and major improvements to MATLAB application toolboxes, among them the introduction of SIMULINK 2. All these new features make programming easier, especially for complex applications. On the other hand, the number of new features is so large that it is impossible to describe all of them adequately in a one-volume textbook. To keep the introductory character of the text, and a reasonable book size, we limited the extent of updating as described below.

We deleted all references to MATLAB 3.5. Where MATLAB 5 commands are different from MATLAB 4 commands, we updated them to version 5. A few new functions and graphic facilities that enhance programming power and graph readability are introduced. Titles, labels and text added to graphs are really improved by using the subset of LaTeX commands admitted by MATLAB 5. For instance, instead of writing *alpha* as previously, we can now write \alpha and obtain the Greek letter α.

From the new data types and structures we chose **multidimensional arrays**, **structures** and **cells** because we found them useful even in simple engineering calculations. Thus, in Chapter 2 we extended the spreadsheet model to represent it by a multidimensional array, and in Chapter 10 we used three-dimensional arrays for the RGB model of additive colour mixing. In Chapter 12 we introduced the new MATLAB **structure** facility to define graphs by a single data structure. In Chapter 17 we used **structures** to store values of constants together with their units, and we introduced new functions operating on character strings and **cells** to operate on those constants and obtain the values and the units of the results.

A major updating is that of the material related to the integration of ordinary differential equations – (**ODEs**). MATLAB 5 introduces new integration routines that solve more difficult problems than those that could be treated in MATLAB 4. Examples of such problems are **stiff equations** and dynamical systems exhibiting discontinuities. Therefore, Chapter 14 underwent an extensive updating.

A few new exercises were distributed among all chapters.

MathWorks, Inc. took care to provide software usable after the year 2000.

While preparing this new edition we received essential help from several people at MathWorks, from Baruch Pekelman and Oren Merom of Omikron Delta, the agents of MathWorks in Israel, and from Emma Mitchell, Bridget Allen and Michael Strang of Addison Wesley Longman.

Preface to *MATLAB for Engineers*

MATLAB is becoming increasingly popular among students, researchers, technicians and engineers because of MATLAB features such as interactive mode of work, immediate graphing facilities, built-in functions, the possibility of adding user-written functions and simple programming. The package provides useful tools for interfacing with external programs and data sets, as well as options for keeping records of calculations which can be later transformed into technical reports. The versatility of the basic MATLAB package can be enhanced by separately-available toolboxes designed for specialized, advanced fields of application.

Our goals in writing this book are to provide a hands-on introduction to MATLAB and to show how to use the package for solving problems in several engineering fields. We hope our examples prove the flexibility and power of MATLAB as a comprehensive computing environment.

This book covers version 4 of MATLAB but also shows how to adapt the text to version 3.5. Wherever possible we have tried to limit the text on the basic MATLAB package. The book is also compatible with the *Student Edition of MATLAB*. Only in Chapter 15, Control, do we refer to a few functions of the *Control System Toolbox*, and in Chapter 16, Signal Processing, we use functions belonging to the *Signal Processing Toolbox*.

Our intended audience includes undergraduate and graduate students from various engineering disciplines, and professional engineers and technicians engaged in design or research work. The first part of the book can be used as a textbook for a first course in MATLAB, or as a supplementary textbook for courses in which calculations are performed in MATLAB. The rest of the book just shows how MATLAB can be used to solve a variety of problems from various science and engineering disciplines.

The text presumes some familiarity with elementary geometry, algebra and calculus. Some linear algebra concepts are introduced in parallel with the MATLAB functions that implement them. The mechanical engineering examples are based on elementary mechanics; those in electrical engineering, on basic electrical circuits. Chapter 14, Modelling and Simulation, requires some knowledge of ordinary differential equations, and Chapters 15, Control, and 16, Signal Processing, presume knowledge of control theory and signal processing. A few mathematical concepts are presented somewhat informally in appendices, at the end of the chapters to which they are relevant, so as to not interrupt the flow of the MATLAB presentation.

About this book

The book is divided into three parts. The first chapter is a concise MATLAB tutorial useful to users who want to get acquainted quickly with the main features of the package. The examples in this chapter are simple and not based on engineering concepts. Section 1.1 should be read because the material in it is not repeated in the rest of the book. Other sections of Chapter 1 are explained again in Chapters 2 to 10, in much more detail.

Part I, 'An introduction for engineers', consists of Chapters 2–10. The material is presented in such a way as to allow the user to perform calculations right from the beginning, and to progressively master techniques for solving more and more complex problems.

Chapter 2 explains how numbers are represented in the computer and how numerical errors originate, and continues with a discussion of vectors. It also introduces the reader to the subject of graphical solutions of equations. Chapter 3 is a painless introduction to two-dimensional arrays and matrices. Chapter 4 covers complex numbers; it shows, that in MATLAB, operations with them are as simple as those with real numbers. This chapter also briefly introduces the user to the subjects of functions of complex numbers, conformal mapping and harmonic motions. The latter material is applied to mechanical vibrations and electric oscillations.

In Chapter 5 simple geometric examples are used to introduce the subjects of matrix inversion and determinants. Chapter 6 shows how to use MATLAB in solving systems of linear equations. Because MATLAB always provides a solution to systems of linear equations, this chapter discusses the conditions for that solution to be correct and unique. The second part of this chapter introduces the MATLAB solution of polynomial equations. Chapter 7 is about programming in MATLAB. Chapter 8 shows how to read data from external files and how to write data to them. Tables of engineering data can be stored as external files and MATLAB provides tools for interpolating over them. The subjects of regression and interpolation are discussed in Chapter 9. Chapter 10 presents a few advanced plotting features.

Part II, 'More applications', contains more advanced material. Chapters 11, 12, and 13 are specialized applications of MATLAB tools learned in Part I, to numerical integration, graphs and dimensional analysis. Chapters 14, 15 and 16 refer to three important fields of engineering, namely modelling and simulation, control, and signal processing. The aim of these chapters is not to teach these fields but to show how MATLAB can be applied successfully to them. The latter three chapters introduce many new functions, some of them belonging to toolboxes that can be acquired in addition to the main package. Chapter 17 shows how to apply MATLAB to a more complicated problem in statics and to a simple partial differential equation, and deals concisely with the MATLAB treatment of tridiagonal and sparse matrices.

Using this book

Within the text we use the following typographical conventions. Emboldened words indicate a key term being defined for the first time in the text, for example **exponential function**. Italics are used to emphasize, for instance *must be given in radians*. Boldface letters are also used to name vectors or matrices where it is usual to write so:

$$\mathbf{X} = \begin{bmatrix} x_1 \\ x_2 \end{bmatrix}$$

Typewriter characters are used for the names of MATLAB functions and command (e.g. `subplot`), program and function listings, and names of files (e.g. `watdens.m`).

Text appearing on the computer screen has a light grey tint printed over the display and thus it is made distinct from the other text.

Wherever possible we intersperse blank spaces within MATLAB commands trying to make them clear and better looking. Thus we write

```
function y = ustep(t, t0)
```

rather than

```
function y = ustep(t,t0)
```

Obviously, this is a matter of style and does not influence calculations.

There are numerous examples appearing throughout the book to illustrate mathematics and mechanical and electrical engineering applications. Examples are used to reinforce ideas learnt within the preceding sections and to make use of the MATLAB tools explained up to that point. Where an example is particularly challenging this has been indicated by referring to it as an *extended example*.

In Parts I and II each chapter contains a number of exercises for the student to work through. As with the examples, the exercises cover mathematics and mechanical and electrical engineering. Detailed solutions to selected exercises appear in an appendix at the back of the book. Those exercises with a solution are listed at the beginning of each exercise section. An *Instructor's manual* is available upon request from Addison–Wesley Publishers Limited.

The listings presented in this book are not always the shortest or the fastest in execution; we try to keep them as clear as possible and so avoid deliberately terse or efficient code that would require long explanations.

A *Quick Reference Guide to MATLAB* is enclosed with this book. This guide is a convenient, portable summary of MATLAB commands and functions.

For more information about MATLAB we encourage you to use the help and demo facilities of the package, the *User's Guide*, especially the reference volume, and the readme files supplied with the software. The MathWorks, the producers of the package, distribute a newsletter and support a user group; also, they can supply information about other MATLAB-related books. Bound with this book is a business-reply card bearing the address of MathWorks. By returning the filled-out card you can receive a diskette distributed free of charge. The diskette contains M-files described or used in the book, and data files for exercises.

If you have any comments about this book please send them to us at ipc@awpub.add-wes.uk

Acknowledgements

We are very grateful to Cristina Palumbo, of The MathWorks Inc., and Baruch Pekelman, of Omikron-Delta Ltd., their agent in Israel, for their invaluable help in keeping us updated with the most recent versions of the software and the related literature. We also wish to express our thanks to those people at MathWorks who reviewed early versions of the book and made useful comments.

Many people helped to make this book what it is, in particular Irina Abramovici, of the Technion Taub Computer Center, who helped us to edit the manuscript in LaTeX. She wrote style and macro files that we used for formatting the text. Other consultants of the same Computer Center who have been helpful are Carla Abulaffio, Susan Feingold and Batia Peri. Per Olof Gutman of the Technion revised an early version of the first chapters and suggested improvements. Isabella Osetinsky, of the Technion, read Chapter 16 and helped us with her comments. Arie Scope, of Microsoft Israel, and Oded Yaniv, of the Tel-Aviv University, provided us with software, literature and information.

We are also grateful to the reviewers whose comments helped in shaping the book and eliminating many errors. We are most grateful to the editors who spared no efforts to see the book published. In the order we met them they are Tim Pitts, Simon Plumtree, Karen Mosman, Susan Keany and Sally Mortimore.

Our wives, Suzi and Aviva, encouraged us to carry on with the job and took over part of our family duties. Finally, our children, Elinor, Ilil, Paul and Amir, did not protest when we neglected them while spending much time in writing this book.

Adrian Biran
Moshe Breiner
May 1995

Chapter 1
MATLAB in a nutshell

1.1   Desktop calculations

1.1.1   Getting started

MATLAB should first be installed as indicated in the MATLAB documentation, for example the *Installation Guide for PC – Release 12*. The usual way to start MATLAB from within Windows is to double-click on the MATLAB icon (see Figure 1.1). Under Unix simply type `matlab`. As MATLAB starts it will open one or more windows. The actual configuration depends on the version of your software and on the previous MATLAB session, if there was one. A default screen is shown in Figure 1.2. You can identify the windows by the names that appear in their title bars: *Launch Pad, Command History, Command Window.* For the moment we are only interested in the

Figure 1.1   The MATLAB icon.

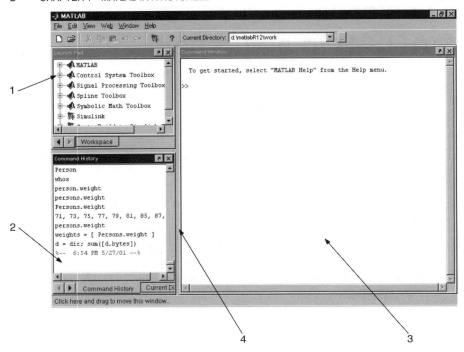

Figure 1.2   The MATLAB desktop.

Command Window. If there are more windows, please close them by clicking on the *close* icon, that is the 'X' that appears in the upper right corner of the window. If necessary, maximize the Command Window by pressing the *maximize* icon, that is the square near the close icon, in the right-hand part of the menu bar.

In the Command Window the **Command prompt** ≫ is waiting for you to enter a command. In the next subsection you will learn the most elementary commands and how to leave the MATLAB environment. Remember that you can view many of the marvelous features of MATLAB by typing demos and selecting items in the interface that will appear on your screen.

1.1.2   Arithmetic operations

The MATLAB operators for the four elementary arithmetic operations are + for addition, − for subtraction, ∗ for multiplication, and / and \ for division. A few examples of using these operators are shown below; try them for yourself.

```
≫ 2 + 3
ans =
    5
```

```
>> 2 - 2
ans =
     0
>> 2*2
ans =
     4
>> 2/3
 ans =
     0.6667
```

You may chain operations; for instance

```
>> 5*5*5
```

Instead of repeating the multiplication we can use the MATLAB power operator '^'; the previous statement can then be written as

```
>> 5^3
```

The power operator can be used with any exponent; try, for example,

```
>> 5^2.5
>> 5^(-3)
```

MATLAB has two operators for division, one for right division

```
>> 6/3
ans =
     2
```

and the other for left division

```
>> 3\6
ans =
     2
```

When the operands are numbers, the two operators, used as in the examples shown above, yield the same result. In Section 1.5 and in Chapter 6 we shall see that MATLAB extends the usual definition of division and allows it also between vectors and matrices. Thus left and right division are no longer exchangeable.

When you want to calculate a more complex expression use parentheses, in the usual way, to indicate precedence. For example:

```
≫ 3*(23 + 14.7 -4/6)/3.5
```

gives the result 31.7429. Or, let us take another look at the expression 5^2.5; it is simply the square root of 5 raised to the 5th power. How would you write the exponent as an ordinary fraction?

If you want to leave MATLAB at this point, enter quit. Alternatively you may open the File menu in the upper left corner of the toolbar, and click on Exit MATLAB. A third possibility is to click on the MATLAB icon in the upper left corner of the screen and click on Close.

We do not want to close this subsection without a few words about the other windows mentioned above. The default configuration is shown in Figure 1.2. The area marked '1' is the **Launch Pad**; it lists all the MATLAB products installed on your system. To get more details double click on the label of the product you are interested in. The area marked '2' is the **Command History**; it contains a log of the commands entered in the **Command Window**, that is the area marked '3'. You can copy commands from area '2' and paste and execute them in area '3' by using regular Windows copy-and-paste procedures. A simpler way is to select a command from the history window by bringing the mouse pointer over it and pressing the left mouse button. While keeping that button pressed, drag the item into the Command Window. Next, press the Enter key to carry out the command.

Commonly you may not need all the windows displayed by the default desktop. In fact, the Command Window is sufficient for all the examples and exercises in this book. There are several possibilities of reconfiguring the windows; we described one above. Another possibility is to move the mouse along the **Separator Bar**, which is marked '4' in Figure 1.2. The cursor will change shape; drag it to the left until the Command Window occupies all your screen. The third possibility is to use the mouse to open the View menu, in the menu bar, and select any window you may be interested in.

1.1.3   Last-line editing

Let us retype the expression

```
3*(23 + 14.7 -4/6)/3.5
```

and carry on with the calculation. Suppose now that you 'misspelled' the expression, as you wanted to write 4.6 and not 4/6. To correct your mistake depress the *Up Arrow*, ↑ or △, to recall the last line, then use the *Left Arrow*, ← or ◁, to bring the cursor onto the division operator. Type the decimal point, '.'. Now you have the group ./ and the cursor is on the slash. On PCs depress the Delete key to remove the unnecessary slash. On workstations it may be necessary to use another command.

In the above example we saw that typing a character inserts it at the cursor position. This means that the MATLAB editor works normally in *insert* mode.

There are more keys for editing; the simplest is the ← Backspace key that can be used for correcting a mistake immediately (that is, before pressing Enter). For the moment, use the *Right arrow*, → or ▷, to navigate from left to right within an expression. Also, depress the *Up Arrow* key several times and see how you recall a whole sequence of previous expressions. What happens if you use the *Down Arrow*, ↓ or ▽, key?

1.1.4   A few built-in functions

A scientific hand-held calculator has keys with names or symbols of functions. Thus, to calculate $\sqrt{4}$, the *argument* value, 4, must be entered first; then the key carrying the square root symbol must be depressed and the display will show the result 2. In MATLAB, the function must be fully spelled out by entering each letter of its name, immediately followed by the argument value enclosed in parentheses. Thus, to calculate the same example as above, type sqrt(4) and press Enter. The screen will show the result 2. Calculate the square roots of 2 and 3 in the same way and see that you get the expected results. What would you obtain by entering sqrt(7)^2?

MATLAB has a useful collection of elementary **transcendental built-in functions**. Let us begin with the **exponential function** e^x, written in MATLAB as exp(x). Try exp(1) to obtain the numerical value of e, the base of natural logarithms.

The **natural logarithm** of x is written as log(x). Experiment with several values for which you may readily check your results, among them log(exp(1)). The obvious answer is 1.

The **decimal logarithm** of x is written as log10(x). Check the following in MATLAB:

$$
\begin{aligned}
log_{10}(10) &= 1 \\
log_{10}(100) &= 2 \\
log_{10}(1000) &= 3
\end{aligned}
$$

and so on. This provides a useful exercise in using the *Up Arrow* key; after calculating $\log_{10}(1)$ depress the ↑ key to retrieve the expression and insert a zero at the position of the right parenthesis. Next press Enter. Proceed in the same way for higher powers of 10. As another exercise, verify in MATLAB that

$$
\begin{aligned}
\log_{10}(5.2 * 7.3) &= \log_{10}(5.2) + \log_{10}(7.3) \\
10^{\log_{10}(100)} &= 100
\end{aligned}
$$

Other transcendental functions provided by MATLAB are the **trigonometric functions** shown in Table 1.1, and the **inverse trigonometric functions** shown in Table 1.2. The argument of all these functions *must be given in radians*. Noting

Table 1.1   Trigonometric functions.

MATLAB name	Meaning
sin(x)	sine of x
cos(x)	cosine of x
tan(x)	tangent of x

Table 1.2   Inverse trigonometric functions.

MATLAB name	Meaning	With image in the range
acos(x)	arccosine of x	0 to π
asin(x)	arcsine of x	$-\pi/2$ to $+\pi/2$
atan(x)	arctangent of x	$-\pi/2$ to $+\pi/2$
atan2(y,x)	four-quadrant arctangent of y/x	$-\pi$ to $+\pi$

that in MATLAB we write pi for π, a few examples of calculating trigonometric functions are

```
≫ sin(pi/6)
ans =
    0.5000
≫ sin(pi)
ans =
    1.2246e-016
≫ cos(0)
ans =
    1
≫ tan(pi/4)
ans =
    1.0000
```

Examples of calculating inverse trigonometric functions are

```
≫ asin(1)
ans =
    1.5708
≫ acos(1)
ans =
    0
```

```
>> atan(1)
ans =
    0.7854
>> atan2(0,(-1))
ans =
    3.1416
```

Sometimes a very small number appears where a zero would be expected; this is caused by errors due to the numerical approximations inevitable in a computer. Thus, in the second example above, the number $1.224\text{e-}016$ must be read as 1.224×10^{-16} and it should have been zero. However, do not generalize and conclude that any very small number should have been zero! Some explanation of errors in numerical calculations can be found in Sections 2.2 to 2.6. Such errors can depend on the computer, so the reader working on a different platform from that used by the authors may get slightly different results.

If we know the angles in degrees we must convert them to radians. There are π radians in 180 degrees, so we calculate the sine of 30 degrees by entering $\sin(30*pi/180)$. For example, verify in MATLAB that

$$\sin(30\pi/180) = 1/2 \tag{1.1}$$

and

$$\sin(30\pi/180)^2 + \cos(30\pi/180)^2 = 1 \tag{1.2}$$

1.1.5   Naming constants and variables

In Equation 1.2 we had to write the same argument twice, first for the sine, then for the cosine. This is tiresome and also a potential source of errors. A better practice is to give the argument a name, define it only once, and call the argument by name each time it is used. MATLAB provides a simple way of doing this. Let us look at a calculation, for instance one of the examples in Subsection 1.1.4. We see that each answer is preceded by ans =, that is, the result is contained in a variable bearing the name *ans*. We can use this feature as follows: first enter $30*pi/180$ and press Enter, then type

```
>> sin(ans)^2 + cos(ans)^2
```

and carry out the calculation.

The contents of the variable *ans* change with each calculation (see the examples in Subsection 1.1.4). You can use this property when you want to carry out a sequence of calculations in which each succeeding calculation uses the value of ans as one of its operands. For example, try $2*9$, then ans^2, and finally $sqrt(ans)/9$. The final result is obviously 2.

MATLAB allows us to give constants and variables names of our choice. This is a powerful facility that can reduce work and help in avoiding **input errors**. When the user begins a session in which the same values must be used several times, the user can define them once and then call them by name. Thus, suppose that we have to calculate trigonometric functions of several angles, let us say $\alpha = 30°$, $\beta = 52°$, $\gamma = 76°$. You may enter them as

```
>> alpha = 30;
>> beta = 52;
>> gamma = 76;
```

When we write the semicolon ' ; ' at the end of a statement, the computer will not display the result of the command, and it will not echo the input. See for yourself what happens if you do not enter the semicolon. Continue by defining a conversion factor conf = pi/180. Now you can calculate trigonometric functions using statements like sin(conf*alpha) and so on:

```
>> sin(conf*alpha)
ans =
    0.5000
>> sin(conf*beta)
ans =
    0.7880
>> sin(conf*gamma)
ans =
    0.9703
```

If you are not interested in keeping angle values in degrees, you can convert them all to radians:

```
>> alpha = conf*alpha;
>> beta = conf*beta;
>> gamma = conf*gamma;
>> sin(alpha)
ans =
    0.5000
>> sin(beta)
ans =
    0.7880
>> sin(gamma)
ans =
    0.9703
```

A more extensive use of named constants is shown in an example in Section 1.1.7 and Examples 2.6 and 2.12.

Above, we have used constant names composed of one or more letters. In fact, such a name may consist of a letter followed by other letters, digits or underscores. However, only the first 19 characters are significant. Take care: by default, MATLAB distinguishes between upper-case and lower-case letters; a and A are different names, for example:

```
≫ a = 2;
≫ A = 3;
≫ 2*a
ans =
     4
≫ 2*A
ans =
     6
```

Later we shall learn how to save the values of constants and variables for use in other sessions. We shall also learn how to program simple trigonometric functions that will allow angle values in degrees as arguments.

To end this subsection let us mention that named constants, variables and intermediate results present another definite advantage: they preserve all the precision of MATLAB calculations. To enter manually, several times, constants, variables and intermediate results with all their digits is simply inconceivable; the job would be terribly tedious and error-prone.

1.1.6   Format

In Subsection 1.1.4 we learned that the value of π is stored in the MATLAB constant pi. We retrieve it with the command

```
≫ pi
ans =
     3.1416
```

The result is displayed with five significant digits; however, the numerical value stored in the machine is much more exact. We can change the format in which numbers are displayed:

```
≫ format long
≫ pi
ans =
     3.14159265358979
```

MATLAB formats for **scientific notation** are

```
≫ format short e
≫ pi
ans =
    3.1416e+000
≫ format long e
≫ pi
ans =
    3.141592653589793e+000
```

A format used for displaying currency values with two decimals, for instance pounds and pence or dollars and cents, is format bank. We can check its action with

```
≫ format bank
≫ pi
ans =
    3.14
```

Obviously, the bank format was not meant for scientific or technical calculations, but it may be useful where it would make no sense to display four decimal digits. For example, when working with building dimensions measured in metres, displaying four decimal digits means a precision of 0.1 mm and this is definitely not realistic; centimetres would be sufficient in most cases.

We return to the default format with

```
≫ format
≫ pi
ans =
  3.1416
```

A useful command is format compact; it suppresses loose lines within the display. Compare, for instance:

```
≫ format compact
≫ x = 4;
≫ y = x^2 + 2*x + 53
y =
    77
```

with

```
≫ format loose
≫ y = x^2 + 2*x + 53

y =
    77
```

For obvious reasons of economy most screen displays in this book were obtained after entering the `format compact` command. More details about the `format` options can be learned by typing `help format`.

Typing `help format` will show more possibilities. Most interesting is the format `rat`: it yields a rational approximation of a real number, that is a fraction that approximates a given number. Try the following sequence of calculations:

```
≫ format rat
≫ pi
ans =
 355/113
≫ format
≫ 355/113
ans =
 3.1416
```

1.1.7   Diary

If you want to keep a log of your MATLAB session you can print it. To do this, open the `File` menu and choose `Print`. You can even print only a fragment of the session; select it with the mouse and click on `Print selection` in the `File` menu. But if you want to process the record of the session, MATLAB provides a better possibility. Calculations performed in MATLAB can be recorded in a simple way by means of the `diary` function. Comments can be interspersed within the record; they are preceded by the per cent sign %. Type the following sequence of commands:

```
≫ format compact
≫ diary
≫ r = 0.1;      % radius of cylinder base, m
≫ h = 2;        % cylinder height, m
≫ S = 2*pi*r*h % lateral surface of cylinder, m^2
S =
     1.2566
≫ V = pi*r^2*h % cylinder volume, m^3
V =
    0.0628
```

and continue with

```
≫ diary off
≫ rho = 0.5;      % average density of fir wood, t/m^3
≫ m = rho*V       % column mass, t
m =
     0.0314
```

The calculations between the statements `diary` and `diary off` are written to a file named `diary` and stored in the same directory from which you invoked MATLAB. Under DOS, for example, you can read this file by means of one of commands `more < diary`, `type diary`, or by opening the file within an editor. An editor is especially useful when long records of calculations must be turned into scientific or engineering reports. For example, the `diary` facility can help students in preparing reports of laboratory experiments.

It is possible to keep several `diaries`, each under its own name chosen for the convenience of the user. Try, for instance, the command

```
≫ diary report1.dia
```

followed by the same calculations as above, or by any other calculations. You will find the record in the file `report1.dia`.

1.2   One-dimensional arrays and graphics

1.2.1   Arrays – elementary operations

An ordered collection of numbers, a_1, a_2, ..., a_n, can be defined in MATLAB as an **array**:

```
≫ A = [ a1 a2 ... an ]
```

Enter, for example, the array of the first six prime numbers:

```
≫ prime = [ 2 3 5 7 11 13 ]
prime =
     2 3 5 7 11 13
```

Instead of separating the elements of the array by blanks, commas can be used:

```
≫ prime = [ 2, 3, 5, 7, 11, 13 ]
prime =
    2 3 5 7 11 13
```

When entering or reading fractional numbers, it is important not to confuse commas with decimal points.

The elements of an array are identified by their **index**. Thus

```
≫ prime(1)
ans =
    2
≫ prime(2)
ans =
    3
```

The indices are sequences of natural numbers *always beginning with 1*. The number of the elements in an array can be retrieved with the length function:

```
≫ length(prime)
ans =
    6
```

It is possible to enter an array element by element; however, this procedure incurs a serious disadvantage and should be used only when there is no other alternative. To illustrate this point, let us first clear the values previously entered:

```
≫ clear prime
```

Next we enter the array as follows

```
≫ prime(1) = 2
prime =
    2
≫ prime(2) = 3
prime =
    2 3
    ⋮
```

```
≫ prime(6) = 13
prime =
      2 3 5 7 11 13
```

We see that at each step MATLAB increments the length of the array by 1. This operation is time consuming, a disadvantage that can become serious when dealing with large arrays. In such cases it is advantageous to allocate the space from the beginning, by defining a matrix of zeros of the correct size. The appropriate command is shown in Section 1.3.2.

The **addition** and **subtraction** operations are defined between two arrays of the same length, $A = [a_1 \ a_2 \ldots \ a_n]$ and $B = [b_1 \ b_2 \ldots \ b_n]$, as follows:

$$
\begin{aligned}
A + B &= [a_1 + b_1, a_2 + b_2, \ldots, a_n + b_n] \\
A - B &= [a_1 - b_1, a_2 - b_2, \ldots, a_n - b_n]
\end{aligned}
$$

To exemplify this, let us define a second array of six elements:

```
≫ natural = [ 1 2 3 4 5 6 ]
natural =
      1 2 3 4 5 6
≫ prime + natural
ans =
      3 5 8 11 16 19
≫ prime - natural
ans =
      1 1 2 3 6 7
```

1.2.2   More operations on arrays

Arrays of equally spaced elements can be entered by stating the first element, the increment, and the last element. Thus, the array of the first six odd numbers is entered as

```
≫ odd = 1:  2:  11
odd =
      1 3 5 7 9 11
```

and the array of the first six even numbers as

```
≫ even = 2:  2:  12
even =
      2 4 6 8 10 12
```

When the increment is 1 it can be omitted; for example, the array of the first six natural numbers can be entered as

```
>> natural = 1:6
natural =
     1 2 3 4 5 6
```

Negative and fractional increments are also permitted. Try, for example,

```
>> inverse_odd = 11:  -2:  1
>> halves = 0:  0.5:  10
```

For the arrays A and B, used above, their **array multiplication**, indicated in MATLAB by '.*', is defined by

$$A.*B = [a_1b_1, \ a_2b_2, \ \ldots, \ a_nb_n]$$

For example, with the two arrays natural and prime defined above, their array multiplication yields

```
>> natural.*prime
ans =
     2 6 15 28 55 78
```

The inverse operation, **array division**, indicated in MATLAB by './', is defined by

$$A./B = [a_1/b_1, \ a_2/b_2, \ \ldots, \ a_n/b_n]$$

For instance, the array division of natural by prime gives

```
>> natural./prime
ans =
     0.5000 0.6667 0.6000 0.5714 0.4545 0.4615
```

We can raise the elements of an array to the same power by using the operator '.^'. For example, the squares of the first six natural numbers are calculated by

```
>> natural.^2
ans =
     1 4 9 16 25 36
```

Many built-in MATLAB functions can be applied to an array simply by using the name of the array as an argument. The functions will operate on all array elements as if called for each element individually. As an example, let us calculate the sine of the angles $0, 10, 20, \ldots, 90$ degrees:

```
≫ angle = [0:10:90];
≫ angle = pi*angle/180;
≫ sin(angle)
ans =
    Columns 1 through 7
    0 0.1736 0.3420 0.5000 ...
```

1.2.3   Row vectors and column vectors

The preceding two sections dealt with 'horizontal' arrays. In geometry the elements of such an array may be the components of a **vector**; in mechanics, the components of a displacement, velocity, acceleration, or force vector. By generalization, horizontal arrays are often called **row vectors**.

It is also convenient to define 'vertical' arrays; they are called **column vectors**. One way of introducing such a vector in MATLAB is analogous to introducing row vectors, with the difference that the elements are separated by semicolons, ';', instead of blank spaces or commas. Thus, the column vector of the first six prime numbers can be input as

```
≫ A = [ 2; 3; 5; 7; 11; 13 ]
A =
    2
    ⋮
    13
```

Another way is to write the name of the array, the equals sign, the opening bracket, '[', and the first number, press Enter, then the second number, press Enter, and so on, until the last number followed by a closing bracket, ']'. As an example, the same column vector as above can be defined in MATLAB by the following sequence:

```
≫ A = [ 2
3
5
7
11
13 ]
```

A row vector of real numbers can be converted into a column vector, and vice versa, by **transposition**. This operation is performed in MATLAB by the apostrophe (prime), ''. As an example, for the array A defined above we obtain the transpose with

```
>> At = A'
At =
     2 3 5 7 11 13
```

and we recover A by

```
>> At'
ans =
     2
     3
     5
     7
    11
    13
```

1.2.4   The scalar product

A row vector

$$A = [a_1 \; a_2 \; \ldots \; a_n]$$

and a column vector with the same number of elements

$$B = \begin{bmatrix} a_1 \\ a_2 \\ \vdots \\ a_n \end{bmatrix}$$

can be **multiplied** by means of the operator '*' with the result

$$A * B = a_1 b_1 + a_2 b_2 + \cdots + a_n b_n$$

This operation corresponds to what is called in various branches of mathematics **scalar product**, **dot product**, or **inner product**, and it is a special case of the multiplication of matrices described in Section 1.3.2 and in Chapter 3. As an example, let us multiply the array of the first six natural numbers by the transposed array of the first six prime numbers:

```
≫ natural*prime'
ans =
    184
```

As a more meaningful example, we can find the sum of the squares of the first six prime numbers by

```
≫ prime*prime'
ans =
    377
```

and the sum of the squares of the first six natural numbers by

```
≫ natural*natural'
ans =
    91
```

We can check our results by using the MATLAB sum function which yields the sum of the elements of the array given as its argument:

```
≫ sum(prime.^2)
ans =
    377
```

The scalar product has important interpretations in geometry and in mechanics, and some of them are illustrated in Chapter 2.

1.2.5   Simple plots

In its simplest form, the plot function produces the graph of the values of the elements of an array against the values of the elements of another array, provided the two arrays *have the same number of elements*. The following sequence of commands plots the graph of the sine function between 0 and π radians:

```
≫ x = 0:  pi/90:  pi;
≫ y = sin(x);
≫ plot(x, y)
```

Now press Enter and type

```
≫ grid
```

Press Enter again and type

```
≫ xlabel('x, radians')
```

and similarly

```
≫ ylabel('sin(x)')
```

The functions xlabel and ylabel take **text strings** as arguments. Text strings are entered by enclosing them between quotes, for example 'x, radians'.

The resulting plot appears in its own window, as shown in Figure 1.3. At the top of the window there is a menu bar, and under it a toolbar. There are two possibilities

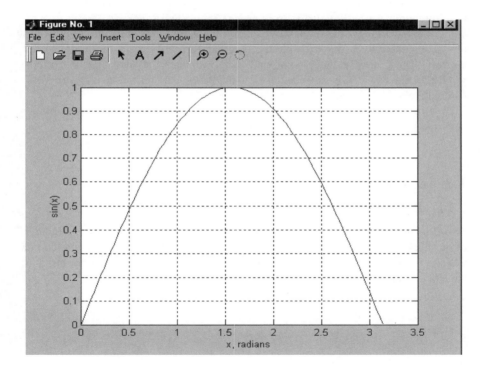

Figure 1.3   A plot window.

of printing the graph:

(1)   click on Print in the File menu;

(2)   click on the printer icon in the toolbar.

It is also possible to print the graph on a file. For example, the following command produces a black-and-white EPS (Encapsulated PostScript) file:

```
>> print -deps Fig03_04.eps
```

It is in this way that we obtained the EPS files that we have embedded in the LaTeX text of this book. For other options of printing on file try help print or consult the manuals.

The toolbar enables you to edit the graph. To do this you should first press the arrow pointing to the left on the toolbar. To the right of this icon and going rightwards you will find icons for text insertion, drawing arrows, drawing lines, zooming in (enlarging), zooming out and rotating the figure. Try these icons for yourself. To close the figure click on Close in the File menu. If you do not close this figure and continue entering commands from the command line, the next time you ask for a plot it will not appear automatically. You should then go to the menu bar and open the Window menu.

When working in the WINDOWS environment, typing a command after invoking the plot function (in our example the command grid), causes the figure to disappear. Then, after the last command that completes the plot (in our example ylabel('sin(x)'), it is sufficient to click the *Window* menu and then *Figure No. 1*. Alternatively, one can enter the command figure(1).

To obtain a hard copy of the graph, type print. To learn about other possibilities enter help print or consult the manuals.

1.3   Matrices

1.3.1   Defining a matrix

Two-dimensional arrays are ordered collections of numbers identified by two indices. In most applications they are **matrices**. Two-dimensional arrays can be entered in a way very similar to entering one-dimensional arrays. Thus, we can either write all the rows in one line and separate them by semicolons:

```
>> A = [ 1 2 3; 4 5 6; 7 8 9 ]
A =
     1    2    3
     4    5    6
     7    8    9
```

or type each row separately and press Enter between consecutive rows:

```
≫ A = [ 1 2 3
4 5 6
7 8 9 ]
A =
        1       2       3
        4       5       6
        7       8       9
```

Of course, we can separate the elements of a row by commas:

```
≫ A = [ 1, 2, 3
4, 5, 6
7, 8, 9 ]
```

As stated above, any element of a matrix is identified by two indices; the first indicates the row, and the second, the column. Try, for example

```
≫ A(2,1)
ans =
    4
```

or

```
≫ A(2, 3)
ans =
    6
```

The number of rows and columns in a matrix is retrieved by the size function, for example

```
≫ size(A)
ans =
    3 3
```

We say that **A** is a *3*-by-*3* matrix. From here on we use bold-face letters to denote vectors and matrices. This is an example of a **square matrix**. It is also possible to define matrices that are not square; two examples follow a few lines below. Let us now enter another array called **B**:

```
≫ B = [ 9 8 7; 6 5 4; 3 2 1 ];
```

We can create a new matrix by putting the two matrices **A** and **B** side by side; this **juxtaposition** can be used for printing a simple table:

```
≫ [ A B ]
ans =
     1    2    3    9    8    7
     4    5    6    6    5    4
     7    8    9    3    2    1
```

The dimensions of this matrix are given by

```
≫ size(ans)
ans =
     3 6
```

that is, a *3*-by-*6* matrix. We can also create a new matrix whose upper rows are those of **A** and lower rows those of **B**:

```
≫ [ A; B ]
ans =
     1    2    3
     4    5    6
     7    8    9
     9    8    7
     6    5    4
     3    2    1
```

It is possible to extract a **submatrix** out of a matrix. For instance, the following command extracts the first row of **A**:

```
≫ A(1, :)
ans =
     1 2 3
```

Above, the number 1 within the parentheses means 'the first row', and the colon after the comma means 'all columns'. Another example of the use of the colon, this time with the meaning 'all rows', is

```
≫ A(:, 1)
ans =
    1
    4
    7
```

In the following example the colon is used to show 'rows from 1 to 2' and 'columns from 1 to 2':

```
≫ A(1:2,1:2)
ans =
    1 2
    4 5
```

1.3.2   Elementary operations with matrices

The sum of two n-by-m matrices, $\mathbf{A}$ and $\mathbf{B}$, whose general elements are a_{ij} and b_{ij}, is a new n-by-m matrix, say $\mathbf{S}$, whose general element is $s_{ij} = a_{ij} + b_{ij}$. As an example, the sum of the two matrices defined in the preceding subsection are

```
≫ S = A + B
S =
    10      10      10
    10      10      10
    10      10      10
```

The difference of the two n-by-m matrices, $\mathbf{A}$ and $\mathbf{B}$, whose general elements are a_{ij} and b_{ij}, is a new n-by-m matrix, say $\mathbf{D}$, whose general element is $d_{ij} = a_{ij} - b_{ij}$. As an example, the difference of the two matrices defined above is

```
≫ D = A - B
D =
    -8      -6      -4
    -2       0       2
     4       6       8
```

An n-by-m matrix can be multiplied by an m-by-p matrix, yielding an n-by-p matrix. With the same notations as above, the product of the matrices $\mathbf{A}$ and $\mathbf{B}$ is a

3-by-3 matrix **P** whose general element is

$$p_{ij} = \sum_{k=1}^{m} a_{ik} b_{kj}$$

With the two matrices used so far we obtain

```
≫ A*B
ans =
        30      24      18
        84      69      54
       138     114      90
```

To exemplify the general case, let us define a new 3-by-2 matrix, multiply **A** by it and get a 3-by-2 matrix:

```
≫ C = [ 10 11; 12 13; 14 15 ];
≫ A*C
ans =
        76      82
       184     199
       292     316
```

A *square* matrix can be multiplied by itself; for instance, the square of the matrix **A** used above is given by

```
≫ A^2
ans =
        30   36   42
        66   81   96
       102  126  150
```

The same operations that work element by element on one-dimensional arrays also work on two-dimensional arrays. As an example, let us calculate the decimal logarithms of the elements of the same array **A**:

```
≫ L = log10(A)
L =
            0 0.3010 0.4771
       0.6021 0.6990 0.7782
       0.8451 0.9031 0.9542
```

We can create a matrix with the same number of rows and columns as **A**, with all the elements equal to one, by the commands:

```
>> [m, n] = size(A); ones(m, n)
ans =
     1 1 1
     1 1 1
     1 1 1
```

The commands can be simplified to

```
>> ones(size(A))
```

We use a matrix of ones to recover **A** from **L**:

```
>> (10*ones(size(A))).^L
ans =
     1.0000 2.0000 3.0000
     4.0000 5.0000 6.0000
     7.0000 8.0000 9.0000
```

To create matrices whose elements are all zeros use the above but insert `zeros` instead of `ones`.

1.3.3   Printing a table

A simple way to build a table from one-dimensional arrays is to use the operations of transposition and juxtaposition. As an example, the table of sines of $0, 10, \ldots, 90$ degrees can be obtained with the following commands:

```
>> angle = 0:10:90;
>> sine = sin(pi*angle/180);
>> [ angle' sine' ]
ans =
          0      0
     10.0000 0.1736
     ...
     90.0000 1.0000
```

1.4   Complex numbers

1.4.1   Complex numbers – elementary operations

The **imaginary unit**, $\sqrt{-1}$, is stored in MATLAB in the constants i and j. Try

```
>> i^2
ans =
    -1
```

and

```
>> j^2
ans =
    -1
```

In electrical engineering the symbol j is preferred to the symbol i, the latter being used for denoting a current. With the aid of the imaginary unit we can define **complex numbers** in the usual way, for example

```
>> z1 = 3 + 4i
z1 =
    3.0000 + 4.0000i
```

The **complex conjugate** is obtained by

```
>> z1_bar = conj(z1)
z1_bar =
    3.0000 - 4.0000i
```

Using the constant j instead of i yields the same result:

```
>> z1 = 3 + 4j
z1 =
    3.0000 + 4.0000i
```

Note that MATLAB always uses the symbol i in the answers it returns, even if we entered the symbol j. We can perform calculations with complex numbers as easily as with real numbers. Let us define a second complex number:

```
>> z2 = 4 + 3i
z2 =
    4.0000 + 3.0000i
```

Now we can add the two numbers

```
≫ z1 + z2
ans =
    7.0000 + 7.0000i
```

multiply them

```
≫ z1*z2
ans =
    0 +25.0000i
```

or divide one by the other

```
≫ z1/z2
ans =
    0.9600 + 0.2800i
```

We can also raise a complex number to a power in the same way we did with real numbers:

```
≫ z1^2
ans =
   -7.0000 +24.0000i
```

The definitions of all the above operations are returned to in Subsection 4.15.1.

1.4.2   Two notes on the use of i and j

In older MATLAB versions it was necessary to write the multiplication sign, '*', before i or j. This option still functions; for example, it is possible to write

```
≫ 3 + 4*i
ans =
    3.0000 + 4.0000i
```

Another important point is that if one of the letters 'i' or 'j' is used to define some constant or variable, it no longer means the imaginary unit. Frequent examples in which such situations inadvertently arise are *FOR loops* (see Subsection 1.7.2).

The following example shows how MATLAB overcomes this difficulty; note the difference in the syntax used to define the numbers a and b:

```
≫ i = 2; a = 3 + 4*i
a =
      11
≫ b = 3 + 4i
b =
      3.0000 + 4.0000i
```

1.4.3   Plotting a complex number

Complex numbers can be represented as points in the complex plane. To do this with the same number used in the preceding section, $z1 = 3 + 4i$, we separate the **real part** of the number:

```
≫ a = real(z1)
a =
      3
```

and the **imaginary part**

```
≫ b = imag(z1)
b =
      4
```

and we plot the latter against the former

```
≫ plot(a, b, '*')
≫ xlabel('Real')
≫ ylabel('Imaginary')
≫ title('z1 = 3 + 4i')
≫ figure(1)
```

The third argument of the plot function, '*', means that the point will be printed as an asterisk. Other possibilities are '.', 'o', +, or 'x'. All these symbols must be enclosed between quotes. We have used the title function to label the figure. The argument to title must be a string variable, which is why 'z1 = 3 + 4i' is written between quote marks. The result is shown in Figure 1.4. For a single number we can type its name directly:

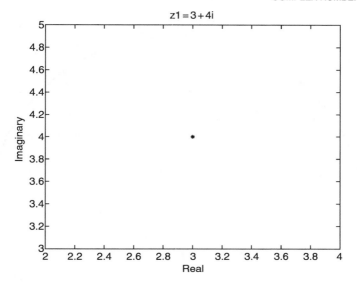

Figure 1.4   Complex number represented as a point in the complex plane.

```
≫ plot(z1, '*')
```

Check this command for yourself.

   If you have continued from the previous figure, you will not see the resulting plot. Thus you must either click *Figure No. 1* in the menu *Window*, or type figure(1). This is not necessary if you clicked *close* in the menu of the previous figure.

   In another geometrical interpretation, a complex number can be represented as a two-dimensional vector whose horizontal component is the real part of the number, and the vertical component is the imaginary part. If we are dealing with only one number, we can use the MATLAB built-in function compass to obtain the graph of such a vector:

```
≫ compass(z1)
```

The result is shown in Figure 1.5.

   One important technical application of the vector representation of complex numbers is the notion of *phasor*; it is introduced in Section 4.9.

1.4.4   Trigonometric and exponential representations

Let us refer again to the vector representation of a complex number, for example the number z_1 used above. The **magnitude** of a complex number can be calculated as

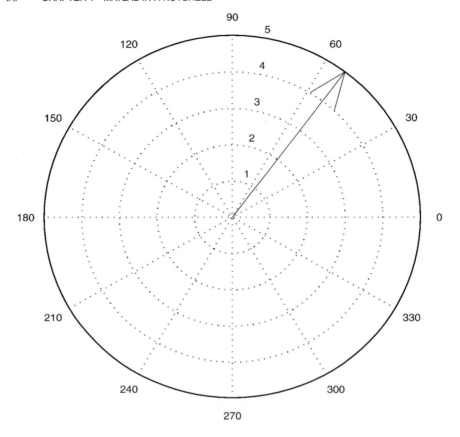

Figure 1.5   Vector representation of a complex number; $z1 = 3 + 4i$.

the square root of the product of the number and its conjugate:

```
>> rho = sqrt(z1*z1_bar)
rho =
    5
```

and the **argument** by

```
>> theta = atan(b/a)
theta =
    0.9273
```

MATLAB provides functions that perform these operations directly: the magnitude is obtained with

```
>> rho = abs(z1)
rho =
      5
```

and the argument with

```
>> theta = angle(z1)
theta =
    0.9273
```

Knowing the magnitude and the argument, the number z_1 can be entered in trigonometric form

```
>> rho*(cos(theta) + i*sin(theta))
ans =
    3.0000 + 4.0000i
```

It is, however, much more convenient to use Euler's formula and enter the number in **exponential form**

```
>> rho*exp(i*theta)
ans =
    3.0000 + 4.0000i
```

A further explanation of this subject can be found in Section 4.5.

1.4.5 Functions of complex variables

Functions of complex variables can be calculated in MATLAB as easily as functions of real variables; for instance, for the number z_1 used above,

```
>> sin(z1)
ans =
    3.8537 -27.0168i
>> cos(z1)
ans =
   -27.0349 - 3.8512i
>> sin(z1)^2 + cos(z1)^2
ans =
      1
```

For more details see Sections 4.6 and 4.7. Functions of complex variables find an important technical application in **conformal mapping**. An introduction to this subject is given in Section 4.8.

1.4.6   Arrays of complex numbers

Complex numbers can be ordered in one- and two-dimensional arrays in the same way as real numbers. As an example, we shall use a vector of complex numbers to illustrate the addition of complex numbers. Using the same numbers we have worked with throughout this chapter we build

```
≫ Z = [ 0, z1, z1+z2 ]
Z =
     0    3.0000 + 4.0000i    7.0000 + 7.0000i
```

Notice that the third argument, $z1+z2$, was entered without any spaces between z1 and the plus sign, or between the plus sign and z2. Using a space would produce a result identical to

```
≫ Z = [ 0, z1, z1, z2 ]
```

We plot the vector Z with

```
≫ plot(Z)
≫ text(real(z1), imag(z1), 'z1')
≫ text(real(z1+z2), imag(z1+z2), 'z2')
≫ xlabel('Real')
≫ ylabel('Imaginary')
```

The vector representing z_1 is drawn from the point 0 to the point z_1. The vector representing z_2 is drawn from the point z_1 to the point z_2. The sum of the two vectors should be a vector drawn from 0 to z_1+z_2. To plot it too, a more elaborate expression is needed:

```
≫ Zsum = z1 + z2;
≫ plot(real(Z), imag(Z), real([ 0 Zsum ]), imag([ 0 Zsum ]))
```

To label the vectors we used the `text` function. The first argument is the x-coordinate of the place where we want to put the text, the second argument is the y-coordinate of the same place, and the third is a string containing the text to be written.

Applying the apostrophe operator to an array of complex numbers results, not in the transpose of the array, but in its **complex conjugate transpose**, for example:

```
>> Z'
ans =
        0
   3.0000 - 4.0000i
   7.0000 - 7.0000i
```

To obtain just the transpose use '.'':

```
>> Z.'
ans =
        0
   3.0000 + 4.0000i
   7.0000 + 7.0000i
```

1.5   Systems of linear equations

1.5.1   Determinants

Let us consider the following system of linear equations:

$$x_1 + 2x_2 + 3x_3 = 4 \tag{1.3}$$
$$2x_1 + 3x_2 + 4x_3 = 5 \tag{1.4}$$
$$4x_1 + 2x_2 + 5x_3 = 1 \tag{1.5}$$

Defining the **coefficient matrix A**

$$A = \begin{bmatrix} 1 & 2 & 3 \\ 2 & 3 & 4 \\ 4 & 2 & 5 \end{bmatrix}$$

and the vector **B**

$$B = \begin{bmatrix} 4 \\ 5 \\ 1 \end{bmatrix}$$

we can write the system in matrix form:

$$AX = B$$

In MATLAB **A** and **B** are entered by

```
≫ A = [ 1, 2, 3; 2, 3, 4; 4, 2, 5 ]
A =
     1 2 3
     2 3 4
     4 2 5
```

and

```
≫ B = [ 4; 5; 1 ]
B =
     4
     5
     1
```

To solve the system by Cramer's rule we must calculate some determinants. Calculating determinants manually is not a pleasant job; in MATLAB, however, it becomes as simple as the following command

```
≫ det(A)
ans =
     -5
```

The rest of the solution is given in the next subsection. Solving a system of linear equations by Cramer's rule is not the most efficient way, especially if the system consists of a large number of equations. The method is presented here just to exemplify a few important notions and to show how working in MATLAB is much easier than calculating by traditional methods. The definition of determinants is recalled in Section 5.6. Determinants have important applications in mathematics; some of their geometrical interpretations are described in Sections 5.10 and 5.11.

1.5.2   Cramer's rule

We recall that the solution, by Cramer's rule, of the system exemplified in the preceding section is:

$$X(1) = \frac{\begin{vmatrix} 4 & 2 & 3 \\ 5 & 3 & 4 \\ 1 & 2 & 5 \end{vmatrix}}{\begin{vmatrix} 1 & 2 & 3 \\ 2 & 3 & 4 \\ 4 & 2 & 5 \end{vmatrix}} = -1.4$$

$$X(2) = \frac{\begin{vmatrix} 1 & 4 & 3 \\ 2 & 5 & 4 \\ 4 & 1 & 5 \end{vmatrix}}{\begin{vmatrix} 1 & 2 & 3 \\ 2 & 3 & 4 \\ 4 & 2 & 5 \end{vmatrix}} = 1.8$$

$$X(3) = \frac{\begin{vmatrix} 1 & 2 & 4 \\ 2 & 3 & 5 \\ 4 & 2 & 1 \end{vmatrix}}{\begin{vmatrix} 1 & 2 & 3 \\ 2 & 3 & 4 \\ 4 & 2 & 5 \end{vmatrix}} = 0.6$$

Let D1 be the matrix whose determinant appears in the numerator of X(1). In MATLAB we derive the matrix **D1**, from **A**, by setting its first column to the vector **B**:

```
≫ D1 = A; D1(:, 1) = B
D1 =
    4 2 3
    5 3 4
    1 2 5
```

Let D2 and D3 be the matrices whose determinants are the numerators of X(2) and X(3). We build the matrices **D1** and **D2** in the same way as we built D1:

```
≫ D2 = A; D2(:, 2) = B
D2 =
    1 4 3
    2 5 4
    4 1 5
≫ D3 = A; D3(:, 3) = B
D3 =
    1 2 4
    2 3 5
    4 2 1
```

The solution by Cramer's rule is

```
≫ X = [ det(D1); det(D2); det(D3) ]/det(A)
X =
    -1.4000
     1.8000
     0.6000
```

To check our solution we multiply **A** by **X**; we do this in MATLAB by

```
≫ A*X
ans =
      4.0000
      5.0000
      1.0000
```

and we recover the vector **B**.

1.5.3   Matrix inversion

The matrix **A** in the preceding example is square and its determinant is different from zero. Such a matrix has an **inverse** which is calculated in MATLAB with

```
≫ A_inv = inv(A)
A_inv =
     -1.4000   0.8000   0.2000
     -1.2000   1.4000  -0.4000
      1.6000  -1.2000   0.2000
```

In this case it is possible to solve the given system of equations by multiplying, at left, the vector **B** by the inverse of the matrix **A**. In MATLAB this is done by

```
≫ X = A_inv*B
X =
     -1.4000
      1.8000
      0.6000
```

1.5.4   Solving systems of linear equations in MATLAB

The usual way of solving systems of linear equations in MATLAB is by **Gaussian elimination**. This algorithm is computationally efficient and it is invoked by the backslash operator, '\':

```
≫ X = A\B
X =
         -1.4000
          1.8000
          0.6000
```

MATLAB always produces a result when we proceed as above, even if the matrix **A** is not invertible. In such cases care must be taken, because the solution can be a particular one or even not true. If the matrix **A** is singular or badly scaled, a warning message is produced. If **A** is not square, MATLAB produces a solution in the *least square sense*.

More about this subject can be learnt by typing the command `help slash`, and especially by reading Chapter 6.

1.6   Polynomials

1.6.1   Polynomial roots

For several operations, polynomials are represented in MATLAB by the array of the coefficients of their terms, in the order of the descending powers of the variable. For example, the polynomial

$$x^2 + 2x + 1$$

is stored in MATLAB as the array

```
>> coeff = [ 1 2 1 ];
```

If this polynomial is the left-hand side of the equation

$$x^2 + 2x + 1 = 0$$

the roots are obtained by

```
>> r = roots(coeff)
r =
    -1
    -1
```

and this is the expected solution because the given polynomial is simply the expansion of $(x + 1)^2$.

As a more interesting example, let us solve the equation

$$x^3 - 15x = 4$$

treated nearly 500 years ago by Bombelli (see Section 4.2). The order of calculations is

```
>> coeff = [ 1 0 -15 -4 ];
>> r = roots(coeff)
r =
     4.0000
    -3.7321
    -0.2679
```

The reader is invited to experiment with more equations.

1.6.2   Retrieving polynomial coefficients from polynomial roots

The coefficients of a polynomial can be retrieved from its roots. Thus, continuing the preceding example,

```
>> p = poly(r)
p =
     1.0000 0.0000 -15.0000 -4.0000
```

As a further example, let us find the coefficients of a polynomial that has three roots equal to one:

```
>> r = [ 1 1 1 ];
>> p = poly(r)
p =
     1 -3 3 -1
```

These are indeed the coefficients of the expansion of

$$(x - 1)^3$$

1.6.3   Polynomial evaluation

Let us suppose that we want to plot the function

$$y = x^3 - 3x^2 - 6x + 8 \tag{1.6}$$

in a range that includes the zeros of y. We begin by entering the array of polynomial coefficients:

```
>> p = [ 1 -3 -6 8 ];
```

The roots are found with

```
>> roots(p)
ans =
     4.0000
    -2.0000
     1.0000
```

Now we can define a domain of x that spans the zeros of y:

```
>> x = -3:  0.1:  5;
```

The values of y at each point contained in the array x are calculated by the MATLAB function `polyval`. We call this function with two arguments: the array of coefficients, and the array of points at which the polynomial will be evaluated. In this example the calculation is

```
>> y = polyval(p, x);
```

and the plot is obtained with

```
>> plot(x, y)
>> grid
>> title('Plot of y = x^3 - 3x^2 - 6x + 8')
>> xlabel('x')
>> ylabel('y')
```

Try it for yourself.

1.6.4   Multiplication and division of polynomials

The multiplication of two polynomials can easily be performed in MATLAB by operating on the arrays of their coefficients. Let us consider, for example, the multiplication

$$(2x^2 + 3x + 1)(5x - 2) = 10x^3 + 11x^2 - x - 2$$

In MATLAB we obtain the same result by **convolution**:

```
>> p1 = [ 2 3 1 ];
>> p2 = [ 5 -2 ];
>> p3 = conv(p1, p2)
p3 =
    10 11 -1 -2
```

The inverse operation, polynomial division, is performed in MATLAB by **deconvolution**:

```
>> [ Q, R ] = deconv(p3, p1)
Q =
    5 -2
R =
    0 0 0 0
```

The array Q contains the coefficients of the quotient polynomial, and the array R contains the coefficients of the remainder polynomial. In the above example p1 divides exactly into p3; Q contains the coefficients of p2 and all the elements of R are zero. Let us substitute p3 to p4 defined as

$$10x^3 + 11x^2 + 2x$$

Dividing by p1 is calculated by

```
≫ p4 = [ 10 11 2 0 ];
≫ [ Q, R ] = deconv(p4, p1)
Q =
    5 -2
R =
    0 0 3 2
```

The remainder of the division of p4 by p1 is indeed $3x + 2$.

The operations of convolution and deconvolution are useful in simulation, control, and signal processing. A few applications can be found in Chapters 14, 15 and 16.

As used above, the deconv function returns two output arguments. More functions with two output arguments will be encountered later in this book.

1.7   Programming in MATLAB

Sequences of MATLAB commands can be written to files with the extension m, appropriately called **M-files**. Entering the name of the file (without the extension!) causes automatic execution of all the statements. In their simplest form, such files are called **script files**. For example, let us write the following lines to a file defined as hello.m.

```
% The program in File HELLO.M greets you and asks for your
% name. Then it greets you by name and tells you the date.
disp('Hello! Who are you?')
name = input('Please enter your name enclosed between quotes ');
d = date;
answer = [ 'Hello ' name '. Today is ' d '.'];
disp(answer)
```

Use the MATLAB **Editor/Debugger** for this. On the toolbar click on the left-most icon. A new window will open and you can type your program into it. The editor automatically provides indentation when you open a for loop or a conditional structure. Figure 1.6 shows the appearance of the editor/debugger with the first lines of listing described in Subsection 1.7.3. Line numbers appear in the grey area at the left of the text. These numbers are used in error messages issued when running the program.

New M–file

M–files

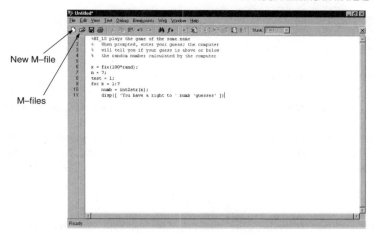

Figure 1.6   The editor/debugger screen.

After completing the first few program lines it is advisable to save your work and give the file a name. To do this use the `Save as` option in the `File` menu of the editor/debugger window. When the file has a name, you can quit the editor/debugger by clicking on `File` and then on `close <filename>` where you substitute the name of your file in `<filename>`. If the file is new, you remain in a window called `Untitled`. To leave it click in the `File` menu on `Close untitled`. Later, if you want to reopen your new file, you can click on the icon next to the right of the `New` icon. A small window will open, listing all the M-files of the directory you are working in. Double click on the filename. If in the meantime you are not working on other M-files, it may be simpler to open the `File` menu and look for the filename.

Returning now to the program described above, the first two lines are comments and are indicated as such by the per cent sign, '%'. The first comments on an M-file can be displayed on the screen by entering the word `help` followed by the name of the file, for example:

```
>> help hello
```

The computer reacts by displaying

```
The program in File HELLO.M greets you and asks for your
name.  Then it greets you by name and tells you the date.
```

This help facility can be used with any M-file available in MATLAB.

The line

```
disp('Hello! Who are you?')
```

displays the string enclosed between quotes. The next line,

```
name = input('Please enter your name enclosed between quotes ');
```

prompts you to write your name as a string and stores your answer in the variable name. The statement d = date; retrieves the current date and stores it in the variable d. The next line,

```
answer = [ 'Hello ' name '. Today is ' d '.'];
```

concatenates the text 'Hello ', the contents of the variable name, the text '. Today is ', the contents of d, and a full stop. The result of the concatenation is assigned to the variable answer and is displayed by the last line in the file. To execute this short program enter the name of the file:

```
>> hello
Hello!  Who are you?
Please enter your name enclosed between quotes
```

If you enter 'Hamlet' you will get

```
Hello Hamlet.   Today is 15-Dec-94.
```

but the date will be, obviously, that of the day you try this program.

1.7.1   Programming a function

We can program our own functions in MATLAB. Like script files, **function files** are also M-files, but the first word (after possible comments) must be function. Function files take external arguments, which are enclosed in parentheses immediately after the function name. For example, to program a function that calculates the hypotenuse of a right-angled triangle, let us write the following code to a file defined as pyt.m:

```
function h = pyt(a, b)
% PYT hypotenuse of a right-angled triangle
%      by Pythagoras' theorem. Input: the sides (legs)
%      of the triangle.

h = sqrt(a.^2 + b.^2);
```

Note the use of the array operations a.^2 and b.^2; they enable the user to input arrays of side (leg) values. After saving the file enter the MATLAB environment and type

```
>> pyt(3, 4)
ans =
     5
```

This is indeed the hypotenuse of the triangle whose sides are 3 and 4.

Function files can accept more than one argument and return more than one output. An example of a function that yields two output values is the `size` function, see Subsection 1.3.2.

1.7.2   Repetitive control structures – FOR loops

Repetitive execution of a statement, or of a block of statements, can be performed in MATLAB in a **FOR loop**. For example, let us write a loop that produces a table of hypotenuses of the triangles whose sides (legs) are equal to one of the first five integers. The resulting table is a 5-by-5 array; we allocate space for it with the command

```
>> P = zeros(5, 5);
```

Next we open the loop with the statement

```
>> for k = 1:5
```

After we press the Enter key, the cursor moves to the next line where it waits for further commands. There is no prompt symbol. For the sake of clarity let us indent the next statements, by means of the tabulator kèy (Tab), and enter them as follows

```
        for l = 1:5
              P(k, l) = pyt(k, l);
        end
end
```

The prompt symbol returns after pressing Enter. To see the table type

```
>> P
P =
     1.4142 2.2361 3.1623 4.1231 5.0990
     2.2361 2.8284 3.6056 4.4721 5.3852
     3.1623 3.6056 4.2426 5.0000 5.8310
     4.1231 4.4721 5.0000 5.6569 6.4031
     5.0990 5.3852 5.8310 6.4031 7.0711
```

The resulting matrix **P** is **symmetric** about its main diagonal; therefore the transpose of **P** is equal to **P**. We can check this with

```
≫ P - P'
ans =
     0 0 0 0 0
     0 0 0 0 0
     0 0 0 0 0
     0 0 0 0 0
     0 0 0 0 0
```

The whole sequence of statements in and around the preceding FOR loop can obviously be written to an M-file.

1.7.3   Conditional control structures

We shall exemplify the use of conditional branching by programming the 'Hi-Lo' game. Write the following listing to a file called `hi_lo.m`.

```
% HI_LO plays the game of the same name.
%      When prompted, enter your guess; the computer
%      will tell you if your guess is above or below
%      the random number calculated by the computer.

x = fix(100*rand);
n = 7;
test = 1;
for k = 1:7
    numb = int2str(n);
    disp([ 'You have a right to ' numb ' guesses' ])
    disp([ 'A guess is a number between 0 and 100'])
    guess = input('Enter your guess ')
    if guess < x
            disp('Low')
    elseif guess > x
            disp('High')
    else
            disp('You won')
            test = 0;
            break
    end
    n = n - 1;
end
if test > 0
    disp('You lost')
end
```

The program again starts with a few lines of comments that help the programmer to remember the purpose of the file, and the user to know how to play the game. As stated above, the comments can be retrieved by typing help hi_lo.

The program begins by 'extracting' a **random number**. The job is done by the rand function which, when invoked as above, outputs a number between 0.0 and 1.0. Called several times within the same MATLAB session, the rand function will produce a sequence of *different* numbers, uniformly distributed in the interval (0.0, 1.0). The random number generated by the program is multiplied by 100 and any decimal digits are dropped by the MATLAB fix function. The result is an integer $0 \leq x \leq 100$.

The maximum number of trials is initialized to $n = 7$, and the current number of the trial is initialized to $i = 1$.

The main part of the program is a FOR loop which is repeated seven times, the maximum number of trials allowed in a play. At each repetition the player is informed of the number of guesses he is still allowed and is prompted to enter a number between 0 and 100. The player's answer is assigned to a variable called guess. The program reacts by displaying 'High' if the guess number is larger than x, and 'Low' if it is smaller. The decision is made by a conditional control structure that has the form

```
if condition
      expressions
elseif condition
      expressions
else
      expressions
end
```

If the guess is exactly the number x, the program displays 'You won' and sets the variable test to zero; execution of the FOR loop is interrupted by the break command. If the guess is not correct, the number n is reduced by 1 and execution of the loop is resumed. After seven unsuccessful guesses a simpler control structure verifies the value of the variable test and, as it is not zero, displays the message 'You lost'.

The beginning of a game may look like

```
≫ hi_lo
You have a right to 7 guesses
A guess is a number between 0 and 100
Enter your guess 50
High
```

The number of trials in the game is limited to seven because, with the correct strategy, it is sufficient for winning. Can you find this strategy?

1.7.4   Repetitive control structures – WHILE loops

Another repetitive control structure is the **WHILE loop**. As an example, let us program a function that performs **integer division**, defined as follows:

Given a dividend, x, and a divisor, y, we are looking for an *integer* quotient, q, and a remainder, r, such that

$$x = qy + r$$

We shall perform this operation in its simplest form, that is, by counting how many times the divisor can be subtracted from the dividend. Write the following listing to a file called divide.m.

```
function [ q, r ] = divide(x, y)
%DIVIDE(X, Y) integer division of x by y.
% The operation is carried out by subtracting
% y from x, until x < y.
% [ q, r ] = divide(x, y) yields the quotient q and
% the remainder r.

q = 0;
c = 1;
k = 1;
if (x == 0)|(x < y)
        q = 0;
        r = x;
end
if y == 0
        error('Division by zero')
end
if x < 0
        x = -x;
        c = -c;
        k = -k;
end
if y < 0
        y = -y;
        c = -c;
end
while x >= y
        x = x - y;
        q = q + 1;
end
q = c*q;
r = k*x;
```

The value of the quotient is initialized to $q = 0$. The algorithm works only between positive numbers; therefore, a coefficient c is initially set to 1 and multiplied by -1, first if x is negative, and second if y is negative. Thus, if necessary, the numbers x and y are converted to positive numbers. At the end of the program c is used to give the quotient its correct sign. Another coefficient, k, is also initialized to 1; it is multiplied by -1 if $x < 0$, and is later used to assign the correct sign to the remainder. Thus the main part of the algorithm is applied to two positive numbers and it is possible to use the whole algorithm with algebraic numbers.

The program checks if x equals zero, or if x is smaller than y. The **relational operator** '==' compares x with y. Another relational operator used immediately afterwards in the program is '<'; it checks if x is smaller than y. Other relational operators provided by MATLAB are '<=', with the meaning *smaller or equal*, '>', meaning *greater than*, '>=', meaning *greater or equal*, and '~=', standing for *not equal*. In conditional structures, if a relation is true, the statements contained between IF and END are executed; if the relation is not true, control is transferred to the statements following END. In a WHILE loop, if the relation acting as the condition is true, the statements within the loop are executed; if not, execution of the loop is stopped.

If x is zero or smaller than y the quotient is set to 0, and the remainder to y. This action is performed after testing a condition that uses the **logical operator** '|'. This operator stands for *or* and here it means that if the relation to its left ($x == 0$) or to its right ($x < y$) is true, or both are true, then the result is 1. Other logical operators provided by MATLAB are '&', meaning *and*, and '~', meaning *not*.

Another conditional structure in the program checks if the divisor, y, equals zero, and if it does execution of the program is stopped and the error message Division by zero is displayed. These actions are carried out by the error function.

The WHILE loop has the form

```
WHILE condition
        expressions
END
```

The expressions between WHILE and END are executed if the condition is fulfilled. After execution the condition is tested again and, if the result is still 'true', the expressions are reiterated. In our example the condition is $x \geq y$. At each execution the value x is substituted by $x - y$, and the value of q is increased by 1. The iterations cease when x becomes smaller than y.

The divide function takes two input arguments, each of which can be either positive or negative; there are, therefore, four possible combinations. Let us try the function in a combination in which both dividend and divisor are positive:

```
>> [ q, r ] = divide(9, 2)
q =
     4
r =
     1
```

Try the other three cases for yourself:

```
≫ [ q, r ] = divide(9, -2)
≫ [ q, r ] = divide(-9, 2)
≫ [ q, r ] = divide(-9, -2)
```

Try also

```
≫ [ q, r ] = divide(0, 2)
≫ [ q, r ] = divide(9, 0)
```

In the program above, we have used relational operators between scalars. Used in this way, relational operators return the value 1 if the relation is true, and 0 if it is not. Used between matrices, relational operators perform element-by-element comparisons and return a matrix with the elements set to 1 where the relation is true, and 0 where it is not.

More about programming in MATLAB can be found in Chapter 7.

1.8   External files and programs

1.8.1   Saving and loading data

In MATLAB there are several ways of saving and loading data; one is by means of the save and load commands. As an example, let us build a table of sine values for angles between zero and 2π, and intervals equal to $\pi/60$. To do this enter

```
≫ x = 0:  pi/60:   2*pi;
≫ y = sin(x);
≫ t = [ x' y' ];
```

Now save the array t in a file called io.mat. To do this use the syntax

```
save <filename.mat> <variable names>
```

Specifying the extension mat produces a **binary** file; in our case

```
≫ save io.mat t
```

Quit MATLAB, start a new MATLAB session and type

```
≫ load io
```

This command **loads** the variables saved above. You may check this fact by typing either who or whos. Now extract the array of angles and the array of sine values:

```
≫ x = t(:, 1);
≫ y = t(:, 2);
```

You can process the loaded data in MATLAB; for instance, you can plot them:

```
≫ plot(x, y)
≫ xlabel('x, rad')
≫ ylabel('y = sin(x)')
```

or you can find the **minimum, maximum** and **mean** values and the **standard deviation**:

```
≫ [ min(y), max(y), mean(y), std(y) ]
ans =
    -1.0000 1.0000 0.0000 0.7071
```

The standard deviation is calculated as in the following expression:

```
≫ sqrt(sum(y.^2)/(length(y)-1))
ans =
   0.7071
```

MATLAB provides many other ways of processing data; some of the more sophisticated are described in Chapter 16, Signal processing. Two simpler operations that roughly approximate numerical integration and differentiation are described in the next subsection. Another way of storing data, and using them when desired, is shown in Subsection 1.8.3.

1.8.2   The CUMSUM and DIFF functions

Applied to a vector y, the cumsum function yields the **cumulative sum** of the elements of y, for example:

```
≫ cumsum([ 1 2 3 4 5 6])
ans =
    1 3 6 10 15 21
```

We can use the cumsum function to calculate a rough approximation of the function

$$\text{inty} = \int_0^y \sin(\tau)\,d\tau$$

by the simplest numerical integration method, that is, **Euler's method**. To do this we multiply the cumulative sum by the *constant* interval that separates the points x. Referring to the example in the preceding subsection, when entering the array x we defined the interval as $\pi/60$. The integral function of the vector y = sin(x) is obtained with

```
>> inty = cumsum(y)*pi/60;
```

Perform this operation and compare the result with the known integral

$$\int_0^{2\pi} \sin(\tau)\,d\tau$$

When applied to a vector $y(x)$, the diff function yields the differences $y_2 - y_1$, $y_3 - y_2$ and so on, for instance

```
>> diff([1 3 5 7 9])
ans =
    2 2 2 2
```

Applying the diff function to the vector y = sin(x) defined in the previous section, and dividing the differences by the interval separating the points x, we obtain the numerical approximation of the derivative of y with respect to x:

```
>> dydx = diff(y)/(pi/60);
```

The result is an array that has one element less than the arrays x and y

```
>> [ size(y), size(dydx) ]
ans =
    1 121 1 120
```

To plot dydx together with y we must add an element; it is dy/dx calculated at the point $x = 0$, that is $d(\sin x)/dx$ at $x = 0$. Type

```
>> dydx = [ 1, dydx ];
```

and plot the sine function, inty and dydx on the same graph:

```
>> plot(x, y, x, inty, x, dydx)
>> grid
>> xlabel('x, rad')
>> gtext('y = sin(x)')
>> gtext('Integral of sin(x)dx')
>> gtext('dy/dx')
```

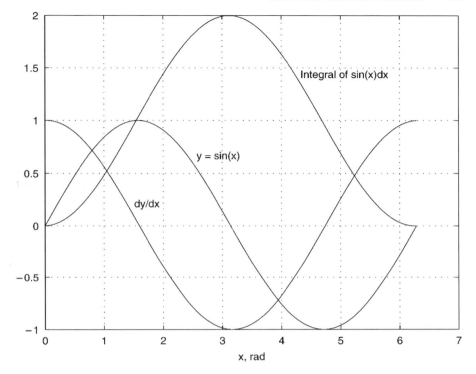

Figure 1.7   The sine function, the integral function and the derivative function.

The function `gtext` produces an arrow or crosshair. Bring it to the position you want in the text and press the mouse button.

The result is shown in Figure 1.7. It is easy to verify visually that when a curve reaches a maximum or a minimum, the curve representing its derivative crosses zero.

More about numerical integration can be found in Chapter 11. Numerical differentiation should be avoided whenever possible because it usually yields results that are not 'smooth'.

1.8.3   Reading data from external files

The commands used at the beginning of Subsection 1.8.1 to create the array `t` can be written to an M-file, let us say `sinfile.m`. In another MATLAB session it is sufficient to type `sinfile` to create the array `t` and use it in that session. Alternatively, you can write the array `t` directly to the file `sinfile`, by means of your favourite editor. Typing `sinfile` loads the array into your workspace and you can use it for further processing. Try these possibilities for yourself. Notice that by proceeding as described in this subsection you will store the data in ASCII, and not in binary format as in Subsection 1.8.1.

Data acquisition systems can store very large arrays in computer files. MATLAB's ability to load and process these data makes possible many important engineering and scientific applications. More about reading data from M-files can be found in Section 8.3.

1.8.4   Issuing commands to the operating system

It is possible to issue commands to the operating system without exiting the MATLAB environment. The commands must be preceded by the exclamation mark '!'. Let us suppose, for example, that we want to write a pyt3 function that extends the pyt function, developed in Subsection 1.7.1, to triangles in three-dimensional space. If our operating system is DOS, we first copy the file pyt.m into a new file pyt3.m

```
>> !copy pyt.m pyt3.m
```

and invoke our editor, for instance KEDIT, to make the required modifications

```
>> !kedit pyt3.m
```

The same operations can be performed under UNIX with the commands

```
!cp pyt.m pyt3.m
!vi pyt3.m
```

Another means of issuing commands to DOS from MATLAB is by using the dos function with string arguments, for example

```
>> dos('kedit pyt3.m')
```

In MATLAB under Windows, the best way of editing an M-file is to click on the first icon on the command window toolbar, for a new file, or on the second icon for an old file.

1.8.5   Writing output to external files

Just as it is possible to read data from external files, it is also possible to write data to external files. As an example, let us enter again the first two commands from Subsection 1.8.1, and create the arrays x and y. We can now output a nice-looking table to an external file by means of the fprintf function. The syntax used in this example is

```
fprintf('filename', 'format', X, Y, Z)
```

Let the name of the external file be sine.out; as we must use it several times, it is convenient to define a shorter form of the filename with

```
>> fn = 'sine.out';
```

To produce the heading of the file type

```
>> fprintf(fn, '          Angle                Sine \n');
>> fprintf(fn, '       degree      radian \n')
>> fprintf(fn, '__ ___ ___ ___ ___ ___ __ ___ _ \n')
```

The character string '\n' means **newline**. The array x contains angle values in radians. To print angle values in degrees as well, enter

```
>> deg = 180*x/pi;
```

We print the values of deg, x and y in a FOR loop:

```
>> for k = 1:  length(x)
fprintf(fn, '%10.5f %10.5f %10.5f\n', deg(k), x(k), y(k));
end
```

If you do not want a verbose screen display, terminate the line beginning with fprintf with a semicolon. The formats in which the data will be printed are specified within a character string. In this example there are three format specifications, corresponding to the three variables enumerated outside the string. The specification %10.5f means fixed point notation, ten-character field width, with five digits after the decimal point. This form of specification is taken from the C language.

We can browse the resulting file without exiting the MATLAB environment:

```
>> !more < sine.out
          Angle                Sine
      degree      radian

__ ___ ___ ___ ___ ___ __ ___ __
  0.00000    0.00000    0.00000
  3.00000    0.05236    0.05234
  ...        ...        ...
360.00000    6.28319   -0.00000
```

Other examples of writing to external files are given in Section 8.6 and in Exercise 8.1.

1.9   Regression and interpolation

1.9.1   Tables with one entry

Let us tabulate the values of

$$y = 2x + 3$$

for $x = 1, 2, \ldots, 10$. We begin by entering the array of coefficients

```
>> c = [ 2 3 ];
```

and the array of independent-variable values

```
>> x = [ 1:10]';
```

The array of y-values is calculated by

```
>> y = polyval(c, x);
```

We produce a table of $x, \ y$ pairs with

```
>> ytable = [ x y ];
ytable =
    1       5
    :       :
   10      23
```

The MATLAB `table1` function interpolates linearly over one-dimensional tables; it is invoked with two arguments: the name of the table, and the independent-variable value for which we want the result. As an example, let us calculate the value of y for $x = 1.5$; we do this with

```
>> yi = table1(ytable, 1.5)
yi =
     6
```

It is easy to check that for the given linear function the result is exact:

```
>> polyval(c, 1.5)
ans =
     6
```

The second argument can be an array. For example,

```
≫ xi = 0.5:  10.5;
```

Try this for yourself. The operation will not succeed because the `table1` function cannot perform extrapolations. Try again with

```
≫ xi = 1.5:  9.5;
```

An engineering application of the `table1` function is shown in Subsection 8.4.1. When linear interpolation is not satisfactory, higher-order interpolations must be used; they are explained in Subsections 1.9.3 and 1.9.4. The `table1` function becomes obsolete, newer interpolating facilities are introduced in Subsections 1.11.1 and 1.11.2.

1.9.2   Tables with two entries

Besides `table1`, MATLAB also provides a function for linear interpolation over tables with two entries. We can regard such a table as a function of two variables, $z(x, y)$. The interpolation (table lookup) is performed by the `table2` function, which must be called with three arguments, for instance `table2(t, xi, yi)`, where t is the name of the table, and `xi, yi` are the entries for which we want to retrieve the value of z.

To exemplify the procedure we turn again to the array P created with the help of the `pyt` function in Subsection 1.7.2. We transform this array into a table by adding first a row containing the y-values 1 to 5, and a column with the x-values 0 to 5. This is done by the following commands:

```
≫ n = 1:5;
≫ T = [ n; P ]
T =
    1.0000 ...  5.0000
    1.4142 ...  5.0990

    ...   ...   ...
    5.0990 ...  7.0711
≫ m = [ 0 n ]';
≫ T = [ m T ]
T =
          0    ...        5.0000
     1.0000    ...        5.0990

     ...     ...        ...
     5.0000    ...        7.0711
```

To find the hypotenuse of a triangle whose sides (legs) are 2.5, 2.5, we enter

```
>> hyp = table2(T, 2.5, 2.5)
hyp =
    3.5705
```

The correct answer is

```
>> pyt(2.5, 2.5)
ans =
    3.5355
```

The error, equal to -0.9902 per cent, is obviously due to the fact that the hypotenuse of a right-angled triangle is not a linear function of its sides.

Check for yourself that the second and third arguments of `table2` can each be an array of numbers. Like `table1`, the `table2` function cannot perform extrapolations. An engineering application of this function is given in Subsection 8.4.2. Also the `table2` function becomes obsolete. Newer interpolating functions are described in Subsections 1.11.1 and 1.11.2.

1.9.3   Polynomial fit and polynomial interpolation

Let us plot the parabola $y = a_1 x^2 + a_2 x + a_3$ that passes through the points $(-1, 0)$, $(0, 2)$, $(1, 6)$. We shall use the MATLAB `polyfit` function which is called with three arguments, for instance `polyfit(x, y, n)`. The result is the array of coefficients of a polynomial of order n that fits the pairs (x, y) in the *least-square* sense.

Returning to our example, we begin the calculations by entering the coordinates of the three desired points

```
>> x = [ -1, 0, 1 ];
>> y = [ 0, 2, 6 ];
```

and continue by invoking the `polyfit` function

```
>> p = polyfit(x, y, 2)
p =
    1.0000 3.0000 2.0000
```

that is, the polynomial $x^2 + 3x + 2$. In this case the solution is exact, because we had precisely the number of points that define the desired polynomial. To check the result we create an array of independent-variable values

```
>> xi = -2: 0.1: 2;
```

and calculate the corresponding dependent-variable values

```
>> yi = polyval(p, xi);
```

We now plot the result as a solid line, and the given three points as asterisks:

```
>> plot(xi, yi, x, y, '*')
>> grid
```

The result is shown in Figure 1.8.

The main use of the polyfit function is in calculating **regressions** over a number of (x, y) pairs that exceeds the number of coefficients of the desired polynomial. To exemplify this procedure let us 'corrupt' the data used above. We use the MATLAB rand function which we call this time with an argument, obtaining thus an array of random numbers uniformly distributed in the interval (0.0, 0.1). The sequence of

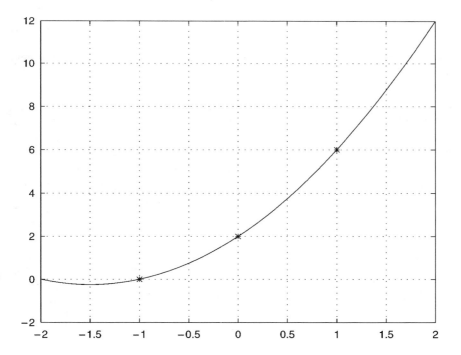

Figure 1.8   Fitting a parabola to a set of points.

calculations is

```
≫ x2 = -2:  2;
≫ y2 = polyval(p, x2) + 2*rand(size(x2));
≫ p2 = polyfit(x2, y2, 2)
p2 =
      1.0319 3.4127 2.9598
```

The random-number generator was called as rand(size((x2)) and it produces an array of the same size as x2. Do not be surprised if the random-number generator will produce other numbers than those in our example.

We see that the coefficients are different from those obtained in the case of the exact solution. Repeating the calculation several times, during the same MATLAB session, will produce different numbers each time because different random numbers will be generated each time. To understand the result better let us plot the resulting polynomial as a solid line, and the given points as '+':

```
≫ y3 = polyval(p2, xi);
≫ plot(xi, y3, x2, y2, '+')
≫ grid
≫ xlabel('x'), ylabel('y')
```

Try the plot for yourself. More about interpolation, regression and their engineering applications can be found in Chapter 9.

1.9.4   Spline interpolation

Cubic spline interpolation is performed by the spline function. If the array y contains values corresponding to the points defined in the array x, and we are interested in the values corresponding to points in the array xi, we obtain them by the command spline(x, y, xi). As an example, let us approximate the hypotenuse of the triangle with both sides (legs) equal to 2.5, by twice performing spline interpolation over the array P calculated in Subsection 1.7.2. The sequence of commands is:

```
≫ x = 1:5;
≫ y = zeros(5, 1);
≫ for k = 1:  5
        y(k) = spline(x, P(k, :), 2.5);
end
≫ y
y =
      2.6913
      3.2007
      3.9049
      4.7170
      5.5902
```

```
≫ yi = spline(x, y, 2.5)
yi =
    3.5345
```

The exact value is

```
≫ ye = pyt(2.5, 2.5)
ye =
    3.5355
```

and the error is now

```
≫ 100*(ye - yi)/ye
ans =
    0.0297
```

much better than in Subsection 1.9.2.

1.10   More about plotting

1.10.1   Function evaluation

Let us suppose that a user-defined function must be evaluated several times, each time for another value or set of values of the independent variable or variables. As an example, let such a function be

$$y = 0.25 + 0.75 \cos x^3$$

(see Example 2.9). A convenient possibility provided by MATLAB consists in entering the function as a character string

```
≫ y = '0.25 + 0.75*(cos(x)).^3';
```

If we want to evaluate and plot this function for the angles 0 to 90 degrees, at 5-degree intervals, we enter

```
≫ angle = 0:  5:  90;
≫ x = pi*angle/180;
≫ z = eval(y);
≫ plot(angle, z)
```

If we later need to plot the same function for angles between −25 and +25 degrees, at one-degree intervals, the commands are

```
≫ angle = -25:   25;
≫ x = pi*angle/180;
≫ z = eval(y);
≫ plot(angle, z)
```

The eval function finds important applications in DO and WHILE loops. An example is given in Section 7.5 where repetitive evaluations of the same function are needed in the iterative solution of equations.

1.10.2   Histograms

Given a one-dimensional array y, the command hist(y) sorts the elements of y into 10 **bins**, according to their numerical value, and draws the histogram that corresponds to the number of elements in each bin (**frequency count**). As an example, let us generate an array of 100 random numbers, *normally* distributed with mean 0 and variance 1, and plot the resulting histogram.

```
≫ y = randn(1, 100);
≫ hist(y)
```

You may try these simple commands for yourself. We prefer to introduce a better version in which the hist function is called with two output arguments: the array of frequency counts, and the array of bin centres. In this case the hist function does not produce a graph; instead we use the bar function. The example begun above is continued with

```
[ n, x ] = hist(y);
S = sum(n);
bar(x, n)
for k = 1:10
        pct = 100*n(k)/S;
        text(x(k), n(k), [ num2str(pct) ' %' ])
end
```

The result is shown in Figure 1.9.

A histogram of engineering data is exemplified in Section 10.2.

1.10.3   Polar plots

Let us suppose that we want to plot a unit-radius arc of 60 degrees. We can certainly use the plot function to obtain the graph in Cartesian coordinates. However, the natural coordinates for such a graph are polar. If we note the magnitude of the radius vector by rho, and its angle to the horizontal by theta, the desired plot is obtained

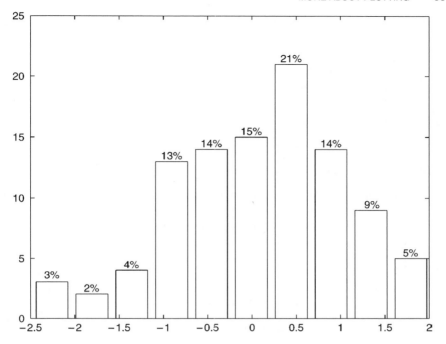

Figure 1.9 A histogram of 100 normal random numbers.

with the following lines

```
≫ a = 60*pi/180;
≫ a1 = (pi - a)/2;
≫ a2 = (pi + a)/2;
≫ theta = a1:  a/60:  a2;
≫ rho = ones(size(theta));
≫ polar(theta, rho, 'r')
```

We can complete the plot to obtain a 60 degrees **sector**. To do this we type hold on to keep the previous plot, and we superimpose on the graph the two sides of the sector:

```
≫ hold on
≫ polar([ a1 a1 ], [ 0 1 ])
≫ polar([ a2 a2 ], [ 0 1 ])
```

If we want to plot the corresponding **segment** of circle, we must first erase the previous graph; we do this with the clf (clear graph) command. Next, we generate the points of the chord and we plot both the arc and the chord by:

```
>> clf
>> rho1 = rho*sin(a1)./sin(theta);
>> polar(theta, rho)
>> hold on
>> polar(theta, rho1)
```

1.10.4   A more elaborate polar plot

For a more elaborate polar plot, write the following to a file called watch.m.

```
% WATCH simulates an analog clock, as an example of a
% polar plot.

clf
hold on
polar(3, 2*pi), axis 'off', axis 'equal'
for n = 0:11
        theta = n*2*pi/12 + pi/2;
        polar([ theta theta ], [ 1.9 2.4 ])
        [ x y ] = pol2cart(theta, 3);
        text(x, y, int2str(12-n))
end
t      = fix(clock);
hour   = rem(t(4), 12);
minute = t(5);
second = t(6);
angle1 = (12-hour)*2*pi/12 + pi/2 - (minute/60)*2*pi/12;
angle2 = (60-minute)*2*pi/60 + pi/2;
angle3 = (60-second)*2*pi/60 + pi/2;
polar([ angle1 angle1 ], [ 0 1.7 ])         % hour hand
polar([ angle2 angle2 ], [ 0 2.4 ])         % minute hand
polar([ angle3 angle3 ], [ 0 2.8 ], 'r')  % minute hand
hold off
```

The clf command clears any existing graph. This enables us to invoke the script file several times during the same MATLAB session. The function pol2cart converts polar to cartesian coordinates. The clock command actually returns an array with six elements:

```
clock = [ year month day hour minute seconds]
```

Writing fix(clock) produces an integer display. Our M-file extracts the values of the hour and the minute.

The `rem` function calculates remainders; invoked as `rem(x, y)`, this function yields $x - yq$, where q is the integer quotient closest to x/y (see Subsection 1.7.4). In this program the `rem` function converts hour values given in the 24-hour system to values in the 12-hour system.

The `hold off` command ensures that subsequent graphs will not be superimposed over the graph produced by the file. Try the file for yourself and you will obtain a display of an analog watch dial showing the time when it was called.

More about polar plots can be found in Section 10.3 and Exercises 10.1 to 10.3.

1.10.5   Three-dimensional plots

The equation

$$-\frac{x^2}{a^2} + \frac{y^2}{b^2} = 2pz \tag{1.7}$$

defines a **hyperbolic paraboloid** (see Figure 1.10). To obtain a three-dimensional graph of this surface we begin by defining the intervals x and y:

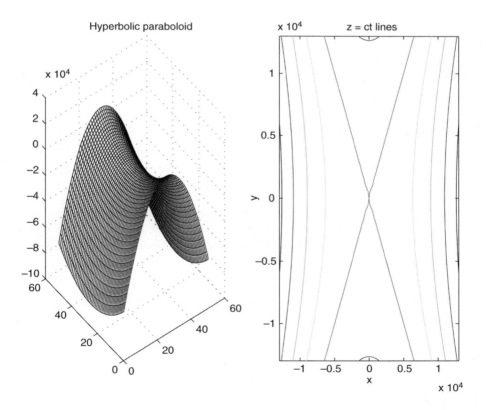

Figure 1.10   A hyperbolic paraboloid.

```
≫ x = -13000:  520:   13000;
≫ y = x;
```

Next we generate two square arrays, X, Y, which define the domain over which we calculate z; we use the meshgrid function for this:

```
≫ [X, Y] = meshgrid(x, y);
```

Continue by typing

```
≫ a = 1; b = 2; p = 1000;
≫ z = (-X.^2/a^2 + Y.^2/b^2)/(2*p);
```

The perspective plot is produced by the mesh function, which we shall use together with subplot:

```
≫ subplot(121), mesh(z)
≫ title('Hyperbolic paraboloid')
```

Contour lines of the surface, that is, lines of constant z, can be obtained with the contour function:

```
≫ subplot(122), contour(x, y, z)
≫ xlabel('x')
≫ ylabel('y')
≫ title('z = ct lines')
```

We can call the mesh function with a second argument, say M = [az el], where az is the **azimuth** and el the **elevation** of the viewing point. The angles are given in degrees. An elevation of 90 is directly overhead; the default values are [-37.5 30]. For example

```
≫ M = [ 0 0 ];
≫ mesh(z,M)
```

shows clearly that the vertical sections are parabolas. Another interesting view is obtained with

```
≫ M = [ 30 -45 ];
```

Another surface can be obtained by simply changing the sign of the term x^2/a^2; this is the **elliptic paraboloid** with the equation

$$\frac{x^2}{a^2} + \frac{y^2}{b^2} = 2pz$$

Try the plot with

```
≫ z = (X.^2/a^2 + Y.^2/b^2)/(2*p);
≫ subplot(1, 2, 1), mesh(z)
≫ subplot(1, 2, 2), contour(x, y, z)
≫ contour(z, x, y)
≫ xlabel('x')
≫ ylabel('y')
```

More about three-dimensional plots can be found in Section 10.4.

1.11   More about interpolation and 3D plots

1.11.1   More interpolating functions

Besides the `table1` and `table2` functions, MATLAB provides the interpolating functions `interp1`, `interp2` and `griddata`. Given an array of values $y(x)$, corresponding to an array of **monotonic** values x, by typing

```
≫ interp1(x, y, xi, 'method')
```

we find the values of y corresponding to the points defined in xi, calculated by the procedure `method`. Thus it is no longer necessary to build a table [x' y'], as required by the `table1` function. Let us return to the example of the array P generated in Section 1.7.2 and show how we use two interpolations to find the value corresponding to the point 2.5, 2.5. The calculations for **linear** interpolation are

```
≫ x = 1:5;
≫ y = pyt(2.5, x)
y =
    2.6926 3.2016 3.9051 4.7170 5.5902
≫ y1 = interp1(x, y, 2.5)
y1 =
    3.5533
```

This is the same as

```
≫ y1 = interp1(x, y, 2.5, 'linear')
y1 =
    3.5533
```

The exact value is given by

```
≫ y0 = pyt(2.5, 2.5)
y0 =
    3.5355
```

so that the error in per cent is

```
≫ e1 = 100*(y0 - y1)/y0
e1 =
    -0.5037
```

A better approximation is obtained with **spline** interpolation:

```
≫ y2 = interp1(x, y, 2.5, 'spline')
y2 =
    3.5350
```

corresponding to an error in per cent equal to

```
≫ e2 = 100*(y0 - y2)/y0
e2 =
    0.0143
```

The third 'method' is **cubic** interpolation and it is performed with

```
≫ y3 = interp1(x, y, 2.5, 'cubic')
y3 =
    3.5344
```

This time the error, in per cent, is

```
≫ e3 = 100*(y0 - y3)/y0
```

```
e3 =
    0.0317
```

The function for interpolation over a table with two entries is `interp2`. For the same example of interpolation over P, having defined the array x (see Subsection 1.7.2), we can proceed in one step with

```
≫ y = x;
≫ PI = interp2(x, y, P, 2.5, 2.5)
PI =
    3.5705
```

The error, in per cent, equals

```
≫ error = 100*(y0 - PI)/P0
error =
   -0.9902
```

Cubic interpolation is performed with

```
≫ PI = interp2(x, y, P, 2.5, 2.5, 'cubic')
PI =
    3.5332
```

The error is

```
≫ e2 = 100*(y0 - PI)/y0
e2 =
    0.0654
```

1.11.2 The GRIDDATA function and 3D plots

The third function, `griddata`, allows more sophisticated processing. We shall use it on the array P. In order to make the example self-contained, we define the arrays x, y again:

```
≫ x = 1:5; y = 1:5;
```

Next we define the points at which we want the values of the hypotenuse, let us say at intervals equal to 0.1:

```
>> xi = 1:  0.1:  5; yi = 1:  0.1:  5;
```

We now form two square arrays with the help of the meshgrid function.

```
>> [ XI YI ] = meshgrid(xi, yi);
```

and call the interpolating function as

```
>> PI = griddata(x, y, P, XI, YI);
```

A first three-dimensional 'mesh' plot is obtained with the mesh function:

```
>> mesh(PI)
```

It is possible to show the axes, if the function is called with three arguments:

```
>> mesh(XI, YI, PI)
>> xlabel('leg')
>> ylabel('leg')
>> zlabel('hypotenuse')
```

We can store the graph in a PostScript file, named pytagrid.ps, with the command

```
>> print -dps pytagrid.ps
```

The last command produces a PostScript file. To send this file to the printer, use the relevant command for the operating system under which you work. The result is shown in Figure 1.11.

A coloured, 'surface' plot is obtained with the surf function:

```
>> surf(XI, YI, PI)
>> xlabel('leg')
>> ylabel('leg')
>> zlabel('hypotenuse')
>> print pytasurf
```

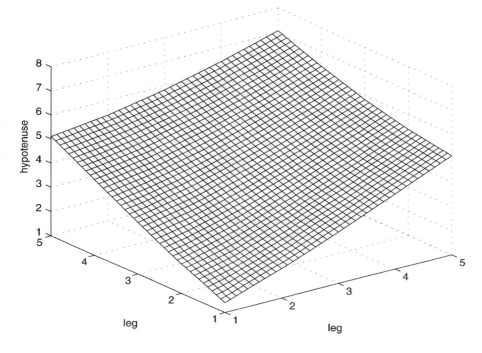

Figure 1.11   Plot obtained with the `mesh` function.

The resulting plot is shown in Figure 1.12 overleaf.

The `surfc` function produces the same plot and also adds the projections of the contour lines on the xOy plane:

```
≫ surfc(XI, YI, PI)
≫ xlabel('leg')
≫ ylabel('leg')
≫ zlabel('hypotenuse')
≫ print pytasurc
```

The graph is shown in Figure 1.13.

1.11.3   The plot of a 3D line

The `plot3` function produces three-dimensional plots of points and lines. As an example, let us plot the edges of a pyramid with the corners of the base at $(-b, b)$, (b, b), $(b, -b)$ and $(-b, -b)$, and the height H. We define two edges as the broken line passing through the points with the coordinates given in two arrays, `x1`, `y1`, and two other edges passing through the points defined in another two arrays, `x2`, `x3`.

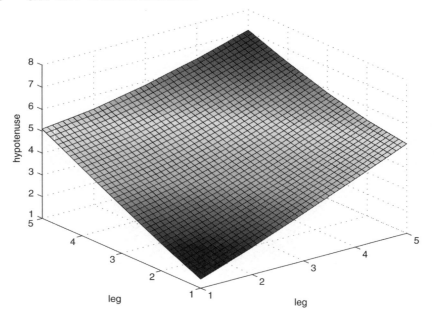

Figure 1.12 Three-dimensional plot obtained with the `surf` function.

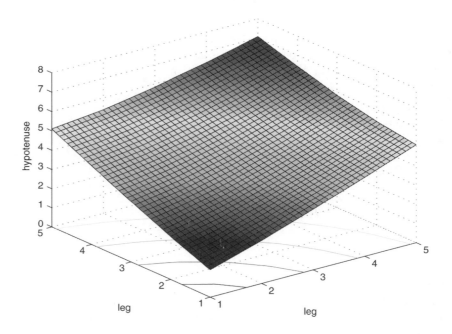

Figure 1.13 Three-dimensional plot obtained with the `surfc` function.

The base is defined as a broken line passing through the points with the coordinates in two arrays x3, y3. The commands are:

```
≫ H = 5; b = 2;
≫ x1 = [ -b, 0, b ];
≫ y1 = [ b, 0, -b ]; z1 = [ 0, H, 0 ];
≫ x2 = [ -b, 0, b ]; y2 = [ -b, 0, b ]; z2 = [ 0, H, 0];
≫ x3 = [ -b, b, b, -b, -b ]; y3 = [ b, b, -b, -b, b ];
≫ z3 = zeros(size(x3));
≫ plot3(x1, y1, z1, '-', x2, y2, z2, '-', x3, y3, z3, '-')
≫ print pyramid
```

The plot is shown in Figure 1.14.

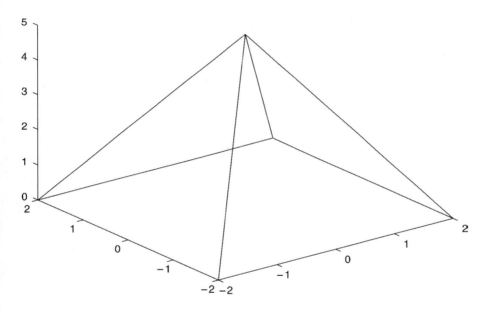

Figure 1.14 Plot of a pyramid.

— PART I —

MATLAB –
An Introduction for Engineers

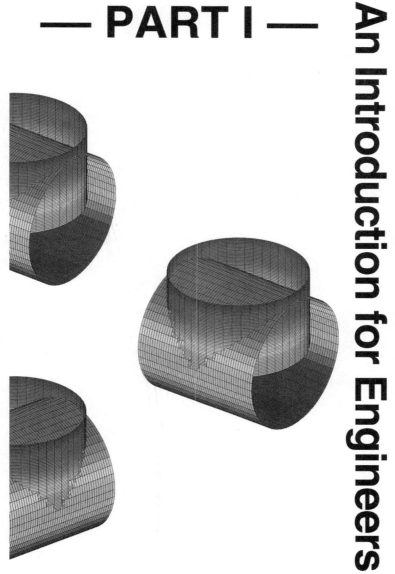

Chapter 2
Desktop calculations with graphics

2.1   Introduction

This chapter continues from the point where Section 1.2 stops. Chapter 1 is a quick guide to MATLAB in which the material is illustrated by simple mathematical examples. Chapter 1 contains no engineering applications and it is assumed that the reader is familiar with the concepts described therein. Chapters 2 to 10 contain a detailed and engineering-oriented introduction to MATLAB, with examples taken mainly from real-life engineering. Some of the mathematical notions involved are introduced in simple terms in the main body of the chapters, or are summarized at the end of the corresponding chapters. More engineering applications can be found in Part II of the book, that is, Chapters 11 to 17.

2.2   Computer-aided mistakes

As computers have entered all fields of science and technology, even invading our private lives, a new mythology has arisen around them. There are people who think that the computer can solve any problem. There are people, and not only laymen

75

among them, who regard the computer as an infallible tool. On the other hand, there are also those who find the computer a convenient scapegoat. Did you make a mistake and someone else found it? Put the blame on the computer; the machine will not defend itself against the accusation.

Probably most 'computer errors' are user errors. The computer works according to the **GIGO** principle: garbage in, garbage out. You feed the computer with wrong data, you get wrong answers. There are also errors due to bad programming. Some of them may be caused by writing computer functions and commands incorrectly; we call them **syntax errors**. Fortunately, the computer objects to most of them by returning **error messages**. Other errors are due to wrong calculations; we call them **logic errors** or, popularly, **bugs**.

There is a further source of errors and it is this that we want to discuss in the following sections: the way in which numbers are represented in the computer. A simple example will help us to introduce the subject. We know that $1 - 5 \times 0.2 = 0$; try, however, the following:

```
>> format long, 1 - 0.2 - 0.2 - 0.2 - 0.2 - 0.2
ans =
     5.551115123125783e-017
```

The result is a very small number, but not exactly zero. For the moment it is sufficient to say that the error is due to the fact that the computer works in the **binary system** of numeration and that the binary representation of 0.2 requires an infinite number of digits. As the computer can store only a finite number of digits, it uses an approximation of the number 0.2 and five times this approximation does not equal exactly 1. Such errors can be very small; however, they can prove disastrous if they are accumulated over long sequences of calculations. Not taking account of the properties of computer numbers can cause the failure of a very costly project, for instance by letting a spacecraft enter the wrong orbit, or may lead to the loss of many lives, for example if a Patriot missile meets a Scud too late.

2.3   Computer representation of numbers

In everyday life we work with numbers represented in the **decimal system**. In this system the value of each digit depends upon its position relative to the decimal point; for example, the meaning of 124.32 is

$$1 \times 10^2 + 2 \times 10^1 + 4 \times 10^0 + 3 \times 10^{-1} + 2 \times 10^{-2}$$

We say that the above number is represented in **fixed point format**. In MATLAB displays the default representation is in fixed point format with four decimal places. We are also familiar with **scientific notation** in which the number 124.32 is represented as 1.2432×10^2. Today computers work with an adaptation of the scientific format called **floating-point representation**; in MATLAB we obtain it with

```
>> format short e, x = 124.32
x =
    1.2432e+002
```

We can return to fixed point notation by

```
>> format short, x
x =
    124.3200
```

To obtain more digits use

```
>> format long, x
x =
    1.243200000000000e+002
```

or

```
>> format long e, x
x =
    1.243200000000000e+002
```

Computers use the floating-point representation, but not the decimal system. Most computers use the **binary system**; some, among them IBM mainframe computers, use the **hexadecimal system**. In the binary system there are only two digits, 0 and 1. As in the decimal system, the value of each digit depends upon its position relative to the decimal point – perhaps it would be better to call it **fractional point** – but it multiplies powers of 2. For example, the meaning of the binary number 101.101 is

$$1 \times 2^2 + 0 \times 2^1 + 1 \times 2^0 + 1 \times 2^{-1} + 0 \times 2^{-2} + 1 \times 2^{-3}$$

The main reason for using binary numbers is that they can be put in correspondence with the *on* and *off* states of physical components; for example 1 for a closed circuit and 0 for an open circuit. Another example: 1 for 'magnetized', 0 for 'demagnetized'.

Putting things together, numbers are represented in the computer in the form $\sigma m b^e$ where σ is the sign, that is, $+$ or $-$, m, the fractional part, or **mantissa**, b the **base** of the number system, and e the **exponent**. The number of digits in m and b is hardware dependent.

In 1985 the Institute of Electrical and Electronics Engineers – an American institute mostly known as IEEE – issued an *IEEE Standard for Binary Floating-Point Arithmetic* (see Bibliography, ANSI/IEEE Std 754-1985). The standard is fully implemented on many computers, partially on a few others. An example of a computer that does not use IEEE arithmetic is DEC's VAX. In the IEEE double-precision standard there are 53 binary digits in the mantissa, and 11 binary digits in the exponent. It is possible to check if the computer works in IEEE arithmetic:

```
≫ isieee
ans =
     1
```

If the answer is 1, the computer uses IEEE arithmetic. Another two MATLAB functions, `realmax` and `realmin`, allow us to find the largest and the smallest number, respectively, that can be stored in the computer. For a computer using the IEEE standard the result of invoking these functions is

```
≫ realmax
ans =
     1.7977e+308
≫ realmin
ans =
     2.2251e-308
```

An indication of the floating-point accuracy of the standard is given by the MATLAB variable eps; as set initially it corresponds to the distance from 1.0 to the next largest floating point number. The following command retrieves eps

```
≫ eps
   eps =
   2.2204e-016
```

This value is also hardware dependent. The value of eps can be changed by the user; in that case eps no longer has the meaning described above.

We can now explain why the computer did not reach zero when subtracting 0.2 from 1 five times. The reason is that the binary number corresponding to the decimal fraction 0.2 is

$$0.00110011001100\ldots \tag{2.1}$$

This representation requires an infinite number of digits. The consequence is that the computer works with an approximate value of 0.2. Subtracting the approximate value of 0.2 from 1 five times does not yield exactly 0.

The computer usage of binary numbers can lead to other unexpected results; as an example, in Chapter 7 we shall illustrate a WHILE loop that does not terminate. Converting back from rounded binary representation to decimal representation can introduce other errors. To illustrate this let us convert the binary number shown in Equation 2.1 back to decimal:

```
>> format long
>> a = 1/2^3 + 1/2^4 + 1/2^7 + 1/2^8 + 1/2^11 + 1/2^12
a =
     0.19995117187500
```

2.4 Roundoff

Arithmetic operations can yield results with many decimal digits. For example, knowing the diameter of a circle, $d = 1.2866$, and using the approximation $\pi = 3.1416$, the circumference is

$$\pi d = 3.1416 \times 1.2866 = 4.04198256 \tag{2.2}$$

that is, a number with eight decimal digits. We get even more digits if we want to find the area of the circle by

$$\frac{\pi d^2}{4} = \frac{3.1416 \times 1.2866^2}{4} = 1.30010369042400$$

Actually, π has an infinite number of digits, and so have numbers resulting from such simple operations as $1/3$, $1/9$, or $\sqrt{2}$. When performing numerical calculations we can deal only with finite numbers of decimal digits. For obvious reasons of convenience, the number of digits considered in manual calculations is small, for example $\pi \approx 3.1416$, more often $\pi \approx 3.14$. Computers can deal with more digital digits, but still with finite numbers of them. Take for instance the number π; the approximation displayed by MATLAB, in the long format, is

$$\pi \approx 3.14159265358979$$

To use an approximation with four decimal digits we could drop all digits to the right of the fourth and retain 3.1415. This is called **chopping**. It can be shown that chopping leads to gross errors which, when accumulated in a long sequence of calculations, can yield catastrophically erroneous results. To minimize errors, most computers use **roundoff** instead of chopping, for example $\pi = 3.1416$ instead of 3.1415.

Rounding rules employed in computers are the same as in manual calculations. The simplest rounding rule is:

For rounding a number to n digits, add half the base, that is, $b/2$, to the digit in position $(n + 1)$ and discard all digits to the right of position n.

In the decimal system the rule for rounding to n digits becomes: if the $(n + 1)$ digit is less than 5 the n-th digit does not change, and if it is 5 or more, the n-th digit is increased by one. Examples in MATLAB are:

```
>> 1/9, 2.2222222222222222/4, 2/3, -2/3
ans =
     0.1111
ans =
     0.5556
ans =
     0.6667
ans =
    -0.6667
```

The reader is invited to repeat the same examples in the long format.

2.5   Roundoff errors

Rounding off a number to n decimal places, following the rule described in the preceding section, produces an error whose absolute value is not larger than $b/2 \times b^{-n}$. Thus, the absolute value of the error in the approximation $\pi = 3.1416$ is not larger than $\rho = 0.5 \times 10^{-4}$. In fact, assuming that the MATLAB value of π is correct, the error is

```
>> E = pi - 3.1416
E =
    -7.3464e-006
```

The error is indeed smaller than the error bound shown above. We used here the definition

$$error = true\ value - calculated\ value$$

Some authors call this **absolute error**; others use the qualifier **absolute** for the absolute value of the error defined above. It makes sense to compare the error, or the absolute error, to the true value of the affected number. To do this we calculate the **relative error**, that is

$$relative\ error = error/(true\ value)$$

or

$$absolute\ relative\ error = (absolute\ error)/(true\ value)$$

In our example we calculate the relative error with

```
≫ E/pi
ans =
    -2.3384e-006
```

Frequently the relative error is expressed in per cent, in our case

```
≫ 100*E/pi
ans =
    -2.3384e-004
```

It can be easily shown that the absolute error of a sum or difference of two numbers is at most equal to the sum of the error bounds of the two numbers. Consider two numbers rounded to n decimal places; the absolute error in their sum or difference is not larger than

$$0.5 * 10^{-n} + 0.5 * 10^{-n} = 10^{-n}$$

When analysing products or quotients it is the relative error that counts. It can be shown that the absolute relative error of the product or quotient of two numbers is not larger than the sum of their relative error bounds. Consider again the example in Equation 2.2:

$$\pi d = 3.1416 \times 1.2866 = 4.04198256$$

or, in MATLAB:

```
≫ format long, circum = 3.1416*1.2866
circum =
    4.04198256
```

In format short the relative error bounds of the two factors are

```
≫ E1 = 0.5*10^(-4)/3.1416
E1 =
    1.5915e-005
≫ E2 = 0.5*10^(-4)/1.2866
E2 =
    3.8862e-005
```

The relative error bound of the product is given by E1 + E2 and the error bound by

```
≫ (E1 + E2)*circum
ans =
     2.2141e-004
```

It follows that only the first three digits of the product are reliable, and the others must be discarded.

A particularly bad error is produced by **cancellation**; it occurs in the addition of two numbers that are nearly equal, but have different signs. Enter, for example, the following numbers:

```
≫ format long e
≫ b = 0.543210987654321*10^2
b =
     5.432109876543210e+001
≫ c = -0.543210987650001*10^2
     c = -5.432109876500009e+001
```

Now try the addition

```
≫ d = b + c
d =
     4.320028779147833e-010
```

The true result is 4.3199×10^{-10}. The digits common to b and c cancelled themselves. The two numbers b, c, have 16 significant digits; the result only 5. The digits beginning in the fifth decimal place of d were 'fabricated' by the computer. The following simple analysis shows that they must be discarded. The maximum error expected in the numbers b, c is 0.5×10^{-15}, that of the result is 10^{-15}. The conclusion is that the digit 5, in the fifth place of the floating-point representation, and those following are unreliable. The relative-error bounds are

```
≫ 0.5*10^(-15)/b
ans =
     9.2045e-018
≫ 0.5*10^(-15)/c
ans =
    -9.2045e-018
≫ 10^(-15)/d
ans =
     2.3148e-006
```

The relative-error bound of the result is larger by 12 orders of magnitude than those of the numbers b and c.

2.6   The set of machine numbers

The preceding sections show that the set of numbers which can be represented on the computer is finite. Let us denote this set by M. Machine numbers are not evenly distributed; it can be shown that the distance between two consecutive machine numbers is smaller in the vicinity of zero.

The computer can only accept data that belong to the set M. Any other number must be approximated to the nearest number in M. Less evident is the fact that operations on numbers belonging to M may yield a result that is not in M. In such cases the computer approximates the result to the nearest machine number.

Depending on the arithmetic of the computer, and the software, certain properties of real numbers do not hold within the set M. We are going to show this in a few examples run in MATLAB, on a computer using IEEE arithmetic. Let us enter the following numbers:

```
≫ format long e, a = 0.123456789012345*10^(-4)
a =
      1.234567890123450e-005
≫ b = 0.543210987654321*10^2
b =
      5.432109876543210e+001
≫ c = -0.543210987650001*10^2
c =
     -5.432109876500009e+001
```

To show that commutativity is not fulfilled, try

```
≫ d = a + b + c
d =
      1.234611090411242e-005
≫ e = c + b + a
e =
      1.234611090411242e-005
≫ d - e
ans =
      2.834290826125505e-015
```

The following calculation shows that the law of associativity is not fulfilled:

```
≫ d = (a + b) + c
d =
```

```
      1.234611090411242e-005
≫ e = a + (b + c)
e =
      1.234611090411242e-005
≫ d - e
ans =
      2.834290826125505e-015
```

Finally, distributivity is checked with

```
≫ d = a*(b + c)
d =
      5.333368815145124e-015
≫ e = a*b + a*c
e =
      5.333298906673445e-015
≫ d - e
ans =
      2.220446049250313e-016
```

If $a + \epsilon = a$, we usually conclude that $\epsilon = 0$. This may be not true within the set of machine numbers, for example:

```
≫ format long, eps
eps =
      2.220446049250313e-016
≫ 1 + eps
ans =
      1.00000000000000
```

We are not going to pursue here the discussion of computer errors. Throughout the book, whenever necessary, we shall point to potential sources of errors. The reader interested in this subject should refer to books on numerical analysis, for example Hartley and Wynn-Evans (1979), Hultquist (1988), Rice (1993), or Gerald and Wheatley (1994).

In the preceding sections we wanted to warn the reader that the computer is not omnipotent and that there are pitfalls that should be avoided. We now want to conclude this discussion by reassuring the user that careful programming can lead to good results. It is also worth mentioning that MATLAB – combined with IEEE arithmetic – is much more efficient in minimizing numerical errors than some older software. We calculated in MATLAB a few problems quoted in books of numerical analysis as examples in which the computer gives wrong results; MATLAB yielded the correct ones!

One final note. The results shown above were obtained in MATLAB 5.2, on a PC provided with a Pentium processor; the last digits differ sometimes from those obtained in MATLAB 4.2, with a 486 PC. In other configurations the reader can obtain slightly different results.

2.7   Vectors

We are familiar with the notion of vectors as directed line segments. Let us begin with vectors in the plane. Thus, **F** in Figure 2.1 may represent a force, a displacement, a velocity or an acceleration (commonly, we would use **F** for forces, and other letters for displacements, velocities or accelerations). Arrays can be used as the simplest way of representing vectors. For example, the vector **F** in Figure 2.1 can be decomposed into two orthogonal components, **F**$_x$ and **F**$_y$, and MATLAB allows us to define it by an array whose elements are the above components

```
>> F = [ Fx Fy ]
```

As shown in Figure 2.2, the sum of two vectors, $\mathbf{P} = [P_x \, P_y]$ and $\mathbf{Q} = [Q_x \, Q_y]$, is a vector $\mathbf{R} = [R_x \, R_y]$ such that

$$\mathbf{R}_x = \mathbf{P}_x + \mathbf{Q}_x$$
$$\mathbf{R}_y = \mathbf{P}_y + \mathbf{Q}_y$$

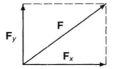

Figure 2.1   The vector **F** and its components, **F**$_x$ and **F**$_y$.

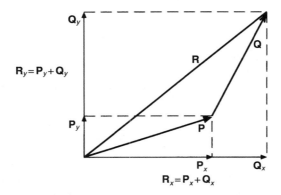

Figure 2.2   Vector addition.

As an exercise, enter

```
≫ P = [ 6 2 ];
≫ Q = [ 2.3 5 ];
≫ R = P + Q
R =
     8.3000 7.0000
```

Sums of vectors can have physical significance. For example, if several forces act on a point of a rigid body, they can be replaced by their sum, in this case called the **resultant**. If an aeroplane flies in wind, its true velocity – that is, the velocity relative to the ground – is the sum of its velocity relative to air and the wind velocity. Other examples come from electrical engineering: the sums of voltages and currents represented as vectors.

The **magnitude** of the vector **R** is given by Pythagoras' theorem (Greek, 6th century BC):

```
≫ magn_R = sqrt(R(1)^2 + R(2)^2)
```

with the result 10.8577. If the vector is a velocity, its magnitude is the **speed**.

The angle between the horizontal and the vector **F** is obtained with

```
≫ angle_R = atan2(R(2), R(1))
```

which yields 0.7006 radians, that is, 40.1434 degrees. If you want to recover the horizontal component of **R** type

```
≫ R(1)
```

and similarly for the vertical component.

As shown in Figure 2.3, the multiplication of a vector **F** by a scalar λ results in a vector whose components are the components of **F** multiplied by λ; try, for example,

```
≫ 2*F3, 3*F3, 4*F3
```

and check the results.

We may readily generalize from two-dimensional to three-dimensional vectors because the real world we are living in is three-dimensional. The term **vector** is often generalized to describe arrays; it will sometimes be used in this way in this book.

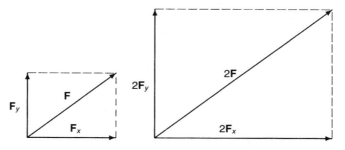

Figure 2.3   Multiplication of a vector by a scalar.

2.8   Column vectors

In Section 1.2.1 we defined arrays by writing their elements in one row. In the previous section we discussed vectors represented by such arrays; they are called **row vectors**. 'Vertical' arrays were introduced in Subsection 1.2.3; an example is

```
≫ B = [ 7
2
4
6.9
10 ];
```

Important engineering applications in which such structures arise are those in which the elements of the array are measurements transferred to a computer file by a data-acquisition system. In linear algebra vertical arrays are used in the notation of systems of linear equations (see Chapter 6). Further, 'vertical' arrays like B are also used to represent the components of other kinds of vectors than those mentioned in the previous section. Consider, first, any example of a row vector; all its components are of the same nature. For instance, the components of a displacement vector are all displacements; the components of a velocity vector are all velocities. In order to fully exploit the possibilities provided by calculating with vectors (and, as we shall see later, with matrices) it is convenient to accept also vectors whose components are of different natures. Thus, it is usual to consider the speed and the acceleration of a material point as the components of the state vector of that point:

$$\begin{bmatrix} x \\ \dot{x} \end{bmatrix}$$

where x is the speed.

Another example comes from strength, when analysing the bending of an elastic beam. Then, the deflection, slope, shear force and bending moment in a given section of the beam are considered as the elements of a state vector characterizing that section. Vectors represented by 'vertical' arrays are appropriately called **column vectors**.

To build a column vector, proceed as shown for vertical arrays, in Subsection 1.2.3. Row vectors can be converted to column vectors, and vice versa, by transposition, as shown in the same Subsection 1.2.3. Vectors of complex numbers have two different transposes, as explained in Subsection 1.4.6.

2.9   A spreadsheet

Let us assume that we would like to purchase a number of objects, as shown in Table 2.1. How much must we pay? This is certainly a good job for a spreadsheet. MATLAB can also solve it quickly. For this we should set up two vectors:

```
≫ price = [ 3.00 1.99 10.99 9.15 1.29 ];
≫ quantity = [ 3 2 1 5 2 ];
```

We can find the costs per item by using the **array product**

```
≫ subtotals = price.*quantity
subtotals =
    9.0000 3.9800 10.9900 45.7500 2.5800
```

Note the use of a point followed by the multiplication sign, that is, '.*'.

The total cost can be obtained by means of the MATLAB sum function which, when applied to a vector, yields the sum of its components:

```
≫ total = sum(subtotals)
total =
    72.3000
```

Table 2.1   A shopping list.

Item no.	Price	Quantity	Subtotals
1	3.00	3	9.00
2	1.99	2	3.98
3	10.99	1	10.99
4	9.15	5	45.75
5	1.29	2	2.58
Totals	–	13	72.30

By using the same function we can also obtain the total number of objects purchased:

```
>> tot_quantity = sum(quantity)
tot_quantity =
    13
```

We can now complete Table 2.1. The main result is the total cost and we obtained it by two operations: an array product and the sum function. In MATLAB, however, we can obtain the same result in one step by

```
>> total = price*quantity'
total =
    72.3000
```

Here we have multiplied the row array `price` by the transpose of the array `quantity`, that is, by a vertical array. In other applications this operation is called the **scalar product** and it amounts to

$$total = 3.00 \times 3 + 1.99 \times 2 + 10.99 \times 1 + 9.15 \times 5 + 1.29 \times 2$$

The scalar product has important geometric and mechanical significance; some examples are given below.

2.10 Geometrical significance of the scalar product

The **scalar product** – also called **dot** or **inner product** – of two vectors, $\mathbf{A} = (a_1, a_2)$, $\mathbf{B} = (b_1, b_2)$, is defined by

$$\mathbf{A} \cdot \mathbf{B} = a_1 b_1 + a_2 b_2 \tag{2.3}$$

It is easy to show (see Example 2.2 and, for instance, Fuller and Tarwater 1992, Section 10.3; Pedoe 1988; or Akivis and Goldberg 1972, page 12) that

$$\mathbf{A} \cdot \mathbf{B} = |\mathbf{A}||\mathbf{B}| \cos \theta , \tag{2.4}$$

where $|\mathbf{A}|$ is the magnitude of the vector $\mathbf{A}$, $|\mathbf{B}|$, that of the vector $\mathbf{B}$, and θ, the angle between the two vectors.

In MATLAB we calculate the scalar product of two row vectors, $\mathbf{A}$ and $\mathbf{B}$, by multiplying $\mathbf{A}$ by the transpose of $\mathbf{B}$, that is

```
>> inner_product = A*B'
```

or by multiplying $\mathbf{B}$ by the transpose of $\mathbf{A}$:

```
>> inner_product = B*A'
```

The commutativity of the scalar product results from its definition. The reason for multiplying one vector, $\mathbf{A}$, by the transpose of another vector, $\mathbf{B}$, and not simply multiplying $\mathbf{A}$ by $\mathbf{B}$, is evident to those familiar with the elements of linear algebra. For others, things will become clearer after reading the next chapter. As an example, let us calculate the scalar product of $\mathbf{A} = (2, 3)$, $\mathbf{B} = (5, 4)$; it is

$$\mathbf{A} \cdot \mathbf{B} = 2 \times 5 + 3 \times 4 = 22 \tag{2.5}$$

In MATLAB we obtain this product by writing

```
>> A = [ 2 3 ];
>> B = [ 5 4 ];
>> A*B'
```

Verify that you obtain the same result by entering

```
>> B*A'
```

A detailed scheme of the calculation is

$$\mathbf{A} \cdot \mathbf{B} = \begin{bmatrix} 2 & 3 \end{bmatrix} \begin{bmatrix} 5 \\ 4 \end{bmatrix} = 22 \tag{2.6}$$

What about the scalar product of two column vectors, for example the scalar product of $\mathbf{At} = \mathbf{A}'$ and $\mathbf{Bt} = \mathbf{B}'$? In order to reach the same scheme as in Equation 2.6 we shall calculate the product by entering At'*Bt. As mentioned, the full rule will be given in the next chapter.

From Equations 2.3 and 2.4 we see that the magnitude of a vector equals the square root of the scalar product of the vector multiplied by itself. Then, from Equation 2.4, the angle between the two vectors $\mathbf{A}$ and $\mathbf{B}$ defined above can be obtained by

```
>> theta = acos(A*B'/(sqrt(A*A')*(sqrt(B*B'))))
```

with the result 0.3081 radians.

The extension to vectors in three-dimensional space is obvious, and for $\mathbf{C} = (c_1, c_2, c_3)$, $\mathbf{D} = (d_1, d_2, d_3)$, the scalar product is

$$\mathbf{C} \cdot \mathbf{D} = c_1 d_2 + c_2 d_2 + c_3 d_3 = |\mathbf{C}||\mathbf{D}| \cos \theta \tag{2.7}$$

where $|\mathbf{C}|$ is the magnitude of $\mathbf{C}$, $|\mathbf{D}|$, that of $\mathbf{D}$, and θ the angle between the two vectors (Pedoe 1988, page 132). As a three-dimensional example let $\mathbf{C} = (2, 2, 2)$ and $\mathbf{D} = (3, 4, 5)$. In MATLAB we calculate

```
≫ C = [ 2 2 2 ];
≫ D = [ 3 4 5 ];
≫ theta = acos(C*D'/(sqrt(C*C')*sqrt(D*D')))
```

the result being 0.2014 radians, that is 11.5370 degrees. Verify that you can equally well write D*C' instead of C*D'.

Can you find other uses of the scalar product? What could be the meaning of the scalar product of vectors having more than three components? More applications of the scalar product can be found towards the end of this chapter.

2.11   Graphical solution of equations

Equations in which the unknown appears as the argument of a transcendental function, such as an exponential function, a logarithm or a trigonometric function, are called **transcendental equations**. A few simple examples are

$$
\begin{aligned}
e^x + x &= 0 \\
\ln x + x &= 0 \\
\sin x + \cos x &= 0
\end{aligned}
$$

Engineering problems often lead to transcendental equations that defy analytical solutions. Sometimes it may even be impossible to formulate an equation and all that can be done is to calculate points on a curve and approximate the point where it crosses zero, or calculate points on two curves and look for their intersection. The MATLAB tools we have learnt so far enable us easily to find graphic solutions of transcendental equations, or of problems that can be defined only numerically.

As an example of a problem leading to a transcendental equation let us consider the segment of circle shown in Figure 2.4. Given the radius of the circle, $r = \overline{OA} = \overline{OB}$, and the angle at centre, $\Phi = \widehat{AOB}$, we calculate the area of the segment enclosed by the arc ACB and the chord AB by

$$A = \frac{r^2}{2}(\Phi - \sin \Phi) \tag{2.8}$$

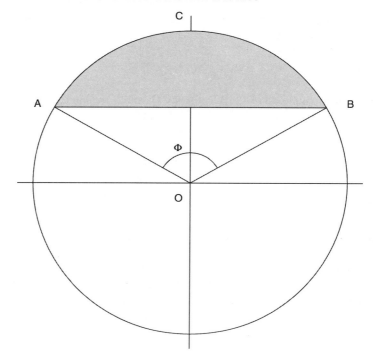

Figure 2.4   A segment of circle.

Let us assume that, given the area A and the radius r, we are looking for a general method of finding the angle Φ. A good practice is to divide both sides of Equation 2.8 by r^2. Then each side has no dimensions in the sense explained in Chapter 13:

$$\frac{A}{r^2} = \frac{\Phi - \sin \Phi}{2} \tag{2.9}$$

To obtain all the solutions of Equation 2.9 graphically, enter the following sequence of commands:

```
>> phi = 0:  pi/180:  2*pi;
>> x = 180*phi/pi;
>> y = (phi - sin(phi))/2;
>> plot(x, y), grid
>> xlabel('Angle at centre, \phi, degrees')
>> ylabel('A/r^2')
```

Above, \phi is a LaTeX command that prints the Greek letter ϕ.

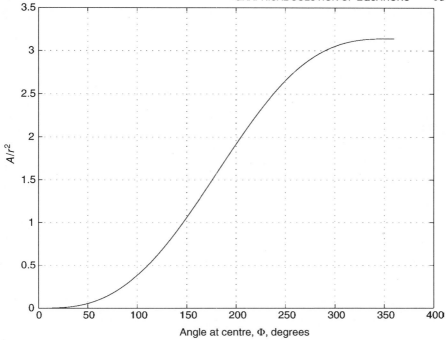

Figure 2.5   To calculate the area of a segment of circle.

The plot is shown in Figure 2.5. Note that, although the area of the segments is a function of two variables, by using nondimensional parameters we could represent the relationship between A, r and Φ by a single curve. If we are interested only in a particular case, we can proceed differently. Let $r = 2\,\text{m}$ and $A = 0.0472\,\text{m}^2$. We can plot the two curves

$$
\begin{aligned}
y1 &= (\Phi - \sin\Phi)/2 \\
y2 &= A/r^2
\end{aligned}
$$

and look for their intersection. The following MATLAB lines will do this:

```
≫ r = 2; A = 0.0472;
≫ phi = 0:  pi/360:  pi/4;
≫ x = 180*phi/pi;
≫ y1 = (phi - sin(phi))/2;
≫ y2 = A/r^2*ones(size(y1));
≫ plot(x, y1, x, y2), grid
≫ xlabel('Angle at centre, \phi, degrees')
```

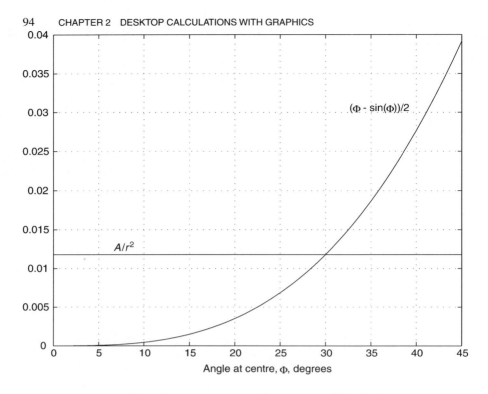

Figure 2.6   Finding the solution at the intersection of two graphs.

To label the two curves use the gtext function:

```
>> gtext('(\phi - sin(\phi))/2')
```

An arrow or a crosshair will appear; by means of the mouse, or the arrow keys, bring it over the place where you want the label to appear and press Enter. Proceed similarly for the other curve with

```
>> gtext('A/r^2')
```

The result is shown in Figure 2.6. Now you can read the solution at the intersection of the two curves. Better still, use the ginput function. An arrow or a crosshair will appear; by means of the mouse, or the arrow keys, bring it as exactly as possible over the intersection and press Enter, for example:

```
>> [phi0 y0 ] = ginput(1)
phi0 =
    29.8669
```

```
y0 =
    0.0119
```

The result can be slightly different, depending on your own appreciation of the inter-section point. Note the use of ginput as a function with two outputs, [phi0 y0].
You can check the solution with

```
≫ A0 = y0*r^2
A0 =
    0.0477
```

With these values, the error, in per cent of the correct value, is

```
≫ error = 100*(A - A0)/A
error =
   -0.9577
```

The result can be improved by 'zooming' the graphs, that is, by plotting y_1 and y_2 in a narrower interval of Φ values, around the previous solution.

2.12   Summary

This section summarizes Sections 1.1 and 1.2, and Chapter 2. In Chapter 1 we learned that a working session begins by clicking the MATLAB icon and ends with the Quit command. We can use the computer as a calculator by means of the operators shown in Table 2.2.

In the following paragraph we shall describe a few last-line editing commands. Under UNIX, the last-line editing commands may be different and the user should consult the relevant manual.

Mistakes made in entering an expression can be immediately corrected by means of the Backspace key. Previously entered expressions can be recovered with the help

Table 2.2   Elementary operators.

Operator	Use	Example
+	Addition	2 + 2 = 4
−	Subtraction	2 − 2 = 0
*	Multiplication	2*2 = 4
/	Right division	2/2 = 1
\	Left division	2\4 = 2
^	Power	2^2 = 4

Table 2.3   A few scientific functions.

Function name	Meaning	Example
sin	sine	$\sin(0.5) = 0.4794$
cos	cosine	$\cos(0) = 1$
tan	tangent	$\tan(\text{pi}/4) = 1.0000$
asin	arcsine	$\text{asin}(\text{sqrt}(2)/2) = 0.7854$
acos	arccosine	$\text{acos}(\text{sqrt}(2)/2) = 0.7854$
atan	two-quadrant arctangent	$\text{atan}(1) = 0.7854$
atan2	four-quadrant arctangent	$\text{atan2}(1,0) = 1.7508$
exp	exponential	$\exp(1) = 2.7183$
log	natural logarithm	$\log(2.7183) = 1.0000$
log10	logarithm in base 10	$\text{log10}(350) = 1.5441$

of the *Up Arrow* and *Down Arrow* keys. The *Left Arrow* and *Right Arrow* keys are used for travelling leftwards and rightwards through the current screen line. The editor is normally in **insert mode**, which means that typing a character inserts it at the current cursor position. On PCs, the `Insert` key is used to switch from **insert** to **overwrite mode** and vice versa, and depressing the `Delete` key deletes the character at the current cursor position.

As is the case with advanced scientific calculators, MATLAB provides many scientific functions, a few of which are shown in Table 2.3. In an expression, the name of a function must be followed by its argument enclosed between parentheses. The arguments of trigonometric functions must be given in radians.

Values to be used repeatedly should be given a name beginning with a letter and containing as many digits and characters as we wish. The computer remembers only the first 19 characters of a name. If no name is given to an expression, its result is stored in the variable *ans* which can be used in the next calculation. The contents of *ans* change with each calculation.

A **row vector** of size n can be defined by entering

```
vector_name = [ a1   a2 ... an ]
```

where $a1, a2, \ldots, an$ are the components. A **column vector** can be defined by

```
vector_name = [ a1
                a2

                 ⋮

                an ]
```

or by

```
vector_name = [ a1;   a2;   ...; an ]
```

The *transposition* operation, indicated in MATLAB by an apostrophe, converts a row vector to a column vector, or vice versa:

Table 2.4   Array operators.

Operator	Use	Example
.*	Multiplication	[2 3] .* [2 4] = [4 12]
./	Division	[2 3] ./ [2 4] = [1 0.7500]
.^	Power	[2 3] . ^ 2 = [4 9]

$$[\text{ a1 a2 } ... \text{ an }]' = \begin{matrix} \text{a1} \\ \text{a2} \\ \vdots \\ \text{an} \end{matrix}$$

See Chapter 4 for transposition of vectors of complex numbers.

Two vectors, **A** and **B**, of the same size, can be added (or subtracted) by writing A+B (or A−B), and a vector **A** can be multiplied by a scalar *lambda* by entering lambda*A. A row vector **A** can be multiplied by a column vector **B** of the same length: A*B. The result is their **scalar product**. The **array product**, A.*B, of two vectors of the same length n, is a vector of length n whose components are the products $a_i b_i$ of the components of **A** and **B**. Table 2.4 describes the array operators used in MATLAB.

Our calculator also has graphic facilities. Thus, the graph of a variable y against another variable x is obtained by the command

```
plot(x, y)
```

We can add a grid, a title, and label the axes of the graph by the commands grid, title('t'), xlabel('xl') and ylabel('yl'), where t, xl and yl are **string variables** of our choice. To define string variables, enclose them in apostrophes.

2.13   Examples

EXAMPLE 2.1   Vectors _____

A vector can define a point, in the sense that each component represents a coordinate of that point. Thus, for Figure 2.7 we can write

```
≫ A = [ 2 3 ];
≫ B = [ 4.1 4.5 ];
```

The distance between the two points A and B is given by

$$d(AB) = \sqrt{(2 - 4.1)^2 + (3 - 4.5)^2} = 2.5807 \qquad (2.10)$$

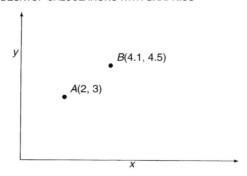

Figure 2.7   Two points in the plane.

which is calculated in MATLAB by

```
>> dist_AB = sqrt(sum((A - B).^2))
```

or, more elegantly, by

```
>> dist_AB = sqrt((A - B)*(A - B)')
```

EXAMPLE 2.2   Vectors

Consider the following two vectors

- **A** of magnitude 5 and at an angle of 15° with the horizontal;
- **B** of magnitude 8 and at an angle of 45° with the horizontal.

We decompose these vectors into their horizontal and vertical components by entering

```
>> alpha = pi*15/180; beta = pi*45/180;
>> A(1) = 5*cos(alpha);
>> A(2) = 5*sin(alpha);
>> B(1) = 8*cos(beta);
>> B(2) = 8*sin(beta);
```

The scalar product of the two vectors **A** and **B** equals

$$
\begin{aligned}
\mathbf{A} \cdot \mathbf{B} &= 5 \cdot \cos\alpha \cdot 8 \cdot \cos\beta \\
&\quad + 5 \cdot \sin\alpha \cdot 8 \cdot \sin\beta \\
&= |\mathbf{A}||\mathbf{B}| \cos(\beta - \alpha) .
\end{aligned}
$$

This result is identical to that in Equation 2.4 and its numerical value is 34.6410. The angle between the two vectors is $45° - 15° = 30°$. In MATLAB we obtain this value by typing

```
>> (180/pi)*acos(A*B'/(sqrt(A*A')*sqrt(B*B')))
```

which does indeed yield 30.0000 degrees.

EXAMPLE 2.3   Orthonormal basis ————————————————————————

Let us enter the three vectors

```
>> e1 = [ 1 0 0 ];
>> e2 = [ 0 1 0 ];
>> e3 = [ 0 0 1 ];
```

The scalar product of two of these vectors, say e_i and e_j, equals 1 if $i = j$, and 0 if $i \neq j$. We verify this property with the commands

```
>> e1*e1', e2*e2', e3*e3'
ans =
     1
ans =
     1
ans =
     1
```

and

```
>> e1*e2', e2*e3', e3*e1'
ans =
     0
ans =
     0
ans =
     0
```

We say that the three vectors e1, e2, e3 form an **orthonormal basis** in three-dimensional space. A geometric interpretation of such a basis is represented in Figure 2.8. Any vector A in the three-dimensional space can be uniquely represented as a linear combination of the basis vectors e1, e2, e3:

$$\mathbf{A} = a_1\mathbf{e}_1 + a_2\mathbf{e}_2 + a_3\mathbf{e}_3$$

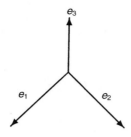

Figure 2.8   Orthonormal basis.

where the '+' sign means vector addition. The scalar product of the vector **A** by a basis vector e_i yields the **projection** of **A** on the direction of e_i; for example, with the basis defined above,

```
≫ A = [ 2 3 4 ];
≫ A*e1', A*e2', A*e3'
ans =
     2
ans =
     3
ans =
     4
```

The generalization of these notions to n-dimensional space is straightforward. This example may help in understanding the meaning of geometrical projections and that of the discrete Fourier transform, as introduced in Chapter 16.

EXAMPLE 2.4   Probabilities _____

Let us toss a pair of dice. The number of ordered pairs of numbers that can be obtained is equal to $6^2 = 36$. Suppose that we are interested in the sum of the numbers obtained. This is a **discrete random variable**, X, that can take the values $2, 3, \ldots, 12$. There is only one possibility of obtaining the sum 2, that is, by tossing 1, 1. Therefore the probability of obtaining 2 is $p(1) = 1/36$. The sum 3 can be obtained by tossing either 1, 2, or 2, 1. The corresponding probability is $p(2) = 2/36$. Continuing this reasoning, we obtain the values shown in Table 2.5 (see, for example, Lipschutz 1965, pages 75–6). The **mean** of X, also called **expectation** or **expected value** of X, is, by definition,

$$E(X) = \sum_{i=1}^{12} X_i \, p(X_i) \,. \tag{2.11}$$

Table 2.5   The sum of two dice.

Sum X	Probability $p(X)$
2	1/36
3	2/36
4	3/36
5	4/36
6	5/36
7	6/36
8	5/36
9	4/36
10	3/36
11	2/36
12	1/36

We enter the vector of the sums by

```
>> X = 2:  12;
```

and the vector of probabilities by

```
>> p = [ 1 2 3 4 5 6 5 4 3 2 1 ]/36;
```

The mean is calculated as a 'scalar product':

```
>> X*p'
ans =
     7
```

We know that we must obtain one of the outcomes in the array X. Therefore, the sum of all probabilities is 1, the probability of certainty. Try sum(p).

It may be interesting to plot the **distribution** of X. Using the plot function would yield a continuous graph, while X has a discrete distribution. The bar function produces a **bar graph** in which for each value of X there is a bar whose height is proportional to p. Try the command bar(X, p) and see the result.

EXAMPLE 2.5   Fourier series _____

Subject to the conditions described in the Appendix to this chapter, a periodic function extending from $-\infty$ to $+\infty$ can be developed into a **Fourier series** (Baron Joseph Fourier, French, 1768–1830). Fourier series (see, for example, Wylie and Barrett

1987 or Ramirez 1985) have an infinite number of terms. On a computer, however, we can generate only a finite number of terms and, therefore, we can **synthesize** only approximations of periodic functions. As an example let us consider a square wave which is symmetric about $t = 0$; it is described by the Fourier series

$$x(t) = \frac{4A}{\pi}(\cos \omega t - \frac{1}{3} \cos 3\omega t + \frac{1}{5} \cos 5\omega t - \frac{1}{7} \cos 7\omega t + \cdots) \qquad \textbf{(2.12)}$$

where A is the **amplitude** of the wave and ω its angular **frequency**. It is also usual to define A as half the **peak to peak amplitude**.

We shall approximate the symmetric square wave by a **truncated** series containing only three terms. The error caused by using only a finite number of terms of the infinite series is called a **truncation error**. Let $A = 1$, $\omega = 2\pi$; the **wave period** is then equal to $T = 2\pi/\omega = 1$. The required MATLAB commands are

```
>> t = -2:  0.05:  2;
>> omega = 2*pi;
>> x1 = cos(omega*t);
>> x2 = -cos(3*omega*t)/3;
>> x3 = cos(5*omega*t)/5;
>> x = 4*(x1 + x2 + x3)/pi;
>> plot(t, x), grid
>> title('Three-term approximation of the square wave')
>> xlabel('t')
```

Once you have written the expression for x1 you can obtain the following two terms more easily by using the *Up Arrow* key to retrieve the previous expression and edit it. Run the commands and check the form, the amplitude and the period of the resulting wave. The graph obtained is shown in Figure 2.9. You may improve the approximation by adding more terms. At this stage, however, this operation would be tedious. It will become much simpler after learning to program functions. Then, writing a *FOR loop*, you can use as many terms as you want, but, obviously, still a finite number of them.

Another point is that the graph may look rather 'broken' because it consists of straight-line segments that connect the calculated points. The resolution can be improved by taking more points, for instance by using

```
>> t = - 2:  0.01:  2;
```

and running the other commands again.

Try other wave forms by using series described in various books, for instance Ramirez (1985) or Spiegel (1968). For more details see also Churchill and Brown (1990). We dealt here with the synthesis of a periodic function; the inverse

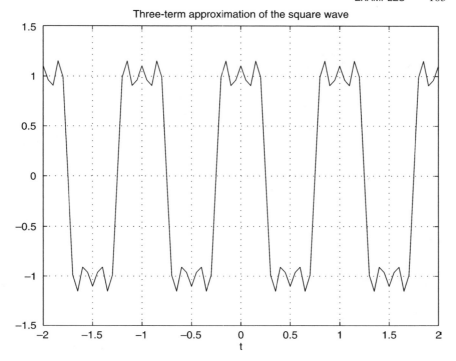

Figure 2.9   A truncated Fourier series.

problem, the decomposition of a periodic function into simple trigonometric terms, is also solvable in MATLAB and is treated in Chapter 16.

EXAMPLE 2.6   Naming constants, mechanical engineering ⎯⎯⎯⎯⎯⎯⎯⎯⎯⎯

Suppose that in a certain project we need a tubular element and we choose, from BS 6323 (abbreviation of *British Standard 6323*, see Bibliography), a tube with outer diameter $D = 139.7$ mm, and wall thickness $t = 6.3$ mm. Most properties of this tube are given in the standard; let us, however, calculate them in MATLAB. Referring to Figure 2.10 we define the constants

```
≫ D = 139.7;
≫ t = 6.3;
```

Then, the inner diameter, in mm, is given by

```
≫ d = D - 2*t
d =
      127.1000
```

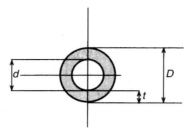

Figure 2.10   Section through a tube.

If the tube is used as a pipe, and we want to calculate the flow through it, we obtain the area of the inner section, in mm^2, by

```
>> A = pi*d^2/4
A =
    1.2688e+04
```

If we are interested in heat transfer through the walls of the pipe we need the external surface; to get it, in mm^2, we calculate the outer circumference

```
>> p = pi*D
p =
    438.8805
```

and multiply it by the pipe length. If the tube is used as a structural member, and it is loaded in tension or compression, we are interested in the **sectional area** of the walls. We obtain this area, in mm^2, by

```
>> a = pi*(D^2 - d^2)/4
a =
    2.6403e+03
```

To check safety with regard to buckling, we calculate the **moment of inertia**, in mm^4, by

```
>> I = pi*(D^4 - d^4)/64
I =
    5.8862e+06
```

For strength in bending we obtain the **sectional modulus**, in mm^3, by

```
≫ Z = 2*I/D
Z =
    8.4269e+04
```

Note that the symbol used in many European countries for the **sectional modulus** is W.

Finally, the pipe mass in kilograms per metre of length is given by

```
≫ m = (a/1000)*7.85
m =
    20.7260
```

Why did we divide a by 1000? We did so because

$$a \text{ mm}^2 \times \left(\frac{1}{10^3} \frac{\text{m}}{\text{mm}} \right)^2 \times 7.85 \frac{\text{t}}{\text{m}^3} \times 1000 \frac{\text{kg}}{\text{t}} = \frac{a}{1000} \times 7.85 \times \frac{\text{kg}}{\text{m}}$$

EXAMPLE 2.7 Moments, centres of gravity ⎯⎯⎯⎯⎯⎯⎯⎯⎯⎯⎯⎯

Figure 2.11 shows, to scale, a system of collinear masses. The masses are given in kg and the distances in mm, as is usual in mechanical drawings. We want to find the centre of gravity of this system. We begin by defining the vectors

```
≫ mass = [ 35 65 45 75 ];
≫ distance = [ 400 580 800 1000 ];
```

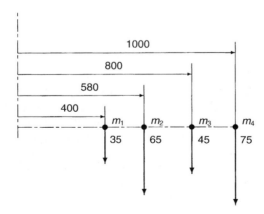

Figure 2.11 A system of collinear masses.

The vector of moments with respect to the reference axis shown in the figure is given by the array product

```
>> moments = mass.*distance
```

with the elements 14000; 37700; 36000; 75000. The total moment is obtained from the scalar product

```
>> t_moment = mass*distance'
```

and is equal to 162 700 kg mm, while the total mass is obtained by using the sum function

```
>> M = sum(mass)
```

that is, 220 kg.

The centre of gravity of the system shown in Figure 2.11 is, by definition, the point in which we can concentrate the total mass M, so that its moment will equal the sum of the moments of the given masses, that is

```
>> cg = t_moment/M
```

which yields 739.5455 mm. We could have obtained the same result directly by

```
>> cg = mass*distance'/sum(mass)
```

or by

```
>> cg = distance*mass'/sum(mass)
```

EXAMPLE 2.8   Opening a door closed by a pneumatic cylinder _____

In Section 2.11 we saw how to use MATLAB in solving transcendental equations. The following example is an application of the method to mechanical engineering. Figure 2.12 shows a door that is closed by a pneumatic cylinder. The hinge is at H. If the sectional area of the cylinder is A, and the initial pressure p_0, a force $p_0 A$ is exerted on the door by means of a roller mounted at the end of the piston rod.

Let us assume that somebody pulls the door with a force F that is directed as shown in the figure, and that the door is thus opened by an angle α; we want to find this angle. The force F pushes the piston a distance

$$c = b \tan \alpha$$

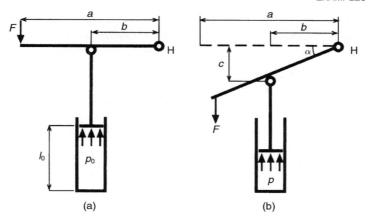

Figure 2.12   A door closed by a pneumatic cylinder. (a) Door closed; (b) door open.

The air volume in the cylinder is reduced to $V = A(l_0 - c)$. The motion is too fast to allow for heat exchanges. Processes that occur without heat exchanges with the environment are called **adiabatic**; a few examples are sound propagation, ignition in diesel engines and shock waves produced by explosions. The relationship between pressure, p, and volume, V, in an adiabatic process is

$$pV^\chi = c_{ad}$$

where χ is called the **adiabatic exponent** and c_{ad} is a constant. Applying these notions to our example we write that the new volume, V, and pressure, p, are related to the initial volume, V_0, and pressure, p_0, by

$$pV^\chi = p_0 V_0^\chi$$

and

$$p = p_0 \left(\frac{l_0}{l_0 - c} \right)^\chi$$

The 'opening' moment is

$$M_O = Fa \cos \alpha$$

and the 'restoring' moment equals

$$M_R = Apb$$

LIVERPOOL JOHN MOORES UNIVERSITY
LEARNING SERVICES

At the point of static equilibrium the opening and the restoring moments are equal. This happens when the following equation is satisfied

$$Fa\cos\alpha = bAp_0\left(\frac{l_0}{l_0 - b\tan\alpha}\right)^x \tag{2.13}$$

This equation in α may seem quite discouraging; however, it can be solved rather easily. To show this, let us assume the following values

```
≫ a = 0.8;          % m, door width
≫ b = 0.25;         % m, piston arm
≫ A = pi*0.04^2;    % m^2, piston sectional area
≫ p0 = 0.1*10^5;    % N/m^2
≫ l0 = 0.50;        % m, open cylinder length
≫ chi = 1.4;        % adiabatic exponent
```

We now plot separately the curves of the opening and the restoring moments:

```
≫ alpha = 0:  pi/90:  pi/6; % opening angle, rad
≫ c = b*tan(alpha); % piston stroke, m
≫ p = p0*(l0*ones(size(alpha))./(l0 - c)).^chi
≫ P = 25; % N, hand force
≫ left = P*a*cos(alpha).^2; % opening moment
≫ right = b*A*p; % restoring mome
≫ angle = 180*alpha/pi; % opening angle, degree
≫ h = plot(angle, left, angle, right, ':'), grid
≫ xlabel('angle, degree'), ylabel('Moments, Nm')
≫ legend(h, 'Opening moment', 'Restoring moment')
```

Above we used two MATLAB commands introduced in version 5.2. We assigned to the variable *h* the **handle** of the *graphic object* produced by the command plot. We use this handle as the first argument of the command legend. The other arguments are strings that we want to print as identifiers of the various curves in the plot. The string arguments appear in the same order of the curves as in the plot command.

The two curves produced by the above commands are shown in Figure 2.13. The angle of equilibrium is found at the intersection of the two curves; we can read it either directly on the graph, or by using the ginput function (see Section 2.11). We must also check the pressure at equilibrium; we do this by producing a second plot

```
≫ plot(angle, p), grid
≫ xlabel('angle, degree')
≫ ylabel('Cylinder pressure, N/m^2')
```

Try the last commands for yourself.

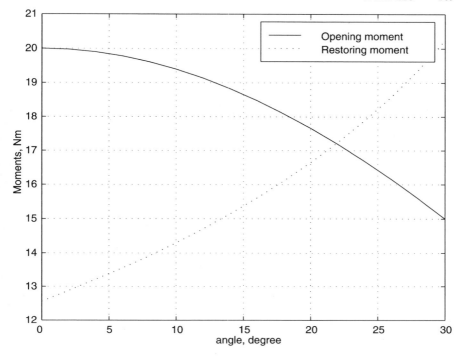

Figure 2.13   Curves of opening and restoring moments.

EXTENDED EXAMPLE 2.9   Ship stability under wind

In the preceding example we solved graphically a transcendental equation. We are going to show now that the same method is applicable when it is not possible to write an equation. In that case, all we can do is define two curves by two sets of calculated points and look for the intersection of those curves. This example is taken from naval architecture, a field in which the method shown here has been in use for a long time. Although this fact is not mentioned in books, we may see the problem as similar to that of a nonlinear spring loaded by a nonlinear force or moment. Then, the method can be easily applied to other instances of nonlinear springs loaded by nonlinear forces or moments.

Figure 2.14 shows a transverse section of a ship. In order to orient this figure, let us assume that we are looking from the stern towards the bow. $W_0 L_0$ is the waterline in the *upright condition*. The projection of the centre of gravity on the given transverse plane is G, and the projection of the centre of the submerged ship volume is B. The resultant of hydrostatic pressures passes through B, a point called the **centre of buoyancy**. K is a reference point on mid-bottom.

Assume now that the ship heels towards *starboard* by an angle ϕ. Instead of drawing the ship again, heeled by an angle ϕ, the ship is considered fixed and the new waterline, $W_\phi L_\phi$, is drawn as inclined at angle ϕ towards port. The vessel's weight, W, acts in G and is vertical, that is, perpendicular to the waterline $W_\phi L_\phi$.

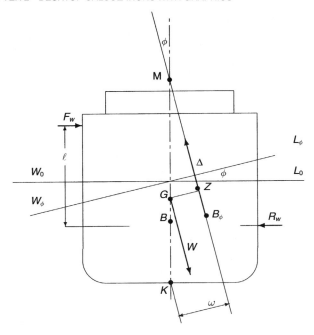

Figure 2.14   Forces acting on a heeled vessel.

Because the ship's weight does not change, part of the submerged volume emerges on the port side – that is, at left – while an equal volume submerges on the starboard side – that is, at right. As a result, the centre of buoyancy moves to starboard to a new position B_ϕ. The force of buoyancy, Δ, passes through B_ϕ and is also vertical, that is, also perpendicular to the waterline $W_\phi L_\phi$. According to Archimedes' principle,

$$W = \Delta \tag{2.14}$$

and we use the name **displacement** for their shared value. The two forces W and Δ form a couple whose lever arm is $\overline{GZ}$, the length of the perpendicular drawn from G on the line of action Δ. The moment $\Delta \cdot \overline{GZ}$ is the **righting moment**. If the vessel is stable, the righting moment returns the vessel to its initial upright condition. $\overline{GZ}$ is called the **righting arm**.

The distance from K to the line of action of the buoyancy force is measured by w, a function of the displacement Δ and the heel angle ϕ. The righting arm is calculated from

$$\overline{GZ} = w - \overline{KG} \cdot \sin\phi \tag{2.15}$$

The plot of $\overline{GZ}$ versus ϕ is called the **diagram of static stability**; we shall use it for the evaluation of the ship's stability under wind. The wind pressure acting on the ship surface above the waterline $W_0 L_0$ generates a force F_W (see Figure 2.14).

This force depends on the lateral projection of the exposed ship surface area, F, called the **sail area**. Under the influence of the force F_W, the ship tends to drift. The drift tendency is opposed by a hydrodynamic reaction, R_W, which acts on the opposite-side submerged hull surface. The forces R_W and F_W are equal; they constitute a **heeling** couple whose lever arm is ℓ. The simplest way of calculating ℓ is based on the assumption that F_W acts in the centroid of the sail area and R_W at half-draft.

Figure 2.14 shows the wind force, F_W, and the hydrodynamic reaction, R_W, corresponding to the upright condition. As the ship heels under the influence of wind, the two forces remain horizontal, that is, for a heel angle ϕ, F_W and R_W are parallel to $W_\phi L_\phi$. The lever arm and the sail area diminish as the heel angle increases. To consider these effects we shall use in this example a formula adopted by the German Federal Navy – and subsequently by a few other navies – which is

$$F_W = pF(0.25 + 0.75\cos^3\phi) \tag{2.16}$$

where p is the wind pressure. The wind heeling moment is

$$M_H = F_W\ell \tag{2.17}$$

The position of static equilibrium under wind is that in which the righting moment equals the heeling moment, that is

$$M_H = \Delta \cdot \overline{GZ} \tag{2.18}$$

Dividing both sides of Equation 2.18 by Δ we reach the conclusion that we must compare the righting arm $\overline{GZ}$ with the **heeling arm** M_H/Δ. Combining this result with Equations 2.16 and 2.17 we calculate the heeling arm, k_w, as

$$k_w = \frac{p \cdot F \cdot \ell(0.25 + 0.75\cos^3\phi)}{\Delta} \tag{2.19}$$

Let us apply the above bit of theory to an actual fishing vessel whose data are

Displacement, Δ . . . . $=$ 402.490 kN
Height of centre of gravity, $\overline{KG}$ $=$ 2.161 m
Sail area . . . . $=$ 35.46 m^2
Lever arm of wind force . . . . . . $=$ 2.120 m

The values of w are given in Table 2.6.

Suppose now that we want to draw the diagram of static stability, to include the curve of the wind heeling lever for a wind of 70 knots, and find the angle of static equilibrium under these conditions. We begin by entering the given data

```
>> delta = 402.49; l = 2.12;
>> KG =    2.161; F    = 35.460;
```

Table 2.6   Fishing vessel, part of the cross-curves of stability.

Heel angle ϕ deg	Lever arm w m	Heel angle ϕ deg	Lever arm w m
0	0.000	35	1.479
5	0.262	40	1.592
10	0.519	50	1.754
15	0.767	60	1.838
20	0.989	70	1.858
25	1.182	75	1.847
30	1.344		

```
>> phi    =    [ 0; 5; ...   75 ];
>> w = [ 0; 0.262; ...   1.847 ];
```

We convert the heel angles to radians and calculate the righting arm according to Equation 2.15:

```
>> heel = pi*phi/180;
>> GZ = w - KG*sin(heel);
```

The wind pressure corresponding to a wind velocity of 70 knots is 1 kN/m^2. The wind arm is calculated from Equation 2.19:

```
>> kw = 1*F*l*(0.25 + 0.75*cos(heel).^3 )/delta;
```

Note the use of the array power operation ' .^ '. We obtain the graph by the commands:

```
>> h = plot(phi, GZ, phi, kw), grid
>> title('Fishing vessel, static stability, 70 knot wind')
>> xlabel('Heel angle, degrees'), ylabel('Lever arms, m')
>> legend(h, 'Righting arm, GZ', 'Wind arm')
```

The result is shown in Figure 2.15. The angle of static equilibrium is approximately 12.2 degrees.

EXAMPLE 2.10   Temperature scales ————————————————————

Some time before 1720, the German physicist Daniel Gabriel Fahrenheit (1686–1736) chose as the zero of his temperature scale the temperature of an ice-salt mixture

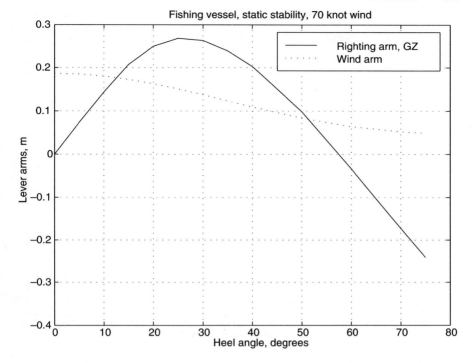

Figure 2.15   A diagram of static stability.

that corresponded to the lowest temperature that occurred in Danzig (today Gdansk) in 1709. In this scale the temperature of the melting ice corresponds to 32 degrees and is denoted by 32 °F. In the same scale, the temperature of boiling water, at sea level, is 212 °F.

In 1742 the Swedish astronomer Anders Celsius (1701–1744) proposed another temperature scale in which the melting point of water corresponds to zero degrees, and the boiling point to 100. These temperatures are denoted by 0 °C and 100 °C.

Let us build a graph that facilitates conversion from one scale to the other. In both scales the interval between the melting point and the boiling point is divided into equal parts. It follows that both scales are linear and the graph will consist of a straight line. Let F be the Fahrenheit axis; C, the Celsius axis. One point on the line has the F coordinate 32 and the C coordinate 0. The second point has the F coordinate 212 and the C coordinate 100. The graph is obtained in MATLAB with

```
>> plot([32 212], [0 100])
>> xlabel('Degrees Fahrenheit')
>> ylabel('Degrees Celsius')
>> grid
```

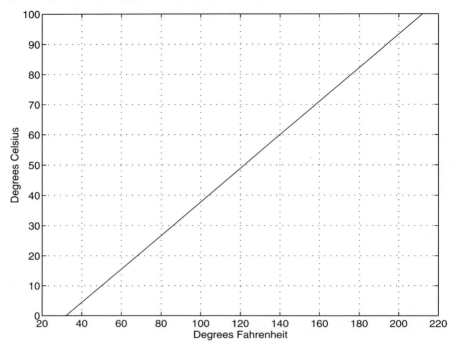

Figure 2.16   The relationship between the Fahrenheit and the Celsius scales.

Such a graph that substitutes calculations is called a **nomogram**: it is shown in Figure 2.16. Fahrenheit indicated 96 °F as the temperature of the human body; this value was corrected later to 98.6 °F. Use the graph to find the Celsius temperatures corresponding to the above values and compare them to what you know today about the temperature of the human body. Also use the mouse and the `ginput` function.

Figure 2.16 represents the relationship within the interval defined by the two given points. Exercise 3.3 deals with an expression that also describes the relationship outside that interval.

Note. The definition of the international temperature scale involves the *triple point* of water instead of the *melting point*. For our purposes the difference between the two definitions can be neglected.

EXAMPLE 2.11   Electrical resistance increase with temperature _____

The resistance, R, of an electrical conductor is directly proportional to its length, L, and inversely proportional to its cross-section area, A:

$$R = \rho \frac{L}{A}$$

The factor of proportionality, ρ, is called **resistivity**. The resistivity of copper, at 20 °C is $\rho = 0.0170 \ldots 0.0178 \, \Omega \text{mm}^2/\text{m}$. The resistivity is a function of temperature and its variation can be described by

$$\rho_\theta = \rho(1 + \alpha\,\Delta\theta) \tag{2.20}$$

where
$\begin{array}{ll} \rho_\theta & \text{is the resistivity at } \theta\,°\text{C,} \\ \alpha & \text{is a temperature coefficient, for copper } \alpha = 0.0039\text{K}^{-1} \\ \Delta\theta & \text{is the temperature difference above } 20\,°\text{C.} \end{array}$

Wiesemann (1989) gives a more detailed relationship

$$\rho_\theta = \rho_{20}(1 + \alpha_{20}\Delta\theta + \beta_{20}\Delta\theta^2) \tag{2.21}$$

where

$$\begin{array}{rcl} \rho 20 & = & 0.017\ \Omega\text{mm}^2/\text{m} \\ \alpha_{20} & = & 4.3 \times 10^{-3}\ K^{-1} \\ \beta_{20} & = & 0.6 \times 10^{-6}\ K^{-2} \end{array}$$

To compare the two relationships graphically, between $20\,°\text{C}$ and $100\,°\text{C}$, we plot them as follows:

```
≫ rho = 0.0178; alpha = 0.0039;
≫ theta = 20:  0.5:  100;
≫ delta = theta - 20;
≫ rho1 = rho*(1 + alpha*delta);
≫ rho_20 = 0.017; alpha_20 = 0.0043; beta_20 = 0.6*10^(-6);
≫ rho2 = rho_20.*(1 + alpha_20*delta + beta_20*delta.^2);
≫ h = plot(theta, rho1, theta, rho2)
≫ xlabel('Temperature, deg C')
≫ ylabel('Copper resistivity, \Omega*mm^2/m')
≫ legend(h, 'Equation 2.20', 'Equation 2.21')
```

Try the plot for yourself. Note that the resistivity is often given in Ωm. In these units the upper limit of copper resistivity is

$$0.0178\frac{\Omega\text{mm}^2}{\text{m}} \times \left(10^{-3}\frac{\text{m}}{\text{mm}}\right)^2 = 1.78 \times 10^{-8}\Omega\text{m}$$

EXAMPLE 2.12 Naming constants, electrical engineering _____

Suppose we have to connect a 12 V dc source to a 25 Ω load situated 100 m away, and we choose a copper conductor with a diameter of 1 mm. To be sure that we made the correct choice we must check the voltage drop caused by the conductor. The resistivity of copper at $20\,°\text{C}$ is 0.0178 Ωmm^2/m. In MATLAB it is convenient to name the various data items and intermediate results and use those names in calculations.

If we want to prepare a note or a report about the following calculations we begin by opening a diary file

```
≫ diary resist.dia
```

Next we enter the data

```
≫ V = 12;           % V
≫ RL = 25;          % ohm
≫ l = 2*100;        % m
≫ rho = 0.0178;     % ohm.mm^2/m
≫ d = 1;            % mm
```

The sectional area of the conductor is

```
≫ A = pi*d^2/4     % mm^2
A =
    0.7854
```

and the resistance,

```
≫ R = rho*l/A      % ohm
≫ R =
    4.5327
```

The total resistance in the circuit equals

```
≫ RT = RL + R      % ohm
≫ RT =
    29.5327
```

and the current

```
≫ I = V/RT          % A
 I =
0.4063
```

The voltage drop across the conductor is given by

```
Vc = R*I            % V
```

```
Vc =
    1.8418
```

which is more than 15% of the available voltage. If this situation is not acceptable the calculations can be repeated with the next higher conductor size. The input data are already defined and this enables an immediate second iteration.

The reader is invited to process the resulting file resist.dia with his or her favourite editor, or word processor, and turn it into a technical report.

EXAMPLE 2.13   A diode circuit _____

Figure 2.17 shows a DC circuit containing a resistor and a semiconductor diode. If the voltage across the diode is v, the current through it can be calculated from

$$i = I_0(e^{40v} - 1) \qquad\qquad\qquad (2.22)$$

where I_0 is a constant called the **reverse saturation current**. For small negative values of v, $i \approx -I_0$. Equation 2.22 is nonlinear and it is valid for voltage values larger than a negative value known as **reverse breakdown** (see, for instance, Carlson and Gisser 1990). Given the value of I_0 we can use MATLAB to view the $i - v$ curve of the diode. Assuming $I_0 = 10^{-6} mA$, a value given by the above-mentioned authors, we enter

```
>> I0 = 1.0E-6;
>> v = -0.05:  0.005:  0.05;
>> i = I0*(exp(40*v) - 1);
>> plot(v, i), grid
>> title('Characteristic of semiconductor diode')
>> xlabel('Voltage v, V'), ylabel('Current i, mA')
```

The result is shown in Figure 2.18 opposite. We obtain thus the characteristic curve of the semiconductor diode within a narrow voltage domain and can see that

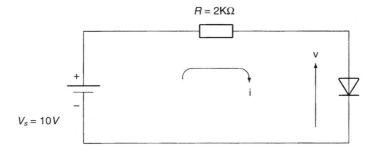

Figure 2.17   A circuit containing a semiconductor diode.

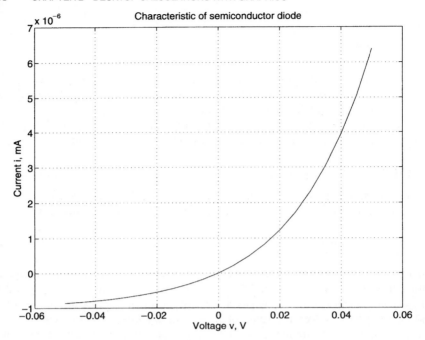

Figure 2.18   Characteristic of semiconductor diode

for any negative voltage a very small negative current will flow, while for positive voltages the current will be positive and increase rapidly with v. The image changes if we plot the curve within broader voltage domains, for instance for

```
>> v = -1.0:  0.05:  0.25;
```

and also for

```
>> v = -10:  0.05:  0.8;
```

Repeat the plots with the v arrays shown above and you will see that the diode is practically *off* for negative voltage values, and *on* for positive ones. The diode acts as a **rectifier**.

   In order to calculate the actual voltage and current values of the circuit, that is, the **operating point**, we must consider the resistance of the circuit. We do this by writing a second equation based on Kirchhoff's law

$$Ri = V_s - v \tag{2.23}$$

We now have two equations in the two unknowns, i and v, and we must find the pair of i, v values that satisfies both. Years ago this was not thought of as an easy task; in a book that appeared as recently as 1981 we can read that 'analysing even a simple circuit with a real diode (or other nonlinear element) is a messy problem'. The authors recommend the reader to approximate the real diode by an ideal one that 'leads to quick but less accurate results'. Today, with software such as MATLAB, finding the exact solution may be simpler than going around through approximate models. Thus, for an exact solution we can combine Equations 2.22 and 2.23 and obtain a single nonlinear equation which can be solved by numerical techniques explained in Chapter 7. For the moment we shall describe a graphical solution which may be slightly less accurate, but easier to understand. We shall plot the lines defined by Equations 2.22 and 2.23 and look for their intersection. This will be the operating point because the values of i and v read there satisfy both equations. For our example we use the values given by Carlson and Gisser (1990):

```
>> Vs = 10; R = 2000;
```

Next we obtain the plot in Figure 2.19 with the commands

```
>> v = 0:  0.05:  0.4; i = I0*(exp(40*v) - 1);
>> vr = [ 0 0.39 ];
>> ir = 1000*(Vs - vr)/R;
>> h = plot(v, i, vr, ir), grid
>> title('Operating point of resistor-diode circuit')
>> xlabel('Voltage v, V'), ylabel('Current i, mA')
>> legend(h, 'Diode characteristic',
   'Circuit characteristic')
```

In the right-hand side of the expression for vr the two voltages Vs and vr are given in V, and the resistance R is measured in Ω. Therefore

```
>> (Vs - vr)/R
```

would yield a current measured in A. Multiplying this result by 1000 we transform to mA which is the unit used in the expression of the current i. The coordinates of the operating point can be read on the graph. Try, however,

```
>> [ v i ] = ginput(1)
```

An arrow or a crosshair will appear on the screen; you can move it either with a mouse or with the arrow keys. Place the arrow as exactly as possible on the intersection and click the mouse or press Enter. The values you are looking for will be displayed on the screen.

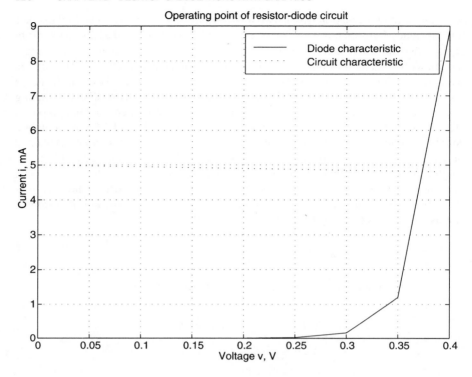

Figure 2.19   Finding the operating point in the diode circuit.

For a good graphic solution the plot must cover as small an area as possible, but still include the operating point. This requires some *a priori* knowledge of the range in which a solution can be expected. The beginner can find the correct range of the plot by trial and error; the guess of the experienced user is usually based on his or her practical experience.

The rectifying function of the diode can be demonstrated if instead of a DC voltage source we supply an alternating voltage, for instance

$$v = 0.4 \sin(2\pi \times 50t) \tag{2.24}$$

The graph of the current passing through the circuit can be obtained by plotting the coordinates of operating points found for several t values. Doing this graphically would be tedious. It would be much more convenient to write a program as shown in Chapter 7. However, to get an idea of what is going on, we can neglect the effect of the resistance R and plot the rectified current by

```
>> t = 0:  0.0001:  0.05;
```

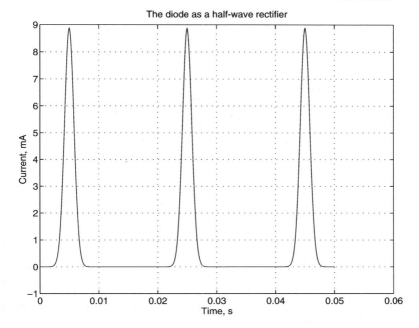

Figure 2.20   The semiconductor diode as a rectifier.

```
≫ v = 0.4*sin(2*pi*50*t);
≫ i = I0*(exp(40*v) - 1);
≫ plot(t, i), grid
≫ title('The diode as a half-wave rectifier')
≫ xlabel('Time, s'), ylabel('Current, mA')
```

The result is shown in Figure 2.20.

2.14   Exercises

Solutions for Exercises 2.3, 2.4, 2.6, 2.9 and 2.11 appear at the back of the book.

■ **EXERCISE 2.1**   Plot an ellipse
The parametric equations of an ellipse with the centre in the origin of coordinates, the major axis $2A$, and the minor axis $2B$, are

$$x \quad = \quad A \cos t \tag{2.25}$$
$$y \quad = \quad B \sin t \tag{2.26}$$

where $0 \le t \le 2\pi$.

Plot an ellipse, for instance with $A = 2$, $B = 1$, and try to understand the meaning of A and B.

Experiment with other curves, for example from Spiegel (1968).

■ **EXERCISE 2.2** Triangular wave

Synthesize a triangular wave, symmetric about $t = 0$, with the Fourier series

$$x(t) = \frac{8A}{\pi^2} (\cos \omega t + \frac{1}{9} \cos 3\omega t + \frac{1}{25} \cos 5\omega t \cdots) , \tag{2.27}$$

where A is the half-amplitude of the wave, and ω its angular frequency. Try, for instance, $A = 1, \omega = 2\pi$.

■ **EXERCISE 2.3** Beats

The superposition of two waves of slightly different frequencies results in a wave with slowly varying amplitude. One easy way of demonstrating this phenomenon is to strike two adjacent piano keys simultaneously.

For simplicity let us consider two waves of equal amplitude

$$x_1 = A \sin \omega_1 t$$
$$x_2 = A \sin \omega_2 t .$$

Adding these two waves and using a formula from trigonometry which transforms the sum of two sine functions into a product (see, for example, Spiegel 1968, page 17) we write

$$x = A \sin \omega_1 t + A \sin \omega_2 t = 2A \cos \frac{(\omega_1 - \omega_2)t}{2} \sin \frac{(\omega_1 + \omega_2)t}{2} \tag{2.28}$$

The result is a wave with angular frequency $(\omega_1 + \omega_2)/2$ and amplitude varying with the angular frequency $(\omega_1 - \omega_2)/2$ (see, for instance, De Facia 1992).

As an exercise generate the two waves

$$x_1 = \sin 2\pi t$$
$$x_2 = \sin 2.2\pi t$$

and simulate their superposition. Identify the two frequencies predicted by Equation 2.28 and the maximum amplitude. Choose the array t so that you will see at least two wave periods of the envelope.

■ **EXERCISE 2.4** Measurement errors

Let us consider a measuring instrument with a scale graduated 0–1000. A few possible examples are

Instrument	Scale	
Thermometer	0–1000	°C
Barometer	0–1000	mm Hg
Ammeter	0–1000	mA
Voltmeter	0–1000	V

If the instrument is guaranteed as belonging to the 3% *class*, the maximum expected error is ±3% of the full-scale deflection, in our case ±30. Then, an indicated value of 1000 corresponds to an actual value lying somewhere between 970 and 1030. If the meter shows 500, the true value can be anywhere in the range 470–530. The corresponding relative error equals $30 \times 100/500 = 6$. This simple calculation shows that the full-scale deflection of the measuring instrument should not be much higher than the range of expected values. One frequently used rule of thumb says that, if one wants to avoid both large relative errors and overloading of the instrument, the expected value should lie between $1/2$ and $2/3$ of full-scale deflection.

To illustrate the preceding considerations, continue the example of the 3% instrument with full-scale deflection equal to 1000 and do the following:

(1)   Calculate and display the per cent error for measured values equal to 100, 200, ..., 1000.
(2)   Plot the per cent error, against the measured values, in the interval 0–1000. For this plot use smaller intervals than at (1), for instance 10.

■ **EXERCISE 2.5**   Instrument calibration
Let us assume that we want to **calibrate** an instrument, such as a barometer, thermometer, ammeter or voltmeter. To do this we measure a few standard values and compare the readings with the known values. For instance, to calibrate a voltmeter we can measure a set of standard voltage sources. Then, we can draw a curve of the readings against the standard values and use the curve to correct the measured values. As an example consider the following table

Reading	Standard
0.500	0
0.633	1
0.767	2
1.167	5
1.833	10
2.500	15

Build a **calibration curve** by plotting the instrument readings against the standard (that is, the true) values. Use the diagram to find out the true value corresponding to a reading of 1.5.

■ **EXERCISE 2.6**   Swimming across a river
In Figure 2.21 a swimmer crosses a river that is 1.1 km wide. The average swimmer speed is $V = 0.9$ km/h and the stream speed is $S = 1.5$ km/h. The swimmer started at A, aiming for B which is exactly opposite, but reaches the other bank at point C.

(a)   Write the swimmer velocity relative to the water as a vector $\mathbf{V}$, the stream velocity relative to the ground as a vector $\mathbf{S}$, and calculate the swimmer velocity relative to the ground as the true-velocity vector $\mathbf{T}$. Find the speed and the angle $\widehat{BAC}$.
(b)   Calculate the distance $\overline{BC}$.

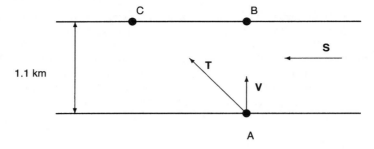

Figure 2.21   Swimming across the river.

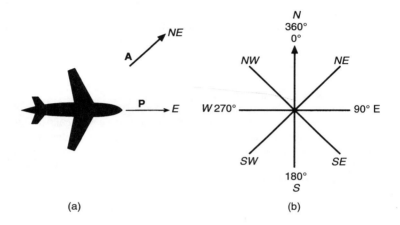

(a)   (b)

Figure 2.22   Aeroplane drifting in wind.

■ **EXERCISE 2.7**   Aeroplane drift
Figure 2.22(a) shows a plane flying east; its speed relative to air is 1000 km/h. The wind blows from SW to NE with a speed over ground equal to 100 km/h.

(a)   Write the aeroplane velocity in air as a vector $\mathbf{P}$, and the wind velocity over ground as a vector $\mathbf{A}$. Find the aeroplane velocity over ground as the true-velocity vector $\mathbf{T}$.

(b)   In navigation it is usual to express directions as angles measured clockwise from the meridian, in degrees, as shown in Figure 2.22(b). Calculate the true aeroplane course (direction of flight) according to this convention.

(c)   How should the aeroplane change its course in order to remain on an eastbound flight? Call the corrected velocity vector $\mathbf{Tc}$ and express the course according to the convention shown in Figure 2.22(b).

(d)   Calculate the vector $\mathbf{Tc}$ and check your results by adding the vectors $\mathbf{Tc}$ and $\mathbf{A}$.

■ **EXERCISE 2.8**   Ship drift
In Figure 2.23 a ship sails on course 315° (that is, towards NW – see Figure 2.22(b)) with a speed of 20 knots. The local current due to tide is 2 knots and has the direction

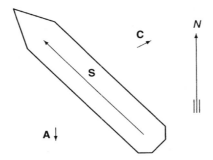

Figure 2.23   Ship drifting in current and wind.

Figure 2.24   Definition of work.

67°30′ (that is, towards ENE). The ship also drifts under wind in the direction 180° (that is, towards S) with a speed of 0.5 knots.

(a)   Represent the ship velocity as a vector **S**, the current velocity as a vector **C**, and the wind-drift velocity as a vector **A**. Calculate the true-velocity vector **T** (velocity over bottom).

(b)   Calculate the true ship speed, that is, the ship speed over bottom.

(c)   Calculate the true ship course, that is, the direction of sailing over bottom, measured clockwise from the meridian.

■ **EXERCISE 2.9**   Mechanical work

In Figure 2.24 the force **F** moves a body along the straight-line path **S**. The **work** done by this force is, by definition, the product of the projection of **F** on **S** and the length of the path **S**, that is the scalar product of **F** and **S** (see, for example, Edward 1964, pages 42–4).

Depending on the problem, the path **S** may be any line in a plane or in space. Then, in order to calculate the work, we must break the path into several straight-line segments, calculate the work done on each of them and add the partial results. In the general case, in which the path is a curve, the process leads to a **line integral**.

If the force fulfils certain conditions, the work done by it will be independent of the path, that is, a function of the initial and end points only (see, for instance, Piskunov 1960, page 672, or Spiegel 1972, page 89). The simplest case is that of a constant force.

As an example consider in Figure 2.25 a force, **F**, whose horizontal component is $2N$, while the vertical component equals $3N$. Let this force act on straight paths from the point A, with coordinates $(1.5, 1)$ m, through the points B, with coordinates

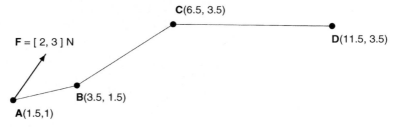

Figure 2.25   Calculating work.

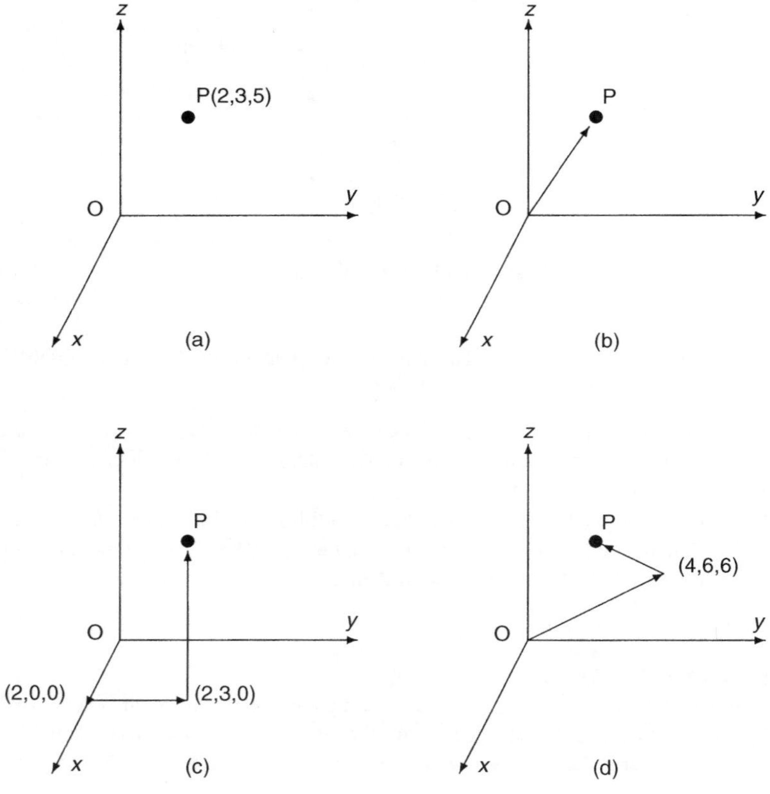

Figure 2.26   Paths for calculating work.

(3.5, 1.5) m, C, with coordinates (6.5, 3.5) m, to D whose coordinates are
(11.5, 3.5) m. To calculate the work in MATLAB we begin by defining the force and
the coordinates of the four points:

```
>> F = [ 2, 3 ];
>> A = [ 1.5 1 ]; B = [ 3.5 1.5 ];
>> C = [ 6.5 3.5 ]; D = [ 11.5 3.5 ];
```

Next we calculate the paths and the work done on each path:

```
≫ P1 = B - A; W1 = F*P1'; % work on path AB
≫ P2 = C - B; W2 = F*P2'; % work on path BC
≫ P3 = D - C; W3 = F*P3'; % work on path CD
≫ work = W1 + W2 + W3  % total work
W =
   27.5000
```

that is, 27.5 Nm. The same work is done if the force **F** acts on the path that connects A directly to D:

```
≫ P = D - A; W = F*P'
W =
   27.5000
```

As an exercise, let us consider now a force equally inclined with respect to the three coordinate planes xOy, yOz, and zOx, and defined by $\mathbf{F} = (2, 2, 2)$ in newtons. Assume that this force moves a body from the origin $O(0, 0, 0)$ to the point $P(2, 3, 5)$, with coordinates in metres – see Figure 2.26(a) – and that the path may be any one of the three:

(1) directly from the origin O to the point P, that is, along the path represented by the vector $(2, 3, 5)$ (Figure 2.26(b)):

(2) along the Ox axis, that is, the path $(2, 0, 0)$, then parallel to the Oy axis, that is, parallel to the vector $(0, 3, 0)$, and finally parallel to the Oz axis, that is, parallel to the vector $(0, 0, 5)$ (Figure 2.26(c));

(3) from the origin to the point $P_1(4, 6, 6)$ and continuing to the point P (Figure 2.26(d)).

Calculate in MATLAB the work done in the three cases and show that the results are identical.

■ **EXERCISE 2.10**   CG of bar with two weights
Figure 2.27 shows a bar with a weight at each end. The length, in mm, and the weights, in N, are given on the figure. If we want to pick up the bar, the easiest way is

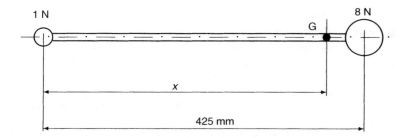

Figure 2.27   Bar with two weights.

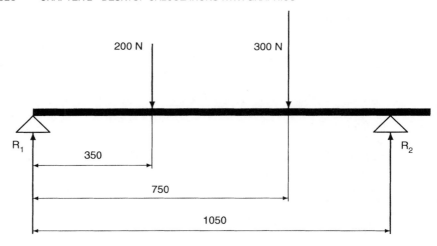

Figure 2.28   Reactions under a simply-supported beam.

to hold it close to its centre of gravity, G. Then the bar will stay horizontal. Using the scalar product and the **sum** function, find the x-coordinate of the centre of gravity, G.

■ **EXERCISE 2.11**   Reactions under a simply-supported beam

Figure 2.28 shows a simply-supported beam loaded by two forces. The levers of the forces are measured in mm, the forces in N. Using the scalar product find the array of reactions $[R_1, R_2]$. Check your results by comparing the sum of reactions with the sum of forces.

■ **EXERCISE 2.12**   Reactions under a simply-supported beam

Figure 2.29 shows a simply-supported beam loaded by three forces. The levers of the forces are measured in mm, the forces in N. Using the scalar product find the array of reactions $[R_1, R_2]$. Verify that the sum of the reactions equals that of the forces acting on the beam.

■ **EXERCISE 2.13**   Balancing an unusual seesaw

Figure 2.30 is a sketch of a seesaw with two children playing on it. The seesaw consists of two planks that make an angle of 120°. The left-hand child weighs 500 N and sits on a plank whose length is 1500 mm; the other child weighs 400 N and sits on a plank 2000 mm long.

Find graphically the angle of equilibrium, α, between the left-hand plank and the horizontal.

Hint: Plot against α the curves of the moments produced by the two children. The problem admits an analytic solution. You may want to find it and use it to check the graphic solution.

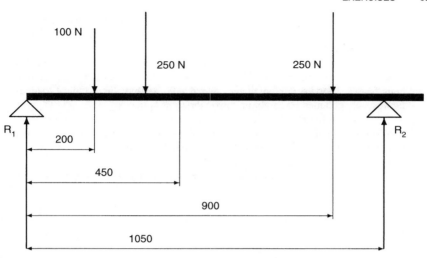

Figure 2.29   Reactions under a simply-supported beam

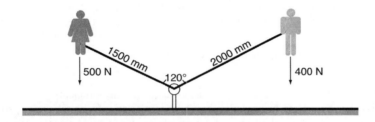

Figure 2.30   Balancing an unusual seesaw.

■ **EXERCISE 2.14**   Aluminium resistivity and temperature
With the same notations as in Example 2.11, the values for aluminium are

$$
\begin{aligned}
\rho &= 0.0286 \ \Omega\text{mm}^2/\text{m} \\
\alpha &= 0.0038\text{K}^{-1} \\
\rho_{20} &= 0.027 \ \Omega\text{mm}^2/\text{m} \\
\alpha_{20} &= 4.3 \times 10^{-3}\text{K}^{-1} \\
\beta_{20} &= 1.3 \times 10^{-6}\text{K}^{-2}
\end{aligned}
$$

Compare graphically the results obtained with Equations 2.20 and 2.21.

■ **EXERCISE 2.15**   Lissajous figures – introduction
Let a point describe a motion in the x, y plane such that

$$x = A \sin(\omega_A + \phi_A) \tag{2.29}$$
$$y = B \sin(\omega_B + \phi_A) \tag{2.30}$$

If the ratio ω_A/ω_B is the ratio of two integers, the resulting curve, $y = f(x)$, assumes certain characteristic forms known as **Lissajous figures** (Jules Antoine Lissajous, French, 1822–1889).

Lissajous figures were first obtained by mechanical means, the first one being **Blackburn's pendulum** devised in 1844. That apparatus consisted of a pendulum hung from a second pendulum that oscillated at $90°$ with the first. Later Lissajous figures were obtained by combining two vibrations optically.

Lissajous figures found an important use with the advent of cathode-ray oscilloscopes. In these instruments the signal x – that is, a voltage having the form of x in Equation 2.29 – is applied to the horizontal deflection plates, while the y signal (Equation 2.30) is applied to the vertical deflection plates.

MATLAB allows us to simulate the response of the oscilloscope. As a simple example assume

$$A = 1, \ B = 1, \ \omega_A = 2\pi, \ \omega_B = 2\pi, \ \phi_A = \pi/2, \ \phi_B = 0$$

and try the following commands

```
t = 0:  0.01:  1;
x = sin(2*pi*t + pi/2); y = sin(2*pi*t);
plot(x, y), axis('square')
```

Explain why you obtained a circle.

■   **EXERCISE 2.16**   Lissajous figures – frequency measurements
Lissajous figures can be used to determine the frequency of a signal by comparing it with a signal generated by the user. Let us assume, for example, that the signal to be analysed,

$$y = A \sin \omega_A t$$

is supplied to the vertical-deflection plates of an oscilloscope. Suppose also that the user tries several known signals on the horizontal-deflection plates until he or she stops at the signal

$$x = A \sin 2\omega_A t$$

Note that during one cycle of y, x executes two cycles. This means that while y reaches the maximum and minimum vertical deflections once, x reaches the minimum and maximum horizontal deflections twice. The resulting oscilloscope picture is shown in Figure 2.31.

Instead of the oscilloscope we can use MATLAB to analyse a signal obtained by a data-acquisition system. To do this:

(1)   Convert the sampled signal into an array called, for instance, y. The job can be done by editing the file of measured values.
(2)   Generate an array of sinusoidal-signal values and call it, for example, x.
(3)   Plot y against x.

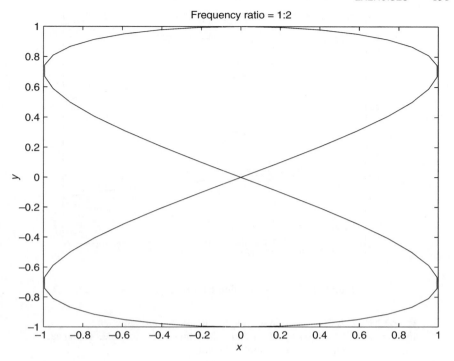

Figure 2.31   Frequency measurement on Lissajous figures.

(4)   If the plotted pattern does not yield the desired information, repeat steps 2 and 3
with another multiple of ω_A.

The rule for comparing the frequencies of two signals having the same phase is:

> Let ω_x be the angular frequency of the signal supplied to the
> horizontal-deflection plates, and ω_y the angular frequency of the signal supplied
> to the vertical-deflection plates. Let n_h be the number of horizontal minima –
> that is, the number of times the figure is tangential at the left to a vertical line –
> and n_v the number of vertical maxima – that is, the number of times the figure is
> tangential at the top to a horizontal line. Then, the ratio of frequencies is equal to
>
> $$\omega_y/\omega_x = n_v/n_h \qquad\qquad (2.31)$$
>
> If the Lissajous figure is open at one end, as in Figure 2.32, add only 0.5 to n_h or
> to n_v.

For example, in Figure 2.32 we count that the Lissajous figure is 0.5 times tangential at
the top to a horizontal line, and 3.5 times tangential at the left to a vertical line. This
yields the frequency ratio 0.5:3.5, or 1:7.

Verify the rule for the frequency ratios 1:1, 2:1, . . . ,5:1.

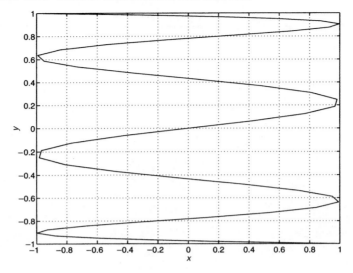

Figure 2.32   Lissajous figure for frequency ratio 1:7.

■ **EXERCISE 2.17**   Lissajous figures – frequency measurements
In Exercise 2.16 the two signals, x and y, had the same amplitude, A. Repeat the
exercise by assuming different amplitude ratios, that is

$$x = A_x \sin \omega_x t$$
$$y = A_y \sin \omega_y t$$

where

$$\omega_x / \omega_y = 1{:}1, \ 2{:}1, \ \ldots, 5{:}1$$

and

$$A_x / A_y = 1{:}2, \ 2{:}1, \ 3{:}1$$

Try to draw a conclusion on the influence of the ratio of amplitudes on the shape
of Lissajous figures.

■ **EXERCISE 2.18**   Lissajous figures – phase measurements
In Exercises 2.16 and 2.17 we saw that Lissajous figures can be used for measuring the
frequency of an acquired signal. In this exercise we shall see that Lissajous figures can
also be used for measuring the phase of a signal. In this application, however, the
answer may not be unique.
    Let us compare the signals

$$x = A \sin(\omega t + \phi_x) \tag{2.32}$$
$$y = A \sin(\omega t + \phi_y) \tag{2.33}$$

by plotting y against x. The maximum y-value is reached for $\omega t + \phi_y = \pi/2$, and it equals

$$y_M = A \qquad\qquad\qquad (2.34)$$

The figure intercepts the y-axis when $x = 0$, that is, when $\omega t + \phi_y = 0$. For this value

$$y_I = A \sin(\phi_y - \phi_x) \qquad\qquad\qquad (2.35)$$

Dividing Equation 2.35 by Equation 2.34 yields

$$\frac{y_I}{y_M} = \frac{A \sin(\phi_y - \phi_x)}{A} \qquad\qquad\qquad (2.36)$$

From Equation 2.36 we conclude that the phase difference equals

$$\phi_y - \phi_x = \arcsin \frac{y_I}{y_M} \qquad\qquad\qquad (2.37)$$

Obviously, the same result will be obtained if y_I is the distance between two intercepts of the y-axis, and y_M, the vertical distance between the minimum and the maximum y-values (that is $y_{max} - y_{min}$).

As an example consider Figure 2.33. The graph corresponds to

$$x = \sin \omega t$$
$$y = \sin(\omega t + \phi)$$

where $\phi = \pi/4$. Let us measure on the figure

- The minimum-to-maximum vertical deflection, $\overline{V_1 V_2}$. It is equal to 2.

- The vertical distance between the two y-axis intercepts, $\overline{I_1 I_2}$. It is approximately equal to 1.4.

We calculate the phase from

$$\sin \phi = \frac{\overline{I_1 I_2}}{\overline{V_1 V_2}}$$

which yields $\phi \approx \pi/4$. Actually it is exactly $\pi/4$.

Build graphs for phase differences equal to $0°$, $45°$, $90°$ and $135°$, and verify that Equation 2.37 holds in all these cases. Verify also that this equation yields for $180°$ the same result as for $0°$, for $225°$ the same result as for $45°$, for $270°$ the same result as for $90°$, and for $315°$ the same result as for $135°$.

There are means for removing the ambiguity but they are beyond the scope of this book.

LIVERPOOL
JOHN MOORES UNIVERSITY
AVRIL ROBARTS LRC
TEL. 0151 231 4022

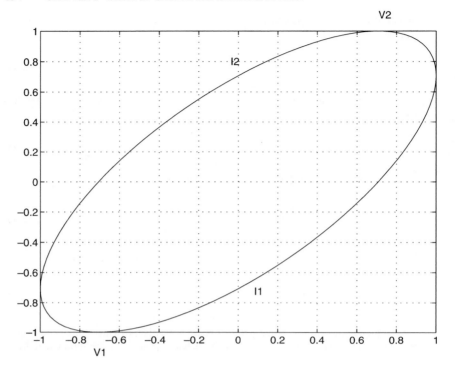

Figure 2.33   Measuring phase on Lissajous figures.

2.15   Appendix – a note on Fourier series

Let us consider a function $f(t)$. If there is a number $T \neq 0$ such that

$$f(t + T) = f(t) \tag{2.38}$$

for any t, we say that f is **periodic with period** T. The smallest positive number T for which Equation 2.38 holds is called the **fundamental period**, or, by abuse of language, simply **period**.

Let us assume now that the function $f(t)$ fulfils the following conditions due to Dirichlet (Peter Gustav Lejeune, born in Germany to a French family, 1805–1859):

(1) $f(x)$ is continuous in an interval $[\theta, \theta + T]$ except possibly for a finite number of finite discontinuities;

(2)   The derivative $\acute{f}(t)$ is similarly piecewise continuous.

Then there exists a number a_0 and two sequences a_n, b_n such that

$$f(t) = \frac{1}{2}a_0 + \sum_{n=1}^{\infty}\left(a_n \cos 2\pi \frac{nt}{T} + b_n \sin 2\pi \frac{nt}{T}\right) \tag{2.39}$$

converges to $f(t)$ at each point of continuity, and to

$$\frac{f(x+0) + f(x-0)}{2}$$

at the points of discontinuity (see, for example, Bronshtein and Semendyayev 1985). Here $f(x+0)$ means the limit of $f(x)$ as x approaches the discontinuity from the left, and $f(x-0)$ the limit as x approaches the discontinuity from the right.

There are other, equivalent formulations of the Dirichlet conditions. A good treatment of Fourier series can be found in Churchill and Brown (1990). More about Fourier series and numerical calculation of their coefficients can be found in Chapter 16.

Chapter 3
Two-dimensional arrays and matrices

3.1 Building a matrix out of vectors

Besides a presentation of elementary matrix operations, this chapter is also a painless introduction to matrices. Matrices are indispensable for an efficient use of MATLAB. Therefore, readers who have not yet learnt this subject, or who have not worked extensively with matrices, could profit from reading this chapter attentively. Readers familiar with matrices may go quickly through the first sections, learn the MATLAB matrix notations and operators from the summary, and study the examples.

Let us return to the shopping list shown in Table 2.1. The quantities indicated there were for one month only. We shall now specify the quantities for three months, as in Table 3.1. Extending the example shown in Chapter 2, we can calculate the expenditures of the three months as follows. We first define the array of prices and the arrays of quantities:

```
>> price = [ 3.00 1.99 10.99 9.15 1.29 ];
>> Jan = [ 3 2 1 5 2 ];
>> Feb = [ 2 3 1 3 3 ];
>> March = [ 1 0 3 3 3 ];
```

Table 3.1   A three-month shopping list.

Item	Price	Quantity			Subtotals			Totals
no.		Jan.	Feb.	March	Jan.	Feb.	March	
1	3.00	3	2	1	9.00	6.00	3.00	18.00
2	1.99	2	3	0	3.98	5.97	0.00	9.95
3	10.99	1	1	3	10.99	10.99	32.97	54.95
4	9.15	5	3	3	45.75	27.45	27.45	100.65
5	1.29	2	3	3	2.58	3.87	3.87	10.32
Totals		13	12	10	72.30	54.28	67.29	193.87

Next we calculate the monthly totals by

```
>> tot_Jan = price*Jan'
>> tot_Feb = price*Feb'
>> tot_March = price*March'
```

which amounts to

$$
\begin{bmatrix} 3.00 & 1.99 & 10.99 & 9.15 & 1.29 \end{bmatrix} \begin{bmatrix} 3 \\ 2 \\ 1 \\ 5 \\ 2 \end{bmatrix} = 72.30 \tag{3.1}
$$

$$
\begin{bmatrix} 3.00 & 1.99 & 10.99 & 9.15 & 1.29 \end{bmatrix} \begin{bmatrix} 2 \\ 3 \\ 1 \\ 3 \\ 3 \end{bmatrix} = 54.28 \tag{3.2}
$$

$$
\begin{bmatrix} 3.00 & 1.99 & 10.99 & 9.15 & 1.29 \end{bmatrix} \begin{bmatrix} 1 \\ 0 \\ 3 \\ 3 \\ 3 \end{bmatrix} = 67.29 \tag{3.3}
$$

Now, instead of proceeding as in the previous section, let us bring together the arrays of monthly quantities into one tabular form, namely the two-dimensional array (we call it a **matrix**) of quantities. We can obtain this by entering

```
≫ quantity = [ 3 2 1
  2 3 0
  1 1 3
  5 3 3
  2 3 3 ];
```

This is done by typing the first line,

```
≫ quantity = [ 3 2 1
```

followed by Enter. The cursor will wait one line down; no prompt will be displayed. Now enter

```
  2 3 0
```

press Enter and continue in the same way to the last row. Better still, we can use the fact that we already have the arrays (*row vectors*) of monthly quantities and simply type

```
≫ quantity = [ Jan' Feb' March' ]
```

Enter this command and you will obtain the same matrix of quantities. Note that you must enter the transposes of **Jan**, **Feb** and **March** and not the respective row vectors directly. We have shown two ways of entering the matrix; both yield the same result:

```
quantity =
  3 2 1
  2 3 0
  1 1 3
  5 3 3
  2 3 3
```

There is even a third way of obtaining the same matrix:

```
≫ quantity = [ Jan; Feb; March ]'
```

We now have not only a more compact and systematic way of storing the quantities than the one shown in the previous chapter, but we can use it to calculate the expenses by the command

```
>> expenses = price*quantity
```

The result is a row vector that contains the sums spent in each month, that is

```
72.30   54.28   67.29
```

where 72.30 is the total for January, 54.28 for February, and 67.29 for March. The total for all three months is given by

```
>> tot_expense = sum(expenses)
```

with the result 193.8700, while the total quantities per month are obtained by

```
>> monthly_q = sum(quantity)
```

The result of this last command is the vector

```
13      12      10
```

Here, 13 is the total quantity for January, 12 for February, and 10 for March. In total, the number of items purchased during the three months is obtained from

```
>> sum(monthly_q)
```

which gives 35.

3.2   Vector-by-matrix multiplication

In the preceding section, the vector **expenses** resulted from the multiplication of a row vector by a matrix. The full scheme is given below:

$$
\begin{bmatrix} 3.00 & 1.99 & 10.99 & 9.15 & 1.29 \end{bmatrix}
\begin{bmatrix} 3 & 2 & 1 \\ 2 & 3 & 0 \\ 1 & 1 & 3 \\ 5 & 3 & 3 \\ 2 & 3 & 3 \end{bmatrix}
$$

$$
= \begin{bmatrix} 72.30 & 54.28 & 67.29 \end{bmatrix} \tag{3.4}
$$

We see that the first component of the resulting row vector is the scalar product of the row vector **price** and the first column of the matrix **quantity**. Similarly, the second component of the vector **expenses** is the scalar product of the row vector **price** and the second column of the matrix **quantity**. In general the i-th component of the resulting row vector is the scalar product of the row vector **price** and the i-th column of the matrix **quantity**. Let us assume that the row vector which is the first multiplicand has m components, in our example

```
>> m = length(price)
m =
     5
```

Then the matrix, which is the second multiplicand, must have m rows, in our example 5. Also, if the matrix has n columns, in our example 3 columns, the result will be a row vector with n columns. We may give a more general formulation of the above remarks if we say that a matrix with m rows and n columns is an m-by-n matrix. Correspondingly, a row vector of length n will be called a 1-by-n matrix. We summarize these remarks by the scheme

$$(1 \ by \ m) * (m \ by \ n) \longrightarrow (1 \ by \ n) \tag{3.5}$$

Checking the schematic representation shown in Formula 3.5 in our example, we see that the 'outer dimensions', *1* and *3*, of the two matrices to be multiplied match the dimensions of the product matrix, while the 'inner dimensions', *5*, are identical for both factors.

The shopping list example allowed us to introduce the concepts of a matrix and of vector-by-matrix multiplication in a simple way. Spreadsheet users may rightly point out that the problem of the shopping list could have been elegantly solved by any spreadsheet program. Among the advantages of such programs are:

- the possibility of producing a display such as Table 3.1 directly;
- the ease of changing data: the spreadsheet will automatically recalculate the results.

Spreadsheet programs are optimized for a particular task and, therefore, they perform this task better than other programs. However, we can reply that:

(1) Results calculated by MATLAB can be used straightforwardly in further calculations; an example will be shown later.

(2) In MATLAB, it is also possible to change data, although the procedure is less elegant than in spreadsheets.

(3) As shown in the next section, when the first factor is a matrix with several rows, and not simply a row vector, MATLAB is a natural environment for this calculation, while a spreadsheet program is an awkward one.

Let us begin with the second point and refer again to the data in Table 3.1. Suppose that we have not ended the session; we still have the data in memory, and we want to change the quantity of item No. 2 bought in January to 5. To do this we type

```
>> quantity(2,1) = 5
quantity =
   3  2  1
   5  3  0
   1  1  3
   5  3  3
   2  3  3
```

We will get the matrix **quantity** with the element in the 2nd row and 1st column changed to 5, while all other elements remain unchanged. Now use the *Up Arrow* to retrieve the operations previously defined and update the results. For example, pressing the *Up Arrow* several times returns the command

```
>> expenses = price*quantity
```

Pressing Enter now produces the updated result

```
expenses =
  78.2700  54.2800  67.2900
```

The results obtained in the above example are stored in the variables named during the calculations, and they can be used in other operations during the same MATLAB session. This possibility is illustrated in Example 3.3. As shown in Chapter 8, results can be also stored in external files for use in other MATLAB sessions. With this facility, for some applications MATLAB may be much more flexible than certain spreadsheet programs.

3.3   Matrix-by-matrix multiplication

Let us return to the example in Table 3.1 and suppose that the items to be purchased are 'raw' machine elements that must be transported and machined. Let us further assume that the full list of costs is as given in Table 3.2; based on it we enter row by row the matrix

$$
\text{costs} = \begin{bmatrix} 3.00 & 1.99 & 10.99 & 9.15 & 1.29 \\ 0.29 & 0.14 & 1.00 & 0.98 & 0.10 \\ 1.29 & 0.89 & 2.30 & 1.98 & 0.00 \end{bmatrix} \tag{3.6}
$$

and we obtain the matrix of expenses by the command

Table 3.2   A table of costs.

| Item | Costs | | | |
no.	Initial	Transportation	Machining	Total
1	3.00	0.29	1.29	4.58
2	1.99	0.14	0.89	3.02
3	10.99	1.00	2.30	14.29
4	9.15	0.98	1.98	12.11
5	1.29	0.10	0.00	1.39

```
>> costs*quantity
```

where the matrix **quantity** is the one defined in the preceding section. The full calculation is shown in Equation 3.7:

$$
\begin{bmatrix} 3.00 & 1.99 & 10.99 & 9.15 & 1.29 \\ 0.29 & 0.14 & 1.00 & 0.98 & 0.10 \\ 1.29 & 0.89 & 2.30 & 1.98 & 0.00 \end{bmatrix} * \begin{bmatrix} 3 & 2 & 1 \\ 2 & 3 & 0 \\ 1 & 1 & 3 \\ 5 & 3 & 3 \\ 2 & 3 & 3 \end{bmatrix} =
$$

$$
\begin{bmatrix} 72.30 & 54.28 & 67.29 \\ 7.25 & 5.24 & 6.53 \\ 17.85 & 13.49 & 14.13 \end{bmatrix} \tag{3.7}
$$

In this example each element of the resulting matrix represents the total monthly expenditure in a particular category of costs. For example, 5.24, the value in the second row and second column, is the total transportation cost in the month of February. As can be easily checked, the element in the i-th row and j-th column of the resulting matrix is the scalar product of the i-th row of the matrix **costs** by the j-th column of the matrix **quantity**. Still more insight can be achieved by arranging the matrices in a way that Dietrich and Stahl (1965) attribute to Falk; this is done in Figure 3.1.

Now, we can generalize Formula 3.5 and write

$$
(\ell \ by \ m) * (m \ by \ n) \longrightarrow (\ell \ by \ n) \tag{3.8}
$$

which for the multiplication shown in Equation 3.7 amounts to

$$
(3 \ by \ 5) * (5 \ by \ 3) \longrightarrow (3 \ by \ 3) \tag{3.9}
$$

With this we have now the explanation promised when the scalar product was introduced in Chapter 2, that is, why the scalar product of the two vectors **A** and **B** is given by A*B' or by B*A'. Indeed, for two row vectors **A** and **B** of length n, that is,

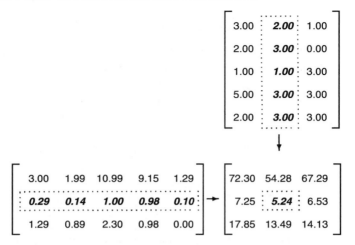

Figure 3.1   Matrix-by-matrix multiplication according to Falk.

Table 3.3   Two sets of results.

Analytic	Numerical
0.0314	0.0389
0.1257	0.1530
0.2827	0.3370
0.5027	0.5642
0.7854	0.8304
0.9998	1.0082

for two 1-by-n matrices, A*B' or B*A' obey Formula 3.8 as

$$(1 \ by \ n) * (n \ by \ 1) \longrightarrow (1 \ by \ 1) \tag{3.10}$$

3.4   Array division

In Chapter 2 we introduced the **array product**, an operation that, when applied to two vectors, $\mathbf{A} = [a_1 \ a_2 \dots a_n]$, $\mathbf{B} = [b_1 \ b_2 \dots b_n]$, of the same length n, yields the vector $\mathbf{P} = [a_1 b_1 \ a_2 b_2 \dots a_n b_n]$. In this section we shall give an example of the 'inverse' operation, which is **array division**. Suppose, for instance, that for a certain problem we could calculate two solutions, one 'exact', obtained from an analytical formulation, the other approximate, obtained by numerical integration. Let the two sets of results be those in Table 3.3. We define the two vectors

```
≫ analytic  = [ 0.0314 0.1257 ...   0.9998 ];
≫ numerical = [ 0.0389 0.1530 ...   1.0082 ];
```

The error is given by

```
>> error = analytic - numerical
error =
  -0.0075 -0.0273 -0.0543 -0.0615 -0.0450 -0.0084
```

The relative error, in %, can be calculated by the MATLAB command

```
>> pct = 100*(analytic - numerical)./analytic
pct =
  -23.8854 -21.7184 -19.2076 -12.2339 -5.7296 -0.8402
```

The point followed by a slash, '$./$', is the array division operator that, for two vectors **A, B**, produces the vector $\mathbf{D} = [a_1/b_1 \ a_2/b_2 \ldots a_n/b_n]$. Further examples of array division are given at the end of this chapter.

3.5 Matrix addition

Let us return to the shopping list shown in Table 3.1 and the costs listed in Table 3.2. Suppose now that the company considered here actually has two departments and that the quantities shown in Table 3.1 are for department I only. Let the quantities required by department II be those shown in Table 3.4. For consistency we shall redefine the matrix **quantity** as **quantityI**. If we still have **quantity** in the memory of our computer, we do this by the command

```
>> quantityI = quantity;
```

and we free the memory space allocated to the matrix **quantity** by the command

```
>> clear quantity
```

Table 3.4 The quantities required by department II.

Item no.	Jan.	Feb.	March
1	4	1	2
2	3	2	0
3	2	0	6
4	6	2	6
5	3	2	6
Total	18	7	20

If the matrix **quantity** is no longer in the memory of our computer, we must enter it again. We also enter the quantities shown in Table 3.4 as the matrix **quantityII**, and we either have, or re-enter, the matrix **costs**. The matrices of expenses for the two departments are obtained by

```
>> deptI = costs*quantityI
>> deptII = costs*quantityII
```

with the results

$$\text{deptI} = \begin{bmatrix} 72.3000 & 54.2800 & 67.2900 \\ 7.2500 & 5.2400 & 6.5300 \\ 17.8500 & 13.4900 & 14.1300 \end{bmatrix}$$

$$\text{deptII} = \begin{bmatrix} 98.7200 & 27.8600 & 134.5800 \\ 9.7600 & 2.7300 & 13.0600 \\ 24.3100 & 7.0300 & 28.2600 \end{bmatrix}$$

We can obtain the total expenses of the company by

```
>> TOTAL = deptI + deptII
```

which gives

$$\text{TOTAL} = \begin{bmatrix} 171.0200 & 82.1400 & 201.8700 \\ 17.0100 & 7.9700 & 19.5900 \\ 42.1600 & 20.5200 & 42.3900 \end{bmatrix}$$

It can be immediately checked that the element in the i-th row and j-th column of TOTAL is the sum of elements in the i-th rows and j-th columns of the matrices **deptI** and **deptII**, for example 171.0200 is the sum of the elements 72.300 and 98.7200.

As an exercise, instead of proceeding as above, first add the quantities for both departments:

```
>> both = quantityI + quantityII
```

and perform the multiplication

```
>> costs*both
```

Compare the result with the matrix **TOTAL** previously obtained.

3.6   Multidimensional arrays

In the previous section we used two arrays to store the quantities required by each department. MATLAB allows us to consolidate the two arrays, quantityI and quantityII, in a single, **three-dimensional array**. Similarly, the results of the multiplication by the array costs can be stored in a single, three-dimensional array, departments. Three-dimensional arrays are an example of **multidimensional arrays**. While the elements of a two-dimensional array are identified by two indices, the number of the **row** and the number of the **column**, the elements of a three-dimensional array are identified by three indices, that is the numbers of the row, column and **page**. Thus, for example, a three-dimensional array containing the costs of all items in the example in Section 3.5 can be represented as in Figure 3.2. The *initial* costs of all items in February, in department II, is 27.86. This value is stored in row 1, column 2 and page 2 of the array departments. Therefore, this element is characterized by the set of indices {1, 2, 2}.

To build the three-dimensional array quantities, we begin by preallocating space for it:

```
>> format bank
>> [ m n ] = size(quantityI);
>> quantities = zeros(m, n, 2);
```

Next, we assign the values in the array quantityI to the first page of the array quantities, and the values in the array quantityII to the second page of the array quantities:

```
>> quantities(:, :, 1) = quantityI;
>> quantities(:, :, 2) = quantityII;
```

Another possibility is to *concatenate* the two arrays, quantityI and quantityII, by means of the function cat:

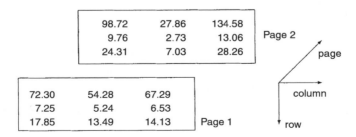

Figure 3.2   A graphic representation of the array departments.

```
>> quantities = cat(3, quantityI, quantityII)
```

The first argument, 3, in the call of the function cat indicates that the arrays identified by the other arguments should be concatenated along the third dimension. In other words, the arrays named by the second and third argument should become *pages* of the resulting array, quantities.

We cannot proceed further by multiplying the array costs by the three-dimensional array quantities because the operation of multiplication is not defined for multidimensional arrays. Therefore, we must multiply the array costs by the pages of the array quantities. We can do this in two operations, one for each page. However, as in other cases the multidimensional array can have more than two pages, we shall show how to perform the operation in a FOR loop.

```
>> [ m n o ] = size(quantities);
>> for k = 1:o
>> departments(:, :, k) = costs*quantities(:, :, k);
>> end
>> departments
 deptI =
     72.30 54.28 67.29
      7.25  5.24  6.53
     17.85 13.49 14.13
 deptII =
     98.72 27.86 134.58
      9.76  2.73  13.06
     24.31  7.03  28.26
```

We can sum directly the costs by

```
>> TOTAL = departments(:, :, 1) + departments(:, :, 2)
TOTAL =
    171.02 82.14 201.87
     17.01  7.97  19.59
     42.16 20.52  42.39
```

For more pages it would be convenient to add the costs in a FOR loop:

```
>> [ m n o ] = size(departments);
TOTAL = zeros(m, n);
```

```
for k = 1:o
        TOTAL = TOTAL + departments(:, :, k);
end
TOTAL
```

Try this loop for yourself. Applying the function sum to the multidimensional array departments results in

```
>> sum(departments)
ans(:,:,1) =
     97.40 73.01 87.95
ans(:,:,2) =
     132.79 37.62 175.90
```

Verify for yourself that these numbers represent the total costs (initial plus transportation plus machining) of all items. per month and per department. For example, 73.01 is the total cost of all items, in the month of February and department I.

Another example employing multidimensional arrays can be found in Chapter 10.

3.7   Summary

In this chapter we have learnt that an m-by-n matrix $\mathbf{A}$ is an array

$$
\begin{bmatrix}
a_{11} & a_{12} & \cdots & a_{1j} & \cdots & a_{1n} \\
\cdots & \cdots & \cdots & \cdots & \cdots & \cdots \\
a_{i1} & a_{i2} & \cdots & a_{ij} & \cdots & a_{in} \\
\cdots & \cdots & \cdots & \cdots & \cdots & \cdots \\
a_{m1} & a_{m2} & \cdots & a_{mj} & \cdots & a_{mn}
\end{bmatrix}
$$

with m rows and n columns. One way of entering a matrix in MATLAB consists in typing its name, the equality sign, and the first row opened by a left bracket

$$A = [\, a_{11}\, a_{12} \ldots a_{1j} \ldots a_{1n}$$

and pressing Enter; next, the second row

$$a_{21}\, a_{22} \ldots a_{2j} \ldots a_{2n}$$

and pressing Enter; and so on until the last row, which is closed by a right bracket:

$$a_{m1}\, a_{m2} \ldots a_{mj} \ldots a_{mn}\,]$$

A row vector of length ℓ is a 1-by-ℓ matrix, and a column vector of length ℓ is an ℓ-by-1 matrix.

Given m row vectors, $\mathbf{A1}$, $\mathbf{A2}$, ..., $\mathbf{Am}$, all of the same length n, we can build in MATLAB an m-by-n matrix $\mathbf{A}$ by the command

```
≫ A = [ A1; A2; ...  Am ]
```

or by

```
≫ A = [ A1
A2
⋮
Am ]
```

Similarly, we can build an m-by-n matrix by placing n column vectors, $\mathbf{A1}$, $\mathbf{A2}$, ..., $\mathbf{An}$, all of the same length m, side by side by the command

```
≫ A = [ A1 A2 ...  An ]
```

A row vector $\mathbf{A}$, of length m, can multiply a matrix $\mathbf{B}$ with m rows. If the matrix has n columns, the result is a row vector $\mathbf{C}$ of length n. In MATLAB we write this operation as C = A*B.

A matrix $\mathbf{A}$ can multiply another matrix $\mathbf{B}$ if the number of columns of $\mathbf{A}$ equals the number of rows of $\mathbf{B}$. If the size of $\mathbf{A}$ is ℓ by m, and the size of $\mathbf{B}$, m by n, then the size of the result is ℓ by n (see the schematic representation in Formula 3.8 above). In MATLAB we perform this operation by the command

```
≫ C = A*B
```

Another MATLAB operation we have learnt in this chapter is array division: for two vectors of the same length and orientation (that is, either both vectors are row vectors, or both are column vectors), $\mathbf{A} = [a_1 \ a_2 \ldots a_n]$, $\mathbf{B} = [b_1 \ b_2 \ldots b_n]$ (change appropriately for column vectors), array division produces the vector $\mathbf{C} = [a_1/b_1 \ a_2/b_2 \ldots a_n/b_n]$. The operation is carried out by the command

```
≫ C = A./B
```

Note the point before the slash.

We have used vector-by-matrix and matrix-by-matrix multiplication in order to calculate several kinds of expenditures in a systematic and concise way. In Example 3.3 vector-by-matrix multiplication is used in the calculation of the centre of gravity of a three-dimensional system of masses, and the results are used in further calculations to check the stability of a self-propelled crane.

In this chapter, one application of array division was in estimating relative errors. In the examples and exercises that follow, array division will be used to calculate equivalent resistances, capacitances and inductances.

As shown in Chapter 12, an interesting application of the repeated multiplication (powers) of square matrices by themselves is in graph theory where it helps to find paths of given length.

An important new feature of MATLAB 5 is the possibility of building multi-dimensional arrays, that is arrays whose elements are identified by more than two indices. Thus, for example, in three-dimensional arrays an element is identified by three indices: the number of the row, the number of the column and the number of the page.

3.8   Examples

EXAMPLE 3.1   Printing a table of sine values ⎯⎯⎯⎯⎯⎯⎯⎯⎯⎯⎯⎯

Let us print a table of $\sin x$ values for $x = 0°, 5°, 10°, \ldots, 90°$. We first define a vector of equally spaced x-values by indicating the first value, the x-step, and the last value:

```
≫ x = 0:  5:  90;
```

Next, we create the desired vector of sine values by the command

```
≫ y = sin(pi*x/180);
```

Note the conversion from degrees to radians. Both **x** and **y** are row vectors. We convert them to column vectors by transposition and we create a matrix by entering

```
≫ [ x' y' ]
```

The resulting display is the table we wanted to print, that is

```
ans =
            0         0
       5.0000    0.0872
      10.0000    0.1736
        . . .     . . .
      90.0000    1.0000
```

EXTENDED EXAMPLE 3.3   Crane stability _____

In the following example a simple problem in mechanical engineering is treated efficiently in MATLAB because it can be formulated in terms of matrices and vectors. This formulation also simplifies calculations when it is necessary to consider several cases of operation and change data from one case to another. This is a situation often encountered in engineering design. Data must also be changed when several variants of the same design must be evaluated and compared.

Figure 3.3 represents a truck crane and Table 3.5 lists the weights of its main components as calculated in the first design stage. There are three crew members, all supposed to be seated in the driver's cabin. The coordinates of the centres of gravity are measured along the axes described below:

- The x-axis lies on the ground, in the plane of symmetry of the right-hand tyres – let us call this plane P – and is positive towards the driver's cabin (forwards).
- The y-axis lies on the ground, in the vertical plane that contains the axis of the rear axle – let us call this plane R – and is positive to the left of the truck.
- The z-axis is the intersection of the planes P and R and is positive upwards.

The crane can travel at a speed of 75 km/h and can follow a circular path having a radius of 8 m. The forces acting on the truck crane, while turning in this circle, are

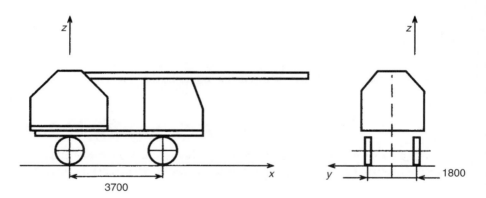

Figure 3.3   A truck crane. Dimensions in mm.

Table 3.5   The weights of the truck crane.

Item	Weight	Centre of gravity, m		
	kN	x	y	z
Truck	42.18	0.89	0.90	1.70
Crane	33.35	0.00	0.90	2.20
Jib	9.81	4.70	0.90	3.70
Crew	2.35	4.20	0.90	2.20

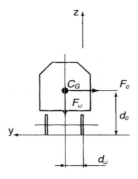

Figure 3.4   Forces acting on the truck crane.

shown in Figure 3.4 where F_w is the total weight, and F_c the centrifugal force. Both F_w and F_c act through the centre of gravity of the truck crane. This centre, C_G, is defined by its coordinates, d_w and d_c, as shown in the figure. The centrifugal force can cause overturning around the right-side wheels. The overturning moment equals $F_c d_c$; it is opposed by the 'stabilizing' moment $F_w d_w$.

The ratio of the stabilizing moment to the overturning moment is a factor of safety for crane stability

$$S = \frac{F_w d_w}{F_c d_c} \tag{3.11}$$

Let us calculate S. We begin by forming a vector of weights

```
>> weights = [ 42.18 33.35 9.81 2.35 ];
```

and a matrix of centres of gravity

```
>> cg = [ 0.89 0.90 1.70
0.00 0.90 2.20
4.70 0.90 3.70
4.20 0.90 2.20 ];
```

The total weight is given by

```
>> Fw = sum(weights)
```

with the result 87.6900 kN. The product weights*cg yields the moments of the weight components in the given system of coordinates. The centre of gravity of the whole crane is obtained with the command

```
≫ CG = weights*cg/Fw
CG =
    1.0665 0.9000 2.1273
```

which yields a vector of three coordinates. The lever arm of the overturning moment is the z-component of $\mathbf{CG}$, that is

```
≫ dc = CG(3)
```

which is 2.1273 m.

We calculate the centrifugal force as

$$mass * speed^2 / radius$$

or, substituting the appropriate values and units,

$$F_c = \frac{F_w}{g} \frac{\text{kN}}{\text{m s}^{-2}} \left[\frac{75 \text{ km/h} * 1000\text{m/km}}{3600 \text{ s/h}} \right]^2 /(8 \text{ m})$$

If we defined somewhere the gravity acceleration $g = 9.8067 \text{ ms}^{-2}$, we carry out the calculation in MATLAB by

```
≫ Fc = (Fw/g)*(75*1000/3600)^2/8
```

obtaining $Fc = 485.1262$ kN. The lever arm of the stabilizing moment is $dw = \text{CG}(2) = 0.9$, and the factor of safety is obtained from

```
≫ S = (Fw*dw)/(Fc*dc)
```

that is, 0.0765. This result simply means that the crane would overturn. In fact, one cannot expect such a vehicle to engage the given circular path successfully at 75 km/h. A speed of 20 km/h seems more reasonable and, indeed, if we use the arrow keys to retrieve the expression of F_c, and we edit it by changing 75 to 20,

```
≫ Fc = (Fw/g)*(20*1000/3600)^2/8
```

we get S = 1.0754. Now the truck crane will not overturn but the factor of safety is too small. Conditions can be improved by lowering the centre of gravity.

Let us now check the case shown in Figure 3.5. The crane handles a load P = 17 kN at a radius of 7 m. Stability is ensured by two outriggers, A and B, extended laterally to each side. It is assumed that one of the crew members operates

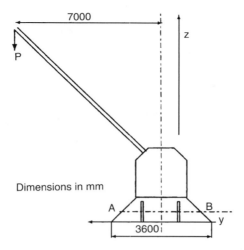

Figure 3.5   Stability, case 1. Dimensions in mm.

the crane from a position approximately at the origin of the x-axis, a second sits in the cabin and operates the engine, and the third is outside the crane and supervises the handling of the load. The corresponding weights and centres of gravity are described in Table 3.6.

We again begin by building a vector of weights, **weight1**, and a matrix of coordinates of centres of gravity, **cg1**. To do so we can either enter **weights1** and **cg1** as new variables, or, better, we can copy **weights** and **cg** and edit them. In the latter case the calculations will look as follows:

```
≫ weights1 = weights;
≫ weights1(4) = 0.78;
≫ weights1(5) = 0.78
weights1 =
      42.1800 33.3500 9.8100 0.7800 0.7800
≫ cg1 = cg;
≫ cg1(3,:)   = [ 0.00 4.40 6.50 ];
≫ cg1(4,:)   = [ 2.35 1.40 2.20 ];
≫ cg1(5,:)   = [ 0.00 0.00 2.50 ]
cg1 =
      0.8900 0.9000 1.7000
           0 0.9000 2.2000
           0 4.4000 6.5000
      2.3500 1.4000 2.2000
           0      0 2.5000
```

Table 3.6   Weights for stability case 1.

Item	Weight	Centre of gravity, m		
	kN	x	y	z
Truck	42.18	0.89	0.00	1.70
Crane	33.35	0.00	0.00	2.20
Jib	9.81	0.00	3.60	6.50
Crew 1	0.78	2.35	0.60	2.20
Crew 2	0.78	0.00	−1.00	2.50

Note the lines that do not end with a semicolon. These lines cause the printing of **weights1** and **cg1**, allowing us to check that we obtained the desired variables. The expression cg1(3,:) means the whole third row of **cg1**. The total weight is given by

```
>> Fw1 = sum(weights1)
```

with the result 86.9000 kN. The centre of gravity is obtained with the command

```
>> CG1 = weights1*cg1/Fw1
CG1 =
    0.4531 1.2915 2.4454
```

The lever arm of the overturning moment is the horizontal distance between the line of action of the load P and the foot of the outrigger A. The lever arm of the stabilizing moment is the horizontal distance between the line of action of the total weight and the foot of the outrigger A. Correspondingly, the factor of safety is obtained from:

```
>> S1 = (Fw1*(3.6/2 + 1.8/2 - CG1(2)))/(1.1*P*(7 - 3.6/2))
S1 =
    1.2587
```

In the above expression $3.6/2 + 1.8/2$ is the distance of the outrigger foot A from the origin of coordinates, and $7 - 3.6/2$ is the horizontal distance between the force P and the same outrigger foot. The factor 1.1 which multiplies P takes into consideration possible overloading, that is, inadvertent lifting of slightly larger loads.

In the case shown in Figure 3.5 we have considered only static forces. Regulations require that inertia forces, produced by load motions and crane turning, and wind forces must be taken into account.

Another case of crane operation is shown in Exercise 3.9.

EXAMPLE 3.3   Parallel connection of resistors

Consider the network of parallel resistors shown in Figure 3.6. Let I_1 be the current passing through R_1, I_2 the current passing through R_2, and I_3 that passing through R_3. Then, according to Ohm's law, the potential difference (voltage drop) between points 1 and 2 equals

$$I_1 R_1 = I_2 R_2 = I_3 R_3 \tag{3.12}$$

According to Kirchhoff's first law (Gustav Robert Kirchhoff, German, 1824–1887), the intensity of the current passing through points 1 and 2 is

$$I = I_1 + I_2 + I_3 \tag{3.13}$$

Let us find the resistance of a single, equivalent resistor R that would cause the same voltage drop as the three resistors R_1, R_2, and R_3, that is

$$I R = I_1 R_1 = I_2 R_2 = I_3 R_3 \tag{3.14}$$

From Equation 3.14 we get

$$I_1 = \frac{R}{R_1}$$
$$I_2 = \frac{R}{R_2}$$
$$I_3 = \frac{R}{R_3}$$

and, after substituting these values into Equation 3.13 and a few algebraical manipulations, we obtain

$$\frac{1}{R} = \frac{1}{R_1} + \frac{1}{R_2} + \frac{1}{R_3} \tag{3.15}$$

(See, for example, Carlson and Gisser 1990, or Nilsson 1993).

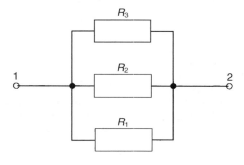

Figure 3.6   Parallel resistors.

Let us assume that $R_1 = 500$ ohms, $R_2 = 1000$ ohms, and $R_3 = 1500$ ohms. In MATLAB 4 we can calculate R by the following sequence of commands

```
>> r = [ 500 1000 1500 ];
>> Rinv = ones(size(r))./r;
>> R = 1/sum(Rinv)
```

which yields 272.7273 ohms. The second command above,

```
>> Rinv = ones(size(r))./r;
```

creates a vector of the same length as r, having all components equal to 1. In general, ones(N), where N is an integer, generates an N-by-N matrix of ones, ones(M, N), where both M, N are integers, generates an M-by-N matrix of ones, and ones(size(A)), where A is a matrix, generates a matrix of ones of the same size as A. In MATLAB 3.5 the latter command should be changed to ones(A).

The array division ones(size(r))./r yields the vector

$$R_{inv} = \left[\frac{1}{R_1} \quad \frac{1}{R_2} \quad \frac{1}{R_3}\right] = [\ 0.0020 \quad 0.0010 \quad 0.0007\ ]$$

and the command sum(Rinv) gives

$$\frac{1}{R_1} + \frac{1}{R_2} + \frac{1}{R_3} = 0.0037$$

The last two commands can be replaced by a single, more compact command that employs a function introduced in one of the following chapters:

```
R = inv(sum(ones(size(r))./r))
```

R as defined by Equation 3.15 is the **harmonic mean** of R_1, R_2 and R_3. In the exercises we shall meet other examples of harmonic means.

EXAMPLE 3.4 A voltage divider _____

In Figure 3.7(a) a potentiometer whose resistance is R is subjected to the voltage U. The cursor divides the total resistance into two partial resistances, R_1 and R_2. The voltage across R_2 is U_2. Without load, the ratio of the voltage U_2 to U equals

$$\frac{U_2}{U} = \frac{R_2}{R} \tag{3.16}$$

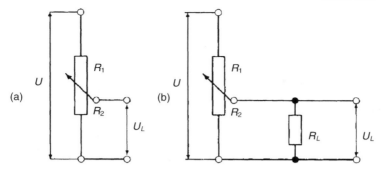

Figure 3.7 A voltage divider.

In Figure 3.7(b) a load whose resistance is R_L is connected across R_2. As shown in the preceding example, the equivalent resistance, R_{eq}, of the parallel connection of R_2 and R_L is given by

$$\frac{1}{R_{eq}} = \frac{1}{R_2} + \frac{1}{R_L}$$

which yields

$$R_{eq} = \frac{R_2 R_L}{R_2 + R_L}$$

The current through R_{eq} is

$$I_{eq} = \frac{U}{R_1 + R_{eq}} = \frac{U}{R - R_2 + (R_2 R_L)/(R_2 + R_L)}$$

and the voltage across R_L, equal to the voltage across R_{eq}, is

$$U_L = I_{eq} R_{eq}$$

The ratio of the load voltage to the source voltage is

$$\frac{U_L}{U} = \frac{R_2/R \cdot R_L/R}{R_2/R - (R_2/R)^2 + R_L/R} \tag{3.17}$$

It follows that the ratio U_L/U is a function of the two ratios R_2/R and R_L/R. The ratio R_2/R can vary between 0 and 1. Let us plot U_L/U against R_2/R, for a small and a large value of R_L/R. For comparison, we shall add on the same graph the characteristic of the circuit without load (Equation 3.16).

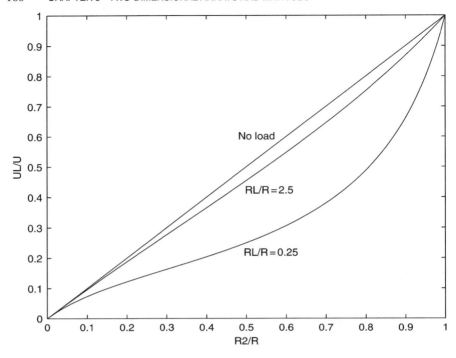

Figure 3.8   The characteristic of a voltage divider.

```
≫ r = 0:  0.01:  1;
≫ rL = 0.25; UL2U1 = (r*rL)./(r - r.^2 + rL);
≫ rL = 2.5; UL2U2 = (r*rL)./(r - r.^2 + rL);
≫ noload= r;
≫ plot(r, UL2U1, r, UL2U2, r, noload)
≫ xlabel('R2/R'), ylabel('UL/U')
≫ text(r(50), noload(60), 'No load')
≫ text(r(50), UL2U1(50), 'RL/R = 0.25')
≫ text(r(50), UL2U2(50), 'RL/R = 2.5')
```

The result is shown in Figure 3.8. The reader is invited to experiment with other values of r_L. There are techniques for easily producing a family of curves corresponding to a larger set of r_L values. Such techniques require a FOR loop, a subject introduced in Subsection 1.7.2 and in Section 4.10.

EXAMPLE 3.5   Load matching in dc _____

In Figure 3.9 R_i is the internal resistance of the dc source, and R_L the resistance of the load. The problem we pose here is to find the load resistance for which the power

Figure 3.9   Load matching.

transferred to the load has a maximum. We begin by calculating the current:

$$I = \frac{U}{R_i + R_L}$$

The power transmitted to the load is

$$P = \left(\frac{U}{R_i + R_L}\right)^2 R_L = \frac{U^2}{R_i} \cdot \frac{R_L/R_i}{\left(1 + R_L/R_i\right)^2} \tag{3.18}$$

With $r = R_L/R_i$, Equation 3.18 can be rewritten as

$$P\frac{R_i}{U^2} = \frac{r}{(1 + r)^2} \tag{3.19}$$

The factor R_i/U^2 represents the short-circuit power; it is a characteristic of the voltage source. By differentiation with respect to r it can be shown that P has a maximum for $r = 1$, that is, when the load resistance equals the source resistance. We are going to show this graphically by plotting $P \cdot R_i/U^2$ against r. To generalize the plot for all similar circuits, we divide P by the **short-circuit power** U^2/R_i. By proceeding thus we obtain **nondimensional quantities** on both sides of Equation 3.19 (more about nondimensional quantities and their use can be found in Chapter 13, Dimensional analysis). To explain completely what happens we shall plot on the same graph the ratio of the current to the short-circuit current

$$I\frac{R_i}{U} = \frac{1}{1 + r} \tag{3.20}$$

and the ratio of the voltage across the load, to the short-circuit voltage

$$\frac{U_L}{U} = \frac{r}{1 + r} \tag{3.21}$$

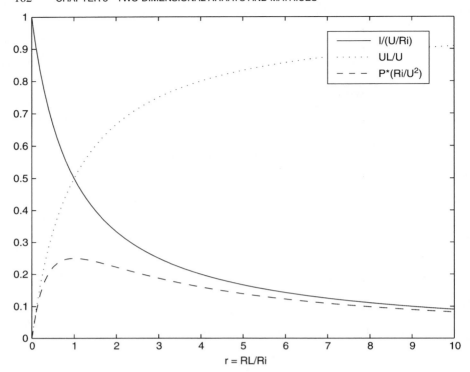

Figure 3.10   Current, voltage, and power in a dc load.

The plot is obtained with

```
>> r = 0:  0.1:  35;
>> i = 1./(1 + r);
>> u = r.*i;
>> p = i.*u;
>> h = plot(r, i, '-', r, u, ':', r, p, '--' )
>> xlabel('r = RL/Ri')
>> legend(h, 'I/(U/Ri)', 'UL/U', 'P*(Ri/U^2)')
```

The result is shown in Figure 3.10.

3.9   Exercises

Solutions for Exercises 3.3, 3.7, 3.9, 3.10, 3.13 and 3.14 appear at the back of the book.

■ **EXERCISE 3.1**   Printing a table of squares and cubes

Use MATLAB to print a table of squares and cubes of the first 15 natural numbers, according to the model

$$
\begin{array}{ccc}
1 & 1 & 1 \\
2 & 4 & 8 \\
\cdots & \cdots & \cdots
\end{array}
$$

■ **EXERCISE 3.2**   Operations with matrices

We have seen that, once we have defined the matrices that interest us, MATLAB allows us to operate on them in much the same way that we would operate on numbers – more exactly, on scalars. This is true if certain conditions are fulfilled, for example two matrices can be added – or subtracted – if they are of the same size, and they can be multiplied if their sizes agree with Equation 3.8. The analogy between operations on numbers and operations on matrices holds good up to a certain point and we shall try to show this in the series of exercises that follow. To start, let us define

$$
\mathbf{A} = \begin{bmatrix} 1 & 3 \\ 2 & 1 \end{bmatrix} \tag{3.22}
$$

$$
\mathbf{B} = \begin{bmatrix} 2 & 1 \\ 3 & 4 \end{bmatrix} \tag{3.23}
$$

$$
\mathbf{C} = \begin{bmatrix} 5 & 6 \\ 6 & 1 \end{bmatrix} \tag{3.24}
$$

(1)   For each matrix of size m by n, there is a matrix that plays in matrix addition the same role that 0 (zero) plays in the addition of numbers; this is the m-by-n **zero matrix**. In this exercise you can get the 2-by-2 zero matrix, **O**, by any of the following expressions:

```
≫ O = A - A
≫ O = B - B
≫ O = C - C
```

MATLAB, however, has more general forms of defining zero matrices. One way is an explicit declaration

```
≫ O = zeros(2,2)
```

which, for a square matrix, simplifies to

```
≫ O = zeros(2)
```

Another way is to build a zero matrix having the dimensions of a given matrix, say **A**: in MATLAB we write

```
≫ O = zeros(size(A))
```

In MATLAB the latter command should be `zeros(A)`.
Check that the two expressions

```
≫ A + O
≫ O + A
```

yield the same result **A**.

(2)   Unlike numbers, the multiplication of matrices is not, in general, commutative. Verify that

$$\mathbf{A} * \mathbf{B} \neq \mathbf{B} * \mathbf{A}$$

where **A** and **B** are the matrices introduced above. One simple way of carrying out this verification in MATLAB is by entering

```
≫ A*B - B*A
```

Note that if the two matrices, **A**, **B**, are not square, one of the products may exist and the other not. Can you give an example?

(3)   For square matrices we can define matrices that play the same role in matrix multiplication that the number 1 plays in the multiplication of numbers; these are the **identity** or **unit** matrices. We usually denote them by **I**. The elements i_{ij}, for $i = j$, constitute the **main diagonal** of the matrix. The elements on the main diagonal of the identity matrix are all equal to 1; all other elements, to zero. For example, the 2-by-2 identity matrix is

$$\begin{bmatrix} 1 & 0 \\ 0 & 1 \end{bmatrix}$$

In MATLAB this matrix can be defined either explicitly, by the command

```
≫ I = eye(2)
```

or by analogy with a given matrix of the size that interests us, for instance, in MATLAB

```
≫ I = eye(size(A))
```

In MATLAB the latter command should be changed to `eye(A)`.
Define the 2-by-2 identity matrix and check that

$$
\begin{array}{ccccc}
\mathbf{A} * \mathbf{I} & = & \mathbf{I} * \mathbf{A} & = & \mathbf{A} \\
\mathbf{B} * \mathbf{I} & = & \mathbf{I} * \mathbf{B} & = & \mathbf{B} \\
\mathbf{C} * \mathbf{I} & = & \mathbf{I} * \mathbf{C} & = & \mathbf{C}
\end{array}
$$

(4)   If the product of two numbers is equal to zero, at least one of the factors is zero. This is not true for matrices: the product of two matrices, neither of which is zero, may be a zero matrix. Angot (1961), paragraph 4.1.17, gives several examples, one of which is

$$\begin{bmatrix} 3 & -2 & -1 \\ 4 & -1 & -3 \\ 2 & -1 & -1 \end{bmatrix} \begin{bmatrix} 1 & 2 & 3 \\ 1 & 2 & 3 \\ 1 & 2 & 3 \end{bmatrix}$$

Dietrich and Stahl (1965) give the following example of a zero product of two non-square, nonzero matrices

$$\begin{bmatrix} 2 & -4 & 8 \\ -4 & 6 & -10 \end{bmatrix} \begin{bmatrix} 1 & 2 \\ 1.5 & 3 \\ 0.5 & 1 \end{bmatrix}$$

Check in MATLAB the two examples shown above. Another example and further explanations can be found in Zurmühl (1961), page 124.

(5)   For the matrix **A** defined in the previous exercise verify in MATLAB that `A^2` and `A.^2` yield different results and indicate what is happening in each case.

■ **EXERCISE 3.3**   Temperature scales

Example 2.10 describes the relationship between the Fahrenheit and Celsius scales by defining the values of the melting and boiling points of water in both scales. It is easy to verify that the relationship is given by the expression

$$C = \frac{5}{9}(F - 32)$$

Calculate and display in MATLAB a table that yields C for

0, 50, ..., 250 F.

Hint: the first row of the table is

```
0   -17.7778
```

■ **EXERCISE 3.4**   Temperature scales

Based on the expression given in Exercise 3.3 calculate and display in MATLAB a table that yields F for

−50, −25, ..., 200 °C.

Hint: the first row of the table is

```
-50    -58
```

■ **EXERCISE 3.5**   Temperature scales

Starting from thermodynamic considerations, the British physicist William Kelvin (Baron Thompson, 1824–1904) defined in 1854 an **absolute zero** point that corresponds to $-273.15\,^\circ$C. This is the basis of the **Kelvin scale** in which the temperature of the boiling point of water equals

$$100 + 273.15 = 373.15\,\mathrm{K}$$

(1)   Calculate and display in MATLAB a table that yields K for

$$-200, \; -150, \; \ldots, \; 200\,^\circ\mathrm{C}$$

(2)   Plot a graph that describes the relationship between the Celsius and Kelvin scales between 0 K and 400 K.

■ **EXERCISE 3.6**   Temperature scales

(1)   Find the relationship between the Fahrenheit and Kelvin scales.
(2)   Calculate and display in MATLAB a table that yields K for

$$-25, \; -50, \; \ldots, \; 200\,\mathrm{F}$$

(3)   Plot a graph that describes the relationship between the Fahrenheit and Kelvin scales between 0 K and 400 K.

■ **EXERCISE 3.7**   Shaft with three sections
Figure 3.11 shows a shaft consisting of three sections, more specifically a central section and two journals. The dimensions are in mm. The material is steel with a density of $7900\,\mathrm{kg\,m^{-3}}$. find:

(1)   the shaft mass;
(2)   the longitudinal coordinate of the centre of gravity;
(3)   the mass moment of inertia.

Hint: the mass moment of inertia of a circular cylinder of mass m and radius r is given by the formula $mr^2/2$.

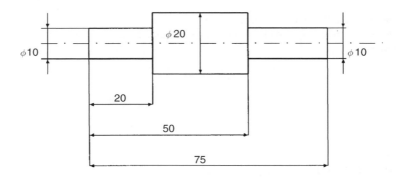

Figure 3.11   A shaft with three sections.

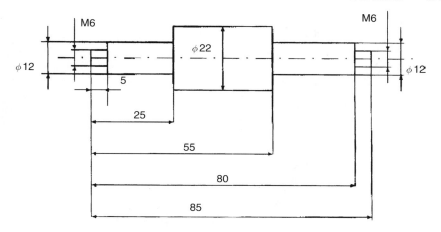

Figure 3.12   A shaft with five sections.

■ **EXERCISE 3.8**   Shaft with five sections

Figure 3.12 shows a shaft consisting of five sections. The dimensions are in mm. The central section is designed to accommodate a gear wheel. At its left and right there are two 12-mm diameter sections for bearings. The latter sections are terminated with M6 threads. The threads are not shown; for the purposes of the following calculations the sections at both ends can be considered as cylinders of diameter 6 mm. The material is steel with a density of 7900 kg m^{-3}. Find:

(1)   the shaft mass;
(2)   the longitudinal coordinate of the centre of gravity;
(3)   the mass moment of inertia.

     Hint: the mass moment of inertia of a circular cylinder of mass m and radius r is given by the formula $mr^2/2$.

■ **EXERCISE 3.9**   Crane stability

This exercise continues Example 3.3. A new case of crane operation is shown in Figure 3.13; corresponding weights and centres of gravity are shown in Table 3.7. The locations of the crew members are described in Table 3.7. The crane can overturn around the line of contact between the rear wheels and the ground.

     Calculate the total weight, the centre of gravity and the factor of safety against overturning. The very small factor of safety you will get indicates that the crane cannot be operated in this mode. You must change something and MATLAB allows you to do this easily. For instance, halve the radius of the load, and at the same time use outriggers extending 1.7 m behind the rear wheels. As the jib is now closer to the truck, change the x-coordinate of its centre of gravity. Calculate the factor of safety again; it will be large so that the load can be lifted at a larger radius.

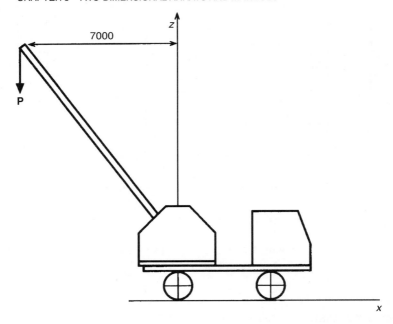

Figure 3.13   Stability, case 2.

Table 3.7   Weights for stability case 2.

Item	Weight	Centre of gravity, m		
	kN	x	y	z
Truck	42.18	0.89	0.00	1.70
Crane	33.35	0.00	0.00	2.20
Jib	9.81	−3.60	0.00	6.50
Crew 1	0.78	2.35	0.60	2.20
Crew 2	0.78	1.30	0.00	2.50

■ **EXERCISE 3.10**   Kinematics of a reciprocating compressor

The mechanism of a reciprocating compressor is shown schematically in Figure 3.14. The length of the crank arm is $\overline{OA} = 100$ mm, and that of the connecting link, $\overline{AB} = 240$ mm.

(1)   Plot the piston stroke, s, as a function of the crank angle α.

(2)   Plot the piston velocity, ds/dt, as a function of the crank angle α. Assume unit crank angular velocity, that is $\omega = d\alpha/dt = 1$.

Hint: use the following properties to derive an equation for s:

•   The projections of the crank arm $\overline{OA}$ and the link $\overline{AB}$ on the Ox axis are equal;
•   The stroke s equals the sum of the projections of $\overline{OA}$ and $\overline{AB}$ on the Oy axis.

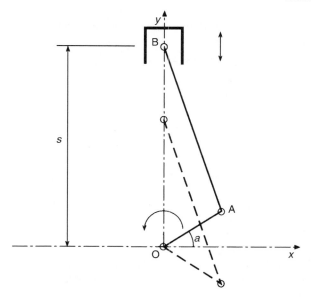

Figure 3.14   The mechanism of a reciprocating compressor. $\overline{OA} = 100$ mm; $\overline{AB} = 240$ mm.

Differentiating s with respect to time yields the equation that answers (b).

■ **EXERCISE 3.11**   Series connection of capacitors

Figure 3.15 represents three capacitors connected in series. At equilibrium the electrical charges of the three capacitors must be equal; let us call their common value q. If the capacitance of the first capacitor is C_1, the voltage across it equals

$$U_1 = q/C_1 \tag{3.25}$$

and, similarly,

$$U_2 = q/C_2 \tag{3.26}$$
$$U_3 = q/C_3 \tag{3.27}$$

The potential difference between points 1 and 2 is

$$U = U_1 + U_2 + U_3 \tag{3.28}$$

If we wish to replace the three given capacitors by a single, equivalent component that would produce the same effect, its capacitance should be

$$C = q/U$$

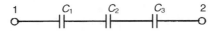

Figure 3.15   Series connection of capacitors.

Show that

$$\frac{1}{C} = \frac{1}{C_1} + \frac{1}{C_2} + \frac{1}{C_3} \tag{3.29}$$

and calculate C, in MATLAB, if

$$\begin{array}{rcll} C_1 & = & 20 & pF \\ C_2 & = & 30 & pF \\ C_3 & = & 40 & pF \end{array}$$

For completeness it may be added that Equation 3.29 can also be derived in alternating current (ac). If we use the concept of **capacitive reactance** (see Chapter 4) we can write

$$X_C = \frac{1}{\omega C} \tag{3.30}$$

where ω is the angular frequency (radian/second) of the alternating current, and C the capacitance defined as above (see Equation 3.25). Then, if the current passing through the three capacitors is I, the voltages across the three capacitors are

$$U_1 \quad = \quad \frac{I}{\omega C_1} \tag{3.31}$$

$$U_2 \quad = \quad \frac{I}{\omega C_2} \tag{3.32}$$

$$U_3 \quad = \quad \frac{I}{\omega C_3} \tag{3.33}$$

The equivalent capacitance that would replace the three given capacitors must fulfil the condition

$$C = \frac{I}{\omega U} \tag{3.34}$$

where U is given by Equation 3.28. From here to Equation 3.29 there is only one step (see also Carlson and Gisser 1990, page 123, and Nilsson 1993, page 242). Show this and calculate C if

$$\begin{array}{rcll} C_1 & = & 400 & pF \\ C_2 & = & 200 & pF \\ C_3 & = & 300 & pF \end{array}$$

■ **EXERCISE 3.12** Parallel connection of inductors

Figure 3.16 shows three inductors connected in parallel. The **inductive reactance** of an inductance L equals

$$X_L = \omega L \tag{3.35}$$

where ω is the angular frequency (radian/second) of the alternating current passing through L. If the intensity of this current is I, the voltage drop caused by L equals

$$U = I X_L \tag{3.36}$$

Referring now to Figure 3.16, the currents passing through the three inductors are:

$$I_1 = \frac{U}{L_1 \omega} \tag{3.37}$$

$$I_2 = \frac{U}{L_2 \omega} \tag{3.38}$$

$$I_3 = \frac{U}{L_3 \omega} \tag{3.39}$$

where U is the voltage drop between points 1 and 2. The current through points 1 and 2 is, according to Kirchhoff's first law,

$$I = I_1 + I_2 + I_3 \tag{3.40}$$

Find the formula that gives the inductance L equivalent to the given parallel connection, and use MATLAB to calculate its value if

$$
\begin{aligned}
L_1 &= 5 \quad mH \\
L_2 &= 8 \quad mH \\
L_3 &= 9 \quad mH
\end{aligned}
$$

(see, for example, Carlson and Gisser 1990, pages 122–3, and Nilsson 1993, page 241).

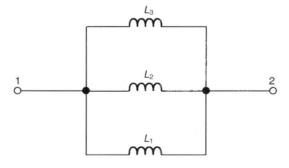

Figure 3.16 Parallel inductors.

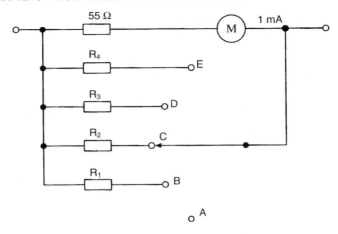

Figure 3.17   Shunts for a multirange ammeter.

■ **EXERCISE 3.13**   Shunts for a multirange ammeter
Figure 3.17 shows a multirange ammeter. The meter movement, denoted by M, has a range of 0 to 1 mA, and an internal resistance of 55 Ω. It is possible to use the same meter in other ranges, with heavier currents, if the movement is *shunted* as shown in the figure. As an example, let us calculate a resistance, R_1, that would allow us to measure currents in the range 0 to 10 mA. The current that must pass through the shunt is $I_1 = 10 - 1 = 9$ mA. The voltage across R_1 must equal that across the movement, that is

$$R_1 I_1 = 55 \times 1$$

which yields $R_1 = 55/9 = 6.1111\,\Omega$.

Let us suppose that, using the same measuring movement as above, we want to specify the shunting resistances of an ammeter defined by the following table

Cursor position	Range mA	Resistor –
A	0–1	–
B	0–10	R_1
C	0–50	R_2
D	0–100	R_3
E	0–500	R_4

Calculate the resistances R_1 to R_4 in a single array operation.

■ **EXERCISE 3.14**   Shunts for a multirange ammeter
Let us suppose that the designer of a multirange ammeter calculated the shunts as in Exercise 3.13 but wanted to use only round-valued resistors. The array of values

chosen by him or her is $R = [6, \ 1, \ 0.5, \ 0.1 \ ]$. What would be the maximum ranges that could be measured with this instrument?

■ **EXERCISE 3.15**   Shunts for a multirange ammeter

Read Exercise 3.13 and assume that we want to define the resistances of a multirange ammeter according to the following table. The movement is rated 0–$100\,\mu A$ and its internal resistance is $825\,\Omega$.

Cursor position	Range μA	Resistor –
A	0–100	–
B	0–200	R_1
C	0–300	R_2
D	0–400	R_3
E	0–500	R_4
F	0–1000	R_5

Calculate the resistances R_1 to R_5 in a single array operation.

■ **EXERCISE 3.16** · Shunts for a multirange ammeter

Let us suppose that the designer of a multirange ammeter calculated the shunts as in Exercise 3.15 but wanted to use only round-valued resistors. The array of values chosen by him or her is $R = [8, \ 4, \ 3, \ 2, \ 1 \ ]$. What would be the maximum ranges that could be measured with this instrument?

■ **EXERCISE 3.17**   Resistances for a multirange voltmeter

In Figure 3.18 a 1-mA ammeter with internal resistance $55\,\Omega$ is used to measure five ranges of voltage, as detailed in the following table. To achieve this, in each range the ammeter is connected in series with a suitable resistance

Cursor position	Range V	Resistor –
A	0–5	R_1
B	0–10	R_2
C	0–140	R_3
D	0–240	R_4
E	0–400	R_5

As an example, let us calculate the resistance R_1 corresponding to the range 0–5 V. At the upper end of the range, a current of 1 mA should cause a voltage drop equal to 5 V; therefore,

$$1 = \frac{5 \times 1000}{55 + R_1}$$

which yields $R_1 = 4945$.

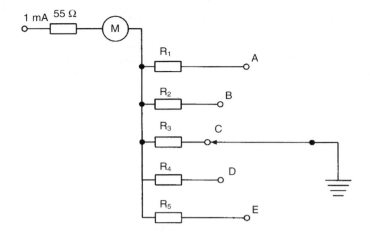

Figure 3.18   A multirange voltmeter.

Calculate in one MATLAB operation the array of resistances that answer the specifications of the above table.

■ **EXERCISE 3.18**   Resistances for a multirange voltmeter
Exercise 3.17 refers to a multirange voltmeter whose circuit is shown in Figure 3.18. Let us add a seventh cursor position, F, and assume the following ranges

Cursor position	Range V	Resistor −
A	0–15	R_1
B	0–25	R_2
C	0–140	R_3
D	0–240	R_4
E	0–400	R_5
F	0–1000	R_6

The range of the instrument, M, is 0–5 mA and its internal resistance is 8.5 Ω. Calculate in one MATLAB operation the array of resistances, **R**, that answers the above specifications.

■ **EXERCISE 3.19**   A Wheatstone bridge
The **Wheatstone bridge** was invented in 1843 by Charles Wheatstone (English, 1802–75). A variant of this instrument is shown in Figure 3.19. The bridge is frequently used to measure resistances by the **null** method that will be described here.

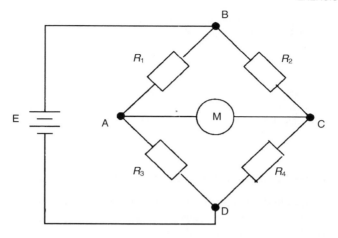

Figure 3.19   A Wheatstone bridge.

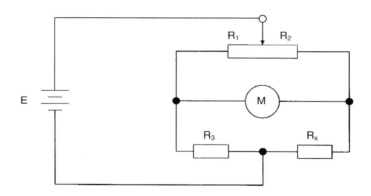

Figure 3.20   A slide-wire Wheatstone bridge.

The bridge is said to be **balanced** if the potential difference between points A and C – that is, the voltage measured by the instrument M – is zero. This happens if the potential at A equals that at C. Formulating this condition as an equation yields

$$\frac{E R_1}{R_1 + R_3} = \frac{E R_2}{R_2 + R_4}$$

or

$$R_1 R_4 = R_2 R_3 \tag{3.41}$$

As seen, Equation 3.41 does not contain the voltage E.

Let us consider a variant of the Wheatstone bridge in which the resistors R_1 and R_2 are parts of a slide-wire potentiometer, as shown in Figure 3.20.

Let $R_1 + R_2 = R$ and the resistance to be measured, R_x. Plot the ratio $R12R = R_1/R$, versus $Rx2R3 = R_x/R_3$, for $Rx2R3 = 0, \ldots, 10$ (read the name $R12R$ as $R1$ to R, and $Rx2R3$ as Rx to $R3$).

■ **EXERCISE 3.20**   Operations with multidimensional arrays
Referring to the example in Section 3.6, apply the function `mean` to the three-dimensional array `departments` and explain the meaning of the result.

3.10   Where to find more examples and exercises

Powers of matrices find an application in **graph theory**; a few examples are given in Chapter 12. If only a few elements of a matrix are not zero, the matrix is called **sparse**. MATLAB provides functions for economically storing such matrices and operating with them; an example is given in Chapter 12 and another in Chapter 17.

Chapter 4
Complex numbers

4.1 Introduction

It has been said that mathematicians are like tailors who cut out and sew clothes without knowing who will wear them. **Complex numbers** constitute a wonderful confirmation of this truth. Complex numbers were invented in order to solve a problem in mathematics; for the past five centuries they have allowed mathematicians to build beautiful, generalized theories. Relatively late, complex numbers found extremely important applications in engineering and physics. Today these numbers have become basic and indispensable tools in such fields as the theory of vibrations, fluid dynamics, heat transfer, alternating current circuits, control theory and signal processing. Other applications can be found in the theory of mechanisms and in electrostatics.

This chapter begins with the definition of complex numbers and a review of their basic properties. MATLAB functions for working with complex numbers are gradually introduced. Examples illustrate applications in the theory of vibrations and alternating current circuits. Conformal mappings are briefly introduced. Their applications can be found in books on heat transfer, electrostatics, and especially fluid dynamics. This chapter also contains a first introduction to programming in MATLAB.

4.2   The introduction of complex numbers

Let us consider the equation

$$x^3 - 15x - 4 = 0 \tag{4.1}$$

which is of the form

$$x^3 + ax + b = 0 \tag{4.2}$$

There are formulae for solving such an equation; they date from the 16th century when they were discovered by Italian algebraists. Applying these formulae we find that one of the three roots of Equation 4.2 is given by (see, for example, Weast and Selby 1970, page 129)

$$x_1 = A + B \tag{4.3}$$

where

$$A = \left(-b/2 + \sqrt{b^2/4 + a^3/27} \right)^{1/3}$$
$$B = \left(-b/2 - \sqrt{b^2/4 + a^3/27} \right)^{1/3}$$

Substituting the coefficients of Equation 4.1 in these formulae we obtain

$$x_1 = \left(2 + \sqrt{-121} \right)^{1/3} + \left(2 - \sqrt{-121} \right)^{1/3} \tag{4.4}$$

Now, the squares of all **real numbers** are positive numbers, for instance $3^2 = 9$, $(-3)^2 = 9$ and so on; therefore, there is no real number whose square could be the negative number -121. At first it was thought that it is not possible to calculate the result of Equation 4.4 and this case was called **irreducible**. Raffaele Bombelli (Italian, 1526–1572) had the courage to work with the square root of a negative number as if it were a 'usual number' and to continue the calculations. The line of reasoning is the following (Dieudonné 1992). Consider first the term $2 + \sqrt{-1}$; raising it to the third power yields

$$\left(2 + \sqrt{-1} \right)^3 = 2^3 + 12\sqrt{-1} + 6\left(\sqrt{-1} \right)^2 + \left(\sqrt{-1} \right)^3 \tag{4.5}$$

With

$$\left(\sqrt{-1} \right)^2 = -1, \ \left(\sqrt{-1} \right)^3 = \left(\sqrt{-1} \right)^2 \sqrt{-1} = -\sqrt{-1}$$

Equality 4.5 becomes

$$\left(2 + \sqrt{-1} \right)^3 = 2 + 11\sqrt{-1} = 2 + \sqrt{-121}$$

This allows us to write

$$2 + \sqrt{-1} = \left(2 + \sqrt{-121}\right)^{1/3} \tag{4.6}$$

Proceeding similarly with the term $2 - \sqrt{-1}$ we obtain

$$2 - \sqrt{-1} = \left(2 - \sqrt{-121}\right)^{1/3} \tag{4.7}$$

Substituting Equations 4.6 and 4.7 into Equation 4.4 we get

$$x_1 = 2 + \sqrt{-1} + 2 - \sqrt{-1} = 4$$

Today we use the symbol i introduced by Euler (Leonhard, Swiss, 1707–1783) for $\sqrt{-1}$ and, following Descartes (René du Perron, French, 1596–1650), we call numbers like $7i$ **purely imaginary**. Note that i is defined as the **positive** square root of -1, and that $(-i)^2$ also equals -1.

Bombelli went even further and worked with linear combinations of the form $a + bi$, where a and b are real. Such numbers can be, for example, solutions of second-degree equations, for instance of the equation

$$x^2 - 4x + 5 = 0 \tag{4.8}$$

which has the roots

$$x_1 = 2 + i$$
$$x_2 = 2 - i$$

(for more details on roots of polynomial equations see Chapter 6). Bombelli called the new numbers **sophistic**, but since Gauss (Carl Friedrich, German, 1777–1855) we call them **complex**.

Working with complex numbers may seem difficult, but this is certainly not the case in MATLAB and we hope that this chapter will show this to be so. To make the chapter as self-contained as possible, some general notions on complex numbers are presented in the following sections.

4.3   Operations with complex numbers

Today we use the notation i for $\sqrt{-1}$, as mentioned, but electrical engineers prefer j instead of i, keeping the latter for the *current* (measured, for example, in amperes).

In older versions of MATLAB the **imaginary unit** had to be defined by entering

```
≫ i = sqrt(-1)
```

or, alternatively,

```
≫ j = sqrt(-1)
```

In newer MATLAB versions these definitions are built in, as can be easily checked by typing i or j. Both commands yield

```
ans =
    0 + 1.0000i
```

Alternatively, try

```
≫ i^2
ans =
    -1.0000 + 0.0000i
≫ j^2
ans =
    -1.0000 + 0.0000i
```

When you want to work with complex numbers take care not to assign the name i, or j, to a variable or constant because otherwise you will have to redefine the imaginary unit.

We can now try a few operations with complex numbers, for example with the numbers

```
≫ z1 = 2 + 3*i; z2 = 3 + 2*i;
```

In MATLAB 4 and later versions it is possible to omit the multiplication symbol and write simply

```
≫ z1 = 2 + 3i; z2 = 3 + 2i;
```

Check that

```
≫ z1 + z2, z1*z2
```

yield in MATLAB the results predicted by Equations 4.59 and 4.60 (see the Appendix of this chapter).

The **opposite** of z_1 is defined by

```
≫ z1opp = -z1
z1opp =
    -2.0000 - 3.0000i
```

The role played by 0 for real numbers is fulfilled for complex numbers by $z_0 = 0 + 0i$. For example, in MATLAB we can get this number by

```
>> z1 + z1opp
ans =
    0
```

By definition, the **conjugate** of $z = a + bi$ is $\bar{z} = a - bi$. In MATLAB we can obtain the conjugates of the numbers z_1 and z_2 by typing

```
>> z1bar = conj(z1), z2bar = conj(z2)
z1bar =
    2.0000 - 3.0000i
z2bar =
    3.0000 - 2.0000i
```

It can be easily checked that the conjugate numbers z1 = 2 + 3i and z1bar = 2 - 3i are the roots of the equation

$$x^2 - 4x + 13 = 0$$

Can you find the equation whose roots are the conjugate numbers z2 = 3 + 2i and z2bar = 3 - 2i?

You can verify immediately that the product of any complex number and its conjugate is a real number. Thus, for the numbers z1, z1bar defined above we get

```
>> z1*z1bar
ans =
    13
```

Using the two complex numbers defined in this section calculate in MATLAB

```
>> z3 = z1/z2
```

and show that z_3 is the complex number expected from Equation 4.63 (see the Appendix of this chapter).

The MATLAB real function extracts the real part of a complex number

```
>> real(z1)
ans =
    2
```

and the `imag` function retrieves the imaginary part

```
>> imag(z1)
ans =
    3
```

4.4   Geometric representation

Complex numbers can be related to the points of the plane by a one-to-one correspondence. The idea was first presented by Wessel (Caspar, Norwegian, 1745–1818), in 1787, but became known after being independently published by Argand (Jean Robert, Swiss, 1768–1822), in 1806. Therefore this representation is known as the **Argand diagram**. figure 4.1 is this diagram for the complex number $z = a + bi$. The real part, a, is measured along the horizontal axis, correspondingly called the **real axis**, and the imaginary part, b, is measured along the vertical axis, called the **imaginary axis**.

Figure 4.1 also shows the opposite, $\hat{z}$, and the conjugate, $\overline{z}$, of z. It can be easily seen that $\hat{z}$ and z are symmetric with respect to the origin, and $\overline{z}$ is symmetric to z with respect to the real axis. All these numbers can be easily displayed in MATLAB: for the complex number $z1$ defined above, for instance, plot its imaginary part against the real part by the command `plot(real(z1), imag(z1))`. Complete the plotting command so as to display also the opposite and the conjugate of $z1$. By the way, for a single complex number it is sufficient to enter `plot(z1)`.

We can also view a complex number as a two-dimensional vector with the horizontal component equal to the real part of the number, and the vertical component equal to the imaginary part. The sum of the two complex numbers, $z1$ and $z2$, is exemplified in Figure 4.2 and the result indeed corresponds to Equation 4.59 (Subsection 4.15.1). From this figure it is evident that the sum of two complex numbers is equivalent to the vector sum of two vectors having the origin at the origin of coordinates and the extremities at the points $z1$ and $z2$. An easy way of illustrating

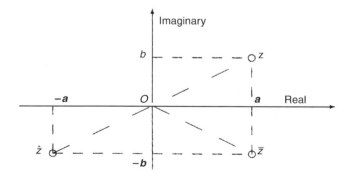

Figure 4.1   Argand diagram.

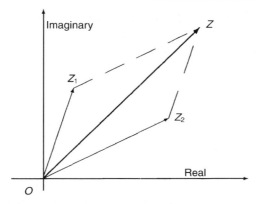

Figure 4.2   The sum of two complex numbers.

the sum of two complex numbers in MATLAB is shown in the following lines

```
>> Z = [ z1, z2, z1+z2 ];
>> compass(Z)
>> text(real(z1), imag(z1), ' z1')
>> text(real(z2), imag(z2), ' z2')
>> text(real(z1+z2), imag(z1+z2), ' z1+z2')
```

The MATLAB compass function displays the elements of the array Z as arrows emanating from the origin. The text function takes three arguments: the first two are the coordinates of the point where the text is to be written, and the third argument is the text itself, presented as a character string and therefore written between quotation marks. Try the plot for yourself.

4.5   Trigonometric representation

In Figure 4.1 the point z can be defined not only by its *Cartesian* coordinates, a and b, but also by its *polar* coordinates $\rho = \overline{OZ}$ and θ, the latter being the angle (in radians) made by $\overline{OZ}$ with the real axis, and measured in the counterclockwise (direct trigonometric) sense. The following relationships are evident:

$$a = \rho \cos \theta \tag{4.9}$$
$$b = \rho \sin \theta \tag{4.10}$$

where a is the real, and b the imaginary part of z. From Equations 4.9 and 4.10 we derive

$$\rho = |z| = \sqrt{a^2 + b^2} \tag{4.11}$$
$$\tan \theta = b/a \tag{4.12}$$

where $|z|$ is known as the **modulus**, or **absolute value** of z, and θ as the **argument** of z.

For θ a real number, *measured in radians*, consider the following series expansions

$$\sin \theta = \frac{\theta}{1!} - \frac{\theta^3}{3!} + \frac{\theta^5}{5!} - \frac{\theta^7}{7!} + \cdots \qquad (4.13)$$

$$\cos \theta = 1 - \frac{\theta^2}{2!} + \frac{\theta^4}{4!} - \frac{\theta^6}{6!} + \cdots \qquad (4.14)$$

$$e^\theta = 1 + \frac{\theta}{1!} + \frac{\theta^2}{2!} + \frac{\theta^3}{3!} + \frac{\theta^4}{4!} + \cdots \qquad (4.15)$$

Starting from them it is possible to deduce the famous **Euler formula**

$$e^{i\theta} = cos\theta + i \sin \theta \qquad (4.16)$$

This gives us an additional representation of the complex number shown in Figure 4.1:

$$z = \rho e^{i\theta} \qquad (4.17)$$

MATLAB provides a set of functions for dealing conveniently with the various representations of a complex number. In order to exemplify them, enter in MATLAB

```
≫ z = 3 + 4i
```

Then use the following commands:

```
≫ rho = abs(z)
≫ theta = angle(z)
≫ z1 = rho*exp(i*theta)
≫ a = real(z1)
≫ b = imag(z1)
```

Compare your results with Equations 4.11, 4.12, 4.17, 4.9 and 4.10, in that order. Type z1 and you will see that, although z_1 was defined in exponential form, you get the answer

```
z1 =
   3.0000 + 4.0000i
```

Let us now consider two complex numbers defined in exponential form

$$z_1 = \rho_1 e^{i\theta1}$$
$$z_2 = \rho_2 e^{i\theta2}$$

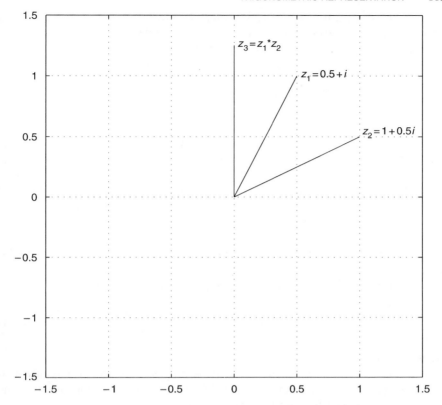

Figure 4.3   The product of two complex numbers.

Their product is given by

$$z_3 = z_1 z_2 = \rho_1 \rho_2 e^{i(\theta_1 + \theta_2)} \tag{4.18}$$

Equation 4.18 has a simple geometric interpretation: multiplying z_1 by z_2 amounts to multiplying the modulus of z_1 by the modulus of z_2, and rotating the result counterclockwise by the angle θ_2 with respect to the direction of z_1. This is illustrated in Figure 4.3 which represents the multiplication

$$(0.5 + i)(1 + 0.5i) = 0 + 1.25i$$

Figure 4.3 was produced in MATLAB by the techniques explained at the end of the preceding section. The graph is to scale; it is easy to measure the angle of rotation of the vector drawn from the origin to z_3 and verify that it is as predicted by Equation 4.18.

Let us see what happens in the particular case in which the second factor is the imaginary unit i. In exponential form

$$i = 1 \cdot e^{i\pi/2}$$

Then, multiplication by i means counterclockwise rotation by $\pi/2$. It follows that multiplication by i^2 means rotation by the angle π, and multiplication by i^3 means rotation by $3\pi/2$. Check these results in MATLAB.

Division of the two complex numbers z_1, z_2 yields

$$z_3 = \frac{z_1}{z_2} = \frac{\rho_1 e^{i\theta_1}}{\rho_2 e^{i\theta_2}} = \frac{\rho_1}{\rho_2} e^{i(\theta_1 - \theta_2)} \tag{4.19}$$

which also has a simple geometric interpretation. In order to divide z_1 by z_2 we divide the modulus of z_1 by that of z_2 and, starting from the direction of z_1, we rotate the result clockwise by an angle equal to the argument of z_2.

Powers of complex numbers are a particular case of multiplication. Repeated application of Equation 4.18 gives **de Moivre's** (Abraham, French emigrated to England, 1667–1754) formula

$$z^n = (\rho e^{i\theta})^n = \rho^n (\cos n\theta + i \sin n\theta) \tag{4.20}$$

Conversely, the n nth roots of the complex number z are obtained from

$$z^{1/n} = \rho^{1/n} e^{i\theta/n} = \rho^{1/n} \left(\cos \frac{\theta + 2k\pi}{n} + i \sin \frac{\theta + 2k\pi}{n} \right) \tag{4.21}$$

where $k = 0, 2, 3, \ldots, n - 1$.

In Section 4.3 we defined in MATLAB two complex numbers z1, z2, and calculated their product, z1*z2, and their quotient, z1/z2. Check now that, for the same numbers, the MATLAB expressions abs(z1*z2), angle(z1*z2), abs(z1/z2), and angle(z1/z2) yield the results predicted by Equations 4.18 and 4.19. Also check that abs(z1^2) and abs(z2^2), angle(z1^2) and angle(z2^2) verify Equation 4.20. Type abs(sqrt(z1)), abs(sqrt(z2)), angle(sqrt(z1)), and angle(sqrt(z2)) and show that the results correspond to Equation 4.21.

Hint: compare, for example, the results obtained with the pair of commands

```
abs(z1)*abs(z2),  abs(z1*z2)
```

4.6   Functions of complex variables

By analogy with Equations 4.13 to 4.15 we can define the following three functions:

$$\sin z = \frac{z}{1!} - \frac{z^3}{3!} + \frac{z^5}{5!} - \frac{z^7}{7!} + \cdots \tag{4.22}$$

$$\cos z = 1 - \frac{z^2}{2!} + \frac{z^4}{4!} - \frac{z^6}{6!} + \cdots \tag{4.23}$$

$$e^z = 1 + \frac{z}{1!} + \frac{z^2}{2!} + \frac{z^3}{3!} + \frac{z^4}{4!} + \cdots \tag{4.24}$$

where z is any complex number. These series converge for all finite z (see, for example, Hille 1959). Several properties, similar to those of the corresponding functions of real variables, can be derived directly from the definitions. Thus

$$e^{z_1} \cdot e^{z_2} = e^{z_1 + z_2}$$

In order to experiment with this relationship try in MATLAB

```
≫ z1 = 1 + i;
≫ z2 = 2 + 3i;
≫ exp(z1)*exp(z2)
ans =
 -13.1288 -15.2008i
≫ exp(z1 + z2)
ans =
 -13.1288 -15.2008i
```

Euler's famous formula becomes

$$e^{iz} = \cos z + i \sin z$$

Using the number z_1 defined above we get

```
≫ exp(i*z1)
ans =
    0.1988 + 0.3096i
```

and this result does indeed equal the result obtained with

```
≫ cos(z1) + i*sin(z1)
ans =
    0.1988 + 0.3096i
```

Relationships known from trigonometry remain valid, for instance

$$\sin^2 z + \cos^2 z = 1$$
$$\sin(pi/2 - z) = \cos z$$

For example, with the same number z_1 defined above we obtain in MATLAB

```
≫ sin(z1)^2 + cos(z1)^2
ans =
    1.0000 - 0.0000i
```

and

```
>> sin(pi/2 - z1)
ans =
    0.8337 - 0.9889i
```

which is equal to the result obtained with

```
>> cos(z1)
ans =
    0.8337 - 0.9889i
```

Another interesting function is the **natural logarithm** of a complex number, $z = r(\cos\phi + i\sin\phi)$. By definition this logarithm is another complex number $a + bi$ such that

$$e^{a+bi} = r(\cos\phi + i\sin\phi)$$

We write $a + bi = \log z$. From the definition we can easily derive

$$e^a = r$$
$$b = \phi + 2k\pi$$

where k is any integer. Then

$$\log z = \log r + (\phi + 2k\pi)i$$

is a **multi-valued function**. In MATLAB we can experiment, for example, with the number z_2 defined above:

```
>> logz = log(z2)
logz =
    1.2825 + 0.9828i
>> r = abs(z2)
r =
    3.6056
>> phi = angle(z2)
phi =
    0.9828
>> log(r) + phi*i
ans =
    1.2825 + 0.9828i
```

which is equal to the previously found value of $\log z$. Now, try also

```
>> exp(logz)
ans =
   2.0000 + 3.0000i
```

which is equal to the given value of z2. Moreover, as the logarithm is a multi-valued function, the expression

```
>> exp(log(r) + (phi + 2*5*pi)*i)
ans =
   2.0000 + 3.0000i
```

also yields the same z2 value.

More about functions of complex variables can be found, for example, in Churchill and Brown (1990), Chapter 9.

4.7   Mapping by functions of complex variables

Let $w = u + iv = f(z)$ be a function of the complex variable $z = x + iy$, where u, v and f are functions of x and y alone. Consider, for example, the function

$$w = Az + B \tag{4.25}$$

where

$$A = a_1 + ia_2 \tag{4.26}$$
$$B = b_1 + ib_2 \tag{4.27}$$

It follows that

$$u = (a_1 x - a_2 y) + b_1 \tag{4.28}$$
$$v = (a_1 y + a_2 x) + b_2 \tag{4.29}$$

These equations show that the function w transforms the coordinates x, y of the point z into two numbers which can be regarded as the coordinates of another point in a new complex plane. We say that w **maps**, or **transforms**, the points of the z-plane into the points of the w-plane. In the particular case considered here, a point z_i in the z-plane is mapped into a point w_i in the w-plane, as shown in Figure 4.4, where the mapping was done in three phases:

(1)   First, the point z_i is mapped in the plane w into the point w_{i1} having the modulus equal to $|A||z_i|$, and the argument equal to the argument of z_i.

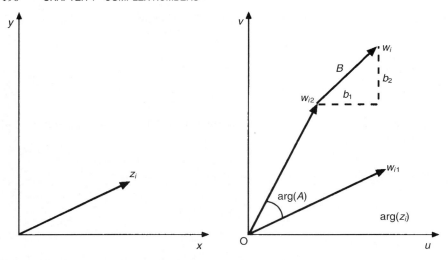

Figure 4.4   Mapping by the function $w = Az + B$.

(2)   Next, the vector from the origin to w_{i1} is rotated counterclockwise (that is, in the direct trigonometric sense) by an angle equal to the argument of A, bringing the point w_{i1} to w_{i2}.

(3)   Finally, the point w_{i2} is translated to w_i by a distance equal to B, that is, by the distance b_1 along the real axis, and by the distance b_2 along the imaginary axis.

As a concrete example, let us consider in Figure 4.5 the following three points of the z-plane:

$$z_1 = 0$$
$$z_2 = 1 + \sqrt{3}\,i$$
$$z_3 = 2$$

These points are the vertices of an equilateral triangle. Let us map the z-plane by means of the function described by Equation 4.25, where $A = 2 + i$, $B = 1 + i$. In MATLAB we can carry out this mapping by the following sequence of commands:

```
>> z(1) = 0;
>> z(2) = 1 + sqrt(3)*i;
>> z(3) = 2;
>> A = 2 + i;
>> B = 1 + i;
>> w = A*z + B
```

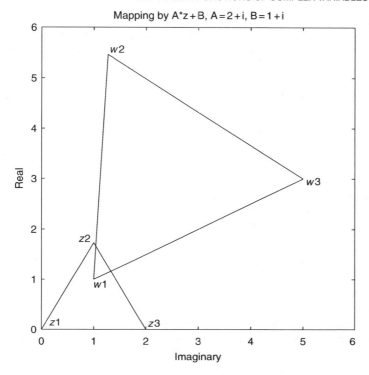

Figure 4.5 Mapping of a triangle by $w = (2 + i) * z + (1 + i)$.

The last command was not followed by a semicolon; therefore, it will cause the display

```
w =
    1.0000 + 1.0000i   1.2679 + 5.4641i   5.0000 + 3.0000i
```

In order to visualize the effect of the transformation we can plot the triangles $z(1)z(2)z(3)$ and $w(1)w(2)w(3)$ on the same figure. first, we must close the two broken lines defined by the above six points. We do this by entering

```
>> z = [ z z(1) ]; w = [ w w(1) ];
```

Next, we produce the plot by typing

```
>> plot(real(z), imag(z), real(w), imag(w))
```

If your computer is connected to a printer, print the plot. The result is distorted. In order to use the full area of the screen MATLAB produced a rectangular frame with the horizontal axis running from 0 to 5, and the vertical axis running from 0 to 6. The scales along the two axes are not equal. The horizontal axis unit is equal to approximately twice the vertical axis unit. We can correct the distortion with the statements

```
≫ axis('square'), axis([ 0 6 0 6 ])
```

The command axis('square') produces a square frame for the plot. The command axis([0 6 0 6]) defines the horizontal axis as running from 0 to 6, and the vertical axis as also running from 0 to 6. Now call the plot function again and see the result.

Let us now apply a few MATLAB facilities that make the plot more readable. first, press Enter to return the text screen, then add a grid with the grid command. Next, we use the title function as follows

```
≫ title('Mapping by A*z + B, A = 2 + i, B = 1 + i')
```

As with all MATLAB functions, the title argument must be enclosed in parentheses. When, as in our case, the argument is a string of characters, it must be enclosed in quotation marks. Two further functions will help us to name the axes; their arguments too are character strings and therefore enclosed in quotation marks:

```
≫ xlabel('Imaginary'), ylabel('Real')
```

Finally, in order to correlate the three given points and their mappings we must mark them with their names. Let us begin with

```
≫ text(real(z(1)), imag(z(1)), 'z1')
```

To continue with the other points we can use the arrows in order to retrieve the last command and modify it to

```
≫ text(real(z(2)), imag(z(2)), 'z2')
```

The remaining commands are

```
≫ text(real(z(3)), imag(z(3)), 'z3')
≫ text(real(w(1)), imag(w(1)), 'w1')
≫ text(real(w(2)), imag(w(2)), 'w2')
≫ text(real(w(3)), imag(w(3)), 'w3')
```

Now type print to send the plot to the printer.

In this section we have worked with arrays of complex numbers, namely z and w. We must point out that the MATLAB procedure used until now for obtaining the transpose of an array yields a different result if the elements of the array are complex numbers. Thus, for the array w considered in this section

```
>> w'
ans =
     1.0000 - 1.0000i
     1.2679 - 5.4641i
     5.0000 - 3.0000i
```

If you continued from the previous calculations, you will see a fourth line equal to the first; it is due to the statement in which you closed the triangle by writing a second time the first point. We started from a row vector and indeed obtained a column vector, but the elements of the new array are the **complex conjugates** of the elements of the array w. We say that we obtained the **conjugate transpose** of w. To obtain the transpose, without conjugation, we must use the point-apostrophe operator:

```
>> w.'
ans =
     1.0000 + 1.0000i
     1.2679 + 5.4641i
     5.0000 + 3.0000i
```

4.8   Conformal mapping

In Figure 4.5 an equilateral triangle was mapped into another equilateral triangle. We can verify this by measuring either the angles or the sides of the triangle $w(1)w(2)w(3)$, in the graph plotted to the correct scales. A better way consists in calculating and comparing the sides of the triangle

```
>> abs(w(1) - w(2))
ans =
     4.4721
>> abs(w(2) - w(3))
ans =
     4.4721
>> abs(w(3) - w(1))
ans =
     4.4721
```

The new triangle is also equilateral and we conclude that the angles between the sides of the triangle $z(1)z(2)z(3)$ were preserved under the given mapping. Mappings that preserve angles between pairs of curves are called **conformal**.

It can be shown that this is the case if the mapping function $w = f(z)$ has a derivative dw/dz at the point z_i to be mapped, and if $dw/dz \neq 0$ at this point. If the derivative of $f(z)$ exists at every point in a neighbourhood of z_i, we say that $f(z)$ is **analytic** at z_i. It can be shown that the mapping $w = f(z)$ is conformal at each point of a domain where $f(z)$ is analytic and $df(z_i)/dz \neq 0$.

A further example of conformal mapping is shown on the left of Figure 4.6 which shows, in the z-plane, an arc ab of a circle with the centre in the origin of coordinates, and the radius 2. The angle subtended by the arc ab equals $\pi/3$. Let us map this arc by the **bilinear** – or **fractional** – transformation

$$w = \frac{z - a}{z - b} \tag{4.30}$$

where a and b are the complex numbers representing the points a and b. Markusevich (1961) shows by elementary means that the circular arc is mapped into a half-straight extending from the origin of the coordinates of the w-plane to infinity. Moreover, the angle made by this half-straight with the real axis, in the w-plane (that is, the angle $\widehat{ROS}$ on the right of Figure 4.6), equals the angle made by the tangent to the circular arc, in a, with the straight line containing the chord of the arc (the angle $\widehat{a_1 a t}$ on the left of Figure 4.6). Let us check this result in MATLAB.

We first calculate a set of points belonging to a circular arc with radius 2, extending from $\pi/3$, and subtending $\pi/3$ radians:

```
>> alpha = pi/3:  pi/90:  2*pi/3; r = 2;
>> z = r*exp(i*alpha);
```

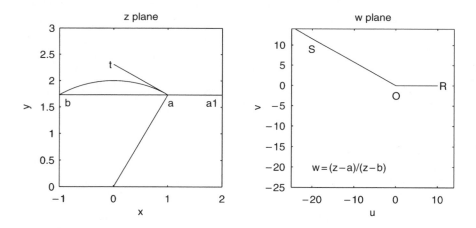

Figure 4.6   Mapping of a circular arc by the bilinear function.

The first number of the array z represents the point a; the last number, the point b. Therefore we type

```
>> a = z(1); b = z(length(z));
```

The radius from the origin of the z-plane to the point a can be represented by its extremities:

```
>> rad = [ 0 a ];
```

Similarly, the chord of the arc ab can be represented by its extremities, that is, by the array

```
>> c = [ a b ];
```

The desired mapping is obtained with

```
>> w = (z - a)./(z - b);
```

In the expression on the right-hand side z is a 1-by-3 array, while a and b are scalars. MATLAB, however, accepts the expression and calculates the equivalent of what should have been

```
>> w = (z - a*ones(size(z)))./(z - b*ones(size(z)));
```

This time let us plot the z- and w-planes in two separate, adjacent graphs. For this purpose we use the MATLAB subplot function. The commands – including those for obtaining graphs with equal scales on the two axes and for writing text – are

```
>> subplot(1,2,1)
>> plot(real(z) ,imag(z),real(rad),imag(rad),real(c),imag(c))
>> axis('square'), axis([ -1 +1 0 2 ])
>> title('z plane')
>> xlabel('x'), ylabel('y')
>> subplot(1,2,2)
>> plot(real(w), imag(w), [ 0 10 ], [ 0 0 ])
>> axis('square'), axis([ -25 14 -25 14 ])
>> title('w = (z - a)/(z - b)')
>> xlabel('u'), ylabel('v')
```

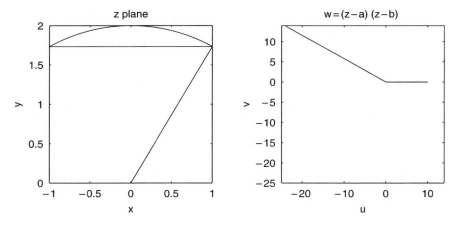

Figure 4.7   Conformal mapping by $w = (z - a)/(z - b)$.

The command subplot(1, 2, 2) should also be changed in a similar way. The arguments of subplot split the display into two graphs, shown in Figure 4.7. The image of b in the w-plane approaches infinity because $z - b = 0$. This produces the messages

```
Warning:  Divide by zero
Warning:  Infinity or NaN found in data and not shown on plot
```

The term relevant here is *Infinity*. The abbreviation *NaN* stands for **Not a number** and it can be caused, for instance, by the division $0/0$. In some computer languages division by zero would stop the calculations and not let us see the rest of the results. As shown by the above example, MATLAB does not stop the calculations; it simply indicates by Inf or NaN the results that could not be represented in the computer, and displays the remaining significant results.

Conformal mappings have many applications in two-dimensional fluid flow, heat flow, and electrostatics (see, for example, Churchill and Brown 1990, Chapter 9; Spiegel 1972, Chapter 9). In these fields, if a solution is found for some simple form or configuration – for instance, flow around an infinite-length circular cylinder – it can be extended to less simple forms by means of an appropriate conformal mapping. More recently, the method has been used in naval architecture to find the potential flow around actual ship sections, by mapping the results obtained for circular sections. Completely new applications of conformal mapping in physics have been found in recent years

4.9   Harmonic motion – phasors

A periodic motion that can be described by a sinusoidal function of time is called **harmonic motion**. One mechanism that produces such a motion is shown in

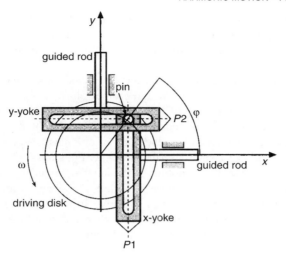

Figure 4.8   Scotch yoke mechanism.

Figure 4.8. The driving element is a rotating disk with a pin mounted a distance A from the centre. The pin can slide in the slot of the element marked *x-yoke*. The motion of the x-yoke is restricted by a guided rod attached to it, so that this yoke can move only horizontally. A similar slotted element, marked *y-yoke*, is assembled above the x-yoke. The motion of the y-yoke is restricted by a guided rod that allows only vertical displacements. Assuming that at time $t = 0$ the position of the pin relative to the x axis is defined by the angle ϕ, the x-coordinate of the point $P1$ is

$$x(0) = A\cos(\phi) \tag{4.31}$$

and the y-coordinate of the point $P2$ is

$$y(0) = A\sin(\phi) \tag{4.32}$$

Let the angular speed of the disk be ω radians per second. Then at time t the abscissa (x-coordinate) of the point $P1$ is

$$x(t) = A\cos(\omega t + \phi) \tag{4.33}$$

and the ordinate (y-coordinate) of the point $P2$ equals

$$y(t) = A\sin(\omega t + \phi) \tag{4.34}$$

Now, if we write

$$z(t) = Ae^{i(\omega t + \phi)}$$

we see that $x(t)$ is the real part and $y(t)$ the imaginary part of z. We can consider the point z to be the end of a vector with the origin in the origin of coordinates and magnitude A. This vector rotates with the angular velocity ω, starting from the angle ϕ.

Scotch-yoke mechanisms, like the one described above, have been used as **function generators** for obtaining sine and cosine values in analog computers (see, for example, Oppelt 1964, Figure 10.3) and as **shakers,** that is, machines for testing the behaviour of equipment subjected to vibrations (Unholz 1988).

Small-amplitude motions of a pendulum, or of a mass suspended by a spring, are also harmonic and they can be described by either Equation 4.33 or Equation 4.34, where A is the amplitude of the motion, ω the angular frequency, and ϕ the phase angle. In one complete rotation the pin in Figure 4.8 covers an angle equal to 2π radians, and in time t the pin covers ωt radians. In the case of mass-spring and pendulum motions we talk about **oscillations** rather than rotations. The number of complete oscillations in one unit of time is the **frequency**

$$f = \omega/2\pi \tag{4.35}$$

The time for one complete oscillation is the **period**

$$T = 1/f = 2\pi/\omega \tag{4.36}$$

If the unit of time is the second – with the SI symbol s – the angular frequency, ω, is measured in radians/s – with the symbol rad s^{-1}, the frequency, f, in hertz (named after Heinrich Rudolf Hertz, German, 1857–1894) – symbol Hz, and the period, T, in s.

If y is the **displacement** of the harmonic motion, the **velocity** is

$$v = \frac{dy}{dt} = \omega A \cos(\omega t + \phi) = \omega A \sin(\omega t + \phi + \pi/2) \tag{4.37}$$

and the **acceleration,**

$$a = \frac{d^2 y}{dt^2} = -\omega^2 A \sin(\omega t + \phi) = \omega^2 A \sin(\omega t + \phi + \pi) \tag{4.38}$$

As explained in the Appendix of this chapter, in electrical engineering, in the study of alternating-current circuits, it is interesting to know the integral of y; it is given by

$$I = \int y\, dt = -\frac{A}{\omega} \cos(\omega t + \phi) = \frac{A}{\omega} \sin(\omega t + \phi - \pi/2) \tag{4.39}$$

We conclude that the velocity of the harmonic motion can be represented by a rotating vector leading the displacement by the phase $\pi/2$, and the acceleration can be represented by another rotating vector, leading the displacement by the phase angle π. The integral of the displacement can also be represented by a rotating vector,

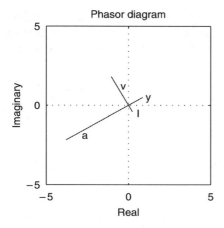
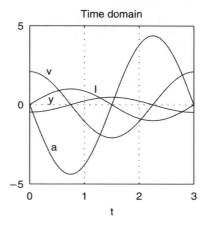

Figure 4.9   Displacement, velocity, acceleration and integral of harmonic motion, as rotating vectors.

this time lagging behind the displacement by $\pi/2$. An example of all four rotating vectors is shown in Figure 4.9. The vectors in such a figure, called a **phasor diagram**, are known as **phasors**. Phasor diagrams can be seen in several books, for instance Rao (1990); in MATLAB we can easily calculate them. Let us try, using a motion that repeats itself every 3 seconds and has unit amplitude and zero phase. Suppose we want to draw the four vectors y, v, a, and I at time $t = 0.25$. We start by entering the definitions

```
≫ T = 3; omega = 2*pi/T;
≫ t = 0.25; A = 1;
≫ y = A*exp(i*omega*t);
```

Instead of using Equations 4.37 to 4.39, we can differentiate and integrate the exponential expression of y and write

```
≫ v = i*omega*y;
≫ a = -omega^2*y;
≫ I = y/(i*omega);
```

It would be interesting to plot side by side the phasor diagram and the time 'stories' of y, v, a and I. So, for the left-hand graph we type

```
≫ subplot(1, 2, 1)
≫ y = [ 0 y ];
≫ v = [ 0 v ];
≫ a = [ 0 a ];
≫ I = [ 0 I ];
```

In order to plot the phasors with a 1:1 aspect ratio, we use the `square` function. The sides of the graph must suit the largest phasor; obviously it is a, and we obtain its length by typing `abs(a)`. Using the result of the preceding command we enter

```
>> ry = real(y); iy = imag(y); rv = real(v); iv = imag(v);
>> ra = real(a); ia = imag(a); rI = real(I); iI = imag(I);
>> plot(ry, iy, rv, iv, ra, ia, rI, iI)
>> axis('square'), axis([ -5 5 -5 5 ])
>> grid, title('Phasor diagram')
>> xlabel('Real'), ylabel('Imaginary')
```

For readability the phasors must be marked with their names. The locations of these names can be decided by visual inspection of the graph. A good placement is obtained with

```
>> text(0.5, 0.5, 'y')
>> text(-0.5, 1, 'v')
>> text(-3, -1.5, 'a')
>> text(0.5, -0.5, 'I')
```

For the right-hand graph we must generate arrays of y, v, a and I values, as functions of time. We begin by defining an array of t values that cover one complete **cycle** of oscillations:

```
>> t = 0:  0.025:  3;
```

and we repeat the definitions of the four phasors by either writing them anew, or by retrieving them with the *Up Arrow*:

```
>> y = A*exp(i*omega*t);
>> v = i*omega*y;
>> a = -omega^2*y;
>> I = y/(i*omega);
```

The right-hand plot is obtained with

```
>> subplot(1, 2, 2)
>> plot(t,imag(y),t,imag(v),t,imag(a),t,imag(I))
axis([ 0 3 -5 5 ])
>> grid
>> title('Time domain'), xlabel('t')
```

One must be able to distinguish between the four time-domain curves; again this is done with the aid of the `text` function. The following text locations were determined by trial and error:

```
≫ text(t(10), imag(y(10)), 'y')
≫ text(t(10), imag(v(10)), 'v')
≫ text(t(14), imag(a(14)), 'a')
≫ text(t(57), imag(I(57)), 'I')
```

The resulting plots are shown in Figure 4.9. Print the pair of graphs, draw horizontal lines through the extremities of the four phasors in the left-hand graph manually and continue them into the right-hand graph. These horizontals must intersect the corresponding time curves at $t = 0.25$.

4.10 A simple MATLAB program – visualizing a rotating vector

The program shown in Figure 4.10 lets us visualize the rotation of a vector represented by a complex number. This example requires a few new MATLAB functions; they will be introduced in this section.

Programs in MATLAB are written to files with the extension m. For example, the program shown in Figure 4.10 has been written to a file called `vecrot.m`.

The first two lines begin with the per cent sign, '%', which indicates that these lines are **comments**. Comments are not executable statements and they are used for explanations and reminders in the same way as in other programming languages – for example, in BASIC comments are preceded by the word REM; in newer FORTRAN versions by C or by *, and in C they appear between /* and */. In Figure 4.10 comments

```
% VECROT Animation program which shows a rotating vector    –  1
% defined as a complex number                               –  2
f=50;           %frequency, Hz                               –  3
omega= 2*pi*f;  % angular frequency,rad/s                    –  4
tmax  = 1/f;    % time for a complete rotation, S            –  5
time    = [];                                                %– 6
motion  = [];                                                %– 7
for t=0: tmax/36:   tmax                                     %– 8
   z       = exp (i*omega*t);  %complex number description   %– 9
   x       = real(z);          %cartesion projection         %– 10
   y       = imag(z);          %cartesian projection         %– 11
   time    = [ time t ];                                     %– 12
   motion = [ motion y ];                                    %– 13
   plot([0,x],[0,y]                                          %– 14
   axis('square'), axis([-1 1 -1 1])                         %– 15
   pause(1.0)                                                %– 16
end                                                          %– 17
```

Figure 4.10   A program that animates a rotating vector.

are also used to assign each line a number to which the following explanations will refer.

The expressions in lines 3, 4 and 5 are explained by the comments that accompany them. The statement in line 6 is the **initialization** of an **empty** array called time. Similarly, the statement in line 7 is the initialization of an empty array called motion.

The statement in line 8 opens a FOR loop. The commands contained between the line beginning with the word for and the line containing the word end – line 17 – will be **iterated**, that is, repeated, until $t = tmax$. In the first iteration $t = 0$, after each iteration t is increased by $tmax/36$. The expression

```
for t = 0: tmax/36: tmax
```

contains the initial value, $t = 0$, the increment, $tmax/36$, and the terminating value, $tmax$, of t.

Line 9 defines the rotating vector as the complex number

$$z = e^{i\omega t}$$

Lines 10 and 11 separate the real and the imaginary parts of z and assign their values to the variables x and y.

In line 12 the array time is augmented with a new element which is the current value of t. Similarly, in line 13 the array motion is augmented with a new element, the current value of the imaginary part of z. At the termination of the loop, the arrays time and motion will contain all the values of t and y produced by the program.

The statement

```
plot([0 x], [0 y])
```

plots a line segment with the origin at $0, 0$ and the end at x, y. Note that, instead of defining the array of horizontal coordinates, $[0\ x]$, and the array of vertical coordinates, $[0\ y]$, by separate statements, the corresponding definitions are enclosed within the plot command.

The projections of the rotating line segment on the real and imaginary axes change at each iteration. When a plot command is invoked, MATLAB provides for automatic adjustment of the axes so that the graph covers the entire plotting area. This means that in this example the axes would change at each iteration, and with them the scale of the line segment representing the rotating vector. In order to visualize the rotating vector correctly, the scale should be constant. Also, as the extremity of the rotating vector describes a circle, the frame of its graph should be a square. The statement

```
axis('square')
```

produces a square plotting area. The statement

```
axis([ -1 1 -1 1 ])
```

defines the axis of abscissae as running from −1 to 1, and the axis of ordinates as also running from −1 to 1. The two calls to the axis function are written in line 15.

Finally, let us look at the last statement of the loop. Each iteration generates a new graph which replaces the preceding one on the screen. Without the command pause(1.0) the screens would change so fast that it would be nearly impossible to follow the rotation of the vector generated by the program. By introducing the statement in line 16, each screen will be presented for one second before the execution of the next iteration.

Use your favourite editor to write the program in Figure 4.10 to a file called vecrot.m. This file may be in the same directory that contains your MATLAB files, but it would be better to store it in a subdirectory reserved for your exercises. In the latter case a proper path specification should be provided.

Now enter the MATLAB environment and type vecrot. You will see a sequence of graphs with the line segment rotating by 10 degrees between two successive screens. Excuse the flicker; MATLAB versions earlier than 4.0 had no facilities meant for animation. You can partially remedy this by inserting the hold on command between lines 14 and 15. Then all the graphs produced during successive iterations will be held and superimposed one upon the other. This will produce a steadier picture that will eventually contain 36 vectors. If you use the hold command, and you want to produce other plots during the same session, type hold off to toggle the hold option, and clf to get rid of the graph.

When the rotating vector is back in its initial position, it stops and you may check that its vertical projection, that is, its imaginary part, has indeed generated a sinusoid. For this purpose, first type Enter, in order to return the MATLAB prompt, and then axis, which will toggle the automatic scaling facility on. Continue by entering

```
>> plot(time, motion)
```

Let us try another MATLAB facility. Type

```
>> help vecrot
```

The screen will display the first two lines of the program, that is, the lines marked as comments. In general, the command help will display all *comment lines that precede the first executable statement.* Try the help command followed by the name of some MATLAB function, for example help plot: you will obtain a short guide to using the plot function. If the help runs on more than one screen, use first the command more on. You will then see one screen; to go to the next, press the space bar. After seeing all the screens, enter more off.

It is good practice to begin each program with a few comment lines that describe its function, input and output.

The way in which the arrays time and motion are built by the program in Figure 4.10 is not the best one. The sizes of these arrays are redefined at each iteration. Thus, after the first iteration their common length is 1, after the second 2, and so on. This resizing consumes time, an effect which may become inconvenient if the number of iterations is large. A better way is to define zero arrays of the final size:

```
time = zeros(1,37); motion = zeros(1, 37);
```

and initialize a **counter**

```
n = 0;
```

Then replace statements 12 and 13 by

```
n = n + 1;
time(n) = t;
motion(n) = y;
```

Copy the file into a new file, called for instance vecrot1.m, modify it as shown above and run it.

4.11   Summary

The **imaginary unit** is $i = \sqrt{-1}$. In older MATLAB versions the user must define this unit by typing i = sqrt(-1). In newer versions the definition is built in and the user may recover the imaginary unit by typing either i or j.

A **complex number** can be defined as a linear combination of its **real** and **imaginary** parts: $z = a + ib$, where a and b are real numbers. In MATLAB the number can be entered as z = a + bi or z = a + bj. Alternatively, the same number can be defined in exponential form: $z = \rho e^{i\theta}$, where ρ is the **modulus**, or **absolute value** of z, and θ the **argument**, with the relationships $\rho = \sqrt{a^2 + b^2}$, $\tan \theta = b/a$. In MATLAB, if the complex number z was defined previously, its real part can be retrieved by typing real(z), the imaginary part by imag(z), the modulus by abs(z), and the argument by angle(z). The conjugate $\bar{z} = a - ib$ of the number z is obtained by conj(z). Table 4.1 contains a list of MATLAB complex number functions.

The arithmetic operations of addition, subtraction, multiplication, division, raising to a power, and root extraction are readily extended to complex numbers; in MATLAB they are carried out by the same commands as for real numbers. For an array w of complex numbers, the transpose is obtained in MATLAB by w.', while w' yields the **conjugate transpose**, that is, the transpose of an array whose elements are the conjugates of the elements of w.

If, in the series expansions of $\sin x$, $\cos x$, and e^x, we substitute the real variable x by the complex variable z, we obtain the definitions of the respective **functions of complex variables**. The **natural logarithm** of a complex number z is another complex number $a + bi$ such that $e^{a+bi} = z$. In MATLAB this function is obtained

Table 4.1 Operations with complex number

Operation	Usage	E
z = a + bi	Cartesian definition	z1 = 3 +
real(z)	a, real part of z	re
imag(z)	b, imaginary part of z	i⟩
+	sum	z1 ⟩
−	difference	z1 − z2 = −₂
*	product	z1*z2 = −9 + 38i
/	quotient	z1/z2 = 0.6393 + 0.03281
abs(z)	$(a^2 + b^2)^{1/2}$, modulus of z	r = abs(z1) = 5
angle(z)	arctan b/a, argument of z	a = angle(z1) = 0.9273 rad
r*exp(i*a)	polar definition	r*exp(i*a) = 3 + 4i
conj(z)	conjugate of z	conj(z1) = 3 − 4i

by log(z). It is easy to check in MATLAB that some well-known properties of $\sin x$, $\cos x$, e^x, and $\ln x$ hold also for $\sin z$, $\cos z$, e^z, and $\ln z$.

A function $w = f(z)$ of a complex variable z can be regarded as a mapping from the complex z-plane to the complex w-plane. When the derivative df/dz exists in a neighbourhood of a point z_i, it is said that $f(z)$ is analytic at z_i. Mappings by analytic functions preserve, in the w-plane, the angles between curves in the z plane, at points at which $df/dz \neq 0$. Such transformations are called conformal mappings; they have applications in two-dimensional fluid flow, heat flow, and electrostatics. Typical cases of applications are the mapping of two-dimensional flow around a circular section to the flow around an actual airfoil or ship section. MATLAB can easily be used to illustrate the results of conformal mappings.

Motions that can be described by a sinusoidal function of time are called harmonic motions. A harmonic motion can be represented by a rotating vector in the complex plane. The velocity and the acceleration of a harmonic motion can also be represented by rotating vectors that lead the displacement by phase angles equal to $\pi/2$ and π. The integral of the displacement is described by a rotating vector that lags $\pi/2$ behind. Examples of phenomena that can be modelled as harmonic motions are the oscillations of a linear mass-spring-dashpot system, the small amplitude motions of a pendulum, and the voltage and the current in alternating-current circuits built with linear elements. Other important applications of complex numbers can be found in Chapter 15, Control, and in Chapter 16, Signal processing.

4.12 Examples

EXAMPLE 4.1 A simple model of car vibrations ⸻⸻⸻⸻⸻⸻

In the section on **harmonic motion** it was mentioned that examples of such behaviour are the motions of linear mass-spring-dashpot systems. As an illustration let us consider, in Figure 4.11, a very simplified model of a car (see also Mitschke 1972).

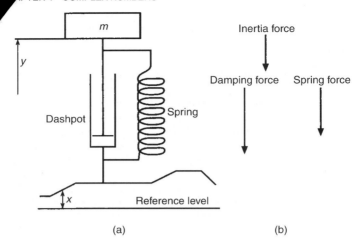

Figure 4.11   Car suspension and damping – a linear mechanical system.

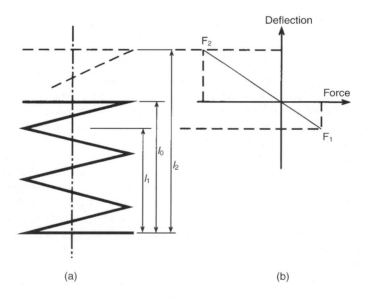

Figure 4.12   A linear spring.

This example will enable us to illustrate the use of phasors and introduce the notions of **frequency response** and **Bode plot** in mechanical engineering. In Figure 4.11(a), the car is represented by its mass m, and the suspension and the tyres by an equivalent **spring** and **dashpot** system. The line marked **reference level** is the horizontal ground under the wheels, when the car is at rest.

For small-amplitude motions we assume a **linear** spring characteristic, such as shown in Figure 4.12. In Figure 4.12(a), l_0 is the length of the spring when loaded by the car weight. We consider this position as the reference and, correspondingly, in the diagram in Figure 4.12(b) the force exercised by the spring is zero. If, following the motions of the mass m, the spring is compressed to the length l_1, a force F_1 directed in the positive sense (that is, directed upwards) appears and its magnitude is

$$F_1 = k(l_0 - l_1)$$

where k is the **spring constant**, here a characteristic of the suspension–tyre system. If the spring is extended to the length l_2, it exerts a force F_2 directed in the negative sense and having the value

$$F_2 = k(l_0 - l_2)$$

The dashpot models the sum of the damping forces developed in the shock absorbers and in the tyres. In this simplified example we consider the force appearing in the dashpot as proportional to the velocity of the mass m. This kind of damping is known as **viscous damping** because it resembles the resistance opposed to *slow* motion by viscous fluids. A graphical representation is shown in Figure 4.13 where c is the **damping coefficient**.

When the car is moving, the ground may change its shape and this change is described by a function of time, $x(t)$, x being measured from the reference level upwards. The vertical position of the car mass, m, is defined by the coordinate y, measured from some convenient reference plane.

Let us now assume that, as the car travels along the line described by $x(t)$, at some instant the mass m moves in the positive y direction. The motion of m is opposed by the forces shown in Figure 4.11(b). According to Newton's second law, the inertia force equals the product of the mass and the acceleration

$$-m\ddot{y}$$

As shown above, the spring force is given by

$$-k(y - x)$$

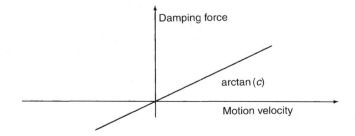

Figure 4.13   A linear damper.

and the damping force, by

$$-c\frac{d(y-x)}{dt} = c\dot{y} - c\dot{x}$$

The sum of all these forces must equal zero, so that the equation of motion is

$$m\ddot{y} + c\dot{y} + ky = c\dot{x} + kx \qquad \textbf{(4.40)}$$

The basic SI units to be used in this equation are the metre (symbol m) for lengths, that is, x and y, the kilogram (symbol kg) for mass, the newton (symbol N) for force, and the second (s) for time. The other quantities are measured in derived units, as follows: $\dot{y}$ in m s^{-1}, $\ddot{y}$ in m s^{-2}, c in N s m^{-1}, k in N m^{-1}.

Equation 4.40 is linear, as y, x and their derivatives appear at the first power. Here x is the **excitation**, or **input**, and y, the **response**, or **output**.

A simple assumption that can be made about x is that it is a sinusoidal function of time, that is, it can be represented, for example, by the imaginary part of

$$x = Be^{i\omega t} \qquad \textbf{(4.41)}$$

This is not an arbitrary assumption, because we can describe any given ground profile by a sum of sines and cosines (see, for example, Genta 1982, page 271). The following **superposition** property can then be used to calculate the car behaviour on any road profile:

If the response of a linear system to an excitation x_i is y_i, the response to an excitation $\sum x_i$ is $\sum y_i$.

In this chapter we shall not make use of this property, but of another one:

Under certain conditions usually fulfilled by technical systems, if the excitation of a linear system is a sinusoidal function of frequency ω, the steady-state response of the system is also a sinusoidal function having the same frequency ω but, in general, different amplitude and phase.

The above property does not refer to **transients**, such as may occur at the beginning and the end of the motion, but to the **steady-state** motion which follows after start-up transients have died out. We conclude that the steady-state response of our car model to the excitation described by Equation 4.41 can be described by the imaginary part of

$$y = ae^{i(\omega t + \phi)} = Ae^{i\omega t} \qquad \textbf{(4.42)}$$

where $A = ae^{i\phi}$ is the output phasor. Substituting the expressions of x and y into Equation 4.40 yields

$$[-m\omega^2 + ic\omega + k]A = [ic\omega + k]B \qquad \textbf{(4.43)}$$

The **complex amplification factor** is

$$Y(i\omega) = \frac{A}{B} = \frac{k + ic\omega}{(-m\omega^2 + k) + ic\omega} \tag{4.44}$$

This is the **frequency response function** and it is related to the **transfer function** of the system.

The **undamped natural frequency** is defined as

$$\omega_n = \sqrt{k/m} \tag{4.45}$$

and the **damping ratio**, as

$$\zeta = \frac{c}{2\sqrt{km}} = \frac{c}{2m\omega_n} \tag{4.46}$$

Using 4.45 and 4.46, Equation 4.44 can be brought to the form

$$Y(\omega) = \frac{1 + i2\zeta(\omega/\omega_n)}{\left[1 - (\omega/\omega_n)^2\right] + i2\zeta(\omega/\omega_n)} \tag{4.47}$$

Equation 4.47 is of the form

$$Y(\omega) = \frac{N_1 + iN_2}{D_1 + iD_2} = \frac{N_1 D_1 + N_2 D_2}{D_1^2 + D_2^2} + i\frac{N_2 D_1 - N_1 D_2}{D_1^2 + D_2^2} \tag{4.48}$$

The real amplification factor equals

$$\left|\frac{A}{B}\right| = |Y(\omega)| = \sqrt{\frac{N_1^2 + N_2^2}{D_1^2 + D_2^2}} \tag{4.49}$$

and the phase shift of the response relative to the input is

$$\arg\left|\frac{A}{B}\right| = \arg|Y(\omega)| = \arctan\frac{N_2 D_1 - N_1 D_2}{N_1 D_1 + N_2 D_2} \tag{4.50}$$

Equations 4.49 and 4.50 allow us to calculate the amplification and the phase shift for any input frequency, ω. In MATLAB, however, we can proceed directly from either Equation 4.44 or Equation 4.47, and use the commands abs(Y) and angle(Y). A numerical example will illustrate this.

The mass of an empty, 1500 cc car is 870 kg; with two passengers it is 1020 kg, and with four passengers and a loaded luggage compartment, 1200 kg. Let the other data be $k = 70000\,\text{N}\,\text{m}^{-1}$ and $c = 5000\,\text{N}\,\text{s}\,\text{m}^{-1}$. Defining in MATLAB the values for the fully loaded car, and using Equation 4.44, for $\omega = 5.7\,\text{rad}\cdot\text{s}^{-1}$ the command

```
>> amplification = abs(Y)
```

yields the answer 1.7944, and the command

```
>> phase = 180*angle(Y)/pi
```

the answer -20.4296 degrees.

Equation 4.43 can be interpreted in terms of phasors. We can draw the phasor diagram as a continuation of the calculations mentioned above. Let us assume that the phase of the response is zero, and that the amplitude of the input is 0.1 m. The response amplitude can be found from

```
>> B = 0.1;
>> A = amplification*B;
```

For our convenience, let the response phasor lie along the real axis and thus the spring-force phasor. The latter can be defined by

```
>> Fs = [ 0 k ]*A;
```

At the extremity of this phasor, and at $90°$ to it, we draw the damping force phasor; its extremity is the point

```
>> Fd = Fs(2) + i*c*omega*A;
```

Starting from this point, we draw the inertia-force phasor, horizontally and oriented in the negative direction; its extremity lies at

```
>> Fi = Fd - m*omega^2*A;
```

The three components of the response form a broken line defined by

```
>> output = [ Fs Fd Fi ];
```

The vector connecting the origin of the coordinates with the point Fi must equal the input phasor, B. We shall not draw it, but instead its two components, that is, the spring component

```
>> Bs = [ 0 k ]*B*exp(-i*phase);
```

and the damping component, whose extremity lies at

```
>> Bd = Bs(2) + i*c*omega*B*exp(-i*phase);
```

The value of the variable **phase** must be given in radians. In calculations we assumed that the phase of B is zero, and that the resulting phase is that of A. As we have drawn $k * A$ with a zero phase, we had to write negative phases for the components of B. The input components form a broken line defined by

```
>> input = [ Bs Bd ];
```

The diagram is obtained with the command

```
>> plot(real(output),imag(output),real(input),imag(input))
```

We see that the graph is closed, that is, the resultant of Bs and Bd is indeed equal to the input phasor. We can also check this numerically: type Fi and Bd and see that in both cases you obtain the same number, $5564.9 + 5114.1i$.

By visual inspection of the graph we can decide the commands that produce the same scale factor on the real and imaginary axes:

```
>> axis('square'), axis([ 0 14000 0 6000 ])
```

Next we retrieve the plot command by means of the *Up Arrow* key, and press Enter in order to see the graph again. Finally, the phasors can be marked with the aid of the text function, for example

```
>> text(Fs(2)/2, 0, 'k*A')
```

The reader is invited to write the other commands that complete the plot, as shown in the upper part of Figure 4.14. To write the Greek letter ω use the LATEX command \omega. When the graph looks satisfactory, the command print -dps vibr1.ps can be entered to store the figure on a PostScript file called vibr1.ps. For colour PostScript use print -dpsc vibr1. To send the file to a local printer, consult the operator.

A second, very important graph can be obtained from Equation 4.47; this is the **frequency response** shown in Figure 4.15: it describes the variation of the amplification and the phase as functions of the **frequency ratio** ω/ω_n. Some of the commands used are

```
>> zeta = c/(2*sqrt(k*m))
>> r = 0:0.05:3;
>> s = 2*zeta*r*i;
>> Y = (1 + s)./(1 - r.^2 + s);
>> axis, axis('normal')
```

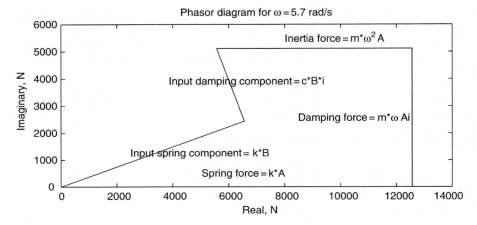

Figure 4.14   Phasor diagram for $\omega = 5.7$ rad/s of the car model.

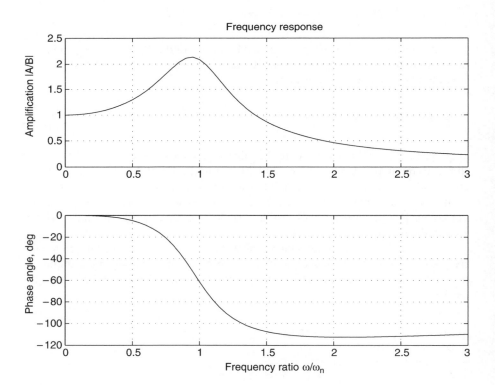

Figure 4.15   Frequency response of the car model.

```
>> subplot(2, 1, 1), plot(r, abs(Y))
>> subplot(2, 1. 2), plot(r, 180*angle(Y)/pi)
```

The `axis` and `axis('normal')` commands restore the automatic scaling facility and the rectangular shape of the graph. The `subplot(2, 1, 1)` and `subplot(2, 1, 2)` commands place the two graphs one above the other. Symbolically we can regard the combined plot as a 2-by-1 matrix of graphs, hence the first two digits of the argument, 2, 1. In the call of the `xlabel` function we used the LaTeX commands `\omega` and `\omega_n`. Both produced the Greek letter ω, and the latter command added the subscript n resulting in ω_n.

In MATLAB under Windows a graph can be printed with the command `print` or by clicking in the menu. The command

```
>> print vibr1 -dps vibr1.ps
```

produces a PostScript file, `vibr1.ps`, that can be sent to the local printer with commands specific to the system, or can be embedded in a document. To learn other printing commands use `help print`.

The frequency response graph shows that the amplification factor reaches a maximum when the excitation frequency, ω, is close to the undamped natural frequency, ω_n. Without damping, the maximum would occur exactly at the frequency ratio 1. This phenomenon is called **resonance**.

There are certain advantages in plotting against a logarithmic scale of frequencies, or frequency ratios, and using a scale in **decibels** for the amplification factor. The resulting plot is known as a **Bode diagram** and the reasons for using it are briefly explained in Example 4.2. The decibel is defined as ten times the decimal logarithm of the ratio of two powers. As powers in harmonic motions are proportional to the square of amplitudes, we can write in our case

$$10 \log_{10} \frac{|A|^2}{|B|^2} = 20 \log_{10} \frac{|A|}{|B|}$$

The use of decibels is explained in many books on control; an interesting explanation in a book on vibrations is given in Broch (1984), Appendix F.

The commands for producing the Bode plot are:

```
>> subplot(2, 1, 1), semilogx(r, 20*log(abs(Y)))
>> grid
>> ylabel('Amplification |A/B|, dB')
>> subplot(2, 1, 2), semilogx(r, 180*angle(Y)/pi)
>> grid
>> xlabel('Frequency ratio \omega/\omega_n')
>> ylabel('Phase angle, deg')
```

and the result is shown in Figure 4.16.

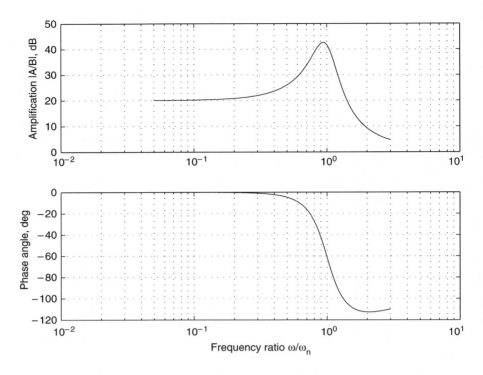

Figure 4.16   Bode plot of the simplified car model.

EXAMPLE 4.2   A lowpass filter

Readers familiar with the elementary principles of AC circuits and with phasors in electrical engineering may read this example and the next one now. Other readers will find a brief introduction to the subject in Subsection 4.15.2.

Figure 4.17 shows a series RC circuit. Let us assume the following values:

V, 10 mV, 50 MHz, zero phase
R, 15 Ω,
C, 100 pF.

The reactance of the capacitor equals:

$$Z_c = \frac{1}{j\omega C} = -j\frac{1}{\omega C}$$

We introduce the values of the elements as follows

```
>> V = 0.01;              % V
>> R = 15;                % ohm
>> omega = 2*pi*50*10^6;  % rad/s
```

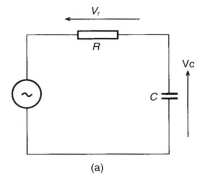 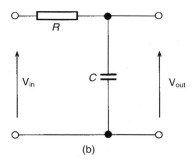

(a) (b)

Figure 4.17 A series *RC* circuit.

```
>> C = 100*10^(-12);      % F
>> Zc = -j/(omega*C);     % ohm
```

Without MATLAB it would be necessary to use algebraic formulae, available in specialized books, and calculate separately the magnitude and the phase of each quantity involved. In MATLAB calculations can be carried out immediately. Thus, the circuit impedance equals

```
>> Z = R + Zc
Z =
     15.0000 -31.8310i
```

and the current,

```
>> I = V/Z
I =
     1.2114e-04+ 2.5707e-04i
```

The voltage across the resistor *R* is given by

```
>> Vr = R*I
Vr =
     0.0018 + 0.0039i
```

and across the capacitor, by

```
>> Vc = Zc*I
Vc =
     0.0082 - 0.0039i
```

Let us plot side by side the phasor diagram and the time story of the calculated voltages. We use the MATLAB `subplot` command to obtain two adjacent plots:

```
>> subplot(1, 2, 1)
```

The argument 1, 2, 1 means that a 1-by-2 'matrix' of graphs is produced, and that the next plot is the first one.

We consider the values V, Vr, Vc as the ends of the phasors. To define the phasors we must also enter their origins. We do this as follows:

```
>> VV = [ 0 V ]; VVc = [ 0 Vc ]; VVr = [ 0 Vr ];
```

Next we plot the given voltage phasor, V,

```
>> plot(real(VV), imag(VV))
```

In order to view the phasors correctly the scale of the real axis should be the same as that of the imaginary axis. This means a square plotting frame which we obtain with

```
>> axis('square')
```

Convenient axes are produced by the statement

```
>> axis([ 0 0.012 -0.006 0.006 ])
```

The extension of both axes is 0.012. This value can be obtained by trial and error, that is, by displaying a first graph, evaluating visually the best axes, and issuing the corresponding `axis` statement. Another possibility is to use the MATLAB abs function in order to get the maximum phasor magnitude and to adjust the axes in accordance with it.

We can use the `hold` function to keep the graph and superimpose on it the other two phasors, Vr and Vc,

```
>> hold on
>> plot(real(VVr), imag(VVr))
>> plot(real(VVc), imag(VVc))
```

The graph is completed with

```
>> title('(a)')
>> xlabel('Real'), ylabel('Imaginary')
```

If we know what we entered in the graph we can identify the phasors ourselves and mark them by means of the `gtext` function. Alternatively, we can let MATLAB identify the phasors; good practice when there are many phasors or the configuration is not very clear. The required statements for the latter procedure are

```
≫ text(real(V), imag(V), 'V')
≫ text(real(Vr), imag(Vr), 'Vr', 'r')
≫ text(real(Vc), imag(Vc), 'Vc', 'g')
```

The argument `'r'` means that the colour of the plotted line should be red, and the argument `'g'`, that the colour should be green. Use `help print'` to learn other possibilities. To allow for further plots we must leave the `hold` on state:

```
≫ hold off
```

The phasor diagram appears in the left-hand side of Figure 4.18. It is easy to check graphically that V is indeed the vector sum of Vr and Vc, and that the latter

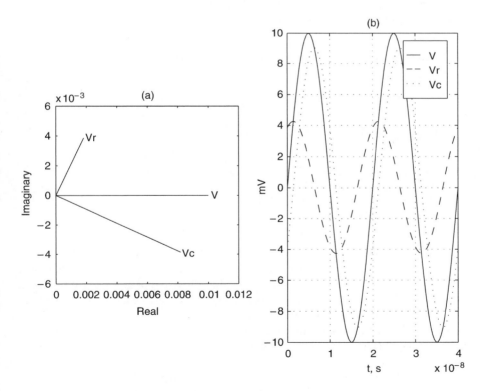

Figure 4.18   Voltages in the series RC circuit.

two phasors are perpendicular to one another. In MATLAB we can verify the above properties as follows:

```
>> Vr + Vc
ans =
    0.0100 - 0.0000i
>> 180*(angle(Vr) - angle(Vc))/pi
ans =
    90
```

To complete Figure 4.18 with the time plots of the calculated voltages we begin as follows:

```
>> f = 50*10^6;          % frequency, Hz
>> T = 1/f;              % period, s
>> omega= 2*pi*f;        % angular frequency, rad/s
>> t = 0: T/50: 2*T;     % array of time values, s
>> v = V*sin(omega*t);
>> vr = abs(Vr)*sin(omega*t + angle(Vr));
>> vc = abs(Vc)*sin(omega*t + angle(Vc));
```

To produce the plot as the second element of the 'graph matrix' we enter

```
>> subplot(1, 2, 2)
```

and the other plotting commands are

```
>> h = plot(t, 1000*v, 'k-', t, 1000*vr, 'r--', t, 1000*vc, 'g:')
>> grid, title('(b)')
>> xlabel('t, s'), ylabel('mV')
>> legend(h, 'V', 'Vr', 'Vc')
```

In the plot, the argument 'k-' means that the first line should be solid and black. The argument 'r--' produces a dashed, red line, and 'g:', a green, dotted line. By writing h = plot(... we assign a **handle** to the plot. We use it in calling the function legend. The latter produces a legend in which each style of line used in the plot is explained by the arguments following the name of the handle, h. Thus, as the first line was solid, the legend contains a sample of solid line followed by the explanation V. It can be checked on the graph that at each instant the voltage V equals the sum of Vr and Vc.

The *RC* circuit studied above functions like a **lowpass filter**. To show this we arrange the circuit as in the right-hand side of Figure 4.17. We consider the given

10 mV voltage as the **input voltage**, and the voltage across the capacitor as the **output voltage**. We mark the former voltage appropriately by V_{in}, and the latter by V_{out}. The following relationships hold in this circuit

$$Z = R + Z_c = R + \frac{1}{j\omega C} = R - j\frac{1}{\omega C}$$

$$I = \frac{V_{in}}{Z} = \frac{1}{R - j/\omega C}V_{in}$$

$$V_{out} = Z_c I = \frac{1}{j\omega C} \cdot \frac{1}{R - j/\omega C}V_{in}$$

The **frequency response function** (related to the **transfer function**) of the filter is by definition the ratio

$$H(j\omega) = \frac{V_{out}}{V_{in}} = \frac{1}{1 + j\omega RC} \tag{4.51}$$

The value $\omega_c = 1/RC$ is called the **cutoff frequency** and we shall soon see what its significance is. With this notation we rewrite Equation 4.51 in nondimensional form

$$H(\omega) = \frac{1}{1 + j\omega/\omega_c} \tag{4.52}$$

or, with

$$\omega/\omega_c = 2\pi f/2\pi f_c = f/f_c$$

we obtain the nondimensional form of the transfer function, in terms of frequency,

$$H(f) = \frac{1}{1 + jf/f_c} \tag{4.53}$$

We shall plot the magnitude and the phase of the transfer function in two graphs. We begin by generating an array of frequency-ratio values, and an array of transfer-function values

```
>> fratio = 0:  0.01:  5;
>> H = ones(size(fratio))./(1 + j*fratio);
```

It is usual to arrange the magnitude plot over the phase plot. In our symbolic description this means a 2-by-1 array of graphs. We again use the `subplot` command, this time with arguments beginning with 2, 1. The sequence of commands is

```
>> subplot(2, 1, 1), plot(fratio, abs(H))
>> grid, ylabel('H(f_ratio)')
>> subplot(2, 1, 2), plot(fratio, 180*angle(H)/pi), grid
>> xlabel('f/f_c'), ylabel('Phase, deg')
```

The result of the commands shown above can be seen in Figure 4.19. Visual inspection of the graph shows that a low-frequency input would produce an output of nearly the same magnitude, while higher-frequency inputs will produce greatly reduced outputs. The circuit acts like a **lowpass filter**. The point at which the frequency equals the cutoff frequency, that is, the point corresponding to $f/f_c = 1$, separates the curves into two regions, on the left the region in which signals pass, and on the right the region in which signals are practically suppressed; hence the name **cutoff frequency**. From Equation 4.53 it is possible to see that at cutoff frequency $|H| = 1/\sqrt{2}$ and the phase equals $-45°$; these values can be read on the graph.

Traditionally, a logarithmic scale is used for frequencies – or frequency ratios – and a decibel scale is used for the magnitude. By definition, the **decibel**, with the symbol *dB*, equals ten times the decimal logarithm of the ratio of two powers.

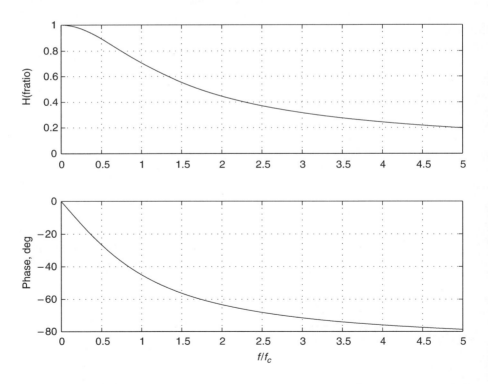

Figure 4.19   Magnitude and phase plots of the series *RC* lowpass filter.

As powers are, in general, proportional to the squares of amplitudes, or magnitudes, in our case:

$$10 \log_{10} \frac{|V_{out}^2|}{|V_{in}^2|} = 20 \log_{10} \frac{|V_{out}|}{|V_{in}|}$$

The use of decibels is explained in many books on control; an interesting explanation in a book on vibrations is given in Broch (1984), Appendix F.

To obtain the plots characterized above we begin by defining an array of logarithmically spaced frequency-ratio values. We use the MATLAB `logspace` function for this and we call it with two arguments:

```
>> fratio = logspace(-1, 2);
```

The result is an array of 50 values extending from 10^{-1} to 10^2. We continue with

```
>> H = ones(size((fratio))./(1 + j*fratio);
>> subplot(2, 1, 1), semilogx(fratio, 20*log(abs(H)))
>> grid, ylabel('Magnitude, dB')
>> subplot(2, 1, 2), semilogx(fratio, 180*angle(H)/pi)
>> grid, xlabel('f/f_c'), ylabel('Phase, deg')
```

The resulting plot is shown in Figure 4.20 and is known as a **Bode plot**. Several properties of this graph can be mentioned here. First of all, the logarithmic frequency scale allows us to 'expand' the graph in the region close to zero. With a linear frequency scale it would be difficult to investigate behaviour close to zero. The logarithmic frequency scale also allows us to extend the scale towards larger frequency values without enlarging the graph too much.

Another important observation is that in logarithmic scales the resulting curves can be approximated, if necessary, by straight-line segments. This procedure, together with the possibility of breaking down a higher-order transfer function into first- and second-order factors, is discussed in most books on control, for instance in d'Azzo and Houpis (1988) or Dorf (1992).

Finally, plotting the magnitude on a dB scale 'compresses' the values in the region of resonance, a phenomenon that does not occur in first-order systems, as discussed here, but in higher-order systems, such as the one described in the next example.

EXAMPLE 4.3 A series *RLC* circuit. Resonance _____

Let us consider a circuit in which all three elements introduced above are connected in series, as in Figure 4.21. All three elements are traversed by the same current i,

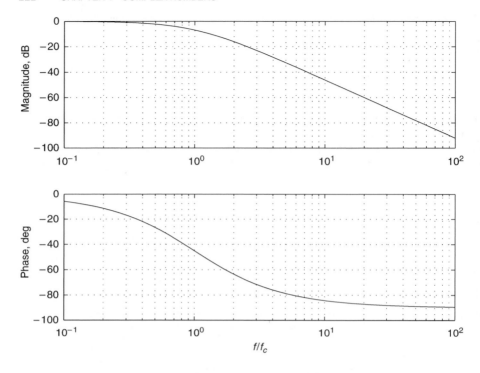

Figure 4.20   Bode plot of the series RC lowpass filter.

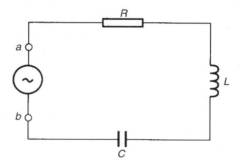

Figure 4.21   An ac series circuit.

and the voltage across the points a and b equals the sum of the voltages across the three elements:

$$v = v_R + v_L + v_C \tag{4.54}$$

In the complex plane Equation 4.54 gives the **complex voltage**

$$\vec{V} = R\vec{I} + jL\omega\vec{I} - \frac{j}{C\omega}\vec{I} = \vec{Z}I \tag{4.55}$$

with

$$\vec{Z} = R + j\left(L\omega - \frac{1}{C\omega}\right) \tag{4.56}$$

The complex number $\vec{Z}$ is called **impedance** and is measured in ohms. The concept of impedance enables the generalization of Ohm's law to ac circuits. Moreover, series and parallel combinations of R, L, and C elements, regarded as complex impedances, can be replaced by equivalent impedances in the same way that series and parallel combinations of resistances are. For instance, n impedances, $Z_1, Z_2, \ldots, Z_n$, connected in series can be replaced by the equivalent impedance

$$Z_s = \sum_{i=1}^{n} Z_i$$

and the same impedances connected in parallel can be replaced by an equivalent impedance Z_p such that

$$\frac{1}{Z_p} = \sum_{i=1}^{n} \frac{1}{Z_i}$$

Any complex impedance, $\vec{Z}$, can be written in the form

$$\vec{Z} = R + jX \tag{4.57}$$

where the real part, R, is the resistance, and the imaginary part, X, is the **reactance**. The argument of $\vec{Z}$ is the phase shift of the voltage relative to the current.

As an example let us consider a series circuit as in Figure 4.21, with $R = 5\,\Omega$, $L = 0.05\,H$, and $C = 100\,\mu F$. Let the voltage across the circuit – that is, between the points a and b – be 220 V and the frequency 50 Hz. In MATLAB, after having defined R, L, C, and the circular frequency omega = 2*pi*50, Equation 4.56 yields $Z = 5.0000 - 16.1230i$ ohms. Further calculations give

```
≫ magnitude = abs(Z)
magnitude =
     16.8805
```

```
≫ phase = 180*angle(Z)/pi
phase =
    -72.7705
≫ I = V/Z
I =
    3.8603 +12.4479i
```

The letter i in the above answer is the symbol for the imaginary unit. Even if we use the letter i for the absolute value of the current, MATLAB will continue to display the results with i in the imaginary part, that is, in the form a + bi. In that case, we must enter complex numbers using the symbol j for the imaginary unit, for example a + bj. The use of j for the imaginary unit is common in electrical engineering; MATLAB, however, always displays the imaginary unit as i.

Taking the phase of the current as a reference, that is, equal to zero, we continue the calculations as follows:

```
≫ i = abs(I)
i =
    13.0328
≫ V_R = i*R
V_R =
    65.1639
≫ V_L = j*L*omega*i
V_L =
    0+ 2.0472e+02i
≫ V_C = -j*i/(C*omega)
V_C =
    0- 4.1485e+02i
```

We can check that the total voltage drop equals the mains voltage, and that the phase shift between current and voltage is the one already calculated:

```
≫ U = V_R + V_L + V_C
U =
    6.5164e+01- 2.1013e+02i
≫ abs(U)
ans =
    220.0000
≫ 180*angle(U)/pi
ans =
    -72.7705
```

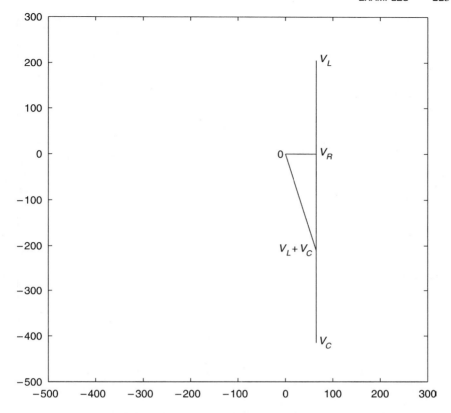

Figure 4.22   Phasor diagram of a series *RLC* circuit.

The interpretation of these calculations in terms of phasors is shown in Figure 4.22 which was produced with MATLAB plotting facilities, among them the commands

```
≫ l(1) = 0; l(2) = V_R;
≫ l(3) = V_R + V_L; l(4) = V_R + V_C;
≫ voltage = [ 0 U ];
≫ plot(real(l),imag(l), real(voltage), imag(voltage))
≫ axis('square'), axis([ -500 300 -500 300 ])
```

The resistive voltage-drop phasor is plotted horizontally, from the origin O to the point marked V_R. The inductive voltage-drop phasor leads the resistive voltage drop by $\pi/2$, and the capacitive voltage-drop phasor lags behind the resistive voltage drop by $\pi/2$. The sum of the two *reactive* voltage drops is the vector from the point V_R to the point $V_L + V_C$. It is easy to check on the graph that the length of the vector connecting the origin O with the point marked $V_L + V_C$ is indeed 220. It is also easy

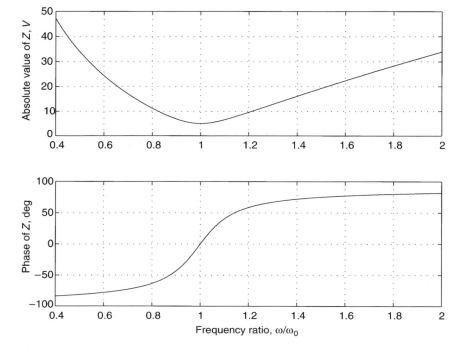

Figure 4.23   Frequency characteristics of a series RLC circuit.

to measure the phase between the resistive voltage, in phase with the current, and the total voltage across the circuit.

From Equation 4.56 we see that the impedance has a minimum when the absolute values of the inductive and capacitive reactances are equal, that is, when

$$\omega_0 = \frac{1}{\sqrt{LC}} \tag{4.58}$$

Continuing the calculations in MATLAB we find this **resonance frequency** to be 447.2136 rad/s, that is, not much above the mains frequency. The reader is invited to obtain the plots shown in Figures 4.23 and 4.24. The first figure represents the behaviour of the impedance Z, as a function of the frequency ratio, ω/ω_0, in the vicinity of resonance. As expected from Equation 4.56, when $\omega = \omega_0$ the impedance equals 5 Ω, that is, R, and the phase is zero. Figure 4.24 represents the variation of the current i, as a function of the frequency ratio, when the applied voltage is 220 V.

4.13   Exercises

Solutions for Exercises 4.5, 4.6 and 4.10 appear at the back of the book.

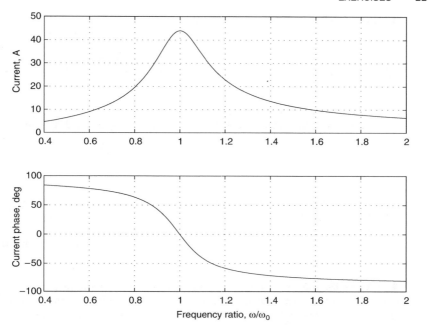

Figure 4.24   The current in a series RLC circuit.

■ **EXERCISE 4.1**   Properties of complex numbers

Complex numbers are a generalization of real numbers, with which they share a number of properties. To show this in MATLAB define three complex numbers $z1, z2, z3$, and verify the statements listed below.

(1)   there exists a 0 such that

$$z1 + 0 = 0 + z1 = z1$$

(2)   For each complex number z there exists an *opposite* (*symmetric*) number $\hat{z}$, $\hat{z}_1 = -z_1$, such that

$$z1 + \hat{z1} = 0$$
$$\hat{z1} + z1 = 0$$

We called this number the **opposite** of $z1$.

(3)   There exists a 1 such that

$$z1 \cdot 1 = 1 \cdot z1 = z1$$

(4)   For each complex number, z, that is not zero, there exists an **inverse** number $\grave{z}$ such that

$$z \cdot \grave{z} = 1$$
$$\grave{z} \cdot z = 1$$

Find the number $\grave{z1}$.

■ **EXERCISE 4.2**   Roots of cubic equation
Calculate the expression in Equation 4.4 in MATLAB and show that it yields 4.

■ **EXERCISE 4.3**   The solutions of a second-degree equation
Substitute the roots indicated for Equation 4.8 in MATLAB and show that they satisfy it.

■ **EXERCISE 4.4**   Cubic roots of unity
Use Equation 4.21 to calculate the three cubic roots, r_1, r_2, r_3 of 1 and show that

$$r_1^2 = r_2$$
$$r_1 \cdot r_2 = r_3$$

Plot the three roots on the complex plane and show that they are the vertices of an equilateral triangle inscribed in the circle with radius 1. Could you generalize for the n n-th roots of 1?

Hint: Use the command `axis('square')` in order to obtain a plot with **aspect ratio** 1:1.

■ **EXERCISE 4.5**   Conformal mapping – the Joukowski transformation
Plot in the z-plane a circle having the centre on the real axis, at -0.5, and passing through 1. Map this circle by means of the **Joukowski transformation** (Nikolai Iegorovitch, Russian, 1847–1921):

$$w = \frac{1}{2}\left(z + \frac{1}{z}\right)$$

Because $dw/dz = 0$ at $z = 1$, the point $z = 1$ is called **critical**. The angle of the tangent to the given circle, at $z = 1$, is not preserved, but doubled under the transformation, and this explains the shape of the mapping at $w = 1$ (see Spiegel 1972, page 223).

Move the centre of the circle – given in the z-plane – above the real axis and see how it is mapped into various *aerofoil* sections.

■ **EXERCISE 4.6**   Swimming across a river
Refer to Exercise 2.6 and write the velocity vectors **V** and **S** as complex numbers. Calculate the velocity relative to ground (**true-velocity**) vector, **T**, as the sum of two complex numbers. Use MATLAB complex-number functions to find the speed, T, and the angle of the velocity over bottom.

■ **EXERCISE 4.7**   Aeroplane drifting in wind
Refer to Exercise 2.7 and express the velocity vectors **P** and **A** as complex numbers.

(a)   Calculate the velocity-over-ground vector, **T**, as the sum of two complex numbers. Use MATLAB complex-number functions to find the speed and the course over ground.

(b)   How should the plane change its course in order to fly on a true eastbound course? Find the new course and, using MATLAB complex-number functions, calculate the speed over ground and verify that the course over ground is the desired one.

Hint: find the angle β shown in Figure 4.25.

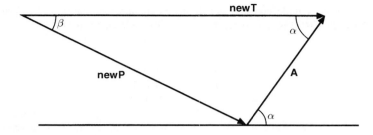

Figure 4.25   Correcting aeroplane drift.

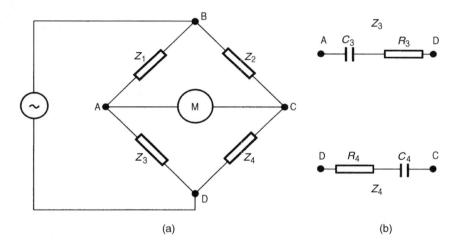

(a)   (b)

Figure 4.26   An ac bridge.

■ **EXERCISE 4.8**   Ship drifting in current and wind
Refer to Exercise 2.8 and define the velocity vectors **A**, **C**, **S** as complex numbers.
Calculate the velocity over bottom as the sum of three complex numbers and, using
MATLAB complex-number functions, find the speed over bottom and the angle of the
true ship course (course over bottom).

■ **EXERCISE 4.9**   An ac bridge
Figure 4.26 is the ac variant of the Wheatstone bridge described in Exercise 3.19.
Instead of resistances, the branches of this bridge can contain impedances, say
Z_1, Z_2, Z_3, Z_4. It is easy to show that the bridge is balanced when

$$Z_1 Z_4 = Z_2 Z_3$$

This is a generalization of Equation 3.41.

As an example, consider that Z_1 and Z_2 are pure resistances, while Z_3 and Z_4 consist of resistances and capacities. Assume the following values:

Frequency	400 Hz
Z_1	2000 Ω
Z_2	400 Ω
R_3	30000 Ω
C_3	0.01 μF

Using the complex-number facilities of MATLAB, calculate the resistance R_4 and the capacitance C_4 that balance the bridge.

■ **EXERCISE 4.10**   A bridge that cannot be balanced
In Figure 4.27 the branch Z_1 consists of a capacity and a resistance; the branch Z_2 of an inductance and a resistance. Gillies (1993) demonstrates that, if Z_3 and Z_4 are pure resistances, this bridge cannot be balanced, whatever the values of the components. As an exercise, verify this property by calculating R_3 for the following sets of values:

	a		b
Frequency	400 Hz	Frequency	50 Hz
R_1	10000 Ω	R_1	30000 Ω
C_1	1 μF	C_1	2 μF
R_2	5000 Ω	R_2	10000 Ω
L_2	0.001 H	L_2	0.002 H

Assume $Z_4 = R_1$.

■ **EXERCISE 4.11**   A bridge that cannot be balanced
Refer again to Exercise 4.10 and assume that $R_3 = 30000$ Ω. To show that the bridge cannot be balanced calculate R_4.

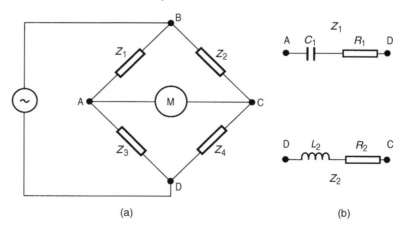

(a)   (b)

Figure 4.27   A bridge that cannot be balanced.

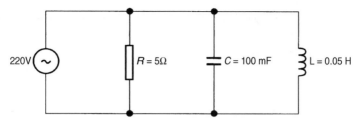

Figure 4.28 A parallel ac circuit, RLC circuit.

■ **EXERCISE 4.12**   A parallel RLC circuit

Analyse the parallel RLC circuit represented in Figure 4.28 and find the expression of the equivalent impedance, Z. Use the same values as in Example 4.3. When the inductive and capacitive reactances are equal, the impedance reaches a maximum and the current a minimum. Find the frequency ω_0 corresponding to this **resonance** (or **antiresonance** as it is called in some books). Plot the absolute value and the phase of the impedance and the current as functions of the frequency ratio ω/ω_0, around $\omega/\omega_0 = 1$.

4.14   Where to find more examples

For more applications of complex numbers see Chapter 15, Control theory, and Chapter 16, Signal processing.

4.15   Appendix

4.15.1   Operations with complex numbers

The sum of two complex numbers, $a + bi$, $c + di$, is defined by

$$(a + bi) + (c + di) = (a + c) + (b + d)i \tag{4.59}$$

and, with $i^2 = -1$, the product of the same numbers yields

$$(a + bi)(c + di) = (ac - bd) + (ad + bc)i \tag{4.60}$$

A complex number $a + bi$ can be divided by another complex, *nonzero* number $c + di$, with the result $e + fi$, if

$$(e + fi)(c + di) = a + bi$$

Developing the left-hand side and equating the real part with a, and the imaginary part with b, we obtain

$$e = \frac{ac + bd}{c^2 + d^2} \qquad\qquad (4.61)$$

$$f = \frac{bc - ad}{c^2 + d^2} \qquad\qquad (4.62)$$

It is easier to reach the same result by multiplying both numerator and denominator by the conjugate of the denominator

$$\frac{a + bi}{c + di} = \frac{a + bi}{c + di} \cdot \frac{c - di}{c - di} = \frac{(ac + bd) + (bc - ad)i}{c^2 + d^2} \qquad (4.63)$$

4.15.2   AC circuits – phasors in electrical engineering

Alternating current is used today in most public electrical networks. The **current** in such a supply can be represented by

$$i = I_m \sin 2\pi f t \qquad\qquad (4.64)$$

where I_m is the maximum instantaneous current, f, the frequency in cycles per second (Hz), and t, the time in s. In North America $f = 60\,\text{Hz}$, in Europe and many other countries, 50 Hz, and on aeroplanes, usually 400 Hz. The **voltage** can be described by a similar sinusoidal function. The basic unit for current is the **ampere** (named after André Marie Ampère, French, 1775–1836) – symbol A, and the unit for voltage is the **volt** (named after Alessandro Volta, Italian, 1745–1827) – symbol V.

The maximum value, I_m, of the current is rarely of interest in electrical engineering, nor is the maximum value of the voltage. The useful quantities are the **effective**, or **rms (root-mean-square) values** of the current and of the voltage. The definition of the effective value of the current is

$$i_e = \left[\frac{1}{T} \int_0^T i^2 \, dt \right]^{1/2} \qquad\qquad (4.65)$$

where $T = 1/f$, and t is the time. The rms values are used in power calculations and they are the values measured by ac ammeters and by ac voltmeters (*ac* is the abbreviation for *alternating-current* used as an adjective). Therefore, when talking about 110 V mains in the USA or Canada, or 220 V in Europe, the numbers refer to rms values.

For i given by Equation 4.64, Equation 4.65 yields

$$i_e = \frac{I_m}{\sqrt{2}} \qquad\qquad (4.66)$$

and Equation 4.64 can be rewritten as

$$i = i_e \sqrt{2} \sin \omega t \qquad\qquad (4.67)$$

with the usual notation $\omega = 2\pi f$.

The simplest element of an electrical circuit is the **resistance**, denoted R. The relationship between the instantaneous values of the voltage across the resistance, v_R, and the current through the resistance, i, is given by the same **Ohm's law** (Georg Simon Ohm, German, 1789–1854) as in direct-current circuits:

$$v_R = iR \qquad\qquad (4.68)$$

A current of 1 A through a resistance of 1 **ohm** – symbol Ω – produces a voltage drop of 1 V. If the current is described by Equation 4.67, the voltage is described by

$$v_R = (i_e \sqrt{2} R) \sin \omega t \qquad\qquad (4.69)$$

We conclude that the voltage across a resistance is in phase with the current through it, and it can be described by a phasor, $\vec{V}_R$, parallel to the current phasor, $\vec{I}$, as at (a) in Figure 4.29.

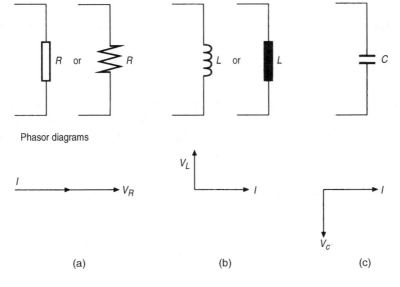

Figure 4.29   Resistance, inductance, and capacitance in ac circuits. (a) Resistance; (b) Inductance; (c) Capacitance.

Another element used in electrical circuits is the **inductor**, a wire coil, with or without a magnetic core. The relationship between the voltage across the inductor and the current through it is

$$v_L = L\left(\frac{di}{dt}\right) \tag{4.70}$$

where L is the **inductance** measured in **henries** (named after Joseph Henry, American, 1797–1878), with the symbol H. For a current as in Equation 4.67

$$v_L = L\omega i_e\sqrt{2}cos\omega t = L\omega i_e\sqrt{2}sin(\omega t + \pi/2) \tag{4.71}$$

so that the voltage across an inductor can be represented by a phasor leading the current by $\pi/2$. In the complex plane, if I is the current phasor, the phasor corresponding to v_L is

$$\vec{V}_L = jL\omega\vec{I} \tag{4.72}$$

where j is the symbol used in electrical engineering for the imaginary unit $\sqrt{-1}$ (see (b) in Figure 4.29) – the symbol i is reserved for current intensity. The quantity $L\omega$ is called the **inductive reactance** and is measured in ohms, like the resistance R.

The third element encountered in ac circuits is the **capacitor**. The voltage across a capacitor traversed by a current i as in Equation 4.67 obeys the law

$$v_C = \frac{1}{C}\int i\,dt = \frac{i_e}{C\omega\sqrt{2}}\sin(\omega t - \pi/2) \tag{4.73}$$

and it can be described by a phasor lagging $\pi/2$ behind the current, as in Figure 4.29(c):

$$\vec{V}_c = \frac{\vec{I}}{jC\omega} = -\frac{j\vec{I}}{C\omega} \tag{4.74}$$

where C is the **capacitance**, measured in **farads** (named after Michael Faraday, English, 1791–1867) – symbol F – and $1/C\omega$ is called the **capacitive reactance** and is measured in ohms. The farad is too large a unit for practical purposes; more common units are the following

microfarad (μF) = 10^{-6} F
nanofarad (nF) = 10^{-9} F
picofarad (pF) = 10^{-12} F

Chapter 5
Geometric calculations

5.1 Introduction

The notions of **matrix inversion** and **determinants** are introduced in this chapter as means for calculating the rotation of coordinate axes in the plane. Determinants and matrix inversion can be used for solving linear equations (see Section 1.5). This solution is not discussed in this chapter because MATLAB uses a more efficient method; it is described in Chapter 6. Rotation in three-dimensional space is treated with the help of **Euler's angles**; they find applicatons in kinematics and dynamics. The examples in this chapter contain a few applications of determinants in geometry and a brief introduction to **affine transformations**. These subjects are applicable in modern engineering fields such as computer graphics and robotics. Determinants have more applications in mathematics than shown here, but they are beyond the scope of this book.

In this chapter the reader will also learn how to write **functions** in MATLAB. This possibility is first illustrated by trigonometric functions that take arguments in degrees. These examples are very simple; the functions, in any case, can be valuable additions for engineers who have to perform many trigonometric calculations. Frequent conversion from degrees to radians and vice versa can be both annoying and a cause of errors.

5.2   Rotation of coordinate axes in the plane

In Figure 5.1 the coordinates of the point P relative to the axes shown in solid lines are x, y. Rotating the axes anticlockwise, by the angle α, we obtain the system shown in dashed lines. The coordinates of the point P relative to the new axes are x_1, y_1. The relationships between the two pairs of coordinates are

$$x_1 \quad = \quad x \cos \alpha + y \sin \alpha \tag{5.1}$$

$$y_1 \quad = \quad -x \sin \alpha + y \cos \alpha \tag{5.2}$$

Let

$$\mathbf{P} = \left[\begin{array}{c} x \\ y \end{array} \right], \; \mathbf{P}_1 = \left[\begin{array}{c} x_1 \\ y_1 \end{array} \right]$$

and

$$\mathbf{A} = \left[\begin{array}{cc} \cos \alpha & \sin \alpha \\ -\sin \alpha & \cos \alpha \end{array} \right]$$

With these notations Equations 5.1 and 5.2 can be rewritten as

$$\mathbf{P}_1 = \mathbf{A}\mathbf{P} \tag{5.3}$$

The **inverse** relationships can also be found from Figure 5.1 and they are

$$x \quad = \quad x_1 \cos \alpha - y_1 \sin \alpha \tag{5.4}$$

$$y \quad = \quad x_1 \sin \alpha + y_1 \cos \alpha \tag{5.5}$$

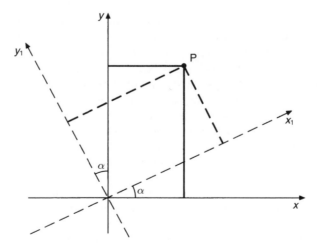

Figure 5.1   Rotation of coordinate axes in the plane.

These equations represent in fact rotation by the angle $-\alpha$, that is, from the coordinate axes x_1, y_1 to the coordinate axes x, y. With

$$\mathbf{B} = \begin{bmatrix} \cos\alpha & -\sin\alpha \\ \sin\alpha & \cos\alpha \end{bmatrix}$$

Equations 5.4 and 5.5 become

$$\mathbf{P} = \mathbf{B}\mathbf{P}_1 \tag{5.6}$$

5.3 Matrix inversion

What is the relationship between the two matrices, $\mathbf{A}$ and $\mathbf{B}$, in the preceding section? The answer to this question can be obtained by substituting, for example, the expression for $\mathbf{P}_1$ given by Equation 5.3 into Equation 5.6:

$$\mathbf{P} = \mathbf{B}\mathbf{A}\mathbf{P}$$

Since this equality must hold for each vector $\mathbf{P}$, we conclude that the product $\mathbf{B}\mathbf{A}$ must equal the identity matrix, and this can be checked directly:

$$\mathbf{B}\mathbf{A} = \begin{bmatrix} \cos\alpha & -\sin\alpha \\ \sin\alpha & \cos\alpha \end{bmatrix} \begin{bmatrix} \cos\alpha & \sin\alpha \\ -\sin\alpha & \cos\alpha \end{bmatrix} = \begin{bmatrix} 1 & 0 \\ 0 & 1 \end{bmatrix}$$

Alternatively, the value of $\mathbf{P}$ given by Equation 5.6 can be substituted into Equation 5.3, yielding

$$\mathbf{P}_1 = \mathbf{A}\mathbf{B}\mathbf{P}_1$$

Again, this equality must hold for each $\mathbf{P}_1$, meaning that the product $\mathbf{A}\mathbf{B}$ must also equal the identity matrix, a conclusion that can be checked directly.

We say that the matrix $\mathbf{B}$ is the **inverse matrix** of $\mathbf{A}$ and we frequently use the notation $\mathbf{A}^{-1}$ for it. A formal definition is:

Given a square matrix $\mathbf{A}$, its inverse is the matrix $\mathbf{A}^{-1}$ such that multiplying it at left or right by $\mathbf{A}$ yields the identity matrix $\mathbf{I}$:

$$\mathbf{A}\mathbf{A}^{-1} = \mathbf{A}^{-1}\mathbf{A} = \mathbf{I} \tag{5.7}$$

The inverse of a 2-by-2 matrix can be easily found as follows. Let a general element of the inverse matrix be b_{ij}. Then, let us write, for example, that left multiplication of this matrix by $\mathbf{A}$ results in the 2-by-2 identity matrix (the reader is invited to obtain the same result by right multiplication):

$$\begin{bmatrix} a_{11} & a_{12} \\ a_{21} & a_{22} \end{bmatrix} \begin{bmatrix} b_{11} & b_{12} \\ b_{21} & b_{22} \end{bmatrix} = \begin{bmatrix} 1 & 0 \\ 0 & 1 \end{bmatrix} \tag{5.8}$$

Equation 5.8 has the solutions

$$b_{11} = \frac{a_{22}}{a_{11}a_{22} - a_{21}a_{12}} \tag{5.9}$$

$$b_{12} = \frac{-a_{12}}{a_{11}a_{22} - a_{21}a_{12}} \tag{5.10}$$

$$b_{21} = \frac{-a_{21}}{a_{11}a_{22} - a_{21}a_{12}} \tag{5.11}$$

$$b_{22} = \frac{a_{11}}{a_{11}a_{22} - a_{21}a_{12}} \tag{5.12}$$

By substituting the matrix $\mathbf{B}$ for $\mathbf{A}^{-1}$ in Equation 5.7 it can be easily shown that $\mathbf{B}$ is indeed the inverse of $\mathbf{A}$.

In MATLAB there is no need to use Equations 5.9 to 5.12 in order to obtain the inverse of a 2-by-2 matrix. The package has a built-in function called inv; using it as inv(A) yields the inverse matrix of $\mathbf{A}$. As an example, consider a rotation of axes by 30°. The matrix of this transformation is calculated with

```
>> alpha = 30;
>> A = [ cos(pi*alpha/180)    sin(pi*alpha/180)
-sin(pi*alpha/180)    cos(pi*alpha/180) ]
A =
    0.8660 0.5000
   -0.5000 0.8660
```

The matrix of the inverse transformation is obtained with the simple command

```
>> B = inv(A)
B =
0.8660 -0.5000
0.5000  0.8660
```

Left multiplication of $\mathbf{B}$ by $\mathbf{A}$ yields

```
>> A*B
ans =
    1.0000 0.0000
   -0.0000 1.0000
```

The same result is obtained by right multiplication.

Let, for instance, the coordinates of the point P in Figure 5.1 be

$$x = 2, \ y = 3$$

After rotation of axes by 30° they become

```
>> P1 = A*[ 2; 3 ]
P1 =
3.2321
1.5981
```

The inverse transformation is, as expected,

```
>> P = B*P1
P =
     2
     3
```

5.4   Programming a function

In the preceding calculation we used the expressions

```
sin(pi*alpha/180), cos(pi*alpha/180)
```

In Section 1.1.5 we learnt a way of avoiding the need to repeat such long arguments: the use of a conversion factor pi/180. A more practical solution is the introduction of trigonometric functions that accept as arguments angles measured in sexagesimal degrees, for instance 30°. This solution is actually used in PL1 and in certain versions of Fortran which, besides functions like *sin* and *cos* which accept arguments in radians, also have functions like *sind* and *cosd*, which accept arguments in degrees. MATLAB allows us to program functions written, like MATLAB programs, to files with the extension *m*. The name of the file should be the name of the function. The first line of the file is the function declaration and must contain the word *function*:

```
function y = sind(x)
```

The second line contains help text and must begin with a per cent sign, '%', followed immediately – that is, without any spaces – by the function name written in upper-case letters:

```
%SIND(X) sines of the elements of X measured in degrees.
```

The second line, called the H1 line, is used by the lookfor function which searches for a given string in the H1 line of all M-files reachable on MATLAB's search path. Write the function sind to a file sind.m, save it, and enter

```
lookfor sind
```

```
function y = sind(x)
%SIND(X) sines of the elements of X measured in degrees.

y = sin(pi*x/180);
```

Figure 5.2   A function that calculates the sine of an angle given in degrees.

You will retrieve the H1 line. If necessary, the H1 line may be followed by other help lines; this book contains many examples of such lines.

As in other programming languages, MATLAB functions are called with arguments, and their internal variables are **local**, that is, they are not effective outside the function. As a first example of a MATLAB function, Figure 5.2 contains the listing of the sine function that accepts as arguments angles measured in degrees. Examples of calling this function are

```
≫ sind(30)
ans =
    0.5000
≫ sind(90)
ans =
    1
≫ sind(180)
ans =
    1.2246e-016
```

The last answer should have been exactly equal to 0; because of numerical errors it is not. The reader is invited to program a function cosd and, using sind and cosd in the transformation matrix, to recalculate the rotation by 30° described above.

A set of functions developed in this book contains the following trigonometric functions of arguments given in degrees: sind, cosd, tand. The set also contains the following inverse trigonometric functions which yield results in degrees: asind, acosd, atand, atan2d. The above set can be downloaded from an address that can be obtained from Pearson Education.

5.5   Euler's angles

Euler's angles are three convenient parameters for describing the rotation of a three-dimensional, orthogonal system of coordinates; these parameters have important applications in mechanics. A few different definitions of Euler's angles are known; the one used here is that found, for example, in Meirovitch (1970), page 141, Guggenheimer (1977), pages 99–100 and Czichos (1989). In our problem, the coordinates of a point P are given in a system x_1, x_2, x_3 and we want to find the coordinates of the same point in a system ξ_1, ξ_2, ξ_3 that has the same origin as the first one, but

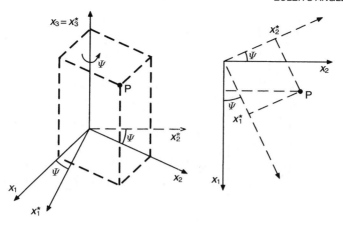

Figure 5.3 Rotation about the x_3 axis.

is rotated with respect to it. Both systems are **right-handed**, that is, rotating a screw in the sense that brings x_1 over x_2 advances the screw in the sense of x_3, and rotating the screw in the sense that brings ξ_1 over ξ_2 advances the screw in the sense of ξ_3. Another popular definition of sense in a right-handed system is the **right-hand rule**: with the fingers of the right hand curved from x_1 to x_2, the thumb points in the sense of x_3.

In Figure 5.3 we begin by rotating the system of coordinates about the axis x_3, by the positive angle ψ. The new coordinates x_1^*, x_2^*, x_3^* of the point P are related to the previous ones by

$$
\begin{bmatrix} x_1^* \\ x_2^* \\ x_3^* \end{bmatrix} = \mathbf{X}^* = \begin{bmatrix} \cos\psi & \sin\psi & 0 \\ -\sin\psi & \cos\psi & 0 \\ 0 & 0 & 1 \end{bmatrix} \begin{bmatrix} x_1 \\ x_2 \\ x_3 \end{bmatrix} = \mathbf{AX} \tag{5.13}
$$

Next, consider in Figure 5.4 the rotation of the system x_1^*, x_2^*, x_3^* about the x_1^* axis, by the positive angle θ. The new coordinates of the point P are related to the previous ones by

$$
\begin{bmatrix} x_1^{**} \\ x_2^{**} \\ x_3^{**} \end{bmatrix} = \mathbf{X}^{**} = \begin{bmatrix} 1 & 0 & 0 \\ 0 & \cos\theta & \sin\theta \\ 0 & -\sin\theta & \cos\theta \end{bmatrix} \begin{bmatrix} x_1^* \\ x_2^* \\ x_3^* \end{bmatrix} = \mathbf{BX}^* \tag{5.14}
$$

The third and final rotation is about the axis x_3^{**}, with the positive angle ϕ (Figure 5.5). The final coordinates of the point P are given by

$$
\begin{bmatrix} \xi_1 \\ \xi_2 \\ \xi_3 \end{bmatrix} = \mathbf{P}_\xi = \begin{bmatrix} \cos\phi & \sin\phi & 0 \\ -\sin\phi & \cos\phi & 0 \\ 0 & 0 & 1 \end{bmatrix} \begin{bmatrix} x_1^{**} \\ x_2^{**} \\ x_3^{**} \end{bmatrix} = \mathbf{CX}^{**} \tag{5.15}
$$

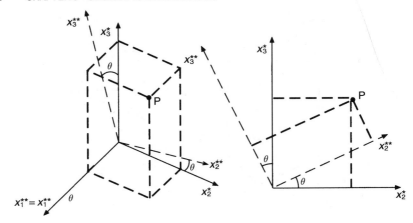

Figure 5.4   Rotation about the x_1^* axis.

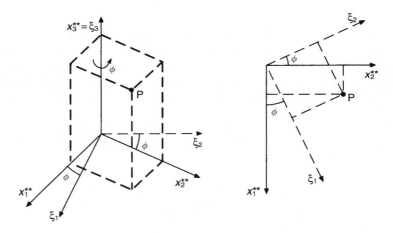

Figure 5.5   Rotation about the x_3^{**} axis.

The **product** of the three rotations is

$$\mathbf{P}_\xi = \mathbf{ABCX} = \mathbf{DX} \tag{5.16}$$

Using, like Czichos (1989), c_θ for $\cos\theta$, s_θ for $\sin\theta$, and so on, the matrix $\mathbf{D}$ can be written as

$$\begin{bmatrix} c_\phi c_\psi - s_\phi c_\theta s_\psi & c_\phi s_\psi + s_\phi c_\theta c_\psi & s_\phi s_\theta \\ -s_\phi c_\psi - c_\phi c_\theta s_\psi & -s_\phi s_\psi + c_\phi c_\theta c_\psi & c_\phi s_\theta \\ s_\theta s_\psi & -s_\theta c_\psi & c_\theta \end{bmatrix} \tag{5.17}$$

Let us program a MATLAB function that takes as arguments the angles ψ, θ, ϕ and builds the transformation matrix $\mathbf{D}$. A possible M-file is shown in Figure 5.6.

```
function D = eulangle(psi, theta, phi)
%EULANGLE matrix of rotations by Euler's angles.
%          EULANGLE(psi, theta, phi) yields the matrix of
%          rotation of a system of coordinates by Euler's
%          angles psi, theta, and phi, measured in degrees.
 A = [    cosd(psi)        sind(psi)        0
         -sind(psi)        cosd(psi)        0
          0                0                1 ];
 B = [    1                0                0
          0                cosd(theta)      sind(theta)
          0               -sind(theta)      cosd(theta) ];
 C = [    cosd(phi)        sind(phi)        0
         -sind(phi)        cosd(phi)        0
          0                0                1 ];
 D = C*B*A;
```

Figure 5.6   A function that receives Euler's angles and builds the rotation matrix.

As an exercise, given the point P(2, 3, 3), let us find its coordinates in a system rotated by the angles 30°, 20°, 15°. The calculations in MATLAB are

```
>> D = eulangle(30, 20, 15)
D =
      0.7149        0.6936        0.0885
     -0.6780        0.6567        0.3304
      0.1710       -0.2962        0.9397
>> Xi = D*[ 2; 3; 3 ]
Xi =
      3.7762
      1.6051
      2.2725
```

The inverse transformation is

```
>> X = inv(D)*Xi
X =
      2.0000
      3.0000
      3.0000
```

as expected. The eulangle function has the internal variables A, B, and C. We can verify that they do not exist outside the function by trying to call them. Then

MATLAB will issue an error message; in the version used by one of the authors it was:

```
≫ A
■     ????  Undefined function or variable 'A'.
```

A better way is to use the MATLAB who function which lists the variables currently held in the memory:

```
≫ who
Your variables are:
    D    X    Xi
```

and we see that the intermediate variables A, B, and C do not appear. The reader is invited to calculate separately the matrices $\mathbf{A}$, $\mathbf{B}$ and $\mathbf{C}$, and to check in MATLAB that

$$\mathbf{D}^{-1} = \mathbf{A}^{-1} * \mathbf{B}^{-1} * \mathbf{C}^{-1}$$

Note the order of multiplication when calculating $\mathbf{D}^{-1}$, as compared with the order in

$$\mathbf{D} = \mathbf{C} * \mathbf{B} * \mathbf{A}$$

5.6   Determinants

Equations 5.9 to 5.12 have the same denominator

$$\Delta_2 = a_{11}a_{22} - a_{21}a_{12}$$

This expression appears in the inversion of a 2-by-2 matrix. If the procedure shown in Section 5.3 is used to obtain the inverse of a 3-by-3 matrix (for example, one of the matrices $\mathbf{A}$, $\mathbf{B}$, $\mathbf{C}$ and $\mathbf{D}$ in Section 5.5), it will be found that the elements of the inverse matrix have the common denominator

$$\Delta_3 \quad = \quad \begin{aligned} & a_{11}a_{22}a_{33} + a_{12}a_{23}a_{31} + a_{13}a_{21}a_{32} \\ & -a_{13}a_{22}a_{31} - a_{12}a_{21}a_{33} - a_{11}a_{23}a_{32} \end{aligned}$$

By definition Δ_2 is the **determinant** of the 2-by-2 matrix with elements a_{ij}, and we write

$$a_{11}a_{22} - a_{21}a_{12} = \det \begin{bmatrix} a_{11} & a_{12} \\ a_{21} & a_{22} \end{bmatrix} = \begin{vmatrix} a_{11} & a_{12} \\ a_{21} & a_{22} \end{vmatrix}$$

Take care with the different notation used for matrices, that is, brackets '[ ]', and determinants, namely vertical bars '| |'.

By definition, Δ_3 is the determinant of the 3-by-3 matrix with elements a_{ij}. If in such a matrix, $\mathbf{A}$, we delete the r-th row and the s-th column we get a 2-by-2 matrix which we call a **minor matrix** of $\mathbf{A}$; let us denote it by M_{rs}. The element of $\mathbf{A}$ common to the deleted row and the deleted column is a_{rs}. We say that the number

$$(-1)^{r+s} \det(M_{rs})$$

is the **cofactor** of a_{rs}. To illustrate these definitions let

$$\mathbf{A} = \begin{bmatrix} a_{11} & a_{12} & a_{13} \\ a_{21} & a_{22} & a_{23} \\ a_{31} & a_{32} & a_{33} \end{bmatrix}$$

Then,

$$\mathbf{M}_{32} = \begin{bmatrix} a_{11} & a_{13} \\ a_{21} & a_{23} \end{bmatrix}$$

is a minor of $\mathbf{A}$. Also

$$A_{11} = \begin{vmatrix} a_{22} & a_{23} \\ a_{32} & a_{33} \end{vmatrix}$$

is the cofactor of a_{11},

$$A_{12} = - \begin{vmatrix} a_{21} & a_{23} \\ a_{31} & a_{33} \end{vmatrix}$$

is the cofactor of a_{12}, and

$$A_{13} = \begin{vmatrix} a_{21} & a_{22} \\ a_{31} & a_{32} \end{vmatrix}$$

is the cofactor of a_{13}. The determinant of the 3-by-3 matrix $\mathbf{A}$ can be defined in terms of cofactors, for example by *expanding it by minors on the first row*

$$\det(\mathbf{A}) = a_{11}A_{11} - a_{12}A_{12} + a_{13}A_{13}$$

or by minors on the second row

$$\det(\mathbf{A}) = -a_{21}A_{21} + a_{22}A_{22} - a_{23}A_{23}$$

or by minors on the first column

$$\det(\mathbf{A}) = a_{11}A_{11} - a_{21}A_{21} + a_{31}A_{31}$$

and so on. To illustrate this, the determinant of

$$\mathbf{A} = \begin{bmatrix} 1 & 3 & 4 \\ 2 & -2 & 3 \\ 4 & -3 & 5 \end{bmatrix}$$

can be calculated as

$$1 \times \begin{vmatrix} -2 & 3 \\ -3 & 5 \end{vmatrix} - 3 \times \begin{vmatrix} 2 & 3 \\ 4 & 5 \end{vmatrix} + 4 \times \begin{vmatrix} 2 & -2 \\ 4 & -3 \end{vmatrix} = 13$$

or as

$$1 \times \begin{vmatrix} -2 & 3 \\ -3 & 5 \end{vmatrix} - 2 \times \begin{vmatrix} 3 & 4 \\ -3 & 5 \end{vmatrix} + 4 \times \begin{vmatrix} 3 & 4 \\ -2 & 3 \end{vmatrix} = 13$$

and so on.

The above definitions can be extended to higher-order determinants. Thus, determinants of 4-by-4 matrices can be defined in terms of their expansion by minors of the third order, which in their turn were defined in terms of expansion by minors of the second order. This way of defining determinants is called **by induction**. The definition by induction will help us to get a few interesting results; however, calculating determinants of higher orders following the above definition is impractical and MATLAB uses another method.

Another way of defining determinants is by **permutations**: the determinant of a square, n-by-n matrix

$$\begin{bmatrix} a_{11} & a_{12} & \dots & a_{1n} \\ \dots & \dots & \dots & \dots \\ a_{n1} & a_{n2} & \dots & a_{nn} \end{bmatrix}$$

is the scalar

$$\det(\mathbf{A}) = \begin{vmatrix} a_{11} & a_{12} & \dots & a_{1n} \\ \dots & \dots & \dots & \dots \\ a_{n1} & a_{n2} & \dots & a_{nn} \end{vmatrix} = \sum (-1)^r a_{1k_1} a_{2k_2} \dots a_{nk_n}$$

with the $n!$ differently-ordered chains $k_1, k_2, \dots, k_n$, where $k_i \in \{1, 2, \dots, n\}$. The exponent r is the number of inversions in the natural order $1, 2, \dots, n$ of k_i.

For instance, in Δ_3 the term $a_{11}a_{22}a_{33}$ has no inversions, as the sequence of second indexes $1, 2, 3$ follows the order of natural numbers. Therefore, for the said term $r = 0$ and the term appears with a plus sign. In the term $a_{13}a_{22}a_{31}$ there are three inversions; they are evident in the three sequences required between $1, 2, 3$ and $3, 2, 1$:

$$2, 1, 3; \quad 2, 3, 1; \quad 3, 2, 1$$

Therefore, for the latter term $r = 3$ and the term is preceded by a minus sign.

Determinants can be used in the solution of linear equations (see Cramer's rule in Chapter 1) and have important applications in geometry. A few of the latter are shown in this chapter. The calculation of determinants is explained in textbooks of algebra and linear algebra (see, for example, Munkres 1964; Fraleigh and Beauregard 1990; Johnson, Riess and Arnold 1993). This subject will not be further discussed in this book because MATLAB has a built-in function, det, for calculating determinants. For instance, for the matrices $\mathbf{A}$ and $\mathbf{B}$, defined in Section 5.2, the MATLAB commands det(A) and det(B) give the result 1. Neither shall we discuss here the use of determinants in the solution of systems of linear equations, because the method is not computationally efficient for large numbers of equations and MATLAB provides a better procedure that will be introduced in the next chapter.

The reader is invited to calculate the determinants of the transformation matrices $\mathbf{A}$, $\mathbf{B}$, $\mathbf{C}$ and $\mathbf{D}$ defined in Section 5.5. All of them equal $+1$ and this is a general property of the matrices governing the rotation of a right-handed system of coordinates into another right-handed system. What would happen for left-handed systems?

The general theory of matrix inversion is also found in books on linear algebra, such as those already cited, and it will not be presented here. One result should however be mentioned: as all the elements of $\mathbf{A}^{-1}$ have det($\mathbf{A}$) in their denominator, it follows that a matrix has no inverse if its determinant equals zero. In the latter case we say that the matrix $\mathbf{A}$ is **singular**.

5.7   Summary

The inverse of a square matrix, $\mathbf{A}$, is a matrix $\mathbf{A}^{-1}$ such that multiplying it at left or at right by $\mathbf{A}$ yields the identity matrix $\mathbf{I}$:

$$\mathbf{A}\mathbf{A}^{-1} = \mathbf{A}^{-1}\mathbf{A} = \mathbf{I}$$

In MATLAB the inverse of a matrix is calculated with the help of the inv function, for instance inv(A).

With each square matrix $\mathbf{A}$ we associate a scalar called **the determinant of $\mathbf{A}$**, and defined by

$$\det(\mathbf{A}) = \sum (-1)^r a_{1k_1} a_{2k_2} \ldots a_{nk_n}$$

with the $n!$ differently-ordered chains $k_1, k_2, \ldots, k_n$, where $k_i \in \{1, 2, \ldots, n\}$. The exponent r is the number of inversions in the natural order $1, 2, \ldots, n$ of k_i. In MATLAB the determinant is obtained by means of the det function, for example det(A).

Like other programming languages, MATLAB accepts user-defined functions; these must be stored in M-files that have the same name as the function and the extension 'm', for example sind.m. The first line of the function begins with the word *function*, for example

```
function y = sind(x)
```

The second line contains help text; it should begin with the per cent sign followed without any spaces by the function name written in upper-case letters, for instance

```
%SIND(X) sines of the elements of X measured in degrees.
```

This line, called H1 in MATLAB jargon, is used by the MATLAB 4 lookfor function which searches for a given string in all H1 lines of the M-files found on the search path. For example, if the above sind function is in the MATLAB directory, the command

```
lookfor sind
```

will retrieve the above H1 line.

5.8   Affine transformations

Geometrical subjects such as those encountered in this chapter have important applications in the modern engineering fields of **computer graphics** and **robotics**. One group of operations frequently used in these applications is **affine transformations**; they include **translation**, **rotation** and **scaling**. In this section we are going to show how to use MATLAB to perform these transformations in the plane.

It is practical to represent affine transformations by transformation matrices. Usually computer graphics and robotics require the **concatenation** of several affine transformations; this is done by multiplying the corresponding matrices. The multiplication of transformation matrices is conveniently done when using **homogeneous coordinates**. To introduce the latter notion, let a point in the plane be defined by the usual Cartesian coordinates x, y; its representation in homogeneous coordinates is

$$\mathbf{P} = \begin{bmatrix} x_1 \\ x_2 \\ w \end{bmatrix}$$

such that $x = x_1/w$, $y = x_2/w$.

One important reason for introducing homogeneous coordinates is that they allow the representation of points at infinity. Thus, in the coordinate system x, y, to represent a point at infinity at least one of its coordinates must be ∞. In homogeneous coordinates it is sufficient to let $w = 0$, while x_1, x_2 remain finite numbers. We shall not pursue this point, but the reader interested in it may consult books on **projective geometry**. Instead we shall show how to write and use functions for two-dimensional affine transformations. The functions will be applied to the square shown in Figure 5.7. The corners of the square are defined in homogeneous coordinates by

$$\mathbf{P_1} = \begin{bmatrix} -0.5 \\ 0 \\ 1 \end{bmatrix}, \; \mathbf{P_2} = \begin{bmatrix} -0.5 \\ 1 \\ 1 \end{bmatrix}, \; \mathbf{P_3} = \begin{bmatrix} 0.5 \\ 1 \\ 1 \end{bmatrix}, \; \mathbf{P_4} = \begin{bmatrix} 0.5 \\ 0 \\ 1 \end{bmatrix}$$

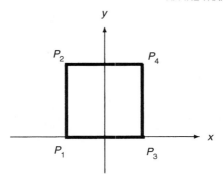

Figure 5.7   A square.

As seen, the third coordinate, w, is set to 1; this is a common practice in computer graphics. In MATLAB we define the corners by

```
≫ P1 = [ -0.5; 0; 1 ]; P2 = [ -0.5; 1; 1 ];
≫ P3 = [ 0.5; 1; 1 ]; P4 = [ 0.5; 0; 1 ];
```

and plot the square with

```
≫ square = [ P1 P2 P3 P4 P1 ];
≫ plot(square(1, :), square(2, :))
≫ axis([-4 4 -1 7]), axis('square')
```

The plot is shown in Figure 5.8.

Note that the matrix P contains twice the vector P1; this closes the square.

A function that performs translation by a distance dx parallel to the x-axis and a distance dy parallel to the y-axis is

```
function T = trlate(dx, dy)
%TRLATE      translation matrix.
%            TRLATE(DX, DY) translates dx along x, dy along y.
%            The translation of an object is performed by
%            multiplying TRLATE by the 3-by-n matrix defining
%            the object, for example:  trlate(dx, xy)*object

T = [ 1  0 dx; 0 1 dy; 0 0 1];
```

To translate the square 0.5 units horizontally and 1 unit vertically enter

```
≫ P = trlate(0.5, 1)*square
≫ plot(P(1, :), P(2, :)), axis([-4 4 -1 7]), axis('square')
```

The result is shown in Figure 5.9.

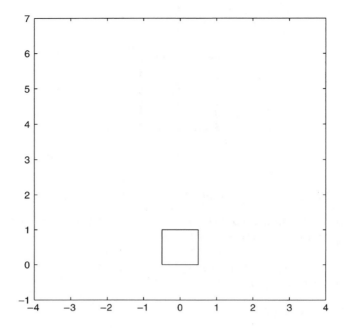

Figure 5.8   A square.

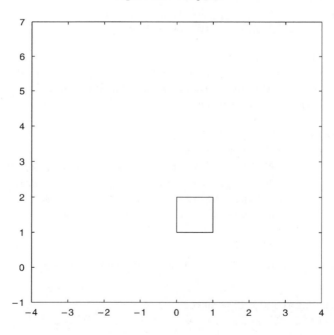

Figure 5.9   Translation.

Rotation around the origin of coordinates, by θ degrees counterclockwise, is performed by the function

```
function T = rtate(theta)
%RTATE      rotation matrix.
%           RTATE(THETA) rotates theta degrees
%           counterclockwise. The rotation of an object
%           is performed by multiplying RTATE by the
%           3-by-n matrix defining the object,
%           for example: rtate(theta)*object

T = [ cosd(theta) -sind(theta) 0
      sind(theta)  cosd(theta) 0
      0            0           1 ];
```

This M-file contains trigonometric functions such as those introduced in Section 5.4. As an example, we rotate our square counterclockwise around the origin of coordinates, by 30°, with the following commands

```
≫ P = rtate(30)*square
≫ plot(P(1, :), P(2, :)), axis([-4 4 -1 7]), axis('square')
```

The result is shown in Figure 5.10.

It is easy to combine translation and rotation:

```
≫ P = rtate(30)*trlate(0.5, 1)*square
≫ plot(P(1, :), P(2, :)), axis([-4 4 -1 7]), axis('square')
```

The result is shown in Figure 5.11.

The following function performs scaling by the factor α in the x-direction, and by the factor β in the y-direction.

```
function S = scale(alpha, beta)
%SCALE   scaling matrix.
%        SCALE(ALPHA, BETA) x scaled by alpha, y scaled by
%        beta. The scaling of an object is performed by
%        multiplying SCALE by the 3-by-n matrix defining
%        the object, for example: scale(alpha, beta)*object

S = [ alpha 0 0 ; 0 beta 0; 0 0 1 ];
```

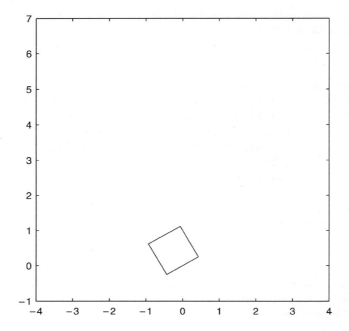

Figure 5.10   Rotation.

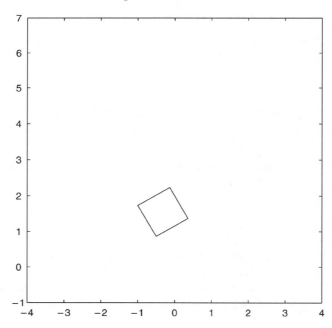

Figure 5.11   Translation and rotation.

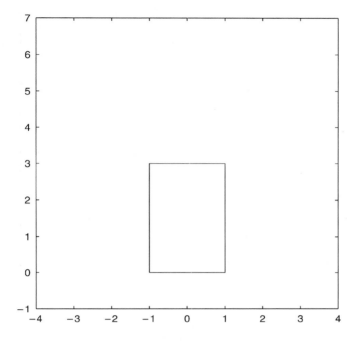

Figure 5.12   Scaling.

As an example, to double dimensions parallel to the x-axis, and to triple dimensions parallel to the y-axis, enter

```
≫ P = scale(2,3)*square
≫ plot(P(1, :), P(2, :)), axis([-4 4 -1 7]), axis('square')
```

The square becomes a rectangle, as shown in Figure 5.12. The function **scale** produces scaling relative to the origin of coordinates. The reader is invited to apply this function to squares placed in other parts of the plane to see what happens.

Translation, rotation and scaling can be combined in a single operation:

```
≫ P = scale(2,3)*rtate(30)*trlate(0.5, 1)*square
≫ plot(P(1, :), P(2, :)), axis([-4 4 -1 7]), axis('square')
```

The result is shown in Figure 5.13. Note that the first transformation performed is that closest to square, and the others are performed reading the other matrices from right to left. In other words the order of transformations is: translation, rotation, scaling. This order is opposed to that in which the names of the matrices are read in English. As we know, in general the product of two matrices is not commutative; therefore, the result of several affine transformations depends on the order of their concatenation.

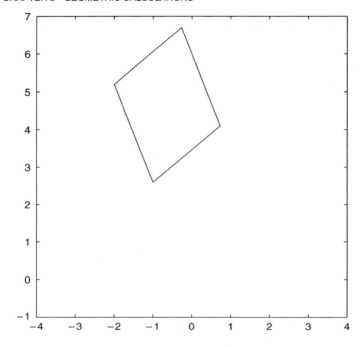

Figure 5.13   Translation, rotation and scaling.

To convince yourself that this is so, try the following commands and compare the plot with Figure 5.13:

```
>> P = trlate(0.5, 1)*rtate(30)*scale(2, 3)*square
>> plot(P(1, :), P(2, :)), axis([-4 4 -1 7]), axis('square')
```

5.9   Inverse affine transformations

To cover all possible situations, the set of affine transformations must also include the inverse transformations. As in Section 5.3, transformation matrices are invertible. We can use the inverses of transformation matrices; however, it is sufficient to apply the functions developed in the preceding section and to change the signs of the calling arguments, for translation or rotation, or to invert those arguments for scaling. In the following we shall compare the two possibilities by applying them again to the square shown in Figure 5.7. To begin, let us repeat the translation:

```
>> P = trlate(0.5, 1)*square
```

The inverse of this operation can be obtained either by inverting the transformation matrix, to obtain the result P1, or by calling `trlate` again, but with the opposites of the arguments, to obtain the result P2:

```
≫ P1 = inv(trlate(0.5, 1))*P
≫ P2 = trlate(-0.5, -1)*P
```

The reader is invited to verify that the two results are identical. To proceed similarly with rotation, enter

```
≫ P = rtate(30)*square;
≫ P1 = inv(rtate(30))*P
≫ P2 = rtate(-30)*P
```

For scaling, the example is

```
≫ P = scale(2,3)*square;
≫ P1 = inv(scale(2,3))*P
≫ P2 = scale(1/2, 1/3)*P
```

For more details on affine transformations in computer graphics, including their applications in three-dimensional space, see, for example, Angel (1990) or Hearn and Baker (1994).

5.10 Bézier curves – subfunctions

In this section we introduce kinds of curves that are extremely useful in computer graphics, and we show how to use **subfunctions**. In the preceding chapters we have learnt how to draw curves that connect given points, and in Sections 1.9 and 1.11 we met functions that draw curves passing close to given points. More explanation about such functions can be found in the following chapters. Here we want to describe a kind of curve defined by points that, excepting those situated at the ends, do not sit on the curve. The idea is due to Paul de Faget de Casteljau who worked for the French company Citroën, and was further developed by Pierre Etienne Bézier (1910–99) who worked for the French company Renault. These curves, known today as **Bézier curves**, are defined by a number of **control points** that form a **control polygon**. Bézier curves emerged from the necessity of drawing and manufacturing faired car surfaces. They have been used in the design of other faired surfaces, such as those of ships and aircraft, and today appear in many graphics programs. Bézier curves are a simple case of more elaborate curves whose treatment is beyond the scope of our book.

Let us begin with a first-degree Bézier curve:

$$\mathbf{P} = (1 - t)\mathbf{P_1} + t\mathbf{P_2} \tag{5.18}$$

where P is a point on the curve, P_1 and P_2 are the end points, and t is a parameter that runs from 0 to 1. For a plane curve we can think of P as representing the column vector $[x; y]$, and similarly for P_1 and P_2. For three-dimensional curves $P = [x; y; z]$. Usually, in the technical literature the indexes of points begin with 0; we prefer to begin with 1 because MATLAB does not accept 0 in array indexing.

For $t = 0$ Equation 5.18 yields the coordinates of the point P_1; and for $t = 1$, those of P_2. This parametric equation describes the straight-line segment connecting the two points; it is also a linear-interpolation formula between the values P_1 and P_2.

If we consider three points, P_1, P_2, P_3, we can define a second-degree curve:

$$\mathbf{P} = (1 - t)^2 \mathbf{P_1} + 2(1 - t)t \mathbf{P_2} + t^2 \mathbf{P_3} \tag{5.19}$$

It can be shown that Equation 5.19 is a parametric representation of a parabola. We invite the reader to choose three points and plot the curve. To do so, one can use the following example of a third-degree curve. We also recommend the reader to prove that the curve passes though the first and the last point, and that it is tangent to the line segments $\overline{P_1 P_2}$ and $\overline{P_2 P_3}$. The second-degree Bézier curve is used in the simplest graphics programs, for example in MS Paint.

Our example refers to a third-degree curve. This is the lowest degree for which a curve can display an **inflection point**, that is a point where the sign of **curvature** changes. Formal definitions of curvature and inflection points can be found in texts on elementary calculus and differential geometry. Intuitively, curvature represents the rate of change of the slope of the tangent to the curve.

A third-degree Bézier curve is defined by four control points and its equation is

$$\mathbf{P} = (1 - t)^3 \mathbf{P_1} + 3(1 - t)^2 t \mathbf{P_2} + 3(1 - t)t^2 \mathbf{P_2} + t^3 \mathbf{P_4} \tag{5.20}$$

To see what such a curve looks like, and to demonstrate how its shape changes when moving one of its control points, we use the program Beziere.

```
%BEZIERE Function that draws a cubic Bezier curve and allows the
%        user to modify it by moving one point of the control
%        polygon. The curve can be modified n times, where n is
%        the input argument.

         function    beziere(n)

%%%%%%%%%%%%%%%%%%%%%%  initialize %%%%%%%%%%%%%%%%%%%%%%%%%%%%%%%%%
t  = [ 0: 0.02: 1 ]';            % parameter
C1 = (1 - t).^3;                 % calculate array of coefficients
C2 = 3*t.*(1 - t).^2;            % in fact, Bernstein polynomials
C3 = 3*t.^2.*(1 - t);
C4 = t.^3;
C  = [ C1 C2 C3 C4 ];
P0 = [ 0 1 3 5; 0 3 5 5.5 ];     % initial control polygon
%%%%%%%%%%%%%%%%%%%%%%%% initial plot %%%%%%%%%%%%%%%%%%%%%%%%%%%%%%%
plotbez(C, P0)
%%%%%%%%%%%%%%%%%%%%%%%% begin loop for changing points %%%%%%%%%%%%%%
```

```
for k = 1:n
    % show crosshair
    [ x1, y1 ] = ginput(1);
    % calculate distance to control points
    d2 = (P0(1, :) - x1).^2 + (P0(2, :) - y1).^2;
    % find closest control point
    dm = min(d2); ii = find(d2 == dm);
    grid on
    % move crosshair to new location of control point
    [ x2, y2 ] = ginput(1);
    % substitute the new coordinates
    P0(1, ii) = x2; P0(2, ii) = y2;
    plotbez(C, P0)    % call plot
end
%%%%%%%%%%%%%%%%%%%%%  define subfunction  %%%%%%%%%%%%%%%%%%%%%%%

    function plotbez(B, P)

% separate coordinates of control polygon
x0 = P(1, :); y0 = P(2, :);
% calculate coefficients of cubic polynomial
xB = B*x0'; yB = B*y0';
% plot control polygon
plot(x0, y0, 'r--', x0, y0, 'r*')
axis([ -1 7 -1 7 ])
title('Cubic Bezier curve')
xlabel('x'), ylabel('y')
hold on
plot(xB, yB, 'k-')
hold off
```

The function beziere (that is, 'Bézier experiment') is the **primary function** in the file. It is invoked with the name of the M-file. We wrote beziere just to allow for the possibility that the user might want to write a more general function bezier. The input argument n defines the number of times that the user wants to change the control points. The primary function calls the subfunction plotbez. The subfunction is written on the same file; therefore, it is visible only to the primary function. The subfunction begins with its own definition line and it must be written after the primary function.

If, for example, we want to modify the control polygon five times, we invoke our function as

```
>> beziere(5)
```

The program starts by plotting an initial control polygon and the Bézier curve defined by it. The function beziere contains a **FOR loop** that is repeated n times. At each repetition a crosshair appears that lets the user choose the control point to be changed. Usually, the user cannot point exactly on a control point. Therefore, the program calculates the distances between the point chosen by the crosshair and the control points and finds the index of the closest one. The grid facilitates dragging the pointer along lines parallel to the coordinate axis, if the user chooses to do so. After the user has clicked on the new position of the chosen control point, the program redraws the control polygon and the corresponding curve. Figure 5.14 shows one plot obtained with the function.

We invite the reader to write the function `beziere` and to play with it. Interesting experiments include:

- the introduction of a point of inflection by dragging the second or the third control point on the other side of the curve;
- placing two control points one above the other;
- closing the control polygon by bringing the last point over the first.

We also invite the reader to check that:

- the curve passes through the first and last control points;
- the curve is tangent to the first and last segments of the control polygon;
- the curve is contained inside the control polygon.

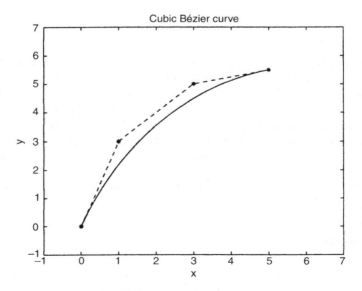

Figure 5.14   A cubic Bézier curve.

5.11   Examples

EXAMPLE 5.1   Area of triangle _____

Consider in Figure 5.15 the triangle with vertices $P_1(x_1, y_1)$, $P_2(x_2, y_2)$, $P_3(x_3, y_3)$. The area of this triangle is given by

$$(x_3 - x_1)\frac{y_1 + y_3}{2} + (x_2 - x_3)\frac{y_2 + y_3}{2} - (x_2 - x_1)\frac{y_1 + y_2}{2}$$

and it can be easily verified that this is the expansion of

$$\frac{1}{2}\begin{vmatrix} x_1 & y_1 & 1 \\ x_2 & y_2 & 1 \\ x_3 & y_3 & 1 \end{vmatrix}$$

In this result it is obvious that the area has a sign which depends on the order in which the points are taken in the determinant. For the significance of this sign see Example 5.2 below.

As a simple example, consider a triangle with the vertices $P_1(1, 1)$, $P_2(3, 1)$, $P_3(1, 8)$. This triangle can be easily drawn and its area is evidently 7. In MATLAB the calculation would be

```
>> area = det([ 1 1 1 ; 3 1 1 ; 1 8 1 ])/2
area =
    7
```

Let us now rotate the system of coordinates by 30°, in the positive trigonometric sense, obtain the new coordinates of P_1, P_2, P_3, and calculate the area of the

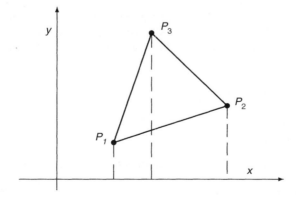

Figure 5.15   Area of triangle.

triangle again:

```
≫ A = [ cosd(30) sind(30) ; -sind(30) cosd(30) ];
≫ p1 = A*[1; 1]
p1 =
    1.3660
    0.3660
≫ p2 = A*[3; 1]
p2 =
     3.0981
    -0.6340
≫ p3 = A*[1; 8]
p3 =
   4.8660
   6.4282
≫ area = det([ p1' 1; p2' 1; p3' 1])/2
area =
     7
```

Intuition tells us that the area must not change with rotation.

EXAMPLE 5.2   Vector product and area of parallelogram ⎯⎯⎯⎯⎯⎯⎯⎯⎯

The **scalar product**, $\mathbf{A} \cdot \mathbf{B}$, was defined in Section 1.2 and studied in more detail in Chapter 2. Another product that can be defined for the same vectors, $\mathbf{A}$ and $\mathbf{B}$, is their **vector**, or **cross product,** written as $\mathbf{A} \times \mathbf{B}$, and by some authors as $\mathbf{A} \wedge \mathbf{B}$. This is a vector having the absolute value $|\mathbf{A}||\mathbf{B}| \sin \theta$, where θ is the angle between $\mathbf{A}$ and $\mathbf{B}$. The product vector is perpendicular to the plane defined by $\mathbf{A}$ and $\mathbf{B}$, and its sense is that in which a right-handed screw would advance when it is turned in a way that would bring $\mathbf{A}$ over $\mathbf{B}$. From Figure 5.16 we see that $|\mathbf{A}||\mathbf{B}| \sin \theta$ is the area of the parallelogram defined by the vectors $\mathbf{A}$ and $\mathbf{B}$ when they have the same origin.

It is convenient to calculate the vector product $\mathbf{A} \times \mathbf{B}$ in terms of the components of $\mathbf{A}$ and $\mathbf{B}$. In order to derive the desired expression we assume a right-handed system of coordinates and three vectors of unit length, $\mathbf{i}$, $\mathbf{j}$ and $\mathbf{k}$, directed along the three axes of coordinates. Then, if a_1, a_2 and a_3 are the projections of $\mathbf{A}$ on the three axes, we can write

$$\mathbf{A} = a_1\mathbf{i} + a_2\mathbf{j} + a_3\mathbf{k}$$

and, similarly,

$$\mathbf{B} = b_1\mathbf{i} + b_2\mathbf{j} + b_3\mathbf{k}$$

From the definition of the vector product it follows that

$$\mathbf{i} \times \mathbf{i} = 0, \ \mathbf{j} \times \mathbf{j} = 0, \ \mathbf{k} \times \mathbf{k} = 0$$

$$\mathbf{i} \times \mathbf{j} = \mathbf{k}, \ \mathbf{j} \times \mathbf{k} = \mathbf{i}, \ \mathbf{k} \times \mathbf{i} = \mathbf{j}$$

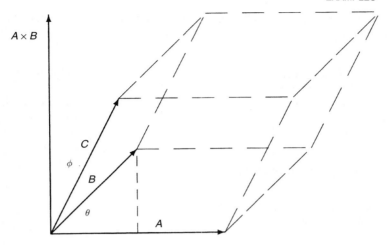

$A \times B$

ϕ

C

B

θ

A

Figure 5.16   Vector product and scalar triple product.

and

$$k \times j = -i, \ i \times k = -j, \ j \times i = -k$$

With these results we can calculate

$$\mathbf{A} \times \mathbf{B} \quad = \quad (a_1\mathbf{i} + a_2\mathbf{j} + a_3\mathbf{k}) \times (b_1\mathbf{i} + b_2\mathbf{j} + b_3\mathbf{k})$$

$$= \quad \begin{vmatrix} a_2 & a_3 \\ b_2 & b_3 \end{vmatrix}\mathbf{i} - \begin{vmatrix} a_1 & a_3 \\ b_1 & b_3 \end{vmatrix}\mathbf{j} + \begin{vmatrix} a_1 & a_2 \\ b_1 & b_2 \end{vmatrix}\mathbf{k}$$

$$= \quad \begin{vmatrix} \mathbf{i} & \mathbf{j} & \mathbf{k} \\ a_1 & a_2 & a_3 \\ b_1 & b_2 & b_3 \end{vmatrix}$$

Let us program a function called vprod that calculates the vector product:

```
function v = vprod(A, B)
%VPROD        vector product of two row vectors.
%             VPROD(A, B) the vector product of
%             the row vectors, A and B.

v = zeros(1, 3);
v(1) = det([ A(2: 3); B(2: 3) ]);
v(2) = -det([ A(1) A(3); B(1) B(3) ]);
v(3) = det([ A(1: 2); B(1: 2) ]);
```

We write this function to a file called vprod.m. As an example of application let **A** have the components $(5, 0, 0)$, and **B** the components $(25, 25, 0)$. The vector representing the area of the parallelogram constructed on the vectors **A** and **B** is given in MATLAB by

```
>> A = [ 5 0 0 ];
>> B = [ 25 25 0 ];
>> area = vprod(A, B)
area =
     0     0    125
```

The absolute value of the area is

```
>> abs_area = sqrt(area*area')
abs_area =
    125
```

In this case it is easy to see that the vector product is perpendicular to the plane of the vectors **A** and **B**. From the definition of the vector product we can find the angle between the vectors **A** and **B**:

```
>> angle = asind(abs_area/(sqrt(A*A')*sqrt(B*B')))
angle =
   45.0000
```

where asind is a user-defined function based on the MATLAB built-in function asin. The output of the latter function is in radians, while the asind function should yield a result in degrees.

EXAMPLE 5.3   Volume of parallelepiped ────────────────────────

The **scalar triple product** $\mathbf{C} \cdot (\mathbf{A} \times \mathbf{B})$ has a simple geometric interpretation that can be found in Figure 5.16. If ϕ is the angle between the vector **C** and the vector $\mathbf{A} \times \mathbf{B}$, then

$$\mathbf{C} \cdot \mathbf{A} \times \mathbf{B} = |\mathbf{C}||\mathbf{A} \times \mathbf{B}| \cos \phi .$$

$|\mathbf{C}| \cos \phi$ is the height of the parallelepiped that has as its base the parallelogram constructed on **A** and **B**, and **C** as edge. It follows that the scalar triple product yields the volume of the parallelepiped defined by the three vectors. We can calculate the scalar triple product in terms of the components of the three vectors as follows:

$$\mathbf{C} \cdot \mathbf{A} \times \mathbf{B}$$
$$= (c_1\mathbf{i} + c_2\mathbf{j} + c_3\mathbf{k}) \left(\begin{vmatrix} a_2 & a_3 \\ b_2 & b_3 \end{vmatrix} \mathbf{i} - \begin{vmatrix} a_1 & a_3 \\ b_1 & b_3 \end{vmatrix} \mathbf{j} + \begin{vmatrix} a_1 & a_2 \\ b_1 & b_2 \end{vmatrix} \mathbf{k} \right)$$

$$= \begin{vmatrix} a_2 & a_3 \\ b_2 & b_3 \end{vmatrix} c_1 - \begin{vmatrix} a_1 & a_3 \\ b_1 & b_3 \end{vmatrix} c_2 + \begin{vmatrix} a_1 & a_2 \\ b_1 & b_2 \end{vmatrix} c_3$$

$$= \begin{vmatrix} a_1 & a_2 & a_3 \\ b_1 & b_2 & b_3 \\ c_1 & c_2 & c_3 \end{vmatrix}$$

For example, if $\mathbf{A}$ and $\mathbf{B}$ are the vectors defined in the previous example, and $\mathbf{C}$ has the components $(25, 0, 40)$, the volume of the parallelepiped constructed on $\mathbf{A}$, $\mathbf{B}$ and $\mathbf{C}$ can be calculated in MATLAB with

```
≫ C = [ 25 0 40 ];
≫ volume = det([ A; B; C ])
volume =
    5000
```

Using the function vprod defined in the previous example, verify that the same result is given by the MATLAB command

```
≫ C*vprod(A, B)'
```

5.12   Exercises

The solution to Exercise 5.7 appears at the back of the book.

■ **EXERCISE 5.1**   The determinant of a product of matrices
Enter in MATLAB the matrices

$$\mathbf{A} = \begin{bmatrix} 2.3 & 7.6 \\ 3.4 & -5.8 \end{bmatrix} ; \mathbf{B} = \begin{bmatrix} 2.4 & 5.9 \\ -6.7 & 9.0 \end{bmatrix}$$

Calculate $\mathbf{C} = \mathbf{A} * \mathbf{B}$ and verify that

$$\det(\mathbf{C}) = \det(\mathbf{A}) * \det(\mathbf{B})$$

This property is general and you may verify it for any pair of square matrices.

■ **EXERCISE 5.2**   Collinear points
Show that the three points $P_1(1, 5)$, $P_2(3, 11)$, $P_3(5, 17)$ are collinear.
    Hint: If the three points are collinear, the area of the triangle $P_1 P_2 P_3$ equals zero.

■ **EXERCISE 5.3**   Parallel vectors

Show in MATLAB that the vectors $\mathbf{A}(2, 3, 5)$ and $\mathbf{B}(6, 9, 15)$ are parallel.

Hint: The area of a parallelogram constructed on two parallel vectors is zero.

■ **EXERCISE 5.4**   Coplanar vectors

Show in MATLAB that the three vectors

$$\mathbf{A} = 2\mathbf{i} + 3\mathbf{j} + 5\mathbf{k}, \ \ \mathbf{B} = 2\mathbf{i} + 8\mathbf{j} + \mathbf{k}, \ \ \mathbf{C} = 8\mathbf{i} + 22\mathbf{j} + 12\mathbf{k}$$

are coplanar.

Hint: If the three vectors are coplanar, the volume of the parallelepiped constructed on them is zero.

■ **EXERCISE 5.5**   Area of triangle

Consider again the points P_1, P_2, P_3 introduced in Example 5.1 and write their homogeneous coordinates as

$$\mathbf{P_1} = \begin{bmatrix} x_1 \\ y_1 \\ 1 \end{bmatrix}, \ \ \mathbf{P_2} = \begin{bmatrix} x_2 \\ y_2 \\ 1 \end{bmatrix}, \ \ \mathbf{P_3} = \begin{bmatrix} x_2 \\ y_2 \\ 1 \end{bmatrix}$$

Show that the area of the triangle having the vertices P_1, P_2, P_3 is

$$\frac{1}{2} \det[P_1 \ P_2 \ P_3]$$

Repeat the calculations in this way with the numerical values given in the above-mentioned example.

■ **EXERCISE 5.6**   Rotating an ellipse

It is easy to plot an ellipse by using the parametric equations

$$x \quad = \quad a \cos t$$
$$y \quad = \quad b \sin t$$

To rotate this ellipse by 90° it is sufficient to exchange the roles of a and b:

$$x \quad = \quad b \cos t$$
$$y \quad = \quad a \sin t$$

In general, for any rotation it is sufficient to multiply the coordinates of the ellipse by the matrix of rotation, as shown in Section 5.8. In this exercise we shall use the `rtate` function developed in the above-mentioned example.

Write an M-file that performs the following:

(1)   Plots the ellipse characterized by $a = 1, b = 2$.

(2)   Plots the ellipse obtained by exchanging a with b.
(3)   Plots the ellipse rotated by 90° with the aid of the `rtate` function.
(4)   Plots the ellipse rotated by 45° with the aid of the `rtate` function.

■ **EXERCISE 5.7**   Swinging pendulum
In this exercise it is required to write an M-file that draws a very simple pendulum, swings it by 30° and draws it again in the new position. The steps are as follows:

(1)   Draw the pendulum weight as a circle with the centre in the origin and diameter equal to 5 units; and the pendulum rod as a line starting from the origin and 32.5 units long – see Figure 5.17(a).
(2)   Translate the pendulum weight to the end of the rod, as shown in Figure 5.17(b).
(3)   Rotate the pendulum by 30° as shown in Figure 5.17(c).

■ **EXERCISE 5.8**   Harmonic mean
In this chapter we learned how to program a function. Let us use this knowledge and write a function that calculates the **harmonic mean** of the elements of an array A. Given these elements, a_i, their harmonic mean, h, is defined by

$$\frac{1}{h} = \frac{1}{a_1} + \frac{1}{a_2} + \cdots \tag{5.21}$$

We have already encountered the harmonic mean in some technical examples. For example, the equivalent resistance of a parallel connection of resistances is their harmonic mean (Example 3.4). Also, the equivalent capacitance of a series connection of capacitors equals their harmonic mean (see Exercise 3.11). A further example is given in this exercise.

(1)   Write a function that calculates the harmonic mean according to Equation 5.21. Check the function with several arrays of your choice.
(2)   The notion of a linear spring was introduced in Example 4.1. Assume now that n linear springs are connected in series, as shown in Figure 5.18. Let the spring

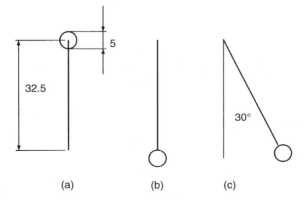

Figure 5.17   Swinging a pendulum by 30°.

k_l k_n

Figure 5.18   A series connection of springs.

constant of the i-th spring be k_i, and its deflection x_i. As the same force, F, acts on each spring, we can write

$$F = k_i x_i$$

for $i = 1, \ldots, n$. The equivalent spring constant, k, is defined by

$$F = k \sum_{i=1}^{n} x_i$$

and conclude that k is the harmonic mean of the spring constants k_i. Consider four springs with the spring constants 1000, 2000, 3000 and 4000 Nm^{-1} respectively. Calculate the equivalent spring constant using the function developed in (1).

■ **EXERCISE 5.9**   More trigonometric functions

(1)   Write a function `cotand` that calculates the cotangent of the argument, the latter being given in degrees.

(2)   Write a function `asind` that calculates the arc sine of the argument and outputs the result in degrees.

Chapter 6
Solving equations

6.1 Systems of linear equations – introduction

A system of equations

$$a_{11}x_1 + a_{12}x_2 + \cdots + a_{1n}x_n = b_1$$
$$\vdots \qquad = \qquad \vdots$$
$$a_{m1}x_1 + a_{m2}x_2 + \cdots + a_{mn}x_n = b_m$$

in which all variables appear only to the first power is, by definition, a **system of linear equations**. We consider the variables as **unknowns** and look for a vector of values that, substituted in place of $x_1, x_2, \ldots$, satisfy simultaneously all equations. If we can find such a vector, it is a **solution** of the system.

Several cases can be distinguished, for instance if the number of equations, m, is smaller than, equal to, or larger than the number of variables (unknowns), n. Another distinction must be made if the terms $b_1, \ldots, b_m$ are not all zero, and if they are. Finally, different cases can be identified according to the values of certain determinants formed with the coefficients $a_{11}, \ldots, a_{mn}$ and the terms $b_1, \ldots, b_m$.

By analysing the different cases it is possible to know if a solution *exists*, and if it does, to determine if it is *unique* or if there are several solutions.

This chapter begins with a non-rigorous discussion of the several cases possible, and of the conditions for existence and uniqueness of solution. This discussion is necessary because the MATLAB method introduced later in this chapter always gives an answer; however, it can be sometimes only a *particular* solution, other times a solution in the *least-squares sense*, and in some cases it may not be a solution at all. Readers interested in a more formal treatment of the subject, and in more details, may refer to textbooks such as Johnson, Riess and Arnold (1993), Fraleigh and Beauregard (1990), Hill (1988), or Wylie and Barrett (1987).

The systems of linear equations are discussed in Sections 6.2 to 6.6 and exemplified in Section 6.11. The other sections of this chapter are about **polynomial equations**, a subject introduced in Section 6.7.

6.2   Inhomogeneous linear equations

An equation of the form

$$a_1 x_1 + a_2 x_2 + \cdots a_n x_n = b$$

is said to be **inhomogeneous** because of the term b which does not multiply any variable (unknown). Consider, as an example, the following equation in two variables:

$$2x_1 - x_2 = 2 \tag{6.1}$$

We can rewrite it as

$$x_1 = 1 + 0.5x_2$$

For each value assigned to x_2 there is a corresponding value of x_1. For a given set of x_2 values we can plot in MATLAB the values x_1 given by Equation 6.1 and obtain the line shown in Figure 6.1(a); it is a straight line (hence the qualifier **linear**). There are an infinite number of x_1, x_2 pairs that are solutions of Equation 6.1; they all lie on the straight line defined by Equation 6.1.

Let us consider now a *system* of two equations in two unknowns, x_1, x_2:

$$2x_1 - x_2 \quad = \quad 2 \tag{6.2}$$
$$x_1 + x_2 \quad = \quad 5 \tag{6.3}$$

The solution of this system is $x_1 = 7/3$, $x_2 = 8/3$. These are the coordinates of the intersection of the two lines corresponding to Equations 6.2 and 6.3, as shown in Figure 6.1(b).

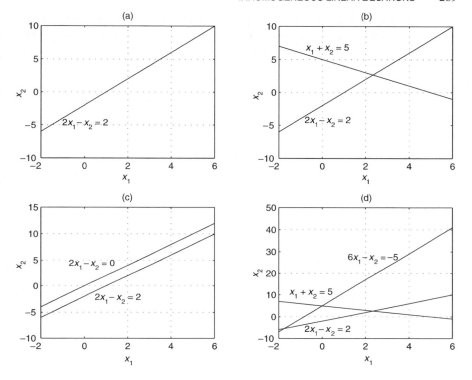

Figure 6.1 Linear equations in two variables.

Not all systems of two equations in two variables (unknowns) have a solution. For example, the system

$$2x_1 - x_2 \quad = \quad 2 \qquad\qquad (6.4)$$
$$2x_1 - x_2 \quad = \quad 0 \qquad\qquad (6.5)$$

cannot be solved. Plotting these equations, as in Figure 6.1(c), we see that the corresponding lines are parallel, that is, they have no point in common; in other words, there is no pair x_1, x_2 that could be a solution of both equations.

Another example of a system that cannot be solved consists of the following three equations in two variables:

$$2x_1 - x_2 \quad = \quad 2 \qquad\qquad (6.6)$$
$$x_1 + x_2 \quad = \quad 5 \qquad\qquad (6.7)$$
$$6x_1 - x_2 \quad = \quad -5 \qquad\qquad (6.8)$$

The graphs of the three equations are shown in Figure 6.1(d). Each pair of lines intersects, and the three intersections do not coincide, so there is no point that satisfies *all* three equations.

The preceding discussion can be generalized to any finite number of variables; it was convenient to begin with two variables because it is easy to find and visualize a geometric interpretation in the plane. In general, a system of m equations in n unknowns can be written as

$$a_{11}x_1 + a_{12}x_2 + \cdots + a_{1n}x_n = b_1$$
$$a_{21}x_1 + a_{22}x_2 + \cdots + a_{2n}x_n = b_2$$
$$\cdots \cdots$$
$$a_{m1}x_1 + a_{m2}x_2 + \cdots + a_{mn}x_n = b_m$$

or, in matrix form,

$$\mathbf{AX} = \mathbf{B} \tag{6.9}$$

where

$$\mathbf{A} = \begin{bmatrix} a_{11}x_1 & a_{12}x_2 & \cdots & a_{1n}x_n \\ a_{21}x_1 & a_{22}x_2 & \cdots & a_{2n}x_n \\ \cdots & \cdots & \cdots & \cdots \\ a_{m1}x_1 & a_{m2}x_2 & \cdots & a_{mn}x_n \end{bmatrix}$$

$$\mathbf{X} = \begin{bmatrix} x_1 \\ x_2 \\ \cdots \\ x_n \end{bmatrix}, \quad \mathbf{B} = \begin{bmatrix} b_1 \\ b_2 \\ \cdots \\ b_m \end{bmatrix}$$

$\mathbf{A}$ is called the **coefficient matrix** and $\mathbf{X}$ the **solution vector**.

If $m = n$, $\mathbf{A}$ is a square matrix, and if det $\mathbf{A}$ is non-zero, $\mathbf{A}^{-1}$ exists; then the solution of the system is given by

$$\mathbf{A}^{-1}\mathbf{AX} = \mathbf{X} = \mathbf{A}^{-1}\mathbf{B} \tag{6.10}$$

For example, for the system consisting of Equations 6.2 and 6.3, we can calculate in MATLAB

```
≫ A = [ 2 -1; 1 1 ];
≫ B = [ 2; 5 ];
≫ X = inv(A)*B
X =
    2.3333
    2.6667
```

It is easy to see that the solution is the one already shown. The MATLAB rats function yields a **rational approximation** of the argument, in this case the exact rational fractions that are the solutions of the system:

```
>> rats(X)
ans =
    7/3
    8/3
```

We cannot proceed in the same way with the system of Equations 6.4 and 6.5 because

$$\begin{vmatrix} 2 & -1 \\ 2 & -1 \end{vmatrix} = 0$$

and the coefficient matrix is not **invertible**, that is, the coefficient matrix has no inverse. Those familiar with the elementary properties of determinants know that this happens because the two rows are identical.

The method given by Equation 6.10 is not computationally efficient if n is large, and MATLAB uses another method which will be presented in Section 6.4. However, from Equation 6.10 it is possible to deduce the once popular method known as Cramer's rule (see Subsection 1.5.2) and also theoretical conclusions. One such conclusion has been reached above: if the number of equations equals the number of variables (unknowns), that is, if $m = n$, and if $\det(\mathbf{A}) \neq 0$, then the system has a unique solution.

Figure 6.1 contains four graphs; they were obtained with the MATLAB subplot function, as follows:

- subplot(2, 2, 1) for the upper left graph,
- subplot(2, 2, 2) for the upper right graph,
- subplot(2, 2, 3) for the lower left graph,
- subplot(2, 2, 4) for the lower right graph
  .

The subplot function was used in Chapter 4 for splitting a plot into two graphs. Now it is used for four graphs, so that a general description of this function would be appropriate. As seen, the argument consists of three digits. The first two digits can be regarded as specifying a 'matrix of graphs'; in our example 2, 2 means a 2-by-2 matrix, that is, 2 rows and 2 columns of graphs. The third digit identifies the place of the graph in the matrix of graphs. For example, 2, 2, 1 means the graph in the first row and first column; 2, 2, 4, the graph in the second row and second column.

6.3   Homogeneous linear equations

A system of linear equations whose right-hand sides are all equal to zero is called **homogeneous**. Such a system can be written in matrix form shown in equation 6.11.

$$\mathbf{AX} = 0 \tag{6.11}$$

LIVERPOOL JOHN MOORES UNIVERSITY
LEARNING SERVICES

If $\det(\mathbf{A}) \neq 0$, the only possible solution is $\mathbf{X} = \mathbf{0}$ (that is, all variables equal zero), called the **trivial solution**. As an example, consider the equations

$$
\begin{aligned}
2x_1 - x_2 &= 0 \\
x_1 + x_2 &= 0
\end{aligned}
$$

represented in Figure 6.2(a). Here $\det(\mathbf{A}) = 3$ and, as also seen in the figure, the solution is $x_1 = x_2 = 0$.

If $\det(\mathbf{A}) = 0$, several solutions may be possible, for example the system

$$
\begin{aligned}
-6x_1 + 3x_2 &= 0 \\
2x_1 - x_2 &= 0
\end{aligned}
$$

represented in Figure 6.2(b). Either equation yields $x_2 = 2x_1$, so that for any value assigned to x_1 there is a corresponding value of x_2. The figure shows that the two equations actually represent one and the same straight line.

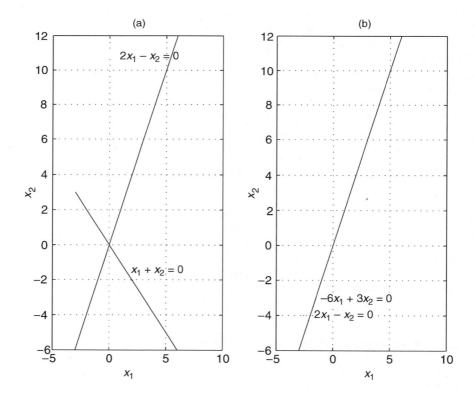

Figure 6.2   Systems of homogeneous equations.

The following system of four homogeneous equations in three unknowns is discussed in Beaumont (1987):

$$3x_1 + 4x_2 - 2x_3 \quad = \quad 0 \tag{6.12}$$
$$-2x_1 + 3x_2 - 4x_3 \quad = \quad 0 \tag{6.13}$$
$$5x_1 + x_2 + 2x_3 \quad = \quad 0 \tag{6.14}$$
$$-9x_1 + 5x_2 - 10x_3 \quad = \quad 0 \tag{6.15}$$

The coefficient matrix is 4 by 3. The largest determinants that can be built from it are of order 3; they are all equal to zero. It is easy to see, however, that it is possible to build determinants of order 2 that are not zero, for example with the elements in rows 1 and 2, and columns 1 and 2:

$$\begin{vmatrix} 3 & 4 \\ -2 & 3 \end{vmatrix}$$

We say in this case that the coefficient matrix has the **rank 2**. More generally, let us assume that we can form a minor, r-by-r matrix by selecting r rows and r columns, not necessarily contiguous, from the matrix $\mathbf{A}$ so that the determinant (of order r) of this minor matrix is not zero, and any determinant of order $r + 1$ built from rows and columns of the same matrix, $\mathbf{A}$, is zero. We say then that the rank of $\mathbf{A}$ is r (more rigorous definitions of rank can be found in textbooks on linear algebra such as Fraleigh and Beauregard 1990, or Johnson, Riess and Arnold 1993). There is a MATLAB function that yields the rank of a matrix directly, in our case

```
>> A = [ 3 4 -2; -2 3 -4
5 1 2; -9 5 -10 ];
>> rank(A)
ans =
    2
```

This means that we can solve a system of two equations in two variables and it remains to assign an arbitrary value to the third variable. In order to do this, let us take the first two equations and rearrange them with the terms in x_3 in the right-hand side:

$$3x_1 + 4x_2 \quad = \quad 2x_3 \tag{6.16}$$
$$-2x_1 + 3x_2 \quad = \quad 4x_3 \tag{6.17}$$

The solutions are

$$x_1 = -\frac{10}{17}x_3, \quad x_2 = \frac{16}{17}x_3$$

It is easy to check that these values are also solutions of the other two equations of the system.

6.4   MATLAB's solution of linear systems

Let us consider again Equations 6.2 and 6.3. We solve them in MATLAB with the aid of the backslash operator, '\':

```
≫ A = [ 2 -1; 1 1 ];
≫ B = [ 2; 5 ];
≫ X = A\B
X =
    2.3333
    2.6667
```

The solution is based on a modification of a technique known as **Gaussian elimination**. A derivation of this theory, illustrated with many MATLAB examples, can be found in Hill (1988).

The backslash operator, '\' , always yields an answer in MATLAB; it is not necessarily the solution of the system, and it may be sometimes only a *particular* one (that is, one solution out of several solutions). The **Kronecker–Capelli theorem** (Leopold Kronecker, German, 1823–1891, Alfredo Capelli, Italian, 1855–1910) tells us if the system has a solution and if this solution is unique. We shall first introduce a new notion: given a system $AX = B$, the **augmented matrix** of the system is the matrix $[A \ B]$. The Kronecker–Capelli theorem states that *a system has a solution if and only if its coefficient matrix – denoted here by* A *– and its augmented matrix have the same rank.* Let this rank be r, and let the number of unknowns be n. If $r = n$ the solution is unique, if $r < n$ the system has an infinite number of solutions: we may solve for r variables (unknowns) as functions of the other $n - r$ variables which can be assigned arbitrary values.

Let us solve a few systems in MATLAB. We have already found the solution of Equations 6.2 and 6.3. The Kronecker–Capelli theorem confirms that the system does indeed have a solution:

```
≫ rank(A), rank([ A B ])
ans =
    2
ans =
    2
```

Let us now consider the **undetermined system**

$$
\begin{aligned}
2x_1 + 3x_2 + 4x_3 &= 4 \\
x_1 + x_2 + x_3 &= 5
\end{aligned}
$$

MATLAB yields:

```
≫ A = [ 2 3 4; 1 1 1];
≫ B = [ 4; 5 ];
≫ rank(A), rank([ A B ])
ans =
     2
ans =
     2
≫ X = A\B
X =
        8
        0
       -3
```

The coefficient matrix and the augmented matrix are both of rank 2; the system has a solution. The rank is smaller than the number of unknowns; we may solve for two variables as functions of the other $3 - 2 = 1$ variables. The solution yielded by MATLAB is a particular one; it can be easily checked that the general solution is

$$x_1 = 11 + x_3; \; x_2 = -6 - 2x_3$$

The solution found in MATLAB corresponds to

$$x_1 = 11 - 3 = 8$$
$$x_2 = -6 - 2 \times (-3) = 0$$
$$x_3 = -3$$

The 2-by-3 matrix $\mathbf{A}$ is not square; therefore, it has no inverse. Without entering into more details, it can be mentioned that one can define a 3-by-2 matrix $\mathbf{P}$, called the **pseudoinverse** of $\mathbf{A}$, such that

$$\mathbf{A} * \mathbf{P} * \mathbf{A} = \mathbf{A}$$
$$\mathbf{P} * \mathbf{A} * \mathbf{P} = \mathbf{P}$$

The pseudoinverse can be calculated in MATLAB by the `pinv` function and thus we can obtain another solution of the system treated above:

```
≫ X = pinv(A)*B
X =
      7.1667
      1.6667
     -3.8333
```

The sum of the squares of roots obtained in this way is smaller than the sum of squares of roots of any other solution of the system. As an exercise, in order to compare the latter solution with the one obtained a few lines above, calculate the sums of their squared roots.

Undetermined systems occur in technical problems, so it is necessary to define supplementary conditions in order to find a unique solution. A simple example can be found in Exercise 6.3.

Returning to Equations 6.12 to 6.15 and using MATLAB we obtain

```
≫ A\B
Warning:   Rank deficient, rank = 2 tol = 9.8903e-15
ans =
     0
     0
     0
```

This is a particular, **trivial** solution; we have found the general solution in Section 6.3. This system is **overdetermined** because there are more independent equations than variables. It could, however, be solved because the rank of the coefficient matrix is equal to that of the augmented matrix. This is always the case with homogeneous systems. Why?

Let us see now what happens with an overdetermined system that does not fulfil the condition required by the Kronecker–Capelli theorem:

$$x_1 + 2x_2 + 3x_3 = 12$$
$$3x_1 + 2x_2 + x_3 = 15$$
$$3x_1 + 4x_2 + 7x_3 = 13$$
$$10x_1 + 9x_2 + 8x_3 = 17$$

The calculations in MATLAB are

```
≫ A = [ 1 2 3; 3 2 1; 3 4 7; 10 9 8 ];
≫ B = [ 12; 15; 13; 17 ];
≫ rank(A), rank([ A B ])
ans =
     3
ans =
     4
≫ A\B
ans =
     1.0887
    -0.2527
     1.5349
```

It is easy to check that this is *not* a solution of the system:

```
≫ A*ans
ans =
      5.1882
      4.2957
     13.0000
     20.8925
```

The result is not equal to **B**!

6.5   Overdetermined systems – least-squares solution

When the number of equations, m, is larger than the number of unknowns, n, we say that the system is **overdetermined**. We mean here m independent equations, that is, none of them can be derived from the others. As an example, let us suppose that we study a phenomenon in which two variables, x and y, are related by

$$y = a + bx \tag{6.18}$$

and that a series of m experiments is performed in order to determine the two coefficients, a and b. In the i-th experiment the input is x_i and the measured output, y_i. The results of experiments are usually affected by various errors, therefore the y values plotted against the x values would not fall exactly on the straight line defined by Equation 6.18, but around it. Defining e_i as the error of y_i relative to the value expected from Equation 6.18, we can write

$$y_i = a + bx_i + e_i, \ i = 1, 2, \ldots, m \tag{6.19}$$

In practice we measure $y_i - e_i$, not y_i, and if $m > 2$, the system of equations

$$(y_i - e_i) = a + bx_i, \ i = 1, 2, \ldots, m \tag{6.20}$$

is usually inconsistent and it has no solution. Instead of an exact solution we must be content with an approximation that would somehow minimize the effect of the errors. It would not be good to minimize the sum of the errors; some errors may have a plus sign, others may have a minus sign, and even if individual errors can be large, they can cancel each other partially in the sum and yield a relatively small number. The usually accepted criterion is the *minimization of the sum of the squares of errors*. The squares are always positive and they do not cancel one another in the sum. Moreover, this **least-squares** criterion leads to an elegant and relatively easy solution. Let us write down the sum of squared errors as:

$$\mathcal{E} = \sum_{i=1}^{m} e_i^2 = \sum_{i=1}^{m} (y_i - a - bx_i)^2 \tag{6.21}$$

We are interested in those values of a and b that minimize $\mathcal{E}$. Let

$$
\mathbf{Y} = \begin{bmatrix} y_1 \\ y_2 \\ \vdots \\ y_m \end{bmatrix}, \quad
\mathbf{A} = \begin{bmatrix} 1 & x_1 \\ 1 & x_2 \\ \vdots & \vdots \\ 1 & x_m \end{bmatrix}, \quad
\mathbf{X} = \begin{bmatrix} a \\ b \end{bmatrix}
$$

Then, as shown in the Appendix of this chapter, the coefficients we seek are given by

$$
\begin{bmatrix} a \\ b \end{bmatrix} = (\mathbf{A}'\mathbf{A})^{-1}\mathbf{A}'\mathbf{Y} \tag{6.22}
$$

In order to experiment with the procedure described above, we may 'create' an example in MATLAB as follows. We assume that in Equation 6.18 a should be equal to 2.5 and b to 3.6 but, instead of measuring points that lie on the line defined by these parameters, we obtained the following x, y pairs:

x	y	x	y
0	2.7190	5.5000	22.9711
0.5000	4.3470	6.0000	24.1077
1.0000	6.7789	6.5000	26.2834
1.5000	8.5793	7.0000	27.7668
2.0000	10.6347	7.5000	29.9175
2.5000	11.8835	8.0000	31.9868
3.0000	13.8194	8.5000	33.6890
3.5000	15.9310	9.0000	35.8304
4.0000	16.9346	9.5000	37.5462
4.5000	18.7535	10.0000	39.0269
5.0000	21.0297		

Above, the x values are equidistant, because this was convenient in the experiment. The procedure described here *does not* require the equidistance of x values. After loading the numbers in MATLAB, with x and y as row vectors, the least-squares solution is obtained by

```
>> A = [ ones(size(x))' x' ];
>> Y = y';
>> X1 = inv(A'*A)*A'*Y
X1 =
    2.8773
    3.6201
```

MATLAB provides an even simpler solution:

```
>> X2 = A\Y
X2 =
    2.8773
    3.6201
```

This means that, as claimed above, the MATLAB operation A\B is always performed, but the meaning of the result may differ from case to case. Thus, in the latter example we obtained a solution *in the least-squares sense.*

The derivation of Equation 6.22 given in the Appendix of this chapter follows Arbenz and Wohlhauser (1986). Another derivation, making appeal to geometrical considerations, may be found in Hill (1988), which also shows how to solve more difficult cases which have not been treated here because they are not frequent in engineering calculations.

As a second example, let us consider again the three equations represented in Figure 6.1(d):

$$2x_1 - x_2 = 2$$
$$x_1 + x_2 = 5$$
$$6x_1 - x_2 = -5$$

The least-squares solution of this system is obtained in MATLAB by:

```
>> A = [ 2 -1; 1 1; 6 -1 ];
>> B = [ 2; 5; -5 ];
>> X = A\B
 X =
    -0.0946
     2.4459
```

Let us write y1 for x_2 in the first equation, y2 for x_2 in the second, and y3 for x_2 in the third. After solving for y1, y2 and y3, we can plot the three straight lines representing the equations, as in Figure 6.3, with the command

```
>> plot(x, y1, x, y2, x, y3, X(1), X(2), '*')
```

The string '*' prints an asterisk in the point X. The solution lies within the triangle whose vertices are the intersections of the three lines taken two at a time.

The problem solved above may have technical applications; some of them are described in Arbenz and Wohlhauser (1986). Thus, the three lines may be **position lines**. For example, let us assume that the position of a certain radio transmitter must be found. The transmitter can be fixed, or it can be carried by a car, aeroplane or ship. In three different locations, radio **direction finders** can be used to find the direction of the transmitter. The next step is to plot on a map lines that pass through

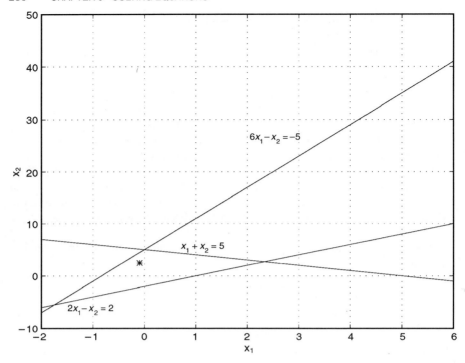

Figure 6.3   Overdetermined system, least-squares solution.

the positions of the three direction finders and have the directions measured by them. The transmitter is located at the intersection of the three lines. Usually, due to various errors, the three lines do not meet in a point, but, as in our example, for each pair of lines there is a different intersection. The method of least squares allows us to find an approximation of the position we seek. Position lines can also be obtained by radar, by optical observation (taking bearings in terrain or in coastal navigation), or in astronomical navigation (for a short, simple description of navigation methods see Moody 1987).

The method of least squares was first used by Gauss, in 1794, in the analysis of astronomical observations. Gauss was then only 17 years old and he did not immediately publish his work. The first publication on a least-squares method is due to Legendre (Adrien-Marie, French, 1752–1833) who dealt with observations on comets.

6.6   Ill-conditioned systems

We say that a problem is **ill conditioned** if small changes in the data produce large changes in the results. The danger in such a problem is that the 'small' data changes can originate from uncertainty and approximations. Most engineering problems are affected by uncertainties because engineers work with data obtained from measurements and with specified dimensions and components. Data obtained from measurements are affected by **measurement errors**. Specified dimensions and components are subject to **tolerances**. As an example, if a technical drawing contains the dimension 100 mm and the tolerance is h6 (see ISO 286), the dimension of the element is acceptable if it lies anywhere between 99.978 and 100 mm. Another example: if a resistor is specified as 1000 Ω, in the tolerance class 5%, its resistance may be any value between 950 and 1050 Ω. Frequently used values, such as those of mains voltage, atmospheric pressure or room temperature, can oscillate considerably even during short time periods. In most engineering calculations it would be impractical to take these variations into acount. Therefore, **standard values** are used instead of the instantaneous, true values and this procedure causes data uncertainties. If such data are the input to an ill-conditioned problem, the results can be disastrous.

A simple example of an ill-conditioned problem arises when we seek the intersection of two straight lines whose slopes are very close to one another. It is easy to imagine technical examples in which such a situation can arise:

- in navigation, finding the position as the intersection of two position lines that make a very small angle one with the other;
- in topography, drawing level lines when the slope is small. The same may happen in bathymetry.

The problem as defined in these examples is equivalent to that of ill-conditioned systems of linear equations; to illustrate it we shall borrow an example from Hartley and Wynn-Evans (1979) and treat it according to our own needs. Consider the system

$$\begin{bmatrix} 1 & 1 \\ 1 & 1.01 \end{bmatrix} \begin{bmatrix} 1 \\ 1 \end{bmatrix} = \begin{bmatrix} 2 \\ 2.01 \end{bmatrix} \tag{6.23}$$

In the short format MATLAB displays the correct solution:

```
≫ A = [ 1 1; 1 1.01 ], B = [ 2; 2.01 ]
X = A\B
   X =
   1.0000
   1.0000
```

A very small error is present in the long format display and this is actually the solution found in MATLAB:

```
≫ format long; X = A\B
X =
   1.00000000000002
   0.99999999999998
```

Let us change one of the elements of **A** by a small amount and see what happens:

```
≫ A(1, 2) = 1.005; X = A\B
X =
   -0.00999999999991
    1.99999999999991
```

Changing A(1, 2) by 0.5% decreased X(1) by approximately 101% and increased X(2) by 100%! Let us restore **A** to its initial value and slightly change one of the elements of **B**:

```
≫ A(1, 2) = 1; B(2) = 2.015;
X = A\B
X =
    0.49999999999999
    1.50000000000001
```

This time we changed B(2) by less than 0.25%. The result is that X(1) decreased by 50% and X(2) increased by 50%.

The sensitivity of the solution to changes in coefficients or right-hand side terms can be estimated with the aid of the **condition number**. The definition and derivation of this concept is based on **norm**, a subject not discussed in this book. In MATLAB the condition number of the matrix **A** is found by

```
≫ cond(A)
ans =
    402.0075
```

A rule of thumb is that when the condition number is expressed in the form

$$a \times 10^k, \quad 1 \le a \le 9$$

the last k significant digits of the result shall be considered as unreliable and dropped. In our example the condition number can be expressed as 4×10^2. This means that the last two digits of the solutions are unreliable.

Another example of an ill-conditioned system of linear equations is given in Exercise 6.4.

6.7   Polynomial equations – introduction

A **polynomial equation of degree** n has the general form

$$a_n x^n + a_{n-1} x^{n-1} + \cdots + a_1 x + a_0 = 0 \tag{6.24}$$

Many physical and engineering problems lead to polynomial equations. As a very simple example, let us suppose that we want to measure the depth of an open, water well. It is sufficient to drop a stone and measure the elapsed time between the stone being released and the sound of the splash being heard. The depth of the well can then be found by solving a quadratic equation. Polynomial equations of various degrees intervene in the solution of linear differential equations with constant coefficients, and in the solution of systems of such equations. One result, for instance, can be the natural periods of oscillating systems.

A solution, or **root**, of the equation is a number x_i, real or complex, such that

$$a_n x_i^n + a_{n-1} x_i^{n-1} + \cdots + a_1 x_i + a_0 = 0 \tag{6.25}$$

The **fundamental theorem of algebra** (postulated earlier by some mathematicians, and demonstrated rigorously by Gauss in 1799) states that *a polynomial equation of degree n has exactly n roots.* Let $x_1, x_2, \ldots, x_n$ be these roots, then the polynomial in Equation 6.24 can be rewritten as

$$a_n(x - x_1)(x - x_2) \cdots (x - x_{n-1})(x - x_n) = 0 \tag{6.26}$$

If several roots are equal, for instance $x_i = x_{i+1} = \cdots = x_{i+m-1} = \xi$, ξ is called a **multiple root**, or, more exactly, a **root of multiplicity** m. Such a root is counted m times in n, so that the number of the remaining roots is $n - m$.

If the coefficients $a_n, a_{n-1}, \ldots, a_0$ of Equation 6.24 are all real, any complex roots appear in conjugate pairs. This property should be evident from Equation 6.26.

Practical solutions of the equation of second degree were known in ancient times, certainly to Babylonian mathematicians. The solutions of the equations of third and fourth degree were found in the 16th century by Italian mathematicians. The formulae giving the solutions are rather complicated and using them without a computer is not a pleasant job. It is surprising how many engineers ignore the existence of these formulae. Efforts to solve equations of higher degrees by formulae including radicals proved unsuccessful. Paolo Ruffini (Italian, 1765–1822) published several proofs of the impossibility of solving equations of the fifth degree by such formulae; those proofs are considered insufficient. A clear proof that there are no formulae for equations of the fifth and higher degrees was published in 1826 by the young Norwegian mathematician Niels Hendrik Abel (1802–1829). These facts explain the interest in having a general function that yields the roots of equations of any degree usually encountered in technical problems. MATLAB provides such a function. Its use will be explained and illustrated without detailing the theoretical background or the algorithm employed.

6.8   Finding roots of polynomials in MATLAB

MATLAB provides a function, `roots`, that yields the solutions of a polynomial equation. The argument of this function is the array of the polynomial coefficients ordered according to descending powers of the variable. For example, for the equation

$$x^5 - 2x^4 + 2x^3 + 3x^2 + x + 4 = 0$$

the array of the coefficients is written in MATLAB as

```
>> c = [ 1 -2 2 3 1 4 ];
```

and the solution is obtained with

```
>> solution = roots(c)
solution =
     1.5336 + 1.4377i
     1.5336 - 1.4377i
    -1.0638
    -0.0017 + 0.9225i
    -0.0017 - 0.9225i
```

Note that while c was a row vector, solution is a column vector.

6.9   Retrieving polynomial coefficients from roots

Given an array of polynomial roots, poly yields the polynomial coefficients in the order of the descending powers of the variable. In our example

```
>> poly(solution)
ans =
     1.0000 -2.0000 2.0000 3.0000 1.0000 4.0000
```

6.10   Summary

Let $\mathbf{A}_r$ be a *submatrix* built with elements from r rows and r columns, not necessarily contiguous, of the matrix $\mathbf{A}$, and let $\det \mathbf{A}_r \neq 0$. If for any submatrix $\mathbf{A}_{r+1}$ built with elements from $r + 1$ rows and $r + 1$ columns of $\mathbf{A}$, $\det \mathbf{A}_{r+1} = 0$, then we say that the matrix $\mathbf{A}$ has the rank r.

A system of m linear equations in n variables (also called **unknowns**)

$$
\begin{aligned}
a_{11}x_1 + a_{12}x_2 + \cdots + a_{1n}x_n &= b_1 \\
a_{21}x_1 + a_{22}x_2 + \cdots + a_{2n}x_n &= b_2 \\
\vdots \quad\quad &= \quad \vdots \\
a_{m1}x_1 + a_{m2}x_2 + \cdots + a_{mn}x_n &= b_m
\end{aligned}
$$

can be written in matrix form as

$$\mathbf{AX} = \mathbf{B}$$

where $\mathbf{A}$ is the **coefficient matrix** and $\mathbf{X}$ the **solution vector**.

The matrix [A B] is called the **augmented matrix of the system**. The Kronecker–Capelli theorem states that *a system of linear equations has a solution if and only if the coefficient matrix and the augmented matrix of the system have the same rank*. If that rank, say r, is equal to the number of the variables, n, the solution of the system is unique. If the rank is smaller than the number of the variables (unknowns), that is, if $r < n$, the system is undetermined and r variables can be expressed as functions of the other $n - r$ variables to which we can assign arbitrary values.

The solution of systems of linear equations is obtained in MATLAB with the backslash operator, '\'. For example, the solution of the system shown above is yielded by the command X = A\B.

If the system has a unique solution, MATLAB will yield it. If the system is **undetermined**, that is, if the common rank, r, of the coefficient matrix and of the augmented matrix is less than the number of variables, n, the backslash operator will yield a particular solution in which $n - r$ variables will be arbitrarily set to zero. A solution which minimizes the sum of squared roots is yielded by the command X = pinv(A)*B. The complete solution must be found by algebraic means.

If the rank of the coefficient differs from that of the augmented matrix, MATLAB's backslash operator will still yield a result; it will not be a solution of the system and this is also what the Kronecker–Capelli theorem predicts.

A system for which the elements of the vector **B** are all zero is called **homogeneous**. A homogeneous system always has a solution. If $\det \mathbf{A} \neq 0$, the solution is the **trivial** one, that is, $\mathbf{X} = \mathbf{0}$. If the determinant equals zero, the system has more than one solution. In this case MATLAB will warn the user that the Matrix is close to singular or badly scaled and it will return only the trivial solution.

If the system is **overdetermined**, that is, if the number of independent equations is larger than the number of variables, the backslash operator will yield the **least squares solution**. The meaning of this notion can be explained by assuming that, for a certain phenomenon, the variables x and y are theoretically related by

$$y = a + bx$$

Experiments yield results affected by errors e_i so that we obtain in reality a number of pairs x_i, y_i related by

$$y_i = a + bx_i + e_i$$

and we actually measure $y_i - e_i$, not y_i. The method of least squares yields a and b which minimize the sum of squared errors, that is, those coefficients for which $\mathcal{E} = \sum e_i^2$ is a minimum.

A polynomial **equation of degree** n has the general form

$$a_n x^n + a_{n-1} x^{n-1} + \cdots + a_1 x + a_0 = 0$$

The **fundamental theorem** of algebra states that such an equation has exactly n roots, real, complex, or multiple.

In MATLAB we represent the polynomial by the array of its coefficients in the order of the descending powers of x, in our example

$$c = [a_n \; a_{n-1} \; \ldots \; a_0]$$

The solution is obtained with the MATLAB `roots` function, in our example:

```
≫ solution = roots(c)
```

The `poly` function yields the coefficients of a polynomial whose zeros are the elements of its argument. In this sense `poly` can be regarded as the inverse of the `roots` function. For instance, `solution` being the array of roots found above,

```
≫ poly(solution)
```

will return the array of coefficients, c, of the initially given polynomial.

6.11   Examples – linear equations

EXAMPLE 6.1   Projection _____

We can find a simple geometric meaning for the concept of rank. Let us consider, for example, the following transformation matrix

```
≫ T = [ 1 0; 0 0 ];
```

It is a 2-by-2 matrix, but its rank is 1. Applying the transformation to the two-dimensional vector

```
≫ B = [ 2.5 7.8 ];
```

we obtain

```
≫ T*B'
ans =
    2.5000
    0
```

The result is actually a one-dimensional vector. If we think of 2.5 as the component parallel to the x axis, and of 7.8 as the component parallel to the y axis, we obtained the **projection** of the vector **B** on the x axis.

Similarly, we may regard the transformation

```
≫ T = [ 1 0 0; 0 1 0; 0 0 0 ];
≫ rank(T)
ans =
     2
≫ B = [ 2.5 7.8 6.9 ];
≫ T*B'
ans =
    2.5000
    7.8000
    0
```

as projecting the three-dimensional vector $\mathbf{B}$ on the xOy plane.

EXAMPLE 6.2   Temperature scales _____

This example is based on data from Example 2.10. It was shown there that the relationship between the Celsius and Fahrenheit scales is linear, that is, it can be represented by an equation of the form

$$C = aF + b \tag{6.27}$$

where C is the temperature in degrees Celsius and F, the temperature in degrees Fahrenheit.

The line described by Equation 6.27 must pass through the melting point of water, with coordinates $F = 32$, $C = 0$, and the boiling point of water, with coordinates $F = 212$, $C = 100$. This means that the coefficients a, b in Equation 6.27 must satisfy the system

$$32a + b \quad = \quad 0 \tag{6.28}$$
$$212a + b \quad = \quad 100 \tag{6.29}$$

or, in matrix form,

$$\begin{bmatrix} 32 & 1 \\ 212 & 1 \end{bmatrix} \begin{bmatrix} a \\ b \end{bmatrix} = \begin{bmatrix} 0 \\ 100 \end{bmatrix}$$

Defining

$$X = \begin{bmatrix} a \\ b \end{bmatrix}$$

the MATLAB solution is

```
>> A = [ 32 1; 212 1];
>> B = [ 0; 100 ];
>> X = rats(A\B)
X =
        5/9
     -160/9
```

In fact we recovered the equation

$$C = \frac{5}{9}(F - 32)$$

shown in Exercise 3.3.

EXAMPLE 6.3   The statics of a ladder ————————————————————

Here is a problem that can be found in one form or another in many textbooks on technical mechanics. Figure 6.4 shows a ladder whose lower end lies on a smooth floor, and upper end on a smooth wall. A man whose weight is W climbs the ladder. Let ℓ be the ladder length, and ℓ_0 the length defining the position of the man as measured from the lower point of the ladder. Assuming equal friction coefficients between ladder and floor, and between ladder and wall, let us find the maximum distance ℓ_0 that the man can climb without causing the ladder to slip.

Figure 6.4(b) is a free-body diagram of the ladder. The reaction of the floor is R_1, that of the wall, R_2. The friction force between ladder and floor is F_1, that between ladder and wall, F_2. With these notations the equations of force equilibrium

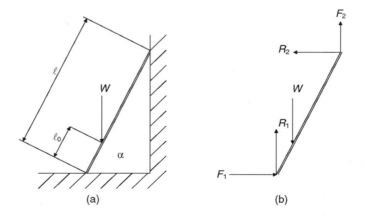

Figure 6.4   Forces acting on a ladder.

are

$$F_1 - R_2 \quad = \quad 0$$
$$R_1 + F_2 \quad = \quad W$$

Just before beginning to slip the coefficient of friction reaches its maximum value for the materials involved. Noting this value by μ, we write $F_1 = \mu R_1$, $F_2 = \mu R_2$ and the equations of force equilibrium become

$$\mu R_1 - R_2 \quad = \quad 0 \tag{6.30}$$
$$R_1 + \mu R_2 \quad = \quad W \tag{6.31}$$

The ladder will not slip if the sum of the moments of F_2 and R_2 about the lower end is larger than the moment of W about the same point:

$$\ell \sin \alpha\, R_2 + \mu \ell \cos \alpha\, R_2 > \ell_0 \cos \alpha\, W \tag{6.32}$$

Dividing both sides by $\cos \alpha$ and rearranging, we obtain

$$\ell(\tan \alpha + \mu) R_2 > \ell_0 W \tag{6.33}$$

Equations 6.30 and 6.31 yield R_2 which can be substituted into Equation 6.33 to obtain

$$\ell_0 < (\tan \alpha + \mu) \frac{\ell \mu}{1 + \mu^2} \tag{6.34}$$

If we use MATLAB to solve this problem numerically, we can avoid part of the algebra by noticing that the limit value of ℓ_0 is given by the system

$$\begin{bmatrix} \mu & -1 & 0 \\ 1 & \mu & 0 \\ 0 & \ell(\tan \alpha + \mu) & -W \end{bmatrix} \begin{bmatrix} R_1 \\ R_2 \\ \ell_0 \end{bmatrix} = \begin{bmatrix} 0 \\ W \\ 0 \end{bmatrix} \tag{6.35}$$

As an illustration let $\mu = 0.8$, $\ell = 2.4\,\mathrm{m}$, $\alpha = 30°$, $W = 800\,\mathrm{N}$. The calculations are

```
>> l = 2.4; W = 800; alpha = pi*30/180; mu = 0.8;
>> A = [ mu -1 0; 1 mu 0; 0 l*(tan(alpha) + mu) -W];
>> B = [ 0; W; 0 ];
>> X = A\B
X =
    487.8049
    390.2439
      1.6125
```

Let us compare our result with that given by Equation 6.34:

```
>> 10 = (tan(alpha) + mu)*l*(mu/(1 + mu^2))
10 =
    1.6125
```

which is the same result and can be rounded off to 1.613 m. A byproduct of the calculations are the reactions $R_1 = 487.8$, $R_2 = 390.2$ N.

EXAMPLE 6.4   Statics – a lifting platform _____

Figure 6.5 is a schematic side view of a lifting platform (scissor lifts). On each side of the platform, two beams, AD and BC, are connected by an articulation, O, so that they form a scissors-like mechanism. Point A is a fixed articulation in the base of the mechanism; point C, a fixed articulation in the load-carrying platform. A wheel at B allows the lower end of the beam BC to slide on the base. Another wheel, at D, allows the upper end of the beam AD to slide under the load-carrying platform. The load to be elevated is represented as a concentrated force W. A hydraulic cylinder is connected between two articulations, one shown at E, on the base, the other at O. The latter articulation is actually placed at half-length of a bar passing through the articulations O of the two sides of the mechanism.

Pumping oil into the cylinder pushes a piston upwards and, with it, the articulation O, thus bringing the mechanism to the position shown in dotted lines. Figure 6.5 is drawn to scale so that the operation of the platform can be checked with a compass. This principle is used in small platforms used for the elevation of weights in workshops or for loading trucks. Much larger scissor tables have been employed for moving helicopters aboard ships and on offshore platforms.

The value of W is specified as a platform performance and the force F, developed by the cylinder, must be calculated. In order to do this we consider the external forces acting on the platform; they are shown in Figure 6.6.

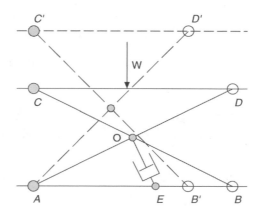

Figure 6.5   A hydraulic lifting platform.

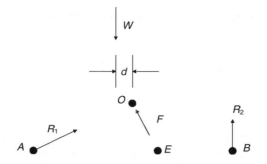

Figure 6.6   External forces acting on the platform.

The force F acts at an angle, $\widehat{AEO}$, which is the angle made by the cylinder axis with the horizontal. The **reaction**, R_1, in the articulation A has both a vertical and a horizontal component. The vertical component opposes that part of the load W that is taken by the articulation. Remember, there are two beams AD, one on each side of the platform; each will take part of W. There is, however, only one cylinder and this will support the reactions discharged through both beams AD, so that we may calculate as if there were only one beam. The horizontal component of R_1 opposes the horizontal component of F. The line of action of R_1 passes through the point O. In the wheel at B there is only a vertical reaction, R_2, because that end can slide without opposition (friction neglected).

We can write three equations of static equilibrium. The first one says that the sum of the horizontal-force components is zero:

$$\cos \widehat{BAD} \cdot R_1 - \cos \widehat{AEO} \cdot F = 0 \tag{6.36}$$

The second equation refers to the vertical force components

$$\sin \widehat{BAD} \cdot R_1 + R_2 + \sin \widehat{AEO} \cdot F = W \tag{6.37}$$

For the third equation we take the moments of the forces about some point and equate them to zero. The equation is simplified if the chosen point is O. Then, with O located at half-beam length, and d the distance between the point where W is concentrated and the centre of the platform, we write

$$\frac{\overline{BC}}{2} \cos \widehat{ABC} \cdot R_2 = -d \cdot W \tag{6.38}$$

from which we conclude that for W placed exactly over O there is no reaction at B.

Equations 6.36 to 6.38 can be combined into one matrix equation which, with $\widehat{BAD} = \widehat{ABC}$, is

$$
\begin{bmatrix}
\cos \widehat{ABC} & 0 & -\cos \widehat{AEO} \\
\sin \widehat{ABC} & 1 & \sin \widehat{AEO} \\
0 & \frac{BC}{2} \cos \widehat{ABC} & 0
\end{bmatrix}
\begin{bmatrix}
R_1 \\
R_2 \\
F
\end{bmatrix}
=
\begin{bmatrix}
0 \\
1 \\
-d
\end{bmatrix}
W \quad \textbf{(6.39)}
$$

For a numerical example, let $W = 20000$ N, $\tan \widehat{AEO} = 2/1$, and $\tan \widehat{ABC} = 1/2$. We cannot be sure that W acts exactly at the centre of the platform; therefore, we assume in this case that d equals 0.5 m. The sequence of calculations in MATLAB is

```
>> AEO = atan(2); ABC = atan(1/2);
>> BC = 3.4; d = 0.5; W = 20000;
>> A = [ cos(ABC) 0 -cos(AEO)
sin(ABC) 1 sin(AEO)
0 BC*cos(ABC)/2 0 ];
>> B = [ 0; 1; -d ]*W;
>> X = A\B
X =
    1.0e+04
    1.1885
   -0.6577
    2.3771
```

The components of the resulting vector are $X(1) = R_1$, $X(2) = R_2$, and $X(3) = F$. The sign of R_2 is opposed to the one assumed in Figure 6.6. Therefore the wheels at B must be guided through slots that will prevent overturning of the platform.

If we want to check the results we can calculate, for instance, the moments about the point B. The horizontal component of R_1 passes through the point B, so that only the vertical component has a non-zero moment about this point:

$$
M_{R_1} = -R_1 \sin \widehat{ABC} \cdot \overline{BC} \cos \widehat{ABC}
$$

Both components of F yield non-zero moments about B and their sum equals

$$
M_F = F \cos \widehat{AEO} \cdot \frac{BC}{2} \cdot \sin \widehat{ABC} - F \sin \widehat{AEO} \cdot \frac{BC}{2} \cdot \cos \widehat{ABC}
$$

The moment of W is

$$
M_W = \left(\frac{BC}{2} \cos \widehat{ABC} + d \right) W
$$

For equilibrium we must have

$$M_{R_1} + M_F + M_W = 0$$

In MATLAB, with the values previously calculated, we obtain

```
>> M1 = -X(1)*BC*sin(ABC)*cos(ABC);
>> M2 = X(3)*(BC/2)*sin(ABC - AEO);
>> M3 = (BC*cos(ABC)/2 + d)*W;
>> M1 + M2 + M3
ans =
    1.4552e-11
```

which is practically equal to zero. The reader is invited to check also the sum of the moments about the point C.

We can continue our exercise by **simulating** the behaviour of the force F as the cylinder EO extends under constant oil flow, that is, with **constant velocity**. We assume that starting from position CD, the platform must reach the position C'D' in 10 seconds. In order to do this the length $\overline{OE}$ must vary from 0.9 to 1.4 m with a speed of 0.05 m/s. We find the angle $\widehat{AEO}$ from the cosine law

$$\overline{AO}^2 = \overline{AE}^2 + \overline{EO}^2 - 2\overline{AE} \cdot \overline{EO} \cos \widehat{AEO}$$

and so the angle $\widehat{ABC} = \widehat{BAD}$

$$\overline{EO}^2 = \overline{AE}^2 + \overline{AO}^2 - 2\overline{AE} \cdot \overline{AO} \cos \widehat{BAD}$$

The following program will do the job:

```
%SCISSOR.M - simulation of a scissor elevating platform.
% program SCISSOR.M simulates the behaviour of the force F
% in a hydraulic cylinder which actuates a scissors-like
% elevating platform.
% declare constants
AO = 1.7;        % m
AE = 1.85;       % m
BC = 3.4;        % m
W  = 20000;      % N
d  = 0.5;        % m
V  = 0.05;       % m/s
a  = 0.9;        % initial cylinder length
% _____
time = [ ];      % initiate array of time values
F  = [ ];        % initiate array of F values
% _____ begin loop _____
```

```
for t = 0: 0.25: 10      % s
    time = [ time t ];  % update array of time values
    EO = a + V*t;       % m
    % calculate angles in radians
    AEO = acos((AE*AE + EO*EO - AO*AO)/(2*AE*EO));
    ABC = acos((AE*AE + AO*AO - EO*EO)/(2*AE*AO));
    % calculate matrix of coefficients
    A = [ cos(ABC) 0 -cos(AEO)
          sin(ABC) 1  sin(AEO)
           0 BC*cos(ABC)/2 0 ];
    % calculate vector B
    B = [ 0; 1; -d ]*W;
    % solve system
    X= A\B;
    F = [ F X(3) ];        % update array of force values
end
plot(time, F)
grid
xlabel('time, t, s')
ylabel('cylinder force, F, N')
```

The program begins with a few comment lines that define its aim. The MATLAB help scissor command displays these lines on the screen, allowing the user to decide whether he is interested in running the program or not. The MATLAB 4 lookfor scissor command searches for the string scissor in the first comment line in all M-files found on MATLAB's search path and displays all lines in which the string is found. In order to use this facility it is good practice to write the first command line as a brief but helpful definition of the program.

Another good practice is to concentrate the definitions of the constants at the beginning of the program. This makes it easy to find them when changes are required.

Write the program to a file named scissor.m and run it. The graph of the force F as a function of time is shown in Figure 6.7. The reader may also try other plots. For instance, as we found that the maximum of F occurs for $t = 0$, it would be interesting to study the influence of the **offset**, d, of W at that moment.

The way in which the array **F** is updated in the program is computationally inefficient because the size of the array is updated at each step. Improve the program in this respect and run it again.

EXAMPLE 6.5   A statically undetermined problem _____

Many structures can be modelled by linear equations. Formulated in matrix form, these equations can be conveniently solved in MATLAB. Some problems lend themselves to systematic treatment, much like electrical networks (see Examples 6.7 and 6.8). We are going to describe just one example; the interested reader may refer to specialized books. This example follows the treatment in Göldner et al. (1979).

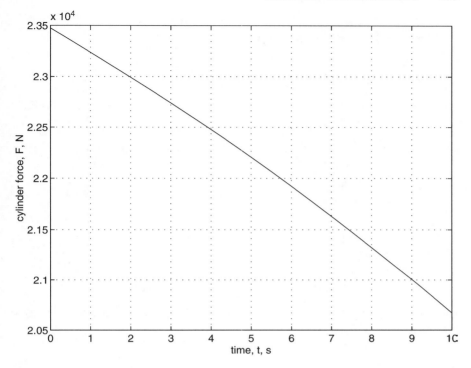

Figure 6.7   Graph obtained with the program SCISSOR.M.

Consider the structure shown in Figure 6.8; it consists of five rods joined by pins at points A, B, C, D, E and O. A vertical force, F, is applied at O. We consider in this example that all rods are made of the same steel with modulus of elasticity (Young's modulus) E, and have the same cross-sectional area, A.

We assume that the articulations allow free rotation; therefore, no moments act on the rods. Let the lengths of the five rods be $\ell_1, \ldots, \ell_5$, where $\ell_1 = \ell_5$ and $\ell_2 = \ell_4$. Five forces, $F_1, \ldots, F_5$, act on the rods, as shown in Figure 6.8(b). The symmetry of the structure implies $F_1 = F_5$ and $F_2 = F_4$. It follows that there are three unknown forces: F_1, F_2, F_3. Let the angle between the rods ℓ_1, ℓ_3 equal $\alpha_1 = \widehat{AOC} = \widehat{EOC}$. Similarly let $\alpha_2 = \widehat{BOC} = \widehat{DOC}$. The equilibrium of forces at O is represented by the equation

$$2F_1 \cos \alpha_1 + 2F_2 \cos \alpha_2 + F_3 = F \qquad (6.40)$$

Statics allow us to write one equation in three variables. We say that the system is **statically undetermined**. To solve the problem we need two additional equations. In practice we add a fourth variable, the elongation of one of the structural members, and this will allow us to write three equations based on elasticity. To do so we consider that, under the force F_1, the length of the rod AO becomes $\ell_1 + \Delta_1 \ell_1$. Similarly, the

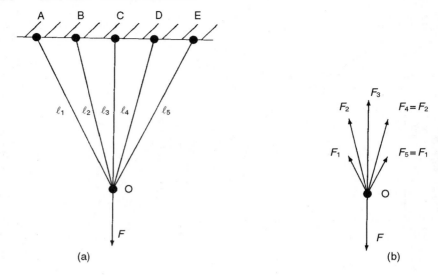

(a)   (b)

Figure 6.8   A statically undetermined structure.

length of the rod BO becomes $\ell_2 + \Delta\ell_2$, and that of CO, $\ell_3 + \Delta\ell_3$. Applying Hooke's law we write

$$\frac{\Delta\ell_1}{\ell_1} = \frac{\sigma_1}{E} = \frac{F_1}{EA} \tag{6.41}$$

$$\frac{\Delta\ell_2}{\ell_2} = \frac{\sigma_2}{E} = \frac{F_2}{EA} \tag{6.42}$$

$$\frac{\Delta\ell_3}{\ell_3} = \frac{\sigma_3}{E} = \frac{F_3}{EA} \tag{6.43}$$

where σ_1 is the stress on the rod AO. Similar notations apply to the rods BO and CO. If $\Delta\ell_1 \ll \ell_3$, and $\Delta\ell_2 \ll \ell_3$, the rotations of the rods around the points A and B are negligible. We can consider then that the angles α_1, α_2 do not change after applying the force F. The situation is shown in Figure 6.9, a zoom of Figure 6.8. Pulled down by the force F, the joint O moves to position O_1 and we can write

$$\Delta\ell_1 = \Delta\ell_3 \cos\alpha_1$$
$$\Delta\ell_2 = \Delta\ell_3 \cos\alpha_2$$

With this assumption Equations 6.41 to 6.43 can be rewritten as

$$\frac{\ell_1}{EA}F_1 - \cos\alpha_1\Delta\ell_3 = 0 \tag{6.44}$$

$$\frac{\ell_2}{EA}F_2 - \cos\alpha_2\Delta\ell_3 = 0 \tag{6.45}$$

$$\frac{\ell_3}{EA}F_3 - \Delta\ell_3 = 0 \tag{6.46}$$

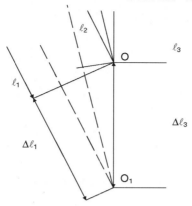

Figure 6.9   Diagram of elongations.

Combining Equation 6.40 and Equations 6.44 to 6.46 in matrix form we obtain

$$
\begin{bmatrix}
2\cos\alpha_1 & 2\cos\alpha_2 & 1 & 0 \\
\ell_1/EA & 0 & 0 & -\cos\alpha_1 \\
0 & \ell_2/EA & 0 & -\cos\alpha_2 \\
0 & 0 & \ell_3/EA & -1
\end{bmatrix}
\begin{bmatrix}
F_1 \\ F_2 \\ F_3 \\ \Delta\ell_3
\end{bmatrix}
=
\begin{bmatrix}
F \\ 0 \\ 0 \\ 0
\end{bmatrix}
=
\quad \textbf{(6.47)}
$$

As a numerical example, let the angles be those shown in the figure, the length $\ell_3 = 1000$ mm, the force $F = 25000$ N, the modulus of elasticity $E = 205000$ N/mm^2, and the cross-sectional area $A = 100$ mm^2. We enter the data in MATLAB by

```
>> alpha1 = atan(1/2); alpha2 = atan(1/4);
>> 13 = 1000; F = 25000; E = 205000, A = 100;
>> 11 = 13/cos(alpha1); 12 = 13/cos(alpha2);
```

and build the matrix of coefficients and the right-hand-side vector with

```
>> C = [ 2*cos(alpha1), 2*cos(alpha2), 1 , 0
   11/(E*A) , 0 , 0 , -cos(alpha1)
   0 , 12/(E*A) , 0 , -cos(alpha2)
   0 , 0 , 13/(E*A), -1 ]
>> B = [ F; 0; 0; 0 ];
```

The solution is obtained with

```
>> X = C \B
X =
    1.0e+003 *
        4.6979
        5.5269
        5.8724
        0.0003
```

It is easy to check that the balance of forces at O is fulfilled by this solution

```
>> 2*X(1)*cos(alpha1) + 2*X(2)*cos(alpha2) + X(3)
ans =
    25000
```

The reader can verify that the equations of elongations also hold. To calculate the rod stresses in N/mm^2 enter

```
>> X(1:3)/A
ans =
    46.9789
    55.2692
    58.7236
```

These values are lower than those admissible; rods with smaller cross-sectional areas can be chosen.

EXAMPLE 6.6   A DC network _____

Figure 6.10 shows a closed dc loop. There are three current sources, which generate the voltage rises U_1, U_2, U_3, and four resistances, R_1 to R_4. Summing the voltage rises and the voltage drops clockwise we can write for the whole loop

$$-U_1 + IR_1 + U_2 + IR_2 + IR_3 - U_3 + IR_4 = 0$$

or

$$U_1 - U_2 + U_3 = IR_1 + IR_2 + IR_3 + IR_4$$

Generalizing, for any independent, closed loop we can write

$$\sum U_i = \sum IR_i \tag{6.48}$$

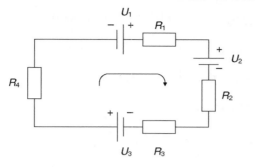

Figure 6.10   Kirchhoff's second law.

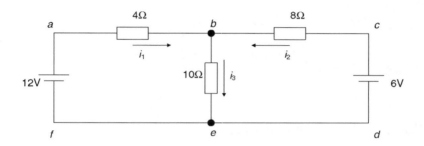

Figure 6.11   A dc network.

Equation 6.48 represents **Kirchhoff's second law** which states that, *in a closed loop, the sum of the instantaneous voltage rises equals the sum of the instantaneous voltage drops, if the summations are carried out in the same direction.*

Kirchhoff's laws – the first of which is described in Example 3.4 and the second in Example 2.13 – yield the equations needed in the analysis of electrical networks. For example, let us consider the network shown in Figure 6.11. Assuming arbitrary senses for the currents, as shown by the arrows, Kirchhoff's second law applied to the closed loop *abef* yields the equation

$$4i_1 + 10i_3 = 12$$

For the closed loop *acdf* the same law gives

$$4i_1 - 8i_2 = 12 - 6$$

Finally, applying Kirchhoff's first law to node *b* we obtain

$$i_1 + i_2 = i_3$$

The system of three equations can be rewritten in matrix form as

$$\begin{bmatrix} 4 & 0 & 10 \\ 4 & -8 & 0 \\ 1 & 1 & -1 \end{bmatrix} \begin{bmatrix} i_1 \\ i_2 \\ i_3 \end{bmatrix} = \begin{bmatrix} 12 \\ 6 \\ 0 \end{bmatrix}$$

The solution in MATLAB is:

```
>> A1 = [ 4 0 10; 4 -8 0; 1 1 -1 ];
>> B1 = [ 12; 6; 0 ];
>> I1 = A1\B1
I1 =
     1.0263
    -0.2368
     0.7895
```

Instead of the closed loop *acdf* it is possible to use the closed loop *cbed* and write the second equation as

$$8i_2 + 10i_3 = 6$$

so that the equation in matrix form becomes

$$\begin{bmatrix} 4 & 0 & 10 \\ 0 & 8 & 10 \\ 1 & 1 & -1 \end{bmatrix} \begin{bmatrix} i_1 \\ i_2 \\ i_3 \end{bmatrix} = \begin{bmatrix} 12 \\ 6 \\ 0 \end{bmatrix}$$

The new MATLAB calculations are

```
>> A2 = [ 4 0 10; 0 8 10; 1 1 -1 ];
>> B2 = [ 12; 6; 0 ];
>> I2 = A2\B2
I2 =
     1.0263
    -0.2368
     0.7895
```

and the results are necessarily the same.

EXAMPLE 6.7 Method of node voltages _____

The electric circuit illustrated in the preceding example is rather simple; electrical networks can be considerably more complex. More systematic approaches are necessary for writing the equations of complex circuits. One method is that of **node currents**; we are going to explain it on the network shown in Figure 6.12.

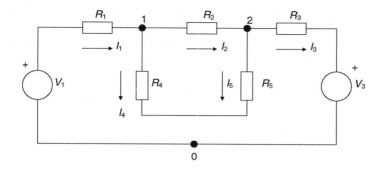

Figure 6.12   An electric network.

We choose node 0 as reference and assume that its voltage is zero. We also assume initially that all currents are directed towards the reference node. Applying Kirchhoff's first law (Kirchhoff's current law) at node 1, and considering the currents that leave the node to be positive, we get

$$-I_1 + I_2 + I_4 = 0 \tag{6.49}$$

Similarly we write for node 2

$$-I_2 + I_3 + I_5 = 0 \tag{6.50}$$

For each current we substitute its value as given by Ohm's law, for example

$$I_1 = G_1(V_1 - U_1)$$

where $G_1 = 1/R_1$ is the **conductance** of the branch between nodes 0 and 1, and U_1 is the voltage of node 1. We obtain in this way a system of linear equations in which the unknowns are the node voltages U_1, U_2 :

$$-G_1(V_1 - U_1) + G_2(U_1 - U_2) + G_4 U_1 \quad = \quad 0$$
$$-G_2(U_1 - U_2) + G_3(U_2 - V_3) + G_5 U_2 \quad = \quad 0$$

or, in matrix form,

$$\begin{bmatrix} (G_1 + G_2 + G_4) & -G_2 \\ -G_2 & (G_2 + G_3 + G_5) \end{bmatrix} \begin{bmatrix} U_1 \\ U_2 \end{bmatrix} = \begin{bmatrix} G_1 V_1 \\ G_3 V_3 \end{bmatrix}$$

In the matrix of conductances the element in position $(1, 1)$ is the sum of all conductances connected to node 1, and the element in position $(2, 2)$ is the sum of all conductances connected to node 2. The element in position $(1, 2)$ is the conductance connecting nodes 1 and 2, with a minus sign. The element in position $(2, 1)$ is equal to that in position $(1, 2)$: the matrix is symmetric. These properties of the matrix of conductances can be easily generalized to more complex networks; they constitute a convenient aid in writing the equations of node voltages directly.

To solve the system in MATLAB we begin by defining the resistances and the voltage sources in the circuit

```
R = [ 4 6 8 10 10 ];
≫ V1 = 12; V3 = 6;
```

We calculate the conductances and build a matrix of conductances by

```
≫ A = 1./R;
≫ G = [ (A(1) + A(2) + A(4)), -A(2)
    -A(2), (A(2) + A(3) + A(5)) ];
```

The vector of current sources is

```
≫ C = [ A(1)*V1; A(3)*V3 ]
```

The node potentials are calculated with

```
≫ U = G\C;
```

Finally, we obtain the branch currents from

```
≫ I1 = zeros(5, 1);
≫ I1(1) = A(1)*(V1 - U(1));
≫ I1(2) = A(2)*(U(1) - U(2));
≫ I1(3) = A(3)*(U(2) - V3);
≫ I1(4) = A(4)*U(1);
≫ I1(5) = A(5)*U(2);
≫ I1
 I1 =
    1.1384
    0.3938
   -0.1146
    0.7446
    0.5084
```

EXAMPLE 6.8   Method of loop currents _____

Another method of analysing networks is that of **loop currents**, also known as **mesh analysis**. We refer again to the network shown in Figure 6.12. We distinguish three independent loops. Let the current in the first loop be J_1, in the second loop, J_2, and

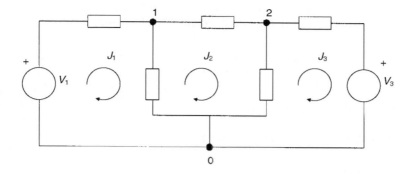

Figure 6.13   An electric network.

in the third loop, J_3, as shown in Figure 6.13. We initially assume that all currents are directed clockwise. For loop 1 we write Kirchhoff's second law (Kirchhoff's voltage law) as follows:

$$R_1 J_1 + R_4(J_1 - J_2) = V_1 \tag{6.51}$$

Similarly for loop 2

$$R_2 J_2 + R_5(J_2 - J_3) + R_4(J_2 - J_1) = 0 \tag{6.52}$$

and for loop 3

$$-R_5 J_2 + (R_3 + R_5)J_3 = -V_3 \tag{6.53}$$

From Equations 6.51, 6.52 and 6.53 we write

$$\begin{bmatrix} R_1 + R_4 & -R_4 & 0 \\ -R_4 & R_2 + R_4 + R_5 & -R_5 \\ 0 & -R_5 & R_3 + R_5 \end{bmatrix} \begin{bmatrix} J_1 \\ J_2 \\ J_3 \end{bmatrix} = \begin{bmatrix} V_1 \\ 0 \\ -V_3 \end{bmatrix}$$

In the matrix of resistances, each element on the main diagonal is the sum of all resistances in a loop. For example, the element in position (1, 1) is the sum of all resistances in the loop of the current J_1. The element in position (1, 2) is the resistance coupling the first and the second loop; it has a minus sign because the currents J_1 and J_2 have opposite directions in R_4. The element in position (1, 3) is zero because no resistance couples the first and the third loop.

The matrix of resistances is symmetric. For example, the element in position (1, 2) is identical to the element in position (2, 1), because what couples the first loop to the second also couples the second loop to the first.

The above properties of the matrix of resistances are general; they can be used for writing the matrix equation of loop currents directly.

In MATLAB, using the same values as in the preceding example, we begin by building the matrix of resistances and the vector of voltage sources:

```
≫ RR = [ (R(1) + R(4)), -R(4), 0
    -R(4), (R(2) + R(4) + R(5)), -R(5)
    0, -R(5), (R(3) + R(5)) ]
≫ V = [ V1; 0; -V3]
```

The loop currents are calculated with

```
≫ J = RR\V;
```

and the branch currents with

```
≫ I2 = zeros(5, 1);
≫ I2(1) = J(1);
≫ I2(2) = J(2);
≫ I2(3) = J(3);
≫ I2(4) = J(1) - J(2);
≫ I2(5) = J(2) - J(3);
≫ I2
I2 =
      1.1384
      0.3938
     -0.1146
      0.7446
      0.5084
```

These are exactly the results obtained by the method of node voltages; in the short format they are identical to the fourth decimal digit, that is, $1/10$ mA, sufficient for most engineering purposes. The reader who likes more precision may try the following test (assuming that the results of the previous example are still available):

```
≫ I2 - I1
ans =
    1.0e-015 *
         0
      0.3331
     -0.3192
         0
     -0.2220
```

Remarkably close, indeed.

EXAMPLE 6.9   A simple ac network _____

The methods described in the preceding two examples can be immediately applied to ac networks. For a simple illustration consider the network shown in Figure 6.14 and the values

$$
\begin{aligned}
R_1 &= 5\,\Omega \\
R_2 &= 6\,\Omega \\
R_3 &= 6\,\Omega \\
L_2 &= 0.06\,\text{H} \\
C_3 &= 100\,\text{pF} \\
V_0 &= 220\,\text{V} \\
&\quad\ 50\,\text{Hz}
\end{aligned}
$$

The branch impedances are given by

$$
\begin{aligned}
Z1 &= R_1 \\
Z2 &= R_2 + jL_2\omega \\
Z3 &= R_3 + \frac{j}{C_3\omega}
\end{aligned}
$$

To apply the method of node voltages we choose node 0 as reference and write Kirchhoff's current law at node 1:

$$-i1 + i2 + i3 = 0 \tag{6.54}$$

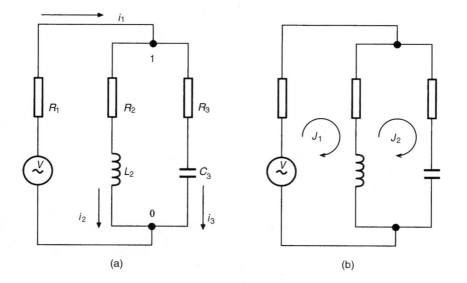

(a)   (b)

Figure 6.14   A simple ac network.

Denoting by U_1 the voltage of node 1, and the branch **admittances** by $Y_1 = 1/R_1$, $Y_2 = 1/Z_1$, $Y_3 = 1/Z_3$, we rewrite Equation 6.54 as

$$-Y_1(V - U_1) + Y_2 U_1 + Y_3 U_1 = 0$$

or

$$(Y_1 + Y_2 + Y_3)U_1 = Y_1 V_0$$

Naturally, the properties of the matrix of conductances described in Example 6.7 also hold for this 1-by-1 matrix of admittances: $(Y_1 + Y_2 + Y_3)$ is the sum of all admittances connected to node 1.

To begin the calculations in MATLAB define the elements of the network:

```
>> R1 = 5; R2 = 6; R3 = 6; L2 = 0.06; C3 = 100*10^(-6);
>> V = 220; w = 2*pi*50;
```

Next calculate the complex impedances and admittances in each branch:

```
>> Z2 = R2 + 0.05*w*j;
>> Z3 = R3 - j/(C3*w);
>> Y1 = 1/R1, Y2 = 1/Z2, Y3 = 1/Z3;
```

The voltage of node 1 and the branch currents are obtained from

```
>> U1 = (Y1 + Y2 + Y3) \Y1*V
>> I1 = Y1*(V - U1)
>> I2 = Y2*U1
>> I3 = Y3*U1
I1 =
    5.6961 - 4.2564i
I2 =
    5.2466 - 10.1885i
I3 =
    0.4496 + 5.9320i
```

It is easy to check that Kirchhoff's current law is fulfilled at node 1:

```
>> -I1 + I2 + I3
ans =
    3.8858e-016
```

For our purposes the result may be regarded as equal to zero; it is not exactly so because of the accumulation of numerical errors. To verify this try (see Section 2.6):

```
≫ I3 + I2 - I1
ans =
    0
```

To analyse the same network by the mesh method we consider the currents J_1, J_2 in the two independent loops, as shown in Figure 6.14(b), and write the two equations

$$
-R_1 J_1 + Z_2(J_1 - J_2) \quad = \quad V_0
$$
$$
Z_2(J_2 - J_1) + Z_3 J_2 \quad = \quad 0
$$

which can be rewritten in matrix form as

$$
\left[\begin{array}{cc} (R_1 + Z_2) & -Z_2 \\ -Z_2 & (Z_2 + Z_3) \end{array} \right] \left[\begin{array}{c} J_1 \\ J_2 \end{array} \right] = \left[\begin{array}{c} V_0 \\ 0 \end{array} \right]
$$

We see immediately that the properties of the matrix of resistances described in Example 6.8 also hold for this matrix of impedances.

In MATLAB we begin by building the matrices of impedance and of voltage sources:

```
≫ Y = [ (R1 + Z2), -Z2; -Z2, (Z2 + Z3) ];
≫ VV = [ V; 0 ];
```

The loop and the branch currents are obtained from

```
≫ J = Y\VV;
≫ I1 = J(1), I2 = J(1) - J(2), I3 = J(2)
I1 =
    5.6961 - 4.2564i
I2 =
    5.2466 - 10.1885i
I3 =
    0.4496 + 5.9320i
```

that is, the same currents as obtained by the node method.

6.12   Examples – polynomial equations

EXAMPLE 6.10   Finding the depth of a well ⸻⸻⸻⸻⸻⸻

In a once popular thriller, a detective was interested in finding the depth of a well. He dropped a stone in it and measured the time that elapsed until he heard the splash. Let t be this time. It is composed of t_1 the time of free fall – that is, the time between the moment the stone was released and the moment it reached the water surface – and t_2, the time the sound took to travel from the water surface to the detective's ear. If g is the acceleration of gravity, d, the well depth (approximately equal to the distance between the hand or the ear of the detective and the water surface), and c, the speed of sound in air,

$$d = \frac{g}{2} \cdot t_1^2$$
$$d = c \cdot t_2$$
$$t = t_1 + t_2$$

In the first equation we obtain the depth, d, as the distance travelled by the freely falling stone during the time t_1. The second equation yields the same depth, d, as the distance travelled by the sound during the time t_2. The third equation says that the total time, t, measured by the detective is the sum of the times t_1 and t_2. Obtaining the values of t_1 and t_2 from the first two equations, and substituting them in the third, we get

$$d^2 - 2(tc + c^2/g)d + c^2t^2 = 0$$

Instead of solving this equation by the well-known formula, let us use the MATLAB roots function. Assuming that the detective counted 2.5 seconds, and taking the speed of sound at atmospheric pressure and 20 °C, we calculate

```
≫ t = 2.5;  % s
≫ g = 9.81;  % m/s^2
≫ c = 343;  % m/s
≫ p(1) = 1;
≫ p(2) = -2*(t*c + c1^2/g);
≫ p(3) = (c*t)^2;
≫ solution = roots(p)
solution =
    1.0e+04 *
    2.5672
    0.0029
```

The first solution corresponds to an impossible well depth; we accept, therefore, the second solution, 29 m. Let us also experiment with the poly function and try to recover the coefficients of the initial equation:

```
>> poly(solution)
ans =
    1.0e+05 *
    0.0000 -0.2570 7.3531
```

This display is obviously inaccurate; we introduced the first coefficient as 1. We can ask for more digits by invoking the MATLAB `format` function:

```
>> format long
>> poly(solution)
ans =
    1.0e+05 *
    0.00001000000000 -0.25700524974516 7.35306250000000
```

For comparison, let us display, in the same format, the coefficients as calculated by us:

```
>> p
p =
    1.0e+05 *
    0.00001000000000 -0.25700524974516 7.35306250000000
```

We can carry out a reverse calculation of the time measured by the detective. We return to the short format and calculate:

```
>> format short
>> depth = solution(2);
>> t1 = sqrt(2*depth/g)
t1 =
    2.4165
>> t2 = depth/c
t2 =
    0.0835
>> t = t1 + t23
t =
    2.5000
```

as initially defined.

EXAMPLE 6.11   Designing a simple float _____

In offshore fish farming fish are grown inside floating cages. One kind of cage consists of a walkway mounted above a number of floats. A net hangs down from the walkway

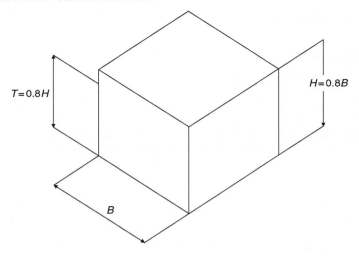

$T=0.8H$

$H=0.8B$

B

Figure 6.15   A simple float.

and fish live in it. The floats must carry the sum of the weights of the walkway, net, farm operators and food containers. Let us suppose that a float of the form shown in Figure 6.15 must be designed in accordance with the following specification:

load	6000 N
base	square, with side B
height	$H = 0.8B$
draught	$T = 0.8H$
plate thickness	3 mm
material	steel
sea water	density $= 1025\,\text{kg/m}^3$

The design equation, based on Archimedes' principle, is

weight of displaced water = own weight + 6000

In order to find the own weight we first calculate the area of the steel plate:

$$\text{area} = 2B^2 + 4BH = 2B^2 + 3.2B^2 = 5.2B^2$$

With a steel density of $7850\,\text{kg/m}^3$, and $g = 9.81\,\text{m/s}^2$, the plate weight in N is

$$W_p = 7850 \times 9.81 \times 0.003 \times \text{area}$$

The weight of the displaced water, that is, the **float displacement**, equals

$$1025 \times 9.81 \times B^2 \times T = 1025 \times 9.81 \times 0.8 \times B^3$$

The design equation becomes

$$c_1 B^3 + c_2 B^2 + c_4 = 0$$

In MATLAB the solution is found with the aid of the `roots` function as follows:

```
>> c(1) = 1025*9.81*0.8;
>> c(2) = -7850*9.81*0.003*5.2;
>> c(3) = 0;
>> c(4) = -6000;
>> B = roots(c)
B =
      0.9595
     -0.4051 + 0.7831i
     -0.4051 - 0.7831i
```

There is only one real solution; the reader may check that it indeed fulfils the specification.

EXAMPLE 6.12   Free vibrations in two degrees of freedom _____

Figure 6.16 shows a system of two masses and two springs. The first spring is hung to a fixed support. The motion of mass m_1 is x_1, that of mass m_2, x_2, and both are measured from the positions of rest of the respective masses. In this position the springs are extended by the weights of the two masses, so that we need not include these weights, $m_1 g$ and $m_2 g$, in the equations to be developed. Two forces act on m_1: one due to the upper spring, which has the **spring constant** k_1, the other due to the lower spring, with spring constant k_2. A deflection x_1, from the position of rest, in the positive sense shown on the figure, causes an upward force, $-k_1 x_1$, in the upper spring. The force exercised by the lower spring on mass m_1 is proportional to the deflection $x_2 - x_1$ of this spring. These considerations allow us to write the equation shown near the first mass, and similar considerations yield the equation written near the second mass. The system is described by two variables, x_1, x_2; therefore, we say that it is a system with **two degrees of freedom**.

Based on experience or on theory we now assume that the motions of the two masses are harmonic, with the same frequency, so that they can be described by

$$
\begin{aligned}
x_1 &= A_1 \sin \omega t \\
x_2 &= A_2 \sin \omega t
\end{aligned}
$$

Substitution in the equations shown in Figure 6.16 gives

$$
\begin{aligned}
-m_1 A_1 \omega^2 + (k_1 + k_2) A_1 - k_2 A_2 &= 0 \\
-m_2 A_2 \omega^2 - k_2 A_1 + k_2 A_2 &= 0
\end{aligned}
$$

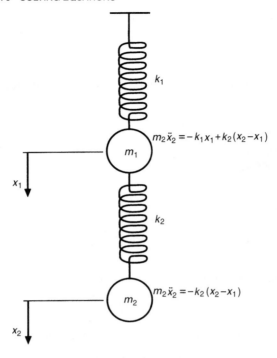

Figure 6.16   A system with two degrees of freedom.

Considering the amplitudes A_1, A_2 as unknowns, we obtain the following system in matrix form:

$$\begin{bmatrix} [(k_1 + k_2) - m_1\omega^2] & -k_2 \\ -k_2 & [k_2 - m_2\omega^2] \end{bmatrix} \begin{bmatrix} A_1 \\ A_2 \end{bmatrix} = 0 \tag{6.55}$$

The homogeneous system in 6.55 has a non-trivial solution only if the determinant of the system is zero, that is

$$\omega^4 - \left[\frac{k_1 + k_2}{m_1} + \frac{k_2}{m_2}\right]\omega^2 + \frac{k_1}{m_1}\frac{k_2}{m_2} = 0 \tag{6.56}$$

Equation 6.56, called the **characteristic equation** of the system, yields, in general, two roots, ω_1^2 and ω_2^2. The **natural frequencies** of the system are ω_1 and ω_2. We use the positive square roots; the negative square roots of the solutions represent the same natural frequencies, but we can think of them as related to vectors rotating in the clockwise sense (see Chapter 4 for the representation of harmonic motions by rotating vectors).

As an example, let us consider the following data

$$m_1 = 0.5\,\text{kg}, \qquad\qquad K_1 = 500\,\text{N/m}$$
$$m_2 = 0.25\,\text{kg}, \qquad\qquad K_2 = 250\,\text{N/m}$$

We introduce these values in MATLAB and calculate the coefficients of the characteristic equation:

```
>> m1 = 0.5; m2 = 0.25;
>> k1 = 500; k2 = 250;
>> c(1) = 1;
>> c(2) = -(k1 + k2)/m1 - k2/m2;
>> c(3) = k1*k2/(m1*m2);
>> c
c =
    1 -2500 1000000
```

The solutions of this equation are obtained with

```
>> omega2 = roots(c)
omega2 =
  2000
   500
```

The natural angular frequencies, in rad/s, are

```
>> omega = sqrt(omega2)
omega =
    44.7214
    22.3607
```

and in Hz

```
>> f = omega/(2*pi)
f =
    7.1176
    3.5588
```

EXAMPLE 6.13   Free oscillations of an electrical circuit _____

Figure 6.17 represents an electrical circuit that can be described by two variables, namely two currents. We say, therefore, that it is a system with **two degrees of freedom**. Assuming that no voltage is impressed upon this circuit, the governing equations are

$$L_1 \frac{di_1}{dt} + \frac{1}{C_1} \int (i_1 - i_2)dt \quad = \quad 0 \tag{6.57}$$

$$\frac{1}{C_1} \int (i_2 - i_1)dt + L_2 \frac{di_2}{dt} + \frac{1}{C_2} \int i_2 dt \quad = \quad 0 \tag{6.58}$$

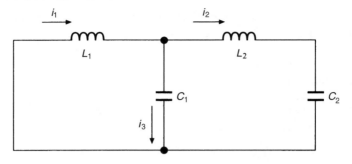

Figure 6.17   An electrical, two-degrees of freedom system.

Substituting

$$i_1 = I_1 \sin \omega t, \quad i_2 = I_2 \sin \omega t \tag{6.59}$$

into Equations 6.57 and 6.58, and considering I_1, I_2 as unknowns, yields

$$\begin{bmatrix} L_1\omega - 1/C_1\omega & 1/C_1\omega \\ 1/C_1\omega & L_2\omega - 1/C_1\omega - 1/C_2\omega \end{bmatrix} \begin{bmatrix} I_1 \\ I_2 \end{bmatrix} = \begin{bmatrix} 0 \\ 0 \end{bmatrix} \tag{6.60}$$

A non-trivial solution is possible only if the determinant of the coefficient matrix is zero, that is

$$\begin{bmatrix} L_1\omega - 1/C_1\omega & 1/C_1\omega \\ 1/C_1\omega & L_2\omega - 1/C_1\omega - 1/C_2\omega \end{bmatrix} = 0 \tag{6.61}$$

This condition leads to the equation

$$\omega^4 - \left(\frac{1}{L_1 C_1} + \frac{1}{L_2 C_1} + \frac{1}{L_2 C_2} \right) \omega^2 + \frac{1}{L_1 C_1} \cdot \frac{1}{L_2 C_2} = 0 \tag{6.62}$$

Let us enter, for example, the following values

```
≫ L1 = 0.05; % H
≫ C1 = 100*10^(-6); % F
≫ L2 = 0.07; % H
≫ C2 = 150*10^(-6); % F (150mF)
```

and calculate the coefficients in Equation 6.62:

```
≫ p2 = 1/(L1*C1) + 1/(L2*C1) + 1/(L2*C2);
≫ p3 = 1/(L1*L2*C1*C2);
```

```
≫ p = [ 1 -p2 p3 ]
p =
    1.0e+10 *
    0.0000 -0.0000 1.9048
```

To read more significant digits we must change the format:

```
≫ format long
≫ p
p =
    1.0e+10 *
    0.00000000010000 -0.00004380952381 1.90476190476191
≫ omega = sqrt(roots(p))
omega =
    1.0e+02 *
    6.23817518338204
    2.21239557741382
```

The natural frequencies, in hertz, are

```
≫ f = omega/(2*pi)
f =
    99.28364163084427
    35.21136922200577
```

EXAMPLE 6.14   Roots of closed-loop transfer functions ⎯⎯⎯⎯⎯⎯⎯⎯⎯

Figure 6.18 shows the basic block diagram of a feedback system. The number K is the **gain**. The transfer function of the closed-loop system is

$$\frac{R(s)}{C(s)} = \frac{KG(s)}{1 + KG(s)H(s)}$$

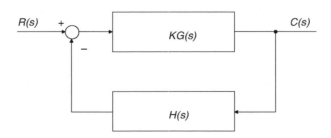

Figure 6.18   A feedback system.

If the transfer function of the forward path, $G(s)$, and the transfer function of the feedback path, $H(s)$, are rational fractions, that is

$$G(s) = \frac{G_{num}}{G_{den}}, \quad H(s) = \frac{H_{num}}{H_{den}}$$

then the transfer function of the closed-loop system is given by

$$\frac{R(s)}{C(s)} = \frac{KG_{num}H_{den}}{G_{den}H_{den} + KG_{num}H_{num}} \tag{6.63}$$

In many cases G_{num}, H_{num}, G_{den}, and H_{den} are polynomials whose roots are known. The denominator in Equation 6.63 has other roots. For denominator degrees higher than 2, finding the roots was once quite a problem; therefore, very ingenious, but tedious, methods were devised for assessing the behaviour of the system in such cases. This is no longer the case with present-day computer facilities. This example, and the following one, show how simple the MATLAB solution is.

Dorf (1992) gives the following example:

$$G(s) = \frac{K}{s(s+2)(s^2 + 4s + 5)}$$
$$H(s) = 1$$

Let us find the roots of the closed-loop transfer function for $K = 6.5$. We enter the data as follows:

```
≫ K = 6.5;
≫ G1 = [1 0]; G2 = [1 2]; G3 = [1 4 5];
```

There is no need to multiply the three factors of the denominator of $G(s)$ manually; let MATLAB do the job. We use for this the convolution operation introduced in Subsection 1.6.4:

```
≫ open = conv(G1, conv(G2, G3))
open =
  1 6 13 10 0
```

In this case the denominator of the closed-loop transfer function is $G_{den} + k$, so that the remaining calculations are

```
≫ closed = open;
≫ l = length(closed);
```

```
≫ closed(1) = K
closed =
    1.0000 6.0000 13.0000 10.0000 6.5000
≫ roots(closed)
ans =
    -2.6507 + 1.2283i
    -2.6507 - 1.2283i
    -0.3493 + 0.7997i
    -0.3493 - 0.7997i
```

According to Dorf, the **dominant roots** are

$$s = -0.35 \pm j0.80$$

The reader is invited to compare the effort required by the MATLAB solution to the effort involved in the conventional **root-locus** method.

EXAMPLE 6.15   Roots of closed-loop transfer functions _____

In a second example, taken from Elgerd (1967), the transfer functions are

$$G(s) = \frac{250K_1}{\pi} \cdot \frac{1}{s^2(s + 10)}$$

$$H(s) = 3\alpha \left(s + \frac{1}{3\alpha} \right)$$

Elgerd assumes the roots $2.65 \pm j3.45$ (the real root is -4.60) and finds the corresponding values

$$\alpha = 0.17, \ K_1 = 1.1$$

We shall start from the latter values and calculate the resulting roots. The following sequence is self-explanatory:

```
≫ alpha = 0.17;
≫ K1 = 1.1;
≫ K = 750*alpha*K1/pi
K =
    44.6430
≫ Gnum = (250*K1/pi)*[1]
Gnum =
    87.5352
```

```
>> Gden = conv([1 0 0], [1 10])
Gden =
     1 10 0 0
>> Hnum = 3*alpha*([0 1 1/(3*alpha)])
Hnum =
     0 0.5100 1.0000
>> Hden = 1;
>> A = conv(Gden, Hden)
A =
     1 10 0 0
>> B = conv(Gnum, Hnum)
B =
     0 44.6430 87.5352
```

At this point we find that the degrees of the polynomials A and B are different. To make addition possible we augment the degree of B and continue as follows:

```
>> closed = A + [0 B]
closed =
     1.0000 10.0000 44.6430 87.5352
>> roots(closed)
ans =
    -4.3673
    -2.8163 + 3.4802i
    -2.8163 - 3.4802i
```

There is a small discrepancy between the roots found above and those assumed by Elgerd. We attribute this to the difference in precision between the methods available in the sixties, and those provided today by MATLAB.

In this, and in the preceding example, we have found the set of roots corresponding to *one K* value. In the root-locus method the roots are determined for a *whole interval* of *K* values. It should not be difficult to do this in the preceding examples; it is sufficient to define an *array* of *K* values at the beginning. For more details, and for the usual MATLAB procedures for calculating and plotting the root locus, see Chapter 16.

6.13   Exercises

Solutions to Exercises 6.2, 6.5, 6.6, 6.8, 6.9, 6.12, 6.14 and 6.18 appear at the back of the book.

■ **EXERCISE 6.1**   Inconsistent linear system
Show in MATLAB that the system

$$4x_1 - 4x_2 = 3$$
$$3x_1 - 3x_2 = 0$$

has no solution. Could you use an elementary property of determinants in order to explain the result? What is the geometric interpretation?

■ **EXERCISE 6.2**   Rational approximations
Find rational approximations of the numbers

$$\pi, \ \sin 30°, \ \sin 45°, \ \tan 45°, \ 0.33333, \ \sqrt{2}\,.$$

Which results are exact? Why are the others not exact?

■ **EXERCISE 6.3**   Problem leading to an underdetermined system
The left-hand part of Figure 6.19 is a schematic drawing of a tank shell. Suppose that we want to obtain the bottom, two faces and the top of the tank by folding a plate, as shown in the right-hand part of the figure. The length of the plate is 12 m, the height, 6 m. Let the length of the tank be $l = 6$ m, the breadth, b, and the height, h. Write the equation whose unknowns are b and h. This is an equation in two variables. To find a unique solution write a second equation, for example one defining the ratio h/b. Alternatively, find the solution for which the cross-section bh is a minimum. Solve the equations in MATLAB.

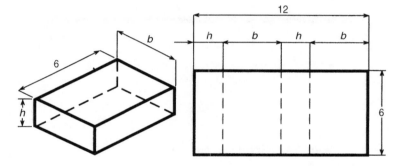

Figure 6.19   A tank and the expansion of four of its faces. Dimensions in m.

■ **EXERCISE 6.4**   An ill-conditioned system of linear equations
The following example of an ill-conditioned system is borrowed from Hartley and Wynn-Evans (1979)

$$\begin{bmatrix} 1/2 & 1/3 & 1/4 \\ 1/3 & 1/4 & 1/5 \\ 1/4 & 1/5 & 1/6 \end{bmatrix} \begin{bmatrix} X(1) \\ X(2) \\ X(3) \end{bmatrix} = \begin{bmatrix} 0.95 \\ 0.67 \\ 0.52 \end{bmatrix}$$

which is of the form

$$AX = B$$

(1)   Calculate the solution of the system as given.
(2)   Change B(3) to 0.53 and calculate the solution again. Compare the relative change in B(3) to the relative change of the solution.
(3)   Calculate the condition number of A and draw conclusions about the solution.

■ **EXERCISE 6.5**   Reactions under a simply-supported beam
Refer to Exercise 2.12, formulate it as a system of two equations and solve it with the MATLAB backslash operation.

■ **EXERCISE 6.6**   Forces on a simply-supported beam
Figure 6.20 shows a simply-supported beam loaded by two unknown forces, F_1 and F_2. The reactions in the two supports were measured and found equal to $R_1 = 500\,\text{N}$ and $R_2 = 980\,\text{N}$.
    Find the forces F_1 and F_2 that caused the above reactions and check your results.

■ **EXERCISE 6.7**   A rope-wheel shaft
Figure 6.21 is a perspective sketch of a shaft carrying a rope wheel. The vertical

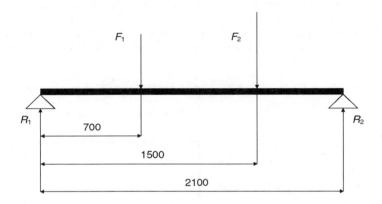

Figure 6.20   Reactions under a simply-supported beam.

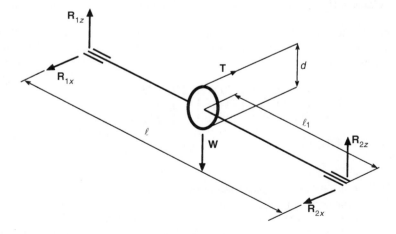

Figure 6.21   A rope-wheel shaft.

vector **W** represents the wheel weight; the horizontal vector **T**, the force transmitted by the rope. The length of the shaft is ℓ, the wheel is placed a distance ℓ_1 from the right-hand bearing, and the wheel diameter is d. The external forces **T** and **W** are opposed in the left-hand bearing by the reaction components $\mathbf{R}_{1x}$, $\mathbf{R}_{1z}$, and in the right-hand bearing by $\mathbf{R}_{2x}$, $\mathbf{R}_{2z}$.

(1)   Write the equilibrium equations in matrix form.
(2)   Solve the equation and find the reactions, assuming the values below.

T	10 N
W	2 N
ℓ	400 mm
ℓ_1	150 mm

(3)   Verify the results by calculating the moments around the left-hand bearing.

■ **EXERCISE 6.8**   Shaping a mooring line
In Figure 6.22 a floating body is held under water by two mooring lines. The floating body has an excess buoyancy (buoyancy force minus weight) $B_f = 10$ kN. In the absence of currents and waves the mooring lines must be symmetric, the angle made by the line segments AB and DE with the horizontal must be 20°, and by the line segments BC and EF, 10° (see Figure 6.22(b) for details). To obtain these angles, two equal weights, W, are hung at points B and E.

Let the tensions in the segments AB and DE be T_1; those in the segments BC and EF, T_2. Then:

(1)   Calculate the line tensions, T_1, T_2, and the weights W;
(2)   Express the external forces (the excess buoyancy force, the weights, and the reactions at A, E, D and H) as vectors and verify your results by showing that the sum of the external forces is null.

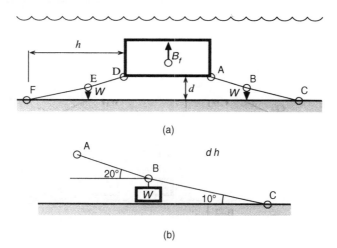

(a)

(b)

Figure 6.22   Mooring lines.

■ **EXERCISE 6.9**   Mooring-line lengths
Calculate the array of lengths

$$L = \begin{bmatrix} \overline{AB} \\ \overline{BC} \end{bmatrix}$$

in Figure 6.22 so that $h = 8$ and $d = 2$.

■ **EXERCISE 6.10**   Shaping a mooring line
In Figure 6.23 a floating body is moored under the water by two lines. The floating
body has an excess buoyancy force (buoyancy force minus weight) $B_f = 10\,\text{kN}$. In the
absence of currents and waves the mooring lines must be symmetric, the angle made
by the line segments AB and EF with the horizontal must be 40°, by the line segments
BC and FG, 30°, and by the segments CD and GH, 20°. To obtain these angles, two
equal weights, W_1, are hung at points B and F, and two other equal weights, W_2, are
hung at points C and G.

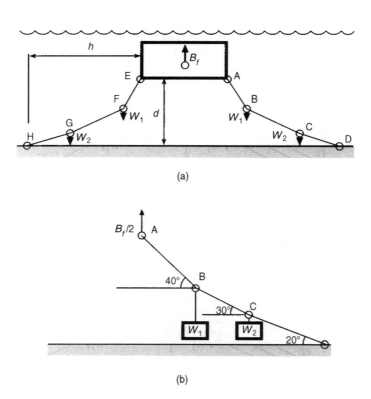

(a)

(b)

Figure 6.23   Mooring lines.

Let the tensions in the segments AB and EF be T_1; those in the segments BC and FG, T_2, and in the segments CD and GH, T_3. Then:

(1)   Calculate the line tensions, T_1, T_2, T_3, and the weights, W_1, W_2;
(2)   Express the external forces (the excess buoyancy force, the weights and the reactions at C and F) as vectors and verify your results by showing that the sum of the external forces is null.

■ **EXERCISE 6.11**   Mooring-line lengths
Calculate the array of lengths

$$L = \begin{bmatrix} \overline{AB} \\ \overline{BC} \\ \overline{CD} \end{bmatrix}$$

in Figure 6.23 so that $h = 9$ and $d = 5$.

■ **EXERCISE 6.12**   Ayrton shunts
In Exercises 3.13 and 3.15 we saw one way of using shunting resistances to extend the range of an ammeter. Proceeding thus, the ammeter can measure currents higher than its rating. The **Ayrton shunt** is another method of achieving the same result.
Figure 6.24 is the diagram of a multirange ammeter that uses Ayrton shunts.
    Calculate the resistances R_1 to R_4 that respond to the following specification

Cursor position	Range mA
A	0–10
B	0–50
C	0–100
D	0–500

The range of the ammeter M is 0–1 mA and its internal resistance equals 55 Ω.

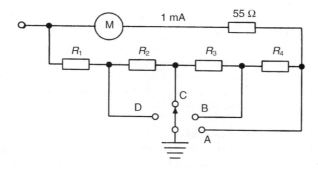

Figure 6.24   Ayrton shunts.

Hint: The voltage across the series connection of resistors at the left of the cursor equals the voltage across the series connection at the right of the cursor. For example, with the cursor in position D the current to be shunted by the resistance R_1 is $500 - 1$ mA and the voltage across it is $499 \times R_1$. The current through the series connection of the remaining four resistances is 1 mA and the voltage across this connection equals $1 \times (55 + R_4 + R_3 + R_2)$ mA. The two voltages must be equal. Reasoning in this way for the whole scheme you get four equations for the four unknown resistances.

■ **EXERCISE 6.13**   Ayrton shunts
Exercise 6.12 refers to a multirange ammeter that uses Ayrton shunts as in Figure 6.24. The diagram suits five measuring ranges. Let us extend the scheme to include a sixth range with a cursor position named F. Calculate the resistances R_1 to R_5 that answer the following specification:

Cursor position	Range mA
A	0–5
B	0–20
C	0–100
D	0–200
E	0–1000
F	0–2000

The range of the ammeter M is 0–5 mA and its internal resistance equals 8.5 Ω.

■ **EXERCISE 6.14**   Designing a weight
Figure 6.25 shows a cylindrical weight; it consists of a cylindrical steel shell, two steel end plates, and a concrete filling. The welds connecting the plates are not shown and their mass may be neglected in calculations. The required mass is 45 kg, the steel-plate thickness is 5 mm. Let the internal diameter of the cylindrical shell be d; the height, $h = 2d$.

Calculate the diameter d that satisfies the specification. Assume a steel density equal to $7850 \, \text{kg m}^{-3}$ and a concrete density equal to $2300 \, \text{kg m}^{-3}$.

■ **EXERCISE 6.15**   Designing a weight
After reading Exercise 6.14 attentively, write a program that will yield the values of the diameter, d, for the thickness values $t = 5, 5.5, 6, \ldots, 10$ mm, and the mass values $M = 50, 75, \ldots, 150$ kg. Plot on one graph the curves of the diameter values as functions of thickness, wit M as parameter. More specifically, on the same graph, for each M value plot a curve of d versus t.

■ **EXERCISE 6.16**   Designing a weight
Repeat Exercise 6.14 for the array of mass values $M = 45, 55, \ldots, 95$ kg. Print a table of diameter values, d, in mm, as functions of the mass values, M, in kg. Plot d against M.

Hint: Take into consideration only real roots.

■ **EXERCISE 6.17**   Designing a weight
Repeat Exercise 6.14 for the array of thicknesses $t = 0.005, 0.006, \ldots, 0.01$ m. Print
a table of diameter values, in mm, as functions of the thickness values, in mm. Plot the
diameter values versus the thickness values.

   Hint: Take into consideration only real roots.

■ **EXERCISE 6.18**   Ayrton shunts
The method of Ayrton shunts is described in Exercises 6.12 and 6.13. Write a function
that, given

- the array of desired current ranges in mA;
- the range of the measuring movement in mA;
- the internal resistance of the movement in Ω,

calculates the array of shunts.

■ **EXERCISE 6.19**   Strange polynomial roots
Numerical calculations can sometimes produce spurious results. To give an example,
consider the polynomial equation

$$(x - 1)^3 = 0$$

It obviously has the triple root $x_1 = x_2 = x_3 = 1$. Expand the expression and you will
obtain the well-known binomial coefficients. Arrange the coefficients, in order of
descending powers of x, in the array c, and try `roots(c)`. In the default `short` format
the results may look OK. However, repeat the calculations after the `format long`
command and you will obtain unexpected results.

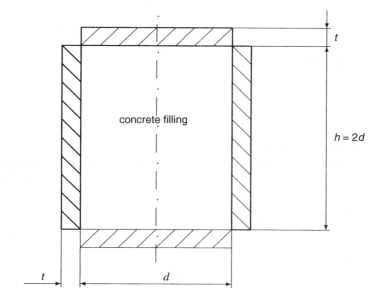

Figure 6.25   A weight.

Without explaining what happens, it may be sufficient to warn the reader again that numerical results are only approximations. It is up to the engineer to appreciate in each case if the approximation is sufficiently good for his particular application.

■ **EXERCISE 6.20**   Strange polynomial roots
Repeat Exercise 6.19 for

$$(x - 1)^4 = 0$$
$$(x - 1)^5 = 0$$

■ **EXERCISE 6.21**   Tank filling
Figure 6.26 is a section through a spherical tank whose inner diameter is $D = 2\,\text{m}$. The tank is filled with sea water of density $1.025\,\text{t m}^{-3}$ up to the height h.

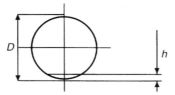

Figure 6.26   Filling height in spherical tank.

(a)   Calculate the filling height h corresponding to the sea-water mass $M = 1\,\text{t}$. Check your result.
(b)   Calculate the filling height h corresponding to the sea-water mass $M = 2\,\text{t}$. Check your result.

Hint: The volume of a spherical cap of height h and a sphere radius r is

$$V = \frac{\pi h^2}{3}(3R - h)$$

■ **EXERCISE 6.22**   Series connection of four resistors
Figure 6.27(a) shows a series connection of four resistors (pure resistances) whose values increase geometrically in the ratio r. Let the first resistance be R_0 and the required, equivalent resistance be R – see Figure 6.27(b).

(a)   Express the problem as an equation in r.
(b)   Solve the equation for $R_0/R = 0.8$ and show that the problem has no solution in this case.
(c)   Show that the proposed problem has only a trivial solution if $R/R_0 = 1.0$.
(d)   Find r for $R_0/R = 2$. Verify your solution.
(e)   Find r for $R_0/R = 4$. Explain this result.
(f)   Find r for $R_0/R = 8$. Verify your solution.

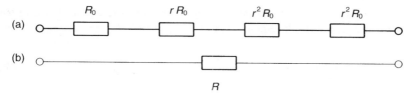

$$R_0 \qquad r\,R_0 \qquad r^2 R_0 \qquad r^2 R_0$$

(a)

(b)

$$R$$

Figure 6.27   Series connection of four resistors.

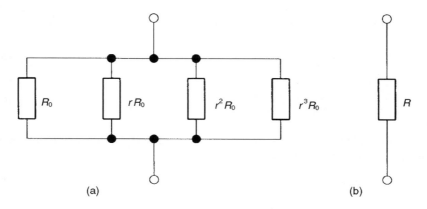

(a)   (b)

Figure 6.28   Parallel connection of four resistors.

■ **EXERCISE 6.23**   Parallel connection of four resistors

Figure 6.28 shows a parallel connection of four resistors (pure resistances) whose values increase geometrically in the ratio r. Let the first resistance be R_0 and the required, equivalent resistance be R (Figure 6.28(b)).

(a)   Express the problem as an equation in r.

(b)   Solve the equation for $R_0/R = 0.8$ and show that the problem has no solution in this case.

(c)   Show that the proposed problem has no solution if $R_0/R = 1.0$.

(d)   Find r for $R_0/R = 2$. Verify your solution.

(e)   Find r for $R_0/R = 4$. Explain this result.

(f)   Find r for $R_0/R = 10$. Verify your solution.

6.14   Appendix – least squares fit

In Section 6.5 we derived the equation

$$\mathcal{E} = \sum_{i=1}^{m} e_i^2 = \sum_{i=1}^{m} (y_i - a - bx_i)^2$$

Looking for a and b values that minimize $\mathcal{E}$, we differentiate $\mathcal{E}$ with respect to a and b and set the results equal to zero:

$$\frac{\partial \mathcal{E}}{\partial a} = -2 \sum_{i=1}^{m} (y_i - a - bx_i) = 0 \tag{6.64}$$

$$\frac{\partial \mathcal{E}}{\partial b} = -2 \sum_{i=1}^{m} x_i (y_i - a - bx_i) = 0 \tag{6.65}$$

This is a system that can be brought to the form

$$n \cdot a + \sum_{i=1}^{m} x_i \cdot b = \sum_{i=1}^{m} y_i \tag{6.66}$$

$$\sum_{i=1}^{m} x_i \cdot a + \sum_{i=1}^{m} x_i^2 \cdot b = \sum_{i=1}^{n} x_i y_i \tag{6.67}$$

Returning now to the system of equations of the type shown in Equation 6.19, we write it in matrix form as

$$\mathbf{Y} = \mathbf{AX} + \mathbf{E} \tag{6.68}$$

where,

$$\mathbf{Y} = \begin{bmatrix} y_1 \\ y_2 \\ \vdots \\ y_m \end{bmatrix} , \quad \mathbf{A} = \begin{bmatrix} 1 & x_1 \\ 1 & x_2 \\ \vdots & \vdots \\ 1 & x_m \end{bmatrix} , \quad \mathbf{X} = \begin{bmatrix} a \\ b \end{bmatrix} , \quad \mathbf{E} = \begin{bmatrix} e_1 \\ e_2 \\ \vdots \\ e_m \end{bmatrix}$$

It can be easily shown that, with the same notations, Equations 6.66 and 6.67 become

$$\mathbf{A'AX} = \mathbf{A'Y} \tag{6.69}$$

where $\mathbf{A'}$ means, as in MATLAB, the transpose of $\mathbf{A}$. Assuming that $\mathbf{A'A}$ is invertible – which usually happens with data obtained from physical problems – the solution of System 6.69 is

$$\begin{bmatrix} a \\ b \end{bmatrix} = (\mathbf{A'A})^{-1} \mathbf{A'Y} \tag{6.70}$$

The **extremum** defined by Equations 6.64 and 6.65 is, indeed, a mimimum. To prove this it is necessary and sufficient to show that

$$\begin{vmatrix} \dfrac{\partial^2 \mathcal{E}}{\partial a^2} & \dfrac{\partial^2 \mathcal{E}}{\partial a\, \partial b} \\[2ex] \dfrac{\partial^2 \mathcal{E}}{\partial b\, \partial a} & \dfrac{\partial^2 \mathcal{E}}{\partial b^2} \end{vmatrix} > 0 \tag{6.71}$$

Calculating the partial derivatives from Equations 6.64 and 6.65, and substituting them into the determinant of 6.71, yields

$$\frac{\partial^2 \mathcal{E}}{\partial a^2} \cdot \frac{\partial^2 \mathcal{E}}{\partial b^2} - \frac{\partial^2 \mathcal{E}}{\partial a\, \partial b}^2 = m \sum_{i=1}^{m} x_i^2 - \left(\sum_{i=1}^{m} x_i\right)^2$$

$$= (x_1 - x_2)^2 + (x_2 - x_3)^2 + \cdots$$

The sum contains all the combinations $(x_i - x_j)^2$, $i < j$, for $i, j = 1, \ldots, m$. The important result is that we got a sum of squares, and as we assumed x_i values different from one another, this sum is always positive. A geometrical proof that the derivation yields a minimum can be found, for example, in Fraleigh and Beauregard (1990), or in Hill (1988).

Chapter 7
Programming in MATLAB

7.1 Introduction

In Chapter 4 we learned how to write simple programs in MATLAB; in Chapter 5, how to write simple functions. In this chapter we shall learn the other control structures provided by MATLAB, namely **conditional branching** and **WHILE loops**. An important application described in this chapter is the solution of equations by **iterations**. A condition under which iterative procedures converge is briefly described in an Appendix.

This chapter also contains a brief introduction to **complexity**, namely the estimation of algorithm performance in terms of the number of elementary operations required to solve a problem, as a function of the number of input data.

7.2 Conditional branching

In the programs we have met so far, a series of statements were executed one after another, in the order in which they were written. Such a simple **control structure**, composed of **serial** or **sequential statements**, can be represented schematically as

```
S1
S2
S3
```

The meaning of this scheme is: the execution of statement S_1 is followed by the execution of statement S_2, which is followed by the execution of S_3.

A different control structure is necessary when a statement, or sequence of statements, should be executed only if a certain condition is fulfilled. If the condition is not fulfilled, another statement, or series of statements, should be executed. The corresponding **conditional branching** structure is programmed in MATLAB as

```
if A
        S1
else
        S2
end
```

Above, and in the following scheme, S1 and S2 may be single statements or sequences of statements.

In the simplest form of a conditional statement the second branching can be omitted

```
if A
        S1
end
```

We shall use the 'if else' control structure to program the **unit step function** defined by

$$y = \begin{cases} 0 \text{ if } t < t_0 \\ 1 \text{ otherwise} \end{cases}$$

Usually t is the time variable, that is, an array of increasing numbers. The graph of this function is shown in Figure 7.1(a). The step function idealizes sudden inputs to processes, for example, the depressing of an electric switch, or the opening of an electromagnetically actuated hydraulic control valve. The verb 'idealizes' is used here because, in reality, the build-up of a physical process requires some time, even if very short. Step functions are used in the study of dynamic systems and in the analysis of automatic control systems.

The following MATLAB code generates the unit-step function:

```
function y = ustep(t, t0)
%USTEP(t, t0) unit step at t0.

[m, n] = size(t);
y = zeros(m, n);   % initialize y array of points
for k = 1: length(t)
        if t(k) < t0
                y(k) = 0;
        else
```

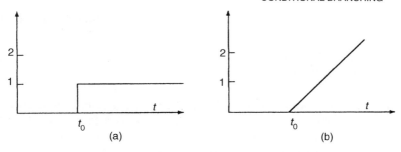

Figure 7.1   (a) Unit step; (b) unit ramp.

```
                y(k) = 1;
        end
end
```

As an exercise generate a suitable time array and plot the function

```
z = ustep(t, 2) - ustep(t, 3)
```

The time, t, is represented in the computer by a finite number of discrete points, namely the elements of the array t. Therefore the graph will not show a perfectly vertical line between the last value $z = 0$ and the first value $z = 1$. The slope of this line will depend upon the spacing of t values, and so will the slope of other theoretically vertical lines.

The output variable y was initialized as an array of zeros; therefore, the first part of the conditional structure may be omitted and the function ustep can be simplified to

```
function y = ustep(t, t0)
%USTEP(t, t0) unit step at t0.

[m, n] = size(t);
y = zeros(m, n);   % initialize y array of points
for k = 1: length(t)
        if t(k) >= t0
                y(k) = 1;
        end
end
```

This is the simplest form of a conditional structure

```
if A
        S1
end
```

The integral of the unit-step function is the **unit-ramp function** defined by

$$y = \begin{cases} 0 & \text{if } t < t_0 \\ t - t_0 & \text{otherwise} \end{cases}$$

The corresponding graph is shown in Figure 7.1(b). The unit-ramp function can be used for the ideal representation of gradual inputs to processes, for example the gradual opening of a valve, pushing an engine throttle lever, or depressing the accelerator pedal in a motor car. The following MATLAB code generates a unit ramp:

```
function y = uramp(t, t0)
%URAMP(t, t0) unit ramp function beginning at t0.

[m, n] = size(t);
y = zeros(m, n);   % initialize y array of proper size
for k = 1: length(t)
        if t(k) >= t0
                y(k) = t(k) - t0;
        end
end
```

As an exercise, using the same time array generated for the example of step functions, plot the function

```
z = uramp(t, 2) - uramp(t, 3)
```

Conditional branching can be more complex, for instance: if the condition A is fulfilled, the sequence S_1 should be executed, if the condition B is fulfilled, the sequence S_2 should be executed, and if neither condition is fulfilled, the sequence S_3 should be executed. Such a control structure is programmed in MATLAB as

```
if A
        S1
elseif B
        S2
else
        S3
end
```

An elaborate example is given in Section 7.5.

In most applications, A is a logical expression having a scalar value, that is, 1 for true and 0 for false. More generally, MATLAB allows A to be a matrix. This is tricky and one must consult the manual carefully. In this context see also the any and all functions.

7.3 WHILE loops

Sometimes it is necessary to repeat the execution of a statement, or of a sequence of statements. This was the case of the program shown in Section 4.10. The control structure employed there was a **FOR loop** in which the number of repetitions was defined from the beginning. In other programs it is necessary to repeat a statement, or a sequence of statements, as long as a certain condition is fulfilled. MATLAB, like some other programming languages, provides a control structure called a **WHILE loop** for this purpose. Before the first execution, and after each subsequent execution of the sequence of repetitive statements, the condition is tested and, if it is still fulfilled, the statements are executed again; if not, the control is passed to the first statement following the end of the loop.

We shall use a WHILE loop in a program that calculates the **greatest common divisor** of two numbers, x and y. In its accepted sense, the definition of the greatest common divisor applies to integers:

If x and y are integers, not both zero, then their greatest common divisor denoted by $\gcd(x, y)$, *is the largest integer that divides both of them (that is, without remainder)* (Alagić and Arbib 1978). MATLAB has a function, gcd, which yields the greatest common divisor of two integers.

In engineering problems it may be useful to extend the definition to numbers that are not integers. Consider, for example, the following problem:

Given a hall 18.6 m long and 7.8 m wide, what is the length of the side of the largest square tile suitable for covering the floor without having to trim any tiles?

The answer is 0.6 m and this number may be considered, in an extended sense, as the greatest common divisor of 18.6 and 7.8.

A systematic approach to the design of a program for finding $\gcd(x, y)$ – obviously for integers – is described at the very beginning of the book by Alagić and Arbib (1978). A program consists of a finite number of instructions to be executed by the computer. The set of instructions that solves a particular problem is called an **algorithm**, a word whose origin is the name of the 9th-century Arab mathematician Muhammad ibn Mūsā al-Khwārizmi. Perhaps the earliest known instance of an algorithm applies to the problem described here and it is attributed to Euclid (Greek, *c*. 300 BC). Given any two numbers, x and y, and assuming for our convenience $x > y$, the following relationship holds

$$x = q \times y + r \tag{7.1}$$

where the **quotient** q is the integer obtained by dividing x by y, and r is the **remainder**. Without restricting Equation 7.1 to integers, for our problem we may write

$$18.6 = 2 \times 7.8 + 3$$

As $\gcd(x, y)$ divides x, it also must divide the right-hand side of Equation 7.1. From here it follows that $\gcd(x, y)$ must divide r and then

$$\gcd(x, y) = \gcd(y, r)$$

We may therefore substitute x by y and y by r without changing the result of the algorithm:

$$7.8 = 2 \times 3 + 1.8$$

Repeating this substitution we shall reach the stage in which the smallest number, that is, the one in the initial place of y, becomes 0. Then, the largest number, namely the one in the place of x, is $\gcd(x, y)$. The continuation of our example is the sequence

$$3 = 1 \times 1.8 + 1.2$$
$$1.8 = 1 \times 1.2 + 0.6$$
$$1.2 = 2 \times 0.6 + 0.0$$

with the result $\gcd(18.6, 7.8) = 0.6$. This algorithm can be implemented in MATLAB by the following function:

```
function z = gcd1(x, y, tol)
%GCD1        greatest common divisor.
% GCD1(x, y, tol)    greatest common divisor of real x, y
%        evaluated with the precision tol. If the third
%        argument is not specified, tol = 1.0E-4.

if nargin == 2
        tol = 1.0E-4;
end
if tol <= 0
        error('Argument tol must be strictly positive')
end
if (sum(size(x) ~= 2)|(sum(size(y)) ~= 2)
      error('Arguments are not scalars, calculation aborted')
end
if x < 0
        x = -x;
end
if y < 0
        y = -y;
end
while y > tol
        r = rem(x,y);
        x = y;
        y = r;
end
z = x;
```

The `nargin` function finds the number of input arguments. If the third argument, `tol`, is specified, the program skips over the first three lines; if not, the condition `nargin == 2` is true and `tol` is set to 0.0001.

The symbol '`|`' stands for the **logical operator** OR; here it means that if either condition (`sum(size(x))` `~= 2`) or (`sum(size(y))` `~= 2`) is true, an error message is issued and the calculation is stopped.

The condition that governs the WHILE loop should be $y > 0$. For engineering purposes the process may be stopped when the remainder becomes smaller than the measurement, or other errors involved in the formulation of the problem. By setting the tolerance argument, `tol`, to 0.0001 we get a fair chance that the first three decimal digits of the result are exact. To be sure, we must examine the convergence of the iterations, as shown, for example in Hartley and Wynn-Evans (1979). Then, if the two numbers, x and y, are lengths measured in metres, the third decimal digit represents millimetres. If this precision is not sufficient, the user may change the value of `tol` by specifying the third input argument.

The MATLAB built-in function `rem(x, y)` yields the **remainder** of the **integer division** of x by y. The reader is invited to experiment with this function, beginning of course with the calculation of gcd 1(18.6, 7.8). The algorithm also functions for negative arguments. Try, for example,

```
gcd1(-18.6, 7.8), gcd1(18.6, -7.8), gcd1(-18.6, -7.8)
```

Can you find the meanings of your results?

7.4   Iterative solution of equations

We return to the problem solved graphically in Section 2.11 and are now going to design a numerical solution. Consider in Figure 7.2 a circle with its centre at O, and the *segment* delimited by the arc ACB and the chord AB. The circle may be, for instance, a wheel, and the segment, a mass assembled on the wheel. The rotation of the wheel will produce a centrifugal force proportional to the mass of the segment. The arrangement is used either for balancing a wheel that is not perfectly symmetric, or for producing a shaking force in vibration-testing machines. The mass of the segment is proportional to the area of the segment and this is given by

$$A = \frac{r^2}{2}(\phi - \sin \phi) \tag{7.2}$$

where $\phi = \widehat{AOB}$ and $r = \overline{OA} = \overline{OB}$. If A and r are given, the angle ϕ must be found; it is the solution of the equation

$$\phi - \sin \phi - \frac{2A}{r^2} = 0 \tag{7.3}$$

Equation 7.3 is called **transcendental**, a term deriving from a Latin expression meaning '*which transcends the powers of algebra*'. We cannot, indeed, solve this

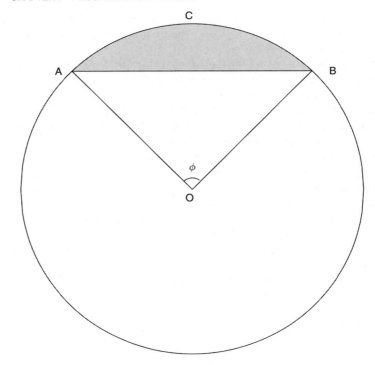

Figure 7.2   A circular segment.

equation by the same means we used for algebraic equations (the solution of polynomial equations is discussed in Chapter 6). Let us rewrite the equation as

$$\phi = \sin \phi + \frac{2A}{r^2} \tag{7.4}$$

Assuming an initial *guess* value, ϕ_0, we calculate

$$\phi_1 = \sin \phi_0 + \frac{2A}{r^2}$$
$$\phi_2 = \sin \phi_1 + \frac{2A}{r^2}$$
$$\dots$$

and hope that the sequence ϕ_i will converge soon enough to a sufficiently good approximation. The following function implements the process in MATLAB:

```
function phi = segment(A,r)
%SEGMENT   angle subtended by a circular segment.
%       SEGMENT(A, r) is the angle subtended by a circular
```

```
%        segment having the area A, and the radius r. The
%        area of the segment equals A = r^2(phi - sin(phi))/2

phi0 = 2*A/r^2;
phi1 = phi0;
phi  = sin(phi1) + phi0;
while abs(phi - phi1) > 0.00001
        phi1 = phi;
        phi  = sin(phi1) + phi0;
end
```

Let us calculate now the area of a segment of a circle having the radius 2 and subtending an angle equal to $\pi/6$:

```
≫ format compact
≫ r = 2;
≫ alpha = pi/6
alpha =
    0.5236
≫ area = r^2*(alpha - sin(alpha))/2
area =
    0.0472
```

With this area and the radius 2 the segment function yields

```
≫ segment(area, r)
ans =
    0.5235
```

that is, practically the angle we assumed. The format compact command was entered at the beginning of the calculation to suppress empty lines between meaningful lines and thus produce a more compact display.

The convergence of the process can be easily visualized. Copy the program segment into a file segment1.m and complete it to become

```
function phi = segment1(A,r)
%SEGMENT1 angle of circular segment, plot of iterations.
%        SEGMENT1(A, r) finds the angle of a circular segment
%        with the area A, and the radius r, and generates a
%        plot showing the evolution of the iterations. The
%        area of the segment equals A = r^2(phi - sin(phi))/2.

phi0 = 2*A/r^2;
phi1 = phi0;
```

LIVERPOOL
JOHN MOORES UNIVERSITY
AVRIL ROBARTS LRC
TEL. 0151 231 4022

```
phi  = sin(phi1) + phi0;
iter = [ phi0 phi1 phi ];
angle = [ 0 phi0 phi0 ];
while abs(phi - phi1) > 0.00001
        phi1 = phi;
        phi  = sin(phi1) + phi0;
        iter = [ iter phi1 phi ];
        angle = [ angle phi1 phi1 ];
end
theta = 0: pi/180: pi/5;
z = sin(theta) + phi0;
lx = [ pi/6 pi/6 ];
ly = [ 0 0.6 ];
plot(theta, z, angle, iter, [0 pi/5], [0 pi/5], lx, ly)
grid
xlabel('\phi')
ylabel('y')
text(-0.1, phi0, '2A/r^2')
text(pi/6 + 0.01, 0.05, '\pi/6')
text(0.63, 0.65, '1')
text(0.05, 0.45, 'curve 1, y = \phi')
lz = length(z);
text(theta(lz), z(lz-0.04), '2')
text(0.05, 0.55, 'curve 2, y = sin(\phi) + 2A/r^2')
```

In this program we used the LaTeX commands introduced in MATLAB 5. Thus, the argument \phi of xlabel types the Greek letter ϕ, and the substring r^2 in the argument of title results in r^2. MATLAB 5 admits only a subset of LaTeX commands. For more details on the latter package the reader is referred to Goossens *et al.* (1994) or to Lamport (1985).

Run the new program with the command segment1(0.0472, 2), print the graph and examine the resulting plot (Figure 7.3). The program was first run without labelling the various lines. This allowed us to appreciate suitable positions for these labels and to write the calls to the text function in the last lines of the function.

Equation 7.3 was solved by an *iterative* method; the term derives from the Latin verb *iterare* that means '*to repeat*'. Why did the method succeed in this case? The answer is given by the **contractive Lipschitz condition** (Rudolf Otto Sigmund Lipschitz, German, 1832–1903). For a brief explanation see the Appendix of this chapter.

7.5   The Newton–Raphson method

The iterations in Figure 7.3 converge rather slowly. One cause is the initial guess, which was rather far from the fixed point. The convergence of iterative methods has been extensively analysed and many procedures have been devised for accelerating

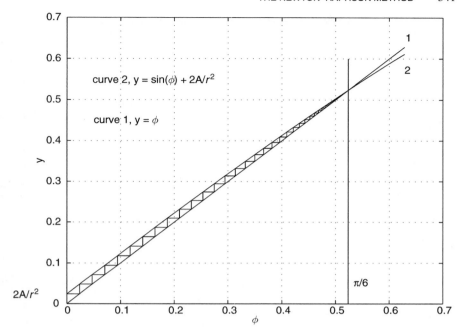

Figure 7.3 Function segment, progress of iterations.

the process in various circumstances (for a comprehensive treatment see Traub 1964). As an example, we shall describe one more procedure, maybe the most popular of all: the **Newton–Raphson method** (Joseph Raphson, English, 1648–1725). In most books originally in languages other than English the procedure is called **Newton's method**.

Given an equation $f(x) = 0$, with $f(x)$ expandable in a Taylor series about an initial guess value x_0, we can write

$$f(x) = f(x_0) + f'(x_0)(x - x_0) + \cdots$$

Neglecting the terms in higher powers of $(x - x_0)$ and remembering that $f(x) = 0$, we get

$$x = x_0 - f(x_0)/f'(x_0)$$

or, as an iteration formula,

$$x_{i+1} = x_i - f(x_i)/f'(x_i)$$

For instance, for the equation solved in the preceding section (angle of circular segment) we should use

$$f(x) = x - \sin x - 2A/r^2$$
$$f'(x) = 1 - \cos x$$

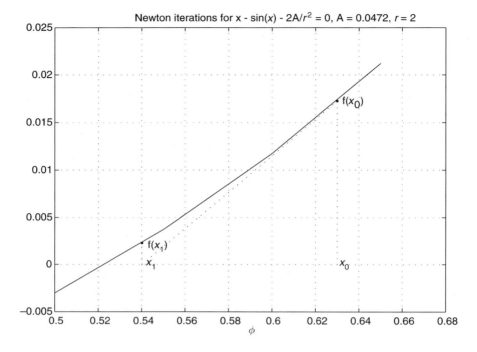

Figure 7.4   Newton–Raphson solution of the segment problem.

Figure 7.4 shows the convergence of the Newton–Raphson method in the example of the segment: it also shows the geometric interpretation of the method.

Using the interactive graphical facilities of MATLAB it is possible to develop an interactive program with the aid of which the user can view a graph of the equation to be solved, change the limits of the graph, choose an initial guess on the graph, and run a Newton–Raphson procedure to obtain the final approximation of the root.

We begin by writing a script file, itermenu.m, that displays a menu; it is called in several places within the program:

```
%ITERMENU displays menu for interactive, iterative root finding

disp('Please choose one of the following:')
disp('   To get a zoom of the plot enter ................. 1')
disp('   To choose an initial guess value and solve enter .. 2')
disp('   To exit the program enter ....................... 3')
```

The listing of the main program follows below, its features are explained after the listing.

```
%NEWTON finds the real zeros of the function y.
%        NEWTON finds real zeros by an interactive Newton procedure.
```

```
tol = 0.00001;
disp('Enter the equation to be solved, y(x), and the derivative')
disp('of y with respect to x as strings variables, for example:')
disp('y    = ''x - sin(x) - c''')
disp('dydx = ''1 - cos(x)''')
disp('When the program returns the prompt k enter the appropriate')
disp('escape command to exit keyboard mode and continue')
disp('the program.')
keyboard
disp('Enter now the range within which you want to plot.')
disp('Then, after viewing the graph press any key to continue')
xmin = input('x min = ')
xmax = input('x max = ')
xx = xmin: (xmax-xmin)/100: xmax;
z = zeros(1, 100);
for k = 1:101
        x     = xx(k);
        yy    = eval(y);
        z(k)  = yy;
end
plot(xx, z)
grid
title('Plot of the equation to be solved')
xlabel('x')
ylabel('y(x)')
pause
real_zeros = [ ];        % initialize array of real zeros
itermenu
answer = input('Enter your choice ')
while answer ~= 3
      if answer == 1
              xmin = input('x min = ')
              xmax = input('x max = ')
              xstep = (xmax - xmin)/100;
              xx = xmin: xstep: xmax;
              z = zeros(1, 100);
              for k = 1: 101
                      x = xx(k);
                      yy = eval(y);
                      z(k) = yy;
              end
              plot(xx, z)
              grid
              xlabel('x')
              ylabel('y')
              pause
```

```
              itermenu
              answer = input('Enter your choice ')
      elseif answer == 2
              disp('Enter initial guess')
              [ x, yg ] = ginput(1)
              for l = 1:100
                      x0 = x;
                      x  = x0 - eval(y)/eval(dydx)
                      if abs(x - x0) < tol
                              break
                      end
              end
              if (l == 100)&(abs(x - x0) >= tol)
                      disp('Procedure did not converge')
              else
                      real_zeros = [ real_zeros x ];
              end
              itermenu
              answer = input('Enter new choice ')
      else
              if answer ~= 3
                      disp('Incorrect answer, please repeat')
                      itermenu
                      answer = input('Enter new choice ')
              end
      end
end
```

At the beginning of the program the MATLAB built-in function disp is used several times to display instructions to the user. The arguments to disp are strings. Following the instructions the control is passed to the user by the built-in function keyboard. The user must now enter $f(x)$ and $f'(x)$ as string variables. When the 'keyboard prompt' k≫ re-appears, the user must enter the system's escape command. This command is not the same in all systems. In MATLAB under Windows the user must write the command return and press Enter. To find out which command applies, the user may consult the manual or type

```
≫ help keyboard
```

Next, the user is prompted to enter the limits of the interval within which the equation will be plotted. Use is made here of the MATLAB built-in function input. The command

```
xmin = input('x min = ')
```

causes the display x min =. The program waits until the user enters the answer, which is assigned to the variable xmin, and the process is repeated for xmax.

After generating an independent-variable array called xx, the program evaluates y (that is, $f(x)$) at the points defined in xx. The task is performed by the MATLAB built-in function eval. This function is used as follows:

- Enter a value, or an array of values, of the independent variable x;
- Enter the function, y, as a string variable, $y = `f(x)$';
- Call z = eval(y); this evaluates y at the given x values, and assigns the result to z.

In our program y is not evaluated once for all the values of the independent variable, but for one value at a time, within a FOR loop. The algorithm was designed in order to avoid complications with expressions that might be interpreted as matrix operations and that would compel the string y to be written in peculiar ways.

After seeing the plot, the user depresses any key and is presented with a menu that provides the following possibilities:

(1) Change the limits of the plot and display again (for zooming the plot, or for looking for possible zeros – roots – in other intervals);

(2) Choose an initial guess and run the Newton–Raphson procedure;

(3) Exit the program.

The main body of the program is a WHILE loop that is repeated as long as the user does not enter the choice '3'. The branch executed after the answer '1' begins with the statement if answer == 1. The *logical* operator '==' compares the value of answer with 1. If the result is *true*, control is passed to the following statements; if not, to the elseif branch. Use of the single equality sign, '=', would have caused an error; '=' is an **assignment operator**.

In the branch corresponding to the answer '2' the user is prompted to enter an initial guess. A crosshair (in some MATLAB versions it may be an arrow) appears on the screen; it can be moved by means of the arrow keys or a mouse. When the arrow keys are used, the step by which the crosshair (or arrow) is moved can be made finer by depressing the '–' key on the numeric keypad, or coarser by depressing the '+' key. The user must bring the crosshair over the point where the function seems to cross the zero line. By depressing Enter the coordinates of that point are assigned to the variables x and yg. The job is done by the MATLAB built-in function ginput. The argument 1 of the function, in this program, means that only one point should be picked up.

After getting the initial guess the program enters a FOR loop; each execution of its statements corresponds to an iteration of the Newton–Raphson procedure. The reason for not using a WHILE loop is the following: we want to impose two **stopping conditions**, and the first one that is fulfilled is executed:

(1) if the program does not converge in 100 iterations – this avoids spending unnecessary time in cases that do not seem to converge;

(2)   if the *distance* between two successive approximations is small enough for the number of significant digits we are interested in. In the listing presented above the chosen stopping distance is 0.00001. The user can change it according to his or her own needs.

Stopping because of the first condition produces the display of an error message followed by the menu. Stopping because of the second condition is implemented by the break command. It causes exiting from the innermost loop, in this case from the FOR loop, and returns control to the first statement following that loop. An array real_zeros is initially in the program. It is designed to accumulate all the roots that the user may find by running the procedure several times before exiting the WHILE loop.

Use the program to solve the problem proposed in Section 7.4. The first command and the first display will be

```
newton
Enter the equation to be solved, y(x), and the derivative
of y with respect to x as strings variables, for example:
y = 'x - sin(x) - c'
dydx = '1 - cos(x)'
When the program returns the prompt k enter the appropriate
escape command to exit keyboard mode and continue the
program.
```

In continuation, one possible dialogue is

```
K >> yA = 0.0472; r = 2;
K >> y = 'x - sin(x) - 2*A/r^2'
y =
    x - sin(x) - 2*A/r^2
K >> ydydx = '1 - cos(x)'
dydx =
    1 - cos(x)
```

In MATLAB under Windows the command for exiting the keyboard mode is

```
return
```

For other MATLAB implementations use the appropriate escape command, as explained above. The following prompt and an example of continuing dialogue is

```
Enter now the range within which you want to plot.
Then, after viewing the graph press any key to continue
x min = 0
```

```
xmin =
     0
x max = pi
xmax =
     3.1416
```

A plot of the function $y(x)$ now appears. Under Windows it may be necessary to click the mouse on the windows menu and the Figure option. After returning to the MATLAB window, the displayed menu and the answer that permits a zoom of the plot are

```
Please choose one of the following:
  To get a zoom of the plot enter ................... 1
  To choose an initial guess value and solve enter .. 2
  To exit the program enter ......................... 3
Enter your choice 1
answer =
     1
```

An example of dialogue continuation is

```
x min = 0
xmin =
     0
x max = 1
xmax =
     1
```

The menu is again presented and the answer for beginning the iterations is

```
Please choose one of the following:
  To get a zoom of the plot enter ................... 1
  To choose an initial guess value and solve enter .. 2
  To exit the program enter ......................... 3
Enter your choice 2
answer =
     2
```

The initial guess is picked up with the mouse, or the arrow keys, on the zoomed plot and the displays, for a particular choice, are

```
Enter initial guess
x =
     0.2784
```

```
yg =
    -0.0194
```

The results of the converging sequence of iterations are:

```
x =
    0.7982
x =
    0.6045
...
    0.5236
```

Obviously, the user can pick up another point and then the displayed values would be different. The menu is presented once again; to exit the user should press 3.

Try to solve several equations with this program. You may encounter one of the following situations:

- If the plotted interval was sufficiently narrow, and the initial guess good, no iteration will be needed.
- If the slope of $f(x)$ is horizontal near a zero, the procedure may not converge.
- For certain combinations of slope and initial guess the procedure may diverge.

MATLAB provides a function, `fzero`, for finding zeros. Use the help facility for learning how to call `fzero` and then experiment with this function.

7.6   Recursion

The function **factorial of** n, denoted $n!$, where n is a positive integer, is defined by

$$n! = 1 \times 2 \times \cdots \times n$$

By convention $0! = 1$.

The factorial of an integer n can be computed in MATLAB with the expression `prod(1:n)`. There is, however, another interesting way of doing the job. Let us note that we can write

$$n! = n \times (n - 1)!$$

This formula can be repeated for decreasing n values, until $n - 1 = 0$, and then, by definition, we set $0! = 1$. Such a definition of the factorial contains a call to itself; we say that it is **recursive**. Some programming languages, including MATLAB, allow the use of **recursion**, that is, programs that call themselves. The following function is an example.

```
function y = fact(x)
%FACT    factorial by a recursive procedure.
%        FACT(X) is the factorial of X by a recursive procedure,
%        where X is an integer scalar

if sum(size(x)) ~= 2
      error('Argument is not a scalar, calculation aborted')
elseif x ~= fix(x)
      error('Argument is not an integer, calculation aborted')
else
      if x == 0
              y = 1;
      else
              y = x*fact(x-1);
      end
end
end
```

The error function returns control to the keyboard and displays the message between parentheses. As an example try

```
>> fact(3)
ans =
    6
```

MATLAB can handle fairly large numbers:

```
>> fact(170)
ans =
    7.2574e+306
```

On the personal computer used to develop this function the limit was reached with fact(171) which yielded the result ∞.

A second example of a recursive program is another function that calculates the greatest common divisor of two integers, x and y:

```
function z = gcd2(x, y, tol)
%GCD2   greatest common divisor by a recursive procedure.
%       GCD2(x, y) recursive greatest common divisor of
%       reals x and y evaluated with the precision tol. If
%       the third argument is not specified, tol = 1.0E-4.

if nargin == 2
        tol = 1.0E-4;
end
```

```
if tol <= 0
        error('Argument tol must be strictly positive')
end
if (sum(size(x)) ~=2)|(sum(size(y))) ~= 2
        error('Arguments not scalars, calculation aborted')
end
if x < 0
            x = -x;
end
if y < 0
        y = -y;
end
if y <= tol
        z = x;
else
        z = gcd2(y, rem(x, y), tol);
end
```

It is sometimes easier to design an algorithm in recursive terms than by means of repetitive statements; for instance in the famous **Hanoi towers** and **Eight queens** problems (Corge 1975; Alagić and Arbib 1978). Recursive formulations of problems may also be interesting from a theoretical point of view. On the other hand, recursive programs require a large memory overhead and are, therefore, often avoided.

7.7   A note on complexity

We have learned how to write programs and functions. A program or function can consist of one or several algorithms. MATLAB functions appear to us as simple expressions; however, calling one of them causes the execution of a particular algorithm. Often a computational problem can be solved by different algorithms. A useful way of choosing the 'best' algorithm is to compare the alternatives in terms of required resources, such as execution time, number of elementary operations, or computer memory. The **complexity** of an algorithm is the difficulty of executing it, as measured in terms of the above resources. Execution time depends on hardware and it can also change with input data. The number of elementary operations appears to be a more convenient measure. In fact, frequently complexity is defined as the relationship between the number of input data and the number of elementary operations required.

To illustrate the idea of counting the number of operations let us consider the two vectors

$$\mathbf{A} = [a_1, a_2, \ldots, a_n]$$
$$\mathbf{B} = [b_1, b_2, \ldots, b_n]$$

The calculation of the sum

$$\mathbf{A} + \mathbf{B} = [a_1 + b_1, a_2 + b_2, \ldots, a_n + b_n]$$

requires n additions. In other words, the number of operations grows linearly when the number of input data, n, increases.

The form of relationship can change in other cases. In general it is less important to know what happens when the number of input data is small; even if the number of operations grows faster, it still may be a bearable cost. What is important is to appreciate how fast the number of required operations grows when the set of input data is large. One way of expressing the growth rate is to say that it is like that of a known function, say $g(n)$. Usual examples of $g(n)$ are $\ln n$, n, n^2, or 2^n. A formal definition of this concept of complexity follows below.

Let A be an algorithm, and $f(n)$ the number of elementary operations required to execute A when the number of input data is n. If we can find a function $g(n)$, a constant $C > 0$ and a number $m > 0$ such that

$$\frac{f(n)}{g(n)} \leq C$$

for all $n \geq m$, we say that $f(n)$ is **of order** $g(n)$, or, in other words, *of the order large O with respect to g* and we write

$$f(n) = O(g(n))$$

Returning to the sum of two vectors of length n we can write

$$\frac{f(n)}{n} = 1$$

for all $n \geq 1$, and say that the addition of the vectors is of order n.

The scalar product of the same vectors, $\mathbf{A}$, $\mathbf{B}$, requires n multiplications plus the addition of the resulting n products $a_i b_i$, in total $2n$ operations. As $2n/n = 2$ for all $n \geq 1$, we can write that the scalar product of two vectors of length n is $O(n)$.

Let us consider now two n-by-n matrices, $\mathbf{A}$, $\mathbf{B}$; each has n^2 elements. Therefore, n^2 operations are required to calculate the sum $\mathbf{S} = \mathbf{A} + \mathbf{B}$ (remember, the general element of the sum is $s_{ij} = a_{ij} + b_{ij}$). We conclude that the sum of two n-by-n matrices is $O(n^2)$.

If we multiply the same matrices $\mathbf{A}$ and $\mathbf{B}$ we obtain a third n-by-n matrix, $\mathbf{P}$, such that each element p_{ij} is the scalar product of the i-th row of $\mathbf{A}$ by the j-th column of $\mathbf{B}$. We already know that each scalar product requires $2n$ operations. There are n^2 elements in $\mathbf{P}$, therefore the product of the two matrices implies $2n^3$ operations and we conclude that this product is of order n^3.

With the aid of the MATLAB `flops` function – which counts floating-point operations – we can verify experimentally the conclusions reached above. To do this write the following program to a file complext.m:

```
x = 1:  5;
% initiate counters
timeav = zeros(1, 5); timemv = zeros(1, 5);
timeam = zeros(1, 5); timemm = zeros(1, 5);
for n = 1 : 5
        v1 = 1: n; v2 = n: -1: 1;    % generate two vectors
        m1 = v1'*v2; m2 = v2'*v1;    % generate two matrices
        flops(0)                     % set counter to zero
        v1 + v2;
        timeav(n) = flops;
        flops(0)                                % set counter to zero
        v1*v2';
        timemv(n) = flops;
        flops(0)                                % set counter to zero
        m1 + m2;
        timeam(n) = flops;
        flops(0)                                % set counter to zero
        m1*m2;
        timemm(n) = flops;
end
[ x' timeav' timemv' timeam' timemm' ], pause
h = plot(x, timeav, '-', x, timemv, '--', x...
    timeam, '-.', x(1:6), timemm(1:6), ':')
xlabel('n'), ylabel('number of flops')
legend(h, 'vector addition', 'vector multiplication', ...
          'matrix addition', 'matrix multiplication')
```

The statement flops(0) sets to zero the counter of floating-point operations. The statement flops retrieves the number of floating-point operations. Running the program will produce the following display:

```
ans =
    1 1  1  1    1
    2 2  4  4   16
    3 3  6  9   54
    4 4  8 16  128
    5 5 10 25  250
    . . .
```

The meanings of the columns can be deduced from the listing of the program and they are

	Number of flops for			
n	Vector sum	Scalar product	Matrix sum	Matrix product

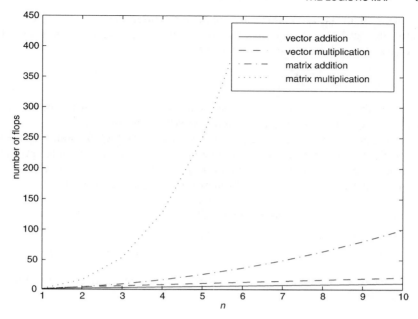

Figure 7.5   Number of flops for vector and matrix operations.

The difference between growth rates can clearly be seen in Figure 7.5.

So far we have only considered real numbers. When applied to complex numbers, the same algorithms require more floating-point operations. More specifically, the sum or the difference of two complex numbers requires two floating-point operations; the product or quotient, six. The reader is invited to verify these facts in MATLAB.

Complexity analysis allows the development and selection of algorithms that work faster and require less computer memory. Algorithms that are $O(\ln n)$ work faster than algorithms that are $O(n)$. Also, algorithms that are $O(n)$ are faster than those that are $O(n^2)$, and so on. Algorithms of exponential order, like $O(2^n)$, require amounts of time that can become prohibitive for large sets of input data. Complexity analysis can indeed identify classes of problems that cannot be solved by even the fastest computers available today.

The subject of complexity belongs to computer science and is treated in specialized books such as Baase (1983), Horowitz and Sahni (1983), or Kronsjö (1987). An instance of application is shown in Example 7.3 which compares the complexity of two algorithms for the evaluation of polynomials.

7.8   The logistic map

We have shown how to use iteration functions for solving equations; the appendix of this chapter contains a condition for convergence of the process. In the following example we shall discuss another aspect of iteration and show how a very simple iteration function enables us to introduce the notions of **bifurcation**, **frequency doubling** and **chaos**. To do this let us consider the equation

$$x_{n+1} = rx_n(1 - x_n) \tag{7.5}$$

where r is the gain. As Bourke (1993) points out, r is 'the growth rate when the equation is being used to model population growth in an animal species'.

The function described by Equation 7.5 is called the **logistic map**; it is treated extensively, but in elementary terms, in Lurçat (1999). A shorter, but more profound treatment can be found in Baker and Golub (1990). The behaviour of the logistic map depends on the value of the gain, r. To show this we plot in Figure 7.6:

- the parabola represented by Equation 7.5;
- the line $x_n = x_{n+1}$;
- horizontal and vertical lines that connect the successive points x_{n+1}.

To start, let us choose a gain $r = 0.5$ and an initial value $x_0 = 0.6$. The first iteration yields

$$x_1 = 0.5 \times 0.6(1 - 0.6) = 0.12$$

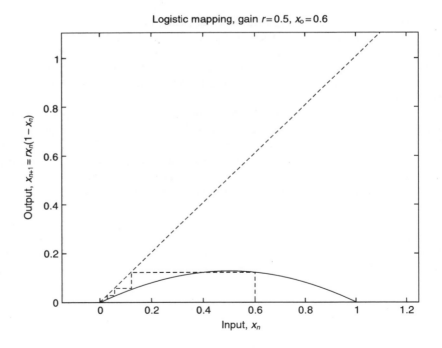

Logistic mapping, gain $r = 0.5$, $x_0 = 0.6$

Figure 7.6   The logistic map – one stable solution.

In Figure 7.6 we find the point $x_1 = 0.12$ on the parabola, then move horizontally to the line $x_{n+1} = x_n$ and from the intercept we descend along the line $x_n = 0.12$ until we reach the parabola at the point $x_2 = 0.528$. Further points are $x_3 = 0.250$, $x_4 = 0.022$, etc. The iterations eventually converge to zero.

Let us now try another gain, for instance $r = 3.2$. As shown in Figure 7.7, this time x_{n+1} oscillates between two values. Actually this phenomenon appears after $r = 3$. We say that a **bifurcation** has taken place. When r passes through approximately 3.4494 another bifurcation occurs and the system oscillates between four values. Further **period doublings** take place at 3.5441 and 3.5644. When r approaches 3.57 the behaviour becomes **chaotic**.

The listing of the file that implements the logistic map is as follows.

```
%CHAOS1 LOGISTIC MAPPING
% see Lurcat Francois (1999), 'Le chaos',
% Presses Universitaires de France,
% Que sais-je No. 3434
r = input('Choose a gain ')
x = input('Choose an input number in the range 0-1, ')
if (x<0)|(x>1)
        error('Chosen input outside legal range')
end
x0 = x;                 % store initial value
xx = zeros(40, 1);      % allocate space for calculated values
X  = 0: 0.01: 1;
Y  = r*X.*(1 - X);      % iteration function
```

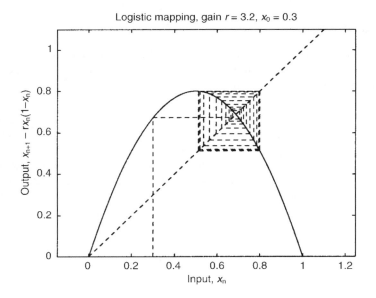

Logistic mapping, gain $r = 3.2$, $x_0 = 0.3$

Figure 7.7 The logistic map - two stable solutions.

```
% plot the iteration function and the line at 45 degrees, Y = X
plot(X, Y, 'k-', [ 0 1.1 ], [ 0 1.1 ], 'k--'),  axis('equal')
hold on
t = ['Logistic mapping, gain r = ' num2str(r) ', x_0 = ' num2str(x0) ];
title(t)
xlabel('Input, x_n')
ylabel('Output, x_{n+1} = rx_n(1-x_n)')
x1 = r*x*(1 - x);     % first iteration
plot([ x x ], [ 0 x1 ], 'r--') % plot result of first iteration
n  = 40;                      % number of successive iterations
for k  = 1:n
    xx(k) = x1;
    plot([ x x1 ], [ x1 x1 ], 'r--')
                              % horizontal leg of iteration path
    x  = x1;
    x1 = r*x*(1 - x);
    plot([ x x ], [ x x1 ], 'r--')
                              % vertical leg of iteration path
end
hold off
disp('Initial value')
x0
disp(' Iteration    Iterated ')
disp('    No.       value   ')
[ [ 1:n ]' xx ]
```

We invite the reader to experiment with the logistic map.

7.9   Summary

Besides simple sequences of statements, MATLAB provides the means of programming some of the **control structures** found in other programming languages. Thus, the simplest **conditional** structure is

```
if A
        S
end
```

where A is an expression. If A is true, the statement, or sequence of statements, S, is executed. If not, control is immediately passed to the first statement following end.

In a case of **conditional branching** the program can execute a statement, or sequence of statements, S1, if a condition A is fulfilled, and another statement, or sequence of statements, S2, if not:

```
if A
        S1
else
        S2
end
```

Three program branches, controlled by two conditions, are obtained with the structure

```
if A
        S1
elseif B
        S2
else
        S3
end
```

More complex programs require the **nesting** of several conditional structures.

MATLAB provides two control structures for repetitive statements. The **FOR loop** was explained in Chapter 4. The **WHILE loop** has the form

```
while A
        S
end
```

The condition A is tested before the first execution and after each subsequent one. The loop will be repeated as long as A is true.

Programs containing repetitive statements can be used for solving equations by **iterations**. Given an **iteration** function, $F(x)$, and an initial **guess**, x_0, a sequence of iterations has the form

$$x_1 = F(x_0)$$
$$x_2 = F(x_1)$$
$$\vdots = \vdots$$
$$x_{n+1} = F(x_n)$$

If the iteration function is differentiable throughout the interval and $|F'(x)| < 1$, the sequence converges to a unique value x^* such that $x^* = F(x^*)$. This value is called a **fixed point** of F. (See the appendix for a more exact statement.)

For practical reasons, computer programs cannot be run until the exact fixed point is reached; the programs are ended when a suitable **stopping condition** is fulfilled. For example, the iterations can be terminated when the *distance* between two successive iterations becomes smaller than a given number.

A popular iterative method is the **Newton–Raphson** method; its iteration function is

$$x_{i+1} = x_i - f(x_i)/f'(x_i)$$

A MATLAB function useful in iterative programs is eval. If a function $f(x)$ is entered as a string variable, y = 'f(x)', eval(y) evaluates $f(x)$ at the x values entered before calling eval.

Three MATLAB functions are useful in interactive computer work. The function keyboard takes control from the program to the keyboard, that is, to the user. Control is returned to the program by entering the escape command (in MATLAB under Windows, it is Return and Enter.

The statement

> ```
> ≫ y = input('s')
> ```

prompts the user by displaying the string s. The program waits for an answer which will be assigned to the variable y.

The statement

> ```
> ≫ [ x y ] = ginput(n)
> ```

displays a crosshair (in some MATLAB versions it can be an arrow), on an existing plot. The crosshair can be moved by means of the arrow keys, preferably by means of a mouse. Pressing Enter assigns the coordinates of the arrow point to x and y. The operation can be repeated for n points.

In general, a computational problem can be solved by different algorithms; these can be compared in terms of required resources such as execution time, number of elementary operations, or computer memory. In a general sense, the **complexity** of an algorithm is the difficulty of executing it as measured by the amount of necessary resources. In a restricted sense, the complexity of an algorithm is the relationship, $f(n)$, between the number of input data, n, and the number of elementary operations required. One way of appreciating the behaviour of this relationship for large sets of data is to compare its evolution with that of some known function. Formally, we say that $f(n)$ is **of order** $g(n)$ if we can find a function $g(n)$, a constant $C > 0$ and a number $m > 0$ such that

$$\frac{f(n)}{g(n)} \le C$$

for $n > m$.

Complexity analysis helps in the development of more efficient algorithms and in the identification of problems that require prohibitive execution times.

7.10   Examples

EXAMPLE 7.1   Random permutations _____

MATLAB provides a function, randperm, which, invoked as randperm(n), yields a random permutation of the integers 1 to n. Instead of using this function, let us consider three functions that, given a row vector of any numbers, yield a permutation of those elements. The three functions perform exactly the same function, but with three different control structures: the first function uses a FOR loop, the second, a WHILE loop, and the third, a recursive algorithm. All three functions use the possibility provided by MATLAB of reducing the length of a vector by excluding some of its elements. Consider, for example, the vector

```
x = [ 5, 7, 8, 2 ];
```

The command

```
>> x(3) = [ ]
```

produces

```
x =
    5 7 2
```

Here, the third element of x was discarded and the length of this vector reduced to 3.

The first function to be described here is

```
function Y = rndprm1(X);
%RNDPRM1 random permutation of row vector using FOR loop.
%        RNDPRM1(X) is a random permutation of the vector X.
%        X is a row vector.
%        Note: This implementation uses a FOR loop.

[m,n] = size(X);
if m > 1
    error('RNDPRM1 accepts as inputs only row vectors');
end
Y = [];                    % start from an empty array;
l = n;                     % number of elements of X
for i = 1:n;
    i = 1+fix(l*rand);     % select at random the position
                           % of the next element of Y
    x    = X(i);           % selected element
    Y    = [Y, x];         % add x to the Y list
    X(i) = [];             % take out x from the X list
    l    = l-1;            % update number of X elements
end % of for block
```

The second function is

```
function Y = rndprm2(X);
%RNDPRM2 random permutation of row vector using WHILE loop.
%        RNDPRM2(X) yields a random permutation of X.
%        X is a row vector. This function returns a random
%        permutation of the elements of X.
%        This implementation uses a WHILE loop.

[m,n]=size(X);
if m > 1
    error('RNDPRM2 accepts as inputs only row vectors');
end
Y=[];                       % start from an empty array;
l = n;                      % number of elements of X
while l > 0
    i = 1+fix(l*rand);      % select at random the position
                            % of the next element of Y
    x = X(i);               % selected element
    Y = [Y,x];             % add x to the Y list
    X(i)=[];               % take out x from the X list
    l   = l-1;             % update number of remaining
                            % elements in X
end % of while block
```

The third function is

```
function Y = rndprm3(X);
%RNDPRM1 random permutation of row vector using recursion.
%        RNDPRM3(X) random permutation of the vector X.
%        X is a row vector. This function returns a
%        random permutation of the elements of X.
%        This implementation uses recursion.

[m,n]=size(X);
if m > 1
    error('RNDPRM3 accepts as inputs only row vectors');
end

if n <= 1
    Y = X;
else
    i = 1 + fix(n*rand);   % select at random the position of
                            % an element of Y
    x = X(i);               % selected element
    X(i) = [];             % take out x from the X list
    Z = rndprm3(X);        % permute remaining elements
                            % at random
```

```
Y = [Z,x];                    % construct output vector
end % of if block
```

Try the functions for yourself. Also, instead of calling the above functions with arguments that are vectors of numbers, try them with character strings, for instance your name. You have a tool for generating *anagrams*! This works because MATLAB stores a character string of length *n* as a vector of length *n*.

EXAMPLE 7.2   Infinite WHILE loop

Write the following program to a file `infloop.m` and run it:

```
x = 1;
while x ~= 0
      x = x - 0.2
end
```

The computer will display

```
x =
    0.8000
    . . .
x =
    5.5511e-017
x =
    -0.2000
    . . .
```

The computer will skip over zero, without meeting it, and the calculations may continue until the whole computer memory is filled, unless we intervene to stop the iterations. On some computers this is done by depressing simultaneously Ctrl and C. The program continued to run because, as explained in Section 2.3, the number 0.2 is represented in the binary system by a fraction with infinitely many places. As the computer cannot store infinitely many digits, it uses an approximation of the number 0.2 and five times this approximation is slightly less than 1. To correct the situation try the following program version:

```
x = 1; tol = 0.001;
while x > tol
      x = x - 0.2
end
```

On the computer used to experiment with this example the program stopped at

```
≫ x =
    5.5511e-017
```

EXAMPLE 7.3   The complexity of polynomial evaluation _____

Let us suppose that we want to evaluate the polynomial

$$p(x) = c_1 x^n + c_2 x^{n-1} + \cdots + c_m x^{n-m+1} + \cdots + c_{n+1}$$

at a real point x_0. In this example we shall program two algorithms that perform this evaluation and count the number of multiplications and additions required by each algorithm. In both we shall use MATLAB's form of describing the polynomials by storing their coefficients, c_i, in an array, say c, in order of descending powers of x, that is

$$c = [c_1\ c_2\ \cdots\ c_m\ \cdots\ c_{n+1}]$$

MATLAB provides an efficient function for the evaluation of polynomials; it is called polyval and it is described in this book in Subsection 1.6.3 and in Section 9.2. This function is used in this example to check the exactitude of the two algorithms. The first algorithm exemplified here evaluates the polynomial term by term; its listing is

```
%EVALPOL1 polynomial evaluation, term by term scheme.
%         EVALPOL1(C, X) evaluates at X the polynomial whose
%         coefficients are contained in the array C.
%         The elements of C are ordered according to
%         descending powers of X.

l = length(c); p = c(1); pow = 1;
for k = l-1: -1: 1
        pow = pow*x;
        p   = p + c(k)*pow;
end
```

Write this function to a file evalpol1.m. It is easy to see that each loop execution requires two multiplications and one addition, that is, three elementary operations. The loop is repeated $l - 1$ times, that is, a total of $3(l - 1)$ elementary operations. Add to this one evaluation of the number $l - 1$ and we get $3 \times (l - 1) + 1$ as the total number of floating-point operations. As $l = n + 1$, we conclude that we need $3n + 1$ floating-point operations.

The second algorithm proposed here is based on a special factorization of the polynomial known as **Horner's scheme**:

$$p(x) = (\ldots ((c_1 x + c_2)x + c_3)x \cdots + \cdots)x + c_{n+1}$$

A simple example of such a factorization is

$$3x^2 + 5x + 3 = (3x + 5)x + 3$$

This time only n multiplications and n additions are needed, in total $2n$ floating-point operations. To implement this scheme write the following function to a file evalpol2.m:

```
function  p = evalpol2(c, x)
%EVALPOL2 Polynomial evaluation by Horner's scheme.
%        EVALPOL1(C, X) evaluates at X the polynomial whose
%        coefficients are contained in the array C.
%        The elements of C are ordered according to
%        descending powers of X.

l = length(c); p = c(1);
for k = 2:l
        p = p*x + c(k);
end
```

To run the two functions described above and count the number of floating-point operations required by MATLAB, write the following program to a script file evalpol.m:

```
%EVALPOL counts operations needed for polynomial evaluation.
%        The program calls the function EVALPOL1 for a term
%        by term scheme, and the function EVALPOL2 for
%        Horner's scheme.

x = 5; count1 = zeros(1, 10); count2 = zeros(1, 10);
value = zeros(1, 10);value1 = zeros(1, 10);
value2 = zeros(1, 10);
for n = 1:10
        c = rand(1, n+1); value(n) = polyval(c, x);
        flops(0), value1(n) = evalpol1(c, x);
        count1(n) = flops;
        flops(0), value2(n) = evalpol2(c, x);
        count2(n) = flops;
end
n = 1: 10;
[ n' count1' count2' ]
pause
plot(n, count1, n, count2)
xlabel('Degree of polynomial'), ylabel('Number of flops')
text(n(5), count1(5), 'simple algorithm')
text(n(5), count2(5), 'Horner''s scheme')
```

Now enter MATLAB, change to the directory that contains the three files described above and invoke them by the command

```
≫ evalpol
```

The computer will display the following answer:

```
ans =
    1   4   2
    2   7   4
    3  10   6
    4  13   8
    5  16  10
    6  19  12
    7  22  14
    8  25  16
    9  28  18
   10  31  20
```

The interpretation of this display is simple; for example, for a polynomial of degree $n = 7$, the term-by-term algorithm requires 22 elementary operations, while Horner's scheme requires only 14. The results confirm the analysis carried out above. Depressing Enter now will produce the graph shown in Figure 7.8.

To verify the exactitude of the results the user is invited to try one of the commands

```
value - value1, value - value2
```

or

```
max(value - value1), max(value - value2)
```

EXAMPLE 7.4   Flow through smooth pipes _____

The flow of fluids through pipes causes a pressure drop that depends upon the fluid density, ρ, the fluid velocity, w, the pipe length, L, the pipe diameter, D, and a frictional coefficient, λ. Dimensional analysis (see Chapter 13) shows that the pressure drop can be expressed by

$$\Delta p = \frac{1}{2}\rho w^2 \frac{L}{D}\lambda$$

where λ is a function of the Reynolds number, $Re = wD/v$, and v, the **kinematic viscosity** (see, for example, Zierep and Bühler 1989, or pages 295–8 in Roberson and Crome 1985).

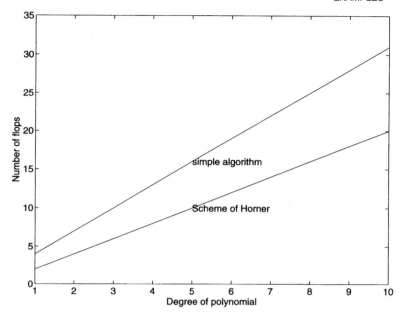

Figure 7.8 Number of flops for polynomial evaluation.

Up to a certain fluid velocity the flow is **laminar**, above it the flow becomes **turbulent**. In laminar flow the stream lines are smooth and well defined. In turbulent flow the velocities at different points vary at random in magnitude and direction, and at the same point they vary in time. If a colouring substance is introduced into the pipe, it is soon diffused throughout the fluid.

Several formulae are used for calculating the frictional coefficient, λ, within various Re intervals. For $Re < 2320$ the flow is laminar and the **Hagen–Poiseuille** relationship is used (Gottfried Heinrich Ludwig Hagen, German, 1797–1889, Louis Marie Poiseuille, French, 1799–1869):

$$\lambda = \frac{64}{Re}$$

Above $Re = 2320$ the flow is turbulent. Two of the equations used in this case are that of **Blasius** (Heinrich, German, 1883–1970):

$$\lambda = \frac{0.3164}{\sqrt[4]{Re}}, \qquad 2320 < Re < 10^5$$

and that of **Prandtl** (Ludwig, German, 1875–1953):

$$\frac{1}{\sqrt{\lambda}} = 2\lg(Re\sqrt{\lambda}) - 0.8, \qquad 10^5 < Re < 10^6$$

where lg means the decimal logarithm. The latter equation is implicit and transcendental; its solution requires an iterative procedure. A function that calculates λ in the *Re* intervals shown above is described below.

```
function lambda = spipe(Re)
%SPIPE   smooth-pipe frictional coefficient.
%        SPIPE(Re) is the smooth-pipe frictional
%        coefficient for Reynolds numbers 0 < Re <= 10^6.

if Re <= 2320
        lambda = 64/Re;
elseif Re <= 10^5
        lambda = 0.3164/Re^0.25;
else
        if Re < 3*10^6
                x0 = -0.8 + 2*log10(Re);
                x  = -0.8 + 2*log10(Re/x0);
                while (abs(x - x0) > 0.000001);
                        x0 = x;
                        x  = -0.8 + 2*log10(Re/x0);
                end
                lambda = 1/(x*x);
        else
                disp('Reynolds number > 10^6')
                disp('Calculation aborted')
        end
end
```

A graph of the frictional coefficient λ can be obtained with the following program:

```
%PIPE plots the diagram of smooth-pipe friction coefficients.

reynolds = logspace(2.5, 6.3, 100);
coeff = zeros(1:100);
for k = 1: 1: 100
        re = reynolds(k);
        co = spipe(re);
        coeff(k) = co;
end
loglog(reynolds, coeff)
grid
title('Frictional coefficient of smooth pipes')
xlabel('Reynolds number, Re')
ylabel('Friction coefficient, \lambda')
```

In the above program the command logspace(2.5, 6.3, 100) creates an array of 100 numbers logarithmically spaced between $10^{2.5}$ and $10^{6.3}$. The statement loglog(reynolds, coeff) plots the elements of the array coeff against the elements of the array reynolds, with logarithmic scales on both coordinate axes.

Compare the resulting graph with Figure 8-33 in Zierep and Bühler (1989).

EXAMPLE 7.5 The operating point of a diode circuit _____

In Example 2.13 we learned how to find graphically the operating point of a circuit containing a semiconductor diode. We shall now solve the same problem by means of the program newton described in Section 7.5. As the currents yielded by Equations 2.22 and 2.23 must be equal at the operating point, we combine both equations into

$$y = I_0(\exp 40 * x - 1) - 1000(V_s - x)/R \tag{7.6}$$

where x stands for the voltage v. The operating point is a solution of $y = 0$. Differentiating Equation 7.6 with respect to x we get

$$\frac{dy}{dt} = 40 I_0 \exp 40x + 1000/R \tag{7.7}$$

Equations 7.6 and 7.7 are the expression to be used in the Newton–Raphson procedure. We begin the calculations by entering the constants

```
≫ I0 = 1.0E-6;
≫ Vs = 10;
≫ R = 2000;
```

Next we invoke the program

```
≫ newton
```

The first display is

```
Enter the equation to be solved, y(x), and the derivative
of y with respect to x as string variables, for example:
y = 'x - sin(x) - c'
dydx = '1 - cos(x)'
When the program returns the prompt k enter the appropriate
escape command in order to get the MATLAB prompt again.
```

We answer the prompt by

```
K ≫ y = 'I0*(exp(40*x) - 1) -1000*(Vs - x)/R';
K ≫ dydx = '40*I0*exp(40*x) + 1000/R';
```

At this point we enter the escape command; in MATLAB under Windows, it is the word `return` followed by the Enter key. The next display is

```
Enter now the range within which you want to plot.
Then, after viewing the graph press any key to continue
    x min =
```

Unlike the graphic procedure described in Example 2.13, it is not necessary to define a narrow voltage interval; therefore, we may answer with 0, and the next prompt with 1. The point where *y* crosses zero is not well defined in the resulting graph. We press Enter and from the menu displayed on the screen we choose 2. The graph is displayed again, together with a crosshair. We bring the crosshair above the point where the curve leaves the *x* axis, for example, and click the mouse. The program displays the first guess – that is, the point picked up with the mouse, the sequence of iterations, and the menu again:

```
Enter initial guess
x = 0.4980
yg =
    1.6478e+08
x =
    0.8157
...
x =
    0.3846
```

To exit the program answer 3. It remains to calculate the current, in mA, for example by means of Equation 2.22:

```
≫ i = I0*(exp(40*x) - 1)
i =
      4.8077
```

We now have the tools for a good solution to the problem posed in the second part of Example 2.13, that is, the simulation of the diode working as a rectifier. Write the following program to a file called `rectify.m`:

```
% RECTIFY.M simulates the rectifying action of a diode
tol = 1.0E-6;
```

```
I0     = 1.0E-8;                     % mA
R      = 2000;                       % ohm
f      = 50;                         % Hz
T      = 1/f;                        % s
t      = 0: T/100: 2*T;              % time array, s
V      = 10*sin(2*pi*f*t);           % ac source
F      = 'I0*(exp(40*x0) - 1) - 1000*(Vs - x0)/R';
F1     = '40*I0*exp(40*x0) + 1000/R';
v      = zeros(1, 201);
x0     = 0.0;      % first initial guess
for k = 1: 201
          Vs = V(k);
          for l = 1:100
                  x = x0 - eval(F)/eval(F1);
                  if abs(x - x0) <= tol
                          break
                  end
                  x0 = x;
          v(k) = x;
          end
end
i = 1000*(V - v)/R;
plot(t, V, t, i)
xlabel('t, s')
text(t( 40), V( 40), 'Source voltage, V')
text(t( 55), i( 55), 'Current, mA')
```

Running the program will produce the plot shown in Figure 7.9.

7.11   Exercises

Solutions for Exercises 7.3, 7.4 and 7.9 appear at the back of the book.

■ **EXERCISE 7.1**   The Newton–Raphson method
An interesting example from Ralston (1965) is

$$x \exp(-x) = 0 \tag{7.8}$$

Solve this equation with the program Newton and verify that the procedure converges if the initial guess is less than 1, and that it diverges for initial guesses larger than 1.

■ **EXERCISE 7.2**   The Newton–Raphson method
Another example is taken from Hartley and Wynn-Evans (1979):

$$x^3 - 3x = 0 \tag{7.9}$$

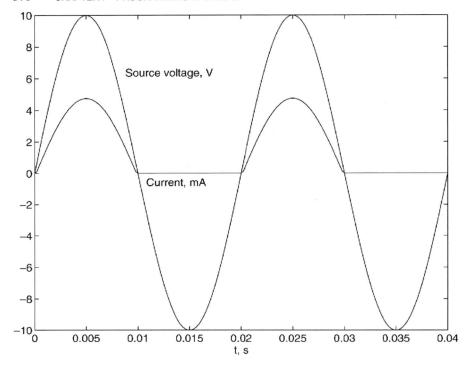

Figure 7.9   The diode as a rectifier.

Study the convergence of the Newton program for different initial guesses. The procedure diverges for $x = 1$, but it is practically impossible to pick up this value exactly with the mouse. Check instead that if the initial guess is close to 1, the number of iterations is large. Compare your results with those obtained with the MATLAB `roots` function.

■ **EXERCISE 7.3**   Step and ramp functions
Describe in terms of unit-step and unit-ramp functions the function shown in Figure 7.10. Check your solution in MATLAB. The graph shown here can represent the position of a gas throttle in a car, the motion of a radio telescope, the position of a radio-volume potentiometer, and so on.

■ **EXERCISE 7.4**   Complexity of sequences of powers
Show that the calculation of the expression

$$\sum_{k=1}^{n} k^2 \tag{7.10}$$

requires $2n$ additions and multiplications. Write a MATLAB function that evaluates the sum, and a MATLAB script file which calls that function and counts the number of floating-point operations. Compare the results with the result predicted by Equation 7.10.

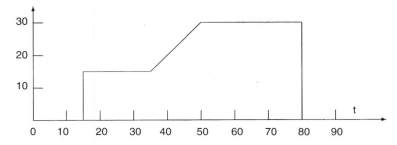

Figure 7.10 A function that can be described by step and ramp functions.

■ **EXERCISE 7.5** Square roots by Newton's method
The calculation of square roots by Newton's method is a classic exercise found in many books on numerical methods or programming. The solution is based on the observation that the square roots of a number n are the solutions of the equation

$$x^2 - n = 0$$

(1)   Write a function that finds the square root of a real number n by Newton's method, starting from an initial guess $x0$. The calculation shall stop when the absolute value of the difference between two successive solutions is smaller than a number *tol*. If this number is not specified, its default value shall be 0.0001.
(2)   Using the above function, calculate $\sqrt{1}$, $\sqrt{2}$, $\sqrt{3}$, $\sqrt{4}$ and check your results by squaring them.

■ **EXERCISE 7.6** Cubic roots by Newton's method
After reading Exercise 7.5 write a function, `cubrt`, that calculates cubic roots of real numbers by Newton's method. Experiment with your function by calculating $1^{1/3}$, $2^{1/3}$, $3^{1/3}$, $27^{1/3}$. Check your results by calculating their cubes.

■ **EXERCISE 7.7** Iterative solution of the seesaw problem
Let us try to solve Exercise 2.13 by an iterative method. The governing equation can be reduced to

$$15\cos\alpha = 16\cos(\pi - (\alpha + 2\pi/3)) \tag{7.11}$$

(1)   From Equation 7.11 deduce the iteration function

$$\alpha_{i+1} = \arccos\left[\frac{16}{15}\cos(\pi/3 - \alpha_i)\right] \tag{7.12}$$

Write a program that asks for the initial guess and solves the problem by means of the iteration function described in Equation 7.12.
(2)   Run the program written at (a). The iterations will not converge. Explain why.
(3)   To try another solution let

$$\gamma = \pi/3 - \alpha$$

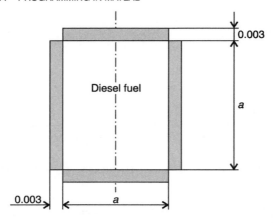

Figure 7.11   A tank for diesel fuel.

Use this substitution in Equation 7.11 and obtain the iteration function

$$\gamma_{i+1} = \arccos\left[\frac{15}{16}\cos(\pi/3 - \gamma_i)\right] \tag{7.13}$$

Write a program that asks for the initial guess and solves the problem by means of the iteration function described in Equation 7.13.
(4)   Run the program and explain why this time the method converges.

■ **EXERCISE 7.8**   Solution of the seesaw problem by Newton's method
Write an M-file that solves the seesaw problem in Exercise 2.13 by Newton's method.

■ **EXERCISE 7.9**   Designing a tank
Engineering problems can lead to expressions in which variables appear with exponents that are rational fractions, for instance $1/3$ or $2/3$. The explanation can be found in Chapter 13, Dimensional analysis. If the expression is an equation in the respective variable, the solution cannot be found by the MATLAB `roots` function or similar procedures. It is sometimes possible to arrange the expression and to raise both its sides to suitable powers, such that the unknown appears only with integer exponents. Then, the `roots` function will work. However, the job may be tedious and it introduces new roots that do not belong to the original problem. Another possibility is to solve the equation by an iterative procedure; an example is given in this exercise.

Let us design a tank for diesel fuel according to Figure 7.11. The shape of the tank shall be that of a cube and it shall be made of steel plate 0.003 m thick. It is required that the total tank mass – that is, fuel plus steel – will equal a given value, M. The steel density is assumed equal to 7.85 t m^{-3}, and the fuel density 0.83 t m^{-3}.

(1)   Let V be the internal tank volume, that is, the diesel-fuel volume. Formulate the problem as an equation in V.
(2)   Find an iteration function that solves the equation written at (a).
(3)   Write a function that uses the iteration found at (b). The input arguments shall be the total mass, M, the initial guess, V_0, and a parameter, `tol`, that stops the iterations. If this parameter is not specified, the default value 0.0001 shall be used.
(4)   Calculate the volume if the total mass is specified as 0.05 t.

7.12   Appendix – the contractive Lipschitz condition

Equation 7.4 is of the form:

$$x = F(x) \tag{7.14}$$

$F(x)$ is an **iteration function**. It is used in the generation of the sequence

$$x_{i+1} = F(x_i)$$

Let us assume that

- for all $x \in [a, b]$, $F(x) \in [a, b]$;
- for any two points x_n and x_m belonging to the closed interval $[a, b]$ the following **contraction** condition holds

$$|F(x_n) - F(x_m)| \le L|x_n - x_m|, \qquad 0 \le L < 1 \tag{7.15}$$

First of all, the second condition implies continuity on the closed interval $[a, b]$. Next, if this condition holds and the first guess is x_0, we can write

$$|F(x_1) - F(x_0)| \le L|x_1 - x_0| \tag{7.16}$$

As $x_2 = F(x_1)$ and $x_1 = F(x_0)$, we conclude that

$$|x_2 - x_1| \le L|x_1 - x_0| \tag{7.17}$$

In the same way

$$|F(x_2) - F(x_1)| \le L|x_2 - x_1| \tag{7.18}$$

leads to

$$|x_3 - x_2| \le L|x_2 - x_1| \le L^2|x_1 - x_0| \tag{7.19}$$

and, in general, to

$$|x_{m+1} - x_m| \le L^m|x_1 - x_0| \tag{7.20}$$

For $n > m$ we can write

$$x_n - x_m = x_n - x_{n-1} + x_{n-1} - x_{n-2} + \cdots - x_m$$

and, using the **triangle inequality,**

$$|x_n - x_m| \leq |x_n - x_{n-1}| + |x_{n-1} - x_{n-2}| + \cdots + |x_{m+1} - x_m|$$
$$\leq (L^{n-1} + L^{n-2} + \cdots + L^m)|x_1 - x_0|$$
$$= L^m(L^{n-1-m} + L^{n-2-m} + \cdots + 1)|x_1 - x_0|$$
$$\leq \frac{L^m}{1 - L}|x_1 - x_0| \tag{7.21}$$

From the inequality 7.21 we conclude that, for $n > m$, the difference $|x_n - x_m|$ can be made as small as we want, provided we choose m large enough. The sequence $x_{i+1} = F(x_i)$ converges to a value x^* such that $x^* = F(x^*)$. This value is called a **fixed point** of F; it is unique. In fact, if there were another fixed point, say y^*, we would have

$$|y^* - x^*| = |F(y^*) - F(x^*)| \leq L|y^* - x^*|$$

As $L < 1$, the only possibility is $y^* - x^* = 0$.

If the function F is differentiable at all points of the interval $[a, b]$, and its derivative is continuous, the Lipschitz condition is satisfied if $|F'(\xi)| \leq 1$ for all $\xi \in [a, b]$. In fact, condition 7.15 can be rewritten as

$$\frac{|F(x_n) - F(x_m)|}{|x_n - x_m|} \leq L < 1 \tag{7.22}$$

On the other hand, under the above conditions, **Lagrange's mean theorem** (Louis de, French, 1736–1813) states that

$$\frac{F(x_n) - F(x_m)}{x_n - x_m} = F'(\xi) \tag{7.23}$$

for at least one point $\xi \in [x_n, x_m]$.

Combining Equations 7.22 and 7.23 we conclude that the contractive condition is satisfied if

$$|F'(x)| \leq L < 1$$

The derivative of the iteration function defined in Equation 7.4 is

$$F'(\phi) = \cos \phi \leq 1 \tag{7.24}$$

for all values of ϕ. This is just a trifle short of the Lipschitz condition. But the latter condition is a sufficient, not a necessary one.

Chapter 8
External files

8.1 Introduction

MATLAB has several facilities for importing data from and outputting data to external files. It is also easy to leave the MATLAB environment, work in the operating system, use an editor or invoke an external program written in another language, and return to MATLAB. Moreover, it is possible to call MATLAB from a program written in Fortran or in C. A few of these facilities will be exemplified in this chapter.

Engineering work is based on many data usually found in tabulated form, in various books. Two functions described in this chapter are used for table lookup; they perform linear interpolation over the data.

This chapter contains several tables of engineering data. They will be used in the examples and exercises of this chapter and the next one. If you write these data to files, keep the files for Chapter 9 too.

8.2 A log-book of calculations

It is good engineering practice to keep records of calculations. Such records can be used for several purposes:

- to prepare drawings of the elements, machines or systems for which the calculations were carried out;

- to prepare lists of materials and components;
- to revise the design at some later stage;
- last but not least, to prepare a report on the project.

Earlier, records of calculations were prepared manually, by writing down the numbers input to, and the results output by, various calculators and computers. A major improvement was the ability to insert computer printouts in reports. MATLAB provides a further facility which enables the user to record automatically and online all calculations made with this package. At the point from which you want to keep the calculations, type diary. From this moment on everything that appears on the screen, graphs excepted, will be dumped in a file called diary.

Next type date: the current date will be printed so that calculations done on different days can be distinguished from one another. A title can be written as a comment, that is, preceded by '%'; explanations can be interspersed in the same way.

After exiting MATLAB, the file diary can be processed with an editor or a word processor. One objective of this operation can be the elimination of records containing erroneous commands and the resulting error messages. The % sign preceding the comments can be erased while editing, so that titles and explanations will appear as normal text. Printing can be done by commands specific to the operating system. Under DOS, for example, the edited diary file can be printed with the command copy diary prn. Example 1 illustrates this simplest way of processing. If the diary file is long, the DOS command shown above will cause an awkward printout with neither top nor bottom page margins. Better alternatives are provided by editors and word processors. An example is provided by Kedit (Kedit is a trademark of Mansfield Software Group): if this editor is invoked for the file diary and the top of the file is made the current line, it is possible to print the diary by means of the command print * 60. The asterisk, '*', means that all lines from the current line to the end of the file are to be printed. The argument 60 indicates that the number of lines per page should be 60. The user can obviously choose another number of lines per page.

A word processor can be used for changing fonts, underscoring, and printing the report with the desired layout, that is, with specified number of lines per page, page margins, page numbering, and so on.

There are word processors and desktop publishing systems that enable the inclusion of diary files and MATLAB graphs into larger documents written with those systems. Many parts of this book were prepared in this way. The main part of the text was written with the aid of the Kedit editor. Diary files containing examples of MATLAB sessions, and program and function listings were *imported* into the text by means of the editor. LaTeX commands were interspersed wherever necessary, including the commands for inserting the graphs obtained in MATLAB, and processed as PostScript files. The work was finished in the LaTeX or TeX environment.

The user may want to have more diary files, one for each project. The relevant operating system command can be used to change the name of the diary file. MATLAB, however, allows the name to be specified directly: simply type at the beginning of the session diary project1, diary project2, or whatever file name you want.

8.3   Reading data from M-files

In Section 6.5 we exemplified the least-squares method on a set of 21 (x, y) pairs. We know how to write the arrays **X** and **Y** directly on the screen during the MATLAB session, but in this mode of working, correcting entry errors is rather awkward. It is much easier to write the input data to a separate file. The processing can then be done with the editor the user is familiar with, and correcting errors or updating data become simple editing matters. The procedure to be followed is the following:

(1)   Open a file with the extension m;

(2)   Write the data as variables bearing the names to be used in your calculations;

(3)   Save the file;

(4)   After opening the MATLAB session, load the data by typing the name of the file.

For example, for the data in Section 6.5 we can open a file named test1.m and write to it

```
x = [ 0:   0.5:   10;
y = [ 2.719
4.347
...
39.0269 ];
```

After entering the MATLAB environment type test1 and wait for the return of the prompt. You may view the data by entering [x y]. Calculate the least-squares solution of this example again.

It is obvious that the above procedure is the only one possible for large sets of data. The most important instances of such cases are input data obtained by computerized **data-acquisition systems**. There are systems that can output data in the format required by MATLAB. Otherwise, if the data are written on a diskette in ASCII code they can be formatted with the help of an editor. Let us assume that the data for our least-squares example have been obtained by means of a data-acquisition system, that they are preceded by a heading and are written in the format

```
0   ,   2.719
0.5 ,   4.347
...
10.0, 39.0269
```

If the file is read by an editor, the heading can be transformed into a comment by typing % before it. Next, we use the editor to replace commas by spaces. Finally, we must transform the data into an array and give it a name, for instance

```
xy = [ 0 2.719
0.5 4.347
...
10.0 39.0269 ];
```

Suppose that these data are in a file xy.m. We begin the calculations by typing the name of the input file and, after the return of the prompt, we separate the variables as shown below:

```
≫ xy;
≫ x = xy(:,1);
≫ y = xy(:,2);
```

8.4   Linear interpolation

8.4.1   Tables with one entry

Table lookup is introduced here by an example taken from mechanical engineering. Example 8.2 illustrates the same subject as applied to electrical engineering/ instrumentation.

Some formulae in Chapters 7 and 13 include fluid density as a variable. Fluid densities are functions of temperature. Let us consider, for example, the density of water. The problem we propose in this example is

Given the temperature(s), find the corresponding water density(ies).

The answer can be usually found in engineering tables; an illustrative segment is shown in Table 8.1. In order to use a formula containing this variable, the engineer

Table 8.1   A table of water densities.

Temperature °C	Density t/m^3
0	0.99987
2	0.99997
4	1
6	0.99997
8	0.99988
10	0.99973
12	0.99953
14	0.99927
16	0.99897
...	...

must look for a suitable handbook, find the table of densities, and identify the value corresponding to a given temperature. If this temperature does not appear in the table, the engineer must interpolate between the two closest values above and below the desired temperature. For example, if we need the water density corresponding to 15 °C, we look in the table and find that

- 0.99927 t/m^3 corresponds to 14 °C;
- 0.99897 t/m^3 corresponds to 16 °C.

A temperature difference of 2 °C results in a change of −0.00030 kg/m^3. We calculate the water density corresponding to 15 °C by

$$0.99927 - 0.00030/2 = 0.99912$$

MATLAB allows for a much simpler solution. First, the table of water densities – like any other tables that may be of interest – should be stored in an M-file. In our example we write the table to a file called watdens.m. The table is entered as an array also called watdens, as shown below:

```
%WATDENS Fresh-water density versus degrees C
% format [ temperature, density ]
% units [ deg C, t/m^3 ]
watdens = [ 0 0.99987
2 0.99997
4 1
6 0.99997
8 0.99988
10 0.99973
12 0.99953
14 0.99927
16 0.99897
...
...   ];
```

Do not forget to type the semicolon, '; ', after the closing square bracket. Without the semicolon the whole table will be displayed when loaded by the user. To obtain the water-density value for a given temperature, the user must first load the table by typing the name of the M-file. Next, he or she should enter a command like table1(tn, x), where *tn* is the name given to the table, and *x* the desired independent-variable value. For instance, the water density at 15 °C is obtained with

```
≫ watdens
≫ table1(watdens, 15)
ans =
   0.9991
```

If more digits are displayed, it is easier to see the effect of the **linear interpolation**:

```
>> format long
>> table1(watdens, 15)
ans =
   0.99912000000000
```

The second argument of the table1 function can be an array:

```
>> temperatures = 1:  2:  31;
>> table1(watdens, temperatures)
ans =
   0.99992000000000
   0.99998500000000
   0.99998500000000
   ...
```

The commands described above can be included in MATLAB programs. Reading tables and interpolating over them will thus be performed automatically. At the point where the table is no longer needed, it is good practice to drop it by means of the clear command; in our example the appropriate command is clear watdens. More memory thus becomes available for running the rest of the program.

There are restrictions on the use of table1:

- The first column of the table on which it acts must be **monotonic**;
- The second argument of the function call must lie between the first and last values in the first column of the table.

The second restriction simply means that table1 cannot **extrapolate**. In order to understand the importance of the first restriction, let us suppose that we want to find the water temperature corresponding to a density of $0.9992 \, \text{t/m}^3$. We may invert the watdens table by the command

```
>> invwat = [ watdens(:,2) watdens(:,1) ]
```

Try the command table1(invwat, 0.9992) and you will obtain an error message. This is due to the fact that water density does not decrease monotonically, but has a maximum at $4\,°\text{C}$ (the so-called **water anomaly**). **Sorting** the inverted table in ascending order of its first column will not help. Indeed, two values in the first column are equal: at $2\,°\text{C}$ and at $6\,°\text{C}$. If you want to see what happens, plot the density against temperature. A MATLAB solution of this problem is shown in Chapter 9.

Table 8.2 A fragment of a table of specific volumes of superheated steam in m^3/kg.

Pressure at abs.	Temperature °C							
	240	260	280	300	320	340	...	550
6	0.393	0.410	0.426	0.443	0.459	0.475	...	0.643
7	0.336	0.350	0.365	0.379	0.393	0.407	...	0.551
8	0.293	0.305	0.318	0.331	0.343	0.355	...	0.482
9	0.259	0.271	0.282	0.293	0.304	0.315	...	0.428
...	...	...	...	...	...	...	...	...
220	–	–	–	–	–	–	...	0.015

8.4.2 Tables with two entries

Frequently an engineer has to find a value in a table with two entries, possibly by interpolating between stored values. One example, from mechanical engineering, is given below and it relates to the *specific volume of superheated steam*. An application from electrical engineering is given in Example 8.3.

Steam is produced in a boiler at a temperature that depends on the prevailing pressure. When the steam is generated in the presence of water with which it is in a state of temperature equilibrium, it is called **saturated steam**. The steam can flow away from the water surface to a place where it can be heated further, under constant pressure. The steam will dry and reach temperatures above saturation, thus becoming **superheated steam**. The specific volume of saturated steam is a function of both temperature and pressure. The problem we propose in this example is:

given the temperature(s) and the pressure(s), find the corresponding specific volume of superheated steam.

Let us assume that the book available on the shelf is an older one containing data in the MKSA (meter, kilogram-force, second, ampere) system, for example, the data in H&B (1961), a fragment of which is shown in Table 8.2. If we want to find, for example, the specific volume of superheated steam at 8.5 bar and 390 °C, we must proceed as follows.

(1)   We must first convert the pressure to at; that is

$$8.5 \text{ bar} \times \frac{10}{9.80665} \frac{\text{at}}{\text{bar}} = 8.66759 \text{ at}$$

(2)   Looking at the table, we find that the value we seek is 'framed' by the following four values

	380 °C	400 °C
8 at	0.380	0.392
9 at	0.337	0.348

The values corresponding to 390 °C are

$$\frac{0.380 + 0.392}{2} = 0.386$$

$$\frac{0.337 + 0.348}{2} = 0.3425$$

And the value corresponding to 390 °C and 8.66759 at is calculated by

$$0.386 + (8.66759 - 8.00000) \times (0.3425 - 0.386) = 0.35696$$

Quite a bit of calculation and some possibilities for errors. To avoid them, the table can be written to an M-file, in the format required by MATLAB, but several problems arise here:

- The pressure is given in **atmospheres**, at, where 1 at equals 1 kg force/cm^2. The SI system used today uses the bar, where

$$1 \text{ bar} = 10\frac{N}{cm^2} \times \frac{1}{g}\frac{kg \text{ force}}{N} = \frac{10}{9.80665} \text{ at}$$

- The table is too wide to be written on an 80-column screen;
- The cells filled with a dash, '–', contain no values because they correspond to points under the saturation curve, not to superheated steam.

To overcome these problems, a file called supsteam.m was built as described below. The table of specific volumes of superheated steam was split into two arrays. The first array, called sv1, contains

- pressures, in at,
- specific-volume values, in m^3/kg force, for temperatures from 240 to 400 °C.

The second array is called sv2 and contains specific-volume values corresponding to temperatures from 420 to 550 °C. In the cells containing points under the saturation line we write NaN, the IEEE representation for *Not-a-Number*. The two arrays are subsequently combined into one array called svol. The values in the first column of this array are converted to values measured in bar. At this stage the arrays sv1 and sv2 are no longer required and they are **cleared**. A partial listing of the file supsteam.m, which contains all these data and operations, is shown below; the complete file can be downloaded from an address that can be obtained from Pearson Education.

```
%SUPSTEAM.M table of superheated-steam specific-volume,
% in m^3/kg.  The first column of the final table contains
% absolute pressures in bar (10^5 bar = 1 Pa = 1 N/m^2).
% The first row of the final table contains temperatures
% in degrees Celsius.
sv1 = [ NaN 240 260 280 300 320 340 360 380 400
6 0.393 0.410 0.426 0.443 0.459 0.475 0.491 0.508 0.524
7 0.336 0.350 0.365 0.379 0.393 0.407 0.421 0.435 0.448
8 0.293 0.305 0.318 0.331 0.343 0.355 0.367 0.380 0.392
...
220 NaN NaN NaN NaN NaN NaN NaN 0.007 0.009 ];
sv2 = [ 420 440 450 460 470 480 490 500 520 540 550
0.540 0.556 0.564 0.572 0.580 0.588 0.596 0.604 0.619 ...
0.462 0.476 0.483 0.490 0.496 0.503 0.510 0.517 0.531 ...
0.404 0.416 0.422 0.428 0.434 0.440 0.446 0.452 0.464 ...
...
0.010 0.011 0.011 0.012 0.012 0.013 0.013 0.013 0.014 ...   ];
svol = [ sv1 sv2 ];
svol(:,1) = svol(:,1)*0.980665;
clear sv1 sv2
```

Now, if we are interested in the specific volume of superheated steam at 8.5 bar and 390 °C, we load the table and interpolate over it by the commands

```
≫ supsteam
≫ table2(svol, 8.5, 390)
ans =
   0.3570
```

Do not try to check the results with the help of Table 8.2; it contains pressure values in at. The values actually used for interpolation can be found by the commands

```
≫ [ svol(4:5,1) svol(4:5,9) svol(4:5,10) ]
ans =
   7.8453 0.3800 0.3920
   8.8260 0.3370 0.3480
```

What happens if we ask for a value under the saturation curve? Try

```
≫ supsteam
≫ table2(svol, 210, 310)
ans =
   NaN
```

The largest pressure for which we can query the table is $220 * 0.980665 = 215.7507$ at; beyond this value MATLAB will issue an error message. Try it for yourself.

There are restrictions on the use of the `table2` function, similar to those imposed by `table1`:

- The first column and the first row of the table on which it acts must be monotonic;
- The second argument of the function call must lie between the first and last values in the first column of the table;
- The third argument of the function call must lie between the first and last values in the first row of the table.

The last two restrictions simply mean that the `table2` function cannot **extrapolate**.

8.5   Switching to the operating system

Let us suppose that we are running a newly written MATLAB program after opening a diary. If error messages are issued, we can exit MATLAB and correct the diary file with the help of our editor. If, during the same session, the invocation of the program was preceded by other calculations, we lose their results. If we want to keep these results we must *save* them, and after re-entering the MATLAB environment we must *load* them. All these operations, including restarting the MATLAB session, are time consuming. The package provides better solutions, the simplest one being the use of the exclamation mark, '!'. For example, if you opened a file `mydiary.dia`, and you want to edit this file using Kedit, type

```
≫ !kedit mydiary.dia
```

When editing is finished, the Kedit command `file` saves the file and returns you to the MATLAB environment. The exclamation mark can be used for invoking any DOS facilities from inside MATLAB. Try, for example, the command

```
≫ !copy mydiary.dia newdiary.dia
```

MATLAB provides another means of issuing DOS commands; for example

```
≫ dos('kedit mydiary.dia')
```

will open a DOS window and the editor invoked will display the file `mydiary.dia` there for editing. Obviously, you can choose another editor in the same way.

If you want to open a new file, click the first button on the toolbar. To edit an existing M-file, click the second button on the toolbar. A window will open and you have to double click the name of the desired file.

What happens if the program you want to run is on a diskette? Let us suppose that you insert that diskette in drive cd a:. Use cd a: and proceed as usual. If the program is, for example, on the hard disk d, in the directory mymatlab, you can reach it by entering cd d:\mymatlab.

8.6   Writing output to external files

Let us return to the program scissor.m described in Example 6.4; its output is a graph. We know how to display numerical output on the screen and how to obtain a hard copy of it. MATLAB also allows us to write numerical output to a file, for example to a file called scissor.out. In order to do so, we insert the following statement before the end of the FOR loop:

```
fprintf('scissor.out', 't = %5.2f F = %5.0f\n', t, X(3))
```

The syntax of the fprintf function is

```
fprintf('file name', 'format', variable names)
```

The file name is given as a string, and so is the format. The format string exemplified above will cause the following:

- 't = ' will be printed as such, including all blanks appearing in the string;
- The first variable will be printed in fixed point notation with five digits, two of which follow the decimal point;
- 'F = ' will be printed as such, including the blanks;
- The second variable will be printed in fixed point notation, in a five-digit wide field, without a decimal point;
- '\n', the *newline escape character* of the C language, causes the next printout to appear on a new line;
- The first variable to be printed is t, the second, $X(3)$. MATLAB allows from zero to three variables in one fprintf statement.

Insert the fprintf statement in the program scissor and run it. You will obtain lines such as:

```
t =   6.50 F = 21778
```

The reference part of the MATLAB manual contains more options and you may combine them in order to obtain clearer and better-looking printouts. As an example, let us improve the format of the file scissor.out. Before the beginning of the FOR loop insert the following statements:

```
fn = 'scissor.out';
ds = fix(clock);
fprintf(fn, '%4.0f %2.0f %2.0f\n', ds(1), ds(2), ds(3))
fprintf(fn, 'Output of program SCISSOR\n')
fprintf(fn, '__ ___ ___ ___ _\n')
fprintf(fn, '      t              F         \n')
fprintf(fn, '__ ___ ___ ___ _\n')
```

The first statement assigns the name of the output file to the string constant *fn*. This constant name will be used later as an argument of the fprnt function, thus eliminating the need to repeat the complete name of the output file several times. The second statement, fix(clock), invokes the clock function and returns the current date and time in decimal form, as an array of six elements: year, month, day, hour, minute and second. The result is assigned to a constant called *ds*. The third statement prints the first three elements of *ds* in the following fields: four characters wide, two characters wide, and two characters wide, all of them obviously without any decimal digits. The fourth statement prints a title, the fifth underscores it, the sixth prints a heading, and the seventh prints a horizontal line under the heading.

Also, replace the fprintf statement before the end of the FOR loop with

```
fprintf(fn, '%6.2f %8.0f\n', t, X(3))
```

The field widths have been increased here for better readability. This also gives us the layout of the heading:

```
(3 blanks)t(6 blanks)F(3 blanks)
```

Run the program again and look at the file scissor.out.

8.7   Exchanging data with Excel

8.7.1   Exporting data from MATLAB to Excel

In Section 3.1 we built a spreadsheet in MATLAB; it is shown in Table 3.1. As acknowledged there, a more natural environment for building a spreadsheet would be to use specialized software, such as MS Excel. If we began the work in MATLAB, could we continue it in Excel? The answer is 'Yes', and one simple way to do this is described below.

Returning to Section 3.1 let us suppose we saved the arrays price and quantity. If not, we may build them again. We open a diary, spread.out, and combine the two arrays into one:

```
>> price = [ 3.00 1.99 10.90 9.15 1.29 ];
>> quantity = [
3 2 1
2 3 0
1 1 3
5 3 3
2 3 3 ];
>> diary spread.out
>> spread = [ price' quantity ]
spread =
     3.0000    3.0000    2.0000    1.0000
     1.9900    2.0000    3.0000    0
    10.9000    1.0000    1.0000    3.0000
     9.1500    5.0000    3.0000    3.0000
     1.2900    2.0000    3.0000    3.0000
diary off
```

Next, we open the file spread.out in an editor and cut out everything that is
not necessary, in our case the line spread = . This work should be done only in a
text editor, not in a word processing program that introduces non-ASCII characters.
We open Excel, click on File on the toolbar and then click on Open. We change the
directory to that in which we edited the file spread.out, and choose All Files in
the Files of type list. What remains now is to double-click on the name of our
file, and the Text Import Wizard will open as shown in Figure 8.1.

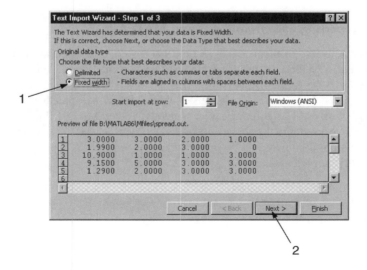

Figure 8.1   The Excel Text Import Data.

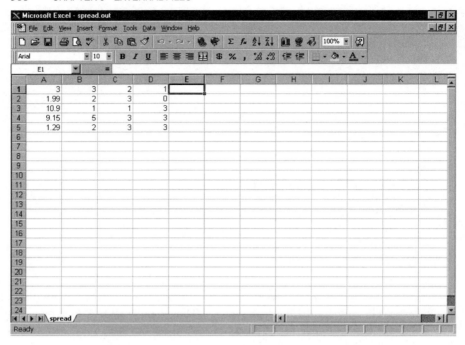

Figure 8.2   Data imported into the Excel spreadsheet.

Figure 8.2 shows the Excel spreadsheet with the imported data. Completing the spreadsheet with the required operations can yield a result like Table 3.1.

8.7.2   Importing data from Excel into MATLAB

And now the inverse problem. Let us assume that we did, indeed, build the spreadsheet in Excel and we called the resulting file Table3_1.xls. Could we import the data into MATLAB for further processing? This is not an exotic question because often an engineer may have made calculations or obtained data in a spreadsheet format and interaction with MATLAB may be advantageous. Today, MATLAB 6.1 allows us to give a positive answer to the above question. Thus, we can call the function xlsread with one output argument and the name of the spreadsheet as input argument, and retrieve only numerical data:

```
>> A = xlsread('Table3_1')
A =
 1.0000 3.0000 ...  18.0000
 2.0000 1.9900 ...   9.9500
 ...
  NaN   ...   NaN 193.8700
```

Calling the function `xlsread` with two output arguments also allows us to retrieve text data:

```
≫ [ B, C ] = xlsread('Table3_1')
B =
  1.0000 ...  3.0000 18.0000
  2.0000 ...  1.9900 9.9500
  ...
  NaN ...    NaN 193.8700
C =
  Columns 1 through 8
  'Item No.'   'Price' ...   [] []
   [] []  ...  'February' 'March'
   ...
   [] [] ...   [] []
  'Totals' [] ...   [] []
  'Totals'
  []
   ...
  []
```

MATLAB 6 also provides a graphical user interface for importing data. This facility also allows the import of data from `xls` files. To see how it functions we go to the `File` menu and click on `Import Data`.

MATLAB responds with

```
Import Wizard created variables in the current workspace.
```

Typing `whos` we obtain the following table:

```
Name Size Bytes Class
A 6x9 432 double array
B 6x9 432 double array
C 8x9 1508 cell array
colheaders 1x9 136 cell array
data 6x9 432 double array
textdata 8x9 1508 cell array
```

The variables *A*, *B* and *C* were built by the command `xlsread`, the variables *colheaders, data* and *textdata* were built by the Import Wizard. We see that *C* and *textdata* are of the **cell array** data type. a subject that will be introduced in Subsection 17.4.2. One can recombine all the data, in the MATLAB environment, as a **structure** data type. This is explained in Chapter 18. However, we think that it may be more interesting for the engineer to build arrays for further calculations. The array `data` contains the input for the Excel spreadsheet, and the results of calculations. If the results are not interesting, the user can extract just the input:

```
>> newdata = data(1:5, 2:5)
newdata =
   3.0000 3.0000 2.0000 1.0000
   1.9900 2.0000 3.0000 0
   10.9900 1.0000 1.0000 3.0000
   9.1500 5.0000 3.0000 3.0000
   1.2900 2.0000 3.0000 3.0000
```

To import data from Lotus 1-2-3 use the function `wklread`.

8.8   Additional input/output functions

Many new interfacing facilities have been added in MATLAB 4; they are described in a separate booklet called *External interface guide*. Other new input/output commands include `fopen`, `fclose`, `fread`, `fwrite`, and `fscanf`. It is beyond the scope of this book to describe all these additions; therefore, the reader is advised either to consult the manuals or to use the `help` facility of the package. MATLAB 4 and 5 also provides more interpolating facilities; they are described in Subsections 1.11.1 and 1.11.2. Other interpolating functions, also available in earlier MATLAB versions, are treated in Chapter 9.

8.9   Summary

Calculations performed in MATLAB can be recorded in a file if they are preceded by the `diary` command. The default name of the resulting 'log-book' file is `diary`. Another file name is used if it is entered as an argument of the command: for example `diary project1` will record the calculations in a file called `project1`. Graphs are not recorded by the `diary` command.

A title can be added to a diary file and explanations interspersed throughout it by means of the MATLAB comment mark, '%'. The current date can be written in the document by using the `date` command. After exiting MATLAB, the diary file can be processed with an editor or word processor and printed in the desired layout. The diary file, together with graphs produced in MATLAB, can be included into larger documents with the aid of more sophisticated systems, such as LaTeX.

When the input to MATLAB consists of large amounts of data it is good practice to write them, using an editor, to an M-file, that is, a file with the extension `m`. The M-file is the only possibility when thousands of numbers are obtained experimentally and recorded by a data-acquisition system. The data should then be grouped into MATLAB-type arrays bearing the names to be used in calculations. The data are loaded simply by typing the name of the file that contains them.

Engineering tables can be stored in M-files by proceeding as above. MATLAB has functions for linear interpolation over tables. For example, consider water density as a function of temperature. If an array called watdens, containing temperatures in °C in the first column and water densities in kg m^{-3} in the second, is written to a file watdens.m, the density corresponding to 15 °C is obtained with the commands

```
>> watdens
>> table1(watdens, 15)
```

Interpolation over tables with two entries is performed by the table2 function. Let the file supsteam.m contain an array svol, its first column containing pressures in bar, the other columns containing specific volumes of superheated steam, in m^3/kg, and the first row temperatures in °C. The specific volume corresponding to 8.5 bar and 390 °C is obtained with the commands

```
>> supsteam
>> table2(svol, 8.5, 390)
```

To issue commands to the operating system from MATLAB, introduce them with the exclamation mark, '!'. For example, assuming that a command XXXX exists, enter

```
>> !XXXX
```

A useful application of this facility is to invoke an editor for editing a diary file without leaving the MATLAB environment. To open a new file or to edit an M-file use the first two buttons on the toolbar.

MATLAB allows not only input to be read from external files, but also output to be written to external files. One possibility is provided by the fprintf function which is invoked with the syntax

```
fprintf('file name', 'format', variable names)
```

For example, the statement

```
fprintf('scissor.out', 't = %5.2f F = %5.0f\n', t, X(3))
```

will print, in the file scissor.out, the value of the variable t in a fixed point format, five characters wide, with two digits after the decimal point, and the value of the variable $X(3)$ in a fixed point format, also five characters wide, but without a decimal point. The value of t will be preceded by 't = ', and that of $X(3)$ by 'F = '. The two characters '\n' advance the printing by one line.

In the above example the name of the output file is the first argument of fprintf and is entered as a string constant. If several print statements refer to the same output file, it is easier to define a string constant containing the file name, and to use the name of this constant as the first argument.

The MATLAB user's guide contains a few more printout options. Also, MATLAB provides more interpolating functions; some of them are introduced in Section 1.11, others in Chapter 9.

8.10   Examples

EXAMPLE 8.1   Report prepared with an editor ＿＿＿＿＿＿＿＿＿＿＿＿＿＿＿＿＿＿＿

Let us return to Example 2.6 and assume that we want to include the calculations in a report. A possible diary file is

```
≫ date
ans =
    12-Oct-91
≫ format short
≫ % Geometrical properties of steel tube, BS 6323
≫ D = 139.7;    % outer diameter, mm
≫ t = 6.3;    % wall thickness, mm
≫ ≫ d = D - 2*t    % inner diameter, mm
d =
    127.1000
≫ A = pi*(D^2 - d^2)/4    % sectional area, mm^2
A =
    2.6403e03
≫ I = pi*(D^4 - d^4)/64    % moment of inertia, mm^4
I =
    5.8862e06
≫ W = 2*I/D    % sectional modulus, mm^3
W =
    8.4269e04
≫ Ip = 2*I    % torsional moment of inertia, mm^4
Ip =
    1.1772e07
≫
≫ S = pi*D/10^3    % superficial area per m length, m^2
S =
    0.4389
≫ quit
20 flop(s).
```

With the help of an editor we correct any mistakes (for example 'Geoemtrical' to 'Geometrical'), eliminate comment marks (%), MATLAB prompts, and superfluous lines ('quit', '20 flop(s)'), centre the title, and align commands and answers. The processed file can look like

```
12-Oct-91
                Geometrical properties of steel tube, BS 6323
D = 139.7;                            outer diameter, mm
t = 6.3;                              wall thickness, mm
d = D - 2*t = 127.1000                inner diameter, mm
A = pi*(D^2 - d^2)/4 = 2.6403e+03     sectional area, mm^2
I = pi*(D^4 - d^4)/64 = 5.8862e+06    moment of inertia, mm^4
W = 2*I/D = 8.4269e+04                sectional modulus, mm^3
Ip = 2*I = 1.1772e+07                 torsional moment of
                                      inertia, mm^4
S = pi*D/10^3 = 0.4389                superficial area per
                                      meter length, m^2
```

EXAMPLE 8.2   Thermocouple

The thermocouple shown in Figure 8.3 consists of two wires of different metals, A and B. The wires are joined together at one end, called the **hot junction**, and maintained at the temperature to be measured. The other end, the **cold junction**, is maintained at some constant, **reference** temperature. The difference in temperature along the wires produces a difference in potential which is a function of the temperature gradient and of the two metals, A and B. The cold junction is connected to a voltmeter that measures the resulting **electromotive force**, **emf** for short. The connection to the voltmeter is represented in the figure as a pair of twisted wires.

Standard reference tables of emf have been established for the calibration of different thermocouple pairs. As an example, let us consider the British Standard BS 4937, Part 1. It contains emf tables for thermocouples type S, one wire of which is made of platinum, the other of a platinum–10%-rhodium alloy. The assumed reference, cold-junction temperature is $0\,°C$. The standard contains emf values, in microvolts, at one-degree-Celsius intervals. For the purpose of this example we shall pick up values at ten-degree intervals and write them to a file s_couple.m.

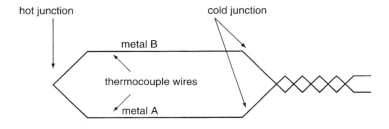

Figure 8.3 A thermocouple.

A fragment of this file is shown below; the full file can be downloaded from an address to be obtained from Pearson Education.

```
% S_COUPLE emf of platinum-10%-rhodium/platinum thermocouples
% Data from BS 4937:Part 1:March 1973
% [ Temperatures in deg C, e.m.f.  in microvolts ]
s_couple = [
-50 -236
-40 -194
-30 -150
-20 -103
-10 -53
 0 0
 10 55
... ...
640 5648 ];
```

Let us find the emf corresponding to 205 °C. We load the table by entering the name of the M-file and invoke the `table1` function with two arguments, the name of the table and the temperature for which we want to interpolate

```
>> s_couple
>> emf205 = table1(s_couple, 205)
emf205 =
   1.4825e+03
```

The value indicated in BS 4937 is 1482 microvolts. We can also interpolate for an array of temperature values, for instance

```
>> ti = 5:  100:  605;
>> emfi = table1(s_couple, ti)
emfi =
   1.0e+03 *
   0.0275
   0.6820
   1.4825
   2.3685
   3.3080
   4.2835
   5.2880
```

Let us enter the values specified in BS 4937 for the temperatures in the array `ti`

```
>> bsi = [27; 682; 1482; 2368; 3308; 4283; 5288];
```

To compare the values in the standard with those interpolated by us we print them side by side, together with the errors and the errors in per cent:

```
>> [ emfi, bsi, (bsi - emfi), (100*(bsi - emfi)./bsi) ]
ans =
    1.0e+03 *
    0.0275 0.0270 -0.0005 -0.0019
    0.6820 0.6820       0        0
    1.4825 1.4820 -0.0005 -0.0000
    2.3685 2.3680 -0.0005 -0.0000
    3.3080 3.3080       0        0
    4.2835 4.2830 -0.0005 -0.0000
    5.2880 5.2880       0        0
```

The restrictions imposed on the table1 function are described at the end of Subsection 8.4.1. In practice, one measures the emf and deduces the temperature from it. As an exercise, try to find the temperature corresponding to a given emf. To do this invert the table with the command

```
inv_couple = [ s_couple(2, :), s_couple(1, :)  ]
```

and interpolate over the new table inv_couple. Unlike in Subsection 8.4.1, you will succeed here. To understand why, plot temperature against emf.

EXAMPLE 8.3   Conductor resistance at different frequencies _____

The flow of alternating current through a conductor produces a magnetic flux. The result is an emf that opposes the current and is greater towards the centre of the conductor. The current density at the centre decreases and increases at the surface. The overall effect is an increase in the effective resistance of the conductor, a phenomenon known as **skin effect**. While negligible at low frequencies, the phenomenon becomes important at higher frequencies. Table 8.3 is the beginning of a list of resistance values for a series of copper conductors at four ac frequencies. The problem we propose here is:

> Given the sectional area, in mm^2, of a copper conductor, and the frequency of the current, in Hz, find the resistance of the conductor in milliohms/metre.

Let us write the table of resistances to a file resist.m as follows

```
%RESIST Copper wire resistance at different frequencies
% Format is [ sectional area, resistance ]
% Units are [ mm^2,  milliohm/m at Hz ]
Cu = [
```

```
0   50   10^5   10^6   10^7
0.03614 554      554     610     1380
0.0707  246      246     340     920
0.126   138      140     245     660
0.196   89       93      178     530
0.283   61.5     67      156     420
0.5     34.6     42.2    110     310
0.75    22.9     33      90      272
1       17.4     28      78.6    210
1.5     11.6     22.6    63      173
2.5     6.95     17      49      138
4       4.35     12.6    36.7    104
6       2.9      10      29.7    83
10      1.74     7.2     23      68
16      1.1      6.6     20      56
25      0.728    NaN     NaN     NaN
35      0.519    NaN     NaN     NaN
50      0.362    NaN     NaN     NaN
70      0.260    NaN     NaN     NaN
95      0.191    NaN     NaN     NaN
120     0.152    NaN     NaN     NaN  ];
```

Table 8.3   Resistance of copper conductors as a function of frequency.

Section	Resistance, milliohms/m			
mm^2	at 50 Hz	10^5 Hz	10^6 Hz	10^7 Hz
0.03614	554	554	610	1380
0.0707	246	246	340	920
0.126	138	140	245	660
0.196	89	93	178	530
...	...	...	...	...

To load the table, and to find the names of the variables it contains, we enter

```
≫ resist
≫ who
Your variables are:
Cu
```

To find the resistance of a conductor having the sectional area 0.75 mm^2, at 20 000 Hz, we call the table2 function with three arguments, namely table name, sectional area, frequency

```
>> table2(Cu, 0.75, 20000)
ans =
   24.9160
```

We can also find the resistance values for an array of sectional-area values, at one frequency. Let us suppose that we are interested only in the areas contained in the table; to isolate them we take the first column without the first row. To do this, we find the dimensions of the table, separate the column vector of areas, and call the function with the name of this vector as its second argument and the desired frequency as the third

```
>> size(Cu)
ans =
   21 5
>> Area = Cu(2:21, 1);
>> table2(Cu, Area, 200000)
ans =
   560.2222
   ...
   NaN
```

As another exercise, let us find the resistance, at different frequencies, of a conductor with a diameter of 3 mm; we do it as follows

```
>> f = Cu(1, 2:5)
>> A = pi*3^2/4
   A =
   7.0686
>> table2(Cu, A, f)
ans =
   2.5901 9.2520 27.9101 78.9928
```

8.11   Exercises

Solutions for Exercises 8.2 and 8.5 appear at the back of the book.

■ **EXERCISE 8.1**   Writing to screen
In the examples described in Section 8.6, substitute `fn = 1` (without quotes) for `fn = 'scissor.out'` and execute the program `scissor`. Then delete `fn = 'scissor.out'` and `fn` everywhere and run the program again. In both cases the output should go directly to the screen.

■ **EXERCISE 8.2**   Fuel consumption
An important measurement of car performance is its fuel consumption per hundred kilometres (see Exercise 8.3 for a number proportional to the reciprocal value, *miles per gallon of fuel*). To calculate this it is sufficient to:

- record the kilometre reading each time when buying fuel;
- calculate the number of kilometres driven between the previous tank replenishment and the present one;
- note the number of litres bought.

In this exercise it is proposed to write a very simple program that does the job. An external file is necessary to keep a record of the previous kilometre reading. The program shall be written to an M-file called `carfuel1.m`; the previous kilometres record, to a MAT-file called `carkm.mat`.

To initialize the file `carkm.mat`, enter MATLAB and define km0 = 0. Save this value in the required MAT-file.

The program shall perform the following steps:

(1)   Load the value km0.
(2)   Prompt the user to enter the present kilometre reading, in km.
(3)   Prompt the user to enter the fuel quantity, ℓ, in l, bought on this occasion.
(4)   Calculate $c = 100\ell/(km - km0)$.
(5)   Display:

Your car consumed c l per 100 km

(6)   Delete the previous file `carkm.mat`.
(7)   Write km0 = km and save this variable on the file `carkm.mat`.

■ **EXERCISE 8.3**   Fuel consumption
Read Exercise 8.2 and design a program that calculates and displays the mileage between two refuellings and the number of miles driven per gallon of fuel.

■ **EXERCISE 8.4**   Looking through a table of atmospheric pressures
When the atmosphere is completely quiet, the relationship between the height above sea level, in m, and atmospheric pressure, in mb (*millibar*), can be represented by Table 8.4. Write the table to an M-file and find, for example, the pressure corresponding to 450 m above sea level.

Table 8.4   Atmospheric pressure.

Height m	Mean pressure mbar
0	1013
100	1001
200	989
300	977
400	965
500	959
600	942
700	932
800	921
900	902
1000	894

One use of the relationship shown is to find the altitude by measuring the pressure; this is the principle of the oldest type of altimeter. As an example, invert the table and find the height corresponding to 956 mb.

■ **EXERCISE 8.5**   Water viscosity
We have seen that water density depends on temperature. Another water property that depends on temperature is **viscosity**; it is important in fluid flow and in some heat transfer problems. Some applications of viscosity are briefly discussed in Chapter 13. Table 8.5 contains a list of fresh-water **kinematic viscosity** values, v, between 1 and 28 °C.

Write the table to a file `kvisc.m` and

(1)   plot kinematic viscosity against temperature;
(2)   find the viscosity values corresponding to the temperatures 0.5, 1.5, 2.5, ..., 27.5 °C;
(3)   invert the table and find the temperature corresponding to $v = 0.9 \, \text{m}^2/\text{s}$. Plot this point over the graph obtained at step 1;
(4)   try to find the viscosity corresponding to 30 °C. What happens?

■ **EXERCISE 8.6**   A table of discharge coefficients
Figure 8.4 shows a tank with an orifice whose diameter is d_0. The **pressure head** h is the height of the free surface above the orifice axis. After leaving the tank the streamlines contract to a diameter $d_1 < d_0$. The phenomenon is known as **vena contracta**. The flow is related to the area of the contracted flow section, $a_1 = \pi d_1^2/4$, and the flow velocity, V, by

$$Q = a_1 V \tag{8.1}$$

Table 8.5   Fresh-water kinematic viscosity.

Temperature °C	v m²/s	Temperature °C	v m²/s
0	1.79	15	1.14
1	1.73	16	1.11
2	1.67	17	1.08
3	1.62	18	1.06
4	1.57	19	1.03
5	1.52	20	1.01
6	1.47	21	0.983
7	1.43	22	0.960
8	1.39	23	0.938
9	1.33	24	0.917
10	1.31	25	0.896
11	1.27	26	0.876
12	1.24	27	0.857
13	1.20	28	0.839
14	1.17		

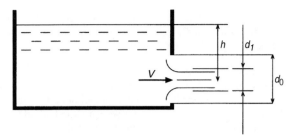

Figure 8.4   Tank discharge.

A consistent set of SI units to be used with Equation 8.1 may be $m^3 \, s^{-1}$ for Q, m^2 for a_1, and $m \, s^{-1}$ for V. Usually it is the orifice area, $a = \pi d_0^2/4$, that is known. Therefore, it is convenient to rewrite Equation 8.1 as

$$Q = caV \qquad\qquad (8.2)$$

where $c = a_1/a$ is known as the **discharge coefficient**. This latter coefficient depends on the orifice diameter, d_0. and the pressure head, h. Tables of discharge coefficients can be found in books on hydraulics; a partial example is shown in Table 8.6.

(a)   Write the data in Table 8.6 to an M-file prepared for table lookup.
(b)   Use the MATLAB `table2` function to find the discharge coefficients corresponding to the orifice diameter 0.25 m and the pressure heads 0.010 and 0.05 m.

■ **EXERCISE 8.7**   Current density
The allowable current density in an electrical conductor is not a constant. The reason is that the flow of current through a conductor generates heat. If the current density were a constant, let us say I_d, the current, I, would be proportional to the sectional area of the conductor, that is, to the square of the diameter, d. The generated heat, H, is proportional to the resistance, R, and the square of the current, so that we can write

$$H = RI^2 = R(I_d \pi d^2/4)^2 \qquad\qquad (8.3)$$

Table 8.6   A table of discharge coefficients.

Pressure	Orifice diameter, d_0, m					
head, h, m	0.39	0.18	0.06	0.03	0.015	0.06
0.21	0.590	0.594	0.601	0.611	0.622	0.651
0.24	0.591	0.594	0.601	0.610	0.620	0.648
0.27	0.591	0.595	0.601	0.609	0.618	0.646
0.30	0.591	0.595	0.600	0.608	0.617	0.644
0.40	0.593	0.596	0.600	0.605	0.613	0.638

Table 8.7   Allowable current in copper conductors.

Sectional area mm^2	Allowable current A	Sectional area mm^2	Allowable current A
0.75	16	50	210
1	20	70	260
1.5	25	95	310
2.5	34	120	365
4	45	150	415
6	57	185	475
10	78	240	560
16	104	300	645
25	137	400	770
35	168	500	880

For unit conductor length, the surface through which heat is transmitted to the air is equal to πd. Thus, at constant current density the generated heat would grow proportionally to the fourth power of the diameter, while the surface through which it was dissipated would grow only proportionally to the first power of the same diameter. This is why the allowable current density decreases with increasing diameter.

Table 8.7 shows the recommended current densities for one-wire copper conductors installed in air with a distance of at least one diameter between them. Write the data to a file `curdens.m`. Then

(1)   plot the allowable current versus sectional area;
(2)   supposing the availability of copper wires with the sectional areas 5, 15, 20, 30, 40, 60, and 100 mm^2, find the corresponding allowable currents;
(3)   plot the values found at (2) over the curve obtained at (1).

■ **EXERCISE 8.8**   Platinum resistance thermometer
Example 8.2 discusses one method of measuring temperature, the thermocouple. This exercise refers to another method, the resistance thermometer. In this instrument the temperature is obtained by measuring the change of resistance with temperature of a conductor or semiconductor. Usually the conductor is connected in a bridge network. One of the metals preferred in resistance sensors is platinum. Table 8.8 is an extract from the British Standard 1904. The original contains values between -200 and $950\,°C$, at one-degree intervals. For the purpose of this exercise Table 8.8 contains values between 0 and $330\,°C$, at ten-degree intervals. The nominal value assumed is $100\,\Omega$ at $0\,°C$.

(1)   Write the data to a file `platin.m` and

    (a)   plot the resistance versus temperature;
    (b)   find the resistances corresponding to the temperatures 5, 15, 25, ..., 325°C.
    (c)   plot the values found at (2) over the curve obtained at (1).

Table 8.8   Resistance of platinum thermometers.

Temperature °C	Resistance Ω	Temperature °C	Resistance Ω
0	100.00	170	164.76
10	103.90	180	168.46
20	107.79	190	172.16
30	111.67	200	175.84
40	115.54	210	179.51
50	119.40	220	183.17
60	123.24	230	186.32
70	127.07	240	190.45
80	130.89	250	194.07
90	134.70	260	197.69
100	138.50	270	201.29
110	142.29	280	204.88
120	146.06	290	208.45
130	149.82	300	212.02
140	153.58	310	215.57
150	157.31	320	219.12
160	161.04	330	222.65

(2)   In practice it is the resistance that is measured, and the temperature is deduced from this measurement. Therefore

    (a)   invert the table;
    (b)   plot temperature against resistance;
    (c)   find the temperatures corresponding to 110 and 150 ohms;
    (d)   plot the values found above over the curve obtained at (2).

Chapter 9
Regression and interpolation

9.1   Introduction

In Chapter 8 we learnt how to interpolate linearly over tables of engineering data. In Section 1.11 we met functions that can be used for linear, cubic, and spline interpolation. In this chapter we shall learn more functions that can be used for interpolation by polynomials of any degree. The same functions can be employed for fitting power and exponential curves. Polynomial interpolation is compared with spline interpolation in this chapter.

The techniques described in this chapter can be used for establishing relationships between experimental data; this is the subject of regression. Economists use regressions for forecasting. In engineering, regressions have important applications that go beyond simple interpolation. For example, the general form of the equation governing a certain process can be known theoretically, but not the values of the coefficients that appear in that equation. Tests are then run for that process and the variables involved are measured. A curve of the theoretically expected form is fitted, by regression, to the experimental data and this defines the parameters of the curve. Models 'calibrated' by regression are used in design calculations and in simulations.

The procedures described in this chapter are first exemplified on simple, easy to understand data sets. Thus, the techniques are not obscured by the details of engineering problems. Further examples, however, use engineering data and are applied to engineering problems. Some sets of engineering data used in this chapter were also used in Chapter 8.

9.2   Polynomial fit

In Subsection 8.4.1 we learnt how to find the density of water, at various temperatures, by interpolating linearly over the table `watdens`. It is easy to check that the actual relationship between temperature and water density is not linear; to see this

(1) | load | the table by entering its name;

(2) | separate | temperature and water density;

(3) | plot | water density against temperature.

The corresponding MATLAB commands are

```
≫ watdens
≫ x = watdens(:, 1);
≫ y = watdens(:, 2);
≫ plot(x, y)
```

Visual inspection of the resulting graph shows that a second-degree, or even a third-degree curve would be more suitable. Such curves can be *fitted* to the given data – that is, the table `watdens` – by the least-squares method. The principle was introduced in Section 6.5, but the equations must be modified to suit higher-degree curves. Thus, assuming that an experiment yielded m pairs of data, (x_i, y_i), and that a second-degree curve seems to fit those data, we must seek the three coefficients, c_1, c_2, c_3, of the equation

$$y = c_1 x^2 + c_2 x + c_3 \tag{9.1}$$

that minimize the sum of squared errors

$$\epsilon = \sum_{i=1}^{m} (y_i - c_1 x_i^2 - c_2 x_i - c_3)^2 \tag{9.2}$$

The common dimension of the arrays x and y is m. Differentiating ϵ with respect to c_1, c_2, and c_3, and equating the derivatives to zero, we obtain the system

$$\begin{bmatrix} \sum x_i^4 & \sum x_i^3 & \sum x_i^2 \\ \sum x_i^3 & \sum x_i^2 & \sum x_i \\ \sum x_i^2 & \sum x_i & m \end{bmatrix} \begin{bmatrix} c_1 \\ c_2 \\ c_3 \end{bmatrix} = \begin{bmatrix} \sum x_i^2 y_i \\ \sum x_i y_i \\ \sum y_i \end{bmatrix} \tag{9.3}$$

where the sums are carried out from $i = 1$ to $i = m$. Obviously, we can build the matrices in Equation 9.3 and use the backslash operator to obtain the matrix of coefficients c_1, c_2, c_3. Alternatively, similarly to the derivation of the least-squares method in Section 6.5 and in the Appendix of Chapter 6, we can define

$$
\mathbf{A} = \begin{bmatrix} x_1^2 & x_1 & 1 \\ x_2^2 & x_2 & 1 \\ \vdots & \vdots & \vdots \\ x_m^2 & x_m & 1 \end{bmatrix}, \ \mathbf{Y} = \begin{bmatrix} y_1 \\ y_2 \\ \vdots \\ y_m \end{bmatrix}, \ \mathbf{C} = \begin{bmatrix} c_1 \\ c_2 \\ c_3 \end{bmatrix} \tag{9.4}
$$

and show that

$$
\mathbf{C} = (\mathbf{A}'\mathbf{A})^{-1}\mathbf{A}'\mathbf{Y}
$$

MATLAB provides a shortcut for performing all these operations. The `polyfit` function builds the matrix $\mathbf{A}$ and solves for $\mathbf{C}$. The `polyfit` function is used with three arguments

(1)   the independent variable,
(2)   the dependent variable,
(3)   the degree of the curve to be fitted.

Thus, continuing the example of the `watdens` table, we fit a second-degree curve to our data by

```
≫ C2 = polyfit(x, y, 2)
C2 =
   -0.0000 0.0000 1.0000
```

This display is not satisfactory; the first two coefficients are so small that they cannot be represented with only four decimal digits. The numbers that were actually calculated can be viewed with the commands

```
≫ format long
≫ C2
C2 =
   -0.00000545123926     0.00002154957057     0.99998997176736
```

These are the coefficients of Equation 9.1 in descending order of the powers of x, that is

$$
c_1 = C2(1), \quad c_2 = C2(2), \quad c_3 = C2(3)
$$

We can substitute the above coefficients in Equation 9.1 and calculate the ordinates of the curve. MATLAB provides a more convenient way: given the array of coefficients, $C2$, the values of the fitted polynomial at the points defined by the array of independent variable values, in our case x, are yielded by the `polyval` function. This function is called with two arguments:

(1)   the name of the array of coefficients,

(2)   the name of the array of independent-variable values.

The command is

```
>> y2 = polyval(C2, x);
```

We went back from the values of y to find the relationship from x to y. The technique is therefore called **regression**, a word derived from a Latin root meaning 'to go back'. With this term we say in the above example that we performed a **second-degree regression.**

Using the same `polyfit` function we can perform regressions of any degree n; the general syntax is `polyfit(x, y, n)`. For example, let us try a third-degree regression

```
>> C3 = polyfit(x, y, 3);
>> C3;
C3' =
    0.00000003751040
   -0.00000770186335
    0.00005668931469
    0.99988734330887
>> y3 = polyval(C3, x);
```

It is left to the reader, as an exercise, to derive the equations for this case and to check in the listing of the `polyfit` function that it implements them.

The given curve of water densities, and the second and third-order **best fits** can be compared by plotting together the three curves

```
>> plot(x, y, x, y2, x, y3)
```

The differences between the three curves are too small to be seen on the resulting graph. We can **zoom** the left segments of the curves

```
>> xx = x(1:10); yy = y(1:10);
>> yy2 = y2(1:10);
>> yy3 = y3(1:10);
>> plot(xx, yy, xx, yy2, xx, yy3)
>> text(xx(1), yy(1), 'y')
>> text(xx(1), yy2(1), 'y2')
```

Zooms of other segments of the curves can be obtained in a similar way.

The reader can try higher-degree polynomial regressions. There is a limit, however, to the degree of the polynomial that can be fitted to a given data set. If the desired degree is n, the number of coefficients to be determined is $n+1$. If the number of *observations,* that is, of (x, y) pairs, is $m < n+1$, the problem is not determined. If $m = n + 1$, and no two x-values are equal, the least-squares procedure yields the polynomial that passes through all given points. In this case the resulting coefficients are the exact solution of a system of $n + 1$ equations in $n + 1$ variables. For example, as the third-degree curve has four coefficients, it is completely defined by four points. A third-degree regression on only four points will result in the exact solution. We can exemplify this by taking, for instance, the first four rows of the `watdens` table:

```
>> c = polyfit(x(1:4), y(1:4), 3);
```

The errors, also called **residuals**, are:

```
>> resid = y(1:4) - polyval(c, x(1:4))
resid =
     0
     0
     0
     0
```

We can talk of a regression only if $m > n+1$. This is important if the regression is applied to experimental data. As discussed in Section 6.5, experimental data are affected by various errors. Therefore, in most cases such data do not fall exactly on the *smooth* line expected from theory. One way of filtering out the error-induced 'noise' is to fit a curve by the least-squares method. If there are m experimental points, and we fit a polynomial of degree $n = m - 1$, the curve will pass through all the m given points and no noise will be eliminated. If n is only slightly smaller than $m - 1$, the curve will be greatly affected by experimental errors and may look 'noisy'. On the other hand, if $n \ll m - 1$, the regression can yield only a very rough description of the phenomenon.

9.3   Polynomial interpolation

The tool we learned in the previous section can be used for interpolation. For instance, in the `watdens` table the entries are $0, 2, \ldots, 40\,°C$. We can use the polynomial coefficients $C3$ – found in the previous section – for calculating water densities at $1, 3, \ldots, 39\,°C$

```
>> xi = 1:39;
>> yi = polyval(C3, xi);
```

The points interpolated in this way can be plotted over the given curve by

```
>> plot(x, y, xi, yi, 'o')
```

This command plots y against x as a solid line, and the xi, yi pairs as points represented by circles. Instead of 'o' we could have used any of the symbols

.   +   *   x

and a few more that can be found by typing `help plot`.

The result of the preceding commands is shown in Figure 9.1. We can compare the values yielded by the third-degree polynomial interpolation with those obtained by linear interpolation (see Subsection 8.4.1)

```
>> yi_lin = table1(watdens, xi);
>> [ xi' yi' yi_lin ]
```

We can now try to solve a problem posed in Subsection 8.4.1: find the temperature corresponding to the water density 0.9992 t/m³. As the water density is not a monotonic function of temperature, the built-in function `table1` was of no help. Unlike this function, the `polyfit` algorithm does not impose any condition on the independent variable. We can, therefore, consider the water density as the

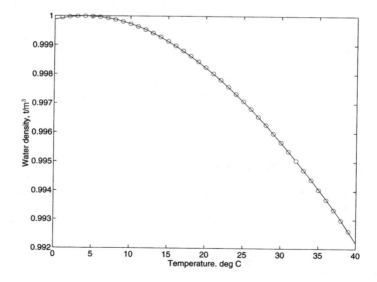

Figure 9.1   Polynomial interpolation of water densities.

independent variable, the temperature as the dependent variable, and perform the regression

```
≫ c3_inv = polyfit(y, x, 3);
≫ wd = polyval(c3_inv, 0.9992)
wd =
   12.7964
```

Notice the order of the arguments: y first, x second. Let us check whether the result of this interpolation is acceptable

```
≫ plot(x, y, wd, 0.9992, 'x')
```

We find that the interpolated point lies rather far from the given curve. We can improve our result if we restrict the interval over which the regression is performed:

```
≫ c3_inv = polyfit(y(5:15), x(5:15), 3);
≫ wd = polyval(c3_inv, 0.9992)
wd =
   14.3924
≫ plot(x(5:15), y(5:15), wd, 0.9992, 'x')
```

We see that the newly interpolated point is sensibly different from the previous result, and lies this time on the curve. We have now obtained a much better approximation; the reason is that as the number of given pairs approaches the number of polynomial coefficients, the result tends to the exact solution.

The points defined in the `watdens` table are 'deterministic' in the sense that we consider them as exact, that is, not affected by experimental errors. We then expect the polynomial line to pass through all of them. The last calculation above suggests a way of doing this: fit lines over restricted intervals. The idea is implemented by **splines**, as shown in Section 9.7.

We have seen how easy it is to fit a polynomial curve to given data, and to use this curve for interpolation. Other advantages of polynomials are that they can be easily differentiated and integrated. Indeed, if $f(x)$ is a polynomial of degree n defined by its array of coefficients C,

$$f(x) = C(1)x^n + C(2)x^{n-1} + \cdots + C(n)x^1 + C(n+1)x^0 \tag{9.5}$$

its derivative is

$$f'(x) = nC(1)x^{n-1} + (n-1)C(2)x^{n-2} + \cdots + C(n)x^0 \tag{9.6}$$

It is defined by the array of coefficients C_D which can be calculated in MATLAB as an array product

```
>> L = length(C) - 1;
>> C_D = C(1: L).*[ L: -1:  1 ]
```

By writing C(1: L) we dropped the last coefficient in C and got an array C_D one shorter than C. The above results can be obtained with the new MATLAB function polyder.

We can calculate in this way, for example, the derivative of water density with respect to temperature. The resulting curve represents the **sensitivity** of water density to changes in temperature.

The integral of the polynomial described by Equation 9.5 is

$$I(x) = \int f(x)\,dx = \frac{C(1)}{n+1}x^{n+1} + \cdots + \frac{C(n+1)}{1} + C_0 \tag{9.7}$$

In order to calculate the **constant of integration** C_0 we must know the value of I at some point in the interval that interests us; the simplest possibility would be $C_0 = I(0)$. The other coefficients can be calculated in MATLAB by the array division

```
>> C_I = C./[ length(C): -1:  1 ]
```

A simple illustration of the above procedures is shown in Example 9.1, an engineering application in Example 9.4.

Polynomials, however, may also have disadvantages. Thus, in certain cases, polynomials fitted over relatively large intervals can oscillate wildly, especially if the degree of the fitted curve is high. An instance of such a behaviour, known as **inflexibility**, is shown in Example 9.3.

9.4   Assessing the quality of a regression

In the preceding section we fitted two curves to the table of water densities. Which one is better, and by how much better? Plotting the regression curves over the given data does not lead to a clear answer, in this case (in other cases this statement can be false). We must look for some other way of comparing the results. The procedures we used minimize the errors relative to the original data, so let us compare the residuals of the two regressions

```
>> resid2 = y - y2;
>> resid3 = y - y3;
>> [ x resid2 resid3 ]
ans =
         0        -0.00011997176736 -0.00001734330887
```

```
2.00000000000000  -0.00004126595144  -0.00000021456804
 ...    ...    ...
40.00000000000000  0.00007002823264  -0.00003260022586
```

It appears that the residuals of the third-degree regression are smaller than those of the second-degree one, but it is rather difficult to follow the differences as displayed above. A better appreciation is possible if we plot the residuals. We can do this versus the independent variable

```
>> plot(x, resid2, 'k-', x, resid3, 'r:')
>> grid
>> legend('residual 2', 'residual 3')
>> xlabel('x')
>> figure(1)
```

Alternatively, the residuals can be plotted versus the given dependent-variable values

```
>> plot(y, resid2, y, resid3)
>> grid
>> text(y(20), resid2(20), 'residual 2')
>> text(y(20), resid3(20), 'residual 3')
```

We clearly see that the third-degree curve is a better approximation than the second-degree one.

A criterion for appreciating, by means of a single number, how well the calculated curves fit the given points is the sum of the squared errors, SSE. For the two regressions

```
>> SSE2 = sum(resid2.^2)
SSE2 =
    5.930157448952528e-08
>> SSE3 = sum(resid3.^2)
SSE3 =
    3.201618175863290e-09
```

As SSE3 < SSE2 we conclude again that the third-degree curve is closer to the given water-density data.

Another criterion is the **coefficient of determination** defined by

$$r^2 = \frac{SS_{yy} - SSE}{SS_{yy}} = 1 - \frac{SSE}{SS_{yy}} \tag{9.8}$$

where

$$SS_{yy} = \sum_{i-1}^{m} (y_i - y_m)^2$$

and y_m is the mean of the given y_i values, that is

$$y_m = \frac{\sum_{i=1}^{m} y_i}{m}$$

SS_{yy} represents the *variance* of y about its mean value, and SSE the *variance* of y about the regression line. SS_{yy} does not depend upon the x values, while SSE does. Therefore, the coefficient of determination measures the extent to which the errors of prediction are reduced by the knowledge of the x values. If, for the regression under consideration, the information provided by the x values does not contribute much to the knowledge of y, SSE does not differ much from SS_{yy} and r is close to zero. The better the regression fits the given data, the smaller the sum of squared errors, SSE, becomes. For a perfect fit SSE = 0 and then $r^2 = 1$.

In our example

```
≫ SSyy = sum((y - mean(y)).^2)
≫ R2 = sqrt(1 - SSE2/SSyy)
R2 =
     0.99977127651426
≫ R3 = sqrt(1 - SSE3/SSyy)
R3 =
     0.99998765283974
```

and we once again see that the third-degree regression fits the data better than the second-degree curve.

All the criteria we discussed consider the errors relative to the given data set. There are, however, other aspects that must be considered too; some of them were briefly mentioned at the end of Section 9.2. Some general advice is given below.

(1)   If there is a **physical model** of the phenomenon under study, fit a curve corresponding to the equations of that model. This is done in Examples 9.4 and 9.5.

(2)   If there is no physical model, build an **empirical model** by fitting a polynomial curve; this was done in Section 9.2. Increase the degree of the polynomial until one of the following happens:

- The SSE or the coefficient of determination ceases to improve visibly;
- The fitted curve begins to exhibit oscillations for which there is no physical explanation;
- The degree of the polynomial approaches the number of data pairs.

(3)   Whenever possible, check your regression on data sets other than that used for computing the coefficients of the regression (but obviously related to the same phenomenon).

9.5   Power regression

Polynomial lines are not the only lines that can be fitted to data. For example, some phenomena can be modelled by a **power function**, that is, an equation of the form

$$y = ax^b \qquad\qquad (9.9)$$

where a and b are constants. Equations like Equation 9.9 usually characterize rapidly growing processes. As shown in the following example, such cases can be easily reduced to linear regressions.

Fish farming in marine floating cages is a branch of *aquaculture* that has expanded rapidly in the past three decades. As an example, data presented in Jones (1987), about the production of yellowtail (*Seriola quinqueradiata*) in cages in Japan are shown in Table 9.1.

We write the data to a file called yellow.m, in an array called fish:

```
%YELLOW production of cultured yellowtail in Japan.
% acc.  to Jones 1987
% The contents are fish = [ year tons ].

fish = [ 1961 1900
...
1984 154500 ];
```

The data are loaded by the command

```
>> yellow
```

Table 9.1   Production of cultured yellowtail in Japan.

Year	Tons	Year	Tons
1961	1900	1976	101600
1964	9500	1979	154900
1967	21200	1982	146300
1970	43300	1984	154500
1973	80300		

Let us suppose that we have forgotten the format of file `yellow.m`. We need this information, but it is not necessary to leave the environment in order to get it; we can use the `help` facility

```
>> help yellow
%YELLOW production of cultured yellowtail in Japan.
% acc.  to Jones 1987
% The contents are fish = [ year tons ].
```

With this information we separate the data by

```
>> year = fish(:, 1); mass = fish(:, 2);
```

Trying a regression with the exact year number as the independent variable leads to some difficulties which will not be explained here. We shall use instead a 'relative' year number; it can be obtained by the subtraction

```
>> x = year - 1960
```

If the data fall around a power-function curve, their representation on log–log axes should be close to a straight line. Indeed, if the data obey Equation 9.9, taking natural logarithms of both sides of Equation 9.9 we obtain

$$\ln y = \ln a + b \ln x \tag{9.10}$$

Let $u = \ln x$, and $v = \ln y$. Then

$$u = \ln a + bv \tag{9.11}$$

is indeed the equation of a straight line in the u, v plane.

We can check the power-function hypothesis by plotting with the use of the `loglog` function

```
>> loglog(x, mass)
```

The result of plotting with log–log scales encourages us to try a power-function regression

```
>> u = log(x); v = log(mass)
>> c = polyfit(u, v, 1)
c =
   1.4761 7.3516
```

```
≫ a = exp(c(2))
a =
    1.5587e+03
≫ b = c(1)
b =
    1.4761
≫ y = a*x.^b;
```

To compare the y-values obtained by regression directly with those given we can enter

```
≫ [ mass y ]
ans =
    1.0e+05 *
    0.0190 0.0156
    0.0950 0.1206
    0.2120 0.2756
    0.4330 0.4665
    0.8030 0.6871
    1.0160 0.9336
    1.5490 1.2031
    1.4630 1.4938
    1.5450 1.6985
```

The values obtained by regression can be plotted over the given graph by

```
≫ plot(year, y, year, mass, 'o')
≫ title('Power function fitted to yellowtail production')
≫ xlabel('Year')
≫ ylabel('Metric tons')
```

Let us write the equation of the curve on the curve itself. If we want to do this approximately in the middle of the curve we must know the length of the plotted vector; we find it by

```
≫ length(y)
ans =
    9
```

The equation will be printed by the text function which requires a string argument. There is no need to remember the values of the constants a and b; we can call them by name and then convert them to string representation by means of the num2str function. The desired text string is obtained by

```
≫ t = [ 'tons = ' num2str(a) 'x^b, b= ' num2str(b) ]
```

The plot is completed by

```
≫ text(year(4), y(4), t)
```

9.6 Exponential regression

The well-known cliché 'exponential growth' is frequently used as a metaphor. However, we can find examples in which this expression is correct, and we shall see in this section that we have the means to check it.

Data obeying approximately the **exponential** law

$$y = ae^{bx} \tag{9.12}$$

can be reduced to a linear regression. Taking natural logarithms of both sides of Equation 9.12, and letting $v = \ln y$, we obtain

$$v = \ln a + bx \tag{9.13}$$

The relationship between x and v is linear. The procedure will be illustrated by the following example, taken again from the field of aquaculture. Poxton and Goldsworthy (1987) present a table of lengths, weights and projected trunk areas of 20 broodstock turbot (*Scophtalmus maximus*). The same authors analyse the data of ten of these fish by plotting them on log–log scales. The values for the selected ten individuals are shown in Table 9.2.

We shall use MATLAB for fitting curves to the length-weight relationship. Let us write the data to a file called turbot.m, in an array turb. We continue by loading

Table 9.2 Data of broodstock turbot.

Length cm	Weight g	Area cm^2	Length cm	Weight g	Area cm^2
34.3	962.3	359.96	36.8	936.0	391.20
38.7	1264.5	448.13	40.0	1490.8	479.79
38.2	1005.5	415.07	40.8	1416.2	478.46
43.8	1879.0	556.30	39.5	1441.0	482.95
41.8	1638.0	518.70	36.3	1089.6	400.67

the data and, if we do not remember the format, we ask for help:

```
≫ turbot
≫ help turbot
TURBOT length and weight data of 10 turbot fish
 as presented in Poxton and Goldsworthy, 1987.
 The data array is called 'turb' with contents:
 [ length, mass, area ]
 in [centimetres, grams, square cm ]
```

Next we separate the arrays and take a first look at them

```
≫ length = turb(:, 1); mass = turb(:, 2);
≫ plot(length, mass)
```

The data are not well ordered and must be sorted. We use the built-in `sort` function and ask for two results: the array *l* of the elements of *length* in ascending order of their values, and the array *i* of the indices of the elements of *length*, in the same order

```
≫ [ l i ] = sort(length)
l =
    34.3000
    :
    :
i =
     1
    :
    :
```

Now we sort also the elements of *mass* by means of the indices, *i*, and check that the sort succeeded

```
≫ for j = 1:10
       m(j) = mass(i(j));
end
≫ [ l m ]
```

The latter command elicits an error message because *l* and *m* have different sizes

```
≫ size(l), size(m)
ans =
```

```
     10  1
ans =
      1  10
```

The correct command is

```
≫ [ l m' ]
ans =
    1.0e+03 *
    0.0343 0.9623
⋮
```

This is OK. We check if a power-function law would be suitable

```
≫ loglog(l,m)
```

The plot does not allow a clear conclusion, but we can try

```
≫ u = log(l); v = log(m);
≫ c = polyfit(u, v', 1)
c =
    3.0631 -4.0634
≫ a = exp(c(2))
a =
    0.0172
≫ b = c(1)
b =
    3.0631
```

Note that in the `polyfit` arguments we have used v' rather than v. We now calculate a few points on the regression line and plot it. For comparison, the initially given points are plotted too, but as circles

```
≫ mi = a*l.^b
≫ plot(l, mi, l, m, 'o')
≫ resid = m - mi'; SSE1 = sum(resid.^2)
SSE1 =
    1.0083e+005
```

The plot looks reasonable. We also try an exponential law

```
≫ semilogy(l, m)
```

The plot looks encouraging and we go on

```
≫ c = polyfit(l, v', 1)
c =
    0.0793 4.0601
≫ a = exp(c(2))
a =
 57.9787
≫ b = c(1)
b =
    0.0793
≫ mi = a*exp(b*l);
≫ plot(l, mi, l, m, 'o')
≫ title('Exponential law fit to turbot-weight data')
≫ xlabel('Turbot length, cm')
≫ ylabel('Turbot weight, g')
≫ resid2 = m - mi'
≫ SSE2 = sum(resid2.^2)
SSE2 =
    9.5505e+004
```

It appears that the exponential law fits the data slightly better than the power-function law.

9.7   Spline interpolation

One example given in Section 9.3 shows us that interpolation over narrow intervals may lead to better results than interpolation over large intervals. Another observation is that higher-degree polynomials can exhibit large oscillations; an illustration is given in Example 9.3. Putting these observations together we are led to the idea of **spline interpolation**. To explain it briefly let us consider a set of pairs (x_i, y_i) in the interval $[a, b]$. We divide the interval into a series of subintervals $[x_{j-1}, x_j]$ such that

$$a = x_0 \le x_1 \le \cdots \le x_{j-1} \le x_j \le \cdots \le x_n = b$$

The coordinates $x_1, \ldots, x_n$ are also called **knots**. In each subinterval $[x_{j-1}, x_j]$ we look for a polynomial s_{j-1}, of degree not larger than k, such that

$$\begin{aligned} s_{j-1}(x_{j-1}) &= y_{j-1} \\ s_{j-1}(x_j) &= y_j \end{aligned}$$

In applications it is often sufficient to choose $k = 3$. Then four equations are needed to find the coefficients of each polynomial s_i. Two of them are the equations shown above. Further equations are obtained by requiring the first and second derivatives of the cubic polynomials to be continuous at each knot, that is

$$s'_{j-1}(x_j) \quad = \quad s'_j(x_j)$$
$$s''_{j-1}(x_j) \quad = \quad s''_j(x_j)$$

The set of equations is completed by defining the first or second derivative at the ends of the interval $[a, b]$.

The set of polynomials s_j, $j = 1, 2, \ldots, n$ is a **cubic interpolating spline**. This name was adopted by I.J. Schoenberg from the name of a tool used in naval architectural drawings and once also on the moulding lofts of shipyards. The splines, once made of wood, more recently of plastic, are flexible rulers. They are forced to pass through a number of points by holding them there under metallic weights called **ducks**. It can be shown that the cubic spline defined above closely approximates the shape taken by a wooden or plastic spline.

A more detailed explanation of spline theory is beyond the scope of this book; it can be found, for example, in Schumaker (1981), Bu-qing and Ding-yuan (1989), and Farin (1993). The MATLAB package includes a `spline` function whose use will be demonstrated below. Many more functions are provided by the `Spline Toolbox` delivered as a separate package by MathWorks (see de Boor 1990).

For illustration we shall again use the example of water densities stored in the file `watdens.m`. We begin by loading the data and separating the vector of water temperatures, x, and the vector of water densities, y

```
≫ watdens
≫ x = watdens(:, 1); y = watdens(:, 2);
```

Before calculating the interpolating spline, we again fit a cubic polynomial line, that is, the one which proved itself better in the previous two sections

```
≫ c3 = polyfit(x, y, 2); y3 = polyval(c3, x);
```

Next, we calculate the spline by calling the function with three arguments:

(1)   the array of given independent-variable values,

(2)   the array of given dependent-variable values,

(3)   the array of independent-variable values at which we want to interpolate.

To make the comparison possible, we make the third argument equal to the first

```
≫ ys = spline(x, y, x);
≫ format long
≫ [ y y3 ys ]
ans =
    0.99987000000000  0.99998997176736  0.99987000000000
```

```
0.99997000000000 1.00001126595144 0.99997000000000
...
0.99299000000000 0.99293726595144 0.99299000000000
0.99220000000000 0.99212997176736 0.99220000000000
```

We clearly see that the spline passes through all given points, while the polynomial line does not. We can strengthen our conviction by checking the residuals:

```
>> resid3 = y - y3; resids = y - ys;
>> plot(x, resid3, x, resids)
>> xlabel('Water temperature, x')
>> ylabel('Residuals of interpolations')
>> text(x(2), resid3(2), 'resid3')
>> text(x(4), resids(4), 'resids')
```

We can also compare the sums of squared errors

```
>> e3 = sqrt(sum(resid3.^2))
e3 =
    2.435191460430273e-04
>> es = sqrt(sum(resids.^2))
es =
    0
```

To see that spline interpolation yields points falling exactly along the given line, we form a new vector of x-coordinates, calculate the corresponding y-coordinates, and plot the newly found points, as circles, over the given line

```
>> xi = 1:  2:  39; yi = spline(x, y, xi);
>> plot(x, y, xi, yi, 'o')
>> title('Spline interpolation of water densities')
>> xlabel('Water temperature, deg C')
>> ylabel('Water density, t/m^3')
```

To see better what is happening, the plot can be zoomed, for example at the left

```
>> plot(x(1:10), y(1:10), xi(1:10), yi(1:10), 'o')
```

Splines are not only used for interpolation; they have important applications in computer graphics where they are used for describing various shapes and surfaces. As mentioned, the name spline was borrowed from an instrument used in naval architectural offices and in shipyard lofting where it was used for drawing ship lines. **Mathematical splines** are extensively used today for other bodies, especially cars and planes. No wonder that some of the most interesting developments come from companies such as Citroën or Renault (see Section 5.10).

9.8   The basic fitting interface

So far we have performed regressions and interpolations by using only the command line facilities. We consider that in this way we can give a better insight into those techniques. Today, MATLAB 6 provides a graphical user interface (GUI) that simplifies the work. In this section we are going to introduce some of the new possibilities.

Let us return to the example of fresh-water, kinematic viscosity shown in Table 8.5. Assuming that the reader saved the data into a file called kvisc, we load and plot them with the commands

```
kvisc; % load data
plot(nu(:, 1), nu(:, 2), 'o')
xlabel('Temperature, degrees Celsius')
ylabel('Kinematic viscosity of fresh water, m^2 s^{-1}')
```

This produces part of Figure 9.2. In the figure window look for the menu bar, open the Tools menu and press Basic fit. A new window will open, as shown in

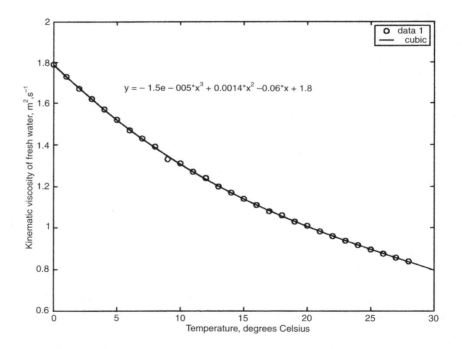

Figure 9.2 Cubic regression of fresh-water kinematic viscosity.

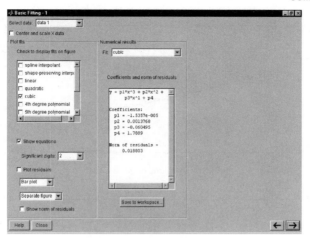

Figure 9.3   GUI for curve fitting.

Figure 9.3. Check the boxes *cubic* and *show equation*. You will see that immediately the figure window is updated and appears as shown in Figure 9.2. If you do not like the position of the expression for the regression equation, you can enable editing and click the mouse on the text of the equation. Use the mouse to drag the rectangle that appears. Now write on the command line

```
plot(nu(:, 1), nu(:, 2), 'o')
title('Kinematic viscosity of fresh water')
xlabel('Temperature, degrees Celsius')
ylabel('Kinematic viscosity, m^2 s^{-1}')
```

and the plots will eventually look as in Figure 9.4.

The interface presents many more possibilities. We are confident that the explanations given in this chapter will enable the reader to explore, understand and implement the new facilities.

9.9   Summary

Given a set of pairs (x, y) we can find the equation of a curve passing close to these points by a procedure called **regression**. The usual criterion is the minimization of the **sum of squared errors**, that is, of the differences between the given and the calculated values of the independent variables, as discussed in Chapter 6. If the equation of the proposed curve is a polynomial, a good order of operations is:

(1)   Plot the given data and check visually what degree of polynomial curve seems to fit them;

(2)   Use the `polyfit` function to obtain the coefficients of the fitted polynomial curve;

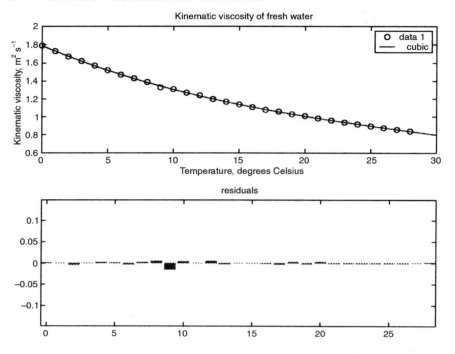

Figure 9.4 Fresh-water,kinematic viscosity – plots of cubic regression and corresponding residuals obtained with the basic fitting interface.

(3) Use the `polyval` function to calculate a set of points as predicted by the regression;

(4) Plot the predicted points over the given curve;

(5) If it is not clear that the regression is satisfactory, try several regressions, of different degrees, and compare them by plotting the **residuals** – that is, the errors – or by comparing the **sums of squared errors** and the **coefficients of determination**. Choose the regression that yields the smallest sum of squared errors or the largest coefficient of determination.

To be more specific, let us suppose that we are given a set of (x, y) pairs and want to fit to them a polynomial of degree n. We do this by

```
C = polyfit(x, y, n)
```

The array C contains the coefficients of the fitted polynomial, in descending order of the powers of x. We can calculate a set of predicted y values, for example for the same set of x values, by

```
yi = polyval(C, x)
```

The residuals are the deviations of the calculated values from the given ones

```
resid = y - yi
```

The sum of squared errors is

```
SSE = sum(resid.^2)
```

and the coefficient of determination is obtained with

```
SSyy = sum(y - mean(y)).^2)
r = sqrt(1 - SSE/SSyy)
```

The better the regression curve fits the given data, the smaller is the sum of squared errors and the larger the coefficient of determination. This coefficient can take values between 0 and 1; the former value occurs when the given data are not correlated at all, the latter when the solution is exact (see, for example, Mendehall and Sincich 1988).

Some phenomena can be described by a **power-function** law

$$y = ax^b$$

Taking natural logarithms of both sides yields

$$\ln y = \ln a + b \ln x$$

If the data fit such a curve well, their plot on log–log axes is close to a straight line. Indeed, with

$$u = \ln x, \quad v = \ln y$$

the curve is reduced to a straight line in the u, v plane, and the array of coefficients, C, can be found by a linear regression, that is, by fitting a first-degree polynomial to the u, v data. Then

$$a = \exp(C(2)), \quad b = C(1)$$

An even simpler case is that of the **exponential** law

$$y = ae^{bx}$$

As, in this case,

$$\ln y = \ln a + bx$$

plotting with a logarithmic y scale produces a nearly straight line. The array of coefficients, C, can be found by fitting a first-degree polynomial to x, $\ln y$ pairs.

Then again

$$a = \exp(C(2)), \quad b = C(1)$$

Better interpolations over large intervals, or for data that do not fall close to any of the curves described above, can be obtained by **cubic splines**. Given a set of pairs $(x_1, y_1), \ldots, (x_n, y_n)$ the MATLAB `spline` function fits a polynomial of degree at most three over each interval $[x_{j-1}, x_j]$, such that the curve described by the set of polynomials passes through all the points and its first and second derivatives are continuous at each knot x_j. The function is invoked as

```
>> spline(x, y, xi)
```

where x is the array of given x-coordinates, y the array of given y-coordinates, and xi an array of x-values at which interpolated ordinates are required.

MATLAB 6 provides a **basic fitting interface** that greatly facilitates the operations of interpolation and regression.

9.10   Examples

EXAMPLE 9.1   Polynomial differentiation and integration _____

Let us consider the polynomial

$$f(x) = 2x^4 + 3x^3 + 2x^2 + 4x + 5 \tag{9.14}$$

Manual differentiation of Equation 9.14 yields

$$\frac{df(x)}{dx} = 8x^3 + 9x^2 + 4x + 4 \tag{9.15}$$

and manual integration,

$$\int f(x)\,dx = \frac{2}{5}x^5 + \frac{3}{4}x^4 + \frac{2}{3}x^3 + \frac{4}{2}x^2 + 5x + C_0 \tag{9.16}$$

In MATLAB, $f(x)$ is defined by the array of coefficients

```
>> C = [ 2 3 2 4 5 ];
```

The array of coefficients of the polynomial obtained by differentiation is calculated by

```
>> C_D = C(1:length(C)-1).*[ (length(C)-1):  -1:  1 ]
C_D =
   8 9 4 4
```

Try also the new MATLAB function `polyder`.

The array of coefficients of the polynomial obtained by integration is calculated as

```
≫ C_I = C./[ length(C): -1:  1 ]
C_I =
    0.4000 0.7500 0.6667 2.0000 5.0000
```

plus a constant of integration to be determined from the data of the problem. We can understand the last result better by rewriting the coefficients in fractional form

```
≫ rats(C_I)
ans =
    2/5 3/4 2/3 2 5
```

EXAMPLE 9.2   Spline interpolation over sine values ⸻

In Table 9.3 y is the value of $\sin x$ for x given in radians. Let us plot y against x. The plot misses the maximum that occurs at $x = \pi/2$. If we had drawn the graph manually, with the aid of french curves, we could have *faired* the curve so as to show that maximum. In MATLAB we can fit a polynomial line or, better still, a spline. The following commands produce both and allow us to compare the results.

```
≫ x = 0:  pi/5:  pi; y = sin(x);
≫ c2 = polyfit(x, y, 2);
≫ xx = 0:  pi/10:  pi;
≫ y2 = polyval(c2, xx);
≫ ys = spline(x, y, xx);
≫ plot(x, y, xx, y2, '+', xx, ys, 'o')
≫ title('sin(x)')
≫ xlabel('x, radians')
≫ text(0.2, 0.2, '+ -- 2nd degree polynomial', 'sc')
≫ text(0.2, 0.3, 'o -- spline', 'sc')
```

Table 9.3   sin(x).

x	y
0.0000	0.0000
0.6283	0.5878
1.2566	0.9511
1.8850	0.9511
2.5133	0.5878
3.1416	0.0000

Run these commands and examine the graph. We first see how the simple plot of the values given in Table 9.3 misses the maximum. The second-degree parabola passes close to the given points and exhibits a maximum; it is not the expected $y = 1$. The spline passes through all the given points and through the correct maximum.

One can argue that a third-degree polynomial fit could give better results. In this case this is not true and the second- and third-degree fits give practically the same results. The following calculations are convincing

```
≫ c3 = polyfit(x, y, 3); y3 = polyval(c3, xx);
≫ plot(xx, y2-y3)
≫ title('sin(x)')
≫ xlabel('x, radians')
≫ ylabel('Differences between 2nd and 3rd degree regressions)
```

EXAMPLE 9.3   Polynomial inflexibility _____

The following example is taken from Section 3.6 in Schumaker (1981) and is treated here in MATLAB. A theorem referring to this case is due to Carl Runge (German, 1856–1927).

Let us consider the function $y = 1/(1 + x^2)$ in the interval $[-5, 5]$. We try first to approximate the function by polynomial interpolation at 5 points

```
≫ x = -5:  0.2:  5;
≫ y = ones(size(x))./(1 + x.^2);
≫ x5 = -5:  2.5:  5;
≫ y5 = ones(size(x5))./(1 + x5.^2);
≫ c5 = polyfit(x5, y5, 4); yc5 = polyval(c5, x);
≫ plot(x, y, x, yc5)
≫ grid
```

The result does not look too good. Let us label and store the graph for comparison with other approximations

```
≫ title('y = 1/(1+x^2), polynomial interpolation, 5 points')
≫ xlabel('x')
≫ ylabel('y')
```

We can try to improve the approximation by interpolating at more points, for example at 15 points

```
≫ x15 = -5:  10/14:  5;
≫ y15 = ones(size(x15))./(1 + x15.^2);
≫ c15 = polyfit(x15, y15, 14);
```

```
≫ y15s = polyval(c15, x);
≫ plot(x, y, x, y15s)
≫ grid
≫ title('y = 1/(1+x^2), polynomial fit, 15 points')
≫ xlabel('x')
≫ ylabel('y')
```

The result is much better in the middle part of the interval, but much worse at the ends. Let us try spline interpolation at 5 points

```
≫ ys = spline(x5, y5, x);
≫ plot(x, y, x, ys)
≫ grid
≫ title('y = 1/(1+x^2), spline interpolation at 5 points')
≫ xlabel('x')
≫ ylabel('y')
```

This spline interpolation is slightly better than the polynomial interpolation at the same number of points, especially at the ends of the interval. It is easier to see this by comparing hard copies of the graphs. We can improve the approximation by taking more points, for example:

```
≫ xi = -5:  1:  5;
≫ yi = ones(size(xi))./(1 + xi.^2);
≫ ys = spline(xi, yi, x);
≫ plot(x, y, x, ys)
≫ grid
≫ title('y = 1/(1+x^2), spline interpolation, 11 points')
≫ xlabel('x')
≫ ylabel('y')
```

Not only is spline interpolation at 11 points better than polynomial interpolation at 15 points, but it is difficult to distinguish between the interpolated and the given curve.

Figure 9.5 shows the four graphs obtained in this example and combined with the aid of the SUBPLOT option. Note that the vertical axes of the four plots are not identical. The curve $y = 1/(1 + x^2)$ is shown as a solid line; the fitted curves, as dashed lines.

EXAMPLE 9.4   Estimating velocity from distance travelled _____

If we throw an object upwards with an initial velocity V_0, the object will travel up, with decreasing velocity, until a maximum height is reached. At this point the velocity will reverse direction and the object will fall down, with increasing velocity, until it

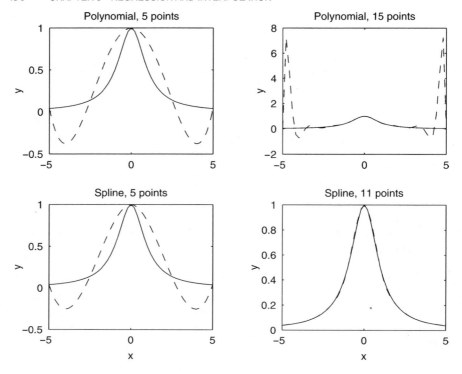

Figure 9.5   Four curves fitted to the function $y = 1/(1 + x^2)$.

hits the ground. If we neglect the resistance of the air, we can write the relationship between height, h, and time, t, as follows.

Space	travelled upwards	–	travelled downwards	=	height
Expression	$V_0 t$	–	$gt^2/2$	=	h
Units	m s^{-1} × s		m s^{-2} × s^2	=	m

Arranging the equation in order of descending powers of t we get

$$h = -\frac{1}{2}gt^2 + V_0 t \tag{9.17}$$

The problem we want to solve here is:

> Measuring the height of the object above ground, at a number of time intervals, estimate the initial velocity, V_0, and the acceleration of gravity, g.

Let us assume $V_0 = 5$ m s^{-1}. We shall 'fabricate' a set of experimental data as follows. First we define V_0 and g, and setting $h = 0$ in Equation 9.17 we calculate how long it will take until our object hits the ground

```
≫ V0 = 5; g = 9.81;
≫ tf = 2*V0/g
tf =
    1.0194
```

We can now define an array of time values and calculate the array of corresponding height values

```
≫ t = 0:  1/100:  1;
≫ h = V0*t - g*t.^2/2;
```

Experimental data are affected by various measurement errors; these errors are usually considered as being *normally distributed*. We generate an array of errors, approximately equal to 2% of the maximum 'measured' height, add them to the theoretical data, and plot the result. The commands are

```
error = 2*max(h)*randn(size(h))/100;
hm = h + error;
plot(t, hm)
```

Based on our knowledge of Equation 9.17, we now fit a second-degree curve to the 'measured' data

```
C = polyfit(t, hm, 2)
C =
   -4.8772 4.9707 0.0071
```

The coefficients C define the polynomial of the height. Differentiating this polynomial yields the expression of the velocity. To get this we use the expression derived in Section 9.3

```
l = length(C) - 1;
C_d = C(1:l).*[ 1:  -1:  1 ]
C_d =
   -9.7543 4.9707
```

We retrieved fairly good estimates of V_0 and g. As part of the variable `error` was produced by a **random generator**, we expect different numbers for successive runs; this is what happened above. Therefore, the reader can obtain results slightly different from those above.

EXAMPLE 9.5   Time constant of first order systems. Decaying curve ——————

This example refers to several systems which, although of different natures, can be modelled by the same equation. In all these systems a variable **decays exponentially**. Consequently we are going to fit an exponential curve to the corresponding data and try to recover the parameters of the decay curve.

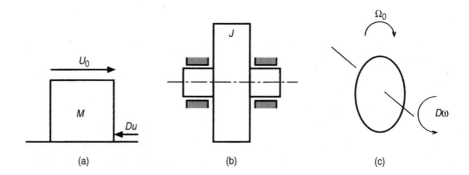

Figure 9.6   First-order mechanical systems.

Figure 9.6 shows two mechanical systems. The system at (a) is **translational**. We assume that the mass M is thrown with the initial velocity U_0 on a flat surface. The motion of the mass is opposed by **viscous friction**, that is, friction proportional to the instantaneous velocity u. The viscous friction coefficient is D. We can write the governing equation with the aid of the following table

Forces	Inertia	+	Viscous friction	=	0
Expression	$M\dfrac{du}{dt}$	+	Du	=	0
Units	$\mathrm{kg \times m\ s^{-2}}$		$\mathrm{kg\ s^{-1} \times m\ s^{-1}}$		

We thus have the governing equation and the initial condition

$$M\frac{du}{dt} + Du = 0, \qquad u(0) = U_0 \tag{9.18}$$

The system in Figure 9.6(b) involves **rotational motion**. We assume that a rotor having the *mass moment of inertia* J is accelerated to an angular velocity Ω_0 and then let free. The rotation is opposed by friction in the bearings and in the air. We assume that the sum of the friction in the bearings and in the air can again be modelled as viscous friction, in this case friction proportional to the instantaneous angular velocity ω. We write the equation of the motion as follows

Torque	Inertia	+	Viscous friction	=	0
Expression	$J\dfrac{d\omega}{dt}$	+	$D\omega$	=	0
Units	kg m^2 × radian s^{-2}		kg m^2 s^{-1} × radian s^{-1}		

We obtained the governing equation and the initial condition

$$J\frac{d\omega}{dt} + D\omega = 0, \qquad \omega(0) = \Omega_0 \tag{9.19}$$

The system shown in Figure 9.7(a) is electrical. The initial voltage across the capacitor C is V_0. At the instant $t = 0$ the switch S is brought from the position S1 to the position S2. A current i will flow through the resistor R. In other words we can say that the capacitance C will discharge a current that will be dissipated in the resistance R. The equation of the system can be written as shown below

Voltage	across resistor	+	across capacitor	=	initial
Expression	Ri	+	$\frac{1}{C}\int i\,dt$	=	V_0
Units	Ω × A		A F^{-1} × s	=	V

The governing equation and the initial condition are therefore

$$\frac{di}{dt} + \frac{1}{RC}i = 0, \qquad i(0) = \frac{V_0}{R} \tag{9.20}$$

The system shown in Figure 9.7(b) involves heat transfer. We assume that a body with *thermal capacity* C and temperature $\theta(0)$ is left at time $t = 0$ in a medium

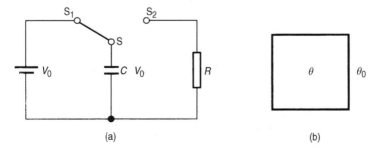

(a)   (b)

Figure 9.7   Two further first-order systems.

whose temperature is $\theta_0 < \theta(0)$. If R is the *thermal resistance* of the body surface, the governing equation can be written with the aid of the following table.

Heat	lost by the body	=	transmitted
Expression	$-Cd\theta$	=	$(\theta - \theta_0)dt/R$
Units	$J\ K^{-1} \times K$	=	$K \times s/(Ks\ J^{-1})$

The resulting equation is

$$\frac{d\theta}{dt} + \frac{1}{CR}(\theta - \theta_0) = 0 \tag{9.21}$$

It follows that all the phenomena discussed above can be described by the following governing equation and initial condition

$$\frac{dy}{dt} + \frac{1}{T}y = 0, \qquad y(0) = y_0 \tag{9.22}$$

with the solution

$$y = A\exp(-t/T), \qquad A = y(0) \tag{9.23}$$

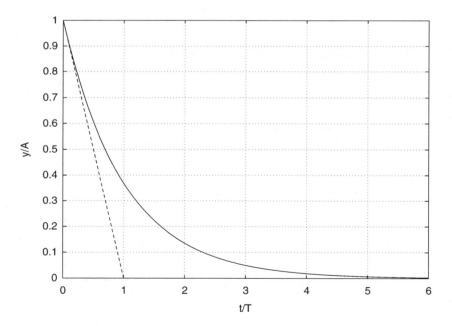

Figure 9.8   Decay curve of first-order systems.

where A is the initial value of y, and T the **time constant**. Figure 9.8 shows the *decay* curve in nondimensional coordinates, that is, t/T on the horizontal axis and y/A on the vertical. The slope of the tangent to this curve is given by

$$\frac{d(y/A)}{d(t/T)} = -\frac{A}{T}exp(-t/T) \tag{9.24}$$

At $t = 0$ the value of the slope is $-A/T$; this is the slope of the line that connects the point $t/T = 0$, $y/A = 1$ with the point $t/T = 1$, $y/A = 0$.

It is interesting to produce a table of y-values, in terms of A, for a few t/T values. We do this by

```
>> x = 0:  6;
>> z = exp(-x);
>> [ x' z' ]
ans =
      0            1.0000
      1.0000       0.3679
      2.0000       0.1353
      3.0000       0.0498
      4.0000       0.0183
      5.0000       0.0067
      6.0000       0.0025
```

The problem we pose here is:

Is it possible to estimate the time constant, T, and the initial value, A, by measuring a number of y values along the decay curve?

If the initial value, A, is known exactly, theoretically one has to look on the curve for one of the y values tabulated above and deduce T. As an example, if $A = 2$, at $y = 2 \times 0.3679 = 0.7358$, we find $t/T = 1$; therefore, the time constant is equal to the time at which the value $y = 0.7358$ was measured.

In practice the knowledge of A can be affected by measuring errors, and so is the knowledge of the various y values. It seems then that some least-squares fit would be in order. In fact, taking natural logarithms of both sides of Equation 9.23, we obtain

$$\ln y = \ln A - t/T \tag{9.25}$$

EXAMPLE 9.6   Fluid dynamics, naval architecture _____

The **total resistance of a body** – in particular of a ship – advancing at the water–air interface with speed V_s can be described by the law

$$R_T = \frac{1}{2}C_T \rho S V_s^2 \tag{9.26}$$

where C_T is called the **total resistance coefficient** and S is the **wetted surface**, that is, that part of the body surface that is in contact with the fluid (see also Chapter 13). C_T is itself a function of the speed V_s. Therefore, the relationship between V_s and R_T cannot be exactly represented by a second-degree curve. In fact, the slopes of curves obtained experimentally seem to increase faster than predicted by a second-degree law. Within not too large speed intervals it is possible to fit **power-function** curves of the form

$$R_T = aV_s^b$$

As shown in Section 9.5, the coefficients a and b can be found by fitting a first-degree polynomial to the pairs $\ln V_s$, $\ln R_T$; the procedure is illustrated by the following example.

Table 9.4 contains the model data of a Bolinder-type fishing vessel with a waterline length equal to 14.251 m, and a volume of displacement equal to 58.356 m^3. The tests were carried out at the Rome test basin (Anon 1962).

With

$$z = \ln y, \quad c_1 = -1/T, \quad c_2 = \ln A$$

we reduce the problem to the linear regression of

$$z = c_1 t + c_2$$

Table 9.4   Test-basin data of a Bolinder-type fishing vessel.

Velocity v m s^{-1}	Total resistance RT kg force	Total-resistance coefficient, CT
0.655	0.230	4.969
0.666	0.250	5.232
0.846	0.420	5.348
0.855	0.465	5.903
1.065	0.780	6.381
1.077	0.805	6.433
1.262	1.200	6.987
1.277	1.245	7.083
1.408	1.650	7.718
1.476	1.900	8.085
1.575	2.330	8.711
1.697	3.090	9.953
1.778	3.910	11.475
1.821	4.600	12.869
1.900	6.000	15.423

Let us assume that the time constant is $T = 5$ seconds; the initial value, $A = 2$. The theoretical decay curve is plotted with the commands

```
>> T = 5; A = 2;
>> t = 0:  T/10:  5*T;
>> y = A*exp(-t/T);
>> subplot(1, 2, 1), plot(t, y, [0 T], [A 0]);
>> title('Theoretical decay curve')
```

Next we 'fabricate' some noise, close to 1% of the initial value A, and add it to the theoretical data. We plot the 'corrupted' curve side by side with the theoretical curve

```
>> noise = A*rand(size(y))/100;
>> ym = y + noise;
>> subplot(1, 2, 2), plot(t, ym, [0 T], [A 0]);
>> title('Noise-affected curve')
```

The graphs obtained above are shown in Figure 9.9. To continue, we perform an exponential regression, estimate the *measured* time constant, Tm, the measured initial value, Am, and the errors in per cent of the true values, T and A

```
>> c = polyfit(t, log(ym), 1);
>> Tm= -1/c(1)
Tm =
     5.4154
>> Am = exp(c(2))
Am =
     1.8639
>> Terror = 100*(T - Tm)/T
Terror =
     -8.3071
>> Aerror = 100*(A - Am)/A
Aerror =
     6.8032
```

In conclusion, we did obtain estimates of the time constant and of the initial value. It is beyond the scope of this book to discuss the errors and ways to decrease them. The reader can obtain slightly different results if the random-number generator was called previously during the same session.

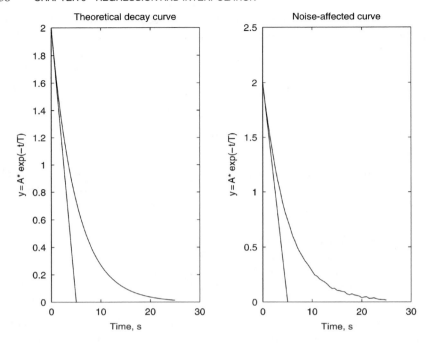

Figure 9.9   Theoretical and experimental decay curve.

In order to process these data let us write them in an array called `bolind1`, to a file called `bolind.m`:

```
bolind1 = [ 0.655 0.230 4.969
...
1.900 6.00 15.423 ];
```

After loading this file we separate out a velocity array and a resistance array

```
>> v = bolind1(:, 1); RT = bolind1(:, 2);
```

The resistance is measured in *kg force*, the unit corresponding to the MKS system previously used in Europe. In the presently employed SI system the recommended unit is the *newton*, with the symbol N. We convert, therefore, from one unit to the other by

```
>> RT = 9.80665*RT;
```

As explained, we assume that the data suit a power function. This assumption can be checked by plotting resistance against velocity on log–log axes

```
≫ loglog(v, RT)
```

With one notable exception, at the highest-velocity point, the resulting graph is approximately a straight line. We can, therefore, perform a power-function regression as follows:

```
≫ x = log(v);
≫ y = log(RT);
≫ c = polyfit(x, y, 1)
c =
   2.8752 1.9258
≫ a = exp(c(2))
a =
   6.8609
≫ b = c(1)
b =
   2.8752
```

Using the following commands we print the graph and verify that, with the exception of the highest-speed point, the curve fits the given data fairly well.

```
≫ RTi = a*v.^b;
≫ [ v RT RTi ]
ans =
   0.6550 2.2555 2.0326
      . . .
   1.9000 58.8399 43.4355
≫ plot(v, RT, v, RTi, 'o')
≫ title('Basin tests of Bolinder-type fishing vessel')
≫ xlabel('Model speed, v, m/s')
≫ ylabel('Model total resistance, RT, N')
```

EXAMPLE 9.7   Thermocouple emf _____

The data used here are taken from Example 8.2; therefore, read that example before going on. Supposing that the file s_couple.m has been loaded, we can get an idea about the relationship between temperature and emf by plotting the latter against the former

```
≫ x = s_couple(:, 1); y = s_couple(:, 2);
≫ plot(x, y), grid
≫ xlabel('Temperature, degrees Celsius')
```

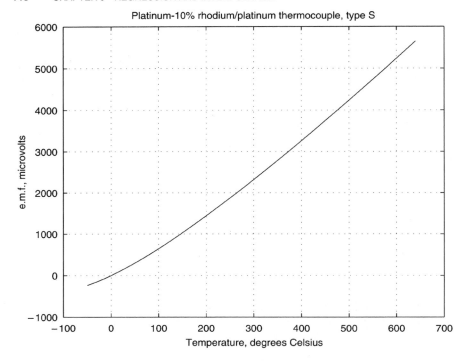

Figure 9.10   Platinum-platinum/rhodium thermocouple-emf curve.

```
≫ ylabel('e.m.f., microvolts')
≫ title('Platinum-10% rhodium/platinum thermocouple, type S')
```

The result is shown in Figure 9.10.

For the interval −50 °C to 630.74 °C we find in BS 4937 the coefficients of a 6th-degree polynomial. We have not loaded all the data contained in that standard, but we can try our own regression

```
≫ c = polyfit(x, y, 6)
Warning:  Matrix is close to singular or badly scaled.
     Results may be inaccurate.  RCOND = 1.799080e-017.
> In C:\MATLAB5\toolbox\matlab\polyfun\polyfit.m at line 52
c = 0.0000 -0.0000 0.0000 -0.0000 0.0125 5.4015 0.0166
```

Obviously, we need more digits to view the result, therefore, try

```
≫ format long
≫ c'
```

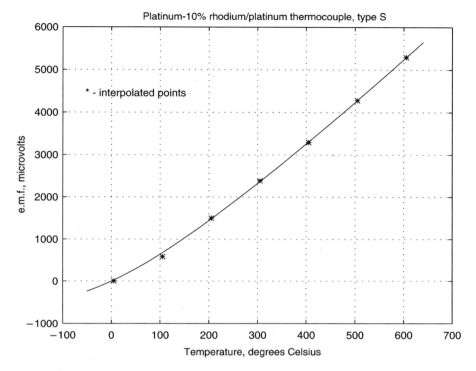

Figure 9.11   Regression over S-type thermocouple data.

To check our results, we evaluate a few points and plot them as asterisks, '*', on the graph obtained above

```
>> xi = 5:100:605;
>> yi = polyval(c, xi);
>> plot(x, y, xi, yi, '*'), grid
>> title('Platinum-10% rhodium/platinum thermocouple, type S')
>> xlabel('Temperature, degrees Celsius')
>> ylabel('e.m.f., microvolts')
>> gtext('* - interpolated points')
```

The last statement causes a crosshair or an arrow to appear. Bring this crosshair to the point where you want the text '* - interpolated points' and press the mouse button. The resulting graph is shown in Figure 9.11.

9.11   Exercises

Solutions for Exercises 9.2, 9.5, 9.8 and 9.11 appear at the back of the book.

Table 9.5 Production of cultured red sea bream in Japan.

Year	Tons	Year	Tons
1964	100	1976	6400
1967	200	1979	12200
1970	500	1982	20200
1973	1300	1984	26100

■ **EXERCISE 9.1** Fourth-degree fit

For the example given in Section 9.3 calculate a fourth-degree fit and compare it with the second- and the third-degree fits. Assess the quality of the fit by all the criteria described in Section 9.4.

■ **EXERCISE 9.2** SSE

Check that SSE2 in Section 9.4 could also have been obtained by

```
SSE2 = resid2'*resid2
```

Why?

■ **EXERCISE 9.3** Cultured red sea bream in Japan

Table 9.5 contains data about the production of red sea bream (*Sparus aurata*) in Japan, as presented by Jones (1987). Fit a power-function and an exponential line to these data and compare the results.

■ **EXERCISE 9.4** Instrument calibration

To calibrate an instrument six standard values were measured with it. The following table shows the instrument readings against the standard (true) values. Carry out a first-degree regression on these data and use the results to plot a calibration curve.

Measured	True
0.5030	0
0.7229	1.0000
0.7802	2.0000
1.2106	5.0000
1.7607	10.0000
2.4649	15.0000

■ **EXERCISE 9.5** Water viscosity

Table 8.5 (Exercise 8.6) contains kinematic-viscosity data of fresh water between $0\,°C$ and $28\,°C$. Find the kinematic viscosities corresponding to $0.5, 1.5, \ldots 27.5\,°C$.

■ **EXERCISE 9.6** Total-resistance coefficient

In Example 9.6 we used the RT data in Table 9.4 to illustrate a power regression. Use the CT data in the same table and fit a power curve to them.

■ **EXERCISE 9.7** Atmospheric pressure

Table 8.4 (Exercise 8.4) contains pressure values of 'stable' atmosphere for 0 to 1000 metres above sea level. Theoretically, these data follow an exponential law of the form

$$p = ae^{-kh}$$

(1)   Perform an exponential regression over these data and find the values of a and k.

(2)   Using the values found at (1), calculate the pressures corresponding to the altitudes 50, 150, 250, . . . , 950 m. Plot these values over the values given in Table 8.4.

(3)   Extrapolate for 1500, 2000 and 2500 m altitude. Compare your values with those indicated in the *U.S. Standard Atmosphere 1962* (published by the U.S. Committee on the Extension of the Standard Atmosphere), that is, 846, 795 and 747 mbar, respectively.

■   **EXERCISE 9.8**   Temperature scales
As shown in Example 2.10, the line representing the relationship between the Celsius and Fahrenheit scales passes through the points (0, 32), (100, 212). Retrieve the formula

$$C = \frac{5}{9}(F - 32)$$

as a linear regression. Then use the `polyval` function to find the Celsius temperature corresponding to 96.8 F (human-body temperature).

■   **EXERCISE 9.9**   Current density in copper conductor
In Exercise 8.8 it was explained why the allowable current density in a copper conductor is not a constant. Table 8.7 contains allowable-current values for sectional areas between 0.75 mm^2 and 500 mm^2. Use the same data for

(1)   a second-degree regression;

(2)   a third-degree regression.

   Compare the results of the two regressions.

■   **EXERCISE 9.10**   Platinum resistance thermometer
Table 8.8 (Exercise 8.8) contains resistance values for platinum resistance thermometers between 0 °C and 330 °C. Usually the resistance is measured and the temperature is deduced. Therefore,

(1)   Carry out a first-degree regression and obtain the coefficients of the equation that yields the temperature as a function of resistance;

(2)   Find the temperatures corresponding to the resistances 125, 150, 175 and 200 ohms;

(3)   Plot the values found above over the graph showing temperature versus resistance;

(4)   Try also a second-degree regression and verify that it does not improve our knowledge significantly.

   Hint: Look at the highest-power coefficient.

■ **EXERCISE 9.11**   A varistor circuit

According to a scientific encyclopedia, a varistor is 'Any two-terminal solid-state device in which the electric current I increases considerably faster than the voltage V'. The relationship between current and voltage can be described by the equation

$$I = aV^n \tag{9.27}$$

where n can usually take values between 3 and 35. Varistors can be considered nonlinear, voltage-dependent resistors. One of their important uses is in the protection of equipment against voltage surges.

Let us assume that the following values were measured for one type of varistor.

Voltage, V	Current, mA	Voltage, V	Current, mA
0	0	30	3.5
12	0.5	35	5.7
18	1	40	8.8
25	2.3	45	12.9

These data and those in the following exercise are borrowed from Niard (1971).

(1)   Plot the measured current against the measured voltage.
(2)   Perform a power regression to find a and n in Equation 9.27.
(3)   Assume that an alternative voltage of 48 V amplitude and 50 Hz frequency is applied to the varistor. Plot the voltage and the current and see how this varistor distorts the current.

Hint: You cannot use u.^n for negative u values; use `sign(u).*abs(u)` or a combination of it. Also, when performing the regression, do not take into account the first pair of measurements, that is, the zero values. Why?

■ **EXERCISE 9.12**   A varistor circuit

Read Exercise 9.11 and assume that the following values were measured:

Voltage, V	Current, mA	Voltage, V	Current, mA
0	0	150	0.65
50	0.03	200	1.5
80	0.11	250	3
100	0.2	300	5

These data are borrowed from Niard (1971).

(a)   Plot the measured current against the measured voltage.
(b)   Perform an exponential regression to find a and n in Equation 9.27.
(c)   Assume that an alternative voltage of 48 V amplitude and 50 Hz frequency is applied to the varistor. Plot the voltage and the current and see how this varistor distorts the current.

Hint: You cannot use u.^n for negative u values; use `sign(u).*abs(u)` or a combination of it.

Chapter 10
More about plotting

10.1 Introduction

This chapter introduces a few additional graphic facilities, mainly histograms, polar plots and animation. Histograms find their uses in the analysis of experimental data. Polar graphs are suitable for functions that are easily described in polar coordinates. Some of those functions cannot be plotted in Cartesian coordinates. The techniques of polar plots are exemplified on a few curves, some of which have very important engineering applications. Conic sections are classic examples. Other curves referred to in this chapter are the involute – the shape used for most gear teeth, and curves representing radiation patterns of antennas. Conic sections are also the subject of an example of a three-dimensional plot in Cartesian coordinates.

A few of the three-dimensional plotting functions were described in Subsections 1.11.2 and 1.11.3; an engineering example is given in Chapter 17. It is beyond the scope of this book to describe all the new, powerful graphing facilities; they certainly deserve a book of their own.

MATLAB 4 and later versions provide tools for animation; a simple example is given in this chapter. Animation requires a 256-colour display.

The chapter ends with a discussion of the additive colour mixing process used, for example, in the computer screen display. This discussion is also a natural application of three-dimensional arrays.

Table 10.1   Breaking strength of 100 steel specimens, kgf/mm^2.

62.382.083.5 54.4 76.8 52.679.161.5 75.875.2
82.753.257.3101.6 85.4102.690.583.4 83.275.6
48.172.298.4 91.5 58.1 75.470.257.1 64.887.3
73.883.086.5 85.4 60.5 60.885.874.2 95.565.1
92.675.843.1 62.5 79.2 75.671.557.6 73.542.6
62.163.472.3 77.6 82.6 89.487.385.1 95.658.4
83.779.663.7 87.5 76.3 43.261.072.6 65.685.5
78.568.275.6 68.3 69.1 78.463.668.2107.274.8
79.593.664.4 74.3107.8 60.594.273.6 89.065.4
105.852.678.2 84.3 93.8 97.053.374.3 85.691.8

10.2   Histograms

Histograms are one of the tools used in the analysis of experimental data. As an example of such data we shall consider the strength of steel samples. Experience shows that if many samples are taken from a certain material, such as a given grade of steel, their strength properties are not identical. The distribution of these properties can be studied with the aid of histograms.

This section follows, with some modifications, an example found in Giardina (1970). Table 10.1 contains the breaking-strength values of 100 steel specimens. To process these data we write them to a file ultim.m, in an array named SU:

```
%ULTIM     Table 1 from Basilio Giardina.  Format is
%          SU = [ Ultimate strength in kgf/mm^2 ]
SU = [ 62.3
...
91.8 ];
```

The notation 'kgf' means 'kilogram force', a unit of force used in the MKS system, previously employed in Europe, which must not be confounded with the unit of mass, kg, used in the SI system. If we receive the file on a diskette and want to know how to use it, we can ask for help in the usual manner, and then load the data:

```
>> help ultim
%ULTIM     Table 1 from Basilio Giardina.  Format is
%          SU = [ Ultimate strength in kgf/mm^2 ]
>> ultim
```

Entering SU would produce a display of 100 numbers; not much information can be obtained in this way. We can try to describe the set of *SU* values by some characteristics, for example by their **mean value**,

$$\bar{x} = \frac{\sum_{i=1}^{i=100} SU(i)}{100} \tag{10.1}$$

obtained in MATLAB with

```
>> mean(SU)
ans =
   75.4980
```

and the **standard deviation**

$$s = \sqrt{\frac{\sum SU(i)^2}{100} - \bar{x}^2} \tag{10.2}$$

yielded in MATLAB by

```
>> std(SU)
ans =
   14.6384
```

We can also find the minimum and maximum values

```
>> min(SU), max(SU)
ans =
   42.6000
ans =
   107.8000
```

A good overall description would be obtained if we could plot the distribution of these data in some way. One possibility is the histogram; to produce it use the following procedure.

(1) ⎕Divide⎕ the interval between the maximum and minimum sample value into n subintervals; let us call them **bins**.

(2) ⎕Group⎕ the samples in the bins corresponding to their values.

(3) ⎕Count⎕ the number of samples in each bin.

(4) ⎕Plot⎕ the number of samples in each bin against the centre of the bin.

Thus, in this example, the interval $107.8 - 42.6 = 65.2$ was divided into ten bins, each 6.52 wide. The first bin is the interval [42.6, 49.12] with its centre at $(42.6 + 49.12)/2 = 45.86$. There are four SU values in this bin: 48.1, 43.1, 43.2, 42.6. The second bin is the interval [49.12, 55.64] with the centre at 52.38; there are five *SU* values in it: 53.2, 52.6, 54.4, 52.6, 53.3. We continue in the same way for the remaining bins. This procedure is implemented in MATLAB by the hist function which, if called with the name of the data vector SU as a single argument, divides the interval [min(SU), max(SU)] into ten bins and yields the output [n, x], where n is a vector whose elements are the number of samples in each bin, and x is a vector whose elements are the **centres** of the bin, that is, the means of their boundaries. For the example in Table 10.1 we obtain

```
≫ hist(SU)
≫ xlabel('Ultimate strength, SU, kgf/mm^2')
≫ [n, x] = hist(SU)
n =
   4 5 11 13 13 17 19 9 4 5
x =
Columns 1 through 7
    45.8600 52.3800 58.9000 65.4200 71.9400 78.4600
84.9800
Columns 8 through 10
    91.5000 98.0200 104.5400
```

We can plot the results in a histogram by means of the MATLAB bar function:

```
≫ bar(x, n)
≫ xlabel('Ultimate strength, SU, kgf/mm^2')
≫ ylabel('Number of specimens')
≫ for i = 1:10
      text(x(i), n(i), int2str(n(i)))
end
≫ title('SU histogram of 100 steel specimens')
```

Try these commands and see what you get.

The histogram would look better with round-valued bin centres. We can force such an output by specifying a second argument of the hist function, namely the vector of bin centres. Another bad feature of the histogram obtained above is that it exhibits a flat segment and a local minimum (we say that the function is not **unimodal**). We can find a remedy for this by defining only seven bins, as in Giardina (1970):

```
≫ nb = 45:  10:   105;
≫ [n, x] = hist(SU, nb)
n =
   4 10 20 29 21 11 5
x =
   45 55 65 75 85 95 105
```

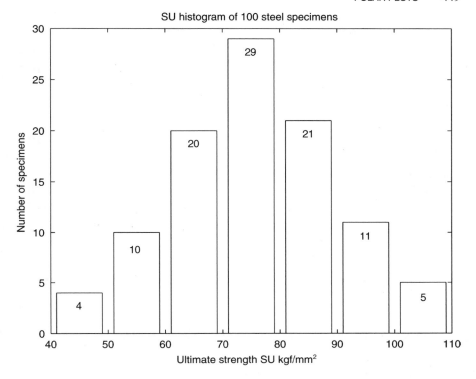

Figure 10.1   Histogram of the ultimate strength of 100 steel samples.

```
≫ bar(x, n)
≫ for i = 1:7
      text(x(i), n(i), int2str(n(i)))
end
≫ title('SU histogram of 100 steel specimens')
≫ xlabel('Ultimate strength SU kgf/mm^2')
≫ ylabel('Number of specimens')
```

The result is shown in Figure 10.1. In the two examples shown above we have used the `text` function with a variable argument supplied by the FOR loop. This argument, the integer `n(i)`, was converted to a string by the `int2str` function (read 'integer to string').

10.3   Polar plots

Certain curves can be easier described in polar coordinates than in Cartesian ones. A simple example is the **spiral of Archimedes**; its equation is

$$\rho = a\theta \tag{10.3}$$

Let

$$x \quad = \quad \rho \cos \theta \tag{10.4}$$
$$y \quad = \quad \rho \sin \theta \tag{10.5}$$

Then, Equation 10.3 can be written in Cartesian coordinates as

$$\sqrt{x^2 + y^2} = a \arctan \frac{y}{x} \tag{10.6}$$

The latter equation is **implicit** and **transcendental**. We cannot express y as an explicit function of x; therefore, we cannot plot the curve by means of Equation 10.6. However, it is very easy to use Equation 10.3 and plot it with the help of the MATLAB polar function:

```
≫ a = 1;
≫ theta = 0:  pi/60:  2*pi;
≫ rho = a*theta;
≫ polar(theta,rho)
≫ grid
≫ title('The spiral of Archimedes, rho = a \theta')
```

In this context the grid command produces a network of circles and radii suitable to polar coordinates. Try this example for yourself.

Another example in which the polar coordinates fit naturally is the **logarithmic spiral** defined by

$$r = e^{m\phi}$$

A plot of such a curve can be produced with the commands

```
≫ m =0.1;
≫ phi = 0:  pi/60:  4*pi;
≫ r = exp(m*phi);
≫ polar(phi, r)
≫ title('Logarithmic spiral')
```

The plot is shown in Figure 10.2.

A recent use of the logarithmic spiral is in the design of a type of **frequency independent antenna**. The curve has an interesting history. The logarithmic spiral was first described by René Descartes (French, 1596–1650) and by Evangelista Torricelli (Italian, 1608–1647). Jacques Bernoulli I (Swiss, 1654–1705) investigated its properties in detail and was known to be so fond of his discoveries that the spiral was engraved on his tombstone. It can be easily checked, both by differentiation and

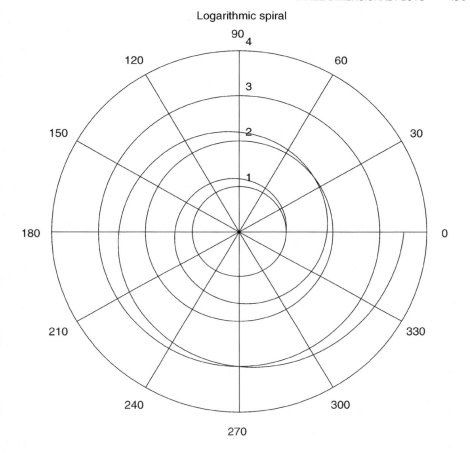

Figure 10.2 The logarithmic spiral.

on the plot, that for a given radius vector the tangents at the points of intersection are all parallel. In other words, the tangents to the logarithmic spiral intersect the radius vector at a constant angle (see, for example, Piskunov 1960, pages 129–30). For this reason the curve is also known as the **equiangular spiral**; more about its properties can be found in Coxeter (1980, Sections 8.7 and 17.36).

10.4 Three-dimensional plots

The MATLAB mesh function generates three-dimensional mesh surfaces.   The graphing possibilities of mesh are limited and it is rather difficult to use them for engineering purposes; therefore, the subject will not be discussed in detail here. The use of mesh will only be described in Example 10.5 for very elementary explanations of conic sections.

Better three-dimensional facilities are described in Subsections 1.11.2 and 1.11.3, and an engineering example is given in Chapter 17.

10.5   Animation

Tools provided by MATLAB 4.0 and above allow animation; they require a 256-colours display.

Let us suppose that we want to visualize the oscillations of a simple coil spring whose shape is that of a helix. The parametric equations of this curve are

$$x = \frac{d}{2}\cos p$$
$$y = \frac{d}{2}\sin p$$
$$z = p$$

where d is the diameter of the helix. To simulate oscillations with amplitude A and angular frequency ω we modify the equation of z to

$$z = (1 + A\cos(\omega(t-1)))p \tag{10.7}$$

where t is the time variable. We begin by plotting a **reference frame**, for example for $t = 1$, and check the appearance of the plot on it:

```
p = 0:  pi/60:  8*pi;
d = 2; A = 0.2; T = 5;
omega = 2*pi/T;
% plot reference frame
x = d*cos(p)/2; y = d*sin(p)/2;
z = (1 + A*cos(omega*1))*p;
plot3(x, y, z)
```

The next step is the generation of a number of frames, say six. We begin by defining axes that will be sufficient for all frames. The statement M = moviein(6) creates a matrix with six columns, one for each frame. The frames themselves are generated within a FOR loop. The getframe function returns a pixel image of the current figure.

```
M = moviein(6);
for t = 1:  6          % record the movie
    x = d*cos(p)/2; y = d*sin(p)/2;
    z = (1 + A*cos(omega*(t-1)))*p;
    plot3(x, y, z)
    axis([-1 1 -1 1 0 10.0*pi]);
    M(:, t) = getframe;
end
```

To play the movie ten times, for example, enter

```
movie(M, 10);
```

10.6   Additive colour mixing

Colours are produced on the computer screen by combining light beams of three colours, namely *red*, *green* and *blue*. The process is appropriately called **additive mixing**. The three colours listed above are the **additive primary colours**. To explain the process we introduce in this section the MATLAB functions cat and image, and use **multidimensional arrays**.

The model described in this section corresponds to the **tristimulus theory** of colour vision. The retina contains cones sensitive to the three additive primary colours. The superposition of red and green light produces the sensation of *yellow*. The addition of green to blue results in *cyan*, and that of blue to red in *magenta*. The superposition of equal amounts of all three primary colours produces *white*. Various hues result if the intensity of the primary colours is varied, as explained in Example 10.9. The absence of all three light beams results in *black*. The name of the process described above derives from the names of the primary colours; it is called the **RGB model**.

To show how colours are produced on the computer screen let us begin with a simple example. The French flag contains three fields, the left one is blue, the middle, white, and the right field, red. To display the left field it is sufficient to project the blue beam. For the middle field we need all three beams, while for the right field we project only the red beam. In MATLAB we construct three arrays, one for each primary colour. Each array contains a number for each flag field. The number 1 means full intensity, while the number 0 means no light in the corresponding beam. The arrays that command the three beams are entered in MATLAB as

```
red   = [ 0 1 1 ];
green = [ 0 1 0 ];
blue  = [ 1 1 0 ];
```

We use the function cat to *concatenate* the three one-dimensional arrays in a **three-dimensional** array. The arguments of cat are the number of dimensions of the new array and the names of the arrays to be concatenated:

```
FLAG = cat(3, red, green, blue);
```

We create now an *image object* by the call

```
image(FLAG)
```

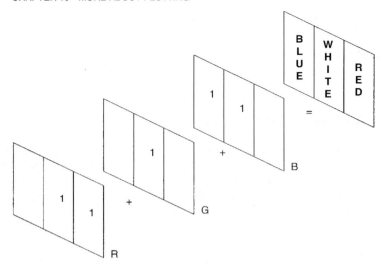

Figure 10.3   Building the French colours by an additive process

Figure 10.3 is a schematic representation of the process.

In drawing, painting and printing colours are produced by another process called **subtractive mixing**. The primary subtractive colours are *magenta*, *yellow* and *cyan*. The reader interested in this subject can consult books such as Hearn and Baker (1994) or Kerlow and Rosebush (1986).

10.7   Handle graphics

10.7.1   Introduction

Let us suppose that we must prepare a transparency to be projected in a classroom or at a conference. Transparencies produced with the *factory-defined* line width and text size cannot yield satisfactory results; it can be difficult to read their projection if the screen is situated a few metres away. However, we can change properties such as line width, text size, and many others, by using **handle graphics**.

MATLAB plots and GUIs (see Chapter 18) are built of **handle graphics objects**. The computer screen is the top object; it is called the **root**. The other objects are its **children**. In the next lower level of children there is a **figure** or several figures. Figures have as children *axes, uicontrols, uimenus* and *uicontexmenus*. A detailed hierarchy of handle graphics objects is shown as a tree graph in Figure 10.4. The objects *uicontrol, uimenu* and *uicontextmenu* are used in GUIs. All other objects may appear in MATLAB plots. When we build a plot by using some high-level command, such as plot(x, y), MATLAB also automatically builds its **parent** object, in this case a **figure**.

A particular implementation of an object is an **instance** of that object. We identify an object instance by its **handle**. Each object has a number of proper-

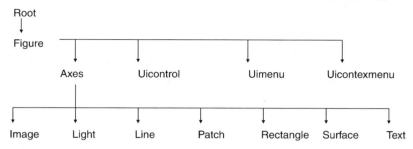

Figure 10.4   The tree of handle graphics objects.

ties whose default values are factory defined. We can modify these properties by low-level commands. A few examples are given in the next two subsections.

10.7.2   Slide prepared with handle graphics

In this subsection we develop a function and a script file that produce a transparency for a lesson in Engineering Graphics. The function, `pline`, plots lines with given width, colour and style properties; it can be called from the command line or from within another M-file. In the example that follows `pline` is invoked in the script file that produces plots explaining the intersection of two pipes.

Let us assume that we want to plot a line between two points and make sure that its width is adequate for overhead projection. To do so we begin by assigning the plot a handle name. Next we call the function `set` and specify the handle name, the property to be changed, written as a character string, and the desired property value:

```
>> Hp = plot([ 0 3 ], [ 0 1 ])
>> set(Hp, 'LineWidth', 2)
```

Above we used a style generally accepted in MATLAB handle graphics. Thus, we begin the name of the handle with an upper-case 'H'. If we do not end the plot command with a semicolon, MATLAB will display the handle allocated by the system. In the `set` command we wrote 'LineWidth' with upper-case 'L' and 'W'. In this context MATLAB is not case sensitive and we could have used lower-case letters. However, we think that the accepted conventions improve readability and we recommend them. Try the above commands and experiment with more line-width values.

We can change more line properties, for instance colour and line style (solid, dotted, etc.). Doing this in the conventional way, for several lines, may become tedious. We show below a function that can simplify the job.

```
%PLINE plots line with given properties, between given points.
%       pline(P, w, c, s) plots a line between the points whose
%       coordinates are described in the array P, the line
%       width being w, the colour c, and the line style s.
```

```
%       The array P has the format
%               [ x1    x2      ...       xn
%                 y1    y2      ...       yn ]
%       where x1, y1 are the coordinates of the first point and
%       so on. For three dimensional plots modify accordingly.

        function        pline(P, w, c, s)

[ m, n ] = size(P);
if m == 2               % two-dimensional plot
    H1 = plot(P(1, :), P(2, :));
    set(H1, 'LineWidth', w, 'Color', c, 'LineStyle', s)
elseif m == 3           % three-dimensional plot
    H2 = plot3(P(1, :), P(2, :), P(3, :));
    set(H1, 'LineWidth', w, 'Color', c, 'LineStyle', s)
else
    error('Input argument P has inadequate dimensions')
end
```

As an example of the application of the above and other handle graphics commands, write the following M-file; it produces a drawing of the intersection of two pipes of equal diameter.

```
%FIG06_98        Intersection of two pipes of equal diameter

r1 = 5;                         % radius of first cylinder
r2 = 5;                         % radius of second cylinder
% front view
% begin horizontal cylinder
P0 = [   0; 0 ];  P1 = [  -5; 5 ];
P2 = [ -13; 5 ];  P3 = [ -13; -5 ];
P4 = [  13; -5 ]; P5 = [  13; 5 ];
P6 = [   5; 5 ];
patch([ P0(1), P6(1), P5(1), P4(1), P3(1), P2(1), P1(1) ],...
      [ P0(2), P6(2), P5(2), P4(2), P3(2), P2(2), P1(2) ], 'y')
axis([ -15 30 -27 18 ]), axis equal, axis off
hold on

P7 = [ 5; 15 ]; P8 = [ -5; 15 ]; % begin vertical cylinder
patch([ P0(1), P6(1), P7(1), P8(1), P1(1) ],...
      [ P0(2), P6(2), P7(2), P8(2), P1(2) ], 'g')
pline([ P0 P1 P2 P3 P4 P5 P6 P0 ], 2.5, 'k', '-')
pline([ P6 P7 P8 P1 ], 2.5, 'k', '-')

% side view
t  = 0: pi/90: 2*pi;    % horizontal cylinder
```

```
xc = 23 + r1*cos(t); zc = r1*sin(t);
patch(xc, zc, 'y')
% begin vertical cylinder
zl = 0;
P11 = [ 28; zl ]; P12 = [ 28; 15 ];
P13 = [ 18; 15 ]; P14 = [ 18; zl ];
% define intersection arc
ti  = 0: pi/90: pi;
xi2 = 23 + r1*cos(ti); zi2 = r1*sin(ti);
%vertical cylinder
patch( [ xi2 P11(1) P12(1) P13(1) P14(1) ],...
       [ zi2 P11(2) P12(2) P13(2) P14(2) ], 'g')
pline([ xc; zc ], 2.5, 'k', '-')
pline([ P11 P12 P13 P14 ], 2, 'k', '-')
ha = plot([ -14 29 ], [ 0 0 ], 'k-.');        % horizontal axis
set(ha, 'LineWIdth', 1.5)
ha = plot([ 0 0 ], [ -6 16 ], 'k-.');        % vertical
axis in front view set(ha, 'LineWIdth', 1.5)
ha = plot([ 23 23 ], [ -6 16 ], 'k-.');        % vertical
axis in side view set(ha, 'LineWIdth', 1.5)
ht = title('Intersection of perpendicular,...
            equal-diameter cylinders');
set(ht, 'FontSize', 14)
t1 = 'horizontal cylinder:              y^2 + z^2 = r^2');
ht = text(-12, -10, t1);
set(ht, 'FontSize', 14)
t2 = 'vertical cylinder:              x^2 + y^2 = r^2');
ht = text(-12, -15, t2);
r^2') set(ht, 'FontSize', 14)
ht = text(-12, -20, 'projection of intersection: z^2 - x^2 = 0');
set(ht, 'FontSize', 14)

hold off
```

We used the function patch above; it plots polygons and fills them with colour. There are several ways of defining patches; we chose the high-level syntax

patch(*x*-coordinates, *y*-coordinates, colour)

It is possible to define three-dimensional patches by supplying *z*-coordinates after the *y*-coordinates.

In the file we modified the *FontSize* property. The default font size is 10 *points*, where a point equals 1/72 inch. Other font units may be chosen, as shown by the MATLAB help facilities.

The result is shown in Figure 10.5.

Intersection of perpendicular, equal-diameter cylinders

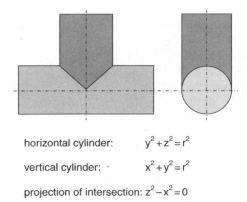

horizontal cylinder: $y^2 + z^2 = r^2$

vertical cylinder: · $x^2 + y^2 = r^2$

projection of intersection: $z^2 - x^2 = 0$

Figure 10.5   Intersection of two pipes of equal diameter – projection on two planes.

10.7.3   Lighting and rendering

In the preceding section we learnt how to show the intersection of two cylinders in orthographic projections. In this subsection we describe a file that produces **axonometric** projections of the same intersections and displays them in realistic ways. This allows us to introduce a few additional graphic features of MATLAB.

```
%PIPES Intersection of two pipes of equal diameter

m     = 50;
z     = 1.2*(0: 1: m)/m;
r     = 1*ones(size(z));
theta = (0: m)/m*2*pi;
x1    = r'*cos(theta); y1    = r'*sin(theta);
z1    = z'*ones(1, m+1);
x     = (-m: 2: m)/m;
x2    = x'*ones(1, m+1); y2    = r'*cos(theta);
z2    = r'*sin(theta);

h = surf(x1, y1, z1);
axis equal, axis off
hold on
h = surf(x2, y2, z2);
axis equal, axis off
t     = [ 'Figure 6.6 - Pipes of equal diameter'];
Ht = title(t);
set(Ht, 'FontSize', 14);
```

```
hold off
pause

% Improved rendering

h = surf(x1, y1, z1);
axis equal, axis off
hold on
set(h, 'FaceLighting', 'phong', 'FaceColor', 'interp',...
       'EdgeColor', 'none')
colormap(spring)
camlight headlight
t    = [ 'Figure 6.6 - Pipes of equal diameter'];
Ht = title(t);
set(Ht, 'FontSize', 14);

h = surf(x2, y2, z2);
axis equal, axis off
set(h, 'FaceLighting', 'phong', 'FaceColor', 'interp',...
       'EdgeColor', 'none')

hold off
```

The first part of the file generates Figure 10.6. The surfaces are **faceted**. Each surface is composed of small patches, each patch in one colour. The network of patch edges describes the surface curvature well.

After viewing the first plot press Enter and look at Figure 10.7. It is produced by the second part of the file in which we assigned handles to the surface objects. This allowed us to specify three surface properties. The property *FaceLighting* determines the way in which light is reflected by the surface object. In our example we invoked a lighting algorithm called *Phong*. For the property *FaceColor* we specified colour interpolation between the faces. For the property *EdgeColor* we specified the value *none*. Thus, the network of face edges no longer appears in the plot.

In this book Figures 10.6 and 10.7 appear in black and white. We strongly recommend the reader to run the files and appreciate the figures in full colour. In our opinion they look great, but this is only the tip of the iceberg. The reader can discover more graphics features by exploring the MATLAB help facilities.

10.8   Examples

EXAMPLE 10.1   The involute of a circle _____

The curve called the **involute of a circle** has a very important engineering application: it is the shape of most gear teeth. The following amusing definition of this curve is due to Markusevich. A goat is tied to a stake whose cross-section is a circle with the centre at O and the radius $\overline{OA} = a$, as shown in Figure 10.8. The rope is fixed at A

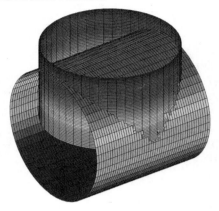

Figure 10.6   Intersection of two pipes of equal diameter–axonometric projection.

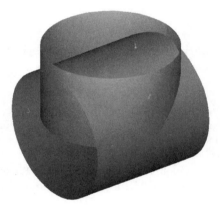

Figure 10.7   Intersection of two pipes of equal diameter – improved rendering.

and its length equals that of the arc AD, that is $AD = a \times \overparen{DOA}$. Stretching the rope taut, the goat moves from B to F, so that part of the rope winds on the stake arc AE. The points B and F lie on a curve which is the involute of the given circle (this circle is the cross-section of the stack).

In Figure 10.9 let $\overparen{BOA} = \alpha$, $\overparen{DOB} = \phi$, and $\overline{OB} = r$. The angle $\overparen{OAB}$ is obviously right. The curve generated by the point B is described in polar coordinates by the equations

$$r = a / \cos \alpha \tag{10.8}$$

$$\phi = \tan \alpha - \alpha \tag{10.9}$$

The derivation of Equation 10.9 is the following: the length of the rope is equal to $\overline{AB} = a \tan \alpha$. When the end of the rope moves from B so that it touches the stake

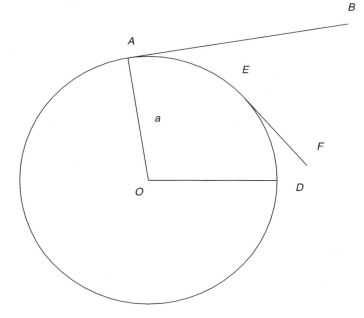

Figure 10.8   The generation of the involute of a circle.

at C, a length of rope equal to $a\alpha$ is wound around the stake, leaving the length $a(\tan \alpha - \alpha)$ free. As this length is exactly equal to the arc CD,

$$a\phi = a \tan \alpha - a\alpha$$

Figures 10.8 and 10.9 were produced in MATLAB by using the `polar` function. Example 10.2 lists the program used for the first of these figures.

The curve defined by Equations 10.8 and 10.9 is the involute of the circle with radius a; as stated above, it is the tooth shape used in most gear designs. Consider two gears in contact, and let $\vec{v}_1$ be the velocity of the point of contact in gear 1, and $\vec{v}_2$ the velocity of the point of contact in gear 2. For 'smooth' operation, the projections of $\vec{v}_1$ and $\vec{v}_2$ on the common normal to the teeth in contact must be equal. This is the **fundamental law of toothed gearing**; it is fulfilled by **involute-** and by **cycloid**-shaped teeth (see, for example, Spotts 1969, Shigley and Mischke 1989, pages 530–2, or Section 13.2 in Dimarogonas 1989). The cycloid is used only in a few special cases.

Figure 10.10 shows how the involute is generated. The listing of the program that produced this figure is given in Example 10.3. Running the program will produce a 'movie'.

The base circle in Figure 10.10 is the **evolute** of the involute represented in the same figure. The mathematical relationship between evolute and involute is defined in differential geometry where it is generalized to other curves besides the circle (see,

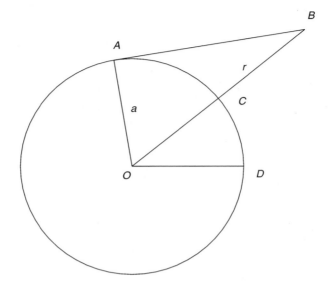

Figure 10.9   The equations of the involute of a circle.

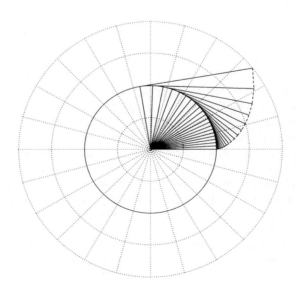

Figure 10.10   The generation of the involute.

for example, pages 219–25 in Piskunov 1960, Chapter 3 in Guggenheimer 1977, and
Section 17.36 in Coxeter 1980).

EXAMPLE 10.2   Listing of the program that generates Figure 10.8 _____

```
%FIG10_03  Draws Figure 10.3, Example 10.1, the generation of
%          the involute of a circle. This M-file is explained
%          in Example 10.2

clf      % clear the screen for new figure
axis('equal'), axis([-1.5 1.5 -1.5 1.5])
axis off, hold on
phi1 = 0: pi/30: 2*pi;
a = 1;
rho = a*ones(size(phi1));
alpha1 = pi/3;
phi2 = tan(alpha1) - alpha1;
phi3 = phi2 + alpha1;
polar(phi1, rho, '-')                    % base circle
polar([ phi3 phi3 ], [ 0 a ])            % radius OA
polar([ phi3 phi2 ], [ a a/cos(alpha1) ]) % tangent AB
text(-0.2, 1.07, 'A')
text(1.4, 1.35, 'B')
polar([ 0 0 ], [ 0 a ])                  % radius vector OD
text(-0.09, -0.09, 'O')
text(-0.05, 0.5, 'a')
text(1.05, 0.0, 'D')
alpha2 = pi/5;
phi4 = tan(alpha2) - alpha2;
phi5 = phi4 + alpha2;
polar([ phi5 phi4 ], [ a a/cos(alpha2) ])  % tangent EF
text(0.75, 0.75, 'E')
text(1.3, 0.2, 'F')
hold off
```

Using the hold on command before any plotting command eliminates the
frame that would otherwise be drawn around the graphs. Also, with hold on invoked,
instead of a single, long polar statement that would produce all figure elements, a
series of short polar statements draw each element in part: first the base circle, next
the radius $\overline{OA}$, and so on. The individual elements are superimposed one upon the
other. Usually, the first polar statement would define the scale and limits of the
graph; they could be insufficient for the other elements. To avoid such a situation, an
axis statement precedes the plotting statements and defines an area sufficient for the
final graph.

EXAMPLE 10.3   A program that generates the involute of a circle _____

```
%INVOLUTE generates the involute of a circle (Figure 10.5).

clf      % begin with a clear screen}
axis('equal'), axis([ -2 2 -2 2 ])
axis('off'), hold on
pni1 = 0: pi/60: 2*pi;
a    = 1;
rho  = a*ones(size(phi1));
polar(phi1, rho)          % base circle}
rad = [ 0 a ]; phi = 0; tang = [ 0 a ];
for alpha = 0: pi/60: pi/3;
        pointa = phi;
        pointr = tang(2);
        phi     = tan(alpha) - alpha;
        phi3    = phi + alpha;
        polar([ 0 phi3 ], rad) % radius vector
        tang    = [ a a/cos(alpha) ];
        polar([ phi3 phi ], tang)
        polar([pointa phi], [ pointr tang(2) ])
        pause(0.5)
end
hold off
```

EXAMPLE 10.4   Orbits of planets and satellites _____

Orbits of planets and satellites are described in polar coordinates by the equation

$$r = \frac{p}{1 + \epsilon \cos \phi} \tag{10.10}$$

where p is known as the **parameter** of the orbit, and ϵ as the **eccentricity** of the orbit (see, for example, Fuller and Tarwater 1992, or Spiegel 1968). The derivation of Equation 10.10 can be found in an Appendix at the end of this chapter. For $0 < \epsilon < 1$ the curve is an **ellipse**; in particular, for $\epsilon = 0$ it is a circle. If $\epsilon > 1$ the orbit is a **hyperbola**, and when ϵ equals exactly 1 the orbit is a **parabola**. Let us program a function conic that plots all these curves by using Equation 10.10; its listing follows.

```
function y = conic(phi, param)
%CONIC     generates a conic section
%     described in polar form with two arguments:
%     phi, the polar angle coordinate, and param = [ p e ],
%     where p is the parameter, and e the eccentricity.
```

```
p = param(1); e = param(2);
r = p*ones(phi)./(1 + e*cos(phi));
polar(phi, r), grid
if e < 1
      t1 = 'Ellipse, ';
elseif e == 1
      t1 = 'Parabola, ';
else
      t1 = 'Hyperbola, ';
end
t2 = 'p = '; t3 = ', e = ';
xlabel([ t1 t2 num2str(p) t3 num2str(e) ]);
```

We can plot an ellipse by the commands:

```
>> phi = 0:  pi/60:  2*pi;
>> parameter = [ 1 0.8 ];
>> conic(phi, parameter)
```

To plot an arc of hyperbola we must redefine the eccentricity and rerun the commands. We can do this by recalling the commands with the arrow keys and modifying them as necessary. A better-looking plot results if we also redefine the range of phi values:

```
>> phi = -pi/2:  pi/90:  pi/2;
>> parameter(2) = 4;
>> conic(phi, parameter)
```

An arc of parabola is obtained when the eccentricity equals exactly 1:

```
>> parameter(2) = 1;
>> conic(phi, parameter)
```

The case of the parabolic orbit is unstable; the smallest perturbation will immediately change the parabola to an ellipse or to a hyperbola. We can check this with the following commands

```
>> phi = -2*pi:  pi/60:  2*pi;
>> parameter(2) = 0.995;
>> conic(phi, parameter)
>> phi = -pi:  pi/90:  pi;
```

```
>> parameter(2) = 1.01;
>> conic(phi, parameter)
```

Geometrically the three curves, ellipse – with the circle as a special case, parabola, and hyperbola, are all **conic sections** or **conics**. The Greeks knew in ancient times that these curves can be obtained by the intersection of a cone with a plane. Credit is given to Apollonius of Perga (c. 262–180 BC) for having written an extensive treatise on conic sections. Figure 10.11 shows a cone and a plane at right angles to the axis of the cone. The intersection of the cone with the plane is a circle. Figure 10.12 shows how to obtain the other curves. We must generalize the notion and assume that the cone extends to infinity in both directions. OZ is the axis of the cone, BC a

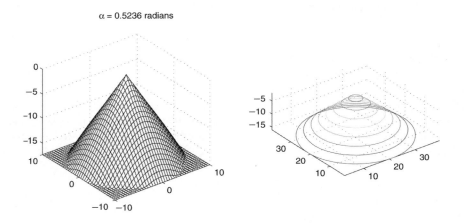

Figure 10.11   The lower nappe of a cone.

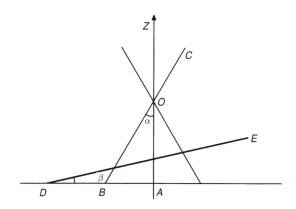

Figure 10.12   Generation of conic sections.

$\alpha = 0.7854$; $\beta = 0.5236$ radians

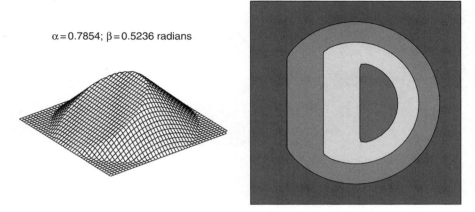

Figure 10.13   The ellipse as a conic section.

generator. $\widehat{AOB} = \alpha$ is the semi-angle of the cone. Let us cut the cone by a plane with the trace DE making an angle $\widehat{ADE} = \beta$ with the planes perpendicular to the axis of the cone. If $\beta = 0$ the intersection curve is a circle, if $0 < \beta < \pi/2 - \alpha$ the curve is an ellipse, if $\beta = \pi/2 - \alpha$, a parabola, and if $\beta > \pi/2 - \alpha$, a hyperbola. The case of the ellipse is shown in Figure 10.13 (Example 10.5). The reader is invited to produce the other conics.

As written above, conics have important applications in engineering and in science; a few of them are listed below.

In graphics. The projection of a circle on a plane not parallel to the plane of the circle is an ellipse.

Mechanics. The trajectory of a projectile in vacuum is a parabola. Orbits of planets and satellites are conic sections.

In optics and communications. Parabolic reflectors and lenses are used for projectors and for antennas. Hyperbolic reflectors are sometimes added.

Power plants. Cooling towers have the shape of hyperboloids of rotation. Sections by planes passing through their axis are hyperbolas; sections through planes perpendicular to their axis are circles.

In navigation. In hyperbolic navigation the position of a plane or ship is found at the intersection of two hyperbolas.

EXAMPLE 10.5   Conic sections

```
function z = cones(alpha)
%CONES       3-D plot of cone.
%CONES(alpha)    plot of cone with semi-angle alpha.
x = -10:0.5:10; y = -10:0.5:10;
```

```
[ X, Y] = meshgrid(x, y);
Z = -sqrt(X.^2 + Y.^2)/tan(alpha); % only lower nappe
i = find(Z<Z(1,21));
for n = i'
   Z(n) = Z(1,21);
end
subplot(1, 2, 1)
mesh(X, Y, Z), axis('equal')
t = [ '\alpha = ' num2str(alpha) ' radians' ];
title(t)
subplot(1, 2, 2)
contour3(Z), axis('equal')
```

Figure 10.11 was plotted by the program listed above.

The expression find(Z < Z(1, 21)) identifies the indices of all elements of Z that are smaller than Z(1, 21); these indices are collected in the array i. Next, all elements with indices in i are made equal to Z(1, 21); they produce the 'reference' plane shown in the figure.

The contour3 function displays lines of equal Z in the surface $Z = f(X, Y)$. In the figure drawn by the cones function the contour lines are intersections with planes perpendicular to the axis of the cone and, therefore, circles. The lines produced by the contour function are similar to the contour lines used in topography.

Cutting the cone by a plane inclined by an angle $\beta < \pi/2 - \alpha$ yields an ellipse. A function that produces such a section, shown in Figure 10.13, is the conecut1 function listed below.

```
function z = conecut1(alpha, beta)
%CONECUT1 3-D plot of a conic section that is an ellipse.
%         alpha is the semi-angle of the cone; beta, the
%         angle of the cutting plane.

b =  1; x =  -10: 0.5: 10;   y =  -10: 0.5: 10;
[ X, Y] = meshgrid(x, y);
z  = -sqrt(X.^2 + Y.^2)/tan(alpha); \% only lower nappe
i = find(z<z(1,21));
for n = i'
   z(n) = z(1,21);
end
a = X(1, 1); b = z(1, 1); c = b - a*tan(beta);
z1 = tan(beta)*X + c;
for j = 1: 41
        for k = 1: 41
                if z(j, k) > z1(j, k)
                        z(j, k) = z1(j, k);
                else
```

```
                        z(j, k) = z(j, k);
                end
        end
end
subplot(1, 2, 1), mesh(X, Y, z), axis('off')
axis('equal')
t1 = [ '\alpha = ' num2str(alpha) '; ' ];
t2 = [ '\beta = ' num2str(beta) ' radians' ];
title([ t1 t2 ])
subplot(1, 2, 2), contourf(z);
axis('square'), axis('off')
```

Note the lines produced in this case by the contourf function. Connecting the left corners of the lines should result in an ellipse; it is the projection – on a plane perpendicular to the cone axis – of the ellipse produced by the intersection with the cutting plane. To improve the form of the projected ellipse and to complete it at left it is necessary to enhance the resolution by asking for more contour lines. This is done by invoking the function as contourf(Z, n), where n is the number of contour levels – when not specified n defaults to 10. Alternatively, the function can be called as contourf(Z, v), with v a vector of specified levels.

EXAMPLE 10.6   Power radiation pattern of antenna _____

Figure 10.14(a) represents a short current filament working as an antenna. The radiation pattern is described by the following equation (Collin 1985):

$$D(\theta) = 1.5 \sin^2 \theta \qquad\qquad (10.11)$$

where the angle θ is defined as in Figure 10.14(a). The angle to be used in MATLAB polar plots is θ_1 and it is defined in the same figure. With $\theta_1 = \pi/2 - \theta$, we obtain

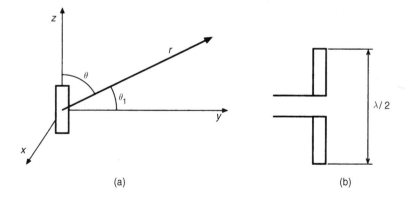

(a)   (b)

Figure 10.14   Definitions of two simple antennas.

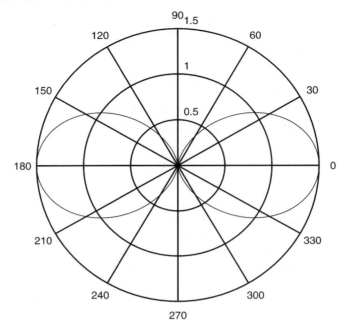

Figure 10.15   Power radiation pattern for short current filament.

the plot of the radiation pattern by the commands

```
≫ theta = 0:  pi/90:   2*pi;
≫ theta1 = pi/2 - theta;
≫ D = 1.5*sin(theta).^2;
≫ polar(theta1, D)
```

The result is shown in Figure 10.15.

EXAMPLE 10.7   Illumination pattern of lamp ──────────────────────────

Consider in Figure 10.16 an ideal lamp that emits uniformly in all directions, and a plane situated a distance h under the lamp. Let P be a point in that plane and r its distance from the lamp. The **angle of incidence** is α. For the intensity, I measured in cd/m^2 – that is, one candela per square metre – the illumination level at P is

$$E = \frac{I}{r^2} \cos \alpha \tag{10.12}$$

and it is measured in lux. With $h = r \cos \alpha$ Equation 10.12 becomes

$$E = \frac{I}{r^2} \cos^3 \alpha \tag{10.13}$$

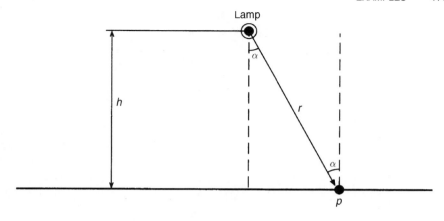

Figure 10.16   Illumination pattern of lamps.

To plot an illumination pattern valid for all similar cases we rewrite Equation 10.13 as

$$\frac{Er^2}{I} = \cos^3 \alpha \tag{10.14}$$

The plot is obtained with

```
≫ alpha = 0:  pi/60:   2*pi;
≫ theta = alpha - pi/2;
≫ e = cos(alpha).^3;
≫ axis square
≫ polar(theta, e)
```

The result is shown in Figure 10.17.   An older possibility is to use `axis('square')` instead of `axis square`.

EXAMPLE 10.8   A grey scale

To display the French colours we used the intensities 0 and 1. Intermediate intensities would result in various hues. In particular, mixing the three primary colours in equal intensities varying between 0 and 1 produces the various 'hues' of grey. To see this, write the following commands on a file `grey.m` and run it.

```
%GREY    Produces the grey scale by an additive process

red   = 0: 0.1: 1;
green = 0: 0.1: 1;
blue  = 0: 0.1: 1;
SCALE = cat(3, red, green, blue);          % build 3d array
```

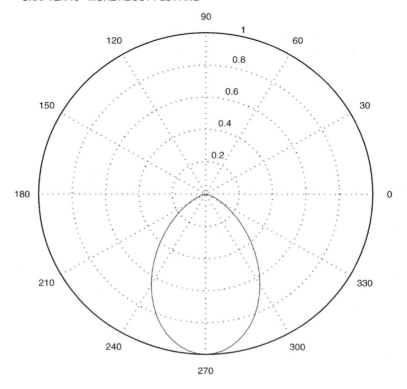

Figure 10.17   Illumination pattern of a lamp that emits uniformly in all directions.

```
image(SCALE)                                    % create image
title('Grey scale')
```

The resulting image is known as the **grey scale**. Unlike in our example, the grey scale is usually displayed with the white end at left and the black end at right. Modify the above listing to produce this display.

EXAMPLE 10.9   The colour cube _____

A schematic representation of the RGB model is the cube shown in Figure 10.18 (Hearn and Baker, 1994). The reader who loves mathematics can imagine the three primary colours, **R**, **G** and **B**, as forming a **vector basis**. Various hues are produced by linear combinations of the form

$$r\mathbf{R} + g\mathbf{G} + b\mathbf{B}$$

where r, g, and b are real numbers in the closed interval $[0, 1]$. In particular, as shown in Example 10.8, if $r = g = b$, we obtain some degree of grey. When $r = g = b = 0$

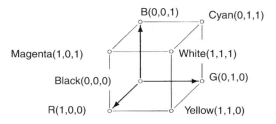

Figure 10.18   The RGB cube.

the result is black, while for $r = g = b = 1$ the result is white. In Figure 10.18, the various degrees of grey are found along the diagonal that connects the *Black* vertex to the *White* vertex. This explains the preceding example and the following M-file that generates the RG plane of the cube:

```
%RGPLANE Generates the RG plane in the RGB cube
red    = zeros(10,10);          % allocate space
green  = zeros(10,10);          % allocate space
blue   = zeros(10,10);          % allocate space
for k = 1: 10
        intensity = (k-1)*0.1;
        red(k, :) = intensity;
        green(:, k) = intensity;
end
RGplane = cat(3, red, green, blue);  % build 3D array
image(RGplane)                       % create image
title('RG plane')
```

10.9   Exercises

Solutions for Exercises 10.2, 10.6, 10.9, 10.11 (partial) and 10.14 appear at the back of the book.

■ **EXERCISE 10.1**   Polar plots
As an exercise, here are a few nice curves to plot in polar coordinates. At least one of them has technical applications. Choose $a = 1$ first and then experiment with other a values.

(1)   **Cissoid of Diocles**

$$r = a \sin^2 \phi / \cos \phi$$

for $-\pi/3 \le \phi \le \pi/3$.

(2)   **Strophoid**

$$r = -a \cos 2\phi / \cos \phi$$

for $-\pi/3 \le \phi \le \pi/3$.

(3)   **Folium of Descartes**

$$r = \frac{3a \sin \phi \cos \phi}{\sin^3 \phi + \cos^3 \phi}$$

for $-\pi/6 \le \phi \le \pi/2$. The name comes from a Latin word meaning 'leaf'.

(4)   **Conchoid**

$$r = b + a/cos\phi$$

for $-\pi/3 \le \phi/3 \le \pi$ and $b = 5$. The name, with Latin and old Greek origins, means 'shell shaped'.

(5)   **The curves of Cassini**

$$r^2 = a^2 \cos 2\phi \pm \sqrt{b^4 - a^4 \sin^2 2\phi}$$

for $-2\pi \le \phi \le 2\pi$ and $b^2 > 2a^2$, $a^2 < b^2 < 2a^2$, $b = a$ (in the latter case the curve becomes a **lemniscate**), $b < a$.

(6)   **Cardioid**

$$r = 2a(1 - \cos \phi)$$

for $0 \le \phi \le 2\pi$. The name comes from the Greek word 'kardia' meaning 'heart'. The cardioid models the radiation pattern of some directional antennas.

■ **EXERCISE 10.2**   Aeroplane in wind – polar plot

The speed relative to air of an aeroplane is 900 km/h. The wind blows from SE to NW and its speed relative to ground is 105 km/h. Draw a polar plot of the aeroplane speed over ground (true speed) as a function of the aeroplane course in air.

Note: the independent variable in the MATLAB polar plot is measured in radians.

■ **EXERCISE 10.3**   Aeroplane in wind – polar plot

An aeroplane flies on a course of 25° relative to air (see Figure 2.22 for the definition of this angle). The aeroplane speed relative to air is 900 km/h. Let us assume that the speed of the wind relative to ground is 105 km/h. To analyse the influence of the wind direction on the aeroplane speed over ground draw a polar plot of this speed as a function of the wind direction.

Note: the independent variable in the MATLAB polar plot is measured in radians.

■ **EXERCISE 10.4**   Conic sections

Complete Example 10.5 by writing functions for generating a parabola and a hyperbola as conic sections.

■ **EXERCISE 10.5**   Radiation pattern of half-wavelength dipole

Figure 10.14(b) represents a half-wavelength dipole antenna. Its radiation pattern is described by the following equation (Collin 1985):

$$D(\theta) = 1.64 \left[\frac{\cos(\pi/2 \cos \theta)}{\sin \theta} \right]^2 \tag{10.15}$$

Plot this equation.

■ **EXERCISE 10.6**   Water waves – animation

In linear water waves the free surface can be described by the equation

$$\zeta = h \cos(kx - \omega t) \qquad (10.16)$$

where

ζ	is the vertical coordinate of the free surface
h	the wave amplitude = half crest-to-trough wave height
k	the *wave number* $= 2\pi/L$
L	the wave length
x	the horizontal coordinate perpendicular to the waves
ω	the wave circular frequency in rad/s
t	the time variable in s

Inspection of Equation 10.16 shows that the form of the waves propagates to the right. However, wouldn't it be easier to build an animation program that lets you visualize the waves?

(1)   Write an M-file that generates the animation starting from the given equation.

(2)   The speed with which the wave form propagates is called **celerity** and it is defined by $c = L/T$, where T is the wave period. As $T = 2\pi/\omega$, and $L = 2\pi/k$, it follows that $c = \omega/k$. This means that changing the sign of k in Equation 10.16 changes the sign of the celerity, that is, the direction of propagation. To see this, change the sign of k in the program you wrote at (1) and run the movie of the waves again.

■ **EXERCISE 10.7**   Standing water waves – animation

If a wave such as described in Exercise 10.6 encounters a vertical wall, it is reflected and travels backwards. The superposition of the **incident** and of the **reflected** wave is a standing wave. To see this, copy the M-file written in the previous exercise, add the expression of the reflected wave and animate the plot of the sum of the two waves.

■ **EXERCISE 10.8**   Standing water waves – animation

In Exercise 10.7 we learnt that, given a linear wave and the corresponding reflected wave, their superposition produces a standing wave. We convinced ourselves that this is so by plotting the sum of the waves and animating the plot. We can obtain the same result by summing the equations of the two waves and writing the sum in a convenient way, that is

$$\zeta = h \cos(\omega t - kx) + h \cos(\omega t + kx) = 2h \cos(kx) \cos(\omega t) \qquad (10.17)$$

Write an animation program based on Equation 10.17.

■ **EXERCISE 10.9**   Swinging pendulum – animation

Read Exercise 5.7 and write an animation program that simulates the swinging pendulum.

■ **EXERCISE 10.10**   Crank-piston kinematics – animation

In Exercise 3.10 we developed the equations that describe the motion of a crank-piston mechanism. Write an animation program that simulates this motion.

Hint: Read Exercises 5.7 and 10.9 and see Figure 10.19.

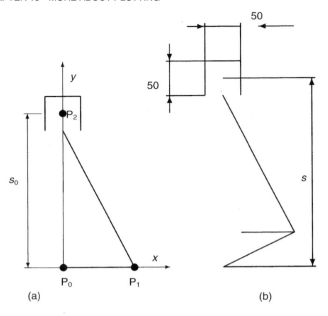

Figure 10.19   Crank-piston kinematics.

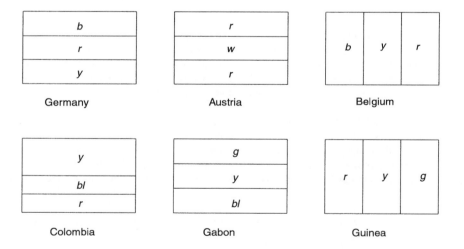

Figure 10.20   A few simple flags.

■ **EXERCISE 10.11**   Some simple flags.

Figure 10.20 shows the colours of a few simple flags. The abbreviation b stands for black, bl, for blue, g, for green, r, for red, w, for white, and y, for yellow. Using the techniques described in Section 10.6 generate the images of those flags.

■ **EXERCISE 10.12**   More simple flags

Relying on the explanations given in the preceding exercise, generate the images of the flags specified in Figure 10.21.

■ **EXERCISE 10.13**   More complex flags
See the explanations given in Exercise 10.11 and generate the images of the flags specified in Figure 10.22.

■ **EXERCISE 10.14**   Colour cube
Write an M-file that generates the RB plane of the colour cube.

■ **EXERCISE 10.15**   Colour cube
Write an M-file that generates the $G = 1$ plane of the colour cube.

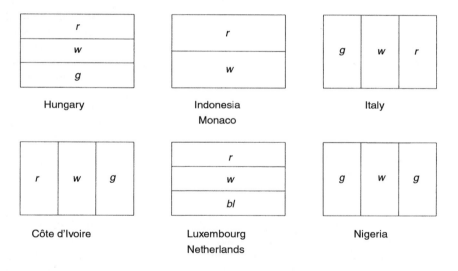

Figure 10.21   More simple flags.

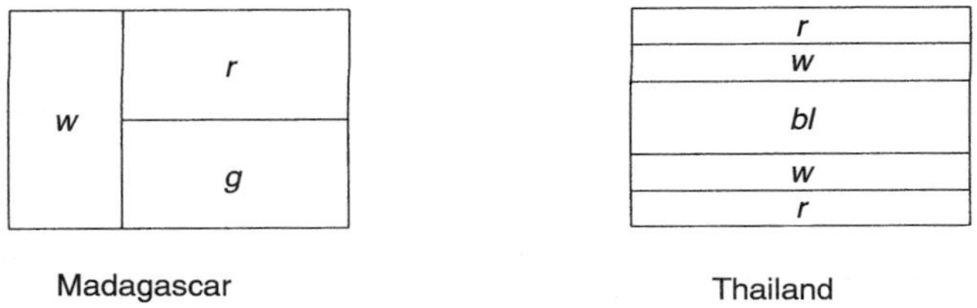

Figure 10.22   More complex flags.

10.10   Appendix – the equation of orbits of planets and satellites

After examining the observations made by the Danish astronomer Tycho Brahe (1546–1601), the German astronomer Johannes Kepler (1571–1630) stated three laws that govern the motions of planets and satellites. Analysing Kepler's laws, Newton deduced his **law of universal gravitation** according to which *two masses, m_1, m_2, attract each other with a force*

$$F(r) = \frac{Gm_1 m_2}{r^2} \tag{10.18}$$

Here r is the distance that separates the centres of the two masses and G, the **universal gravitation constant** ($G = 6.67259 \cdot 10^{-11} \mathrm{Nm^2\ kg^{-2}}$). $F(r)$ acts along the line that joins the two masses (see Figure 10.23).

Assuming $m_2 \gg m_1$ we can consider m_2 as immobile. While the mass m_1 moves along its path, the force $F(r)$ acting on it is always directed towards the centre of m_2. We say, therefore, that the motion of m_1 is a particular case of the **central force problem.** In Figure 10.24 let C be the centre of m_2, and $\vec{r}$ the radius vector defining the position of m_1 with respect to C. The acceleration of m_1 is $\ddot{\vec{r}}$ and, as the force acting on the mass is always directed towards C, the two vectors $\vec{r}, \ddot{\vec{r}}$ are collinear. The velocity of m_1 is the vector $\dot{\vec{r}}$, and the **angular momentum** of m_1 is, by definition, the vector product

$$\vec{M} = \vec{r} \times m_1 \dot{\vec{r}} \tag{10.19}$$

The time derivative of $\vec{M}$ is

$$\dot{\vec{M}} = \dot{\vec{r}} \times m_1 \dot{\vec{r}} + \vec{r} \times m_1 \ddot{\vec{r}} = 0$$

because $\dot{\vec{r}}$ is collinear with itself, and $\vec{r}$ is collinear with $\ddot{\vec{r}}$. We conclude that the angular momentum is a constant in the central force problem.

By definition, $\vec{M}$ is perpendicular to the plane containing $\vec{r}$ and $\dot{\vec{r}}$. As $\vec{M}$ is a constant, it follows that the plane defined by $\vec{r}$ and $\dot{\vec{r}}$ is always the same plane: the motion is two-dimensional.

Figure 10.23   Newton's law of universal gravitation.

Let $\vec{u}_r$ be a unit vector collinear with $\vec{r}$, and $\vec{u}_\theta$ a unit vector tangential to the orbit of m_1. The vector product

$$\vec{u}_n = \vec{u}_r \times \vec{u}_\theta$$

is a unit vector normal to the plane of the orbit (see Figure 10.24). Decomposing the velocity $\dot{\mathbf{r}}$ into its *radial* and *tangential* components we can rewrite Equation 10.19 as

$$\vec{M} = \vec{r} \times m_1 \dot{\vec{r}} = r\vec{u}_r \times m_1(\dot{r}\vec{u}_r + r\dot{\theta}\vec{u}_\theta) = m_1 r^2 \dot{\theta}\vec{u}_n$$

As $\vec{M}$ and m_1 are constants,

$$r^2\dot{\theta} = r^2\frac{d\theta}{dt} = \text{constant} \tag{10.20}$$

Referring again to Figure 10.24 we can see that, in polar coordinates,

$$dA = \frac{1}{2}r^2 d\theta$$

is the element of area described by the radius vector during the time dt. Equation 10.20 states that this element is a constant, and from here follows **Kepler's second law**: *The areas swept by the radius vector in equal times are equal.*

Summing up, the governing equations of the motion can be written as

$$\ddot{r} = -k/r^2 \tag{10.21}$$
$$r^2\dot{\theta} = M \tag{10.22}$$

Let us represent the vector $\vec{r}$ in exponential form

$$\vec{r} = re^{i\theta} \tag{10.23}$$

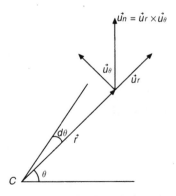

Figure 10.24   Kepler's second law.

Differentiating Equation 10.23 twice we obtain

$$\ddot{\vec{r}} = (\ddot{r} - r\dot{\theta}^2)e^{i\theta} + (2\dot{r}\dot{\theta} + r\ddot{\theta})ie^{i\theta} \tag{10.24}$$

The terms between the first pair of parentheses multiply $e^{i\theta}$, that is, they belong to a vector in phase with the radius vector $\vec{r}$. The terms between the second pair of parentheses multiply $ie^{i\theta}$; they belong to a vector perpendicular to the radius vector. The first term between these parentheses is the **Coriolis acceleration** (Gaspard Coriolis, French, 1792–1843). Projecting Equation 10.19 on the direction of $\vec{r}$ we get

$$\ddot{r} - r\dot{\theta}^2 = -k/r^2 \tag{10.25}$$

With $\dot{\theta}$ given by Equation 10.20 we can write

$$\dot{r} = \frac{dr}{d\theta}\dot{\theta} = \frac{dr}{d\theta}\frac{M}{r^2} = -M\frac{d(1/r)}{d\theta} \tag{10.26}$$

Substituting $u = 1/r$ and differentiating with respect to time yields

$$\ddot{r} = -M^2 u^2 \frac{d^2 u}{d\theta^2}$$

With this value, and the value of $\dot{\theta}$ given by Equation 10.20, Equation 10.25 yields

$$\frac{d^2 u}{d\theta^2} + u = \frac{k}{M^2} \tag{10.27}$$

with the solution

$$u = [1 + \epsilon\cos(\theta - \delta)]\frac{k}{M^2}$$

or

$$r = \frac{M^2/k}{1 + \epsilon\cos(\theta - \delta)} \tag{10.28}$$

where ϵ, δ are two constants of integration. If we choose $\theta = 0$ where r is minimum (that is, at the **pericentre**, or **perihelion**, of the orbit), then $\delta = 0$. Equation 10.28 can be rewritten as

$$r = \frac{p}{1 + \epsilon\cos\phi} \tag{10.29}$$

where p is known as the **parameter** of the orbit, and ϵ as the **eccentricity** of the orbit (see, for example, Fuller and Tarwater 1992, or Spiegel 1968).

Physically the distinction between the different curves is determined by the total energy (potential plus kinetic) of the moving mass. The derivation of the equations follows the lines of Wittenburg *et al.* (1989). Other derivations, making use of the notions of energy, can be found, for example, in Arnold (1984) and Meirovitch (1970).

— PART II —

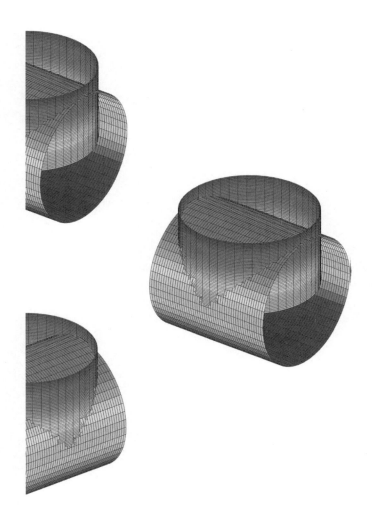

More Applications

Chapter 11
Numerical integration

11.1   Introduction

Two functions for integration are introduced in this chapter: `trapz`, introduced in MATLAB 4 and further developed in MATLAB 5, and `simp`, developed within this chapter. These functions are first exemplified on integrands defined by mathematical expressions; this is done to convince the reader that the functions are efficient, and to allow an evaluation of errors. The first examples are followed by engineering applications to functions which are presented in tabular form and are not defined by mathematical expressions.

Many engineering problems require the calculation of the definite integral

$$\int_a^b f(x)\,dx,$$

of a function bounded in the finite interval $[a, b]$. Often it is difficult or even downright impossible to calculate this integral analytically. In such cases we can approximate the definite integral by the weighted sum of a number of function values, $f(x_0)$, $f(x_1)$, ..., $f(x_n)$, evaluated, or measured, at n points $x_i \in [a, b]$, $i = 1, 2, \ldots, n$, that is

$$\int_a^b f(x)\,dx \approx \sum_{i=1}^n a_i f(x_i) \qquad \textbf{(11.1)}$$

485

The coefficients a_i are called **multipliers** by some authors, **weights** by others. Some instances in which we must resort to numerical integration are described below.

(1)   The integrand is given as a mathematical expression, but its integral cannot be expressed in terms of elementary functions. A few examples in this category are

$$\int_0^1 e^{-x^2}\,dx, \quad \int_0^{\pi/2} \sqrt{1 + \cos^2 x}\,dx$$

$$\int \frac{\sin x}{x}\,dx, \quad \int \frac{\cos x}{x}\,dx, \quad \int \frac{dx}{\ln x}, \quad \int \frac{dx}{\sqrt{1 - x^4}}$$

The first integral above is a case of the **error function** defined as

$$\mathrm{Erf}(x) = \int_0^x e^{-u^2}\,du$$

The second integral represents the length of an arc of the **sine function**, between 0 and $\pi/2$ radians.

(2)   Integrals that can be expressed in terms of elementary functions, but their evaluation is too tedious. In this category we include the numerous cases in which we cannot even know whether a closed-form integral exists or not. The search for this integral requires time and effort, and as success is not assured it is much more practical to revert to numerical methods.

(3)   Integrals of functions defined by tables of values evaluated, or measured, at a number of points, and not by mathematical expressions. For this case we shall use the term **integrand given in tabular form**.

The third category is of special interest in engineering and it includes the integration of functions measured experimentally, for example the evaluation of the area in an indicator diagram (in order to obtain the work done by an internal combustion engine), the evaluation of land areas in surveying, and the calculation of geometrical properties (areas, centroids, moments of inertia, volumes and centres of volumes) of figures and solids that cannot be defined by a mathematical expression, such as car, ship and aeroplane hulls.

There are several ways of deriving formulae for numerical integration – also called **quadrature formulae** – of the form shown in Equation 11.1; three of them are mentioned below.

(1)   By geometrical reasoning, considering $\int_a^b f(x)\,dx$ as the area under the curve $f(x)$, between $x = a$ and $x = b$. This is the approach adopted in Gerald and Wheatley (1994), pp. 288–9, Hartley and Wynn-Evans (1979), pp. 317–18, Kaplan (1991), pp. 167–72, Piskunov (1960), and Thomas and Finney (1992), pp. 178–80.

(2)   By approximating the function $f(x)$ by an interpolating polynomial, $P(x)$, and integrating the latter instead of the given function, so that

$$\int_a^b f(x)\,dx \approx \int_a^b P(x)\,dx$$

In many cases $P(x)$ is chosen to be a Legendre polynomial. This second approach can be found in Arbenz and Wohlhauser (1986), pp. 319–21, Hartley and Wynn-Evans (1979), and Ralston (1965). A general discussion can be found in Gerald and Wheatley (1994).

(3)   By developing the given function into a Taylor or MacLaurin series and integrating this series. Quadrature formulae are developed in this way in Hartley and Wynn-Evans (1979), pp. 319–21.

The first approach yields a simple intuitive interpretation of the rules for numerical quadrature and of the errors involved. This interpretation enables the user to derive the rules for himself whenever required, and to apply them according to his needs, for instance when changing the integration step, or when the integrand vanishes between two evaluation points. On the other hand, each rule must be derived separately. The advantages of the other approaches are:

• The derivation is common to a group of rules which thus appear as particular cases of a more general method.

• The derivation yields an expression of the error involved.

In the next two sections we shall use the geometrical approach to derive the two most popular rules, namely the **trapezoidal** and **Simpson's rules**. These two methods are sufficient for solving many problems encountered in engineering. The error terms will be given without derivation; the user may find the proofs in the books referred to above. However, short interpretations of the error expressions will follow their presentation.

11.2   The trapezoidal rule

Let us consider the function $f(x)$ represented in Figure 11.1. We assume that we know the values $f(x1)$, $f(x2)$, ..., $f(x7)$ and we want to calculate the definite integral

$$I = \int_{x1}^{x7} f(x)\,dx \tag{11.2}$$

The integral in Equation 11.2 represents the area under the curve $f(x)$. Let us connect the points $f(x1)$, $f(x2)$, ..., $f(x7)$ by straight-line segments (the dashed lines in the figure). We approximate the area under the curve by the sum of the areas of six trapezoids, that is, the area of the trapezoid with the base $x1x2$ and the

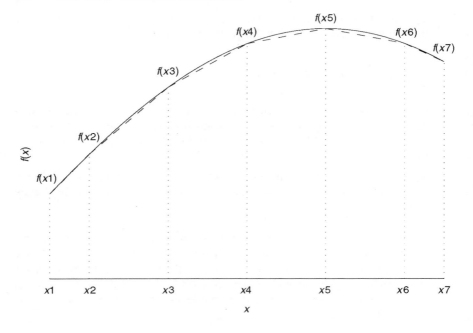

Figure 11.1   The derivation of the trapezoidal rule.

heights $f(x1)$, $f(x2)$, plus the area of the trapezoid with the base $x2x3$ and heights $f(x2)$, $f(x3)$, and so on. We obtain

$$I \approx (x2 - x1)\frac{f(x1) + f(x2)}{2} + (x3 - x2)\frac{f(x2) + f(x3)}{2} + \cdots \qquad \textbf{(11.3)}$$

For constant x-spacing, $x_2 - x_1 = x_3 - x_2 = \cdots = h$, Equation 11.3 can be reduced to a simpler form:

$$I \approx h \left[\frac{1}{2} f(x_1) + f(x_2) + f(x_3) + \cdots + f(x_{n-1}) + \frac{1}{2} f(x_n) \right] \qquad \textbf{(11.4)}$$

As an example let us calculate manually

$$\int_{0^0}^{90^0} \sin x \, dx$$

The calculation presented in tabular form is as follows:

Angle degrees	$\sin x$	Multiplier	Product
0	0	1/2	0
15	0.2588	1	0.2588
30	0.5000	1	0.5000
45	0.7071	1	0.7071
60	0.8660	1	0.8660
75	0.9659	1	0.9659
90	1.0000	1/2	0.5000
Sum	–	–	3.7979

The calculations were performed with MATLAB and the precision of the display was retained. To obtain the approximation of the integral we multiply the sum in column 4 by the constant subinterval, h:

$(\pi * 15/180) * 3.7979 = 0.9943$

Equation 11.3 in matrix form yields

$$I \approx [(x2 - x1),\ (x3 - x2), \ldots, (x7 - x6)] \begin{bmatrix} y1 + y2 \\ y2 + y3 \\ \vdots \\ y6 + y7 \end{bmatrix} /2 \qquad \textbf{(11.5)}$$

The generalized form of Equation 11.5 is implemented in MATLAB by the trapz function as

$z = \text{diff}(x)'*(y(1:m-1,:) + y(2:m,:))/2;$

where m is the common number of rows of x and y. The trapz function can be called with two arguments

(1)   the column vector x,

(2)   the column vector y, of the same length as x, or a matrix y, with the same number of rows as x.

If the points $x1, x2, \ldots, xn$ are equally spaced, that is, if

$x2 - x1 = x3 - x2 = \cdots = h$

the trapz function can be called with one argument, namely the column vector (or matrix) y. In this case, the result must be multiplied by the common x-interval, h.

As an example let us calculate with one command the integrals

$$\int_{0°}^{90°} \sin x \, dx, \quad \int_{0°}^{90°} \cos x \, dx \tag{11.6}$$

We know that the exact result of both integrals is 1. In MATLAB we can proceed as follows

```
>> angle = 0:  15:  90; x = (pi*angle/180)';
>> y = [ sin(x) cos(x) ];
>> trapz(x, y)
ans =
    0.9943 0.9943
```

The error equals 0.57% of the true value; as will be shown below, it can be reduced by making the x-interval smaller. As we used $\sin x$ and $\cos x$ values calculated at equally spaced x points, we could have called the `trapz` function with only one argument, and multiplied the result by the x spacing *in radians*

```
>> h = pi*15/180;
>> h*trapz(y)
ans =
    0.9943 0.9943
```

To improve the result try a smaller x step, for example

```
>> angle = 0:  5:  90;
```

The `trapz` function does not require constant x spacing. We could have used, for example,

```
>> x = [ 0 5 10 20 30 40 50 55 65 75 80 90 ];
```

Try this for yourself.

11.3   Error of integration by the trapezoidal rule

In any subinterval $[x_i, x_{i+1}]$, the error of the approximation, I_i, obtained by the trapezoidal rule equals

$$I_i - \int_{x_i}^{x_{i+1}} f(x) \, dx = h^3 \frac{d^2 f(\xi_i)}{dx^2} \Big/ 12 \tag{11.7}$$

where ξ_i is a point in the interval (x_i, x_{i+1}) and $h = x_{i+1} - x_i$. Usually, the interval of integration, $[x_1, x_m]$, is divided into several subintervals; if we assume that they are equal, and note by I the trapezoidal approximation over the whole interval, we can write

$$\left| I - \int_{x_1}^{x_m} f(x)\, dx \right| \quad = \quad \left| \sum_{i=1}^{m-1} \frac{h^3}{12} \frac{d^2 f(\xi)}{dx^2} \right| \tag{11.8}$$

$$\leq \quad \frac{x_m - x_1}{12} h^2 \max_{\xi \in [x_1, x_m]} \left| \frac{d^2 f(\xi)}{dx^2} \right| \tag{11.9}$$

We do not know the maximum value of the derivative in Equation 11.9; otherwise we would have been able to calculate the exact value of the integral. We can, however, say the following:

- By substituting in Equation 11.9 the maximum value of $df^2(x)/dx^2$ in the interval $[x_1, x_m]$ we can calculate an upper boundary of the error.
- The error is proportional to the square of h: if we halve the subinterval, the error is reduced approximately in the ratio $1/4$.
- The method is exact if $df^2(x)/dx^2 = 0$. This is the case for linear functions. As a matter of fact, the derivation of the trapezoidal rule was based on a linear approximation of $f(x)$.

EXAMPLE 11.1

In this example we are going to use the long format; this will allow us to visualize better the convergence of the integral when the subinterval h is being reduced. Let us calculate analytically the integral

$$\int_0^{\pi/2} \{1 + \sin(x)\}\, dx \quad = \quad [x - \cos(x)]_0^{\pi/2}$$

$$= \quad \pi/2 + 1 = 2.57079632679490$$

To calculate the same integral numerically, by means of the trapz function, we first form a vector of integrand values. We begin by dividing the interval $[0, \pi/2]$ into two subintervals

```
>> x = 0:  pi/4:  pi/2;
>> y = 1 + sin(x);
```

and next we call the function by

```
>> area = trapz(x, y)
```

obtaining 2.51885577576342. The error equals -0.05194055103148, or -2.02% of the correct value. Let us compare this result with the upper bound predicted by Equation 11.9. With

$$x_3 - x_1 = \pi/2 - 0, \; h = \pi/4, \frac{d^2 f(\xi)}{dx}^2 = -\sin(x)$$

In the interval $[0, \pi/2]$ the maximum value of $\sin x$ is 1. Therefore the upper bound of the error is calculated in MATLAB as

```
(pi/2 - 0)*(pi/4)^2*(-1)/12
ans =
    -0.0807
```

This is, indeed, more than the effective error. In Figure 11.1 the error is represented by the sum of the small areas contained between the dotted line (the trapezoids) and the solid line (the given curve). This area looks really small.

We can reduce the error by halving the subinterval h. Experimenting with subintervals equal to $\pi/8, \pi/16, \dots, \pi/128$, we obtain the results shown in Table 11.1 where they are compared with the results yielded by Simpson's rule (see the following sections). The errors are shown in Table 11.2 and the errors in per cent of the true value

Table 11.1   Results by trapezoidal and by Simpson's rule.

Subinterval	Integral	
	Trapezoidal rule	Simpson's rule
$\pi/4$	2.51885577576342	2.57307620428711
$\pi/8$	2.55791212776767	2.57093091176909
$\pi/16$	2.56758149868107	2.57080462231886
$\pi/32$	2.56999300727997	2.57079684347960
$\pi/64$	2.57059552111492	2.57079635905990
$\pi/128$	2.57074612688700	2.57079632881103

Table 11.2   Errors by trapezoidal and by Simpson's rule

Subinterval	Error	
	Trapezoidal rule	Simpson's rule
$\pi/4$	-0.05194055103148	0.00227987749221
$\pi/8$	-0.01288419902722	0.00013458497419
$\pi/16$	-0.00321482811383	0.00000829552397
$\pi/32$	$-0.80331951492774e{-}3$	$0.00051668470613e{-}3$
$\pi/64$	$-0.20080567998138e{-}3$	$0.00003226500089e{-}3$
$\pi/128$	$-0.50199907899007e{-}4$	$0.00002016129486e{-}4$

Table 11.3   Per cent error by trapezoidal and by Simpson's rule.

Subinterval	Per cent error	
	Trapezoidal rule	Simpson's rule
$\pi/4$	−2.0204	0.08868371
$\pi/8$	−0.5012	0.00523515
$\pi/16$	−0.1251	0.00032268
$\pi/32$	−0.0312	0.00002010
$\pi/64$	−0.0078	0.00000126
$\pi/128$	−0.0195	0.00000008

in Table 11.3. As predicted by Equation 11.9, each time we divide the subinterval h by 2, the error is divided by approximately 4. It is easy to see that as $h \rightarrow 0$, the trapezoidal approximation of the integral tends to the true value. On computers this limit generally cannot be reached because

- we can add only a finite number of terms;
- the numbers are represented in the calculator by a finite number of digits (round-off and truncation errors).

In this example, by reducing the size of the subinterval h we could make the error negligible. This was easy because we had an analytic expression for $f(x)$ and we could evaluate as many values of $f(x)$ as we wanted. When there is no mathematical definition, the number of function values that can be measured, or evaluated, is restricted by practical limitations. In such cases we must be satisfied if the precision of the integration is consistent with the precision of the measurements, or the simplifying assumptions of the mathematical model on which calculations are based. To understand this point better, let us suppose that we want to calculate the mass of a 'fancy' steel plate whose form cannot be described in simple mathematical terms. It makes no sense to worry too much about the precision of integration when

(1) for technical reasons the thickness of the plate is given with a certain tolerance;

(2) the specific gravity of steel quoted in handbooks is an average value affected by tolerances in the composition of the steel and by the manufacturing process.

If the plate outline is described by enough tabulated values, the error of integration may be less than the uncertainty in the two factors enumerated above.

The example was based on a function for which we had a mathematical definition. Thus we could know the exact value of the integral and compare it with the results obtained numerically. It should be clear, however, that the mathematical expression was not used in any way in the process of integration: the two arguments of the `trapz` function were vectors of numerical values! These vectors could have been obtained by measuring a curve such as that in Figure 11.1, or by measuring the output of some instrument, or it could have resulted from a previous numerical calculation.

11.4   Simpson's rule

In Figure 11.2 the solid line passing through the points B, C and D represents the integrand $f(x)$. We want to calculate the integral of $f(x)$ between $x = A$ and $x = E$, that is, the area $ABCDEFA$. This time we shall approximate $f(x)$ by a parabola whose equation has the form

$$f(x) = a_0 + a_1 x + a_2 x^2 \tag{11.10}$$

The parabola is represented by a dashed line in Figure 11.2. We need three points to define this curve; therefore, in addition to the values of $f(x)$ calculated at the two extremities, that is, at the points B and D, we shall also evaluate $f(x)$ at the half-interval, obtaining the point C. Let

$$\overline{AB} = f(x_1), \ \overline{FC} = f(x_2), \ \overline{ED} = f(x_3)$$

$$h = \overline{AE}/2 = (x_3 - x_1)/2$$

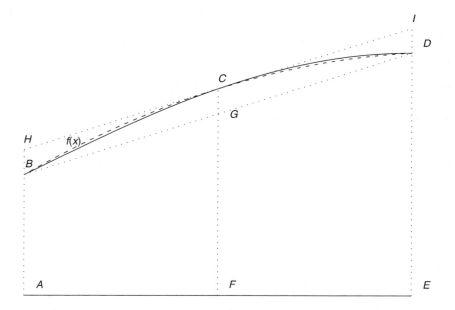

Figure 11.2   The derivation of Simpson's rule.

We decompose the total area under $f(x)$ into two partial areas:

(1)   the trapezoid $ABDEA$;

(2)   the parabolic segment $BCDGB$.

The first area equals

$$\overline{AE} \cdot \frac{\overline{AB} + \overline{ED}}{2} = 2h \cdot \frac{f(x_1) + f(x_3)}{2}$$

For the second area we use a result from geometry which says that the area of a parabolic segment equals two thirds of the area of the circumscribed parallelogram. Correspondingly we calculate the second area as 2/3 of the circumscribed parallelogram $BHID$, that is

$$\frac{2}{3} \cdot \overline{AE} \cdot \overline{CG} = \frac{2}{3} \cdot 2h \left(f(x_2) - \frac{f(x_1) + f(x_3)}{2} \right)$$

Adding the two partial sums yields

$$\int_{x_0}^{x_2} f(x)dx \approx \frac{h}{3} \left[f(x_1) + 4f(x_2) + f(x_3) \right] \tag{11.11}$$

which is the elementary form of **Simpson's rule.**

Usually we have to integrate the function $f(x)$ over a larger interval $[a, b]$. Then we achieve a better approximation by dividing the given interval into more subintervals. From the way we derived Equation 11.11 we see that the number of subintervals must be even, say $n = 2k$, where k is a natural number. Let

$$h = \frac{a - b}{n} = x_2 - x_1 = x_3 - x_2 = \cdots = x_{n+1} - x_n$$

Applying Equation 11.11 for each pair of subintervals, and adding all partial sums, we get

$$\int_{x_1}^{x_{n+1}} f(x)\, dx \quad = \quad \frac{h}{3}[f(x_1) + 4f(x_2) + 2f(x_3) + $$
$$4f(x_4) + \cdots + 4f(x_n) + f(x_{n+1})] \tag{11.12}$$

which is the extended form of Simpson's rule, for equal subintervals. This form was very helpful when calculations were carried out manually. As an example, let us calculate manually

$$\int_{0°}^{90°} \sin x \, dx$$

In tabular form the calculation is

Angle degrees	$\sin x$	Multiplier	Product
0	0	1	0
15	0.2588	4	1.0353
30	0.5000	2	1.0000
45	0.7071	4	2.8284
60	0.8660	2	1.7321
75	0.9659	4	3.8637
90	1.0000	1	1.0000
Sum	–	–	11.4595

To obtain the approximation of the integral we multiply the sum in column 4 by the constant subinterval:

$$(\pi * 15/180) * 11.4595/3 = 1.0000$$

When a computer is used there is no need to have all subintervals equal and it is sufficient to have **pairs of equal intervals**. A MATLAB function called simp which implements Equation 11.11 is shown below.

```
function z = simp(x, y)
%SIMP(X, Y) Simpson integration of tabular data y(x).
% Z = SIMP(X, Y) integrates Y with respect to X using
% Simpson's first rule. X and Y are column vectors of the
% same length, or X is a column vector and Y a matrix
% with the same number of rows as X. In the latter
% case Z is a row vector containing the integrals of
% each column of Y.  If either or both X and Y are
% row vectors, they are converted to column vectors.
%
% Z = SIMP(Y) integrates Y assuming that the X intervals
% are constant. The user must multiply the result by the
% value of the constant X interval.

% Check that x and y are column vectors, or y is a
% matrix with the same number of rows as x.
if nargin < 2, y = x; end
[ n, m ] = size(y);
if n == 1, y = y(:); n = m; end
if nargin < 2, x = 1:n; end
x = x(:);
% [ n, m ] = size(y);
if length(x) ~= n
```

```
                error('Input arguments must be of same length')
end
% n = length(x);
if rem(n, 2) == 0
        error('Uneven number of intervals')
end
c = [ 1 4 1 ];
dx = diff(x);
z = 0;
for i = 1: 2: (n-2)
        if abs(dx(i) - dx(i+1)) > 0.00001
                error('Two sequential intervals not equal')
        end
        z = z + c*[ y(i,:); y(i+1,:); y(i+2,:)]*dx(i);
end
z = z/3
```

As with `trapz`, the function is called as

```
>> simp(x, y)
```

where x is the column vector of x-values and y the column vector of y-values. If the x-spacing is constant, the first argument, x, can be omitted and the result multiplied by the constant value of the x-spacing. The function checks if the number of ordinates supplied in the argument is uneven, and if not it stops the execution and displays an error message.

As an example, let us calculate the same integral that we exemplified in Section 11.2

```
angle = 0:  15:  90; x = (pi*angle/180)';
y = sin(x);
simp(x, y)
ans =
   1.0000
```

In this case the result is much better than the one obtained with the trapezoidal rule in Section 11.2. In fact, in `short format` precision, the result is exact.

11.5   Error of integration by Simpson's rule

Noting by I_i the approximation obtained by Simpson's rule in the interval $[x_1, x_3]$, the error equals

$$I_i - \int_{x_1}^{x_3} f(x)\,dx = h^5 \frac{1}{90} \frac{d^4 f(\xi)}{dx^4} \tag{11.13}$$

where $x_1 \leq \xi \leq x_3$. Summing up the errors in all pairs of intervals, and noting by I the approximation obtained with Simpson's rule, we obtain

$$\left| I - \int_{x_1}^{x_n} f(x)\,dx \right| \quad = \quad \left| \sum_{1}^{n/2} \frac{d^4 f(\xi)}{dx^4} \cdot \frac{h^5}{90} \right| \tag{11.14}$$

$$\leq \quad \frac{x_n - x_1}{180} h^4 \max_{\xi \in [x_1, x_n]} \left| \frac{d f^4(\xi_m)}{dx^4} \right| \tag{11.15}$$

At this point we can say the following about Simpson's rule:

(1)   If we divide h by 2, the error decreases approximately in the ratio $1/16$.

(2)   Simpson's rule yields the exact result if $d^4 f/dx^4 = 0$. This is certainly true for second-degree parabolas, which is not surprising because we assumed such a curve when we developed the rule. It is interesting that the method is also exact for cubics (third-degree curves).

(3)   For an equal number of subintervals, Simpson's rule yields better results than the trapezoidal rule. On the other hand, Simpson's rule imposes a serious constraint: the number of subintervals must be even – or, equivalently, $f(x)$ must be evaluated at an uneven number of equally spaced points.

EXAMPLE 11.2 _____

In Figure 11.2 $f(x) = 1 + \sin(x)$, as in Example 11.1. We shall now integrate $f(x)$ by means of Simpson's rule using the commands

```
>> t = 0:  pi/4:  pi/2;
>> z = 1 + sin(t);
>> format long
>> area = simp(t, z)
   area =
       2.57307620428711
```

The error relative to the true value, at the maximum precision displayed by MATLAB, is shown in Table 11.2. We can calculate an upper bound of this error by means of Equation 11.15 where

$$x_3 - x_1 = \pi/2, \ \ h = \pi/4, \ \ \frac{d^4 f(\xi_m)}{dx^4} = \sin x$$

In the interval $[0, \pi/2]$ the maximum value of $\sin x$ is 1. Therefore, we calculate the upper bound in MATLAB as

```
(pi/4)^5*1/90
ans =
    0.0033
```

This is, indeed, above the effective error. We can experiment with smaller subintervals and obtain the results shown in Table 11.1, where they are compared with the results obtained with the trapezoidal rule. The convergence is considerably faster than that obtained with the trapezoidal rule. The errors with respect to the exact value, at the maximum precision yielded by MATLAB, are compared in Table 11.2, and the per cent errors in Table 11.3. As predicted by Equation 11.15, each time we divided the subinterval h by 2, the error decreased approximately in the ratio $1/16$. Note also that only two subintervals yielded better results with Simpson's rule than with the trapezoidal rule.

11.6   MATLAB quadrature functions – function handles

Older versions of MATLAB provided two functions for numerical integration, quad and quad8. Recent MATLAB documentation describes those functions as obsolescent and recommends the use of the new function quadl. A discussion of the first two functions and the background of the third can be found in Gander and Gautschi (2000). Further, the function for double integration is dblquad. Because of the restrictions imposed on the latter, however, we find it of little use in engineering calculations.

All cited MATLAB quadrature functions take as arguments an explicit expression that allows the calculation of the function for any value of the independent variables, and the limits of integration. It is possible to add other arguments, as documented in the MATLAB help facilities. The procedures iterate the numerical integration, reducing at each iteration the subinterval of integration, until the difference between two evaluations reaches a given tolerance value. Obviously, this is only possible when the integrand is defined explicitly in terms of computable functions. On the other hand, many real-life engineering problems require the integration of a function whose explicit expression is not known. Therefore, we preferred to introduce and exemplify in the previous sections the MATLAB trapz function and our own simp function. These functions work on integrands given in tabular form; such tables can be obtained by measurement, including measurement by data-acquisition systems, or by evaluation at a limited number of points.

The syntax of quadrature functions provided by MATLAB can be found with the help facilities of the software. We exemplify one implementation here because it allows us to introduce the notion of **function handles**. In Section 11.4 we used a result from geometry that says that the area under a segment of a parabola equals two-thirds of the area of the circumscribed parallelogram. A parabola representation convenient for our purpose is

$$y = -\frac{b}{a^2}x^2 + b \tag{11.16}$$

The curve crosses the x-axis at $x = -a$ and $x = a$, and reaches the maximum, $y = b$, at $x = 0$. Let us check numerically that the area above the x-axis equals two-thirds of $2ab$. For illustration we assume $a = 1$, $b = 3$. Equation 11.16 becomes

$$y = -3x^2 + 3 \tag{11.17}$$

and we call the function quadl with a string argument defining the integrand, and the limits of integration

```
area = quadl('-3*x.^2 + 3', -1, 1)
area =
 4.0000
```

The result is the expected one, but the procedure preferred today is the following. First, we define the integrand as a function:

```
%HPARABOLA   Defines a function for a parabola used in a QUADL
% example
        function y = hparabola(x)
a = 1;
b = 3;
y = -(b/a^2)*x.^2 + b;
```

Next, we assign a **function handle** to our function and we use it as the argument of quadl;

```
hp = @hparabola;
area = quadl(hp, -1, 1)
area =
 4.0000
```

Notice that the function handle was defined by attaching the character '@' before the name of the function.

A function handle is a MATLAB **data type**, a concept briefly discussed in Chapter 18. The function handle stores all the information about the function and allows its execution or evaluation by other functions. For example, plot for yourself the parabola segment with the command

```
>> fplot(hp, [ -1 1 ])
```

A shortcut is possible:

```
area = quadl(@hparabola, -1, 1)
```

However, it will then not be possible to supply the function handle to other functions, as we did above.

Function handles are presently used in the integration of ordinary differential equations (ODEs) as shown in more detail in Chapter 14.

A further possibility provided by MATLAB is to define the function as an **inline function**. The reader may care to look up the MATLAB documentation on inline functions. An example of using an inline function for the same purpose as above is

```
>> ip = inline('-3*x.^2 + 3', 'x')
>> fplot(ip, [ -1, 1 ])
>> area = quadl(ip, -1, 1)
```

We do not find inline functions very useful in engineering applications because:

- they are saved in the workspace like variables and are, therefore, lost at the end of the session;
- the syntax is only suitable for defining very simple functions, namely one-line functions;
- there are no tools for debugging them.

We decided nevertheless to include this short description in the book because occasionally inline functions can be handy when you need to define a simple function, for one-time use, and prefer to avoid the trouble of going through the editor.

11.7   Examples

EXAMPLE 11.3   Energy required for heating 1 kg of water ⎯⎯⎯⎯⎯⎯⎯⎯

Trapezoidal rule

The heat required to raise the temperature of one unit of mass of a given substance, by a small temperature difference dT, under constant pressure, equals

$$dQ = c_p dT \tag{11.18}$$

where c_p is called **specific heat** (see, for example, Janna 1986). The specific heat is itself a function of temperature, as we can see, for example, in Table 11.4. The SI units to be used in Equation 11.18 are J (Joule) for heat, $J \cdot kg^{-1} \cdot K^{-1}$ for specific heat, and K (Kelvin) for temperature differences.

Table 11.4   Specific heat of saturated water.

Temperature °C	c_p J/(kg · K)	Temperature °C	c_p J/(kg · K)
0	4217	160	4342
20	4181	180	4417
40	4178	200	4505
60	4184	220	4610
80	4196	240	4756
100	4216	260	4949
120	4250	280	5208
140	4283	300	5728

Let us calculate the heat necessary to raise the temperature of 1 kg of saturated water from 0 °C to 300 °C. We begin by writing the contents of Table 11.4 to a file `watercp.m`:

```
%WATERCP specific heat of water
% Format is [ Temperature, Specific heat cp ]
% Units are [ degree C, J/(kg.K) ]
cp = [
0 4217
20 4181
...
300 5728 ];
```

Next, we load the data and separate the column vectors of temperature and specific capacity by

```
>> watercp
>> temp = cp(:, 1);
>> spec = cp(:, 2);
```

To calculate the energy required to raise the temperature from 0 °C to 300 °C we must integrate Equation 11.18 numerically. In MATLAB we do this by

```
>> trapz(temp, spec)
>> ans =
   1344950
```

Suppose now that we want to calculate the energy necessary to raise the temperature to 140 °C only and we know that Table 11.4 contains the specific heat corresponding to this temperature. We must first find the index of 140 in the column vector `temp`; to do this we use the `find` function as follows:

```
>> ind = find(temp == 140)
ind =
     8
```

and call the `trapz` function as

```
>> trapz(temp(1:ind), spec(1:ind))
ans =
     589100
```

Simpson's rule

We assume that the data are loaded and that temperature and specific capacity are separated as above. Let us try to calculate by Simpson's rule the heat required to raise the water temperature from $0\,°C$ to $300\,°C$:

```
>> Q = simp(temp, spec)
???  Error using ==> simp
Uneven number of intervals
```

Indeed, we have 15 x-intervals, as can be checked with

```
>> length(temp)
ans =
    16
```

Calculating instead the heat required to raise the temperature to $280\,°C$ would yield

```
>> Q = simp(temp(1:15), spec(1:15))
Q =
    1.2349e+006
```

And what if we still want to calculate by Simpson's rule the heat required to raise the temperature to $300\,°C$? One way of doing this is to use the `table1` function to obtain by interpolation a value of specific capacity for $290\,°C$, and to insert this temperature in the vector `temp` and the corresponding specific capacity in the vector `spec`. The new vectors suit Simpson's rule. Try this solution for yourself.

EXAMPLE 11.4   Switzerland's area _____

Numerical integration is frequently used for approximating areas enclosed by outlines that cannot be defined mathematically. As an example, let us calculate the area of some 'small' country, say Switzerland (Figure 11.3). To do so we **digitize** a map that can be copied from an encyclopaedia or atlas. Maps are produced by various kinds of projections of the earth's surface on a plane; some of these projections distort areas and this effect becomes important for large areas. It is beyond the scope of this book to explain which projections can be used and which cannot. A simple means of avoiding serious distortions is to consider only relatively small areas, hence the choice of Switzerland.

For a numerical approximation of Switzerland's area it would be sufficient to divide its west-to-east extension into a number of subintervals defined by x-coordinates measured from some convenient origin, and measure the 'breadths' b_i as in Figure 11.4(a). The area would then be yielded by integrating b with respect to x. However, using this method it is not possible to plot and check the digitized outline. Therefore, at each x_i we shall measure two south-to-north coordinates: y_{down_i}, belonging to the southern border, and y_{up_i}, belonging to the northern border, as in Figure 11.4(b). The outline can be visualized by plotting y_{down} and y_{up} against x on the same graph. The area is obtained by integrating $b = y_{up} - y_{down}$ with respect to x.

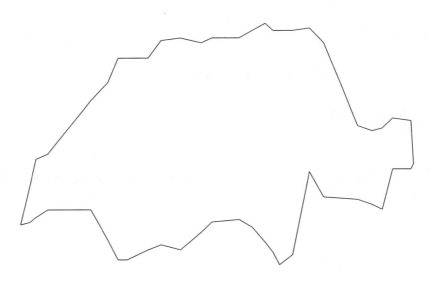

0 ————— 40 km

Figure 11.3   Outline of Switzerland.

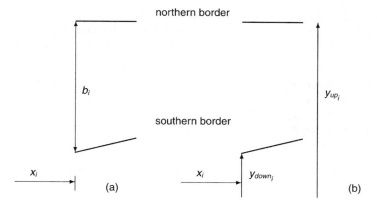

northern border

southern border

b_i

y_{up_i}

x_i

x_i y_{down_i}

(a)

(b)

Figure 11.4   How to digitize the map.

Table 11.5   Coordinates of Switzerland's outline.

x	y_{down}	y_{up}	x	y_{down}	y_{up}
7.0	44	44	96.0	43	121
10.5	45	59	101.0	37	124
13.0	47	70	104.0	33	121
17.5	50	72	106.5	28	121
34.0	50	93	111.5	32	121
40.5	38	100	118.0	65	122
44.5	30	110	123.5	55	116
48.0	30	110	136.5	54	83
56.0	34	110	142.0	52	81
61.0	36	117	146.0	50	82
68.5	34	118	150.0	66	86
76.5	41	116	157.0	66	85
80.5	45	118	158.0	68	68
91.0	46	118			

It is not always possible to find a ruler for the scale at which a particular map is printed; therefore, the coordinates can be read, for instance, in mm and transformed to actual values by one computer command. The measurements, in mm, are presented in Table 11.5. We begin by writing them to a file swiss.m, in an array swiss:

```
swiss = [
7 44 44

...

158 68 68 ];
```

On the map, 18 mm corresponds to 40 km. Therefore we convert the measurements to km and separate the coordinates by the following commands, which can be either introduced through the keyboard or written to the same file swiss.m:

```
swiss = 40*swiss/18;
long = swiss(:, 1);
lat_down = swiss(:, 2);
lat_up = swiss(:, 3);
```

A plot of the outline, together with a scale, is obtained with the commands

```
≫ plot(long, lat_down)
≫ axis('off'), axis('equal')
≫ hold on
≫ plot(long, lat_up)
≫ scale = 40*[ 10 28 ]/18;
≫ plot(scale, [10 10])
≫ text(15, 10, '0')
≫ text( 70, 10, '40 km')
```

An approximation of Switzerland's area is given by

```
breadth = lat_up - lat_down;
area = trapz(long, breadth)
area =
    4.2414e+004
```

The true area is 41 288 km^2; our error equals 2.73% of the true value. To improve the precision it is necessary to employ a larger map and digitize it at each point where the borderline changes direction. The subintervals of integration chosen in this example do not correspond to Simpson's rule. Try to use the simp function and observe the computer's reaction.

EXAMPLE 11.5   Indicator diagram _____

One way of measuring the power of an internal-combustion engine is by means of an **indicator diagram**; the method has also been used for steam engines. The diagram is obtained by plotting the pressure, p, measured in the cylinder, against the volume, V, swept by the piston. A possible form of this diagram is shown in Figure 11.5. The area enclosed by the curve, that is

$$W = \int p\, dV \tag{11.19}$$

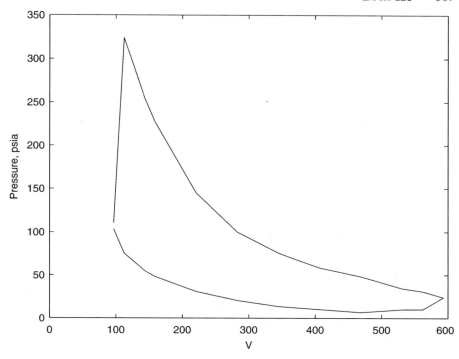

Figure 11.5   Indicator diagram.

has the dimensions of force times length and it represents the work done per engine cycle. For two-stroke engines a cycle is completed at each crankshaft rotation; for four-stroke engines a cycle requires two crankshaft rotations.

An important quantity derived from the indicator diagram is the **indicated mean effective pressure** defined by

$$imep = \frac{W}{V_{swept}} \tag{11.20}$$

With this notation the power of a two-stroke engine equals

$$W = \frac{imep V_{swept} Nn}{10^{-2}}$$

and that of a four-stroke engine is

$$W = \frac{imep V_{swept} Nn}{2 \times 10^{-2}}$$

Table 11.6   Coordinates of indicator diagram.

V	p_down	p_up	V	p_down	p_up
14.00	15.0	16.0	50.00	2.0	11.0
16.25	11.0	47.0	59.00	1.5	8.5
18.50	9.5	42.0	68.00	1.0	7.0
20.75	8.0	37.0	77.00	1.5	5.0
23.00	7.0	33.0	81.50	1.5	4.5
32.00	4.5	21.0	86.00	3.5	3.5
41.00	3.0	14.5			

where N is the number of revolutions per second, and n the number of cylinders. The SI units to be used in the above equations are kW for W, bar for $imep$ and m^3 for V_{swept}.

Table 11.6 contains the data obtained by a rough digitization of an indicator diagram found in Taylor (1966). The x-axis was divided into a number of subintervals suitable for Simpson's rule. Like Example 11.4, and as explained in Figure 11.4, two pressure coordinates were measured for each V-value: p_{down} for the lower arc of the curve, and p_{up} for the upper arc. This allows the visualization of the diagram by plotting the arrays of the two pressure coordinates against V on the same graph. The area is obtained by integrating the difference $p_{up} - p_{down}$ with respect to V. The measurements are in mm, as read on the figure. The plot obtained with this data is shown in Figure 11.5. We begin the calculations by writing the data to a file indicat.m, in an array indicator:

```
indicator = [
14 15 16
...
86 3.5 3.5 ];
```

In the figure used for this example, 14.5 mm represents 100 psia; therefore, we convert the data to psia, separate the volume coordinates and the pressure coordinates, and plot with the commands

```
indicator = 100*indicator/14.5;
v = indicator(:, 1);
p_down = indicator(:, 2); p_up = indicator(:, 3);
plot(v, p_down)
hold on
plot(v, p_up)
plot([v(1) v(1)], [p_down(1) p_up(1)])
xlabel('V'), ylabel('Pressure, psia')
```

Loan Receipt
Liverpool John Moores University
Library Services

Borrower Name: Allsopp,John
Borrower ID: **********3113

MATLAB 6 for engineers /
31111010753265
Due Date: 10/01/2014 23:59

Total Items: 1
13/12/2013 10:04

Please keep your receipt in case of
dispute.

The chosen spacing allows us to call both the `trapz` and the `simp` functions to calculate the area enclosed by the curve

```
breadth = p_up - p_down;
area = [ trapz(v, breadth) simp(v, breadth) ]
area =
    1.0e+004 *
    4.0612 4.1130
```

The swept volume spanned 72 mm on the figure. To calculate the indicated mean effective pressure, imep, we must first convert the scale of the swept volume and then divide the area by the result

```
V_swept = 100*72/14.5;
imep = area/V_swept
imep =
    81.7888 82.8305
```

The area indicated in the book is 4.40; the imep, 88.0 psia. The discrepancies can be attributed to

- the reduced size of the diagram, as reproduced in the book;
- the small number of points at which the diagram was digitized.

Most probably the original of the diagram used in this example was recorded at a larger scale and the area measured with the help of a **planimeter**, a very simple but ingenious mechanical computer invented in 1856 by the Swiss Amsler. Today, the points of the diagram can be recorded by computerized data-acquisition systems, and the resulting file can be fed to a quadrature function such as `trapz` or `simp`.

EXAMPLE 11.6   Work done by capacitor discharge _____

Figure 11.6 is reproduced from Example 9.5. It was shown there that the current that flows through R, after moving the switch from S_1 to S_2, is given by

$$i = \frac{V_0}{R} e^{-\theta/RC} \tag{11.21}$$

where θ is the time in seconds when V_0 is measured in volts, R in ohms and C in farads. The power generated by the discharge across the resistor R is

$$P = i^2 R = \frac{V_0}{R} e^{-2t/RC} \tag{11.22}$$

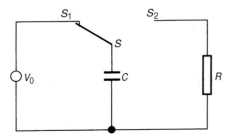

Figure 11.6   An RC circuit.

in watts, and the work produced between 0 and θ seconds,

$$W = \int_0^\theta P\,dt = \frac{V_0^2 C}{2}\left(1 - e^{-2\theta/RC}\right) \tag{11.23}$$

The current tends to 0 when θ tends to infinity; thus the complete discharge produces the work

$$W_{max} = \lim_{t \to \infty} W = \frac{V_0^2 C}{2} \tag{11.24}$$

Equation 11.24 is a closed formula for calculating the work done by the complete discharge. As an exercise, let us calculate the same work by numerical integration of the power given by Equation 11.22, where the current is that yielded by Equation 11.21. Numerical integration can be performed for a finite time interval only. We can be satisfied by this because for most practical purposes the current can be considered negligible after five time constants, that is, after $5RC$ seconds, *a fortiori* the square of the current.

Let us assume the following values for the circuit:

$$V_0 = 24\,\text{V}, \ \ R = 500\,\text{k}\Omega, \ \ C = 1000\,\text{pF}$$

The commands for integration by the trapezoidal rule are

```
V0 = 24; R = 500000; C = 1000*10^(-12);
tau = R*C
tau =
    5.0000e-004
t = 0:  tau/10:  5*tau;
i = V0*exp(-t/tau)/R;
W = trapz(t, R*(i.^2))
W =
    2.8895e-007
```

The commands needed in MATLAB for Equation 11.24 are

```
>> Wmax = V0^2*C/2
Wmax =
   2.8800e-007
```

The results are fairly close to one another. Let us also try Simpson's rule

```
Ws = simp(t, R*(i.^2))
Ws =
   2.8799e-007
```

The per cent error is

```
error = 100*(Ws - Wmax)/Wmax
error =
    -0.0037
```

remarkably small, indeed.

This example illustrates numerical integration in a case in which the answer is given by a closed equation. True, to reach this exact answer we had to perform some simple analytical integration. In some instances an analytical solution may not be possible, for instance when the current values are measured and not given by an expression. It is in such cases that numerical integration is unavoidable and the procedure to be followed is that exemplified above.

11.8   Exercises

Solutions to Exercises 11.1, 11.4, 11.11 and 11.13 appear at the back of the book.

■ EXERCISE 11.1
Calculate

$$\int_0^2 x \, dx$$

by the trapezoidal rule, using three ordinates, and show that the result is exact. Why?

■ EXERCISE 11.2
Calculate

$$\int_0^2 x^2 \, dx$$

by the trapezoidal rule and by Simpson's rule, using five ordinates, and show that the trapezoidal rule yields an error, while Simpson's rule gives the correct result. Why?

■ **EXERCISE 11.3**

Calculate

$$\int_0^2 x^3 \, dx$$

by the trapezoidal rule and by Simpson's rule, using five ordinates, and show that the trapezoidal rule yields an error, while Simpson's rule gives the correct result. Why?

■ **EXERCISE 11.4**

Try to calculate the previous integral by means of the `simp` function, with an uneven number of subintervals. Compare the result with the true value.

■ **EXERCISE 11.5**   Simpson's rule subintervals

Use the MATLAB `diff` function to show that the subintervals used in Example 11.4 are not suitable for Simpson's rule.

■ **EXERCISE 11.6**   Simpson's rule subintervals

Use the MATLAB `diff` function to show that the subintervals used in Example 11.5 are suitable for Simpson's rule.

■ **EXERCISE 11.7**   Switzerland's area

Convert the measurements given in Example 11.4 to statute miles, plot the outline with a scale in miles, and use the `trapz` function to calculate the area in mi^2. The value quoted as true is $15\,914\,mi^2$.

   Note that a *statute mile*, or land mile, equals 1609.3 metres, and is not to be confused with the *nautical mile* which measures 1852 metres.

■ **EXERCISE 11.8**   Areas of countries

Copy from an encyclopaedia or atlas the map of a small county, state or country. Digitize it as explained in Example 11.4 and calculate the area. Compare the result with the area stated in the map's source.

■ **EXERCISE 11.9**   Indicator diagram

Convert the measurements given in Example 11.5 to the SI bar unit and use the `trapz` and `simp` functions to calculate the *imep* in bar.

   Note that the volume scale must be converted too – see Example 11.4.

■ **EXERCISE 11.10**   Wind data

Meteorological data, such as wind velocities, are important in the design of air conditioning and heating systems. Table 11.7 contains the average wind velocities measured in January each year from 1969 to 1974, at Berlin-Tempelhof. The data, in m/s, are reproduced from the German standard DIN 4710.

Table 11.7   Average wind velocities at Berlin-Tempelhof in January, in m/s,

			Direction					
N	NE	E	SE	S	SW	W	NW	Mean
3.4	3.5	4.0	3.6	3.3	3.6	3.8	4.6	

(1)   Complete the table by calculating the arithmetic mean of the velocities for all directions.

(2)   Considering that the wind velocities, V, are samples from continuous functions of the direction α, calculate the mean as

$$m_\alpha = \frac{\int_0^{2\pi} V\, d\alpha}{2\pi}$$

where α is obviously measured in radians. Which quadrature function can you use?

Compare the results obtained by (1) and (2).

■ **EXERCISE 11.11**
Repeat Example 11.6 with the following values

$$V_0 = 12\,\text{V}, \quad R = 790\,\text{k}\Omega, \quad C = 1500\,\text{pF}$$

■ **EXERCISE 11.12**   RMS value of sinusoidal voltage
The **rms value** of a sinusoidal current i was defined in Subsection 4.15.2 as

$$i_e = \left[\frac{1}{T} \int_0^T i^2\, dt\right]^{1/2} \tag{11.25}$$

where T is the period, and t the time. Correspondingly, the rms value of a voltage u is given by

$$u_e = \left[\frac{1}{T} \int_0^T u^2\, dt\right]^{1/2} \tag{11.26}$$

Evaluation of the integral in Equation 11.25 yields

$$i_e = \frac{I_m}{\sqrt{2}} \tag{11.27}$$

where I_m is the maximum value of i, that is, the current amplitude. A similar result is obtained for the rms voltage calculated according to Equation 11.26.

As mentioned in Subsection 4.15.2, rms values are used in power calculations. Consider, for example, the power delivered by a dc current, i_e, to a resistance R; it is equal to Ri^2. It is easy to see that the energy delivered by an ac current of intensity i_e as given by Equation 11.25, to a resistance R, over a period T, is equal to the energy delivered to the same resistance, over the same time T, by the ac current i whose square is integrated in Equation 11.25.

(1)   Evaluate the integral in Equation 11.26 numerically and verify that you obtain the result predicted by Equation 11.27. Assume an amplitude of 170 V.

(2)   It can be easily seen that the definition of the rms current can be generalized to

$$i_e = \left[\frac{1}{T} \int_{t_0}^{t_0+T} i^2\, dt\right]^{1/2} \tag{11.28}$$

and the result shown by Equation 11.27 obtained again. In other words, the integration can begin at any instant, provided that it is carried out over a period. Verify this property by repeating the calculations done in (1), but starting at another instant.

■ **EXERCISE 11.13**   RMS value of current in varistor circuit

The definition of rms value as given in Equation 11.28 can be generalized to any periodic current, for example to the current obtained in a varistor circuit subjected to a sinusoidal voltage input. As an exercise, write an M-file that repeats Exercise 9.11 and allows you to calculate the rms value of the current in the circuit.

■ **EXERCISE 11.14**   RMS value of current in varistor circuit

Read Exercise 11.13 and write an M-file that repeats Exercise 9.12 and allows you to calculate the rms value of the current in the circuit.

■ **EXERCISE 11.15**   Using a function handle and `quadl`

To compute

$$\int_0^{\pi/6} \sin x \, dx$$

numerically, define a handle for the sine function and invoke `quadl`. Compare your result with the value obtained analytically.

■ **EXERCISE 11.16**   Using a function handle and `quadl`

Compute

$$\int_0^{\pi/6} e^{2x} \sin x \, dx$$

numerically in the following steps:

(1)   define a function called `expsin`;
(2)   define a function handle, `hexpsin`, for `expsin`;
(3)   invoke the function `quadl`;
(4)   to check if the function `expsin` was correctly defined plot it with the function `fplot` called with the argument `hexpsin` and the vector of the limits of integration;
(5)   compare the result obtained with the result calculated analytically. *Hint*: you may find the exact solution by applying the method of integration by parts twice.

Chapter 12
Graph theory

12.1   Definitions

This chapter illustrates a simple application of MATLAB in graph theory without going deeper into this branch of mathematics, which is treated in books dedicated to this subject.

Consider the set of *vertices* $V = \{V_1, V_2, V_3, V_4\}$ and the set of *edges* E connecting the vertices, that is, the set of **unordered pairs**

$$E = \{(V_1, V_2), (V_2, V_3), (V_3, V_4), (V_2, V_4)\}$$

We used the term **unordered pairs** because we could equally well have taken the set

$$E = \{(V_2, V_1), (V_3, V_2), (V_4, V_3), (V_4, V_2)\}$$

or any other permutation within the same pairs of vertices. The mathematical structure defined by the two sets V, E is a **graph**. A pictorial representation of a graph is obtained by displaying the vertices as points and the edges as lines connecting the vertices, as shown in Figure 12.1.

Graphs are used to represent various relationships, for instance transportation networks, flow of information, flow of materials in manufacturing plants, electrical circuits, or family relationships.

A useful way of storing the data of a graph is by means of the **adjacency matrix**. For a graph with n vertices the adjacency matrix is an n-by-n matrix $\mathbf{A}$ in which the element a_{ij} in the i-th row and j-th column is equal to 1 if the vertices V_i and V_j are connected by an edge – that is, if they are *adjacent* – and 0 otherwise (see, for example, Prather 1976, pp. 140–1, or Dierker and Voxman 1986, pp. 83–9). Table 12.1 shows

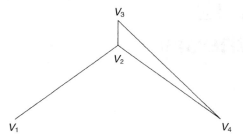

Figure 12.1   A graph.

Table 12.1   An adjacency matrix.

	V_1	V_2	V_3	V_4
V_1	0	1	0	0
V_2	1	0	1	1
V_3	0	1	0	1
V_4	0	1	1	0

how to obtain the adjacency matrix of the graph represented in Figure 12.1. Let us call the resulting matrix **A**; it is

$$A = \begin{bmatrix} 0 & 1 & 0 & 0 \\ 1 & 0 & 1 & 1 \\ 0 & 1 & 0 & 1 \\ 0 & 1 & 1 & 0 \end{bmatrix} \tag{12.1}$$

The matrix is symmetric about its *main diagonal*, that is, $a_{ij} = a_{ji}$. This means that the transpose of **A** equals **A**, a property that can be easily checked in MATLAB.

A **path** in a graph is a sequence of edges in which the end of one edge is the beginning of the next one. The **length** of a path is the number of edges in it. Thus, for example, $V_1 - V_2 - V_4$ in the graph shown in Figure 12.1, that is, the sequence of edges $V_1 V_2$, $V_2 V_4$, is a path of length 2. Following this definition we can say that the element a_{ij} in the i-th row and j-th column of the matrix **A** is equal to the number of paths of length 1 that join the vertices V_i, V_j.

From the way that the adjacency matrix is defined, it follows that the number of its rows is equal to the number of its columns. We say that such an n-by-n matrix is **square**. We can define **powers** of square matrices by $A^2 = A * A$, $A^3 = A * A * A$, and so on.

It can be shown (see Dierker and Voxman 1986, pp. 96–7) that, when **A** is an adjacency matrix, the element b_{ij} in the i-th row and j-th column of the matrix $B = A^2 = A * A$ gives the number of paths of length 2 that join the vertices V_i and V_j. Thus, for the graph shown in Figure 12.1, the number of paths of length 2 is given by

$$A^2 = \begin{bmatrix} 1 & 0 & 1 & 1 \\ 0 & 3 & 1 & 1 \\ 1 & 1 & 2 & 1 \\ 1 & 1 & 1 & 2 \end{bmatrix} \tag{12.2}$$

Let us analyse this result. The element in the 1st row and 1st column equals 1, which means that there is a path of length 2 connecting V_1 to V_1. This is the path $V_1 - V_2 - V_1$. The element in the 1st row and the 2nd column equals zero, that is there is no path of length 2 between V_1 and V_2. The element in the 2nd row and 2nd column is equal to 3. There are, indeed, three paths of length 2 that join the vertex V_2 to itself and they are: $V_2 - V_1 - V_2, V_2 - V_3 - V_2$ and $V_2 - V_4 - V_2$. The reader is invited to check the other elements of the matrix A^2.

Similarly, the number of paths of length 3 is given by

$$A^3 = \begin{bmatrix} 0 & 3 & 1 & 1 \\ 3 & 2 & 4 & 4 \\ 1 & 4 & 2 & 3 \\ 1 & 4 & 3 & 2 \end{bmatrix} \tag{12.3}$$

Let us check a few elements, for example the element in the 1st row and 1st column: it is 0. Indeed, there is no path of length 3 connecting V_1 to itself. The element in the 3rd row and 2nd column is 4. This means that there are four paths of length 3 connecting V_3 to V_2; they are $V_3 - V_2 - V_1 - V_2, V_3 - V_2 - V_4 - V_2, V_3 - V_2 - V_3 - V_2$ and $V_3 - V_4 - V_3 - V_2$. We leave to the reader the interpretation of the other elements of the matrix A^3.

A graph with n vertices is **connected** if each pair of vertices V_i, V_j is connected by a path. It can be easily proven (for example by induction on the number of vertices) that if a graph with n vertices is connected, any two vertices can be connected by a path shorter than n. Then, it can be deduced that a graph with n vertices is connected if and only if all elements of the matrix

$$A + A^2 + \cdots + A^{n-1} \tag{12.4}$$

are different from zero. In our example this property is easily checked in Equation 12.5:

$$A + A^2 + A^3 = \begin{bmatrix} 1 & 4 & 2 & 2 \\ 4 & 5 & 6 & 6 \\ 2 & 6 & 4 & 5 \\ 2 & 6 & 5 & 4 \end{bmatrix} \tag{12.5}$$

More about graphs and their treatment in MATLAB can be found in Hill (1988), pp. 378–86.

12.2   Graph of a railway network

This example illustrates a very simple application of graph theory to a traffic problem. The corresponding adjacency matrix has 144 elements; only 24 of them are not zero. We call such a matrix **sparse**. MATLAB provides tools for dealing efficiently with sparse matrices; we shall encounter them here. Another facility we are going to learn in this example is the gplot function which draws a graph from its adjacency matrix and a matrix of vertex coordinates. A simple trick will allow us to label the graph.

In this example we are going to consider the graph of British Rail's Intercity network. From this graph we choose a subgraph of the maximum size that can be easily visualized both in the book and in MATLAB. To do so, we disregard the network south of Preston and York and consider only the northern part, as shown in Figure 12.2.

We now build a graph with the twelve vertices listed in column 'Station' of Table 12.2. Next, we write the adjacency matrix of this graph; let us call it BR1. Fort William is connected only to Glasgow; therefore, we write '1' at the intersection of row 1 and column 2. All other elements in the row are zeros. Glasgow is connected to Fort William, Edinburgh and Carlisle. In row 2 we write three '1's, namely at the intersections with columns 1, 3 and 6. Continuing in this manner we obtain a 12-by-12 matrix which we write to the file br.m:

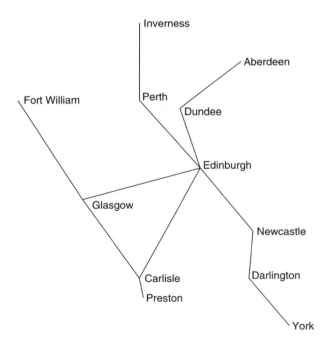

Figure 12.2   Part of the British Rail Intercity network.

Table 12.2   Table describing Figure 12.2.

No.	Station	1	2	3	4	5	6	7	8	9	10	11	12
1	Fort William	0	1	0	0	0	0	0	0	0	0	0	0
2	Glasgow	1	0	1	0	0	1	0	0	0	0	0	0
3	Carlisle	0	1	0	0	0	1	0	0	0	0	0	1
4	Inverness	0	0	0	0	1	0	0	0	0	0	0	0
5	Perth	0	0	0	1	0	1	0	0	0	0	0	0
6	Edinburgh	0	1	1	0	1	0	0	1	1	0	0	0
7	Aberdeen	0	0	0	0	0	0	0	1	0	0	0	0
8	Dundee	0	0	0	0	0	1	1	0	0	0	0	0
9	Newcastle	0	0	0	0	0	1	0	0	0	1	0	0
10	Darlington	0	0	0	0	0	0	0	0	1	0	1	0
11	York	0	0	0	0	0	0	0	0	0	1	0	0
12	Preston	0	0	1	0	0	0	0	0	0	0	0	0

```
% BR1 adjacency matrix of northern British-Rail network
BR1 = [
0  1  0  0  0  0  0  0  0  0  0  0
1  0  1  0  0  1  0  0  0  0  0  0
0  1  0  0  0  1  0  0  0  0  0  1
0  0  0  0  1  0  0  0  0  0  0  0
0  0  0  1  0  1  0  0  0  0  0  0
0  1  1  0  1  0  0  1  1  0  0  0
0  0  0  0  0  0  0  1  0  0  0  0
0  0  0  0  0  1  1  0  0  0  0  0
0  0  0  0  0  1  0  0  0  1  0  0
0  0  0  0  0  0  0  0  1  0  1  0
0  0  0  0  0  0  0  0  0  1  0  0
0  0  1  0  0  0  0  0  0  0  0  0 ];
```

We now write a second matrix, BR2, to the same file, br.m; this matrix contains the names of the twelve railway stations given in Table 12.2. We keep the same order as in that table. The rows of BR2 are character strings. Each string begins with a blank space, so that the printing of names will not begin exactly on the vertices. All the rows of a matrix must have the same length, in this case 13 as defined by the longest name, ' Fort William'. Therefore we **pad** the shorter names with blanks so that all quotes are aligned under one another. The resulting 12-by-13 matrix is

```
% BR2 matrix of station names
BR2 = [
' Fort William'
' Glasgow      '
' Carlisle     '
' Inverness    '
' Perth        '
' Edinburgh    '
' Aberdeen     '
' Dundee       '
' Newcastle    '
' Darlington   '
' York         '
' Preston      '
```

A third matrix, BR3, is written to file br.m; it contains a set of coordinates of the twelve stations, again in the same order as in Table 12.2:

```
% BR3 matrix of vertex coordinates
BR3 = [
25 180
41 155
55 135
55 200
55 180
70 163
80 190
65 178
83 147
82 135
92 123
56 130 ] ;
```

We now have an interesting **data structure** consisting of three matrices related by their row indices. Thus, row 1 in all three matrices refers to Fort William; row 2, to Glasgow, and so on. We load the whole data structure by one command

```
>> br
```

To plot the graph we use the MATLAB gplot function called with two arguments:

(1)   the adjacency matrix of the graph;

(2)   the array of vertex coordinates.

The set of commands is:

```
>> gplot(BR1, BR3)
>> axis('equal')
>> axis('off')
```

Above, `axis('equal')` produces equal scaling for the x- and y-coordinates, and `axis('off')` eliminates the axes as we are not interested in them. If you want to understand the effect of the last two commands better, try the plot without them. The labelling of the vertices is done in the following FOR loop

```
for i = 1:12
    text(BR3(i, 1), BR3(i, 2), BR2(i, :))
end
```

Notice that the third argument of `text` is `BR2(i, :)`, that is, the i-th row with all its columns. The resulting plot is shown in Figure 12.2. Raising the matrix to its third power yields

```
B3 = BR1^3
B3 =
0    3    1    0    1    1    0    1    1    0    0    1
3    2    5    1    1    7    1    1    1    1    0    1
1    5    2    1    1    7    1    1    1    1    0    3
0    1    1    0    2    0    0    1    1    0    0    0
1    1    1    2    0    6    1    0    0    1    0    1
1    7    7    0    6    2    0    6    6    0    1    1
0    1    1    0    1    0    0    2    1    0    0    0
1    1    1    1    0    6    2    0    0    1    0    1
1    1    1    1    0    6    1    0    0    3    0    1
0    1    1    0    1    0    0    1    3    0    2    0
0    0    0    0    0    1    0    0    0    2    0    0
1    1    3    0    1    1    0    1    1    0    0    0
```

The matrix B3 contains the paths of length 3 between the twelve railway stations considered in this example. A path of length 3 exists, for instance, between Fort William and Preston; therefore, `B3(1,12) = 1`, while `BR1(1,12) = 0`. The element `B3(1,2)` is equal to 3. This means that there are three paths of length 3 between Fort William and Glasgow; they are

(1)   Fort William – Glasgow, Glasgow – Edinburgh, Edinburgh – Glasgow;

(2)   Fort William – Glasgow, Glasgow – Carlisle, Carlisle – Glasgow;

(3)   Fort William – Glasgow, Glasgow – Fort William, Fort William – Glasgow.

The reader is invited to interpret the other elements of the matrix B3.

12.3   Sparse matrix

In the preceding section we stored BR1 as a **full matrix**. The memory used for this is revealed by

```
whos
    Name    Size     Bytes Class
    BR1     12x12     1152 double array
```

All 144 elements of BR1 are stored in 1152 bytes of memory. Let us calculate BR1^3 and find out how much time and how many **flops** – floating-point operations – are needed for this operation.

```
>> flops(0)
>> tic
>> B3 = BR1^3
>> t1 = toc;
>> f1 = flops;
```

The command flops(0) sets the counter of floating point operations to zero; the expression f1 = flops retrieves the contents of the counter and assigns them to f1. The command tic starts a **stopwatch**; the expression t1 = toc assigns the reading of this watch to t1.

MATLAB 4 allows us to take advantage of the many zero elements of BR1 and to store this matrix as a **sparse matrix** in fewer bytes of memory. To do this we use the sparse function called as follows:

```
>> Bs = sparse(BR1)
Bs =
    (2,1) 1
    (1,2) 1
    ...
    (3,12) 1
```

As we see, only the non-zero elements are stored, together with their indices. Thus '(2,1) 1' corresponds to BR1(2,1) = 1, and '(1,2) 1' to BR1(1,2) = 1. Let us compare the memory requirements of the two types of storage:

```
whos
    Name    Size     Bytes    Class
    B3      12x12     1152     double array
    BR1     12x12     1152     double array
    BR2     12x13      312     char array
    BR3     12x2       192     double array
    Bs      12x12      340     sparse array
```

We see that the memory requirements for the storage of the sparse matrix decreased from 1152 to 340 bytes. Working with matrices in sparse form can also reduce the number of operations and the time required to perform them. To see this, let us find out the number of flops and the time required to raise Bs to its third power.

```
>> flops(0)
>> tic
>> Bs3 = Bs^3
Bs3 =
   (2,1) 3
   ...
   (8,12) 1
   (9,12) 1
>> t2 = toc;
>> f2 = flops;
```

We can now compare the time and the flops required for the full matrix with those necessary for the sparse form:

```
>> [ t1 t2 ], [ f1 f2 ]
ans =
   29.6000 18.6200
ans =
   6930 454
```

For larger matrices, with lower densities, the advantages obtained by working with sparse forms become important. An example is given in Chapter 17.

12.4   MATLAB 5 new features

A few new features introduced in MATLAB 5 can be exemplified on the railway graph described in Section 12.2. First, let us return to the BR2 array. All rows of the array must be of the same length. Therefore, we padded with trailing blanks the names of all stations except the longest, Fort William. The new function char does this job for us:

```
BR2 = char(' Fort William', ' Glasgow', ' Carlisle',
' Inverness', ...
'Perth', ' Edinburgh', ' Aberdeen', ' Dundee',
' Newcastle', ...
'Darlington', ' York', ' Preston')
```

Try for yourself. The three periods, ..., allow us to continue a statement on another line.

Structure   Field   Arrays

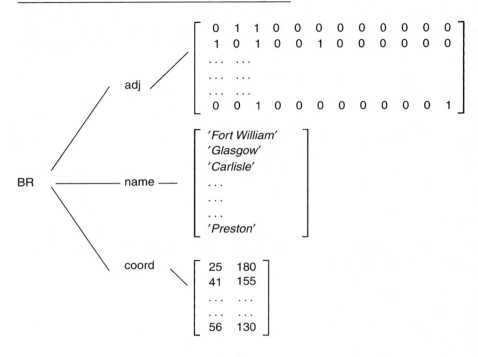

Figure 12.3   A graphic description of the structure BR.

In Section 12.2 we used three arrays, BR1, BR2, and BR3. We had to do so because the three arrays are of different sizes and types: BR1 is a 12-by-12 array of numbers, BR2, a 12-by-13 array of characters, and BR3, a 12-by-2 array of numbers. MATLAB 5 enables us to consolidate the three arrays into a single **structure**. Let us use the function struct to build a structure with three **fields**: adj, containing the adjacency matrix, name, containing the array of station names, and coord, containing the array of vertex coordinates. The syntax is:

```
BR = struct('adj', BR1, 'name', BR2, 'coord', BR3)
```

Figure 12.3 is a graphic description of the resulting structure, BR. Typing BR we obtain a summary of the structure contents:

```
BR
BR =
    adj:   [12x12 double]
    name:  [12x13 char ]
    coord: [12x2 double]
```

Detailed information can be retrieved by typing the name of each field separately. To do so, we write the name of the structure, a point, and the name of the field:

```
BR.adj
  ans =
     0 1 0 0 0 0 0 0 0 0 0 0
     1 0 1 0 0 1 0 0 0 0 0 0
     . . .
     0 0 1 0 0 0 0 0 0 0 0 0

BR.name
ans =
     Fort William
     Glasgow
     . . .
     Preston

BR.coord
ans =
     25 180
     41 155
     . . .
     56 130
```

We plot the graph of the railway network with the commands

```
gplot(BR.adj, BR.coord), axis('equal'), axis('off')
for i = 1:  12
       text(BR.coord(i, 1), BR.coord(i, 2), BR.name(i, :))
end
```

12.5   Exercises

The solution for Exercise 12.2 appears at the back of the book.

■ **EXERCISE 12.1**   Railway network
Choose a subgraph with 12 vertices from a railway network and treat it as in Section 12.2. Use both the full and the sparse forms.

■ **EXERCISE 12.2**   Digraph
If we assign a direction to each edge of a graph we obtain a **directed graph** or, for short, a **digraph**. In this way we can transform, for example, the graph shown in Figure 12.1 into the digraph represented in Figure 12.4. The adjacency matrix of a digraph is defined in the same way as that of a graph. Correspondingly, for the digraph

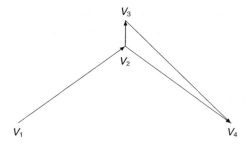

Figure 12.4   A digraph.

	V_1	V_2	V_3	V_4
V_1	0	1	0	0
V_2	0	0	1	1
V_3	0	0	0	1
V_4	0	0	0	0

Figure 12.5   The adjacency matrix of a digraph.

presented here we form the adjacency matrix as shown in Figure 12.5. Let us call the resulting matrix **A**; it is equal to

$$A = \begin{bmatrix} 0 & 1 & 0 & 0 \\ 0 & 0 & 1 & 1 \\ 0 & 0 & 0 & 1 \\ 0 & 0 & 0 & 0 \end{bmatrix} \tag{12.6}$$

Unlike the adjacency matrix of a graph, the adjacency matrix of a digraph is not symmetric. In set-theoretical terms the digraph in this example is a representation of the relation constituted by the set of **ordered pairs**

$$E = \{(V_1, V_2), (V_2, V_3), (V_2, V_4), (V_3, V_4)\} \tag{12.7}$$

For the digraph shown here, calculate the matrices $A^2 = A * A$ and $A^3 = A * A * A$ and check their significance. Also, calculate the matrix

$$C = I + A + A^2 + A^3 \tag{12.8}$$

where **I** is the 4-by-4 **identity matrix**

$$\mathbf{I} = \begin{bmatrix} 1 & 0 & 0 & 0 \\ 0 & 1 & 0 & 0 \\ 0 & 0 & 1 & 0 \\ 0 & 0 & 0 & 1 \end{bmatrix} \tag{12.9}$$

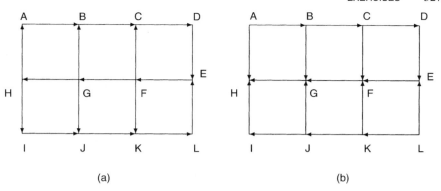

Figure 12.6   Two street networks.

Check that there is a path from V_i to V_j if c_{ij}, that is, the element in the i-th row and j-th column of C, is non-zero. Explain why it was necessary to add the identity matrix I as well.

■ **EXERCISE 12.3**   A street network

Let us assume that all the streets in a small neighbourhood are one-way and the correct directions are those indicated in Figure 12.6(a). Show, with the aid of the adjacency matrix of the graph, that any point in the neighbourhood can be reached from any point in the same neighbourhood.

If the directions are changed as shown in Figure 12.6(b) it is evident that there is no possibility of reaching the points A and L. Analyse the graph of this neighbourhood by means of Equation 12.8 and interpret your results.

Repeat the exercises using the sparse forms of the adjacency matrices. Compare the memory resources, the time and the number of flops required for the full form with those necessary for the sparse form.

■ **EXERCISE 12.4**   The graph of a street network

Build a **structure** that contains all the information of the graph in Figure 12.6(a) and plot the graph using that structure.

Chapter 13
Dimensional analysis

13.1 Introduction

This chapter contains a very specialized application of the solution of systems of linear equations. Among other things, it shows that the MATLAB backslash operator can be used to solve several systems of equations and yield a matrix of solutions, using only one command. Dimensional analysis is a fundamental subject in fluid mechanics and heat transfer. These fields sometimes deal with phenomena so complex that the equations governing them cannot be found analytically. Dimensional analysis can be used to find the form of the equations and to determine the conditions under which those phenomena can be investigated experimentally. The method involves building and solving systems of linear equations, operations that can be efficiently performed in MATLAB.

13.2 Dimensional analysis

Let some physical quantity p be related to other quantities x, y, z by a function

$$p = F(x, y, z)$$

For two different sets of values x_1, y_1, z_1, and x_2, y_2, z_2, we obtain

$$p_1 = F(x_1, y_1, z_1)$$
$$p_2 = F(x_2, y_2, z_2)$$

529

If the unit used to measure x is reduced in the proportion $1/a$, the **measure** of x increases to ax. Let us also suppose that the unit of y is reduced in the proportion $1/b$, and the unit of z, in the proportion $1/c$. Then the values of p_1 and p_2 change to

$$p_1 = F(ax_1, by_1, cz_1)$$
$$p_2 = F(ax_2, by_2, cz_2)$$

We expect that

$$\frac{F(x_1, y_1, z_1)}{F(x_2, y_2, z_2)} = \frac{F(ax_1, by_1, cz_1)}{F(ax_2, by_2, cz_2)} \tag{13.1}$$

It can be easily shown that Equation 13.1 is satisfied if the function F is of the form

$$F = Cx^\alpha y^\beta z^\gamma$$

where C is a constant. The exponents α, β, γ are called the **dimensions** of p. Actually, Equation 13.1 is another way of saying that the laws of physics should not be influenced by the choice of units used to measure the quantities involved.

Three **fundamental quantities** are necessary to define all the quantities appearing in the laws of mechanics. The usual choice of fundamental quantities is *mass*, denoted by M, *length*, denoted by L, and *time*, denoted by T. A few examples of *derived* mechanical quantities and their dimensions are shown below, where, for example, the notation $[v]$ means *dimension of v*.

Velocity	$[v]$	=	$[LT^{-1}]$
Acceleration	$[a]$	=	$[LT^{-2}]$
Force	$[F]$	=	$[MLT^{-2}]$
Energy	$[E]$	=	$[ML^2T^{-2}]$
Power	$[P]$	=	$[ML^2T^{-3}]$

The study of the dimensions of physical quantities and the dimensional structure of physical relationships is called **dimensional analysis**. The techniques of dimensional analysis have several important applications, as will be seen below.

(1)   The most striking application consists in establishing the form of relationships governing phenomena that are too complicated to be obtained by regular mathematical techniques. As will be seen below, the resulting equations are not complete; usually one constant, or the exact form of a function, remains to be determined by experiments or by other means.

(2)   The equations obtained as at (1) show how to extrapolate to full scale the results obtained with scaled-down models.

(3)   The techniques of dimensional analysis allow a reduction of the number of parameters required to describe a physical law.

(4)   Dimensional analysis yields a *necessary* condition for the correctness of mathematical expressions that govern physical phenomena or technical relationships.

Explaining the last point first may help in understanding the others. Dimensional analysis shows that relationships that do not depend upon the choice of units must be **dimensionally homogeneous**, that is, all terms on both sides of any equation must have the same dimensions. As a simple example, let us check the dimensions of the following equation which governs rotational motion:

$$I\frac{d^2\alpha}{dt^2} = \sum F_i r_i,$$

where

$$
\begin{aligned}
I &= \text{moment of inertia, dimensions } [ML^2] \\
\tfrac{d^2\alpha}{dt^2} &= \text{angular acceleration, dimensions } [T^{-2}] \\
F_i &= \text{force, dimensions } [MLT^{-2}] \\
r_i &= \text{lever arm of } F_i, \text{ dimensions } [L]
\end{aligned}
$$

The dimensions of the left-hand side are $ML^2 \cdot T^{-2} = ML^2T^{-2}$; those of the right-hand side, $MLT^{-2} \cdot L = ML^2T^{-2}$. The equation is dimensionally homogeneous; it can be used with any *consistent system of units*, for example kg m^2, radian/s^2, N, m in the SI system.

Obviously, in dimensionally homogeneous equations, only terms having the same dimensions can be added or subtracted. This means that the arguments of trigonometric, logarithmic and exponential functions must be dimensionless, otherwise their series expansions would consist of terms with different dimensions (the radian is a dimensionless unit). There is no restriction on multiplication or division.

Checking the dimensions of the results of long calculations is usually easy and it should always be done. If the results are not dimensionally homogeneous, something is definitely wrong. If the results are dimensionally homogeneous, this does not necessarily mean that they are correct.

The applications listed under (1) to (3) are based on the following powerful theorem. *Let us assume that n physical quantities, $x_1, x_2, \ldots, x_n$, are related by an expression $\Phi(x_1, x_2, \ldots, x_n) = 0$. If the number of fundamental quantities is m, $m < n$, then the expression can be transformed into another one containing $n - m$ dimensionless groups $\pi_1, \pi_2, \ldots, \pi_{n-m}$, formed with the n given quantities:*

$$f(\pi_1, \pi_2, \ldots, \pi_{n-m}) = 0$$

The term **dimensional group** describes a quantity obtained by multiplication and division of physical quantities in such a way that all its dimensions are zero. The first rigorous proof of this theorem, known as the π **theorem**, was given by E. Buckingham. In French books the result sometimes appears as the theorem of **Vaschy**.

An elementary example, used by several authors for explaining the techniques of dimensional analysis, is that of a simple pendulum (see, for example, Stewart 1987).

Let us suppose that we want to find the structure of a formula defining the period of oscillation, τ, of the pendulum. A list of the quantities that can influence this period, together with their dimensions, is

Quantity	Symbol	Dimensions
Mass	m	M
Length	ℓ	L
Acceleration of gravity	g	LT^{-2}
Swing amplitude	θ	$M^\circ L^\circ T^\circ$
Period of swing	τ	T

We are looking for a relationship of the form

$$m^{\alpha_1} \ell^{\alpha_2} g^{\alpha_3} \theta^{\alpha_4} \tau^{\alpha_5} = k$$

where k is some dimensionless constant. Substituting the dimensions of the five quantities we obtain

$$M^{\alpha_1} L^{\alpha_2} (LT^{-2})^{\alpha_3} (M^\circ L^\circ T^\circ)^{\alpha_4} T^{\alpha_5} = M^\circ L^\circ T^\circ$$

Collecting the exponents of each fundamental quantity, and equating the sums on both sides of the equation, yields the following system of linear equations

$$\alpha_1 = 0$$
$$\alpha_2 + \alpha_3 = 0$$
$$-2\alpha_3 + \alpha_5 = 0$$
$$\alpha_4 = undetermined$$

We actually obtained three equations in five unknowns. The rank of the coefficient matrix is 3, and therefore we can solve for three unknowns, if we assign arbitrary values to the other 2. This result is in agreement with the π theorem: the number of dimensionless groups that can be formed equals the number of quantities minus the number of fundamental quantities, that is, $5 - 3 = 2$. One dimensionless group is naturally θ. The other is obtained by assigning, for example, the value 1 to α_5 and solving the system. This yields $\alpha_1 = 0$, $\alpha_2 = -1/2$, $\alpha_3 = 1/2$. The second dimensionless group is $m^0 \ell^{-1/2} g^{1/2} \tau^1 = \tau \sqrt{g}/\sqrt{\ell}$, so that the required relationship is

$$\tau \sqrt{g/\ell} = Cf(\theta)$$

Assuming that the amplitude is so small that $f(\theta)$ is constant, the relationship becomes

$$\tau = k\sqrt{l/g}$$

The constant k equals 2π; this value cannot be obtained by dimensional analysis.

The example discussed above allows us to state the π theorem in more rigorous terms: *Let us assume that n physical quantities, $x_1, x_2, \ldots, x_n$, are related by an expression $\Phi(x_1, x_2, \ldots, x_n) = 0$. Let us form the matrix of dimensions in which the element a_{ij} is the exponent of the i-th fundamental quantity in the j-th quantity. If the rank of this matrix is m, then the expression can be transformed into another one containing n–m dimensionless groups $\pi_1, \pi_2, \ldots, \pi_{n-m}$, formed with the n quantities:*

$$f(\pi_1, \pi_2, \ldots, \pi_{n-m}) = 0$$

A fairly complete treatment of the subject of dimensional analysis can be found in Fahidy and Quairashi (1986). An extensive list of dimensionless groups appears in Catchpole and Fulford (1987). Three more complex examples, solved with MATLAB's facilities, follow. They belong to the fields in which dimensional analysis finds most of its applications: fluid dynamics and heat transfer.

13.3   Examples

EXAMPLE 13.1   Wave resistance ——————————————————————

The motion of a body – for instance a ship – at the surface of water is opposed by a **resistance** force. Part of the resistance force is due to friction. The other part is due to several phenomena, the most important of them being the generation of waves. The work of the water particles moving up in the waves is done against the force of gravity, therefore one important quantity intervening in the phenomenon is the acceleration of gravity, g. Other quantities involved are a characteristic length of the body, L_s, the density of the water, ρ, the speed of the body, V_s, and its **wetted surface**, S (the area of the body surface in contact with the water). The **wave resistance** force, R_W, is the required result. In total there are six quantities. The fundamental quantities are the mass, M, length, L, and time, T. We can form a 3-by-6 matrix containing the dimensions of the six quantities:

	g	L_s	ρ	V_s	S	R_W
M	0	0	1	0	0	1
L	1	1	−3	1	2	1
T	−2	0	0	−1	0	−2

In MATLAB the matrix of dimensions is entered as

```
>> D = [ 0 0 1 0 0 1; 1 1 -3 1 2 1; -2 0 0 -1 0 -2 ];
```

It has the rank

```
>> rank(D)
ans =
    3
```

This means that for the six quantities involved there are three independent equations. By assigning arbitrary exponents to three quantities it is possible to find the exponents of the other three. According to the π theorem it is possible to form three nondimensional groups; their exponents are the solutions of *three* systems of linear equations. It follows that we must assign *three* sets of arbitrary exponents to the qualities chosen as 'independent'. Let the vector $C = [c_1, c_2, c_3]$ be any of these sets, and $X = [x_1, x_2, x_3]'$ the vector of exponents to be determined. The system of equations to be solved for each nondimensional group is

$$0 \times x_1 + 0 \times x_2 + 1 \times x_3 + 0 \times c_1 + 0 \times c_2 + 1 \times c_3 = 0$$
$$1 \times x_1 + 1 \times x_2 + -3 \times x_3 + 1 \times c_1 + 2 \times c_2 + 1 \times c_3 = 0$$
$$-2 \times x_1 + 0 \times x_2 + 0 \times x_3 + -1 \times c_1 + 0 \times c_2 + -2 \times c_3 = 0$$

We can rewrite the system in matrix form as

$$\mathbf{AX} = \mathbf{BC'}$$

where $\mathbf{A}$ and $\mathbf{B}$ are 3-by-3 matrices such that $\mathbf{D} = [\mathbf{A} - \mathbf{B}]$, that is:

$$\mathbf{A} = \begin{bmatrix} 0 & 0 & 1 \\ 1 & 1 & -3 \\ -2 & 0 & 0 \end{bmatrix}, \quad \mathbf{B} = \begin{bmatrix} 0 & 0 & -1 \\ -1 & -2 & -1 \\ 1 & 0 & 2 \end{bmatrix},$$

In MATLAB we begin by

```
≫ A = D(:, 1:3);
```

The command A = D(:, 1:3) means that the elements of the matrix $\mathbf{A}$ are taken from all the rows of matrix $\mathbf{D}$, but only from its columns 1 to 3. Using the same MATLAB facility, we form the matrix $\mathbf{B}$ from the remaining three columns of $\mathbf{D}$ as follows:

```
≫ B = -D(:, 4:6)
```

The minus sign appears when the affected columns are transferred to the right-hand sides of the equations we intend to solve.

Usually it is necessary to find R_W as a function of the other quantities; it is therefore natural to assign the value 1 to the exponent of R_W in the first set of arbitrary values, and the value 0 in the other two sets. Then, in the second set we can assign the value 1 to the exponent of S, and in the third to that of V_s. Let the full choice for the first set be

```
≫ C1 = [ -2 -1 1];
```

This is an educated guess. The vector in the right-hand side of the first system of three equations is given by

```
>> B1 = B*C1'
B1 =
    -1
     3
     0
```

and the exponents of g, L_s, and ρ are obtained by solving the system

$$\mathbf{AX}_1 = \mathbf{B}_1,$$

which is done in MATLAB by

```
>> X1 = A \B1
X1 =
     0
     0
    -1
```

For the second set of arbitrary exponents we choose

```
>> C2 = [ 0 1 0 ];
```

and calculate

```
>> B2 = B*C2';
>> X2 = A \B2
X2 =
     0
    -2
     0
```

The choice for the third set of arbitrary exponents and the calculations are

```
>> C3 = [ 1 0 0 ];
>> B3 = B*C3';
>> X3 = A \B3
X3 =
    -0.5000
    -0.5000
          0
```

Table 13.1   Dimensionless groups.

	g	L_s	ρ	V_s	S	R_W
π_1	0	0	-1	-2	-1	1
π_2	0	-2	0	0	1	0
π_3	$-1/2$	$-1/2$	0	1	0	0

In expressions that are dimensionally correct the exponents are rational numbers; therefore we change the format of the results by

```
≫ X3 = rats(X3)
X3 =
   -1/2
   -1/2
      0
```

After all this work we may ask ourselves whether MATLAB allows a short-cut. The answer is *yes*, we could have solved the three systems of linear equations simultaneously, which amounts to finding a 3-by-3 matrix $\mathbf{X}$ that satisfies

$$\mathbf{AX} = \mathbf{BC} \tag{13.2}$$

where

$$\mathbf{A} = [\mathbf{X1}\ \mathbf{X2}\ \mathbf{X3}], \quad \mathbf{C} = [\mathbf{C1}'\ \mathbf{C2}'\ \mathbf{C3}']$$

The calculations in MATLAB are

```
≫ C = [ C1; C2; C3 ];
≫ BB = B*C';
≫ X = rats(A \BB)
X =
    0  0 -1/2
    0 -2 -1/2
   -1  0   0
```

The results are summarized in Table 13.1 and the three dimensionless groups we sought are

$$\pi_1 = \frac{R_W}{\rho V_s^2 S}, \quad \pi_2 = \frac{S}{L_s^2}, \quad \pi_3 = \frac{V_s}{\sqrt{gL_s}}$$

The third group, π_3, is called the **Froude number**, in honour of William Froude (1810–1879) who established in England principles and techniques of ship-model testing that are in use to this day. Some of these principles had been proposed earlier, but not applied, by the French naval architect Frédéric Reech (1805–1879). In some French books the number $V_s/\sqrt{gL_s}$ is called the **Reech–Froude** number.

The second group, π_2, gives the ratio of two geometrical characteristics. For **geometrically similar (geosim)** bodies this ratio is obviously a constant and we shall neglect it.

Combining the first and the third group we get

$$\frac{R_W}{\rho V_s^2 S} = f\left(\frac{V_s}{\sqrt{gL_s}}\right)$$

The relationship is usually written as

$$R_W = \frac{1}{2} C_R \rho S V_s^2 \qquad\qquad (13.3)$$

where C_R, a function of the Froude number, is called the **coefficient of residual resistance**. Obviously C_R is the same for a ship and its model if their Froude numbers are equal. Let λ be the geometrical scale of the model, that is

$$\lambda = \frac{L_m}{L_s}$$

where L_m is the model, and L_s, the ship's length. From the condition

$$\frac{V_s}{\sqrt{gL_s}} = \frac{V_m}{\sqrt{gL_m}}$$

it follows that the model-to-ship-speed ratio must be

$$\frac{V_m}{V_s} = \sqrt{\frac{L_m}{L_s}} = \sqrt{\lambda}$$

This is an example of how dimensional analysis yields the laws governing experiments with models.

One can object that in the above example the choice of the exponents in the first set, $C1$, was an educated guess based on *a priori* knowledge of what some of the exponents should be. Is it not possible to proceed without such knowledge? In fact, the simplest choice of exponents would be

	V_s	S	R_w
First set	1	0	0
Second set	0	1	0
Third set	0	0	1

This is the identity matrix and multiplying $\mathbf{B}$ by it leaves $\mathbf{B}$ unchanged. It is left as an exercise for the reader to obtain in this way, in MATLAB, the nondimensional groups:

	g	L_s	ρ	V_s	S	R_W
π_1	$-1/2$	$-1/2$	0	1	0	0
π_2	0	-2	0	0	1	0
π_3	-1	-3	-1	0	0	1

$$\pi_1 = \frac{V_s}{\sqrt{gL_s}}, \quad \pi_2 = \frac{S}{L_s^2}, \quad \pi_3 = \frac{R_W}{\rho g L_s^3}$$

With these groups, we can retrieve the result found the first time by looking at tables of nondimensional groups and trying to obtain one of them by multiplication and division of the groups we have obtained. In our case we return to the first result by

$$\frac{\pi_3}{\pi_1^2 \cdot \pi_2} = \frac{R_W}{\rho S V_s^2}$$

EXAMPLE 13.2   Aerofoil drag and lift _____

This example refers to the aerodynamic forces that act on an **aerofoil**, such as the cross-section of an aeroplane wing, or a boat sail. Usually the forces are decomposed into two perpendicular components: **lift**, denoted L, and **drag**, denoted D. As the analysis is the same for both lift and drag, we shall talk about **force** in general and use the symbol F for it. Thus, during the discussion we can keep the symbol L for length as one of the three fundamental dimensions in mechanics.

By simple intuition the force F can be related to the quantities listed below.

Angle of attack, α. This is by definition a dimensionless quantity; by considering it from the beginning as one of the dimensionless groups, we can omit it from the discussion that follows.

Free-stream viscosity, μ_∞. The qualifier **free-stream** refers to quantities measured theoretically at infinity, practically far enough not to be affected by the presence of the aerofoil.

Air compressibility. This air property is described by the **free-stream sound velocity**, a_∞.

Aerofoil surface, S.

Free-stream velocity, V_∞.

Free-stream viscosity, μ_∞.

Table 13.2 contains the dimensions of the last five parameters listed above, plus the force F.

Table 13.2 Dimensions of quantities related to aerofoil lift and drag.

	μ_∞	a_∞	S	V_∞	ρ_∞	F
M	1	0	0	0	1	1
L	−1	1	2	1	−3	1
T	−1	−1	0	−1	0	−2

The matrix of dimensions is

$$D = \begin{bmatrix} 1 & 0 & 0 & 0 & 1 & 1 \\ -1 & 1 & 2 & 1 & -3 & 1 \\ -1 & -1 & 0 & -1 & 0 & -2 \end{bmatrix}$$

We write it in MATLAB and obtain its rank by

```
≫ D = [1 0 0 0 1 1; -1 1 2 1 -3 1; -1 -1 0 -1 0 -2];
≫ rank(D)
ans =
   3
```

It follows that the number of dimensionless groups to be determined is $6-3 = 3$. To find them we must separate a matrix of coefficients

$$A = \begin{bmatrix} 1 & 0 & 0 \\ -1 & 1 & 2 \\ -1 & -1 & 0 \end{bmatrix}$$

and a matrix containing the vectors in the right-hand sides of the equations

$$B = \begin{bmatrix} 0 & -1 & -1 \\ -1 & 3 & -1 \\ 1 & 0 & 2 \end{bmatrix}$$

The corresponding MATLAB commands are

```
≫ A = D(:, 1:3);
≫ B = -D(:, 4:6);
```

Without any *a priori* knowledge we assume that the powers of the three quantities V_∞, ρ_∞ and F appear in the three dimensionless groups as

$$\begin{bmatrix} 1 & 0 & 0 \\ 0 & 1 & 0 \\ 0 & 0 & 1 \end{bmatrix}$$

This is an identity matrix; multiplying $\mathbf{B}$ by it leaves $\mathbf{B}$ unchanged. Then, the solution is given by

```
≫ X = A \B
X =
           0 -1.0000 -1.0000
     -1.0000  1.0000 -1.0000
           0  0.5000 -0.5000
≫ rats(X)
ans =
      0 -1   -1
     -1  1   -1
      0 1/2 -1/2
```

Table 13.3 contains the dimensions of the resulting three nondimensional groups. The groups themselves are

$$\pi_1 = \frac{V_\infty}{a_\infty}, \quad \pi_2 = \frac{a_\infty S^{1/2} \rho_\infty}{\mu_\infty}, \quad \pi_3 = \frac{F}{\mu_\infty a_\infty S^{1/2}}$$

The inverse of π_1, that is

$$M = \frac{a_\infty}{V_\infty}$$

is called the **Mach number** and is a well-known parameter in aerodynamics. The other two groups, π_2 and π_3, are not used as such. To retrieve two known groups from them we proceed as follows:

$$\frac{\pi_3}{\pi_1^2 \pi_2} = \frac{F}{\rho_\infty V_\infty^2 S}$$

$$\pi_1 \pi_2 = \frac{V_\infty S^{1/2}}{\nu_\infty}$$

where $\nu_\infty = \mu_\infty / \rho_\infty$ is the free-stream kinematic viscosity. In aerodynamics the quantity

$$q_\infty = \frac{1}{2} \rho_\infty V_\infty^2$$

Table 13.3 Dimensionless groups involved in aerofoil forces.

	μ_∞	a_∞	S	V_∞	ρ_∞	F
π_1	0	−1	0	1	0	0
π_2	−1	1	1/2	0	1	0
π_3	−1	−1	−1/2	0	0	1

is called the **dynamic pressure**; its meaning can be easily understood from Bernoulli's equation. With this notation, the group $\pi_3/(\pi_1^2\pi_2)$ yields the **force coefficient**

$$C_F = \frac{F}{q_\infty S} = \frac{F}{\frac{1}{2}\rho_\infty V_\infty^2 S}$$

In the group $\pi_1\pi_2$ the factor $S^{1/2}$ has the dimensions of length. The **characteristic length** to be considered in this group is the **chord length**. Thus, the third dimensionless group is the Reynolds number, Re, referred to the aerofoil chord (named after Osborne Reynolds, British, 1842–1912).

The preceding analysis leads to the equations

$$L = \frac{1}{2}\rho_\infty V_\infty^2 S C_L \tag{13.4}$$

$$D = \frac{1}{2}\rho_\infty V_\infty^2 S C_D \tag{13.5}$$

where

$$C_L = f_L(\alpha, \ Re, \ M_\infty) \tag{13.6}$$

is called the **lift coefficient**, and

$$C_D = f_D(\alpha, \ Re, \ M_\infty) \tag{13.7}$$

is the **drag coefficient**.

To illustrate one important consequence of these results let us assume that five points are needed to define the curves of lift and drag as functions of the governing parameters. At the beginning of this example we identified six governing parameters: $\alpha, \mu_\infty, a_\infty, S, V_\infty$ and ρ_∞. Without dimensional analysis $6^5 = 7776$ tests would be necessary. Dimensional analysis shows that only three nondimensional parameters govern drag and lift: α, Re and M_∞. In consequence, it is necessary to perform only $3^5 = 243$ experiments.

Another consequence is the definition of the conditions for model tests: the results of wind-tunnel tests can be extrapolated to real-life size if the following necessary, but not sufficient, conditions are fulfilled:

- The model aerofoil and the real-size aerofoil are geometrically similar.
- The Reynold's number and the Mach number are the same in the wind tunnel and in real life.

EXAMPLE 13.3   Heat transfer

Another major area in which dimensional analysis finds natural applications is heat transfer. In order to take into account the fact that heat-transfer phenomena are different from mechanical phenomena, it would be sufficient to introduce one additional fundamental quantity, usually the temperature, denoted in this example by θ. It is usual, however, to consider a further quantity as fundamental, even if derived from previous quantities. In the following example the additional quantity is energy, bearing here the symbol W. Energy, as a derived quantity, has the dimensions $[ML^2T^{-2}]$. Considering energy as a fundamental quantity increases the rank of the dimensional matrix, thus reducing the number of exponents that must be determined arbitrarily.

This example deals with heat transfer from a fluid forced to flow through a pipe. It is assumed that the temperatures of the pipe wall and the fluid are different. Thus defined, our problem is one of **forced convection**. The interested reader may find a good, short description of convection phenomena in Giedt (1987). For our purposes the process can be quantified by a **convection heat transfer coefficient**, h_c, defined as energy transferred per unit area, unit time, and unit difference of temperature. **Newton's law of cooling** can be used for a simple, formal definition of this coefficient:

$$q = h_c A(t_{wall} - t_{fluid})$$

where q is the heat flow, that is, the energy transfer per unit time, A, the area perpendicular to the heat flow, t_{wall}, the wall temperature, and t_{fluid}, the fluid temperature.

Seven other factors are thought to affect the process. These include the fluid properties: density, ρ, viscosity, μ, specific heat at constant pressure, C_p, and thermal conductivity, k.

Viscosity is a measure of the resistance opposed to a flow which produces shear stresses. Let us assume that, given a system of orthogonal coordinates, the fluid flows in the direction of the x axis. In the presence of viscosity the fluid velocity varies along the y axis, that is, there exists a **velocity gradient** dV/dy. The resistance force on an area A, parallel to the direction of flow, is given by **Newton's equation**

$$f = \mu A \frac{dV}{dy}$$

which yields the physical interpretation of **dynamic viscosity** μ.

The **specific heat** is the energy required to raise the temperature of a unit mass of fluid by one degree. In the case of gases the temperature rise can occur at either constant pressure or constant volume. For forced flow through a pipe the transfer is done under constant pressure, hence the symbol C_p used here.

Thermal conductivity, k, is the rate of heat flow per unit area, normal to the direction of flow, for a unit difference of temperature per unit length. This definition may be better understood with the help of Figure 13.1. If θ_1 is the wall temperature, and θ_2 the fluid temperature at a small distance from the wall, the heat flow through the fluid, in the y direction, through a perpendicular area A, is related to the temperature gradient by **Fourier's law**:

$$\frac{q}{A} = -k \frac{d\theta}{dy}$$

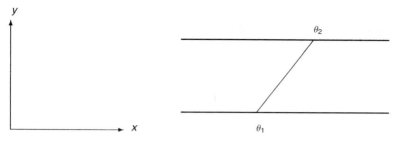

Figure 13.1   The definition of thermal conductivity.

Table 13.4   Matrix of dimensions.

	ρ	C_p	μ	V	δt	D	k	h_c
M	1	−1	1	0	0	0	0	0
L	−3	0	−1	1	0	1	−1	−2
T	0	0	−1	−1	0	0	−1	−1
θ	0	−1	0	0	1	0	−1	−1
W	0	1	0	0	0	0	1	1

Other quantities involved in the convection process may be the fluid velocity, V, the temperature difference between wall and fluid, δt, and the pipe diameter, D.

The dimensions of the eight quantities described above are shown in Table 13.4. From the first five columns we form the coefficient matrix, **A**, of a system of five equations with eight unknowns. The last three columns, with changed signs, yield the matrix **B**, which contains the three vectors that constitute the right-hand sides of the equations.

The rank of the matrix **A** is 5, equal to the rank of the augmented matrix [**AB**], and therefore we can form $8 - 5 = 3$ dimensionless groups. For the first group we choose the exponents 1 for D, 0 for k, and 0 for h_c. For the second group the exponent of k is 1 and the other two are 0. In the third group the exponent of h_c is 1; the others are 0. The calculations in MATLAB are

```
>> A = [ 1 -1 1 0 0
 -3 0 -1 1 0
 0 0 -1 -1 0
 0 -1 0 0 1
 0 1 0 0 0 ];
>> B = [ 0 0 0; -1 1 2; 0 1 1; 0 1 1; 0 -1 -1 ];
>> A \B
ans =
   1.0000        0  -1.0000
        0  -1.0000  -1.0000
  -1.0000  -1.0000  -0.0000
   1.0000        0  -1.0000
        0        0        0
```

Table 13.5   Dimensionless groups.

	ρ	C_p	μ	V	δt	D	k	h_c
π_1	1	0	-1	1	0	1	0	0
π_2	0	-1	-1	0	0	0	1	0
π_3	-1	-1	0	-1	0	0	0	1

The resulting exponents of the eight quantities, in the three dimensionless groups, are shown in Table 13.5, and the groups are

$$\pi_1 = \frac{V D \rho}{\mu} = \frac{V D}{\nu}, \ \pi_2 = \frac{k}{C_p \mu}, \ \pi_3 = \frac{h_c}{\rho C_P V}$$

where $\nu = \mu / \rho$ is called the **kinematic viscosity**.

The first dimensionless group, π_1, is known as the **Reynolds number** and its usual symbol is Re.

The second group, π_2, is the inverse of the **Prandtl number** $Pr = C_p \mu / k$ (named after Ludwig Prandtl, German, 1875–1953). The third dimensionless group, π_3, is not one of those listed in tables of dimensionless numbers. In order to obtain one of the commonly used groups we multiply π_3 by the Reynolds and Prandtl numbers and get

$$\pi_3 \times Re \times Pr = \frac{h}{\rho C_p V} \times \frac{\rho V D}{\mu} \times \frac{C_p \mu}{k_f} = \frac{h D}{k_f}$$

We obtain thus the **Nusselt number**, with the symbol Nu, and we can write

$$Nu = f(Re, Pr)$$

More about dimensional analysis in heat transfer can be found in specialized textbooks, such as Janna (1986), Gröber *et al.* (1961).

13.4   Summary

Dimensional analysis can be used to find the forms of relationships between the physical quantities that influence a phenomenon. The analysis leads to **dimensional groups** obtained by multiplying and dividing several of the quantities involved. The study of dimensionless groups yields information important for experiments and especially for model experiments. The steps required in the solution of a problem by dimensional analysis are described below.

(1)   Using as much as you know about the phenomenon, list the physical quantities that can influence it. Let the number of these quantities be n.

(2)   Write the matrix of dimensions, **D**, of the quantities listed at (1). Take care to ensure that the quantity you want to express as a function of the others is in the right part of the matrix.

(3)   Find the rank of the matrix of dimensions. Let this rank be m. It follows that the number of dimensionless parameters is $p = n - m$.

(4)   From the matrix of dimensions, **D**, choose an m-by-m matrix of coefficients, **A**.

(5)   From the remaining columns of the matrix of dimensions, **D**, form a matrix, **B**, containing the right-hand terms of the equations. Do not forget to change the signs of the elements.

(6)   Assign arbitrary exponents to the independent quantities, that is, to those corresponding to the columns of **B**. In the simplest choice, in each set of exponents one exponent equals 1 and all the others are 0.

(7)   Find the solution matrix by the MATLAB operation

$$\mathbf{X} = \mathbf{A} \backslash \mathbf{B}$$

(8)   Write the matrix of exponents of the dimensionless groups and form these groups.

(9)   If a dimensionless group found at the previous step is not usual, multiply or divide this group by some of the others and try to obtain a known group.

13.5   Exercises

The solution for Exercise 13.1 appears at the back of the book.

■ **EXERCISE 13.1**   Beam deflection
In Figure 13.2 a cantilever beam of span ℓ is subjected to a load P. Let the moment of inertia of the beam cross-section be I, the modulus of elasticity E, and the deflection y.

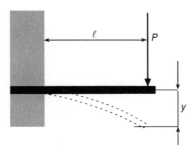

Figure 13.2   Bending of a cantilever beam.

(1)   Show by dimensional anlysis that the relationship between deflection and the other quantities is of the form

$$\frac{y}{\ell} = f\left(\frac{P\ell^2}{EI}\right)$$

(2)   Find the exact relationship in a book on strength or structures and compare it with your result.

Hint: Use force, F, and length, L, as fundamental dimensions.

■ **EXERCISE 13.2**   Period of oscillation
Consider a system composed of a mass, m, and a spring with a spring constant k. The deflections of this system are governed by the equation

$$m\ddot{x} + kx = 0$$

(1)   Assuming that the system oscillates with period T, show that the relationship between this period and the other variables is of the form

$$T = f(\sqrt{k/m})$$

(2)   Compare your result with the exact relationship.

Hint: If a row of the matrix of dimensions contains only zeros, the corresponding fundamental quantity must be ignored.

■ **EXERCISE 13.3**   Moment coefficient of aerofoil
Show by dimensional analysis that the moment acting on an aerofoil can be calculated from

$$M = \frac{1}{2}\rho_\infty V_\infty^2 ScC_M$$

where c is the chord length and

$$C_M = f_M(\alpha, Re, M_\infty)$$

is the moment coefficient.

Chapter 14
System modelling and simulation

14.1   Introduction

A large number of physical models can be described by means of an ordinary differential equation. We have already met in Chapter 4 the example of a mass attached to a spring (see Figure 4.11) and the RLC model described in Example 4.3.

MATLAB uses five common methods to describe a dynamic system, and, although most systems can be represented in all of them, there is sometimes a distinct advantage in choosing a particular one, either because it is conceptually simpler, or because it provides more accurate numerical results. Fortunately, the conversion from one representation to another is not difficult to perform manually. Moreover, if you have access to the Control Toolbox, you are provided with a number of useful functions, such as `tf2ss`, `zp2tf`, and a few more that perform most of these conversions automatically.

The five methods are **transfer functions**, **zero-pole-gain**, **partial fractions**, **state space representations** and **Cauchy form**. We are now going to show how the model of a linear spring is expressed in each of these forms. Remember that the motion of the spring is governed by the differential Equation 4.40. Since the letters x and y that appear there have an established conventional meaning in state space theory, in order to avoid confusion we are going to rewrite that equation in terms of the quantity $\ell = y - x$, which represents the distance of the mass from its point of equilibrium. For the same reason, as k in control theory usually indicates a gain, we shall use the letter h for the spring constant. With these notations and the introduction of an additional symbol F, to indicate the sum of all external forces applied to the mass, Equation 4.40 becomes

$$m\ell'' + c\ell' + h\ell = F \tag{14.1}$$

In this chapter we shall use Equation 14.1 with the following constants

$$m = 2\,\text{kg}$$
$$c = 1.4\,\text{N s m}^{-1}$$
$$h = 0.1\,\text{N m}^{-1}$$

14.2   Five ways of modelling dynamic systems

14.2.1   Transfer functions

This representation is very common in the electrical engineering community. Noting the complex frequency by s, the Laplace transform of any variable q, by $\hat{q}$, and assuming zero initial conditions, Equation 14.1 can be rewritten as

$$(ms^2 + cs + h)\hat{\ell} = \hat{F} \tag{14.2}$$

which yields

$$\hat{\ell} = \frac{1}{ms^2 + cs + h}\,\hat{F} \tag{14.3}$$

The expression

$$H(s) = \frac{1}{ms^2 + cs + h} \tag{14.4}$$

is called the **transfer function** of the system. Frequently, as in this case, H is the ratio of two polynomials in s, say num and den, that can be defined in MATLAB (see Section 1.6) by the array of coefficients ordered according to the decreasing powers of s, that is

```
>> num = 1; den = [2 1.4 0.1];
```

This is an accepted form of representing H when using it in conjunction with many MATLAB functions, such as `rlocus` in the Control System Toolbox.

The transfer function representation is very convenient for **single-input single-output (SISO)** systems, but cannot be easily generalized to the **multiple-input multiple-output (MIMO)** case. While transfer functions are capable, in principle, of describing **single-input multiple-output (SIMO)** systems, we suggest that the reader interested in the analysis of any SIMO or MIMO system should use the state space representation.

14.2.2 Zero-pole-gain models

This is a simple variation of the previous representation. In a zero-pole-gain model the transfer function $H(s)$ is written in the form

$$H(s) = K\frac{(s - Z_1)(s - Z_2) \cdots (s - Z_M)}{(s - P_1)(s - P_2) \cdots (s - P_N)} \tag{14.5}$$

where K is the **gain**, the elements of the column vector Z are the **zeros**, and the elements of the column vector P, the **poles** of H.

The spring-mass system exemplified in the previous section, and defined by the transfer function in Equation 14.5

```
num = 1;    den = [ 2 1.4 0.1 ];
```

has no zeros, its gain, $K = 1/m$, equals 0.5, and its poles are given by

```
>> P = roots(den)
```

The system is therefore represented in zero-pole-gain form by

```
Z =[]
P = [ -0.6193;
       -0.0807];
K = 0.5000;
```

If you have installed the Control Toolbox, you can obtain Z, P and K with the command

```
>> [Z,P,K] = tf2zp(num,den)
```

Algorithms applied to the zero-pole-gain representation are often simpler and numerically more precise than algorithms that use transfer functions.

Let us consider, for example, two systems connected in cascade, as in Figure 14.1. In the transfer function representation, let the first system be described by the arrays of coefficients num1, den1, and the second by num2, den2.

In the zero-pole-gain representation, let the first system be described by Z1, P1, K1, and the second, by Z2, P2, K2.

In the transfer function representation, the transfer function of the whole system is obtained with

```
>> num = conv(num1, num2); den = conv(den1, den2);
```

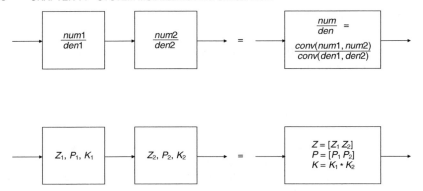

Figure 14.1   Two systems connected in series: (a) transfer-function representation;
(b) zero-pole-gain representation.

The convolution is a potential source of numerical imprecision. The zero-pole-gain model, on the other hand, requires only one multiplication,

```
>> K = K1*K2
```

and two composition operations

```
>> Z=[Z1; Z2]; P= [P1; P2];
```

This is clearly preferable from the numerical point of view.

14.2.3   Partial fractions

The rational function $H(s)$ can be represented as a **partial-fraction expansion**

$$H(s) = \frac{R_1}{s - P_1} + \frac{R_2}{s - P_2} + \cdots + \frac{R_M}{s - P_M} + k(s) \qquad (14.6)$$

where P is the column vector of the poles, as in the zero-pole-gain representation, R is a column vector, called the vector of the residues, and k is a polynomial, expressed, as usual, by the row vector of its coefficients.

The MATLAB residue function converts in both directions, from polynomial to residue representation and back, depending on the number of right-hand parameters. For example, for the arrays num and den defined in the previous section, the command

```
>> [R,P,k] = residue(num, den)
R =
     -0.9285
      0.9285
```

```
P =
      -0.6193
      -0.0807
k =
      []
```

decomposes $H(s)$ into partial fractions, while the command

```
>> [num1, den1] = residue(R,P,k)
num1 =
      0 0.5000
den1 =
      1.0000 0.7000 0.0500
```

reconstructs the polynomials representing the numerator and the denominator of $H(s)$. You can verify that [num1, den1] coincides with [num, den] up to a coefficient of proportionality.

14.2.4 State space

A system is represented in state space form, when it can be written as

$$x' = Ax + Bu$$
$$y = Cx + Du \tag{14.7}$$

for suitable column vectors x, the **vector of the states**, and u, the **vector of inputs**, and for suitable matrices A, B, C and D. The column vector y represents the **outputs**.

The second-order differential equation of the spring, that is, Equation 14.1, can be transformed into a state space form in many ways. We can, for example, let x_2 be equal to ℓ, x_1 to ℓ', u to F, and y also to ℓ. The reader is invited to verify that the following matrices A, B, C and D describe the proposed system:

$$A = \begin{bmatrix} -c/m & -h/m \\ 1 & 0 \end{bmatrix}, \quad B = \begin{bmatrix} 1/m \\ 0 \end{bmatrix}$$

$$C = \begin{bmatrix} 0 & 1 \end{bmatrix}, \quad D = \begin{bmatrix} 0 \end{bmatrix}$$

If you have access to the Control Toolbox you can obtain the conversion from transfer function to state space representation by means of the tf2ss function. Thus, for the same example as above:

```
>> num = 1; den = [ 2 1.4 0.1 ];
>> [ A1, B1, C1, D1 ] = tf2ss(num, den)
```

```
A1 =
     -0.7000  -0.0500
      1.0000        0
B1 =
      1
      0
C1 =
      0  0.5000
D1 =
      0
```

The state space representation is probably the most common. It is sufficiently general for most practical purposes, it has good numerical properties, and there are many control functions, not only in MATLAB, that expect the system to be described in this form. A further positive aspect of the state space representation is that it is equally well suited to describing both SISO and MIMO systems.

14.2.5   Cauchy form

A large number of dynamic systems can be represented in a standard mathematical form, called the **Cauchy form**, as a system of n first-order differential equations that looks like

$$\left\{ \begin{array}{rcl} w'_{(1)}(t) & = & f_{(1)}(t, w) \\ & \vdots & \\ w'_{(n)}(t) & = & f_{(n)}(t, w) \end{array} \right. \tag{14.8}$$

where t is the independent variable, usually the time, $w(t)$ is a vector of n components, and the derivative with respect to the independent variable is indicated by a prime sign as in $w'_{(1)}$. In vector notation, this system can be written as

$$\mathbf{w}'(t) = \mathbf{f}(t, \mathbf{w}) \tag{14.9}$$

This form of describing a system is probably the most common in the simulation community.

The function $\mathbf{f}(t, \mathbf{w})$ is usually contained in a separate unit, such as a MATLAB M-file or a Fortran subroutine. The MATLAB ode23 and ode45 functions, which we discuss in the next section, require the model to be described in this form, and so do most popular packages (for example, IMSL and NAG). There are many reasons why this form is so popular. First of all it is very general, as $\mathbf{f}(t, \mathbf{w})$ can be any reasonably smooth function of t and $\mathbf{w}$. There are no requirements on linearity, time invariance, and so on. Secondly, once the model is defined, it can often be submitted in this form to different solving routines, based on very different strategies, such as Runge–Kutta, predictor-corrector, Gear, and so on, which we discuss later in this chapter.

14.3   Numerical solution of ordinary differential equations

Numerical strategies for solving differential equations are often selected according to the underlying physical properties of the problem, and while most of them *do often produce* a solution, it is not uncommon to encounter real-life problems where one routine is faster than another by several orders of magnitude.

We are now going to write in Cauchy form the equation of a spring subjected to a force of $a \sin t$ newton, where $a = 2\,\text{N}$. Let us choose for states $w_1 = \ell'$ and $w_2 = \ell$. The equation can then be written in Cauchy form as

$$w_1' = -c/m w_1 - h/m w_2 + a/m \sin(t) \tag{14.10}$$
$$w_2' = w_1 \tag{14.11}$$

This system has a unique solution for each set of initial conditions. Let us choose to start the simulation at $t_0 = 0$, with initial conditions

$$w_1(0) = 0$$
$$w_2(0) = 0$$

We are going to use the ode23 routine to solve the differential system thus obtained. If you were to write

```
≫ help ode23
```

you notice, in the list of inputs, the presence of a parameter called options, followed by a number of parameters P1, P2, etc. We will not worry for the time being about these parameters, which are optional, and will simply omit them. MATLAB will assign them a reasonable value. The first step necessary to compute the dynamics of the spring is to write a function file that describes the system, like the following file springb.m. We named this file springb.m for spring-basic version. We plan to modify this function later and will call the variations springg.m, springp.m. Such a function is called, in the MATLAB jargon, the **odefile**. An odefile is a function that, in its simplest form, accepts as inputs a scalar (most often time, t in the following example), a column vector of states (w in the following example) and returns a vector (wd in the following example) that represents the derivative of w at time t. Here is the source of springb.m:

```
function wd=springb(t,w);
% This function defines the dynamics of a
% mass-spring-damper system, subject
% to an external sinusoidal force.
% It is written according to the syntax required by odesolvers.

% --- assign values to the constants that define the system:
a = 2.0;                    % N
m = 2.0;                    % kg
```

```
c = 1.4;                          % Ns/m
h = 0.1;                          % N/m
om= 1.0;                          % rad/s
% --- allocate space for wd
wd = zeros(size(w));
% --- compute derivatives
wd(1) = -c/m*w(1) -h/m*w(2) + a/m*sin(om*t);
wd(2) = w(1);
```

To see how the mass oscillates, define the initial and final time and the initial values of the states:

```
>> t0 = 0.0; tf = 100; w0 = [0; 0];
```

The old syntax required the name of the odefunction to be passed as a string:

```
>> [ t, w ] = ode23('springb', [ t0, tf ], w0)
```

The new syntax requires the handle of the odefunction (see Section 11.6) to be passed as shown in the following example. In MATLAB 6 both forms are supported. If you develop new code we strongly recommend you use the new syntax, that is to use function handles.

```
>> [t,w] = ode23('@springb', [t0, tf], w0)
t =

 0
 0.0195
 0.0391
 0.0684
 .
 .
 .
100.0000
w =

 0 0
 0.0002 0.0000
 0.0008 0.0000
 0.0023 0.0001
 .
 .
 .
-0.8430 -0.0873
```

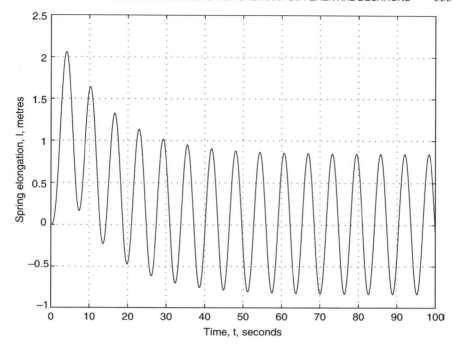

Figure 14.2   Simulation of spring-mass system.

You can now plot the position, as a function of time, with the command:

```
>> plot(t,w(:,2); % position is the second state
>> grid on;
>> xlabel('Time, t, seconds');
>> ylabel('Spring elongation, l, meters');
```

The result is shown in Figure 14.2. We are going now to examine some alternative commands to solve the same problem, namely:

- specifying the times of the solution;
- using alternative odesolvers;
- passing parameters to the model.

14.3.1   Specifying the times of the solution

In the previous example, the function ode23 computed the array of times t, and correspondingly the values of the vector of the states, w. The values of t were produced by MATLAB, in a way that make the computation most efficient. Often we want to be able to specify the vector t, for example at constant steps. A possible strategy is to solve the equation as before, and then use some form of interpolation to produce w at the assigned values of time, but it is much better, and simpler, to define the vector *tspan*, for example as in the following line:

```
>> tspan=0.0:0.1:100;
```

and pass it directly to ode23. The command to solve the differential equation is, in this case:

```
>> [t,w] = ode23('@springb', tspan, w0)
t =

0
0.1000
0.2000
0.3000
.

.

.
100.0000
w =
0  0
0.0049  0.0002
0.0190  0.0013
0.0417  0.0043
.

.

.

-0.8430 -0.0873
```

The array span was, in our example, an arithmetic sequence, but it can be more generally any monotonic sequence of numbers.

14.3.2   Using alternative odesolvers

Your package of MATLAB contains a number of routines that solve ordinary differential equations. We are not going to list them, as their number increases with each new release. To obtain the list of odesolvers available on your installation, type

```
>> help ode23
```

Each of these routines is, in principle, capable of solving any differential system, but the performance and the precision is different for each of them. Choosing the correct routine is usually not a simple task, and requires a fair knowledge of the underlying mathematical theory, which is probably beyond the interest of the occasional user. If you are interested in going deeper on this subject, please read Section 14.5, otherwise we can only suggest you experiment with different odesolvers. The syntax of all odesolvers is identical, so if you want to submit the odefile `springb` to a new solver, like `ode45`, the syntax is (assuming `springb`, *tspan* and $w0$ defined from the previous section):

```
>> [t,w] = ode45('@springb', tspan, w0)
```

14.3.3   Passing parameters to the model

In this section we want to consider a very common situation. We have the odefile `springb.m`, but we would like to examine how the solution changes if we modify one or more parameters that define the system, like the damping coefficient, c, or the parameter *om* that changes the frequency of the external force. In the following example, for the sake of simplicity, we are going to vary only one parameter, c. We have three possibilities, which we are going to examine in the following example.

Example

Solve the differential equation of the mass-spring-dumper system described in the file `springb.m`, with the new values $c = 2.5\,\mathrm{N\,s\,m^{-1}}$.

Solution 1

The first solution is to edit the file `springb.m`. Change the line

```
c = 1.4;                    % Ns/m
```

to the new line

```
c = 2.5;                    % Ns/m
```

Call the new file `springb1.m`:

```
function wd=springb1(t,w);
% This function defines the dynamics of a
% mass-spring-damper system, subject
% to an external sinusoidal force.
% It is written according to the syntax required by odesolvers.

% --- assign values to the constants that define the system:
a = 2.0;                    % N
m = 2.0;                    % kg
c = 2.5;                    % Ns/m
h = 0.1;                    % N/m
om= 1.0;                    % rad/s
```

```
% --- allocate space for wd
wd = zeros(size(w));
% --- compute derivatives
wd(1) = -c/m*w(1) -h/m*w(2) + a/m*sin(om*t);
wd(2) = w(1);
```

You can now compare the original system, where $c = 1.4$, with the new system, where $c = 2.5$, with the commands:

```
>> tspan=[0,100]; w0=[0;0];
>> % solve original system
>> [t,w]=ode23('@springb',tspan,w0);
>> % solve modified system
>> [t1,w1]=ode23('@springb1',tspan,w0);
>> % compare results
>> plot(t,w(:,2),t1,w1(:,2))
>> grid on
>> xlabel('Time, t, in seconds')
>> ylabel('Spring elongation, l, meters')
```

The resulting plot is shown in Figure 14.3.

While this method works well, it is a little inconvenient because it requires the use of the editor for each new value of the parameter you want to test.

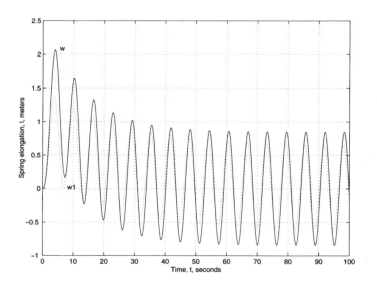

Figure 14.3   Plot produced by springb1.

Solution 2

We can define the varying parameter as **global**. The second solution is to change in springb.m the line

```
c = 1.4;                        % Ns/m
```

to the new line

```
global c                        % Ns/m
```

Call the new file springg.m, for 'spring with global':

```
function wd=springg(t,w);
% This function defines the dynamics of a
% mass-spring-damper system, subject
% to an external sinusoidal force.
% It is written according to the syntax required by odesolvers.

% --- assign values to the constants that define the system:
a = 2.0;                        % N
m = 2.0;                        % kg
global c;                       % Ns/m
h = 0.1;                        % N/m
om= 1.0;                        % rad/s
% --- allocate space for wd
wd = zeros(size(w));
% --- compute derivatives
wd(1) = -c/m*w(1) -h/m*w(2) + a/m*sin(om*t);
wd(2) = w(1);
```

You can now compare the original system, where $c = 1.4$, with the new system, where $c = 2.5$, with the commands:

```
t≫ span = [0,100]; w0=[0;0];
t≫ global c
t≫ % solve original system
t≫ c = 1.4; [t,w] = ode23('springg',tspan,w0);
t≫ % solve modified system
t≫ c = 2.5; [t1,w1] = ode23('springg',tspan,w0);
t≫ % compare results
t≫ plot(t,w(:,2),t1,w1(:,2)); grid on
```

This solution does not require that we edit the file for each new value of the parameter, but we still need to define a global parameter, in our case c. Generally speaking, defining global parameters is a potential source of nasty bugs. Imagine what happens if some other program defines as global a different variable c! We strongly advise you to avoid this practice, except for very short programs, and employ the solution described below.

Solution 3

We can place the varying parameter in the list of the input parameters of the odefile. This alternative syntax of the odefile uses as third parameter the variable flag. We are not going to use this parameter, which was introduced for compatibility with Simulink, but must nevertheless put it in the list of input parameters. From the fourth place on, we are free to put as many optional parameters as we like. We therefore modify the function springb.m to the new file springp.m (spring with parameters). The changes are in the first line and the line that originally defined c which is now deleted:

```
function wd=springp(t,w,flag, c);
% This function defines the dynamics of a
% mass-spring-damper system, subject
% to an external sinusoidal force.
% It is written according to the syntax required by odesolvers.

% --- assign values to the constants that define the system:
a = 2.0;                        % N
m = 2.0;                        % kg
% c now appears in the list of input parameters
h = 0.1;                        % N/m
om= 1.0;                        % rad/s
% --- allocate space for wd
wd = zeros(size(w));
% --- compute derivatives
wd(1) = -c/m*w(1) -h/m*w(2) + a/m*sin(om*t);
wd(2) = w(1);
```

The commands to run the simulation for an odefile with parameters are also slightly different:

```
>> tspan=[0,100]; w0=[0;0];
>> % solve original system
>> c=1.4; [t,w]=ode23('springp',tspan,w0,[],c);
>> % solve modified system
>> c=2.5; [t1,w1]=ode23('springp',tspan,w0,[],c);
>> % compare results
>> plot(t,w(:,2),t1,w1(:,2));grid on
```

Observe the list of input parameters to ode23. The fourth place is occupied by a parameter, called **options**, or by a couple of empty brackets, as in the example above. In this case the optional parameters are assigned their default values. The user-defined parameter or parameters, like c in our example, start from the fifth place.

14.4 Alternative strategies to solve ordinary differential equations

In this section we are going to define what it means to solve numerically an ordinary differential equation in Cauchy form, and what tools MATLAB provides to obtain such a solution. We are fully aware that the rest of this chapter is less easy to read than the rest of the book. We have tried to simplify it, by providing most formulae just for single equations, instead of for systems of equations. Generalizing the proofs for systems of equations is just a technicality that contains no new ideas, but makes the notation a lot heavier. With this compromise, we feel more comfortable about inserting this section in a book not written for numerical analysis specialists, particularly for the following reasons:

(1) It requires no more mathematical knowledge than the Taylor-McLaurin expansion.

(2) It can be skipped without compromising the understanding of the following chapters.

On the other hand, if you feel uneasy, like the authors of this book, about using a routine without understanding it, we encourage you to make the effort and read this chapter to the end.

In exchange, we promise you that:

• your simulations will run much faster;

• you will be able to understand and assign correctly the values of the parameters that define the precision of the results.

We have seen in the previous section that a differential system of equations is expressed in Cauchy form as:

$$w'_{(1)}(t) = f_{(1)}(t, w)$$

$$\vdots$$

$$w'_{(n)}(t) = f_{(n)}(t, w)$$

or, in vector notation,

$$\mathbf{w}' = \mathbf{f}(t, \mathbf{w})$$

From now on, we shall consider for a while only single equations, that is the particular case when $n = 1$, and just state the results for the general case. Solving a differential equation means, by definition, producing a function Φ such that

$$\Phi'(t) = f(t, \Phi(t))$$

It can be proven that, under very modest conditions of regularity on f, for any initial condition $w_0 = w(t_0)$, there exists, in the neighbourhood of the point (t_0, w_0), a unique function $\Phi(t)$ that solves the equation and such that $\Phi(t_0) = w_0$. The proof can be found in the literature, for example in Brauer and Nohel (1967). We will make our life a bit easier by assuming that f has infinitely many continuous derivatives. The theorem of existence is, unfortunately, not a constructive one. It states that a solution exists, but gives no indication on how to find it. A numerical solution to the Cauchy problem, on the other hand, is a sequence of values $[w_0, w_1, \ldots w_n]$ corresponding to an increasing sequence of time points $[t_0, t_1, \ldots, t_n]$, such that w_i approximates $\Phi(t_i)$. The points t_i are sometimes selected by the user, but it is usually preferable, for the sake of efficiency, to let the routine define them. If one needs the solution at specific points, the standard practice is to let the routine find the solution at the point it selects, and then apply some interpolation formula.

Given the initial value w_0 at time t_0, the basic algorithm must be able to produce, in correspondence of the time $t_1 = t_0 + \Delta t$, the value of $w_1 = w(t_1)$. In the process we are aware of introducing a **local error**, which in most cases decreases if we take smaller steps. This local error has two main components, the first one due to the arithmetic precision of the processor, the other one to the algorithm itself, which substitutes, as we shall see in a moment, a differential equation with an approximate algebraic expression. We can repeat the algorithm to produce, from the new initial condition w_1 corresponding to time t_1, a new point, w_2, which approximates Φ at $t_2 = t_1 + \Delta t$ (either the same Δt, in which case the algorithm is called a **fixed step algorithm**, or possibly a different Δt, in which case the algorithm is called a **variable step algorithm**). In this way we produce, step by step, a numerical solution to the Cauchy problem. But when computing w_2, in addition to the local error, we introduce a new error which was not present at step 1. In fact, the correct initial condition for the interval $[t_1, t_2]$ is $\Phi(t_1)$, which we don't know, and we start instead from the point w_1, which is just an approximation of $\Phi(t_1)$. This **cumulative error** grows, in general, as the number of steps increases.

The conceptually simplest (and probably computationally hardest) way to compute $w(t + \Delta t)$ is by Taylor expansion. Notice that, once we know $\Phi'(t) = f(t, w)$, we potentially know *all* the derivatives of the solution. In fact:

$$\Phi''(t) = \frac{d}{dt} f(t, w)$$
$$= \frac{\partial f(t, w)}{\partial t} + \frac{\partial f(t, w)}{\partial w} \cdot \frac{dw}{dt} = \frac{\partial}{\partial t} f(t, w) + \frac{\partial f(t, w)}{\partial w} f(t, w)$$

and, by taking successive derivatives of f, it is possible, in principle, to compute all the derivatives of Φ. We can then compute $\Phi(t_0 + \Delta t)$ using the first n terms of the Taylor expansion. By doing so, we contribute to the local error with a term proportional to $(\Delta t)^{n+1}$. This term is called **truncation error**, because it is the consequence of truncating the infinite Taylor expansion after a finite number of terms. For example, if we take into account the first two terms of the Taylor expansion of f, we obtain the following formula:

$$w_1 \approx \Phi(t_0 + \Delta t) \approx w_0 + \left[f + \frac{1}{2} \left(\frac{\partial f}{\partial t} + \frac{\partial f}{\partial w} f \right) \Delta t \right]_{(t_0, w_0)} \Delta t$$

with an error proportional to $(\Delta t)^3$. The term that appears in square brackets can be interpreted as the average slope of the solution in the interval $[t_0, t_0 + \Delta t]$, and we are going to refer to it as the **Taylor slope**.

Applying this method requires, in all practical cases, an incredibly long preliminary work to compute the formulae for the successive derivatives but, until the end of the last century, there was no better way to compute the numerical solution of an ordinary differential equation. The rest of this chapter will be devoted to explaining alternative methods to solve numerically a differential equation, namely **Runge–Kutta methods, predictor-corrector methods** and special methods for **stiff equations**.

14.4.1   Runge–Kutta methods

Around the turn of the century Carl Runge (German, 1856–1927) and Wilhelm Kutta (German, 1867–1944) independently developed a number of algorithms based on the observation that, instead of computing $f(t, w)$ and its derivatives at the point t_0, one can compute only the slope, at different points in the interval $[t_0, t_0 + \Delta t]$, and produce an approximation of $\Phi(t_0 + \Delta t)$ comparable to that obtained by Taylor expansion.

For example, by computing $f(t, w)$ for two different values of t and w, one can write a formula for $w(t_0 + \Delta t)$ that differs from the true solution $\Phi(t_0 + \Delta t)$ by no more than a constant times $(\Delta t)^3$, like the approximation obtained by the second-order Taylor expansion. At each step we compute

$$k_1 \quad = \quad f(t_0, w_0) \tag{14.12}$$

$$k_2 \quad = \quad f(t_0 + \alpha \Delta t, \ w_0 + \alpha k_1 \Delta t) \tag{14.13}$$

and the **average slope** for the interval,

$$k = \lambda_1 k_1 + \lambda_2 k_2$$

For analogy with the Taylor slope introduced in the previous section, we shall call this k the **Runge–Kutta slope**. We use the Runge–Kutta slope to produce $w(t_0 + \Delta t)$ as

$$w(t_0 + \Delta t) = w_0 + k \Delta t$$

As long as we choose the parameters, λ_1, λ_2, α, such that:

$$\lambda_1 + \lambda_2 \quad = \quad 1$$

$$\alpha\lambda_2 \quad = \quad \frac{1}{2}$$

the Runge–Kutta slope k coincides, up to higher order terms, with the Taylor slope, as one can easily verify by writing the Taylor expansion of k. This method can be generalized to higher orders. For example, it is possible to write a fourth order Runge–Kutta algorithm that requires four calls of $f(t, w)$ at each step, and produces results accurate to a constant times $(\Delta t)^5$, like the Taylor expansion truncated after the fourth term. Probably the most complete collection of Runge–Kutta algorithms is contained in Rosser (1967).

Runge–Kutta methods were the most popular for the numerical solution of ordinary differential equations for more than half a century, mainly because they were easy to use with hand calculators first, and to implement on electronic computers later. Their main drawback was the lack of an intrinsic evaluation of their accuracy. The typical method of checking accuracy was to recompute the solution using twice as many points, and accept the solution if the two results were close enough. This implied, in the best case, an overhead of 200%. And, if you were unlucky, that is, if the discrepancy between the two solutions was unacceptable, you could restart the game anew with a smaller Δt.

In the fifties a new family of algorithms was developed, called predictor-correctors (see next section). These algorithms were more efficient than comparatively precise Runge–Kutta methods, and, in particular, by comparing the result of the predictor with the corrector, were able to estimate the truncation error. Eventually, in the seventies, a little modification of the Runge–Kutta method was proposed by Fehlberg (see Fehlberg, 1970). The second-order Runge–Kutta procedure, as we have seen, requires two computations of $f(t, w)$ per integration step. Fehlberg observed that an extra computation, representing a 50% overhead, allows an estimate to be made of the factor η that appears in the computation of the truncation error formulated as

$$error \approx \eta(\Delta t)^3 \tag{14.14}$$

The situation is even better for the fourth order Runge–Kutta, that requires at each step four calls to $f(t, w)$. In this case a fifth call, representing a mere 20% overhead, produces an estimate of the truncation error. At each step we test the estimated local error and consider the integration step as successful if it is smaller than the value

$$\max(RelTol \cdot \|w\|, AbsTol)$$

where $RelTol$ and $AbsTol$, the relative and absolute tolerance parameters, are constants that, as we shall see in a moment, have small default values or can alternatively be defined by the user.

In the case of a system of n equations, *RelTol* and *AbsTol* can either be vectors of length n, or scalars. In the latter case that scalar value is common for all states. *RelTol* and *AbsTol* have default values, and we, in fact, used them until now. If you want to set different values, you should use the parameter *options*. This parameter is usually defined with the function odeset. For example, if you want to define $RelTol = 0.0001$ and $AbsTol = 0.000001$ (one tenth of their default values), the syntax is:

```
>> options = odeset('RelTol',1e-4,'AbsTol',1e-5);
```

and this parameter, *options*, is then passed to the odesolver. So, if we want to solve the problem of the spring with these values for *RelTol* and *AbsTol* we should write, instead of the command

```
>> c=2.5; [t1,w1]=ode23('springp',tspan,w0,[],c);
```

seen at the end of Subsection 14.3.3, the new command

```
>> c=2.5; [t1,w1]=ode23('springp',tspan,w0,options,c);
```

Formula 14.14 does not just satisfy our legitimate curiosity for estimating the truncation error, it makes it possible to create very efficient algorithms, by reducing the integration steps when the error is large and increasing them when the error is small.

A last note of caution. The reader should be careful not to assign to *AbsTol* and *RelTol* too small values. This would be a penny-wise, pound-foolish strategy. If the tolerances are too small, MATLAB will be forced to chose too small integration steps over a given interval; this will result in a large number of steps and possibly in large errors of a different type (finite arithmetic errors, cumulative errors, etc.) that the algorithm does not take into account.

Methods based on the Runge–Kutta algorithm are ode23, ode45 and other solvers, which are not supplied with the basic package, like ode2, ode4 that come with some editions of Simulink.

14.4.2   Predictor-corrector methods

Let us consider again the problem of finding $w_{k+1} \approx \Phi(t_{k+1})$, but this time assuming that we know the past history of t and w, namely the points $[t_1, t_2, \ldots, t_k]$ and $[w_1, w_2, \ldots, w_k]$. Let us also define $\dot{w}_i = f(t_i, w_i)$, which is approximately equal to $\dot{\Phi}(t_i)$. Then

$$w_{k+1} = w_k + \int_{t_k}^{t_{k+1}} \dot{\Phi}(s)\, ds \tag{14.15}$$

We can decide to compute the integral using some numerical routine like trapezoidal approximation, Simpson's rule (Section 11.4) or some higher order formula. To illustrate the idea, let us choose the trapezoidal approximation. Then Formula 14.15 becomes

$$w_{k+1} \approx w_k + \frac{\dot{w}_k + \dot{w}_{k+1}}{2} \Delta t = w_k + \frac{\dot{w}_k + f(t_{k+1}, w_{k+1})}{2}(t_{k+1} - t_k)$$

$$\textbf{(14.16)}$$

So w_{k+1} can be obtained by solving the equation:

$$w_{k+1} = w_k + \frac{\dot{w}_k + f(t_{k+1}, w_{k+1})}{2} \Delta t \qquad \textbf{(14.17)}$$

There are various methods which find the value of w_{k+1} that solves this implicit equation. The predictor-corrector idea is to substitute the w_{k+1} that appears on the right-hand side of Equation 14.15 with a predicted value $w_{k+1}^{(p)}$ obtained by substituting the integrand in Formula 14.15 with an appropriate polynomial approximation. For example, if we decide to use parabolic approximation, we would use the polynomial of degree 2 that passes through the points $(t_{k-2}, \dot{w}_{k-2})$, $(t_{k-1}, \dot{w}_{k-1})$. and $(t_k, \dot{w}_k)$. Since this is not a book on numerical analysis but a section of a book for non-specialists and our purpose is just to illustrate the idea of the predictor-corrector, we shall just use linear approximation, and our polynomial P will be simply the line that passes through $(t_{k-1}, \dot{w}_{k-1})$ and $(t_k, \dot{w}_k)$, that is the polynomial:

$$P(s) = \dot{w}_k + \frac{\dot{w}_k - \dot{w}_{k-1}}{t_k - t_{k-1}}(s - t_k)$$

Having so defined $P(s)$, $w_{k+1}^{(p)}$ can be expressed as

$$w_{k+1}^{(p)} = w_k + \int_{t_k}^{t_{k+1}} P(s)\, ds = w_k + \int_{t_k}^{t_{k+1}} \left[\dot{w}_k + \frac{\dot{w}_k - \dot{w}_{k-1}}{t_k - t_{k-1}}(s - t_k) \right] ds$$

and finally:

$$w_{k+1}^{(p)} = w_k + \dot{w}_k(t_{k+1} - t_k) + \frac{\dot{w}_k - \dot{w}_{k-1}}{t_k - t_{k-1}} \cdot \frac{(t_{k+1} - t_k)^2}{2}$$

Now we can use this value on the right-hand side of Formula 14.17 and eventually get the new value for w_{k+1} corrected, or simply w_{k+1}, as:

$$
\begin{aligned}
w_{k+1} \quad &= \quad w_k + \frac{\dot{w}_k + \dot{w}_{k+1}}{2}(t_{k+1} - t_k) \\
&= \quad w_k + \frac{\dot{w}_k + f(t_{k+1}, w_{k+1}^{(p)})}{2}(t_{k+1} - t_k)
\end{aligned}
$$

Predictor-corrector methods are usually very efficient, because a comparison between the value of the predictor and the value of the corrector leads to a good estimate of the local error introduced at each integration cycle, without requiring an extra evaluation of the odefile as done in the Runge–Kutta–Fehlberg algorithm. As in the latter methods, this estimate can be used to determine dynamically the next integration step. Moreover, at each cycle, we can also change the *order* of the predictor (linear, parabolic, etc.) and the integration formula for the corrector (trapezoidal, Simpson, etc.). The current version of MATLAB comes with a variable-step, variable-order predictor-corrector algorithm, ode113.

14.4.3 Stiff systems

In previous sections, when we illustrated the ideas of Runge–Kutta and predictor-corrector odesolvers, we were concerned with the precision of the algorithm but we carefully avoided another minefield, the problem of **stability**. Stability is a qualitative property rather difficult to define. Formal definitions are complicated, and not very illustrative.

Let us agree to use the term **precision** when dealing with an algorithm that produces a solution differing only a little from the true one, and the term **instability**, when the algorithm produces a numerical solution that is very far from the true one. For example, in the latter case the error can grow to infinity or oscillate widely. In other words, we speak of instability in such cases when the error becomes so large that the numerical solution is useless for every practical purpose, as the following example shows.

To illustrate instability we shall develop a simple implementation of the second-order, fixed-step Runge–Kutta algorithm that solves differential equations, not systems. Let us call it rk2fxeq:

```
function [t,w]=RK2fxeq(odefun,tspan,w0);
% This is the implementation of the second order
% Runge-Kutta algorithm for functions. User defines:
% - the name of the odefile F (a scalar function!!!)
% - the points of integration tspan
% w0 - the initial state
% The outputs t (equal to tspan) and the solution w:
% Calling syntax : [t,w]=RK2fxeq('F',tspan,w0);

% --- define parameters of integration routine;
la1 = 1/4;
la2 = 3/4;
al  = 2/3;

l  = length(tspan);
t = zeros(l,1);  % allocate space for times
w = zeros(l,1);  % allocate space for the solution;
% assign initial conditions:
```

LIVERPOOL JOHN MOORES UNIVERSITY
LEARNING SERVICES

```
t(1) = tspan(1);
w(1) = w0;
% start cycle
for i= 1:(l-1);
    T = tspan(i);    % initial time of the cycle
    W = w(i);        % initial value of the cycle
    del_t = tspan(i+1)- tspan(i);
    k1 = feval(odefun,T,W);
    k2 = feval(odefun,T+al*del_t, W+al*k1*del_t);
    k   = la1*k1+la2*k2;
    t(i+1) = tspan(i+1);
    w(i+1) = W+k*del_t;
end
```

Lets us now apply this new odesolver to the simplest equation we can think of:

$$w' \quad = \quad -\left(\frac{1}{\tau}\right)w$$
$$w(0) \quad = \quad 1$$

for which we know the algebraic solution

$$\Phi(t) = e^{-t/\tau}$$

Let us assign to τ the value 0.1 second, and write the odefile deq.m:

```
function wd = deq(t,w);
% odefile for the diff. eq. w'=-w/tau
tau=0.1;  % time constant
wd = -(1/tau)* w;
```

Let us solve this equation, at fixed, constant steps of 0.1 seconds, and plot the results with the following commands:

```
≫ % define constants;
≫ tau=0.1; w0=1;
```

and find the numerical solution, using different integration steps. For example, for an appropriate integration step, like $\tau/4$, the numerical solution agrees quite well with the algebraic solution:

```
≫ tau = 0.1;
≫ w0 = 1.0;
≫ step = tau/4;
≫ tspan = 0:  step:  5;
```

```
>> [t,w] = rk2fxeq('deq',tspan,w0); % numerical solution
>> walg = exp(-t/tau); % algebraic solution
>> h = plot(t,walg,'-',t,w,':'); grid on;
>> legend(h,'Analytic solution','numerical solution')
>> title('Integration steps:  \tau/4');
```

The result is shown in Figure 14.4.

The reader is invited to experiment to see what happens when we increase the steps. Gradually the solution becomes less precise and, when the step is larger than 2τ, it becomes unstable:

```
>> step = 2.01*tau;
>> tspan = 0:step:5;
>> [t,w] = rk2fxeq('deq',tspan,w0);
>> walg = exp(-t/tau);
```

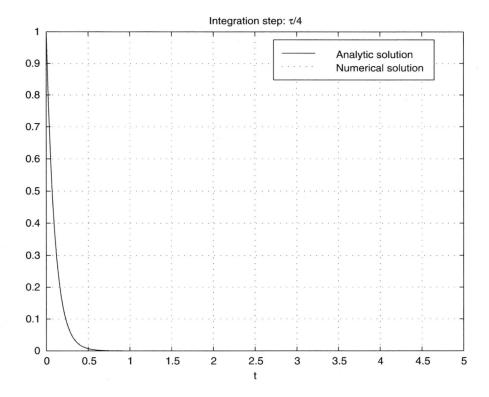

Figure 14.4 Small integration steps: the system is stable.

```
≫ h = plot(t,walg,'k -',t,t,w,':'); grid on;
≫ legend(h,'Analytic solution','Numerical solution');
≫ title('Integration steps:  2.01\tau')
```

The result is shown in Figure 14.5. At this point, the reader must trust us that this phenomenon is quite typical, non only for differential equations, but for differential systems as well. Each second-order Runge–Kutta algorithm becomes unstable as soon as the integration step exceeds twice the minimum time constant of the system. Higher-order Runge–Kutta algorithms can take slightly larger steps. For example, fourth-order Runge–Kutta algorithms can take steps up to four times the minimum time constant of the system. Similar results apply to predictor-corrector algorithms. Treating this fascinating subject in more depth is beyond the scope of this book and we must refer the interested reader to specialized books like Henrici (1962) and Ralston (1965). Now we have the background necessary to analyze what happens if we try to use either a Runge–Kutta or a predictor-corrector algorithm to solve a system like:

$$\dot{w}_1 = (a-2)w_1 + 2(a-1)w_2$$
$$\dot{w}_2 = (1-a)w_1 + 2(1-2a)w_2$$

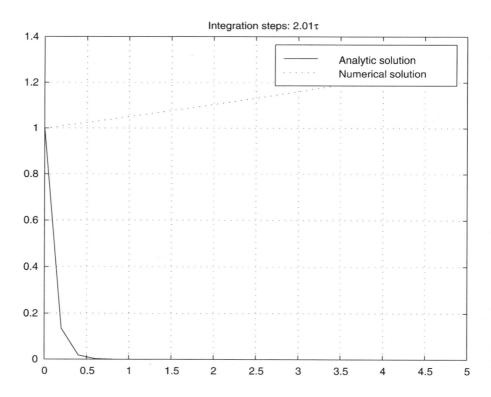

Figure 14.5 Large integration steps: the system is unstable.

with initial conditions

$$w_1(0) = 1$$
$$w_2(0) = 0$$

The solution, as the reader can easily verify, is

$$w_1 = 2e^{-t} - e^{-at}$$
$$w_2 = -e^{-t} + e^{-at}$$

that is, the solution is the sum of two exponentials, the first one with time constant $\tau_1 = 1$, and the second one with time constant $\tau_2 = 1/a$. As long as τ_1 and τ_2 are of the same order of magnitude, the system can be efficiently solved with an algorithm like ode23. For this purpose we must prepare the odefile

```
function wd = stiff(t,w,flag,a);
A =   [a-2, 2*(a-1);
        1-a, 1-2*a];
wd = A*w;
```

and run the simulation with the commands:

```
≫ tspan = [0,10];
≫ w0 = [1;0];
≫ a = 2; tic; [t,w] = ode23('stiff',tspan,w0,[],a); toc
```

So far so good, the numerical solution is correct (you are invited to compare it with the analytic solution) and the computation time reasonable. Let us now change the value of a from 2 to 2000:

```
≫ a=2000; tic; [t,w] = ode23('stiff',tspan,w0,[],a); toc
```

Now the solution takes much longer; on our computer more than 100 times longer. To add insult to injury, a simple investigation reveals that the term responsible for the extremely large number of integration cycles and therefore for the length of the computation, is $-e^{-at}$, a component whose contribution to the solution, for such a large value of a, soon becomes insignificant. Such a system is said to be **stiff**. It is hard to give a precise definition of stiffness, since this is a qualitative, not a quantitative property. Stiff subsystems are not always easy to recognize from their mathematical formulation. A useful definition of stiffness should take into account not only the equations that define the system, but also the time frame we want to analyse. Our example is stiff if we want to study its solution in the interval [0, 5] but is not stiff if we want to analyse it in the first few thousands of a second.

Runge–Kutta and predictor–corrector methods are incapable of treating efficiently stiff problems, since the length of the integration steps they can take is bounded by the time constant of the fast subsystem. To solve a stiff system we need an algorithm that is capable of taking integration steps much, much larger than the minimum time constant of the system. The first algorithm of this kind was devised by William Gear (English, 1935). Its strategy is to solve Equation 14.17 by an implicit method, like the Newton–Raphson method show in Section 7.5. We have seen there that the solution to the equation

$$\phi(x) = 0$$

can often be obtained by starting with a good guess and then solving iteratively the linear equation:

$$0 = \phi(x_i) + \phi'(x_i)(x_{i+1} - x_i)$$

The method maintains its validity also when x, instead of a scalar, is a vector of n components, $[x_1, x_2, \ldots, x_n]$, and ϕ, instead of a single equation, is a system of equations:

$$
\begin{aligned}
\phi_1(x) &= 0 \\
\phi_2(x) &= 0 \\
\vdots\;\; &= \vdots \\
\phi_n(x) &= 0
\end{aligned}
$$

The role of the derivative, in this case, is played by the **jacobian**, which is defined as the matrix, $\partial\phi/\partial x$, of the (i, j) component:

$$\left(\frac{\partial\phi}{\partial x}\right)_{i,j} = \frac{\partial\phi_i}{\partial x_j}$$

The equation we want to solve is then (replace w_{k+1} simply by x):

$$\phi(x) = -x + w_k + \frac{\dot{w}_k + f(t_{k+1}, x)}{2}(t_{k+1} - t_k)$$

and the jacobian of ϕ is

$$\frac{\partial\phi}{\partial x} = \left[-I_n + \frac{\partial f(t_k, x_k)}{\partial w} \cdot \frac{t_{k+1} - t_k}{2}\right]$$

where I_n denotes the n-by-n identity matrix.

The Newton–Ralphson method directs us to solve the implicit equation by iteratively computing x_{i+1} as the solution of the linear system

$$0 = \phi(x_i) + \frac{\partial\phi}{\partial x}(x_i)(x_{i+1} - x_i) \tag{14.18}$$

The first guess is not a problem. Many stiff routines use the predictor to produce a reasonable first guess, the same one used by the predictor-corrector. Also, the
number of times to repeat the iteration varies from implementation to implementation. Solving the linear equation is an operation that today can be performed quite
efficiently, so most time is usually spent in the computation of the jacobian. It is
true that stiff algorithms allow us to take large integration steps, but if we had to
perform at each step the complete computation of finding numerically the jacobian
(for instance by numerical perturbation) and solving the linear system described by
Equation 14.18, the computation would probably be so slow that we would be better
sticking to old faithful Runge–Kutta.

In practice good implementations of this strategy compute the jacobian not
at each step, but only when necessary. At each step the algorithm tries to use the
previous jacobian, and only if some accuracy test fails it computes the jacobian anew.
MATLAB, in addition, lets you:

- inform the solver that the jacobian has special properties, like being vectorized
  or sparse;

- inform the solver that the system is linear, i.e. that the jacobian remains constant
  and never needs to be recomputed;

- pass the jacobian to the solver, if you can compute it, for example, in closed
  form.

For an explanation of this, and other less common properties, we refer the reader
to the manual or to the text displayed when you type

```
>> help odeset
```

Stiff odesolvers in our version of MATLAB are ode23s and ode15s.

14.5 Conclusion: how to choose the odesolver

In this section you receive the rewards for having read the previous one. So, how
do you choose the odesolver? There is no general rule valid in every case, and what
follows is a list of suggestions derived mainly from our experience.

The first and most critical decision is whether to use a stiff solver, or a non-
stiff one, like those based on Runge–Kutta and predictor-corrector methods. There is
usually little advantage in choosing a stiff odesolver, unless our system is composed of
subsystems whose time constants differ by at least two or three orders of magnitude.
To find these time constants, it can be useful to compute the eigenvalues of the
linearized system, but it is usually your engineering intuition that should suggest to you
whether the system described can be broken down into subsystems of different time
constants. Answering affirmatively to this question is a necessary but not sufficient
condition to opt for a stiff solver. Stiff solvers take large integration steps, at the
expense of introducing large errors in the description of the fast subsystem. If you
are not interested in taking large steps, or if this error is unacceptable for the kind of
analysis you are performing, do not choose a stiff solver.

The second factor you should take into account is that the cost of each full integration step is usually very large, so choose a stiff solver only if you think that there will be no need to recompute the jacobian at each step (this happens if your system is linear or quasi-linear). This condition can certainly be mitigated, if you can and are willing to compute the jacobian and provide it to the solver. If you decide that you are going to use a stiff solver, please go carefully through all the options offered to you by odeset and activate those that apply to your case. If you decided not to use a stiff solver, you are left with less critical decisions.

Generally, it can be said that a predictor-corrector is superior to a Runge–Kutta routine in the absence of discontinuous phenomena, i.e. when the polynomial extrapolation represents a good prediction. On the other hand, when the prediction is misleading, the predictor-corrector is usually inferior to a Runge–Kutta solver. Such is the case in the well-known example of simulating a ball bouncing on a table. Here the predicted trajectory of the ball is to penetrate the table. The MATLAB algorithm based on a predictor-corrector is capable of coping with a discontinuity of this kind, but only at the price of a loss of efficiency. Alternatively, you could write some extra code, to help MATLAB treating the discontinuity present when the ball hits the table. Such a phenomenon is called, in MATLAB language, an **event**, but we feel that event handling is a subject beyond the scope of this book, and we refer you to the MATLAB manual. To simulate this or similar systems, unless you want to learn how to describe events efficiently, it is probably better just to use a Runge–Kutta algorithm.

A last advice about the order of integration. Higher-order algorithms, like ode45, are usually superior to the corresponding lower-order ones, like ode23, when describing smooth systems. Lower-order algorithms are sometimes more efficient, especially in the presence of discontinuities, or when the precision requirements are less stringent.

Before ending this chapter, we want to mention SIMULINK. This is a MATLAB toolbox, developed by MathWorks to simulate dynamic systems. It allows you to describe the system also in graphic form, it contains a number of additional odesolvers and is fully integrated with MATLAB. For more information, you should contact a MATLAB distributor.

14.6   Exercises

Solutions for Exercises 14.2, 14.3, 14.4, 14.7, 14.10 and 14.12 appear at the back of the book.

■ **EXERCISE 14.1**   Linear, time-invariant system
Using the ode23 or ode45 function, solve the system of differential equations

$$\mathbf{w}' = \mathbf{A}\mathbf{w}$$

in the interval $[t_0, t_f]$, with initial condition $\mathbf{w}(t_0) = \mathbf{w}_0$, and plot the results.
Parameters:

$$\mathbf{A} = \begin{bmatrix} -0.5 & 1 \\ -1 & -0.5 \end{bmatrix}, \quad t_0 = 0, \quad t_f = 4\pi, \quad \mathbf{w}_0 = \begin{bmatrix} 0 \\ 1 \end{bmatrix}$$

■ **EXERCISE 14.2**   Linear, time-varying equations
Using the `ode23` or `ode45` function, solve the following differential equations with given initial conditions, in the interval $[t_0, t_f]$, and plot the results:

(1) $$w' + (1.2 + \sin 10t)w = 0, \quad t_0 = 0, \quad t_f = 5, \quad w(t_0) = 1$$

(2) $$3w' + \frac{1}{1 + t^2}w = \cos t, \quad t_0 = 0, \quad t_f = 5, \quad w(t_0) = 1$$

■ **EXERCISE 14.3**   Linear, higher-order equations
Using the `ode23` or `ode45` function, solve the following differential equations with given initial conditions, in the interval $[t_0, t_f]$, and plot the results:

(1) $$(1 + t^2)w'' + 2tw' + 3w = 2, \quad t_0 = 0, \quad t_f = 5, \quad w(t_0) = 0, \quad w'(t_0) = 1$$

(2) $$w''' - 5\frac{\cos 2t}{(t + 1)^2}w'' + w' + \frac{1}{3 + \sin t}w = \cos t, \quad t_0 = 0,$$

$$t_f = 5, \quad w(t_0) = 1, \quad w'(t_0) = 0, \quad w''(t_0) = 2$$

Hint: Rewrite an equation of order n as a first-order system in the vector

$$\mathbf{z} = \begin{bmatrix} w \\ w' \\ w'' \\ \vdots \\ w^{(n-1)} \end{bmatrix}$$

■ **EXERCISE 14.4**   Dog chasing his master
A number of interesting curves are the trajectories of a point D moving at constant speed while always pointing towards another point M that moves along a known path. Such a method of tracking is known as **dog-tracking** because it resembles the path followed by a dog chasing his master. Similar curves are those followed by a vessel chasing another vessel and by some ground-to-air or air-to-air missiles.

Figure 14.6 shows the trajectory of the master (upper curve) and that of the dog (lower curve). Then, at each instant the velocity vector v_D of the dog has constant magnitude vel_D and is directed from the position of the dog, indicated by a star, to that of the master, indicated by a small circle. Thus, in vector notation we write

$$\vec{v}_D = vel_D \frac{\vec{M} - \vec{D}}{|\vec{M} - \vec{D}|}$$

Compute and plot the trajectories of the dog in the following two cases.

(1)   The master moves on a straight line and the parameters of the problem are:
Initial dog position $(x_0, y_0) = (0, 0)$.
Dog speed $vel_D = 10 \, \mathrm{m \, s^{-1}}$.
The position of the master at time t is $x_M = vel_M t$, $y_M = 100 \, \mathrm{m}$, and the master speed $vel_M = 5 \, \mathrm{m \, s^{-1}}$.
Initial and final time $t_0 = 0, t_f = 10 \, \mathrm{s}$.

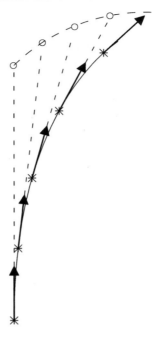

Figure 14.6   The curve described by a dog chasing his master.

(2)   The dog is in the centre of a circular pond of radius r, while his master M walks
on the bank at a constant velocity vel_M. The dog swims at a constant speed
vel_D, always pointing towards his master, as shown in Figure 14.6. Plot the
trajectory of the dog in the interval $[t_0, t_f]$. The parameters of the problem are:
$r = 15$ m.
Initial dog position $(x_0, y_0) = (0, 0)$.
Dog speed $vel_D = 2.5$ m s^{-1}.
Master speed $vel_D = 2$ m s^{-1}.

■ **EXERCISE 14.5**   Cats chasing each other
Four cats are in the four corners of a square room of unitary base. At time $t = 0$ they
start chasing each other at unitary velocity, so that cat No. 1 runs in the direction of cat
No. 2, cat No. 2, in the direction of cat No. 3, cat No. 3, in the direction of cat No. 4
and cat No. 4, in the direction of cat No. 1, until they meet in the centre of the room.
Figure 14.7 shows the trajectories followed by the four cats. In particular, it can be
seen how cat No. 1 always points in the direction of cat No. 2.
    Using ODE23, compute and plot the trajectories of the cats. If you are
mathematically oriented, you can enjoy computing the length of the trajectories
analytically, generalize the problem to rooms of different shape, like a regular polygon,
or in higher dimensions (flying cats in a tetrahedral room), and so on.

■ **EXERCISE 14.6**   Foxes and rabbits
A well-known ecosystem due to Vito Volterra (Italian, 1860–1940; see, for example,
Kahaner, Moler and Nash, 1989 or Giordano and Weir 1991) considers two

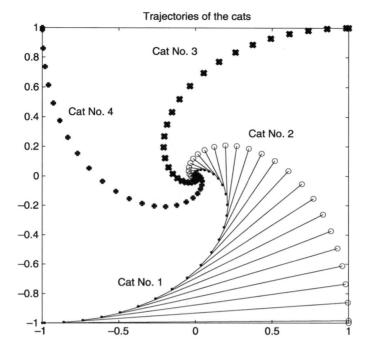

Figure 14.7   The curves described by the four cats.

populations of rabbits and foxes, related by the equations

$$\frac{dr}{dt} = 2r - \alpha r f$$

$$\frac{df}{dt} = -f + \alpha r f$$

where r is the number of rabbits, f, the number of foxes and the time, t, is given in
years. Using `ode23`, compute and plot the solution of the differential system, for
$\alpha = 0.01$ and initial conditions $r_0 = 300$ and $f_0 = 150$, over the time interval $[0, 25]$.

■ **EXERCISE 14.7**   Pendulum
The motion of an ideal pendulum of length l (see Figure 14.8) is governed by the
equation

$$\theta'' = -gl \sin \theta \tag{14.19}$$

where θ is the angle of the pendulum from the vertical. Find θ as a function of t, in the
time interval $[0, 10]$, and plot θ and θ' as functions of time. Parameters:
$g = 9.81 \, \text{m s}^{-2}, l = 0.5 \, \text{m}$. Initial conditions: $\theta(0) = 1$ radian, $\theta'(0) = 0 \, \text{rad s}^{-1}$. Do
not be surprised if the graphs of θ and θ' look like sinusoids. The sinusoid is the
solution of the linearized model obtained by substituting $\sin \theta$ by θ in Equation 14.19.
The linearized model is an excellent one, as long as the angle θ and its derivative

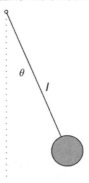

Figure 14.8   A pendulum.

remain in the neighbourhood of 0. To see that θ and θ' are not sinusoids, repeat the simulation with a large value of $\theta'(0)$.

■ **EXERCISE 14.8**   Ballistics
A simple ballistic model assumes that only two forces act on the projectile, namely gravity and drag. According to this model, the equations of motion are

$$m v'_x = -W v_x/v$$
$$m v'_y = -W v_y/v - mg$$

Here v_x, v_y are the components of the velocity and v its magnitude. The drag W is given by the equation

$$W = c_w \frac{\rho}{2} v^2 \frac{\pi}{4} d^2$$

The symbol c_w is called the **drag coefficient** and is nearly constant as long as the flight is at subsonic speed, ρ is the air density and d, the diameter of the projectile.

(1)   Plot the trajectory, using the following parameters: $g = 9.81 \text{ m s}^{-2}$, $m = 10 \text{ kg}$, $c_w = 0.2$, $\rho = 1.225 \text{ kg m}^{-3}$, $d = 0.050 \text{ m}$. The initial conditions are $x_0 = 0 \text{ m}$, $y_0 = 0 \text{ m}$, $v_0 = 250 \text{ m s}^{-1}$ and the gun elevation equals $\pi/6$.

(2)   If you used `ode23` with the default value of `tol`, the graph of the trajectory is unpleasant, due to the small number of resulting points. Repeat the problem at (a), but produce a smoother graph by defining the parameter `tol` to be 5e–4, instead of the default tolerance, which is equal to 1e–3.

■ **EXERCISE 14.9**   Discharge from tank
A cylindrical tank of radius R is filled with water as shown in Figure 14.9. The water spills from a large orifice of radius r. Let h be the water level above the orifice axis. At each instant, h satisfies the following differential equation

$$h' = C\sqrt{2gh}\left(\frac{r}{R}\right)^2 \tag{14.20}$$

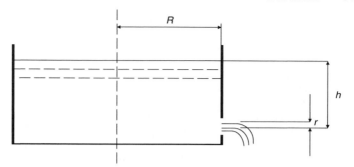

Figure 14.9 Flow from tank.

where g is the gravity acceleration and C the discharge coefficient. For the purpose of this exercise, assume C to be constant.

Plot the height of the liquid as a function of time, for t from 0 to 100 seconds.

Parameters: $R = 1.0$ m, $r = 0.1$ m, $g = 9.81$ m s^{-2}, $C = 0.6$. Initial condition: $h_0 = 1$ m.

■ **EXERCISE 14.10** Pliny's intermittent fountain

Legend says that Pliny the Elder (Gaius Plinius Secundus, Roman, 23–79) had an intermittent fountain in his garden. It is fun to construct a model of such a fountain, schematically depicted in Figure 14.10. The water enters the cylindrical tank of radius R with constant flow ϕ_{in}, and fills it until it reaches the level h_{hi}. Then the water discharges through a pipe ending with a circular nozzle of radius r, until the water level in the tank decreases to the value h_{lo} and the syphon fills with air. The fountain then remains dry until the water in the tank again reaches the level h_{hi} and the cycle repeats itself.

The inflow, ϕ_{in}, is constant, while the outflow is either zero, when the syphon is empty, or equal to the following expression

$$\phi_{out} = C\sqrt{2gh}\,\pi r^2 \qquad\qquad (14.21)$$

when the syphon is full.

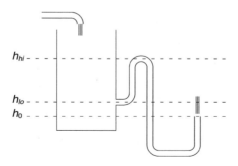

Figure 14.10 Intermittent fountain.

The parameters of the problem:

Radius of the base of the tank	$R = 0.05$ m
Radius of the discharge nozzle	$r = 0.005$ m
Maximum level of the syphon	$h_{hi} = 0.1$ m
Minimum level of the syphon	$h_{lo} = 0.025$ m
Discharge coefficient	$C = 0.6$
Gravity acceleration	$g = 9.81$ m s^{-2}
Flow of water entering the tank	$\phi_{in} = 50\mathrm{e}{-6}$ m^3 s^{-1}

Initial conditions: $t_0 = 0$, $h_0 = 0$. At time t_0 the syphon is empty.

Find and plot the level of the water in the tank, as a function of time, running ode23 or ode45 over 100 seconds. You can neglect the volume of water in the pipe.

Hint: This problem is very similar to the preceding one, but an additional variable is needed to keep track of whether the syphon is full or empty. The value of this variable must be preserved from one integration step to the next, and the way to achieve this in MATLAB is to define it as global or persistent.

■ **EXERCISE 14.11**   RLC circuit

Figure 14.11 represents a simple electric circuit consisting of a voltage source, E, a resistor, R, an inductance, L, and a capacitance, C. The voltage source produces ac current with

$$E = E_0 \sin(2\pi f t)$$

From zero initial conditions, compute the charge q of the capacitance and the current i that circulates in the circuit, and plot q and i as functions of time, from 0 to 100 milliseconds. Use ode23 with tol = 1.0e-4. Parameters: $E_0 = 5$ V, $f = 400$ Hz, $R = 20$ ohm, $C = 100$ mF, $L = 50$ mH.

Hint: By Kirchhoff's second law

$$L\frac{di}{dt} + Ri + \frac{q}{C} = E$$

Also, $i = q'$.

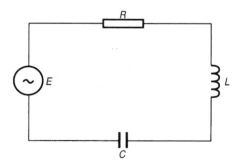

Figure 14.11   An ac series circuit.

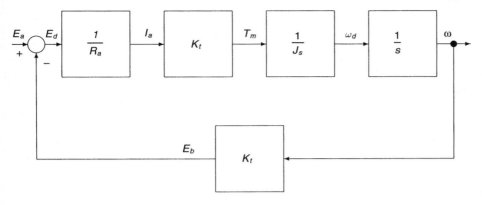

Figure 14.12   Simplified model of dc motor.

■ **EXERCISE 14.12**   DC motor

Figure 14.12 shows the block diagram of the simplified model of a dc motor, with a flywheel attached to its rotor.

E_a is the applied voltage, R_a denotes the armature resistance, so $I_a = (E_a - E_b)/R_a$ is the armature current, K_t denotes the torque sensitivity, so T_m is the torque, J_s denotes the inertia (rotor + flywheel) and finally E_b is the back emf. The model neglects the armature inductance, frictional losses and so on, but is certainly adequate for many applications.

(a)   From initial conditions $\omega_0 = 0$, we apply constant voltage $E_a = 15\,\text{V}$. Compute and plot ω as a function of time, for t from 0 to 2 seconds. Parameters: $R_a = 20\,\text{ohm}$, $K_t = 0.03\,\text{volt/rad/s}$, $J_s = 10^{-5}\,\text{kg m}^2$.

(b)   Using `ginput`, find the approximate time constant of the system.

   Hint: Compute the asymptotic velocity ω_∞, the one that produces a back emf equal to the applied voltage. Plot the graph of ω together with that of the horizontal line at

$$\left(1 - \frac{1}{e}\right)\omega_\infty$$

and read the coordinates of the point where the two curves meet.

Chapter 15
Control

15.1 Introduction

The basic MATLAB package contains a number of functions that are very useful for designing feedback control systems. There are also specialized toolboxes that provide more functions. Some of them, such as the MATLAB Control Toolbox, are available from MathWorks, the distributor of MATLAB. Whether you like classical approaches like root locus, frequency analysis and optimal control, or more recent methods, such as robust control, μ-analysis and quantitative feedback, you will be surprised how MATLAB will shorten the time required to analyse or design a control system. Days of cumbersome computations, often aided by graphical and mechanical accessories like the **Spirule**, are replaced by the time necessary to write a few lines of code. This chapter assumes that the reader is familiar with the basic concepts of control theory; the purpose is not to teach control, but to show how the use of MATLAB can help in solving control problems.

We have tried as much as possible to use only MATLAB functions that are part of the basic package. Only a few examples require access to M-files that belong to the Control Toolbox. We have purposely avoided any reference to the Robust Control, Quantitative Feedback Theory and μ-analysis Toolboxes. They are based on advanced theories, which are not yet widely known. A good indication of the validity of MATLAB in these fields is given in the preface of one of the best books on control theory which has appeared recently, *Multivariable Feedback Design*, by Jan Maciejowski (1991), where the author states that all examples and exercises have been solved with the help of MATLAB or one of the Toolboxes.

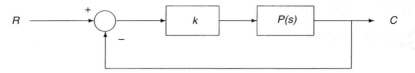

Figure 15.1   Canonical configuration of a feedback plant.

The rest of this chapter is divided into three sections, each showing how MAT-LAB can be used effectively in solving control problems, using different design approaches.

15.2   Root locus design

The basis of the root-locus synthesis technique is the observation that often the transient response of a system is largely determined by the position of the poles of the closed-loop transfer function in the complex plane. It is then imperative for the control engineer to place such poles in the positions that ensure the desired response. A common method is to construct a number of compensating networks, depending on a continuous parameter k, construct the root locus of the closed-loop system corresponding to each k, and then select the one that best meets the specifications of the system. Very often, as in Figure 15.1, such a parameter is the gain, and in this case the method is called **gain-factor compensation**.

We shall only consider the particular, but by no means uncommon, case where $P(s)$ is a rational function. This allows us to express $P(s)$ as the ratio of two polynomials, $N(s)$ and $D(s)$. In this case the poles of the closed-loop system are simply the roots of $D(s) + kN(s)$. The control engineer, who used to compute the approximate position of these poles by time-consuming methods (computation of break-away points, breakaway directions, asymptotic behaviour, and so on) will certainly appreciate the benefits of using MATLAB, as the following example shows.

Let us consider a plant having the following open-loop transfer function

$$P(s) = \frac{1}{s(s+2)(s+4)}$$

Our goal is to find a gain compensator, so that the complex pair of closed-loop poles have a damping ratio $\zeta = 0.5$. First of all, we display the root locus of the system

```
≫ den = [1 6 8 0]; % define den
≫ num = [0 0 0 1]; % define num, fill with 0's
≫ k = logspace(-2, 2, 50)'; % define significant gains
≫ for n = 1:50
        r(:,n) = roots(den + k(n)*num);
  end
```

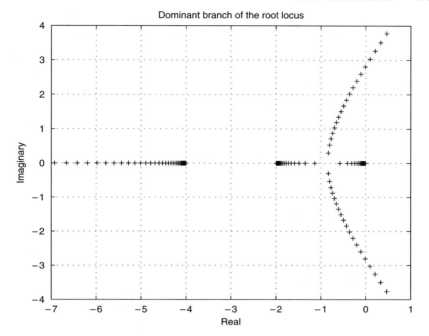

Figure 15.2   Root locus.

We find the real parts of the roots with

```
≫ rr = real(r);
```

and their imaginary parts with

```
≫ ri = imag(r);
```

The commands for plotting are

```
≫ plot(rr, ri, 'b+')
≫ xlabel('Real')
≫ ylabel('Imaginary')
```

The resulting graph is shown in Figure 15.2. A preliminary inspection shows that the damping ratio is determined by the second root

```
≫ plot(rr(2,:),ri(2,:),'b+'); % plot the second root
≫ title('Dominant branch of the root locus');
```

The design specifications can be translated into the problem of determining the value of k, such that the corresponding root, in MATLAB notation `r = rr + sqrt(-1)*ri`, on the dominant branch satisfies the relation

$$\frac{|rr|}{|r|} = \zeta \tag{15.1}$$

The proof can be found, for example, in the chapter on **root locus** in d'Azzo and Houpis (1988).

Let us display in tabular form, for each gain, k, the corresponding damping ratio, ζ:

```
≫ [k, abs((rr(2,:))./abs(r(2,:)))']
ans =
       0.0100        1.0000
       0.0121        1.0000
        . . .
       5.9636        0.6433
       7.1969        0.5592
       8.6851        0.4817
        . . .
      82.8643        0.0943
     100.0000        0.1222
```

We can plot these data by

```
≫ plot(k, abs(rr(2,:))./abs(r(2,:)));
≫ grid
≫ xlabel('k'); ylabel('Damping ratio');
```

The results are shown in Figure 15.3.

From here we see, by visual inspection, that the design specification is met when the value of the gain is slightly larger than 8. Alternatively you can use the mouse and pick up the value of k, from the graph, by means of the MATLAB `ginput` function. If you have the Control Toolbox, you can obtain a more precise value for the gain, using the `rlocfind` function.

If you often have to compute root loci, it may be convenient for you to have access to the `rlocus` function in the Control Toolbox. It performs essentially the same computation that we have shown in this chapter, but it accepts other definitions of the plant besides its transfer function (see the preceding chapter) and uses an algorithm that, while somewhat more complicated, is both faster and more precise.

15.3   Design in the frequency domain

When designing a control system in the frequency domain, a great deal of information on performance and stability can often be obtained from examining its Bode diagrams for the open-loop, total-loop and closed-loop transfer functions.

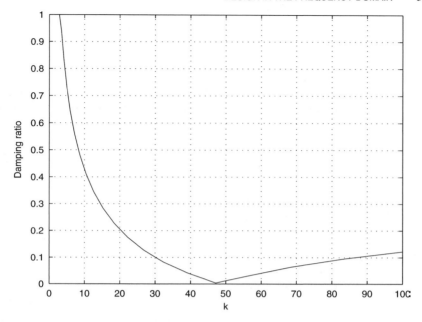

Figure 15.3 Damping ratio versus gain.

If the plant is defined by a transfer function, $P(s)$, that is, a quotient of two polynomials, $N(s)$ to $D(s)$, as in the great majority of practical engineering cases, the Bode diagram of the **open-loop transfer function** is composed of two curves. The x-axis of both curves represents the significant frequencies ω, either in hertz or in rad s^{-1}, usually on a logarithmic scale. The y-axis of the first curve represents the magnitude of the transfer function, in decibels, and the y-axis of the second curve is the phase, usually in degrees.

Consider, for example, the plant defined by the transfer function

$$H(s) = 2\frac{1}{s(s/3+1)(s/4+1)} \tag{15.2}$$

The open-loop Bode diagram is obtained by the commands

```
≫ pk = 2;
≫ pnum = [0 0 0 1];
≫ pden = [1/12 7/12 1 0];
```

where pk is the Bode gain, pnum, the vector of numerator coefficients, and pden, the vector of denominator coefficients. We could have simply defined pnum as

```
≫ pnum = 1
```

instead of

```
>> pnum = [0 0 0 1]
```

but, as we shall shortly see, it is good practice to pad pnum with zeros, and have the two arrays pnum and pden of the same size. We build a scale of significant frequencies in rad s^{-1} by

```
>> om = logspace(-2, 2);
```

The numerical values, ol, and the corresponding magnitudes of the open-loop transfer function, in decibels, olmag, are obtained from

```
>> s = sqrt(-1)*om;
>> ol = polyval(pk*pnum, s)./polyval(pden, s);
>> olmag = 20*log10(abs(ol));
```

The phase angles, in degrees, olpha, are calculated by

```
>> olpha=180/pi*angle(ol);
```

Finally we plot the magnitude curve with the commands

```
>> semilogx(om, olmag);
>> grid
>> xlabel('Frequency (rad/sec)')
>> ylabel('Magnitude (db)')
>> title('Bode magnitude plot - open loop')
```

The results are shown in Figure 15.4. The phase curve is obtained with

```
>> semilogx(om, olpha);
>> grid
>> xlabel('Frequency (rad/sec)')
>> ylabel('Phase (degrees)')
>> title('Bode phase plot - open loop')
```

and it is shown in Figure 15.5.

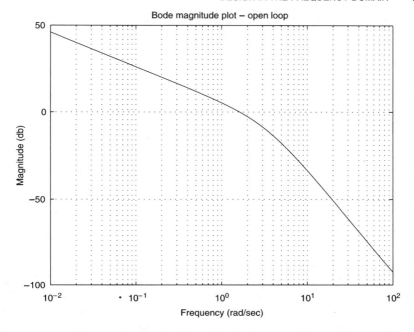

Figure 15.4   Bode magnitude plot.

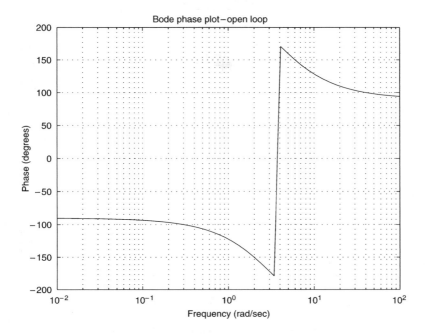

Figure 15.5   Bode phase plot.

The phase plot is not a continuous line, as its graph jumps from -180 to $+180$ degrees. If you have access to the unwrap function, you can change the definition of olpha to

```
>> olpha = 180/pi*unwrap(angle(ol));
```

and plot the result

```
>> semilogx(om, olpha);
>> grid
>> xlabel('Frequency (rad/sec)')
>> ylabel('Phase (degrees)')
>> title('Bode phase plot - open loop')
```

The results are shown in Figure 15.6.

Let us embed the plant just defined in a unit feedback system, like that in Figure 15.7. There are a number of quantities commonly used by control engineers to define different characteristics of the system, such as **gain crossover frequency**, **gain margin**, **phase crossover frequency**, **phase margin**, **bandwidth**, **resonant**

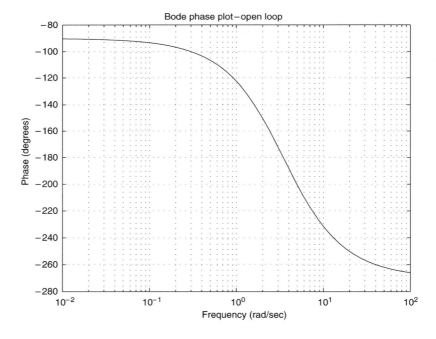

Figure 15.6 Unwrapped Bode phase plot.

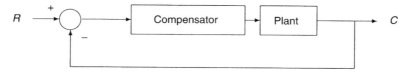

Figure 15.7 An automatic plant with compensator.

peak, **resonance frequency**, and so on, defined in virtually any book on control, for example in d'Azzo and Houpis (1988). All these quantities can be easily determined with the help of MATLAB. Let us compute a few of them.

First, let us recall that, for most systems encountered in practice, it is possible to define the **gain crossover frequency**, ω_1, as the frequency for which $|H(i\omega_1)| = 1$, and the **phase crossover frequency**, ω_π as the frequency for which $\arg |H(i\omega_\pi)| = -\pi$. Then, the **gain margin** is the inverse of $|H(i\omega_{pi})|$, that is, the largest gain k we can put in cascade in front of the plant before the system becomes unstable. Similarly the **phase margin** is the number of degrees the argument of $H(i\omega_1)$ is above $-\pi$.

The values of ω_1 and ω_π can be read from the Bode diagrams just produced, either by visual inspection, or with the help of the ginput function. Alternatively, we can display the values of om and olmag with the command [om' olmag'] and read the value of ω_1, namely om, in the row where olmag is closest to 0 db. We obtain $\omega_1 \approx 1.6666$ rad/s.

If you have the Control Toolbox, a faster and more precise way to compute the stability margins is by invoking the bode and margin functions with the commands

```
>> [mag, pha, w] = bode(pk*pnum, pden);
>> [Gm, Pm, Wcg, Wcp] = margin(mag, pha, w)
```

This produces the gain margin, Gm, the phase margin, Pm, the gain crossover frequency, $\omega_1 =$ Wcp, and the phase crossover frequency $\omega_\pi =$ Wcg. For the plant examined, MATLAB gives $\omega_1 = 1.6248$.

The resonance peak and resonance frequency are usually given for the closed-loop function. We begin by calculating the closed-loop transfer function

```
>> cl = ol ./ (1+ol);
```

and obtain the closed-loop magnitude, in db, and the phase, in degrees,

```
>> clmag = 20*log10(abs(cl));
>> clpha= 180/pi*unwrap(angle(cl));
```

The approximate peak magnitude, 3.4633 db, and resonance frequency, 1.9307 rad/s, can be read from the graph with the help of the ginput function, or, alternatively, displayed by

```
>> [Mp, Mppos] = max(clmag)
>> om(Mppos)
```

Another way to compute the closed-loop values of a given plant is by means of its transfer function. Here the advantage of having pnum and pden of the same size is apparent. The closed-loop transfer function is defined by its gain, clk, and the coefficients clnum and clden of the numerator and denominator polynomials. They are given by the following simple formulae:

```
>> clk = pk;
```

for the gain,

```
>> clnum = pnum;
```

for the numerator, and

```
>> clden = pk*pnum + pden;
```

for the denominator. We can now plot the Bode diagram as we did for the transfer function of the open loop.

There is another way to produce Bode diagrams. So far we have called the bode function with three left-hand-side arguments. The same bode function, when called without left-hand-side arguments, plots a Bode diagram. Thus, the results of the command line

```
>> num = clk*clnum; den = clden; bode(num, den)
```

are shown in Figure 15.8.

Besides Bode diagrams, there are other common graphic representations of transfer functions; the Control Toolbox contains functions to display them with minimum effort. In particular, the nichols and nyquist functions compute and display Nichols charts and Nyquist diagrams with a syntax similar to that of the bode function already encountered. For example, the Nichols chart of the plant described in Equation 15.2 can be produced by the command

```
>> num = 2; den = [ 1/12 7/12 1 0 ]; nichols(num, den)
```

The results are shown in Figure 15.9.

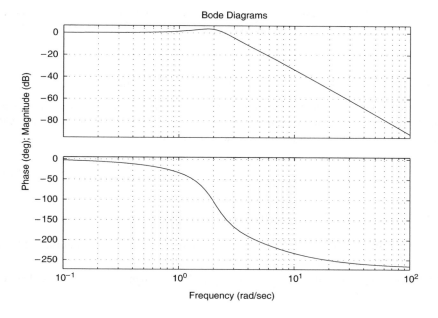

Figure 15.8 Closed-loop Bode diagram.

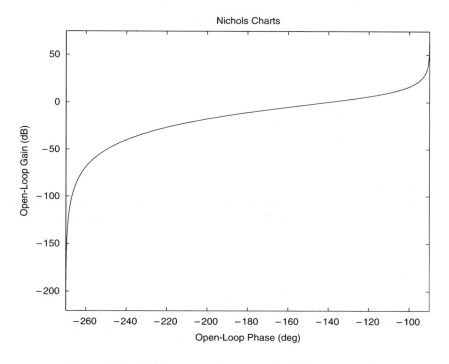

Figure 15.9 Nichols chart of plant described by Equation 15.2.

From now to the end of the chapter, we shall assume that the user has access to the Control Toolbox, as we are going to use some functions that are not part of the basic MATLAB package.

EXAMPLE 15.1   A control design in the frequency domain _____

We want to embed the plant defined by Equation 15.2 in a feedback control design as shown in Figure 15.7. We are requested to stabilize the plant by means of a gain-lead compensator which, by definition, has the transfer function

$$G(s) = ck\frac{1 + s/Z}{1 + s/P} \tag{15.3}$$

and need to meet the following design requirements:

Error condition – the position error for a ramp input should be smaller than 25% of the slope of the ramp;

Stability condition – the phase margin should be approximately equal to 40 degrees (± 5 degrees).

It is convenient to express Z as $Z = \omega_M/\alpha$, and P as $P = \omega_M \cdot \alpha$. Here ω_M is the frequency where the lead compensator produces the maximum lead angle, and such a lead angle is usually indicated as Φ_M. It is well known that Φ_M is related to α by the relation

$$\alpha = \left[\frac{1 + \sin \Phi_M}{1 - \sin \Phi_M}\right]^{1/2}$$

or, equivalently,

$$\Phi_M = \arcsin \frac{\alpha^2 - 1}{\alpha^2 + 1}$$

For the proof, see, for example, Dorf (1992).

The design is usually accomplished as follows: first ck is determined, from the error condition, then α and, finally, Φ_M. We begin by defining the plant, but this time we let MATLAB do the algebra of the coefficients

```
≫ pk = 2;              % plant Bode gain
≫ pnum = [0 0 0 1];    % coefficients of plant numerator
≫ pden1 = [1 0];       % plant denominator factor
≫ pden2 = [1/3 1];     % second plant denominator factor
≫ pden3 = [1/4 1];     % last plant denominator factor
```

Remember that the coefficients of a polynomial which, like our denominator, is the product of a number of terms, are obtained as the convolution of the coefficients of the individual factors (see Subsection 1.6.4). Therefore pden is given by

```
>> pden = conv(pden1, conv(pden2, pden3));
```

The error condition requires that the open-loop Bode gain, $ck \cdot pk$, be greater than or equal to 4, that is, ck is greater than or equal to 2. Let us choose the value 2:

```
>> ck = 2;
```

Let us now examine the stability of the plant, compensated only with the gain ck. The numerator with the new Bode gain is given by

```
>> num = ck*pk*pnum;
```

while the denominator remains unchanged

```
>> den = pden;
```

We can now compute the phase margin

```
>> [mag, pha, w] = bode(num, den);
>> [Gm, Pm, Wcg, Wcp] = margin(mag, pha, w);
```

The phase margin Pm is approximately 17 degrees, which is 23 degrees short of the requirements.

Books on classical control, such as Dorf (1992), suggest the design parameter α should be chosen so that it provides a lead of slightly more than 23 degrees, say 30 to 35 degrees, and give practical rules for the determination of ω_M, in MATLAB wm.

The reader will find it advantageous to use a slightly different strategy, made possible only by the efficient way in which MATLAB computes the **margins**. In the following M-file, we invite the user to select the lead angle Φ_M and then plot, for a large number of values of wm, the phase margin as a function of candidate ω_M values.

Assume that ck, pk, pnum and pden are defined in the workspace, as we did at the beginning of the section. Now prepare an M-file fndwma1.m (abbreviation of 'find wm and alpha'), containing the following lines

```
num = ck*pk*pnum;          % numerator with new Bode gain
den = pden;                % denominator
% --- compute phase margin
```

```
[mag, pha, w] = bode(num, den);
[Gm, Pm, Wcg,Wcp] = margin(mag,pha,w);

% --- display results and prompt user for lead angle phimax

str1   =' Phase margin = ';
str    = [str1 num2str(Pm)] % display the string

phimax = input(' Please enter phimax  --- > ');
% --- compute al from phimax

leadrad = pi/180*phimax;    % phimax in radians
sn  = sin(leadrad);         % its sine
al  = sqrt ((1+sn)/(1-sn));
% --- wm is the frequency where the maximum lead angle is
%     produced and is certainly larger than Wcp.

% --- Plot the phase margin versus wm
nwm = 50;                   % number of wm
awm = linspace(Wcp, 10*Wcp, 50); % array of wm-s.

% make space for array of phase margin
[ rows, cols ] = size(awm); apm = zeros(rows, cols);

% --- next big loop prepares the data for the graph of
%     phase margin as a function of wm

for l=1:nwm,
    wm = awm(l);
    cnum = [1/(wm/al) 1];% numerator 1 + s/Z (Z=wm/al)
    cden = [1/(wm*al) 1];% denominator + s/P (P=wm*al)
    num  = ck*pk*conv(cnum, pnum);
    den  =     conv(cden, pden);
    % --- Compute and save phase margin for this design

    [mag, pha, w]=bode(num, den);
    [Gm, Pm, Wcg, Wcp] = margin(mag,pha,w);
    apm(l) = Pm; % array of phase margins, relative to wm
end
plot(awm, apm);
str = ['phi-max = ' num2str(phimax)];
title(str);
grid
pause
```

```
% --- inform designer of maximum phase margin and prompt
%     him for wm

[maxpm, ipm]=max(apm);
str1 =['Phase margin = ' num2str(maxpm)];
str2 =['  at wm = ' num2str(awm(ipm))];
str = [str1 str2]
wm = input('Please enter wm --- > ');

% --- test result

cnum = [1/(wm/al) 1];  % numerator 1 + s/Z (Z=wm/al)
cden = [1/(wm*al) 1];  % denominator + s/P (P=wm*al)
num  = ck*conv(cnum, pnum);
den  = conv(cden, pden);

[mag,pha,w]  = bode(num,den);
[Gm, Pm, Wcg, Wcp] = margin(mag,pha,w);
% --- Display result and Bode diagram
str  =['Phase margin = ' num2str(maxpm)]
pause;
bode(num,den)
```

Now run the script file:

```
>> fndwmal
```

Whenever the computer pauses, giving you the opportunity to look to the results, press Enter in order to continue. We suggest you answer 40 to the first prompt, asking for the lead angle, and accept the suggestion of 5.822 for wm. If you are not satisfied with the results, or if you just want to get a better 'feeling' for the parameters, you can obviously rerun the script file and try different values.

15.4   Optimal design

For the control of plants defined in state space form (see Chapter 14), the Control Toolbox provides a number of functions that allow quick design of a compensation network. Let us recall the state space definition of the spring-mass system defined in Section 14.2.4.

$$\dot{x} = \mathbf{A}x + \mathbf{B}u$$
$$y = \mathbf{C}x + \mathbf{D}u$$

$$\mathbf{A} = \begin{bmatrix} -c/m & -h/m \\ 1 & 0 \end{bmatrix} \quad \mathbf{B} = \begin{bmatrix} 1/m \\ 0 \end{bmatrix} \tag{15.4}$$

$$\mathbf{C} = \begin{bmatrix} 0 & 1 \end{bmatrix} \quad \mathbf{D} = \begin{bmatrix} 0 \end{bmatrix} \tag{15.5}$$

With the following constant values

$$m = 2\,\mathrm{kg}$$
$$c = 1.4\,\mathrm{N\,s\,m^{-1}}$$
$$h = 0.1\,\mathrm{N\,m^{-1}}$$

the system is represented by the matrices

$$\mathbf{A} = \begin{bmatrix} -0.7 & -0.1/2 \\ 1 & 0 \end{bmatrix} \quad \mathbf{B} = \begin{bmatrix} 1/2 \\ 0 \end{bmatrix} \tag{15.6}$$

$$\mathbf{C} = \begin{bmatrix} 0 & 1 \end{bmatrix} \quad \mathbf{D} = \begin{bmatrix} 0 \end{bmatrix} \tag{15.7}$$

We want to define the external force u as a linear function of $\mathbf{x}$ in the form $\mathbf{u} = -\mathbf{kx}$, where $\mathbf{k}$ is a row vector, in this case a 1-by-2 vector.

The approach of optimal control is to define a **performance index**, that is, a function that represents the quality of our system. We shall then try to find the k that maximizes such a function.

Defining the performance function, or equivalently its opposite, the **penalty function**, is often a major problem. On the one hand, such a function should really be indicative of the quality of the control, and this usually leads to very complex functions; on the other, it should be mathematically treatable and this restricts us to simple functions.

The Control Toolbox `lqr` function, for **linear quadratic regulator**, solves the optimal control problem, when the performance is defined by quadratic functions.

Recall that a square matrix $\mathbf{M}$ is said to be **positive definite** if, for any vector $\mathbf{z} \neq 0$, the number $\mathbf{zMz'}$ is positive. Similarly, it is **semi-positive definite** if $\mathbf{zMz'} \geq 0$.

The MATLAB `lqr` function solves the problem of finding the vector k when the penalty function is given in the form

$$\int_0^\infty (\mathbf{xqx'} + \mathbf{uru'})\,dt \tag{15.8}$$

where $\mathbf{q}$ is a semi-positive definite **hermitian matrix** and $\mathbf{r}$ a positive definite hermitian matrix. The first term under the integral sign is the penalty for $\mathbf{x}$ not being zero, the second, the cost of the external force applied. The optimal $\mathbf{k}$ for a given choice of $\mathbf{q}$ and $\mathbf{r}$ is usually not optimal for a different pair of matrices.

We expect that, when $\mathbf{q}$ is small with respect to $\mathbf{r}$ (that is, the penalty for $\mathbf{x}$ not being zero is small with respect to the cost of the energy), an optimal control will try to save energy and produce a sluggish response. In the opposite case the controller will infuse energy generously into the system and the response will be faster.

It is interesting to keep one of the matrices, say $\mathbf{q}$, fixed, and study how the response changes when we change the value of $\mathbf{r}$. For this purpose we have to write a short M-file `cspring.m`:

```
function xd=cspring(t,x,flag,k);
% This function defines the spring system.
% The external force is defined with
% the help of the parameter k.

% --- assign values to the constants that define the system
m = 2.0;                    % kg
c = 1.4;                    % Ns/m
h = 0.1;                    % N/m

% --- define "A" and "C" matrices of state space representation.
a = [-c/m        -h/m;
    1            0];
c = [1;
      0];
% --- define external force u
u = -k*x;
% --- compute derivatives xd of the state x
xd =a*x+c*u;
```

and perform comparative simulation runs. We define a, b, c and d in the workspace:

```
≫ a = [-.7 -.05; 1 0];
≫ b = [0.5; 0];
≫ c = [0 1];
≫ d = 0;
```

The initial and final time of the simulation are entered as

```
≫ t0 = 0; tfin = 5;
```

and the initial conditions as

```
≫ y0 = [0; 1];
```

We define a performance matrix which remains constant for all the runs

```
≫ q =[0 0; 0 1];
```

We can now perform a sequence of simulation runs and display the results:

```
≫ for r = logspace(-1,1,5),
≫       k = lqr(a,b,q,r);
≫       [t,y] = ode23('cspring',t0,tfin,y0);
```

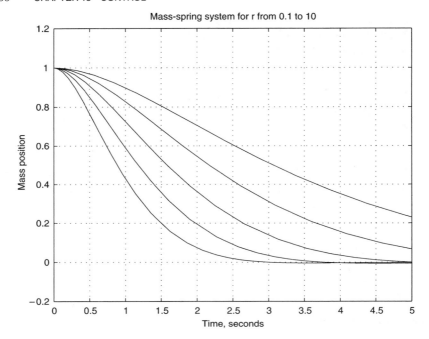

Figure 15.10   Mass displacements for different performance specifications.

```
>>          plot(t,y(:,2)); hold on;
>> end
>> xlabel(' Time, seconds');
>> ylabel(' Mass position');
>> title('Mass-spring system for r from 0.1 to 10')
```

The results are shown in Figure 15.10.

We have shown with a few examples how MATLAB helps the control engineer in the synthesis and the analysis of continuous feedback systems. Discrete systems are usually simpler to treat on a digital computer than continuous ones. For such systems, the Control Toolbox provides a number of script files, analogous to their continuous counterparts. They usually have the prefix letter d, for digital, such as dbode and dlqr.

15.5   Exercises

The solutions for Exercises 15.3, 15.5, 15.7, 15.8, 15.9, 15.11, 15.14 and 15.16 appear at the back of the book.

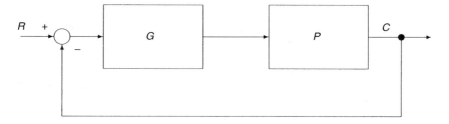

Figure 15.11   Control plant in Exercise 15.1.

■ **EXERCISE 15.1**   Simple root locus
A plant of transfer function

$$P(s) = \frac{s+2}{s^3 + 4s + 5}$$

is embedded in a canonical unity negative feedback system as shown in Figure 15.11 where the compensating network G is simply a gain k. Plot its root locus, for k in the range $[10^{-2}, 10^2]$.

■ **EXERCISE 15.2**   Root locus and convolution
A plant of transfer function

$$P(s) = \frac{20}{s(s+1)(s+2)(s+4)}$$

is embedded in a canonical unit negative feedback system, where the compensating network G is simply a gain k. Plot the root locus of the closed-loop system.

■ **EXERCISE 15.3**   Root locus, convolution, gain margin
A plant, defined by the transfer function

$$P(s) = \frac{10}{(s+1)(s+2)(s+4)}$$

is embedded in a canonical unit negative feedback system with gain compensator k. Find the value of k, so that the resulting closed-loop system is stable with gain margin equal to 4.

■ **EXERCISE 15.4**   Root locus and damping ratio
A plant of transfer function

$$P(s) = \frac{15}{(s+1)(s+3)(s+4)}$$

is embedded in a canonical unit negative feedback system, where the compensating network G is simply a gain k. Using root locus methods, find the value of k for which the closed loop system has a damping ratio $\zeta = 0.60$.

Hint: Plot the root locus adding one root at a time, and indicate in the title the values of k. It is then easy to identify the value of k for which we have the first root that crosses one of the lines $y = \pm\sqrt{1 - \zeta^2}x$.

■ **EXERCISE 15.5**   Bode grid
Prepare a 4-decade Bode grid, for ω from 0.01 to 100 rad s^{-1}, magnitude from -20 to 20 db, phase from -360 to 0 degrees.

Hint: Use the `subplot` and `axis` functions. The only non-trivial point is to have the y-axis of the phase plot marked in multiples of 90 degrees, and not in the defaults -300, -200, -100 and 0 degrees, which are much less meaningful. Use the command `set(gca,'Ytick' ...)`.

■ **EXERCISE 15.6**   Bode plot, open loop
A plant is defined by the transfer function

$$P(s) = \frac{1}{1 + s/P_1} \cdot \frac{1}{1 + s/P_2} \cdot \frac{\omega_n^2}{\omega_n^2 + 2\zeta\omega_n s + s^2}$$

with $P_1 = 6$ rad s^{-1}, $P_2 = 40$ rad s^{-1}, $\omega_n = 15$ rad s^{-1} and $\zeta = 0.6$. Plot its Bode diagram for the frequencies 0.1 to 100 rad s^{-1}.

■ **EXERCISE 15.7**   Bode plot, closed loop
A plant is defined by the transfer function

$$P(s) = k\frac{1 + s/R/\alpha}{1 + s/(R\alpha)} \cdot \frac{1}{s} \cdot \frac{\omega_n^2}{\omega_n^2 + 2\zeta\omega_n s + s^2}$$

with $k = 5$, $R = 6$ rad s^{-1}, $\alpha = 4$, $\omega_n = 20$ rad s^{-1} and $\zeta = 0.6$. The plant is embedded in a canonical unit negative feedback system. Compute and plot the Bode diagram of the resulting closed-loop system for the frequencies 0.1 to 1000 rad s^{-1}.

■ **EXERCISE 15.8**   Bode plot, gain and phase margin
A plant of transfer function

$$P(s) = \frac{4}{s(s + 1)(s/3 + 1)}$$

is embedded in a canonical unit feedback system. Plot its Bode plot, and, using your mouse and the `ginput` function, determine its gain and phase margins. If you have access to the `margins` function from the Control Toolbox, use it to check your answer.

■ **EXERCISE 15.9**   Bode plot, compensation lead
A **lead compensator** is a network of transfer function

$$\frac{s + \omega_n/\alpha}{s + \omega_n\alpha}$$

where α is a parameter > 1. It is often useful to have its Bode plot available, for different values of α. Plot the magnitude and phase of the lead compensators with parameters $\omega_n = 1$, $\alpha = \sqrt{2}, 2, 2\sqrt{2}, 4, 4\sqrt{2}$, and ω from 0.01 to 100.

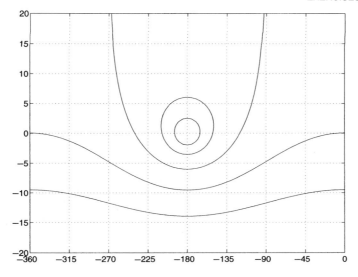

Figure 15.12   A Nichols plot.

■ **EXERCISE 15.10**   Bode plot, compensation lag
A **lag compensator** is a network of transfer function

$$\frac{1 + s/(\omega_n \alpha)}{1 + s/(\omega_n/\alpha)}$$

where α is a number larger than 1. It is often useful to have its Bode plot available, for different values of the parameter α. Plot the magnitude and phase of the lead compensators with parameters $\omega_n = 1$, $\alpha = \sqrt{2}, 2, 2\sqrt{2}, 4, 4\sqrt{2}$, and ω from 0.01 to 100.

■ **EXERCISE 15.11**   Plotting a Nichols chart with assigned M-circles
Plot the Nichols chart shown in Figure 15.12. Using the `contour` function show the M-circles of constant closed-loop magnitude relative to -12, -6, 0, 6 and 12 decibel.

   Hint: This is not an easy exercise. Before you attempt to solve this problem, we suggest you read carefully the documentation on the `meshgrid`, `contour`, `gca` and `set` functions.

■ **EXERCISE 15.12**   Plotting the Nichols chart of a plant
A plant P has the transfer function

$$P(s) = \frac{1}{s} \cdot \frac{1}{1 + s/10} \cdot \frac{20^2}{s^2 + 2(0.5)(20)s + 20^2}$$

(1)   Using the Nichols chart constructed in the previous exercise (or, if you have access to the Control Toolbox, using the `ngrid` function), construct and plot its Nichols chart, and verify the graph against our solution (Figure 15.13).
(2)   Annotate the Nichols chart for the frequencies $\omega = 0.25, 0.5, 1, 2, 5$ rad s^{-1}.

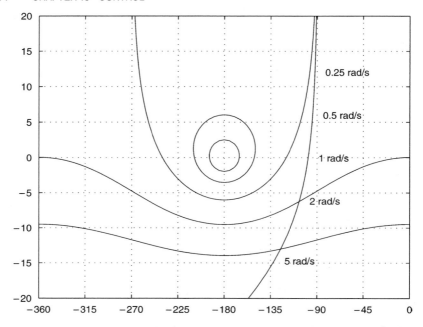

Figure 15.13   A Nichols plot.

(3)   For the same frequencies print, in tabular form, the frequency, the phase in degrees and the magnitude in decibels.

■ **EXERCISE 15.13**   Plotting the Nichols chart of a plant

$$P(s) = \frac{1}{s} \cdot \frac{1}{1 + s/10} \cdot \frac{20^2}{s^2 + 2(0.5)(20)s + 20^2}$$

The plant is embedded in a canonical unit feedback system with compensating network

$$G(s) = 0.75 \frac{10^2}{s^2 + 2(0.65)(10)s + 10^2}$$

(1)   Plot the Nichols chart for the uncompensated and the compensated networks.
(2)   Mark on the graph the points that correspond to the frequencies $0.25, 0.5, 1, 2, 5 \, \text{rad s}^{-1}$.
(3)   Using the `ginput` function, compute the gain and phase margins of the compensated plant (approximately 56 degrees and 5.65 db).
(4)   If you have access to the `margin` function of the Control Toolbox, verify your answer against that produced by `margin`.
Note: The `margin` function produces G_m, the *numerical* value of the gain margin. If you want the value in decibels, you have to compute 20 `log10(Gm)`.

■ **EXERCISE 15.14**   Gain and phase margins from Nichols chart
A plant of transfer function

$$P(s) = \frac{5}{s(s/10 + 1)} \cdot \frac{15^2}{s^2 + 2(0.7)s + 15^2}$$

is embedded in a canonical unit negative feedback system. Plot its Nichols chart and, using your mouse and the `ginput` function, determine its gain and phase margins. If you have access to the `margin` function, use it to check your answer.

■ **EXERCISE 15.15**   Simple lqr design
A linear system is described in state space form by the matrices

$$\mathbf{A} = \begin{bmatrix} 1 & 0 \\ -1 & 2 \end{bmatrix}, \quad \mathbf{C} = \begin{bmatrix} 1 \\ 1 \end{bmatrix}$$

We want to regulate the system by embedding it in a canonical unit feedback system. Find the optimal gain $K = [k_1, k_2]$ such that the feedback $u = -Kx$ minimizes the cost function

$$\int_0^\infty (\mathbf{x}'\mathbf{Q}\mathbf{x} + \mathbf{u}'\mathbf{R}\mathbf{u})\, dt$$

for

$$\mathbf{Q} = \begin{bmatrix} 1 & 0 \\ 0 & 4 \end{bmatrix}$$

and $\mathbf{R} = 5$.
    Hint: Use the `lqr` function.

■ **EXERCISE 15.16**   Stabilizing an inverted pendulum
A classical problem in control courses is to find a regulator for the system in Figure 15.14 which shows an inverted pendulum of length l and mass m mounted on a cart of mass M, by means of a force u applied to the cart.
    We choose the states as

$$
\begin{array}{rcl}
w(1) & = & x \\
w(2) & = & \dot{x} \\
w(3) & = & \theta \\
w(4) & = & \dot{\theta}
\end{array}
$$

If you are familiar with basic analytic mechanics, you can prove, for example from Lagrange equations in x and θ, that the system is governed by the equations

$$
\begin{array}{rcl}
(M + m)\ddot{x} + ml\cos\theta\,\ddot{\theta} & = & ml\sin\theta\,\dot{\theta}^2 + u \\
ml\cos\theta\,\ddot{x} + ml^2\ddot{\theta} & = & mgl\sin\theta
\end{array}
\tag{15.9}
$$

Otherwise, just accept them and continue with the exercise.

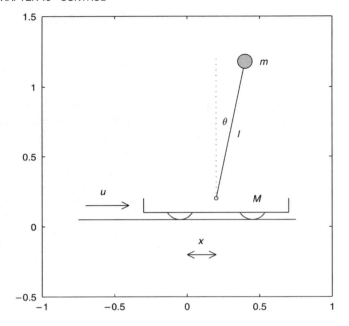

Figure 15.14   An inverted pendulum.

Our purpose is to find the constant gain array $\mathbf{K} = [k1, k2, k3, k4]$ such that the force $\mathbf{u} = -\mathbf{Kw}$ will minimize, or nearly minimize, the penalty function

$$\int_0^\infty (\mathbf{x}'\mathbf{Qx} + \mathbf{u}'\mathbf{Ru})\, dt$$

Our grand strategy will be to

(1)   linearize the system;

(2)   find the optimal $\mathbf{K}$ for the linearized system;

(3)   test the controller on the original nonlinear system.

This strategy is quite common for defining controls when the system operates in the neighbourhood of a point where its behaviour is nearly linear.

(1)   Linearize the system in the neighbourhood of the operating point
        $\mathbf{w} = [0; 0; 0; 0]$. You are requested to find the matrices $\mathbf{A}$ and $\mathbf{B}$, such that the
        equation $\dot{\mathbf{w}} = \mathbf{Aw} + \mathbf{Bu}$ describes the linearized system, that is, the system
        obtained from Equation 15.9 by neglecting second-order terms.
        Hint: Substitute θ for $\sin\theta$, 1 for $\cos\theta$ and 0 for $\dot{\theta}^2$.

(2)   Using the matrices $\mathbf{A}$ and $\mathbf{B}$ defined at (a) and $\mathbf{Q}$ and $\mathbf{R}$ defined below in the
        parameter list, find, by means of the MATLAB `lqr` function, the gain K that
        minimizes the integral

$$\int_0^\infty (\mathbf{x}'\mathbf{Qx} + \mathbf{u}'\mathbf{Ru})\, dt$$

(3)   Given the following initial conditions

$$x(0)   =   0.2$$
$$\dot{x}(0)   =   0.5$$
$$\theta(0)   =   0.1$$
$$\dot{\theta}(0)   =   0.15$$

simulate the system for 5 seconds and plot x_{lin} and θ_{lin} versus the time t.
Hint: Use the MATLAB ode23 function.

(4)   Simulate the original nonlinear system from the same initial conditions and plot x and θ against the time t.

(5)   Compare the solutions of the linearized and the nonlinear system graphically by plotting the corresponding states on the same graph.

(6)   Away from the linearization point, the two systems behave quite differently. The reader is invited to repeat (3), (4) and (5) while experimenting with various sets of initial conditions and find one for which this difference is appreciable.
System parameters: $g = 9.81\,\mathrm{ms}^{-2}$, $l = 0.5\,\mathrm{m}$, $M = 1\,\mathrm{kg}$, $m = 0.1\,\mathrm{kg}$, $\mathbf{Q}$ = 4-by-4 identity matrix, $\mathbf{R} = 0.1$.

Chapter 16
Signal processing

16.1 Signals and signal processing

The word *signal* has several meanings; the one that interests us is defined in Webster (1988) as 'a detectable physical quantity or impulse (as a voltage, current, or magnetic field strength) by which messages or information can be transmitted'. For example, the desired information can be a temperature, and the signal a voltage proportional to this temperature.

Many books refer to signal variation as a function of time. Measuring the sea elevation at one point would generate such a signal; it represents the evolution of the sea wave at that point. We may, however, be interested in signals that vary spatially. Examples of these are the roughness of a surface, and the grey intensity across an image. It is also possible to find signals that are functions of both time and space.

Many signals are continuous: the air temperature, the sea elevation at one point, the surface roughness. Other signals are discrete, for example letters transmitted in Morse code. Signals may be discrete because they are obtained by **sampling** continuous information, for example atmospheric temperature and pressure as transmitted at regular intervals by radio. The computer can process only discrete signals; therefore, signals intended for this purpose, unless discrete by nature, must be obtained by sampling.

To be processed by a computer, most signals can be conveniently represented by either one-, two- and less often multi-dimensional arrays. Signals produced by sensors, such as thermometers and tachometers, produce one-dimensional arrays of real numbers when sampled at constant intervals. The digitization of an image produces a two-dimensional array, each entry representing, for example, the grey level of a picture element. Three-dimensional arrays appear naturally if we want to describe the temperature of a room. We can think of dividing the room into little boxes, using three indexes for the three spatial dimensions. A four-dimensional array is the obvious way to store data, if we want to study how the temperature of the same room varies with time. Such arrays and matrices are usually manipulated in various ways; they can be filtered to attenuate noise, can be modulated, and can be processed to enhance the contrast of images, or to compress the dynamic range. While such operations can be performed in most cases either in the time or in the frequency domain, selecting the correct domain and the correct algorithm often results in a considerable increase of efficiency. MATLAB provides very fast and precise algorithms for switching back and forth from the time to the frequency domain.

In this chapter we are going to examine some typical problems, and see how they can be solved with the help of MATLAB. The Signal Processing Toolbox provides about 70 useful functions for analysing digital signals and building digital filters with given characteristics. Many of them duplicate each other with minor variations. Instead of going superficially through many functions, we decided to select a few of them, the most important ones in our opinion, and study them in depth. We believe that a good understanding of a few basic tools is more important for the nonspecialist than a superficial knowledge of a large number of functions, and that it will allow him or her to solve most problems encountered.

16.2   The FILTER function

One of the most useful functions for processing an array is the `filter` function. Digital filters appear almost anywhere in signal processing. A simple case occurs when a signal x is corrupted by the addition of noise. We can, to a certain extent, reconstruct the original signal with an appropriate filter.

Let us consider the case when the signal is to be displayed on an instrument that will be read by a human operator. Reading can be difficult in this case because the numbers change all the time, due to sensor noise, but can be improved if we decide to display, at constant intervals, not x itself but a weighted average of the last value displayed and the new input, that is

$$y_n = k_1 y_{n-1} + k_2 x_n$$

where y_{n-1} is the last value displayed, and x_n the new input. For example, if we choose $k_1 = 0.9$ and $k_2 = 0.1$

$$y_n = 0.9 y_{n-1} + 0.1 x_n$$

This relation uniquely defines y_n for $n > 1$. Let us not worry how the initial value y_1 is determined (we shall discuss initial conditions later in this chapter), and just let y_1 be equal to x_1. The following MATLAB commands produce y:

```
≫ t = linspace(0,10,100);   % time base
≫ s = sin(2*pi/5*t)         % signal
≫ [r,c] = size(t); n = 0.1*rand(r,c);    % noise
≫ x = s + n;                % input
≫ y(1) = x(1);             % initial condition
≫ for i = 2:100            % FOR loop to smooth x
        y(i) = 0.9*y(i-1) + 0.1*x(i);
  end
```

Above, the comments are for the sake of clarity only and you do not have to type them when you reproduce this or any of the following examples on your computer.

We can now compare x and y with the command

```
≫ plot(t, x, t, y)
```

The result is shown in Figure 16.1.

We could also decide that the value to output should be 0.9 times the last output value plus 0.1 times the average of the last two inputs so that y_n is given by the formula:

$$y_n = 0.9y_{n-1} + 0.05x_n + 0.05x_{n-1}$$

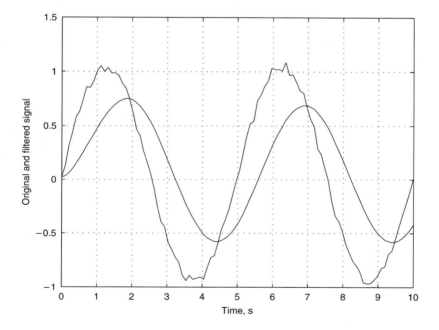

Figure 16.1   Smoothing a noisy signal – first example.

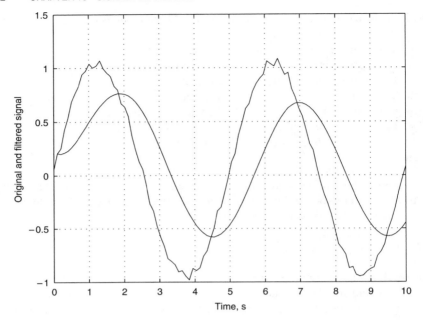

Figure 16.2   Smoothing a noisy signal – second example.

In this case we have the freedom to define y_1 and y_2. Now y is produced by the commands

```
>> t = linspace(0,10,100);   % time base
>> s = sin(2*pi/5*t)         % signal
>> [r,c] = size(t); n = 0.1*rand(r,c);     % noise
>> x = s+n;                  % input
>> y(1) = x(1);              % initial condition
>> y(2) = x(2);              % initial condition
>> for i = 3:100             % FOR loop to smooth x
      y(i)=0.9*y(i-1)+0.05*x(i)+0.05*x(i-1);
end
```

As in the previous case, the plot is obtained by

```
>> plot(t, x, t, y)
```

and is shown in Figure 16.2.

Digital filters can also be easily introduced by starting from a simple, analog filter. Let us thus consider, for instance, the RC low-pass filter analysed in Example 4.2. It is governed by the differential equation

$$\frac{L}{R}\frac{di}{dt} + i = \frac{v}{R}$$

With $\tau = L/R$ – this is the *time constant of the circuit* – $y = i$, and $x = v/R$, the previous equation becomes

$$\tau \frac{dy}{dt} + y = x \tag{16.1}$$

We assume that y is sampled at intervals T_s which are small compared to the time constant τ. Then the time derivative of y can be approximated by

$$\frac{dy}{dt} \approx \frac{y_n - y_{n-1}}{T_s}$$

where y_n is again the n-th measured value of y, and y_{n-1} the previous one. The differential Equation 16.1 can thus be replaced by the **finite difference** equation

$$\tau \frac{y_n - y_{n-1}}{T_s} + y_n = x_n \tag{16.2}$$

which can be further brought to the form

$$y_n = \frac{b_1}{a_1} x_n - \frac{a_2}{a_1} y_{n-1} \tag{16.3}$$

Equation 16.3 describes a **first-order filter**.

The examples just given can be generalized into the problem of producing, from a given array, x, a new array, y, related to x by an expression of the form

$$a_1 y_n + a_2 y_{n-1} + \cdots + a_{n_a} y_{n-n_a+1} = b_1 x_n + b_2 x_{n-1} + \cdots + b_{n_b} x_{n-n_b+1} \tag{16.4}$$

or

$$y_n = \frac{b_1}{a_1} x_n + \frac{b_2}{a_1} x_{n-1} + \cdots + \frac{b_{n_b}}{a_1} x_{n-n_b+1} - \frac{a_2}{a_1} y_{n-1} - \cdots - \frac{a_{n_a}}{a_1} y_{n-n_a+1} \tag{16.5}$$

This equation describes a filter of order N, where $N = \max(n_a, n_b) - 1$. In MATLAB this filter is defined by the two arrays

$$A = [a_1, a_2, \ldots, a_{n_a}]$$
$$B = [b_1, b_2, \ldots, b_{n_b}]$$

It is easy to verify by visual inspection that this filter can be represented by the diagram in Figure 16.3 where the coefficients a_i and b_i were normalized by dividing them by a_1, the coefficient of y_n. In this figure z is the symbol for the **unitary time shift operator**. Let x be the discrete version of a signal $f(t)$ sampled at rate T_s, so that $x(n) = f(n \cdot T_s)$. Then zx is, by definition, the sequence whose k-th component is $zx(k) = x(k+1)$. Similarly, the k-th component of $z^{-1}x$ is $x(k-1)$. The z-notation provides a convenient way to express digital operators, and we refer the interested

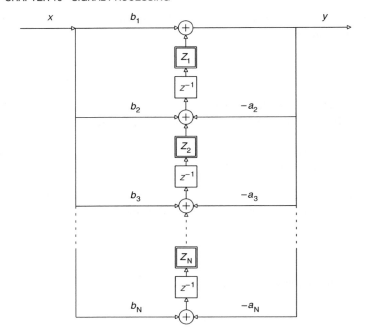

Figure 16.3   Transposed direct form II.

reader to textbooks on signal processing, such as those of Rabiner and Gold (1975), or Oppenheim and Shafer (1975).

The representation shown in Figure 16.3 is called the **transposed direct form II** and is one of the many possible algorithms that requires the minimum amount of storage. In fact, at each step we must store only the values of the states $Z_1, Z_2, \ldots, Z_N$, represented in the diagram by the double-framed boxes in the central line.

The filter is implemented as follows:

(1)   Initialization.

   (a)   The vector of initial conditions, usually denoted by Zi, is stored in the delays Z_j. If Zi is not supplied, all Z_j-values are set to zero.

   (b)   The values of A and B are normalized by the factor a_1.

(2)   The main loop. At each step, the `filter` function performs the following operations:

   (a)   it produces y_n from the relation $y_n = b_1 x_n + Z_1$

   (b)   it updates Z_j, for j from 1 to $N - 1$ as in

$$Z_j = b_j x_n + Z_{j+1} - a_j y_n$$

   and for $j = N$ as in

$$Z_N = b_N x_n - a_N y_n$$

The loop continues until the array x is exhausted.

(3)   Final step. The values Z_j are copied to the output vector Zf.

Equation 16.5 can be implemented in MATLAB by the `filter` function. There are four ways of calling the `filter` function:

```
y = filter(B, A, x);
y = filter(B, A, x, Zi);
[y, Zf] = filter(B, A, x)
[y, Zf] = filter(B, A, x, Zi);
```

where Zi and Zf are arrays of optional parameters, related to the initial and final conditions, and were described above. The `filter` function can return the final values of Z as the array Zf, if it is called with two left-hand-side arguments

```
>> [y, Zf] = filter(B, A, x)
```

For example, let

```
>> x = [ 1, 2, 1, 2, 1, 2, 1, 2, 1, 2 ];
>> B = [ 0.5 ];
>> A = [ 1, -0.25, -0.25 ];
```

Calling the filter as above

```
>> [y, Zf] = filter(B, A, x)
```

produces the following sequence of calculations

Step	Input	Output	Z_1	Z_2
1	1	0.5	0.125	0.1250
2	2	1.125	0.4063	0.2813
3	1	0.9063	0.5078	0.2266
4	2	1.508	0.6035	0.3770
5	1	1.104	0.6528	0.2759
6	2	1.653	0.6891	0.4132
7	1	1.189	0.7105	0.2973
8	2	1.71	0.7249	0.4276
9	1	1.225	0.7338	0.3062
10	2	1.734	0.7397	0.4335

In this table, produced by a MATLAB M-file, the numbers are rounded off at four digits after the decimal point. The reader is invited to repeat the calculations manually, following the scheme described above and Figure 16.3. At the end, after defining the arrays x, A, and B as above, and invoking the `filter` function as shown, try also

```
>> y(:)
ans =
     0.5000
     1.1250
     0.9063
     1.5078
     1.1035
     1.6528
     1.1891
     1.7105
     1.2249
     1.7338
```

and

```
>> Zf
Zf =
     0.7397
     0.4335
```

We recognize the array y calculated by the M-file, and the last values of Z_1 and Z_2 in the table.

16.3   Calling the filter with initial conditions

If we know the initial conditions to be stored in the delays, we can call the filter by

```
>> [Y,Zf] = filter(B,A,x,Zi)
```

This is particularly useful if we have a long signal x that cannot be stored in the memory of our computer. We can split x into smaller chunks, say $x_1, x_2, \ldots, x_n$, such that, in MATLAB

```
>> x = [x1; x2; ...; xn]
```

and filter them separately, without loss of precision. The final values, Zf, of the delays at each step are used as the initial values, Zi, for the next one. To exemplify this, let us create an array of 100 random numbers

```
>> x = rand(100,1);
```

We split it into four subarrays by

```
≫ x1 = x(1:25);
≫ x2 = x(26:50);
≫ x3 = x(51:75);
≫ x4 = x(76:100);
```

We now create a filter and invoke it for each subarray in part. When doing this we use the values of the final conditions, Zf, produced by the first call, as initial conditions, Zi, for the second call, and so on:

```
≫ a = [1 0.5]; b = [0.5 0.3];
≫ [y1,Zf1] = filter(b,a,x1);     Zi2 = Zf1;
≫ [y2,Zf2] = filter(b,a,x2,Zi2); Zi3 = Zf2;
≫ [y3,Zf3] = filter(b,a,x3,Zi3); Zi4 = Zf3;
≫ [y4,Zf4] = filter(b,a,x4,Zi4);
```

As a check, we now invoke the `filter` function for the whole array x:

```
≫ y = filter(b,a,x);
```

and we verify that the results produced by the 'partial' calls are identical to those produced by the last call:

```
≫ max(max( abs(y-[y1;y2;y3;y4])))
ans =
    0
```

As we have seen, the vector Zi is optional and can be omitted. In this case the `filter` function uses by default a vector of length N filled with zeros. If Zi is supplied, it must be of the correct length N, which is equal to the order of the filter, and not $1 + N$, as stated in the MATLAB manuals.

In order to define a filter of order N uniquely, we must supply N conditions, like the values of the vector Zi, in addition to the arrays A and B. Alternatively, we can give N initial conditions for the output, in the form of a vector y_i of length N, and require that the first N values of y coincide with y_i.

If we write the first N equations of the `filter` algorithm, we obtain the relations

$$y_1 = Zi_1 + b_1 \cdot x_1 \tag{16.6}$$

$$y_2 = Zi_2 + [b_1 \cdot x_2 + b_2 \cdot x_1] - [a_2 \cdot y_1] \tag{16.7}$$

$$y_3 = Zi_3 + [b_1 \cdot x_3 + b_2 \cdot x_2 + b_3 \cdot x_1] - [a_2 \cdot y_2 + a_1 \cdot y_3] \tag{16.8}$$

$$y_k = Zi_k + \sum_{i=1}^{k} b_i \cdot x_{k+1-i} - \sum_{i=1}^{k-1} a_{i+1} \cdot y_{k-i} \qquad (16.9)$$

$$\vdots \qquad\qquad\qquad\qquad (16.10)$$

$$y_N = Zi_N + \sum_{i=1}^{N} b_i \cdot x_{N+1-i} - \sum_{i=1}^{N-1} a_{i+1} \cdot y_{N-i} \qquad (16.11)$$

If we want the first N values of the filter to agree with y_i, we can substitute y_i for y in the N equations above, and solve them for Zi. The filteric function has been written to perform this task; please prepare the following file and call it filteric.m.

```
function Zi =filteric(B,A,X,Y)
%FILTERIC - digital-filter initial conditions.
% The function Y=FILTER(B,A,X,Zi) is defined by the
% coefficients A and B of the filter and the vector Zi of
% the initial delays, of length N = max(length(A), length(B))-1.
%
% Given B,A,X,Y, this function produces the vector Zi
% such that the output of filter(B,A,X,Zi) agrees with
% Y in the first N terms.
%
% WARNING: The length of each of the vectors X and Y must
%          be at least N.
%

% test that X and Y contain enough terms
lB = length(B);
lA = length(A);
nst  = max(lA,lB) - 1;
if ((length(X) < nst) | (length(Y) < nst)),
     error('Not enough initial conditions');
end;

% check validity of the coefficients. A(1) must be non-zero
if(A(1)==0),
     error('First denominator coefficient must be non-zero.');
end;

% normalize filter coefficients by A(1)
factor=A(1);
A=A/factor;
B=B/factor;

% Truncate X and Y to length nst and make them into
```

```
% column vectors
XIc=X(1:nst);    XIc=XIc(:);
YIc=Y(1:nst);    YIc=YIc(:);


% Build auxiliary variables for the computation of Zi and
% truncate them to length nst

B      = B(:);
cnvbx = conv(B,XIc);
cnvbx = cnvbx([1:nst]');


A(1)=0;
A=A(:);
cnvay = conv(A,YIc);
cnvay = cnvay([1:nst]');
% Compute Zi
Zi = YIc - cnvbx + cnvay;
```

As an example, let X represent the first 1000 points of a signal sampled at 100 Hz. We want to pass the signal through a 30 Hz Butterworth low-pass filter, of order 5, and obtain a signal Y such that $Y(i) = X(i)$ for $i = 1$ to 5.

First we construct the signal by

```
≫ X = rand(1000,1);
```

Next, we define the parameters of the filter following the first example in the Tutorial section of the Signal Processing Toolbox (Section 5.1):

```
≫ [b,a] = butter(5,30/50)
b =
    0.1084 0.5419 1.0837 1.0837 0.5419 0.1084
a =
    1.0000 0.9853 0.9738 0.3864 0.1112 0.0113
```

The initial conditions are defined by

```
≫ Yi = X(1:5);
```

and the initial conditions of the delays by

```
≫ Zi = filteric(b,a,X,Yi);
```

We invoke the `filter` function by

```
>> Y = filter(b,a,X,Zi);
```

We can now display the first five terms of the input and output arrays and verify that they are equal:

```
>> [X(1:5), Y(1:5)]
ans =
    0.2190 0.2190
    0.0470 0.0470
    0.6789 0.6789
    0.6793 0.6793
    0.9347 0.9347
```

16.4   Design of digital filters

16.4.1   Definitions

One of the most common problems encountered in digital signal processing is that of constructing a filter with given magnitude characteristics at different frequencies. A number of tools are available in the Signal Processing Toolbox, and we are going to concentrate on two that, if properly understood, should suffice for most problems one is apt to encounter in practice, namely the `yulewalk` and `fir2` functions.

We recall that a rational digital filter H of order N, applied to a sequence x of sampled data, produces a new sequence y, related to x by the equation

$$a_1 \cdot y_n + a_2 \cdot y_{n-1} + \cdots + a_{N+1} \cdot y_{n-N} =$$
$$b_1 \cdot x_n + b_2 \cdot x_{n-1} + \cdots + b_{N+1} \cdot x_{n-N} \tag{16.12}$$

The coefficients $B = [b_1, b_2, \ldots, b_{N+1}]$ and $A = [a_1, a_2, \ldots, a_{N+1}]$ are uniquely defined up to a multiplicative nonzero coefficient, so we can assume without loss of generality that they are normalized by a_1. Moreover, at least one of the coefficients a_{N+1} or b_{N+1} should be different from 0, otherwise the filter could be defined by shorter vectors A and B, and it would be of order strictly lower than N. The functions in the MATLAB toolbox that produce the coefficients of the filter (`yulewalk`, `cheb1`, and others) always produce normalized coefficients, consistent with the `filter` function.

Using the time shift operator z defined in the previous section, the filter H can be represented by the rational function

$$H(z) = \frac{B(z)}{A(z)} = \frac{b_1 + b_2 z^{-1} + \cdots + b_N z^{-(N-1)}}{a_1 + a_2 z^{-1} + \cdots + a_N z^{-(N-1)}} \tag{16.13}$$

with $a_1 = 1$ and at least one of the coefficients a_N or b_N different from zero.

If the terms $a_2, a_3, \ldots, a_N$ are all equal to zero, the filter is called **FIR (finite impulse response)**, otherwise **IIR (infinite impulse response)**. The yulewalk function is used to synthesize IIR filters, while the fir2 function is used for FIR filters.

16.4.2   Defining the frequency characteristics of the filter

MATLAB allows us to define a number of frequencies, $fr_1, fr_2, \ldots, fr_i, \ldots, fr_k$, and corresponding magnitudes, $mag_1, mag_2, \ldots, mag_i, \ldots, mag_k$, and design a digital filter that approximates the ideal analogue filter.

The frequency response of a digital filter depends on the sampling rate. Half the sampling frequency is called the **Nyquist** frequency and some MATLAB functions are expressed in terms of **normalized frequency**, that is, by definition, the frequency in Hz divided by the Nyquist frequency. So, for example, if the sampling rate is 1000 Hz, the frequency of 50 Hz will correspond to the normalized frequency $50/(1000/2) = 0.1$, and 150 Hz will correspond to $150/(1000/2) = 0.3$.

In order to define the characteristics of the filter, we must therefore give two arrays, one of normalized frequencies, $f = [f_1, f_2, \ldots, f_k]$, and one of corresponding magnitudes $m = [m_1, m_2, \ldots, m_k]$. MATLAB requires f_1 to be 0 and f_k to be 1.

As an example, let us assume that a signal x is sampled at 500 Hz, and we want to construct a filter with the following frequency–magnitude relationship:

From Hz	To Hz	Magnitude
0	100	1.0
100	150	Decreasing linearly from 1 to 0.5
150	200	Remains constant at 0.5
200	225	Increasing linearly from 0.5 to 1
200	250	1

We enter the desired filter characteristics in MATLAB by

```
>> fHz0 = [  0 100 150 200 225 250];
>> m0    = [1.0 1.0 0.5 0.5 1.0 1.0];
```

To check that we did not make a mistake, we can plot the graph that appears in Figure 16.4:

```
>> plot(fHz0,m0);
```

MATLAB provides the tools to construct IIR and FIR digital filters with given specifications. Moreover, in the tutorial to the Signal Processing Toolbox, there is a concise but useful discussion on their relative advantages and disadvantages. We are now going to construct an IIR version of the filter, using the yulewalk function, and will later use the fir2 function for the synthesis of a similar FIR filter.

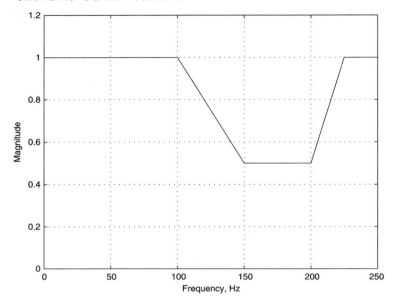

Figure 16.4   Frequency characteristic of the filter.

In order to use the `yulewalk` function, we must normalize the frequencies to non-dimensional units:

```
>> fs = 500;
>> f0 = fHz0/(fs/2);
```

where `fs` is the sampling frequency and `fHz0` is normalized by the Nyquist frequency, `fs/2`.

The `yulewalk` function yields the best approximation, in the sense of minimum square error, among all filters of a given order.

Let us try a filter of order 6:

```
>> [bIIR, aIIR] = yulewalk(6,f0,m0);
```

We can check how good our approximation is by comparing the response of the filter defined by `[bIIR,aIIR]` to the desired response. It is well known that the response of a digital filter $H(z)$ at the frequency ω rad/sec is given by the value of $H(z)$ for $z = \exp(i*\omega/fs)$, where fs is the sampling frequency. For our purpose we need a fine resolution on the x-axis, such as 50 points from 0 to the Nyquist frequency, expressed in rad/sec. In MATLAB we obtain this axis, in Hz, with

```
>> fHz1 = linspace(0, 250, 50);
```

and convert it to rad/s by

```
>> om1 = 2*pi*fHz1;
```

We can compute the magnitude response of the filter with the commands

```
>> z = exp(sqrt(-1)*om1/fs);
>> mIIR = abs(polyval(bIIR,z)./polyval(aIIR,z));
```

We can now compare the fit between the desired and actual magnitude response:

```
>> plot(fHz0, m0, fHz1, mIIR)
```

The result is shown in Figure 16.5. If the approximation is not good enough for our purposes, we can try a higher-order filter.

Let us now solve the same problem using an FIR filter. FIR filters must be of higher order than IIR filters in order to achieve comparable performance, so we try a filter of order 20:

```
>> bFIR=fir2(20, f0, m0);
```

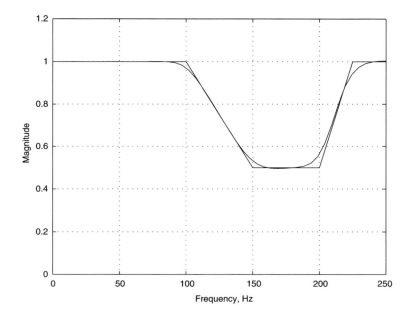

Figure 16.5   Definition and realization of the IIR filter.

The `fir2` function returns only the vector b, since for all FIR filters $a = [1]$. We can check our results graphically by

```
>> mFIR = abs(polyval(bFIR,z));
>> plot(fHz0, m0, fHz1,mFIR);
```

The resulting graph is shown in Figure 16.6.

The Signal Processing Toolbox has a number of additional functions designed to help in the synthesis of IIR filters: `cheby1`, `cheby2`, `ellipt`, among others. The `yulewalk` function requires that the characteristics of the filter be defined by two arrays, one of frequencies, the other of magnitude responses. We could instead define the filter as **high-pass**, **low-pass**, **band-pass**, or **band-stop** and assign conditions on the transients (**ripple**). In this case the synthesis is simpler if we use the other functions, such as `cheby1`, `cheby2` and `ellipt`. Similarly, for the synthesis of FIR filters, the Symbolic Toolbox contains, in addition to the function `fir2` described in the text, a few more functions like `fir1`, `remez`, `cremez`, `firls`, etc.

For the computation of the frequency response of a digital filter, MATLAB provides the `freqz` function, which is generally faster than the direct computation of `H(sqrt(-1)*om/fz)`.

For all these alternative methods, we refer the reader to the manual.

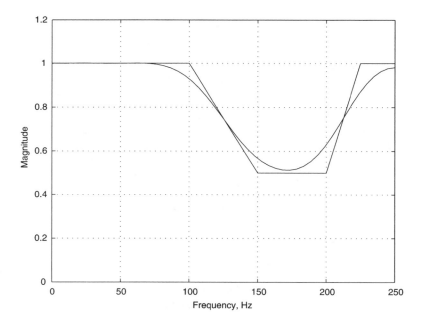

Figure 16.6   Definition and realization of the FIR filter.

EXAMPLE 16.1   Extracting two sinusoidal waves from their sum _____

Filters are frequently used to separate or to reject sinusoidal components from a composite signal. As an example, let us build a simple signal from two sinusoidal waves, one with the frequency 100 Hz, the other with the frequency 400 Hz, over an interval of 0.1 seconds. Let the sampling frequency be 2000 Hz.

```
>> fs = 2000;
>> t = 0:(1/fs):0.1;
>> x1 = sin(2*pi*100*t);
>> x2 = sin(2*pi*400*t);
>> x = x1+x2;
```

The signal x appears in the upper subplot of Figure 16.8. We now use `yulewalk` to design a low-pass and a high-pass filter. The base of significant frequencies is defined by

```
>> fHz0 = [0 225 275 1000];
```

The magnitude specification of the low-pass filter is

```
>> ml0 = [1 1 0 0];
```

and that of the high-pass filter is

```
>> mh0 = [0 0 1 1];
```

The normalized significant frequencies are obtained with

```
>> f0 = fHz0/(fs/2);
```

The parameters of the low-pass filter are calculated by

```
>> [bl, al] = yulewalk(6, f0, ml0);
```

and those of the high-pass filter by

```
>> [bh, ah] = yulewalk(6, f0, mh0);
```

In order to check the quality of the filters we calculate and plot their frequency characteristics with the commands

```
>> fHz1 = linspace(0, fs/2, 50);
>> om1 = 2*pi*fHz1;
>> z = exp(sqrt(-1)*om1/fs);
>> ml = abs(polyval(bl,z)./polyval(al,z));
>> mh = abs(polyval(bh,z)./polyval(ah,z));
```

We can compare the characteristic of the high-pass filter with its specification:

```
>> plot(fHz0, ml0, fHz1, ml);
```

Similarly, we can compare the characteristic of the low-pass filter with its specification:

```
>> plot(fHz0, mh0, fHz1, ml);
```

The frequency characteristics of the two filters can be seen in Figure 16.7. Satisfied with the result so far, we filter the given signal

```
>> y1 = filter(bl,al,x);
```

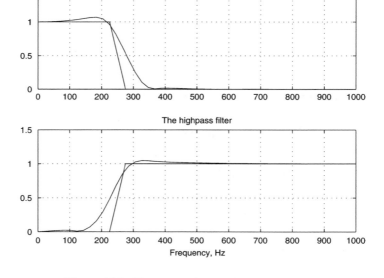

Figure 16.7   Frequency characteristics of the filters.

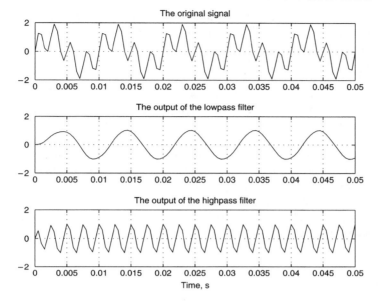

Figure 16.8 Separating two sine waves.

and, by plotting y_1, we can see that only the 400 Hz component passes. We now do the same thing with the high-pass filter

```
>> y2 = filter(bh,ah,x);
```

and, plotting y_2, can see that we recovered the 100 Hz component.

Figure 16.8 shows the original signal x and the outputs of the two filters, y_1 and y_2, for a time interval of 0.05 seconds.

16.4.3   The Tustin bilinear transformation

Sometimes we already have the transfer function $H(s)$ of an analog filter defined in the frequency domain, and want to approximate it with a digital filter $H_d(z)$. There are a number of different strategies commonly employed to transform an analogue filter into a digital 'equivalent', and the interested reader is referred to Chapter 4 of Franklin, Powell and Workman (1990).

One of the possible approaches is to find a function $s = s(z)$ in the variable z, that closely approximates the differential operator, and construct

$$H_d(z) = H(s(z)). \tag{16.14}$$

The transformation

$$s(z) = \frac{2}{T_s}\frac{z - 1}{z + 1} \tag{16.15}$$

is called **Tustin's bilinear transformation**, and is performed by the MATLAB bilinear function.   In Equation 16.15 T_s is the sampling interval and z, the unitary time shift operator.

This transformation is closely related to the trapezoidal integration rule (see Section 11.2) and is valid within the limits in which integration can be substituted by its trapezoidal approximation, which is often the case if the functions involved are smooth and the sampling time short enough. Tustin's transformation has the merits of involving relatively simple algebraic operations and mapping stable continuous filters into stable digital filters.

Its drawback is that, as the sampling rate decreases, it introduces phase distortion, which can only partially be corrected with prewarping. Again we must refer the reader willing to go deeper into the subject to a text in signal processing, such as Franklin, Powell and Workman (1990), or Gabel and Roberts (1973).

As an example, let us design a digital filter with characteristics similar to those of the second-order, low-pass filter with the transfer function

$$H(s) = \frac{\omega_n^2}{s^2 + 2\zeta\omega_n s + \omega_n^2} \tag{16.16}$$

where $\omega_n = 30\,\text{rad/s}$, $\zeta = 0.6$, and the signal is sampled at $100\,\text{Hz}$. To solve the problem in MATLAB we begin by defining the sampling frequency

```
>> fs = 100;
```

and the parameters of the filter

```
>> wn = 30; zi=0.6;
```

The numerator is

```
>> num = [wn^2];
```

and the terms of the denominator, in the order of the descending powers of s, are

```
>> den =[1 2*zi*wn wn^2];
```

We obtain the digital filter equivalent to the given analogue one by

```
>> [b,a] = bilinear(num,den,fs);
```

In order to compare the original analogue filter, defined by [num,den], with the digital filter, defined by [b,a], we generate an array of linearly spaced significant frequencies in rad/s

```
>> om = linspace(0, 300);
```

Next, we compute the frequency response of the analogue filter with the commands

```
>> s  = sqrt(-1)*om;
>> hs = polyval(num,s)./polyval(den,s);
```

We compute the frequency response of the digital filter by

```
>> z  = exp(s/fs);
>> hz = polyval(b,z)./polyval(a,z);
```

and we compare the magnitudes of the two responses by

```
>> subplot(2, 1, 1)
>> plot(om, abs(hs), om, abs(hz))
>> grid on
>> title('Comparing magnitudes');
```

and the phases by

```
>> subplot(2, 1, 2)
>> plot(om, 180/pi*angle(hs), om, 180/pi*angle(hz))
>> grid on
>> title('Comparing phases');
```

The resulting graphs are shown in Figure 16.9.

16.5   The Discrete Fourier Transform

A signal $f(t)$ of a continuous variable t is said to be **periodic of period** T if, for each t, $f(t + T) = f(t)$. If there is a minimum real positive period, this period is called the **fundamental period** of f.

Similarly, a digital signal $d = [\ldots, d(-1), d(0), d(1), d(2), \ldots]$ is said to be **periodic of period** P if, for each integer k, $d(k + P) = d(k)$.

If we sample a periodic function f of real period T at constant sampling intervals T_s, and T_s is a submultiple of T, say $T_s = T/N$, the sampled version d of f is a

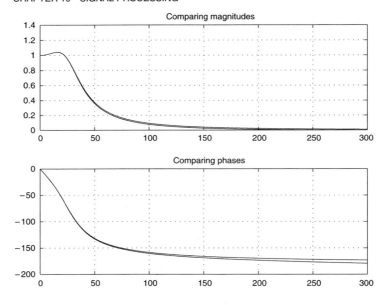

Figure 16.9   Approximation of an analogue filter by an IIR filter.

periodic digital signal of period N. Recall that, by definition of the sampled version, $d(k) = f(k \cdot T_s)$ and, therefore,

$$
\begin{aligned}
d(k + N) &= f((k + N) \cdot T_s) \\
&= f((k + N) \cdot T/N) \\
&= f(k \cdot T/N + T) \\
&= f(k \cdot T/N) \\
&= f(k \cdot T_s) \\
&= d(k)
\end{aligned}
$$

A periodic signal of period N is uniquely represented by any N consecutive terms, for example the terms with indices 1 to N, and can, therefore, be conveniently represented in MATLAB by a vector x of length N. The vector x is called the **time domain representation** of the signal d, and is simply defined by the array of components $x(h) = d(h)$, for $h = 1$ to N.

From the time domain representation x of d, using the periodicity of the signal, it is easy to reconstruct the signal itself, by means of the relation $d(h) = x(k)$, for the only k that simultaneously satisfies the following two conditions:

(1) $1 \le k \le N$

(2) $h - k$ is divisible by N.

With a slight abuse of notation, we shall identify the signal d with its time domain representation x.

Each entry $x(k)$ of the signal x can be either a real or a complex number. Actually, as we shall see in a moment, there is little advantage in considering real signals separately, either from the computational or the theoretical point of view, and it is probably more convenient to study only the general case when each $f(k)$ is complex, and consider real signals as a particular case, when all imaginary parts just happen to be equal to zero.

The **Discrete Fourier Transform, DFT**, of an array x of length N is another array, X, of the same length N. The Fourier transform is invertible, its inverse usually being denoted as **IFT**, that is, **Inverse Fourier Transform**. The mathematical definitions of the DFT and IFT functions will be given later in this section.

The vector X is also called the **frequency domain representation** of the signal x.

IFT and DFT are implemented in MATLAB very efficiently, using the algorithm known as the **Fast Fourier Transform**, or **FFT**. The Fast Fourier Transform is an algorithm that became popular after a famous article by Cooley and Tukey (1965). This algorithm requires approximately $N \log(N)$ arithmetic operations to compute the DFT, in comparison to approximately N^2 operations required by the routines in use until then.

Fourier transforms have two main families of applications. The first is transparent to the user. Many operations on a signal are much faster when implemented in the frequency domain. Some 15 functions in the Signal Processing Toolbox alone, instead of applying a function directly in the time domain, follow the scheme of transforming the original vector to the frequency domain, applying the appropriate function there, and then transforming the result back to the time domain. This leads to a great improvement in efficiency.

The second use of the DFT is to identify the frequency components of a signal, as we shall see in the next section.

16.6   A short introduction to the DFT

The reader is certainly familiar with the fact that in the N-dimensional space R^N (or C^N), a vector is the sum of its projections on the coordinate axes. This property is sometimes called the **decomposition property** of the vectors in R^N (or C^N).

In C^N, for example, we have a **natural basis**, denoted by the symbols $i_1, i_2, \ldots, i_N$, and defined by

$$i_1 = (1, 0, 0, \ldots, 0)$$
$$i_2 = (0, 1, 0, \ldots, 0)$$
$$i_3 = (0, 0, 1, \ldots, 0)$$
$$\vdots =$$
$$i_N = (0, 0, 0, \ldots, 1).$$

C^N, moreover, has a **dot product**, denoted by the symbol $\langle | \rangle$ and defined as follows. If

$$x = [x_1, x_2, \ldots, x_N]$$
$$y = [y_1, y_2, \ldots, y_N]$$

their dot product is

$$\langle x | y \rangle = \sum_{h=1}^{N} x_h \overline{y_h}$$

where $\overline{y_h}$ means, as explained in Chapter 4, the complex conjugate of y_h. The particular definition of the dot product in R^N and its MATLAB implementation are introduced in Subsection 1.2.4 and in Sections 2.9 and 2.10.

We also recall that the projection of the vector x on a non-zero vector y is the vector

$$x_y = \langle x | y \rangle \frac{y}{\langle y | y \rangle}$$

This vector is also called the **component** of x in the direction of y.

A basis of R^N (or C^N) is said to be **orthogonal** with respect to a dot product $\langle | \rangle$ if the dot product of any two distinct elements of the basis is equal to 0. For example, the vectors $i_1, i_2, \ldots, i_N$ just defined are an **orthogonal basis** of R^N (or C^N).

The decomposition property can be generalized into the following theorem:

For any orthogonal basis of R^N (or C^N), a vector is equal to the sum of its components in the direction of the vectors of the basis.

In other words, the decomposition property holds not only for the natural basis, but also for *any* orthogonal basis.

It is well known that the family of N vectors, each of length N, $e_m = [e_m(h)]$, defined as

$$e_m(h) = \exp\left(2\pi i \frac{(m-1)(h-1)}{N}\right) \qquad 1 \le m \le N$$

form an orthogonal basis for C^N with respect to the dot product previously defined. Moreover, for each h, $\langle e_h | e_h \rangle = N$. The proof of these two facts can be found in virtually any book on signal processing, such as Oppenheim and Shafer (1975). We will verify this result using MATLAB in a particular case, say for $N = 16$.

In the matrix **E** we are about to create, the m-th row represents the vector e_m. Please type the following MATLAB commands:

```
>> N = 16;
>> for m = 1:N
```

```
        for n = 1:N
                E(m,n) = exp(2*pi*sqrt(-1)*(m-1)*(n-1)/N);
        end
end
```

Let us now construct the matrix $\mathbf{D}$ that has the dot product of e_h and e_k in position (h, k). Verify that D is given in MATLAB by the expression

```
≫ D = E*E'
```

and is equal to `N*eye(N, N)`.

The Discrete Fourier Transform, X, of a vector x of length N, is defined as $X(h) = \langle x | e_h \rangle$. Therefore $X(h)$ represents, up to a multiplicative coefficient, the magnitude of the projection of x in the direction of e_h. The operation of reconstructing x from X, called the inverse Fourier transform, is performed in MATLAB by the `ifft` function. As a consequence of the decomposition property, `ift` performs the algebraic operation

$$x = \sum_{h=1}^{N} \frac{X(h)}{N} e_h \tag{16.17}$$

EXAMPLE 16.2

Let us verify Formula 16.17 for a random vector of 128 terms.

```
≫ N = 128;
≫ x = rand(1,N);
≫ X = fft(x);
≫ t = (0:(N-1))/N;
≫ for h=1:N
        yy(h,:)  = X(h)/N*exp(2*pi*sqrt(-1)*(h-1)*t);
end
≫ y = sum(yy);
```

Now compare x and y, either graphically

```
≫ plot(1:N, x, 1:N, y)
```

or numerically

```
≫ max(abs(x-y))
```

EXAMPLE 16.3   A digression on code efficiency —————————————

Because of the large size of the arrays considered, solving problems with MATLAB in the field of signal and image processing requires a higher degree of skill than many other fields. Two operations, in particular, are very inefficient and should be avoided whenever possible, namely dynamic memory allocation and FOR loops. Memory allocation takes place whenever we ask the operating system for space to store a new matrix, or when we increase the dimension of an existing one. Each such request is extremely time consuming. FOR loops should be avoided and replaced as often as possible by array operations, such as +, -, :, which are faster by several orders of magnitude.

To illustrate these ideas let us return to the example in Section 16.6 in which, when creating the matrix E, we sacrificed code efficiency for the sake of clarity. A faster solution is obtained by allocating space for the solution matrix and eliminating one loop by vectorization. Write the following M-file and run it.

```
N  = 16;
P1 = zeros(N, N);
l  = [ 0: (N-1)]/N;
for m = 1:N
        P1(m, :) = exp(2*pi*sqrt(-1)*(m-1)*l);
end
```

Type

```
>> P1 - E
```

and you will obtain the zero 16-by-16 matrix.

We can eliminate FOR loops completely by calculating the transpose-conjugate of the FFT of the identity matrix:

```
>> P2 = fft(eye(N, N))';
```

We can again verify the result with

```
>> P2 - E
```

This time, instead of zeros we get very small differences due to numerical errors.

The reader is invited to assign a larger value to N, and compare the time needed for calculations in the three ways described above.

16.7   The power spectrum

Let x be the time-domain representation of a periodic signal of period T, sampled at intervals $T_s = T/N$, and X its discrete Fourier transform.

The base vector e_h defined in the previous section is the sampled version of the continuous signal

$$\exp\left(2\pi i \frac{h-1}{T}t\right) \tag{16.18}$$

of frequency $(h-1)/T$ Hz.

The vector $(X(h)/N)e_h$ is the projection of x in direction of e_h. For $h > 1$, this vector is often referred to as the **component** of x of frequency $(h-1)/T$ Hz. The h-th entry of the vector X, that is, $X(h)$, is sometimes called **the h-th bin of X**, especially in the signal processing community.

The average of x is $X(1)/N$ and is sometimes called the **DC component** of the signal x, especially by electrical engineers; $(X(2)/N)e_2$ and $(X(N)/N)e_N$, which are associated to the period T, are called the **fundamental components** of the signal.

Figure 16.10 shows the relationship between the components of $X = \text{fft}(x)$ and the frequency components of x. If you are familiar with the literature on the subject, please notice that MATLAB notation is slightly different from that used in many books.

For each $h = 1, 2, \ldots, N-1$, the terms $X(1+h)$ and $X(1+N-h)$ are called **conjugate terms**. Exercise 16.1 justifies this definition.

The array of elements $|X(h)|^2/N$ is called the **power spectrum** of x, as for many phenomena the square of the signal, or a multiple of it, represents its power. If this is the case, the decomposition theorem has an important physical interpretation.

The square of the magnitude of the vector x, by definition equal to

$$\langle x|x\rangle = \sum_{h=1}^{N} |x_h|^2$$

MATLAB index convention

If x is the discrete version of a periodic signal of period T sampled at frequency $f_s = N/T$ Hz and X is its Fourier transform,

1. X(1)	is associated with the DC component of the signal
2. For $b \leq N/2 + 1$ $X(b)$	is associated with the frequency $\frac{b-1}{T} = \frac{b-1}{N}f_s$ Hz
3. For $f \leq f_s/2$ The frequency f Hz	is associated with the bin $b = \frac{N.f}{f_s}$

Figure 16.10 Relationship between the frequency components of a signal and its DFT.

can be computed using Equation 16.17:

$$\langle x | x \rangle = \sum_{h=1}^{N} \frac{|X_h|^2}{N} \qquad\qquad (16.19)$$

as all the mixed products $\langle e_h | e_k \rangle$ are equal to 0 when $h \neq k$. The term $|X_h|^2/N$ represents the power of the component of x of frequency $f = (h - 1) f_s / N$. So Equation 16.19 states that *the power of a signal is equal to the sum of the powers of its individual components*. This is one of the forms of Parseval's theorem (Marc Antoine, 1755–1836).

EXAMPLE 16.4   Extracting the spectral frequencies of a signal _____

We are going to sum two signals of different frequencies and amplitudes, and see how each contributes to the power spectrum. The only difficulty in this example is to keep track of which bin of the power corresponds to which frequency, and how the magnitude of the power relates to the amplitude of the signal. We begin by creating a signal x_1 of amplitude $a_1 = 7$ and frequency $f_1 = 16$ Hz and a second signal x_2 of amplitude $a_2 = 3$ and frequency $f_2 = 48$ Hz, sampled at 128 Hz, and call x their sum

```
>> N = 512;                  % number of points
>> b = 1:N;                  % bins
>> Ts = 1/128;               % sampling interval in seconds
>> fs = 1/Ts;                % sampling frequency in hertz
>> ts = Ts*(b-1);            % sampling instants
>> a1 = 7; f1 = 16;
>> x1 = a1*sin(2*pi*f1*ts);  % 1st signal
>> a2 = 3; f2 = 48;
>> x2 = a2*sin(2*pi*f2*ts);  % 2nd signal
>> x = x1+x2;
```

If you want to see the resulting signal (Figure 16.11) enter the commands

```
>> plot(ts, x)
>> xlabel('Time, s'), ylabel('x')
```

We can now construct and plot the power spectrum:

```
>> X = fft(x);              % DFT of x
>> pwr = X.*conj(X)/N;      % power of the signal
>> frs = (b-1)/N*fs;        % frequencies
>> subplot(2,1,1);
```

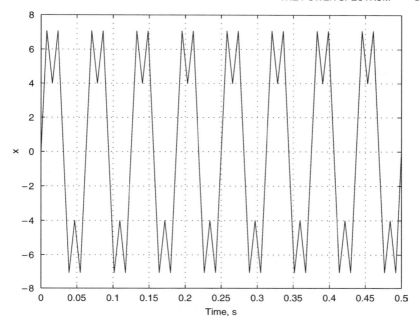

Figure 16.11   The sum of two sinusoids.

```
>> plot(b, pwr)          % plot power spectrum
>> grid on; xlabel('bin number'); ylabel('Power');
>> axis([ 1 N 0 8000 ])
>> subplot(2,1,2);
>> plot(frs, pwr);
>> grid on; xlabel('Frequency, Hz'); ylabel('Power');
>> axis([ 1 frs(N) 0 8000 ])
```

The resulting plot appears in the upper graph of Figure 16.12. The signal x_1 contributes to the power at bin 65, associated with the frequency $f_1 = 16\,\text{Hz}$ ($65 = 1 + 512 \times 16/128$, see Figure 16.10) and at bin 449, the latter because the conjugate of the number found in bin $65 = 1 + 64$ is stored in bin $449 = 1 + 512 - 64$.

The power spectrum is shown in the lower graph of Figure 16.12. The reader is invited to verify that pwr(65) is equal to $(a_1/2)^2 N$. Similarly, the second sinusoidal signal x_2 contributes its power to bins 193 and 321, and pwr(193) = pwr(321) is equal to $(a_2/2)^2 N$.

EXAMPLE 16.5   Identification of the frequencies that contain most power _____

In this example we are going to decompose a triangular signal of period $T = 5$ seconds and peak-to-peak amplitude 1 into its frequency components, using 512

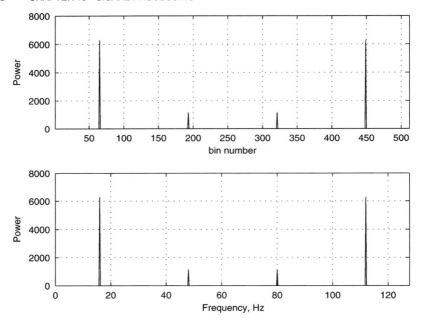

Figure 16.12   Power spectrum of the signal $x = x1 + x2$.

sampling points. We are interested in finding what percentage of the total power is contained in a signal obtained from the original, by neglecting all components except the four most significant ones. We also want to know how close the approximating signal is to the original. First of all, we are going to construct the discrete version x of the signal, by sampling it at 512 equally spaced points:

```
≫ T = 5;
≫ N = 512;
≫ t = linspace(0, T, N+1); t = t(1:N);
≫ x1 = 2*t/T-1/2 ; x2 = 2*(T-t)/T-1/2;
≫ x = min(x1,x2);        % the triangular signal
```

and construct its power spectrum:

```
≫ b = 1:N;                     % bin sequential number
≫ X = fft(x);
≫ Ts = T/N; fs = N/T;         % sampling interval and frequency
≫ frs = (b-1)/T;              % equal to (b-1)/N*fs;
≫ pow = X.*conj(X)/N;
```

To check our results so far, we can now verify Parseval's equality. The following two numbers should be equal, up to the numerical precision of the computer:

```
>> [sum(pow) norm(x)^2]
ans =
    42.6680    42.6680
```

It is easy to identify the frequencies that contain the largest part of the power, using the sort function which returns the elements of pow in increasing order:

```
>> [spow, spos] = sort(pow);
```

Let us find the indices of the four frequencies that contain most power:

```
>> m = 4; spos(N: -1:  (N-m+1))
```

We see that these frequencies are contained in bins 512, 2, 510 and 4. Let us now construct the approximating signal:

```
>> X4 = zeros(X); % allocate space for approximated X
>> h = [512 2 510 4];
>> X4(h) = X(h); % copy the bins that contain most power
```

The percentage of the power contained in the four most significant terms is then given by

```
>> perc = 100*(norm(X4)/norm(X))^2
```

In conclusion, 99.7698% of the power is contained in just four terms, those corresponding to the fundamental frequency 0.2 Hz, associated with bin number 2, its conjugate frequency, associated with bin 512, the second harmonic, 0.6 Hz, associated with bin 4, and its conjugate, associated with bin 510. We will use this result in Example 16.8.

The following lines show how closely the original triangular signal is approximated; they produce the graph shown in Figure 16.13.

```
>> x4 = ifft(X4);
>> plot(t, [x; x4]);
>> grid on
>> xlabel('t');
>> ylabel('Triangular signal and its approximation')
```

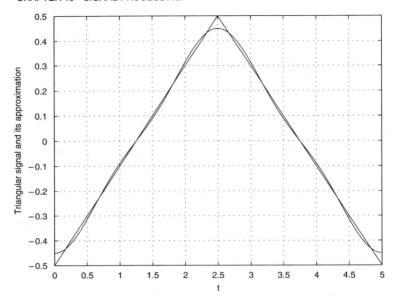

Figure 16.13   Approximation of a triangular signal.

16.8   Trigonometric expansion of a signal

The purpose of this section is to show how the discrete version of a real signal, periodic of period T, and sampled at intervals $T_s = T/N$, can be expressed as a linear combination of sines and cosines in the form

$$x = \sum_{h=1}^{N} \left(A_h \cos \left(2\pi (h-1) \frac{t}{T} \right) + B_h \sin \left(2\pi (h-1) \frac{t}{T} \right) \right) \qquad (16.20)$$

for each t multiple of T_s. We have seen that, if X denotes the Fourier transform of x, Equation 16.17 implies

$$x = \sum_{h=1}^{N} \frac{X(h)}{N} \exp \left(2\pi i (h-1) \frac{t}{T} \right) \qquad (16.21)$$

Using Euler's identity, and calling R and I, respectively, the real and imaginary parts of X, Equation 16.21 can be rewritten as

$$x = \sum_{h=1}^{N} \left(\frac{R_h}{N} \cos \left(2\pi (h-1) \frac{t}{T} \right) - \frac{I_h}{N} \sin \left(2\pi (h-1) \frac{t}{T} \right) \right)$$

$$+ i \sum_{h=1}^{N} \left(\frac{R_h}{N} \sin \left(2\pi (h-1) \frac{t}{T} \right) + \frac{I_h}{N} \cos \left(2\pi (h-1) \frac{t}{T} \right) \right) \qquad (16.22)$$

This identity holds for each x, but can be further simplified when x is real. In this case we know *a priori* that the imaginary part of Equation 16.22 must vanish, proving Identity 16.20 for

$$A_h = R_h/N$$
$$B_h = -I_h/N$$

and each h from 1 to N.

Formula 16.20 is called the **trigonometric expansion** of x.

EXAMPLE 16.6

In the following example we shall verify Formula 16.20 for a 5-second interval and a random vector of 128 terms.

```
≫ T = 5;                % time interval, seconds
≫ N = 128;              % length of the vector
≫ t = linspace(0,T,N+1);
≫ t = t(1:N);           % sampling time
≫ x = rand(t);          % a random vector
≫ X = fft(x);           % its DFT
≫ A = real(X)/N;        % cosine coefficients
≫ B = -imag(X)/N;       % sine coefficients
≫ sumcos = zeros(N, N);
≫ sumsin = zeros(N, N);
≫ for h=1:N
        sumcos(h,:)  = A(h)*cos(2*pi*(h-1)*t/T);
        sumsin(h,:)  = -B(h)*sin(2*pi*(h-1)*t/T);
end
≫ y = sum(sumcos + sumsin);
```

Now compare x and y, either graphically

```
≫ plot(t,x,t,y)
```

or numerically

```
≫ max(abs(x-y))
```

In our version of MATLAB the result was 2.242e-14, which is 0 within the arithmetic precision of our processor.

EXAMPLE 16.7   Trigonometric decomposition of a triangular signal _____

We now want to decompose the triangular signal x defined in Example 16.5 into its trigonometric components and check the results. If the number N = 512 that appears in the next block of commands is too large for the memory of your computer, you may want to reduce it to a smaller one, such as 32.

```
≫ T = 5;
≫ N = 512;
≫ t = linspace(0, T, N+1); t = t(1:N);
≫ x1 = 2*t/T - 1/2 ; x2 = 2*(T-t)/T - 1/2;
≫ x = min(x1, x2); % the triangular signal
≫ plot(t, x)
```

Let us now compute the coefficients of the sines and the cosines:

```
≫ X = fft(x);
≫ A = real(X)/N;    % cosine coefficients
≫ B = -imag(X)/N;   % sine coefficients
≫ sumcos = zeros(N,N);
≫ sumsin = zeros(N,N);
≫ for h=1:N
        sumcos(h,:)  = A(h)*cos(2*pi*(h-1)*t/T);
        sumsin(h,:)  = B(h)*sin(2*pi*(h-1)*t/T);
end
≫ y = sum(sumcos + sumsin);
```

We can now check the results by comparing x and y, either graphically

```
≫ plot(t,x,t,y);
```

or numerically

```
≫ max(abs(x-y))
```

16.9   High frequency signals and aliasing

Figure 16.10 shows the correspondence between the power of a signal and its discrete Fourier transform for frequencies up to the Nyquist frequency. It is interesting to investigate what happens when we sample at constant intervals T_s a continuous periodic signal of frequency higher than the Nyquist frequency $N_f = 1/(2T_s)$. As we shall see in a moment, the sampled version of such a signal is identical to that of another signal of lower frequency. This phenomenon is called **aliasing**, from 'alias', which comes from a Latin root meaning 'other'. A complete discussion of aliasing can be found, for example, in Oppenheim and Shafer (1975). With the help of MATLAB, we are going to show in an intuitive, if not rigorous, fashion, why aliasing occurs.

To fix the ideas, let us choose a time interval T of 5 seconds, $N = 16$ samples per period, and indicate the sampling interval with $T_s = T/N$ and the sampling frequency with $f_s = 1/T_s$.

A continuous periodic signal of period T has as its fundamental period a sub-multiple of T, say T/k, for a suitable k. Let us indicate its frequency, k/T, with the letter f. Such signals are, for instance, $\sin(2\pi ft)$ and $\cos(2\pi ft)$. The frequency f can always be written as

$$f = f_{app} + nf_s$$

where n is an integer and $0 \leq |f_{app}| < N_f$. It is then easy to verify that, at each t multiple of T_s, say $t = hT_s$, $\sin(2\pi ft) = \sin(2\pi f_{app}t)$. In fact,

$$
\begin{aligned}
\sin(2\pi ft) &= \sin(2\pi(f_{app} + nf_s)t) \\
&= \sin(2\pi(f_{app} + nf_s)hT_s) \\
&= \sin(2\pi f_{app}hT_s + 2\pi nf_shT_s) \\
&= \sin(2\pi f_{app}hT_s + 2\pi nh) \\
&= \sin(2\pi f_{app}t)
\end{aligned}
$$

So the signal $x = \sin(2\pi ft)$, of frequency f, when sampled at frequency f_s, is indistinguishable from the signal $x_l = \sin(2\pi f_{app}t)$ of a lower frequency f_{app}.

MATLAB allows us to produce an illustrative plot of aliasing. Please prepare the following M-file, `alias.m`:

```
T = 5;                    % fundamental period
Np = 512;                 % number of points for plotting
t = linspace(0,T,Np+1);
t = t(1:Np);              % fine resolution time,
                          % for plotting

N = 16;                   % number of sampling points
Ts = T/N;                 % sampling interval
fs = 1/Ts;                % sampling frequency
ts = Ts*(0:(N-1));        % sampling instants
Nf = 1/(2*Ts);            % Nyquist frequency

f  = k/T;                 % frequency of the continuous
                          % signal
x  = sin(2*pi*f*t);       % signal, high resolution
xs = sin(2*pi*f*ts);      % signal, sampling resolution
```

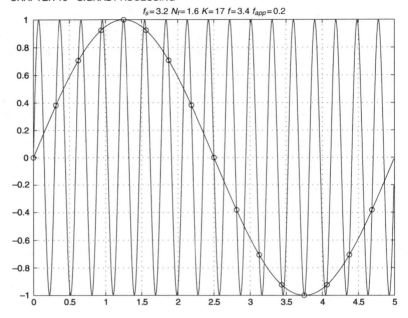

Figure 16.14   A high frequency signal sampled as a low frequency one.

```
% find fapp, such that f = n*fs+fapp
n    = round(f/fs);
fapp = f-n*fs;
xa   = sin(2*pi*fapp*t);

plot(t,[x;xa],ts,xs,'o');
str1 = ['fs = ',num2str(fs),' Nf = ',num2str(Nf)];
str2 = ['k = ',num2str(k),' f = ',num2str(f),'];
str3 = [ fapp = ',num2str(fapp)];
str  = [ str1, '    ',str2, '    ', str3 ];
title(str);
```

and run the file with the command

```
≫ k = 17; alias
```

You may compare the results with Figure 16.14.

EXAMPLE 16.8   A vibrating platform _____

The calculations in Examples 16.5 and 16.7 can find an interesting technical application in the design of a vibration testing machine. A simple reaction type testing

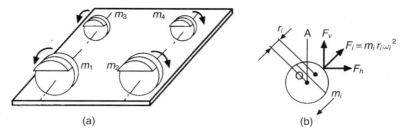

(a)   (b)

Figure 16.15   A vibration testing machine.

machine is shown in Figure 16.15 (for more examples and details see Unholz (1988)).
The active components of the machine are four rotating, unbalanced masses m_1 to m_4.
As illustrated in Figure 16.15(a), the unbalanced masses can be segments of circles
made of steel and assembled on rotating disks. The masses m_1 and m_2 are equal, but
rotate in opposite directions, and so are the smaller masses m_3 and m_4.

One of the components is shown in detail in Figure 16.15(b). Let the distance
between the axis of rotation, passing through O, and the centre of the unbalanced
mass, m_i, be r_i. Let us assume that the mass turns around O with an angular velocity
ω_i. The centrifugal force developed in the centre of the unbalanced mass equals
$F_i = m_i r_i \omega_i^2$. If the motion starts from the vertical axis OA and the sense of rotation
is clockwise, after a time interval t the angle between OA and the direction of F
equals $\omega_i t$. The vertical component of the centrifugal force is $F_v = m_i r_i \omega_i^2 \cos \omega_i t$,
and the horizontal component is $F_h = m_i r_i \omega_i^2 \sin \omega_i t$. To the left of this mass there is
an equal mass which rotates in the opposite sense, also starting from a vertical axis.
It will develop a centrifugal force whose vertical component is equal to F_v, while the
horizontal component is $-F_h$. The horizontal components balance each other, while
the vertical components add up, producing a vibrating force equal to $2m_i r_i \omega_i^2 \cos \omega_i t$.
It is important to observe that, in the expressions of the forces and their components,
the product $m_i r_i$ represents the static moment of the mass about the axis of rotation.

If two pairs of counter-rotating masses are arranged on the same vibrating
table, and the ratios between their moments and their angular velocities are properly
established, it is possible to synthesize vibrating pulses of various shapes. We shall try
in this way to approximate the wave shape analysed in Examples 16.5 and 16.7. We
recall that only four components contained almost all the energy. These were the first
harmonic, of frequency 0.2 Hz, its conjugate, the third harmonic, of frequency 0.6 Hz,
and its conjugate. The conjugates correspond to rotations in the opposite direction,
with frequencies 0.2 and 0.6 Hz. This means that a pair of unbalanced masses rotating
in opposite directions, as in Figure 16.15, will generate the forces corresponding to a
pair of conjugate terms in the trigonometric expansion of the force. The amplitudes
of the components are proportional to the coefficients in the trigonometric expansion;
let them be 0.2026 N, for the frequencies 0.2 and -0.2 Hz, and 0.0225 N, for the
frequencies 0.6 and -0.6 Hz.

We begin the design of the vibrating machine by entering the angular velocities
of the unbalanced masses, in rad/s,

```
>> omega1 = 2*pi*0.2, omega2 = 2*pi*0.6
omega1 =
    1.2566
omega2 =
    3.7699
```

Next, we enter the magnitudes of the forces to be generated by the unbalanced masses:

```
>> F1 = 0.2026; F2 = 0.0225;
```

The mass moments, $m_1 r_1$, $m_2 r_2$, in kgm, that must generate these forces are

```
>> r1m1 = F1/omega1^2
r1m1 =
    0.1283
>> r2m2 = F2/omega2^2
r2m2 =
    0.0016
```

We assume that the unbalanced masses are segments of a circle of thickness 0.02 m, made of steel whose density is 7850 kg/m^3. The static moments of the segment areas, in m^3, are given by

```
>> s1 = r1m1/(0.02*7850)
s1 =
    8.1718e-04
>> s2 = r2m2/(0.02*7850)
s2 =
    1.0084e-05
```

It can be shown that the moment of the area of a segment of a circle depends only on its chord, t, and is equal to $t^3/12$. Using this formula we calculate the chords of the segments of the circle, in m, by

```
>> t1 = (12*s1)^(1/3)
t1 =
    0.2140
>> t2 = (12*s2)^(1/3)
t2 =
    0.0495
```

Let us check if we can reduce the chord of the masses m_1, m_2, by increasing their thickness to 0.03 m:

```
≫ s1 = r1m1/(0.03*7850)
s1 =
    5.4479e-04
≫ t1 = (12*s1)^(1/3)
t1 =
    0.1870
```

We can now show that the designed unbalanced masses indeed produce a vertical force whose time graph closely approximates the desired triangular form. We begin by defining a time axis

```
≫ t = 0:  0.02:  10;
```

and continue by writing the expressions of the dominant harmonics

```
≫ f1 = 2*r1m1*omega1^2*cos(omega1*t);
≫ f2 = 2*r2m2*omega2^2*cos(omega2*t);
```

The plot is obtained with

```
≫ plot(t, (f1+f2))
≫ grid
≫ title('Synthesis of triangular vibrating force')
≫ xlabel('t, s')
≫ ylabel('F, N')
```

Try it for yourself and verify on the graph that the period of the triangular wave is indeed 5 seconds, and the amplitude of the vibrating force is 0.45 N, close to 0.5 N. A sketch of the masses designed in this example is shown in Figure 16.16. The figure was produced in MATLAB, and the dimensions are indicated in mm, as preferred in mechanical drawings.

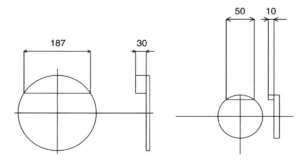

Figure 16.16   Dimensions of unbalanced masses.

16.10   Exercises

Solutions for Exercises 16.2, 16.3, 16.7, 16.10 and 16.12 appear at the back of the book.

■ **EXERCISE 16.1**   The conjugation proposition

(1)   Verify the following proposition for the vector x defined in MATLAB by `N = 128; x = rand(1,N)`:
        If x is a real signal of length N and X its Direct Fourier Transform, for each h in the range $[1, N - 1]$, $X(1 + N - h)$ is the complex conjugate of $X(1 + h)$.

(2)   If you are mathematically oriented, prove the proposition for each real vector x.
        Hint: By assumption $\bar{x} = x$ and $\overline{e_{1+h}} = e_{1+N-h}$.

■ **EXERCISE 16.2**   Define filter frequency characteristics
Some MATLAB functions, like `yulewalk` and `fir2`, build the coefficients of a digital filter that approximates a given one with assigned frequency characteristics.

(1)   Build a function `deffiltm.m` that allows the user to define the frequency characteristics of a filter by clicking the points in the frequency–magnitude plane with the mouse and returns the arrays of normalized frequencies (that is, frequencies normalized by the Nyquist frequency), `f0`, and magnitudes, `M`.

(2)   Test the function. Define, by means of `deffiltm` which you created at (1), the digital filter that, on a sequence sampled at 100 Hz (that is, for a Nyquist frequency of 50 Hz), has the following characteristics:

Magnitude	At frequency (Hz)
1.0	0
1.0	10
0.5	20
0.5	30
1.0	40
1.0	50

■ **EXERCISE 16.3**   Design IIR – `yulewalk`
A signal is sampled at 800 Hz. We want to use the `yulewalk` function to design an IIR digital filter which approximates the filter `F`, defined by the following frequency characteristics:

(1)   Write two arrays `f0` and `m0` that define the characteristics of the filter in the form required by `yulewalk`.
        Hint: Write the frequencies as multiples of the Nyquist frequency.

(2)   Verify the correctness of your solution to (1) by plotting `m0` versus `f0`.

(3)   Using the `yulewalk` function, find the coefficients of the filters of order 6, 8, 10 (call them respectively `bIIR6`, `aIIR6`, `bIIR8`, `aIIR8`, `bIIR10`, `aIIR10`) that approximate the given filter.

From Hz	to Hz	Magnitude
0	100	0
100	150	Increases linearly from 0 to 2
150	180	2
180	200	Decreases linearly to 0.5
200	240	0.5
240	300	Increases linearly from 0.5 to 1
300	400	1

(4)   Compare graphically the characteristics of the filters obtained with those of F.

■ **EXERCISE 16.4**   Testing a filter with sinusoidal inputs
While solving Exercise 16.3, you produced two arrays,

```
bIIR6 =[0.5169 -0.7337  0.6589 -0.6989  0.4929 -0.1354  0.1355]
```

and

```
aIIR6 =[1.0000 -0.3217  1.2452 -0.0819  0.5872  0.0185  0.1643]
```

which represent the coefficients of a digital filter. If you did not save them, please enter them manually. You want to check that the filter has the frequency characteristic required, by testing it on a number of sinusoidal inputs, as follows.

(1)   Create the discrete version of the signal $s = \sin(2\pi f t)$ sampled at 800 Hz, over a time interval of 1 second, for $f = 100$ Hz.
(2)   Using the `filter` function pass s through the filter defined by the coefficients bIIR6 and IIR6 and call the result fs. Plot fs as a function of time, for t in the interval [0.5, 0.6], after enough time for the effects of initial conditions to have faded away.
(3)   Check whether the filter has the desired frequency characteristic. (Observe, for example, that for a signal of 100 Hz, the amplification factor appears to be close to 0.5.)
(4)   Verify that the filter has the frequency characteristic we would expect from Exercise 16.3.
(5)   Repeat the exercise at (3) for the frequencies 100, 150, 180, 200, 240 and 300 Hz.

■ **EXERCISE 16.5**   Design FIR – `fir2`
A signal is sampled at 400 Hz. We want to use the `fir2` function to design an FIR digital filter which approximates the filter F, defined by the following frequency characteristics:

(1)   Write two arrays f0 and m0 that define the characteristics of the filter in the form required by `fir2`.

From Hz	to Hz	Magnitude
0	25	1
25	50	decreases linearly from 1 to 0
50	100	0
100	150	increases linearly from 0 to 1
150	200	1

(2) Verify the correctness of your solution to (1), by plotting m0 versus f0.
(3) Using the fir2 function, find the coefficients of the filters of order 10, 20, 30 (call them respectively bFIR10, bFIR20, bFIR30) that approximate the given filter.
(4) Compare graphically the characteristics of the filters obtained with those of F.

■ **EXERCISE 16.6** Bilinear function with assigned sampling rate
The following is the transfer function of a low-pass filter, defined in the s-plane:

$$H(s) = \frac{1}{1+s/P} \cdot \frac{\omega_n^2}{\omega_n^2 + 2\zeta\omega_n s + s^2}$$

with $P = 6\,\text{rad/s}$, $\omega_n = 15\,\text{rad/s}$ and $\zeta = 0.6$.

(1) Write $H(s)$ as the ratio of two polynomials, num and den, and express them according to the usual MATLAB convention (an array of coefficients of decreasing powers of s).
   Hint: Use the conv function.
(2) Plot the magnitude response of the filter defined by the rational function $H(s)$, in the range 0.1 to 100 rad/s, by displaying the frequencies in logarithmic scale and the magnitude in db.
(3) Plot its phase response in the same range, by displaying the frequency in rad/s and the phase in degrees (use the unwrap function, if it is available on your installation).
(4) Find the coefficients of its digital equivalent, assuming a sampling frequency of 50 Hz.
   Hint: Use the bilinear function.

■ **EXERCISE 16.7** Appropriate sampling rate for the bilinear function
The following is the transfer function of a low-pass filter, defined in the s-plane:

$$H(s) = \frac{1}{1+s/P} \cdot \frac{\omega_n^2}{\omega_n^2 + 2\zeta\omega_n s = s^2}$$

with $P = 8\,\text{rad/s}$, $\omega_n = 20\,\text{rad/s}$ and $\zeta = 0.65$. You want to realize an equivalent digital filter, and want to determine the sampling frequency with the help of MATLAB. Write an interactive MATLAB program that:

(1) prompts the user for a sampling frequency fs;

(2)   using the `bilinear` function, constructs the equivalent digital filter relative to `fs`;

(3)   displays the magnitude and phase characteristics of the original analogue and the equivalent digital filters;

(4)   repeats steps (1), (2), (3) until the user is satisfied, then exits the loop;

(5)   upon terminating the loop, displays the sampling frequency and the parameters of the digital filter.

(6)   Compare graphically the responses of the digital filter constructed at (4) with those of the original analogue filter.

■ **EXERCISE 16.8**   FFT and bins

X is a 256-point FFT, obtained by applying the Direct Fourier Transform to an array x of 256 points, obtained by sampling a periodic signal at 64 Hz. Looking at the power spectrum, we see a peak at the 33rd bin. This indicates a probable (that is, if aliasing can be excluded) component of which frequency in the original signal?

Hint: Use the formula in Figure 16.10.

■ **EXERCISE 16.9**   Aliasing

Consider again the signal x defined in the previous exercise. If aliasing is present, which other frequencies could produce the same peak?

■ **EXERCISE 16.10**   Power spectrum of rectangular signal

A rectangular periodic signal is sampled at 256 Hz over a time interval of 0.5 seconds, producing an array x that alternates 48 points of value 0 with 16 points of value 1.

(1)   Plot x as a function of time, over an interval of 0.5 seconds.

(2)   Compute and plot the power spectrum of x.

(3)   Indicate the first five frequencies that contain the most power.

Hint: Use the `sort` function.

(4)   Approximate x by these five harmonics (call the result `xappr5`) and plot x and `xappr5`.

■ **EXERCISE 16.11**   Filtering a signal

A low-pass filter F is defined by the arrays of coefficients a and b, obtained by the MATLAB command

```
≫ [b,a]=butter(5, 0.5)
```

The signal x, defined as

```
≫ Ts = 1/100; t = Ts*(1:500);
≫ f = 25;   x = sin(2*pi*f*t);
```

is the discrete version of $\sin(2\pi ft)$ sampled at 100 Hz over the time interval [0, 5].

Using the `filter` function without defining the initial states `Zi` (that is, letting MATLAB set them to 0, by default), find the signal y, obtained by passing x through the filter F, and observe the effect of transients by plotting y as functions of t over the interval $[0, 0.2]$.

■ **EXERCISE 16.12**   Filter with assigned initial conditions
A low-pass filter F is defined by the arrays of coefficients a and b, obtained with the MATLAB command

```
>> [b,a] = butter(5, 0.5)
```

The signal x is defined as

```
>> Ts = 1/100; f = 25; x = sin(2*pi*f*Ts*(1:500));
```

Find the vector `Zi` such that the command

```
>> y = filter(b,a,x,Zi);
```

produces a vector y that starts with 5 zeros. Check your answer by plotting the first 30 terms of y.
   Hint: Use the `filteric` function, described in the text.

Chapter 17
Case studies in mechanical engineering

17.1 Bending moment caused by a moving vehicle

This chapter contains two case studies that illustrate graphic facilities, economic storage of sparse matrices, and two new powerful features introduced in MATLAB 5, that is **structures** and **cells**. In the first section we shall analyse the bending moment of a simply-supported beam, under the influence of a moving, twin-axle vehicle. The results will be presented in three-dimensional plots.

The beam is shown in Figures 17.1 and 17.2. Let the span be s. The distance between the two vehicle axles is d; the distance of the forward axle from the left-hand support, x. We shall write a function that calculates the bending moments acting on the beam as the vehicle moves from left to right. We assume two independent variables: x, defined as above, and y, the coordinate of the beam section in which we calculate the moment.

It is possible to distinguish three cases, as shown in Figures 17.1 and 17.2. In the first case (see Figure 17.1(a)), only the forward axle of the vehicle entered the

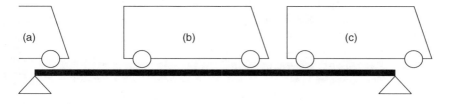

Figure 17.1   Vehicle moving along a simply-supported beam.

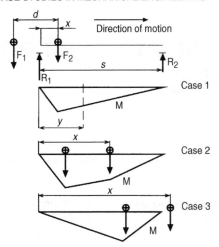

Figure 17.2   Bending moment produced by a vehicle moving along a simply-supported beam.

beam, while the rear axle is still moving on another beam, not connected to the one for which calculations are performed. In the second case (Figure 17.1(b)), both axles are within the beam span. In the third case (Figure 17.1(c)), the forward wheel moves on another beam, so that the bending moments are entirely due to the rear-axle load. Different equations must be used in the three cases.

The following listing yields the bending moments. The function is explained by the comments included. We named this function bending1, thus allowing the interested reader to develop further functions, for other bending situations, and name them bending2, bending3, and so on. The listing should be written to a file bending1.m. It is possible to write a more compact and elegant code, but we preferred to write clear statements whose significance can be easily appreciated by the reader.

```
function M = bending1(s, d, F1, F2)
%BENDING1 bending moments caused by vehicle moving on beam.
%    Bending moments caused vehicle by moving on
%    simply-supported beam.
%    The  input arguments and their SI units are:
%    s  - beam span, m
%    d  - axle distance, m
%    F1 - forward-axle load, N
%    F2 - rear axle load, N
%    The output is
%    M, m-by-n matrix of bending moments, Nm
%    Internal variables are:
%    x - position of forward axle relative to left-hand
```

```
%     support, positive forward, m
%     y - coordinate where M is calculated, measured from
%        the left-hand support, positive forward, m
%     R1 - reaction in left-hand support, N
%     R2 - reaction in right-hand support, N

s, d, F1, F2              % display the input
disp('Press ENTER to continue')
pause
step = d/10;
m = fix(s/step)            % number of y steps
n = fix((s + d)/step)      % number of x steps
x = [0: n]*step;           % equally spaced points
x = [ x (s+d) ]            % include last point
y = [0: m]*step;           % equally spaced points
y = [ y s ]                % include last point of span
M = zeros((m+2), (n+2));   % space for array of moments

for k = 1:(n+1)
        % case 1
        if x(k) < d
                disp('case 1')          % shows where we are
                R1 = (1 - x(k)/s)*F1;
                for l = 1:(m+1)
                    M(l,k) = y(l)*R1;
                    if y(l) >= x(k)
                        M(l,k) = M(l,k) - (y(l) - x(k))*F1;
                    end
                end
        % case 2
        elseif x(k) < s
                disp('case 2')          % shows where we are
                R1 = (1 - x(k)/s)*F1 + (1 + (d - x(k))/s)*F2;
                for l = 1:(m+1)
                    M(l, k) = y(l)*R1;
                    if y(l) >= x(k) - d
                        M(l,k) = M(l,k) - (y(l) - (x(k)-d))*F2;
                    end
                    if y(l) >= x(k)
                        M(l,k) = M(l,k) - (y(l) - x(k))*F1;
                    end
                end
        % case 3
        else
                disp('case 3')          % shows where we are
                R1 = (1 + (d - x(k))/s)*F2;
```

```
            for l = 1:(m+1)
                    M(l,k) = y(l)*R1;
                    if y(l) > x(k) - d
                        Mdiff  = (y(l) - x(k) + d)*F2;
                        M(l,k) = M(l,k) - Mdiff;
                    end
            end
        end
    end
Mmax = max(M)              % displays maximum for
                           % each vehicle position
Mmaxmax = max(Mmax)        % maximum maximorum moment

% 3-D MATLAB4 plot
surf(x, y, M)
xlabel('Position of forward axle, m')
ylabel('Position of section, m')
zlabel('Bending moment, Nm')
disp('Press ENTER to continue')
print
pause
contour3(x, y, M)
xlabel('Position of forward axle, m')
ylabel('Position of section, m')
zlabel('Bending moment, Nm')
print
```

As an example, let us call the bending1 function as follows:

```
>> S = 10; D = 3.42;
>> f1 = 1800; f2 = 2400;
>> moment = bending1(S, D, f1, f2);
```

If you want to see the entire array of bending-moment values, do not terminate the preceding statement with a semicolon. Then you will get many screens of data because M is, in this case, a 29-by-39 matrix. Whether you type the semicolon or not, the display will include the following information

```
Mmax =
    1.0e+03 *
 Columns 1 through 7
    0     0.5945    1.1470    ...
  ...
Mmaxmax =
 7.6364e+03
```

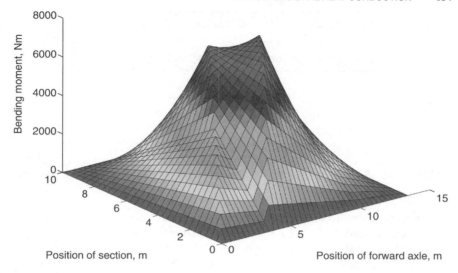

Figure 17.3   Surface of bending moments produced by a moving vehicle.

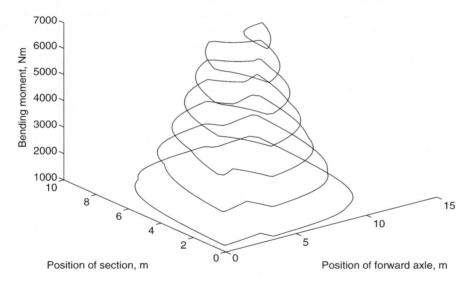

Figure 17.4   Contours of bending moments produced by a moving vehicle.

The graphic output is shown in Figures 17.3 and 17.4.

17.2   One-dimensional heat conduction

In this section we shall show how to use MATLAB for the integration of a relatively simple partial differential equation. In this case study we must build a matrix with

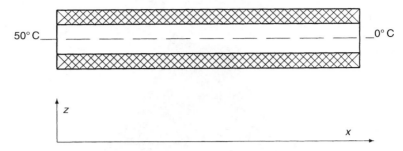

Figure 17.5   A section through a rod thermally insulated everywhere except at its ends.

many zero elements. To store it economically, we shall use the sparse-matrix facilities. Sparse matrices and the MATLAB functions dealing with them were introduced in Chapter 12; the reader is referred to Section 12.3 for details.

This case study follows an example given in Chapter 24 of Chapra and Canale (1989), with some modifications. Figure 17.5 shows a rod with 'perfect' thermal insulation everywhere except at its ends. We assume that these ends are held at two different, constant temperatures. Under these conditions heat is conducted from the hot to the cold end. We want to study the distribution of the temperature along the rod, as a function of time, for given initial and boundary conditions.

The governing equation is obtained from an energy balance: for each small element of the rod, the heat energy stored until time $t + \Delta t$ equals the energy stored until time t plus the energy that entered during the interval $[t, t + \Delta t]$ minus the energy exiting the element in the same time interval. The resulting equation is

$$q(x)\Delta y \Delta z \Delta t - q(x + \Delta x)\Delta y \Delta z \Delta t = \Delta x \Delta y \Delta z \rho C \Delta T \tag{17.1}$$

where

$\quad q(x)$ is the heat flux at x, in $\mathrm{cal} \cdot \mathrm{cm}^{-2} \cdot \mathrm{s}^{-1}$.
$\quad \Delta x,$ the longitudinal dimension of the element, in cm,
$\quad \Delta y,$ the vertical dimension of the element, in cm,
$\quad \Delta z,$ the transversal dimension of the element, in cm,
$\quad t,$ the time, in s,
$\quad \rho,$ the density of the rod material, in $\mathrm{g} \cdot \mathrm{cm}^{-3}$,
$\quad C,$ the heat capacity of the material, in $\mathrm{cal} \cdot \mathrm{g}^{-1} \cdot {}^{\circ}\mathrm{C}^{-1}$, and
$\quad u,$ the temperature in $^{\circ}\mathrm{C}$.

Dividing by the volume of the element, $\Delta x \Delta y \Delta z$, and by the element of time, Δt, and taking limits we obtain

$$-\frac{\partial q}{\partial x} = \rho C \frac{\partial u}{\partial t} \tag{17.2}$$

Substituting Fourier's law of heat conduction

$$q = -k\rho C \frac{\partial u}{\partial x} \tag{17.3}$$

into Equation 17.2 yields

$$\frac{\partial u}{\partial t} = k \frac{\partial^2 u}{\partial x^2} \tag{17.4}$$

where k is the coefficient of thermal diffusivity. For a rod built of aluminum let us assume $k = 0.835 \, \text{cm}^2\text{s}^{-1}$. Actually the value of k depends on the exact composition of the metal and on the temperature; it can be calculated from data found in tables of properties, such as those in Eckert and Drake (1972) or Holman and White (1992).

We approximate the governing, partial differential equation, by its **difference-equation analogue**:

$$u(x, t + \Delta t) = u(x, t) + k \frac{u(x - \Delta x, t) - 2u(x, t) + u(x + \Delta x, t)}{(\Delta x)^2} \Delta t \tag{17.5}$$

Instead of the continuous function $u(x, t)$ we work with a discrete function, U, such that

$$U(i, \ell) = u((i - 1) * \Delta x, (\ell - 1) * \Delta t) \tag{17.6}$$

Using Equation 17.6, and noting $\lambda = k\Delta t / (\Delta x)^2$, Equation 17.5 yields

$$U(i + 1, \ell + 1) = \lambda U(i, \ell) + (1 - 2\lambda)U(i + 1, \ell) + \lambda U(i + 2, \ell) \tag{17.7}$$

Let the initial temperature of the whole rod be $0\,^\circ\text{C}$. Let us calculate the evolution of the temperature, at each point of the rod, if one extremity is kept at $0\,^\circ\text{C}$ and the other one at $50\,^\circ\text{C}$.

$$U(1, \ell) = 50$$
$$U(Nx, \ell) = 0$$

for all ℓ. The initial conditions are

$$U(i, 1) = 0$$

for $i > 1$. It is easy to see that $U(:, \ell + 1)$ is related to $U(:, \ell)$ by the linear expression

$$U(:, \ell + 1) = \mathbf{T} * U(:, \ell)$$

where the colon ':' means, as in MATLAB, *all k*. The matrix $\mathbf{T}$ is called the **transition matrix** of the system and it is a **tridiagonal matrix**.

LIVERPOOL
JOHN MOORES UNIVERSITY
AVRIL ROBARTS LRC
TEL. 0151 231 4022

To fix the ideas let the rod length be $\ell = 10$ cm, and let the number of sections used in calculation be $N_x = 50$. The following program, stored in ROD1.M, yields the solutions for the first 50 seconds:

```
%ROD1 solves PDE of heat transmission along insulated rod.

k = 0.835;                    % thermal diffusivity, cm^2/s
L = 10;                       % rod length, cm
Nx = 50;                      % number of nodes along the rod
x = linspace(0, L, Nx);
dt = 0.01;                    % time step
dx = L/(Nx-1);                % length step
la = k*dt/(dx*dx);
% build tridiagonal matrix T
A = la*ones(Nx-1, 1);
D = (1-2*la)*ones(Nx, 1);  % main diagonal
B = la*ones(Nx-1, 1);
T = diag(A, -1) + diag(D, 0) + diag(B, 1);
clear A D B
T(1, 1) = 1;
T(1, 2) = 0;
T(Nx, Nx-1) = 0;
U = zeros(Nx, 1);
U(1) = 50;
% calculate
m = 1;
for n = 1:10
        if n <= 5
                s = 1;
        elseif n == 6
                s = 5;
        else
                s = 10;
        end
        for l = m:(m + s*100)
                UU = T*U;
                U = UU;
        end
        m = l;
        plot(x, UU)
        grid
        text(x(10+2*n), UU(10+2*n), num2str((m-1)/100))
        hold on
end
hold off
```

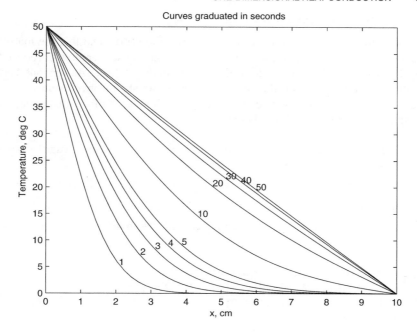

Figure 17.6   Temperature distribution in the rod. First program.

In the above program we have used the `diag` function to define the diagonals of the matrix T. Thus, as we declared A as a column vector of length $N_x - 1$, the statement `diag(A,-1)` generates a square matrix of order $Nx - 1 + |-1| = Nx$, with the elements of A on the diagonal under the main diagonal. For more details try `help diag` and examine Example 17.1. Only the values of U at the last time instant are stored, and they are used to plot the temperatures, against the rod length, at predetermined time instants. As can be seen in Section 17.3, storing all U values would require considerable memory resources.

The results are shown in Figure 17.6. In this solution all the elements of the transition matrix **T** were specified and stored. To find the memory resources employed for this we use the MATLAB `whos` facility. The corresponding display in MATLAB 5 is

```
Name      Size       Bytes     Class
   T      50x50      20000     double array
   U      50x1         400     double array
```

Most elements of **T** are equal to zero, that is, the transition matrix is **sparse**. As shown in Chapter 12, MATLAB provides a better way of storing sparse matrices; we shall use it in the next section.

17.3   Using a sparse matrix

In this section we are going to rewrite the script file ROD1.M so that the matrix **T** is defined and stored as a sparse matrix. This program uses features introduced in MATLAB 4 and will not run with earlier versions of the package. As versions 4 and 5 usually require more powerful computer resources, we shall store all values of **U** up to a certain time, let us say 5 seconds, and thus allow for further processing. The listing of the script file is shown below.

```
% ROD2.M solves PDE of heat transmission along insulated rod.
k = 0.835; L = 10; Nx = 50;
x = linspace(0, L, Nx);
dt = 0.01;
dx = L/(Nx - 1);
la = k*dt/(dx*dx);    % coefficient lambda
% build matrix T
e = ones(Nx, 1);
A = la*e; D = (1 - 2*la)*e; B = la*e;
T = spdiags([A, D, B], -1:1, Nx, Nx);
T(1, 1) = 1; T(1, 2) = 0;
T(Nx, Nx - 1) = 0;
% define initial conditions
T(Nx, Nx) = 1;
U = zeros(Nx, 1);
U(1) = 50;  % temperature at hot end, deg C
% simulate evolution of rod temperature
for k = 1:501
    U(:, k+1) = T*U(:, k);
end
% plot results
plot(x, U(:, 101), x, U(:, 201), x, U(:, 301),...
x, U(:, 401), x, U(:, 501))
xlabel('x')
ylabel('Temperature, deg C')
for m = 1:5
    text(x(10+2*m), U(10+2*m, (1+100*m)), num2str(m))
end
```

The sparse matrix T was generated using the spdiags function in the statement

```
T = spdiags([A, D, B], -1:1, Nx, Nx);
```

The diagonals are the columns of the matrix [A, D, B]. The argument -1:1 shows that column A contains the elements of the diagonal immediately under the main diagonal, column D, those in the main diagonal, and column B, the elements of the diagonal immediately above the main diagonal. The two arguments Nx define T as an N_x-by-N_x matrix.

Running the program produces the curves of temperature versus rod length, for the first five seconds; try the program for yourself. The memory allocations for the matrices T and U are again obtained with whos:

Name	Size	Bytes	Class
T	50x50	1980	sparse array
U	50x502	200800	double array

The difference is really tremendous, and it would have been even more impressive for more x-steps. Note that, while much memory was saved by defining T as sparse, considerable memory was required for storing U. As an exercise, fix the first program – that is, the one in Section 17.2 – by defining T as sparse, run the program again, and compare the memory resources needed in the three cases.

EXAMPLE 17.1   Building tridiagonal matrices ―――――――――――――

The following example is meant to clarify the way in which the tridiagonal matrix was defined in the first script file, that is, in Section 17.2, and in the second script file, in Section 17.3. To define a *full* matrix we begin by entering the vectors of diagonal elements:

```
≫ V1 = ones(5,1);
≫ V2 = 2*ones(4,1);
≫ V3 = 3*ones(4,1);
```

and we combine them by

```
≫ M = diag(V1, 0) + diag(V2, -1) + diag(V3, 1)
M =
    1    3    0    0    0
    2    1    3    0    0
    0    2    1    3    0
    0    0    2    1    3
    0    0    0    2    1
```

To define the same matrix as sparse we need three vectors of the same length; we enter them as

```
≫ V1 = V1;
≫ V2 = 2*ones(5, 1);
≫ V3 = 3*ones(5, 1);
```

and we combine them by

```
>> N = spdiags([V1 V2 V3], [0 -1 1], 5, 5)
N =
   (1,1)      1
   (2,1)      2
   (1,2)      3
   (2,2)      1
   (3,2)      2
   (2,3)      3
   (3,3)      1
   (4,3)      2
   (3,4)      3
   (4,4)      1
   (5,4)      2
   (4,5)      3
   (5,5)      1
```

Only the non-zero elements are stored now, together with their indices. We can convert a sparse matrix to a full matrix with the `full` command:

```
>> N1 = full(N)
N1 =
     1     3     0     0     0
     2     1     3     0     0
     0     2     1     3     0
     0     0     2     1     3
     0     0     0     2     1
```

and back to the sparse form with the `sparse` command:

```
>> N2 = sparse(N1)
N2 =
   (1,1)      1
   ...
   (5,5)      1
```

We can easily find the memory space required by the sparse and full matrices:

```
>> whos
```

```
Name          Size         Bytes     Class
...
  N           5x5           180      sparse array
  N1          5x5           200      double array
...
```

17.4   Operations on unit-affected quantities

17.4.1   Introduction

In Chapter 12 we introduced the new MATLAB 5 feature **structure**. As briefly explained there, a structure can include arrays of different sizes, as well as arrays of numbers and arrays of characters. This possibility of combining numerical and character-string data under one name allows us an interesting application that will be described in this section. The idea is to store values of constants together with their units. Moreover, when performing operations on those constants, we want to recover not only the value of the result, but also its unit.

To explain what we are going to do, let us suppose that we must find the base area and the volume of a parallelepiped whose length is 2 m, breadth, 0.5 m, and height, 3 m. A good manual practice is to write

$$L = 2 \ m$$
$$B = 0.5 \ m$$
$$H = 3 \ m$$
$$base \ area = L \times B = 2 \ m \times 0.5 \ m = 1 \ m^2$$
$$volume = base \ area \times H = 1 \ m^2 \times 3 \ m = 3 \ m^3$$

The above example may look simple. In complex calculations, however, writing the units and performing operations on them enables us to check if the resulting units are the expected ones. This can help to detect some errors, a point related to the explanations in Section 13.2.

To computerize operations like those exemplified above, we begin by writing a function that assigns to a constant both a value and the corresponding unit. The following function, udef, stores the constant as a **structure** with two **fields**: one field called value, the other, unit. While the first field contains a number, the second stores a character string.

```
function       y = udef(v, u)

%UDEF    Assigns value and unit to a physical quantity
%        Example:
%                L = udef(23, 'm')
```

```
%         Now, typing L results in
%              L =
%                   value: 23
% =                 unit: 'm'


y         = struct('value', 'unit');
y.value = v;
y.unit   = u;
```

Use the above function to store the constants L, B and H of the manual example.

Units are usually written as strings of characters with numerical exponents, for example m^2, $kg\ m^{-3}$, $m\ s^{-2}$. Let us agree to write the exponents in line with the characters. For the above examples this means: m2, kgm−3, ms−2.

The simplest operation we can perform on physical constants is **addition**. Addition has a physical meaning only when carried on between quantities having the same units. The following function, uadd, implements the operation.

```
function        y = uadd(x1, x2)

%UADD   Addition of unit-affected quantities
%       Examples:
%               a = udef(2, 'm');
%               b = udef(3, 'm');
%               c = udef(4, 'm2');
%               uadd(a, b)
%               ans =
%                       value: 5
%                        unit: 'm'
%               uadd(a, c)
%               ??? Error using ==> uadd
%               Quantities measured in different units

if strcmp(x1.unit, x2.unit) == 1    % if units are identical
        y.value = x1.value + x2.value;
        y.unit  = x1.unit;
else
        error('Quantities measured in different units');
end
```

We called above the MATLAB 5 function strcmp; it compares two strings. If the two strings are equal, strcmp outputs 1, otherwise 0. Use the function uadd to calculate the perimeter of the base in the manual example, as

$$perimeter = L + B + L + B$$

Subtraction has a meaning only when both operands have the same units. We leave to an exercise the definition of a function, `udif`, that performs the operation.

17.4.2   Transition tables

In this section we introduce a programming paradigm that we shall later use for the multiplication of unit-affected quantities and for the conversion of units. The device used by this technique is sometimes called a **transition table**, in other contexts it appears as a **decision table**. We exemplify the method in the simple case of conversion of time units shown in Table 17.1. A function that performs the conversion is:

```
function         y = utime(x, u)

%UTIME   Conversion of time units
%UTIME(X, U)     Converts the value X to the units U
%                Argument X must be predefined by UDEF

% build cells that contain time units
unit     = cell(1, 3);
unit(1) = {'s'};
unit(2) = {'min'};
unit(3) = {'h'};
% build table of conversion factors
convert = [
    1        1/60      1/3600
    60       1         1/60
    3600     60        1 ];
i        = find(strcmp(unit, x.unit) == 1);
if isempty(i) == 1
         error('Unit of first input argument not defined')
end
j        = find(strcmp(unit, u) == 1);
if isempty(j) == 1
         error('Output unit not defined')
end
y.value = convert(i, j)*x.value;
y.unit  = u;
```

The second argument can be chosen from a set of character strings of unequal lengths: {'s', 'min', 'h'}, where the abbreviations mean, as usual, *second*, *minute* and *hour*. In MATLAB 5 such a set can be stored in a **cell array**, a structure consisting of 'bins', or **cells**, in which we store dissimilar classes of arrays.

In the following listing we build a cell array in two stages. First, we preallocate space for an array of empty cells by invoking the MATLAB function `cell`, for example:

Table 17.1   A transition table for conversion of time units.

from	To convert to		
	s	min	h
	multiply by		
s	1	1/60	1/3600
min	60	1	1/60
h	3600	60	1

```
unit = cell(1, 3);
```

Next, we use **assignment statements** for the cells that are not empty, for instance:

```
unit(1) = {'s'};
```

Notice that the cell contents are enclosed between curly brackets. For another possible syntax consult the MATLAB manuals or use the help facilities.

In the above function, `utime`, the matrix `convert` plays the role of the transition Table 17.1. This is a table with two entries. One entry is the unit of the quantity, x, on which we operate; the other, the desired output unit.

The MATLAB function `find` looks into the array `unit` for the index of the element that matches the content of `x.unit`. We cannot use directly the function `find` with a cell array; therefore, it is necessary to appeal to the function `strcmp` that compares the given output unit with the elements of the array `unit`. If the compared strings are identical, `strcmp` returns 1, otherwise 0. When an element equal to the given unit is found, its index is assigned to `i`. If no match is found, the MATLAB function `isempty` detects that the array `i` is empty, stops the operation and issues the error message 'Unit of first input argument not defined'. If the unit of x is defined, `utime` calls again the functions `find` and `strcmp` to obtain the index, j, of the element of `unit` that matches the argument `u`. If `u` is not contained in `unit`, the operation ceases and the screen displays the error message 'Output unit not defined'. If both `x.unit` and `u` are defined, the conversion factor is the element of the matrix `convert` found in row i and column j.

In an exercise appearing at the end of this chapter we invite the reader to extend the function `utime` by adding *day* as a time unit.

17.4.3   Multiplication

Multiplication can be carried on between physical quantities having different units, but not all multiplications have physical meanings. To define a function, `umul`, that performs multiplication of unit-affected quantities, we must use the convention of exponents defined in Subsection 17.4.1. Next, to exemplify here a function of reasonable size, let us limit the set of allowable units to the set of base **SI** mechanical units and their derivatives (see Table 17.2). Later we shall show how to extend

Table 17.2   Base mechanical units.

Quantity	Unit	Symbol
length	metre	m
mass	kilogram	kg
time	second	s

Table 17.3   Multiplication of mechanical units.

	m	m^2	m^3	s	$m\,s^{-1}$	$m\,s^{-2}$	kg	N	Pa	w	$kg\,m^{-3}$
m length	m^2	m^3	m^4				kg m	N m J			
m^2 area	m^3	m^4	m^5				$kg\,m^2$		N		
m^3 volume	m^4	m^5									kg
s time					m	$m\,s^{-1}$				J	
$m\,s^{-1}$ velocity				m				$N\,m\,s^{-1}$			
$m\,s^{-2}$ acceleration				$m\,s^{-1}$			N				
kg mass	kg m	$kg\,m^2$				N					
N force	J, Nm				$N\,m\,s^{-1}$						
Pa pressure stress		N									
w power				J							
$kg\,m^{-3}$ density			kg								

the definition by including the base electrical units. The multiplication of the base mechanical units is shown in Table 17.3. This **multiplication table** is by no means comprehensive. The reader can extend it by consulting a textbook of mechanics, or specialized articles such as Chertov (1997) or Weil (1997). Table 17.4 explains the meanings of some derived units appearing in Table 17.3.

Table 17.4   Some derived mechanical units.

Unit	Physical quantity
m^3	volume or 1st moment of area
m^4	1st moment of volume or 2nd moment of area
m^5	2nd moment of volume
kg m	moment of mass
N m	moment of force
$kg\,m^2$	mass moment of inertia
$N\,m\,s^{-1}$	momentum

In this section we exemplify a function, umul, that performs multiplication using a transition table. We leave to an exercise another method, based on vectors of exponents of units. We prefer here the former method for the reasons shown below.

- Not all multiplications of physical quantities have physical meanings. In a table of transitions the position corresponding to an undefined operation can be easily marked.

- Sometimes the name of the resulting unit is not a combination of the units of the multiplicands. For instance, work is the result of multiplying a force, measured in newtons (N), by a distance, measured im metres (m). The unit of work, like that of energy, is the joule (J). In electricity, the multiplication of a current, measured in amperes (A), by a resistance, measured in ohms (Ω, or ohms), is a voltage measured in volts (V).

In Subsection 17.4.2 the transition table was a 3-by-3 array of numbers. Here, the table should be an 11-by-11 array of chracter strings, a structure that cannot be built directly in MATLAB. In fact, in a MATLAB array of strings, the number of columns is the number of characters, necessarily equal in all strings. Therefore, if we try to combine two character strings, A and B, by writing [A B], the result is the concatenation of the two strings. For example, let us try to build the submatrix corresponding to the upper left corner of Table 17.3. The result would be

$$\begin{vmatrix} \text{'m2m3'} \\ \text{'m3m4'} \end{vmatrix}$$

Moreover, the elements of the table should have different numbers of characters, for example 'm' and 'm2'. MATLAB 5 allows us to solve the problem by storing Table 17.3 as a cell array.

As in the example in Subsection 17.4.2, the entry vectors of the transition table consist of character strings of different lengths. Therefore, it is convenient to build the vector unit again as a cell array.

A listing of a function, umul, that performs the multiplication of two physical quantities is:

```
function        y = umul(x1, x2)
%UMUL    Multiplication of unit-affected quantities
%        Examples
%                a = udef(2, 'm');
%                b = udef(3, 'm');
%                c = udef(4, 'N');
%                umul(a, b)
%                ans =
%                    value: 6
%                     unit: 'm2'
%                umul(a, c)
%                If product is work enter w,
%                if moment (torque) enter t
%                 w
%                ans =
%                    value: 8
%                     unit: 'J'

y.value = x1.value*x2.value;

% -------------- define vector of input units ---------------
unit    = cell(1, 11);  % preallocate empty 1-by-11 cell array
unit(1) = {'m'};   unit(2)  = {'m2'};   unit(3) = {'m3'};
unit(4) = {'s'};   unit(5)  = {'ms-1'}; unit(6) = {'ms-2'};
unit(7) = {'kg'};  unit(8)  = {'N'};    unit(9) = {'Pa'};
unit(10) = {'w'}; unit(11) = {'kgm-3'};
% ----------------- define transition table ------------------
mtable  = cell(11, 11); % preallocate empty 11-by-11 cell array
mtable(1,1)  = {'m2'};    mtable(1,2) = {'m3'};
mtable(1,3)  = {'m4'};    mtable(1,7) = {'kgm'};
mtable(1,8)  = {'x0'};
mtable(2,1)  = {'m3'};    mtable(2,2)  = {'m4'};
mtable(2,3)  = {'m5'};    mtable(2,7)  = {'kgm2'};
mtable(2,9)  = {'N'};
mtable(3,1)  = {'m4'};    mtable(3,2) = {'m5'};
mtable(3,11) = {'kg'};
mtable(4,5)  = {'m'};     mtable(4,6) = {'ms-1'};
mtable(4,10) = {'J'};
mtable(5,4)  = {'m'};     mtable(5,8) = {'Nms-1'};
mtable(6,4)  = {'ms-1'}; mtable(6,7) = {'N'};
mtable(7,1)  = {'kgm'};  mtable(7,2) = {'kgm2'};
mtable(7,6)  = {'N'};
mtable(8,1)  = {'x0'};    mtable(8,5) = {'Nms-1'};
mtable(9,2)  = {'N'};
mtable(10,4) = {'J'};
mtable(11,3) = {'kg'};
```

```
% --------------- choose row of transition table --------------
i = find(strcmp(unit, x1.unit) == 1);
if isempty(i) == 1
    error('Unit of first input argument not defined')
end
% ------------- choose column of transition table -------------
j = find(strcmp(unit, x2.unit) == 1);
if isempty(j) == 1
    error('Unit of second input argument not defined')
end
if isempty(mtable{i, j}) == 1
    error('Multiplication not defined')
end
% ------------------ identify unit of product -----------------
y.unit  = mtable{i, j};
if strcmp(y.unit, 'x0') == 1
    disp('If product is work enter w,')
    disp('if moment (torque) enter t')
            I = input(' ', 's');
            if I == 'w';
                    y.unit = 'J';
            elseif I == 't'
                    y.unit = 'Nm';
            else
                    error('Try again')
            end
end
```

We leave to an exercise the definition of a function that performs the division of physical quantities.

17.4.4   Electrical units

Table 17.5 contains a multiplication table for a subset of the units used in electricity. We invite the reader to write a function that performs multiplication over the above subset. More elegantly, it is possible to extend the function umul introduced in the preceding subsection. We can give a few hints here. First, change the preallocation of the entry array unit to that of a 1-by-15 cell array. Second, change the preallocation of the transition table, mtable, to that of a 15-by-15 array. Finally, complete the assignments of elements in unit and mtable according to Table 17.5.

17.5   Exercises

The solution for Exercises 17.4, 17.7 and 17.15 appear at the back of the book.

Table 17.5 A multiplication table of electrical units.

	s	A	V	Ω	S
s time		C			
A current	C		w	V	
V voltage		w			A
Ω resistance		V			
S conductance		A			

■ **EXERCISE 17.1** Bending moments in a springboard
Figure 17.7(a) shows a springboard, such as is found near swimming pools. From the point of view of the strength of the materials it is a **cantilever beam**. The force F represents the weight of a man. The bending moment in the section of restraint is $M = aF$. Plot the curve of bending-moment values as functions of a. Use the following values:

$$\ell = 4000\,\text{mm}$$
$$F = 700\,\text{N}$$

■ **EXERCISE 17.2** A springboard – bending stresses and deflection
Let us reconsider the springboard shown in Figure 17.7. The maximum stress in the section of restraint equals

$$\sigma = \frac{M}{Z} \tag{17.8}$$

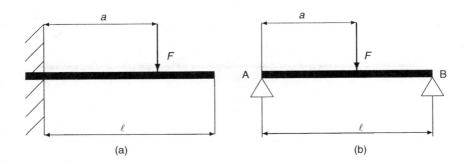

Figure 17.7 (a) Cantilever beam; (b) simply-supported beam.

where σ is measured in MPa (equal to N/mm^2), M is the bending moment as given in Exercise 17.1, and Z, the section modulus. For a rectangular section of breadth b and height d, $Z = bd^2/6$.

The maximum deflection of the beam in Figure 17.7(a) is

$$D = \frac{Fa^3}{3EI} \tag{17.9}$$

where E is the modulus of elasticity, and I the moment of inertia of the section in which the stresses are calculated. For a rectangular section $I = bd^3/12$.

Using the MATLAB `subplot` function, plot a graph of the stress, σ, and a graph of the deflection, D, as functions of a. Assume the following values

$$
\begin{aligned}
b &= 500\,\text{mm} \\
d &= 40\,\text{mm} \\
\ell &= 4000\,\text{mm} \\
E &= 10000\,\text{MPa} \\
F &= 700\,\text{N}
\end{aligned}
$$

■ **EXERCISE 17.3**   A simple bridge – bending moment
Write a program that calculates and plots the bending moment produced by the force F as it moves along the simple bridge shown in Figure 17.7(b). Assume that the force F is the weight of a man, namely 700 N, and the span $\ell = 4$ m. Use the `subplot` function to show the two diagrams one under the other.

■ **EXERCISE 17.4**   A simple bridge – animation
Consider again the simple bridge shown in Figure 17.7(b) and the values given in Exercise 17.3. Write an animation program that shows how the diagram of bending moments changes while the load moves along the bridge.

Hint: See Section 10.5.

■ **EXERCISE 17.5**   Truck on a simple bridge
Figure 17.8 shows a truck travelling along a simply-supported beam. The span, s, equals 12 m, the load on each axle, F, 100 kN. Following the example in Section 17.1, write a program that calculates the bending moment in each beam section as a function

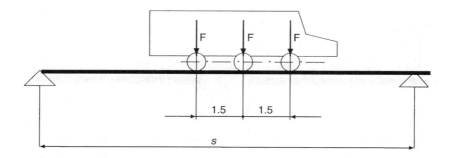

Figure 17.8   Truck travelling along a simply-supported beam. Dimensions are given in metres.

of the truck position. Plot the surface of these moments. The distance between the axles and the load on each axle correspond to the recommendations of the German standard DIN 1072.

■ **EXERCISE 17.6**   Truck on a simple bridge
Repeat the preceding exercise for a span $s = 10$ m and axle load $F = 200$ kN.

■ **EXERCISE 17.7**   Display value and unit on same line
We are accustomed to write the units of a physical quantity on the same line with its numerical value. Keeping the convention of writing exponents as accepted in Subsection 17.4.1 , write a function that, for a constant stored by means of udef, displays in the same line the numerical value and the corresponding units, for example:

```
a = udef(2, 'ms-1');
udis(a)
    2 ms-1
```

■ **EXERCISE 17.8**   Subtraction
Write a function, udif, that calculates the difference of two quantities and checks the compatibility of their units.

■ **EXERCISE 17.9**   Time units
Extend the function utime described in Section 17.4.2 by adding the unit *day*. Why would it be difficult to add the time units *month* and *year*?

■ **EXERCISE 17.10**   Time units
We refer to the function utime developed in Subsection 17.4.2. The elements of the array convert are actually powers of 60. Rewrite the function utime so as to use a table of exponents of 60.

■ **EXERCISE 17.11**   Division
Write a function, udiv, that performs the division of two quantities and assigns the units of the result.

■ **EXERCISE 17.12**   British to SI units conversion
Write a function, uSI, that performs the conversion from British to SI units according to Table 17.6. For example:

```
a = udef(2, 'ft');
usi(a)
ans =
    value:  0.6096
    unit:   'm'
```

The function should issue an error message if the input unit is not defined.

Table 17.6 Conversion of British to SI units.

from	To convert to	multiply by	Notes
in	mm	25.4	
ft	m	0.3048	
yd	m	0.9144	
mile	m	1609.344	
nautical mile	m^2	1852	
in^2	cm^2	6.4516	
ft^2	m^2	0.092903	
yd^2	m^2	0.836127	
mi^2	km^2	2.58999	
in^3	cm^3	16.3871	
ft^3	dm^3	28.3168	
yd^3	m^3	0.764555	
gall	m^3	3.785×10^{-3}	
lb	kg	0.453592	mass
long ton	t	1.016047	mass
short ton	t	0.907185	mass

■ **EXERCISE 17.13** SI to British units conversion
Write a function that converts from SI to British units according to the table in
Exercise 17.12.

■ **EXERCISE 17.14** Angle units
Write a function that converts degrees to radians and radians to degrees, for example:

```
a = udef(20, 'deg'); b = udef(0.5, 'rad');
uang(a)
ans =
    value:   0.3491
    unit:    'rad'
uang(b)
ans =
    value:   28.6479
    unit:    'deg'
```

The function should issue an error message if the input unit is not defined.

■ **EXERCISE 17.15** Exponents of units
In Subsection 17.4.3 we wrote that there may be an additional method of multiplying
units, namely that of using **vectors of exponents of units**. To exemplify this, let us
first assume that the order of presenting mechanical units is [kg m s]. Then, to the
unit $kg^\alpha\, m^\beta\, s^\gamma$ we assign the vector $[\alpha\ \beta\ \gamma]$. Thus, for example, to a velocity

measured in m s^{-1} we assign the vector [0 1 − 1], and to a time interval measured in s, the vector [0 0 1]. A velocity cannot be added to a time interval because

$$[0 \ 1 \ -1] \neq [0 \ 0 \ 1]$$

However, a velocity can be multiplied by a time interval and the resulting vector of exponents is the sum of the vectors correponding to the two multiplicands:

$$[0 \ 1 \ -1 \ ] + [0 \ 0 \ 1 \ ] = [0 \ 1 \ 0 \ ]$$

This is, indeed, the result expected for the unit of distance, m.

   Write a function that adds two physical quantities defined by a structure with two fields: the numerical value, and the vector of exponents.

■ **EXERCISE 17.16**   Subtraction
Write a function that performs the subtraction of physical quantities defined as in Exercise 17.15.

■ **EXERCISE 17.17**   Multiplication
Write a function that performs the multiplication of physical quantities defined as in Exercise 17.14.

■ **EXERCISE 17.18**   Division
Write a function that performs the division of physical quantities defined as in Exercise 17.15.

Chapter 18
Advanced features

18.1   Introduction

In this chapter we discuss some advanced features of MATLAB. There are not many engineering problems that one can solve after reading this chapter, and that cannot be solved otherwise, but if you master the concepts discussed here you will be able to develop your programs faster, reduce the debugging time and create software that is easier to modify and maintain. In this chapter we give more details about the concept of structures introduced in Section 12.4 and Subsection 17.4.1, and that of cell arrays introduced in Subsection 17.4.2, and the use of functions with a variable number of inputs and/or outputs that appeared earlier in the book but were not dealt with as such. We introduce **graphical user interfaces**, a term abbreviated to **GUIs**, and define briefly the concept of **object-oriented programming**. The reason for not expanding the latter subject is that it belongs to the realm of software developers, not practising engineers, and a good treatment would require an extent that goes beyond the limits of this book.

This is the last chapter of the book and, until now, there has been no need to define the notion of **data type**. At this point, however, things may become clearer if we introduce the concept of data type as a *set of values defined by the operations that apply to them*. In the documentation provided by The MathWorks, the distributors of MATLAB, we read, 'There are 14 fundamental data types (or classes) in MATLAB.' By adding the term **classes**, albeit within parentheses, the above sentence includes object-oriented terminology.

All data types admitted by MATLAB are arrays, the simplest instance being the void array [ ]. An array such as BR2 in Section 12.2

```
BR2 = [
' Fort William'
.................
```

is an **array of characters** and belongs to the char data type. The array BR3 in the same section

```
BR3 = [
25 180
......
```

belongs to one of the several numeric data types defined in MATLAB. The character and numeric data types were the subjects of the preceding chapters. Two further data types, structures and cells, were introduced by a few examples and, as mentioned above, more operations allowed on them will be detailed in this chapter. Both these data types can store non-homogeneous data, but do this in different ways. In other words, with structures or cells the user can collect under one name arrays of the char type, and numeric arrays of different sizes.

There are two further data types, **Java** and **function handles**. The former is beyond the scope of this book, the latter was introduced in Chapter 11 and is briefly exemplified in this chapter, in Subsection 18.5. Today MATLAB enables the user to define further data types, and this feature is exemplified in the section on object-oriented programming.

18.2   Structures

18.2.1   Where structures can help

Let us start with a simple example. We have seen in Section 14.2.4 that a system can be described in space state form by four matrices, conventionally called **A**, **B**, **C**, **D**, and we described there the example of a simple spring–mass–damper system represented by those matrices. In practice, we may prefer more descriptive names, like spring_A, spring_B, spring_C and spring_D, defined by

```
≫ spring_A = [  -0.7, -0.05; 1, 0  ];
≫ spring_B = [  1; 0  ];
≫ spring_C = [ 0 0.5  ];
≫ spring_D = 0;
```

Beginning with version 5, MATLAB allows a better alternative and this is

```
>> spring.A = [  -0.7, -0.05; 1, 0  ];
>> spring.B = [  1; 0  ];
>> spring.C = [  0 0.5  ];
>> spring.D = 0;
```

In this case, spring is said to be a variable of the type **structure** and A, B, C and D are the **fields** of the variable spring. We can operate on the individual fields of a structure exactly as we are accustomed to operate on any array. For example, the following commands are legal:

```
>> a(1,1) = spring.A(1,1);
>> spring.A(1, 1) = -0.65;
```

So, where is the advantage of this alternative notation? As shown in Section 12.4, the main advantage is that a structure allows us to organize diversified information under one name. We are going to give some more examples here. If we just compare the two sets of assignments, we see very little, but suppose now that we are required to write a function showsys that displays the values of **A**, **B**, **C** and **D**. If we use regular numerical arrays, the function showsys could look like:

```
function showsys1(A, B, C, D)
% show the matrices that represent a system
% in state space form.
% Version 1 - without using structures
A, B, C, D
```

To see the values of the matrices **A**, **B**, **C** and **D** we invoke this first version of showsys with the command

```
>> showsys1(spring_A,spring_B,spring_C,spring_D)
A =
 -0.7000  -0.0500
  1.0000   0
B =
  1
  0
C =
  0  0.5000
D =
  0
```

On the other hand, using structures, we can rewrite showsys as follows:

```
function showsys2(sys)
% show the matrices that represent a system
% in state space form.
% Version 2 - using structures
sys.A, sys.B, sys.C,sys.D
```

This second version of showsys is invoked with the command

```
>> showsys2(spring)
ans =
 -0.7000  -0.0500
  1.0000  0
ans =
  1
  0
ans =
  0  0.5000
ans =
  0
```

There are several reasons for preferring the second version of showsys. First of all, we must pass to the function a smaller number of parameters, one instead of four. This reduces the number of possible errors, like forgetting a parameter or getting their order wrong. There are functions, like ode23, which we met in Chapter 14, that take more than 10 parameters. In this and similar cases it is much easier to pass, say, four structures of four fields each, than 16 different parameters.

Another reason to use structures is to reduce the amount of housekeeping. If we use four matrices to describe our system, it is the responsibility of the user to keep them together and not mix the **A**-matrix of one system with the **B**-matrix of another. In earlier versions of MATLAB, which did not support structures, this was usually done by saving related matrices in separate sub-directories, or by choosing long names. Both solutions require more work and are more likely to introduce errors than using a single structure. When we use structures, each field of a variable (in the example above, spring) is identified by a field name, which is a string (like 'A').

An alternative possibility is to identify the field by an index as shown in Section 18.3 on cell arrays. Structures and cell arrays contain the same information and, as we shall see shortly, it is easy to convert back and forth from structures to cell arrays. Generally speaking, identifying a field by a name, that is using structures, is clearer than identifying the same field by an index, as cell arrays do. On the other hand the use of cell arrays may be preferable if you plan to loop over indexes.

Each individual field of a structure can refer to any MATLAB object; in other words, there are no restrictions against collecting under the same name, spring, four numerical arrays and a string. If we decide to attach an explanation line to spring, we could just write

```
>> spring.comment = 'Spring in state space representation';
```

18.2.2   Working with structures

As mentioned, structures allow us to collect in a single variable objects of different types. A structure variable can be defined by direct assignment, as we saw in the first section of this chapter, with commands like

```
>> spring.A = [  -0.7, -0.05; 1, 0  ];
```

as well as by means of the function struct that we have already met in Chapter 17:

```
>> spring = struct('A', [  -0.7, -0.05; 1, 0  ],...
          'B', [  1;   0  ],...
          'C', [  0, 0.5  ],...
          'D', 0);
```

The function struct takes as input a list of parameters consisting of the strings for field names and their corresponding values. If you are familiar with the terminology of object-oriented programming, you will certainly have noticed that, from this point of view, struct is a **constructor** of the variable spring of class struct. This is very similar to what we are accustomed to doing with regular numerical arrays. Numerical arrays can be defined by direct assignment, like

```
>> a(1)= 11; a(2) = 12; a(3) = 13; a(4) = 14;
```

or by constructing the array from a list of numbers:

```
>> a = [  11, 12, 13, 14  ];
```

The square brackets are actually a constructor. They look typographically different from a constructor like struct, but perform exactly the same operation as a hypothetical function array:

```
>> a = array(11, 12, 13, 14);
```

Some assignment and retrieval operations of the value of fields, that can be performed by means of the equals sign, can also be performed by built-in MATLAB

functions defined for specific operations on structures. For example, you can use the
function `getfield`

```
>> blockA = getfield(spring, 'A')
blockA =
 -0.7000  -0.0500
  1.0000   0
```

which is equivalent to

```
>> blockA = spring.A;
```

The function `rmfield` does not actually remove a field from a structure variable,
as the name suggests, but rather makes a copy of the variable, without a specific field.
For example

```
>> noD = rmfield(spring, 'D');
noD =
 A: [2x2 double]
 B: [2x1 double]
 C: [0 0.5000]
```

leaves `spring` unchanged, but creates a new variable `noD`, identical to `spring` except
for the fact that it does not contain the field D. Similarly, the function `setfield` does
not add a field to a variable, but creates a copy of the given structure with an additional
field, according to the paradigm

```
newspring = setfield(spring, 'newfield', < field value >);
```

For example,

```
newspring = setfield(spring,...
'info', 'Spring in Chapter 14')
newspring =
A: [2x2 double]
B: [2x1 double]
C: [0 0.5000]
D: 0
info:  'Spring in Chapter 14'
```

The last function we want to introduce in this section is `fieldnames`. This
function returns the field names of a variable, arranged as a vertical cell array, the
contents of each cell being a string, the name of a field. For example, if you write

```
>> namelist = fieldnames(spring);
namelist =
 'A'
 'B'
 'C'
 'D'
```

the resulting namelist is a cell array of four rows and one column, and namelist{1}
is the string 'A', namelist{2} is the string 'B', etc.

It is possible to create arrays of structures, like the following structure called
persons:

```
>> persons(1).name='Avi';     persons(1).weight=71;
>> persons(2).name='Beni';    persons(2).weight=73;
>> persons(3).name='Charles'; persons(3).weight=75;
>> persons(4).name='David';   persons(4).weight=77;
>> persons(5).name='Eytan';   persons(5).weight=79;
>> persons(6).name='Fritz';   persons(6).weight=81;
>> persons(7).name='Gidi';    persons(7).weight=83;
>> persons(8).name='Hava';    persons(8).weight=85;
>> persons(9).name='Ilana';   persons(9).weight=87;
>> persons(10).name='Joe';    persons(10).weight=89;
```

For further processing we write the above lines into a file called person. In
this way, we have actually built a small **database** containing information about a
number of persons. We can **query** this database by means of some MATLAB built-in
fuctions. Here are a few examples:

```
>> mean([ persons.weight ])
ans =
 80
>> std([ persons.weight ])
ans =
 6.0553
>> min([ persons.weight ])
ans =
 71
>> max([ persons.weight ])
ans =
 89
```

Note the use of square brackets; this is explained again in Subsection 18.4.5.
We can build our own query functions. For instance, the following function

weight retrieves from the structure persons the weight corresponding to a given name:

```
%WEIGHT QUERIES WEIGHT OF PERSON 'MAN' IN STRUCTURE 'PERSONS'

        function        W = weight(firstname)
person                  % load data from M-file person
lp    = length(persons);
k     = 0;              % initialize index
found = 0;              % initialize control flag
while (found == 0) & (k < lp)
        k = k + 1;      % begin while construct
        if strcmp(persons(k).name, firstname)
                W = persons(k).weight;
                found = 1;
        end
end                             % end while construct
if found == 0
        error([ 'Name ' firstname ' not in data base' ])
end
```

In the above function, the statement person loads the file containing the structure persons; thus the data will be available in the scope of the function.

```
>> W_Charles = weight('Charles')
W_Charles =
 75
```

Before ending this section, we want to present here the function deal. This function is almost useless (although legal) as long as one works only with scalars or numerical arrays, but will become important when manipulating structures and cells. In its simplest form, deal distributes values to variables. For example

```
>> [x,y,z] = deal(1,2,3)
x =
 1
y =
 2
z =
 3
```

distributes the values 1, 2 and 3 to the variables x, y, z, and is therefore equivalent to the following line:

```
>> x = 1; y = 2; z = 3;
```

Another example is given in Subsection 18.4.6. Here we show how we can use the function `deal` to assign to the variables `name1`, `name2`, `name3`, `name4` the contents of the first four names in structure `persons`:

```
>> [ name1, name2, name3, name4 ] = deal(persons(1:4).name)
name1 =
Avi
name2 =
Beni
name3 =
Charles
name4 =
David
```

18.3   Cell arrays

Like structures, cell arrays can be defined by **direct assignment**

```
>> cspring{1} = [-0.7, -0.05; 1, 0];
>> cspring{2} = [1;0];
>> cspring{3} = [0 0.5];
>> cspring{4} = 0;
```

In this case the curly brackets are placed around the index. This method is called **content indexing**. An alternative, and entirely equivalent, way of defining the same cell array is by enclosing the indexes in regular parentheses and placing the curly brackets on the right-hand side of the equals sign:

```
>> cspring(1) = {[-0.7, -0.05; 1, 0]};
>> cspring(2) = {[1; 0]};
>> cspring(3) = {[0 0.5]};
>> cspring(4) = { 0 };
```

This method of notation is called **cell indexing**. Let us examine for a moment how MATLAB interprets this sequence of commands. When you write

```
>> cspring(1) = {[ -0.7, -0.05; 1, 0 ]};
```

MATLAB requests from the operating system the amount of memory necessary to store the array [−0.7, −0.05; 1, 0] and the space to store a cell array of length 1 that points to it. When you write

```
>> cspring(2) = {[1; 0]};
```

MATLAB must request from the operating system the memory to store [1; 0]. Now it finds out that cspring is a cell array of length 1, which is not sufficient to contain two references. It must therefore request memory for a new cspring, this time of length 2, make a copy of the existing cspring into the new array, assign the value of cspring(2), call the new cell variable cspring, instead of the old one of length 1, and release the memory occupied by the old cspring. This operation is repeated each time you add a new cell to a variable, and is quite time consuming. If you are concerned about writing efficient code, you should pre-allocate the space for a cell array of four rows and one column, with the command

```
>> cspring = cell(1,4);
```

This creates a cell array with empty contents that you can fill later without having to interact so much with the operating system. In conclusion, you should create cspring with the following sequence of commands:

```
>> cspring = cell(1,4); % pre-allocate the memory
>> cspring(1) = {[-0.7, -0.05; 1, 0]};
>> cspring(2) = {[1; 0]};
>> cspring(3) = {[0 0.5]};
>> cspring(4) = { 0 };
```

We can display the resulting cell array by means of the function celldisp:

```
>> celldisp(cspring)
cspring1 =
 -0.7000  -0.0500
  1.0000   0
cspring2 =
1
0
cspring3 =
0   0.5000
cspring4 =
0
```

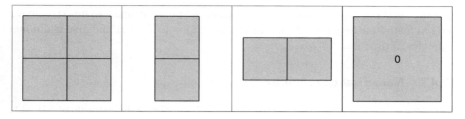

Figure 18.1 Graphic description of the cell array `cspring`.

The function `cellplot` produces the graphic description of the cell array shown in Figure 18.1:

```
>> cellplot(cspring)
```

We can see, indeed, that the first cell contains a 4-by-4 array, the second a 2-by-1 array, and so on.

A few MATLAB built-in functions can be applied to cell arrays by means of the function `cellfun`. For example, let us invoke the function `ndims`, which yields the number of array dimensions, and the function `prodofsize`, which shows the number of elements in the cell array:

```
>> cellfun('ndims', cspring)
 ans =
   2  2  2  2
>> M = cellfun('prodofsize', cspring)
 M =
   4  2  2  1
```

We extract the contents of individual cells by calling them with the cell index enclosed between curly brackets. Also, we can apply operators on individual cells:

```
>> AA = 2*cspring{1}
AA =
   -1.4000   -0.1000
    2.0000    0
```

Similarly to what we did with structures, we are going to exemplify in Section 18.8 how we can *query* an array of cells.

18.4 Conversions

We have seen in the previous section that often the same information can be stored in different ways, for example in a cell array, in a structure or in a numerical array.

In some cases one representation is more convenient than another. In this section we want to learn how to convert from one representation to another and give additional examples of their use.

18.4.1   Numerical to cell array

A numerical array can be converted to a cell array by means of the function num2cell. For example, let us consider the array A defined below and its simplest conversion:

```
≫ A = [ 1 2; 3 4; 5 6 ]:
≫ Ac = num2cell(A)
Ac =
   [1]   [2]
   [3]   [4]
   [5]   [6]
```

In this case, we were converting a numerical array into a cell array of the same size, by placing each number into a different cell. The same function num2cell can be used to convert a numerical array into a cell array by placing entire rows or columns into each individual cell, instead of just numbers. To do this the function num2cell requires a second parameter that indicates which dimension must be placed in the same cell. The general syntax is

```
≫ Xc = num2cell(X, dim)
```

According to the MATLAB convention, dim = 1 refers to rows, dim = 2 refers to columns, and so on. Thus, if you apply the function num2cell to the same array A, and specify dimension 1, MATLAB collects the entries of A in the direction of rows, and the result, Ac1, is a horizontal array of length 1, where each cell contains a column of the original numerical array, A:

```
≫ Ac1 = num2cell(A, 1)
Ac1 =
 [3x1 double]   [3x1 double]
≫ celldisp(A1)
Ac1{1} =
   1
   3
   5
Ac1{2} =
   2
   4
   6
```

If you specify dimension 2, MATLAB collects the elements of A in the direction of columns, and the result, Ac2, is a vertical cell array of dimension 3, where each cell contains a row of the original array, A.

```
≫ Ac2 = num2cell(A, 2)
Ac2 =
 [1x2 double]
 [1x2 double]
 [1x2 double]
≫ celldisp(Ac2)
Ac2{1} =
   1    2
Ac2{2} =
   3    4
Ac2{3} =
   5    6
```

Figure 18.2, produced with the function cellplot, can provide more insight.

We suggest the reader saves the array A and its conversions and proceeds immediately to the following subsection in which we show how to recover the initial numerical array from the cell arrays just produced.

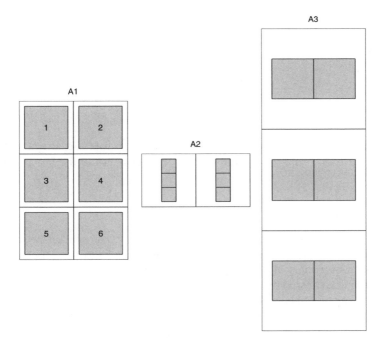

Figure 18.2   Converting a numerical array to a cell array.

18.4.2   Cell array of numbers to numerical array

To convert a cell array in which every cell contains a number, to a numerical array, we use the colon operator. Let us first observe that the command A1{:} produces the same result as entering the list 1, 2, 3, 4, 5, 6. Including this 'list' within square brackets we reconstruct the numerical array:

```
>> Acopy = zeros(size(Ac))
>> Acopy(:)  = [ Ac{:} ]
Acopy =
  1  2
  3  4
  5  6
```

The situation is slightly more complicated when each cell of the array does not contain just a number, but an entire row or column. Here, in addition to the colon operator, we need the function cat. Thus, the inverse conversions of the second and third conversion in the last subsection are

```
>> Acopy1 = cat(2, Ac1{:})
Acopy1 =
  1  2
  3  4
  5  6
>> Acopy2 = cat(1, Ac2{:})
Acopy2 =
  1  2
  3  4
  5  6
```

This time, for example, the command Ac2{:} lists the arrays [1 2], [3 4], [5 6] and we use the function cat to return to the initial numerical array.

18.4.3   Structure to cell array

As we have already pointed out, structures and cell arrays can contain the same information. The difference between them is that in the case of structures the information is addressed by means of a string, the field name, while in the case of cells the information is addressed by means of an integer, the index.

Let us again consider the structure array persons defined in Subsection 18.2.2. If you followed our suggestion and saved this structure in the file person, just type person to retrieve the data into your working space. Otherwise, retype the definitions.

The structure persons is a horizontal vector of length 10, as you can convince yourself if you type

```
≫ size(persons)
size =
   1   10
```

It is quite easy to translate persons into a cell array, cpersons, using the following conventions. The first index of cpersons substitutes the field name, that is cpersons(1, :, :) are the names, and cpersons(2, :, :) are the weights. The remaining indexes are shifted to the right. In this case the second index of cpersons is always 1, as the first index of persons, and the third index of cpersons corresponds to the second index of persons. The conversion is performed by the function struc2cell. You are invited to type

```
≫ cpersons = struct2cell(persons)
```

and verify the results. For example,

```
≫ cpersons(1, 1, 3)
ans =
 'Charles'
≫ cpersons(2, 1, 5)
ans =
```

Figure 18.3, produced with the function cellplot, shows that the cell array has 10 pages, and on each page two cells. The figure helps to understand how the contents are arranged in three dimensions.

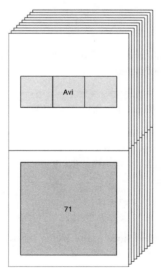

Figure 18.3   Graphic description of the cell array cpersons.

18.4.4   Cell array to structure

This operation is performed by `cell2struct`. This function requires three inputs, namely the cell array, the names of the fields, and the number of the dimension which is converted into fields. The names of the fields must be supplied as a cell array of strings. The following example shows how to convert the cell array `cpersons` created in the previous section into a structure array identical to the structure array `persons` defined in the same section.

```
>> fn = {'name'; 'weight'} % field names
fn =
  'name'
  'weight'
>> dim = 1; % rows are converted into fields
>> personscopy = cell2struct(cpersons, fn, dim);
>> isequal(persons, personscopy)
ans =
  1
```

18.4.5   Numerical field of structure to numerical array

Let us again consider the structure `persons` defined in Subsection 18.2.2. The command

```
>> persons.weight
```

displays the values in the field `names`. If you type this command, MATLAB produces the same output as if you had typed

```
>> 71, 73, 75, 77, 79, 81, 83, 85, 87, 89
```

From a comma-separated list, we can create a numerical array by enclosing the list within square brackets, as the following line shows:

```
>> weights = [persons.weight];
```

As an exercise let us find how many bytes the files in your current directory occupy. To do this, write

```
>> d = dir
```

This command creates a variable d, which is an array of structures, with fields name, date, bytes, isdir. Therefore, d.bytes is a comma-separated list, [d.bytes], a numerical array that indicates the size of each file in the current directory, and the solution to the problem is simply

```
>> d = dir; sum([d.bytes] )
```

18.4.6   Numerical array to numerical field of structure

This is the opposite situation to that seen in the previous section. Let us go back to the variable persons defined in Subsection 18.2.2. Suppose this time we have a numerical array like

```
>> ages = 35:2:53;
```

and we want to add to persons a new field age, so that persons(k).age is equal to ages(k). First of all we must create an intermediate cell array agesc, as we saw in Subsection 18.4.1,

```
>> agesc = num2cell(ages);
```

and then distribute the values of this cell array to persons.age:

```
>> [persons.age] = deal(agesc);
```

18.5   Functions with variable number of input/output arguments

Admittedly, there are few functions that accept a variable number of inputs and outputs. Still, this feature is useful in some cases, and we therefore decided to write this section, which incidentally provides a good example of the use of cell arrays. Let us write a function whose declaration is

```
function [pout1, pout2] = myfun(pin1, pin2, pin3);
```

Here pout1 and pout2 are the output parameters and pin1, pin2 and pin3 the input parameters. We invoke such a function with the call

```
>> [vout1, vout2] = myfun(vin1, vin2, vin3)
```

where vout1, vout2 are the output variables, and vin1, vin2, vin3 are the input variables. The compiler associates vin1 to pin1, vin2 to pin2, vin3 to pin3 and, after the function has run, returns the value of pout1 as vout1 and that of pout2 as vout2.

Some languages require that the number of input and output variables at invocation time exactly match the number of input and output arguments in the function definition, but MATLAB is more permissive. If you invoke a function with more input variables than those in the function definition, MATLAB complains with the message

```
???  Error using ==> myfun
Too many input arguments.
```

On the other hand, it is perfectly legal to invoke a function with fewer input variables than the number of parameters that appear in the definition. For example, you might invoke myfun with a call like

```
>> [vout1, vout2] = myfun(vin1, vin2)
```

The value of vin1 is passed to pin1, that of vin2 to pin2, and pin3 is undefined. MATLAB then starts executing the function myfun, and will complain only if you try to compute an expression that involves pin3.

The function nargin tells us how many input variables are passed to myfun at invocation time. If the function finds out that too few parameters are passed and defines them before they are used, MATLAB will not complain. We can start the code of myfun with the lines

```
if nargin < 3
    pin3 = 1.0e-3; % default value for pin3
end;
```

Now the function myfun can be invoked with either three or two input parameters. If the third input parameter is not provided, it is given the default value 0.001. This mechanism is quite common for defining computing tolerances and other optional parameters.

A similar situation occurs when the number of output arguments at invocation time does not match the number of output arguments in the function definition. If you invoke a function with more output variables than the number of input arguments that appear in the definition, MATLAB issues an error message, but it is perfectly legal, for example, to call myfun as

```
>> vout1 = myfun(vin1, vin2, vin3)
```

In this case, the second output argument is simply ignored. If you are interested only in the second output variable, there is no way to ask MATLAB to return it alone, and you should use a call like

```
>> [junk, vout2] = myfun(vin1, vin2);
```

and ignore the output corresponding to junk.

Corresponding to the function nargin there is a function nargout that returns the number of output variables at invocation time. Suppose we expect the function myfun to be called most of the time with only one output variable and only rarely with two output variables, and that the computation of the second output variable will be very long. We can than make our code more efficient by writing myfun as the following skeleton code suggests:

```
[vout1, vout2] = myfun(vin1, vin2, vin3);
% STEP 1 : compute vout1 in any case
vout1 = < expression for vout1 >
% STEP 2 : compute vout2 only if requested
if nargout > 1,
    vout2 = < expression for vout2 >
end;
```

This feature, of performing different operations according to the number of inputs and/or outputs, is called **arity** and is not uncommon. Here are some examples that use MATLAB built-in functions. If **M** is a two-dimensional matrix, you use the function size to find how many rows and columns it has. You can invoke size as

```
>> [m,n] = size(M)
```

and the output consists of two numbers, or as

```
>> dims = size(M)
```

and the output is one array.

The function sort can be called with either one or two outputs. If **A** is an array of numbers, the invocation

```
>> A_sorted = sort(A)
```

returns the values of A arranged in ascending order. If, on the other hand, your call is

```
>> [A_sorted, pos] = sort(A)
```

it returns, in addition, the array pos, where pos(k) indicates the position of A_sorted(k) in the original array **A**.

We have seen above how MATLAB deals with functions at invocation time when we provide or request a different number of input and/or output parameters than the number that appears in the function definition. A more general situation is when the developer must write a function that will be invoked with any number of inputs and outputs. Such functions are rare, but do exist, even in languages that provide you with no mechanism to develop a function of this kind. For example, in Pascal, you can use the function write to write a string (one input), or a string and an integer (two inputs), or more generally any number of inputs. You might be interested in writing a hypothetical function slideshow that can be invoked in one of the following ways:

```
>> slideshow(image1)
>> slideshow(image1, image2)
>> slideshow(image1, image2, image3)
```

and so on.

Functions with a variable number of outputs are even more uncommon in engineering applications, but we can think of a function powers that computes the powers of the input argument. So, invocating the function as shown below should yield the results indicated after the call:

```
>> vout1 = powers(5)
vout1=5
>> [vout1, vout2] = powers(5)
vout1=5, vout2 = 25
>> [vout1, vout2, vout3] = powers(5)
vout1=5, vout2 = 25, vout3 = 125
```

As a first approach to developing functions with a variable number of inputs, let us write the code of the function proposed above. The declaration line is

```
function     varargout = powers(x);
```

The name varargout is a reserved name of a cell array. We must return the output as varargout{1}, varargout{2}, etc. The function nargout, introduced in the previous section, tells us how many output arguments we must define. Here is the code for powers:

```
function varargout = powers(x);
for k = 1:nargout,
    varargout{k} = x^k;
end;
```

More generally, a function can have a number of fixed output parameters, followed by an unlimited number of additional output parameters. Its declaration line will be like

```
function [pfout1, pfout2, varargout] = myfun(pin1, pin2, pin3)
```

If you call this function with the statement

```
>> [out1, out2, out3, out4] = myfun(vin1, vin2, vin3);
```

the output will be as follows:

- out1 is assigned the value of pfout1;
- out2 is assigned the value of pfout2;
- out3 is assigned the value of varargout{1};
- out4 is assigned the value of varargout{2}.

Note that varargout always follows the list of fixed parameters. It collects in a single cell array all parameters that follow the fixed variables required at invocation time. The situation is entirely symmetrical for functions with a variable number of inputs. The declaration line of such a function looks like

```
[pout1, pout2] = myfun(pin1, pin2, pin3, varargin)
```

When invoked with a call like

```
>> [vout1, vout2] = myfun(vfin1, vfin2, vfin3, vin4, vin5)
```

it assigns to the function parameter pin1 the value of the variable vfin1, to pin2 the value of vfin2, to pin3 the value vfin3, and collects all remaining input parameters in the cell array varargin. Thus, varargin{1} receives the value of vin4, varargin{2} the value of vin5, and so on.

As an example, let us write a function showall that displays the values of the input parameters

```
function showall(varargin);
for k = 1:nargin,
    display(varargin{k});
end;
```

With the help of varargin and varargout we can develop a function without knowing with how many input or output parameters it will invoke, for example the following function dummy:

```
function varargout = dummy(varargin);
varargout = varargin;
```

The latter was a very simple, and useless, example, but this technique of transmitting the input variables can be useful in some practical applications. Suppose we want to compare two functions, fun1 and fun2, that receive the same number of input arguments and produce the same number of output parameters, like ode23 and ode45. We could certainly write a function that calls ode23, runs it and saves the results. Then, using a text editor, we could change each appearance of ode23 to ode45, rerun the function and compare the results. Alternatively, we could modify the function dummy and run both functions, without the need to modify the source code, as the following example shows.

Let us compare the solutions of the differential equation described by the following function derv, for t from 0 to 2π, and use it with ode23 and ode45. We can write derv:

```
function wd = derv(t,w);
wd = zeros(size(w));
wd(1) =   w(2);
wd(2) = -w(1);
```

Continuing, we write the function derv to the file derv.m, and define a function test as

```
function varargout = test(h, varargin);
% create output cell to store results
varargout = cell(1, nargout);
% run function of handle h and store results in varargout
[varargout{:}] = feval(h, varargin{:});
```

Now we can integrate the equation using ode23 with the following commands:

```
>> h=@ode23; [t23, w23]=test(h, @derv,[0 2*pi], [0;1]);
```

If we want to solve the same system using ode45, we do not have to modify a single line of code; it is sufficient to enter the command

```
>> h=@ode45; [t45, w45]=test(h, @derv,[0 2*pi], [0;1]);
```

In fact, here we used function handles, a subject introduced in Chapters 11 and 14.

18.6   GUIs

18.6.1   What are GUIs?

The acronym **GUI** stands for 'Graphical User Interface'. This acronym is usually pronounced 'gooey'. If you work in Windows, for instance in Word, you use a graphical interface consisting of a title bar, a menu bar, toolbars, scroll bars and a status bar. If you work with any CAD program, your graphical interface allows you to choose between various drawing possibilities, such as lines, circles or splines, and enables you to zoom in to and out of the picture, to change line styles, line widths and colours, and apply many other features. All these interfaces are actually GUIs and the main way of using them is by clicking or double clicking on buttons and menus, and dragging scroll bars.

MATLAB windows also contain GUIs and you have used them throughout this book. However, in addition to those GUIs provided with the software, MATLAB allows you to build your own GUIs for specific tasks. Some excellent examples can be viewed after entering

```
≫ demo
```

You can find more listings in the subdirectories

- matlabR12 \matlab\toolbox\demos
- matlabR12\signal\sigdemo

If you want to build such a demo, to explain to your audience a particular phenomenon or a complex calculation, say, a GUI could help greatly. GUIs find another application where calculations and plotting must be repeated many times while changing variable values. On the other hand, rarely repeated calculations do not justify the effort involved in building a GUI.

GUIs make extensive use of handle graphics. A thorough treatment of handle graphics and of the many features GUIs can have would require a dedicated book. Nevertheless, those subjects can greatly enhance the work in MATLAB and we feel that by the end of this book the reader should be aware of their existence. Therefore, we present two examples here.

18.6.2   A simple example

As a relatively simple example, let us build a GUI that shows the interference of two sinusoidal waves having the same amplitude. While the circular frequency of the first wave is fixed and equal to one, and its phase set to zero, the user can define the ratio of the frequency of the second wave to that of the first wave, and the phase of the second wave. We want to show how the shape of the resulting wave changes with the frequency and phase of the second component. Obviously, we could write a regular MATLAB function and call it several times, each time with other argument

values. We think that an appropriate GUI can demonstrate in a more pleasant way
the influence of the various parameters.

A GUI can be built in several ways; we shall describe a model here that we
recommend for its advantages over other models. In the first place, we store the
whole GUI in one file only. Next, the structure of the GUI is clearly shown, its parts
being well and logically separated. Finally, passing parameter values from one part
of the program to another is done in a way that avoids confusion and errors. The
interface is programmed as a recursive function, interfer, of an argument named
flag here. As shown in Section 7.6, a recursive function can call itself. The complete
GUI listing appears below.

```
%INTERFER    GUI that demonstrates the interference of two
%            sinusoidal waves
%       Possible actions:
%           'init'      -   initializes the graphical user interface
%           'Ch_omega2' -   defines the frequency of the second wave
%           'Ch_phase'  -   defines the phase of the second wave
%           'refresh'   -   plots the superposition of the two waves

            function        interfer(flag)

if nargin < 1           % called without argument
        flag = 'init';
end

switch flag

        case 'init'                         % initialize GUI
            H_fig = figure;
            omega1 = 1;                % 1st wave frequency, rad/s
            T      = 2*pi/omega1;      % 1st wave, period s
            t      = 0: T/30: 3*T;     % time scale, s
            w1     = sin(omega1*t);    % first wave
            multipl = 1;               % second-to-first
                                       % wave-frequency ratio

            set(H_fig, 'NumberTitle', 'off',...
                    'Name', 'Interference of two sinusoidal waves')

            Hedit1 = uicontrol(H_fig, 'Units', 'normalized',...
                    'Position', [ 0.05 0.07 0.15 0.05 ],...
                    'Style', 'Edit', 'String', num2str(multipl),...
                    'Tag', 'edit1',...
                    'CallBack', ('interfer(''Ch_omega2'')'));

            Htext1 = uicontrol(H_fig, 'Units', 'normalized',...
```

```
                'Position', [ 0.05 0.13 0.15 0.08 ],...
                'Style', 'Text', 'String', 'Frequency multiplier');

phase  = 0;         % second-wave phase-to-period ratio

Hedit2 = uicontrol(H_fig, 'Units', 'normalized',...
                'Position', [ 0.3 0.07 0.15 0.05 ],...
                'Style', 'Edit',...
                'String', num2str(phase), 'Tag', 'edit2',...
                'CallBack', ('interfer(''Ch_phase'')'));

Htext1 = uicontrol(H_fig, 'Units', 'normalized',...
                'Position', [ 0.3 0.13 0.15 0.08 ],...
                'Style', 'Text', 'String', 'Phase(w2)/T2')

H_button1 = uicontrol(H_fig, 'Units', 'normalized',...
                'Position', [ 0.55 0.07 0.15 0.14 ],...
                'Style', 'pushbutton', 'String', 'Refresh',...
                'CallBack', ('interfer(''Refresh'')'));

H_button2 = uicontrol(H_fig, 'Units', 'normalized',...
                'Position', [ 0.8 0.07 0.15 0.14 ],...
                'Style', 'pushbutton', 'String', 'Restore',...
                'CallBack', ('interfer(''init'')'));

H_text1 = uicontrol(H_fig, 'Units', 'normalized',...
                'Position', [ 0.8 0.71, 0.15 0.14 ],...
                'Style', 'text',...
                'String', 'Component waves, w_1 and w_2');
H_text2 = uicontrol(H_fig, 'Units', 'normalized',...
                'Position', [ 0.8 0.36, 0.15 0.14 ],...
                'Style', 'text',...
                'String', 'Resultant wave, w_1 + w_2');

Ha_up = axes('Position', [ 0.05 0.71 0.65 0.21 ]);
H_w1 = plot(t, w1, 'r-');

Ha_down = axes('Position', [ 0.05 0.36 0.65 0.21 ]);
H_w2    = plot(t, w1, 'r-');
Hlx     = xlabel('Time, s');

Mydata    = cell(7);  % pre-allocate space
Mydata{1} = omega1;
Mydata{2} = t;
Mydata{3} = w1;
Mydata{4} = multipl;
```

```
        Mydata{5} = phase;
        Mydata{6} = Ha_up;
        Mydata{7} = Ha_down;
        set(gcf, 'UserData', Mydata);

    case 'Ch_omega2'
        edit1    = findobj(gcf, 'Tag', 'edit1')
        multipl  = str2num(get(edit1, 'String'))
        Mydata   = get(gcf, 'Userdata');
        omega1   = Mydata{1}
        t        = Mydata{2};
        w1       = Mydata{3};
        omega2   = omega1*multipl
        w2       = sin(omega2*t);
        Ha_up    = Mydata{6};
        axes(Ha_up)
        H_w1 = plot(t, w1, 'r-', t, w2, 'b--');
        Mydata{4} = multipl;
        set(gcf, 'UserData', Mydata);

    case 'Ch_phase'
        edit2    = findobj(gcf, 'Tag', 'edit2')
        phase    = str2num(get(edit2, 'String'))
        Mydata   = get(gcf, 'Userdata');
        omega1   = Mydata{1}
        t        = Mydata{2};
        w1       = Mydata{3};
        multipl  = Mydata{4};
        omega2   = omega1*multipl
        2        = 2*pi/omega2;
        delta    = phase*T2;
        w2       = sin(omega2*t + delta);
        Ha_up    = Mydata{6};
        axes(Ha_up)
        H_w1 = plot(t, w1, 'r-', t, w2, 'b--');
        Mydata{5} = phase;
        set(gcf, 'UserData', Mydata);

    case 'Refresh'
        Mydata   = get(gcf, 'Userdata');
        omega1   = Mydata{1}
        t        = Mydata{2};
        w1       = Mydata{3};
        multipl  = Mydata{4};
        omega2   = omega1*multipl
        T2       = 2*pi/omega2;
```

```
phase      = Mydata{5};
delta      = phase*T2;
w2         = sin(omega2*t + delta);
w          = w1 + w2;
Ha_down    = Mydata{7};
axes(Ha_down)
H_w2       = plot(t, w, 'b-');
```

```
end
```

We invoke the function without arguments. Then, the MATLAB built-in function `nargin` detects that the number of input arguments is smaller than one and sets `flag` to the string *init*. The main part of the GUI is built as a **switchyard**, that is as the structure

```
switch flag

        case 'init'
                              % segment 1
        case 'Ch_omega2'
                              % segment 2
        case 'Ch_phase'
                              % segment 3
        case 'Refresh'
                              % segment 4
    end
```

As the conditional structure at the beginning of the file sets the flag to the value `init`, the first program segment is executed, initializing the GUI. The figure is assigned the handle `H_fig` and the first wave is defined. The lines

```
set(H_fig, 'NumberTitle', 'off',...
    'Name', 'Interference of two sinusoidal waves')
```

define a title, rather than letting MATLAB give the figure a number. The next block of statements defines the first **control** element of the interface, an **editable text box**. The respective lines are

```
Hedit1 = uicontrol(H_fig, 'Units', 'normalized',...
        'Position', [ 0.05 0.07 0.15 0.05 ],...
        'Style', 'Edit','String', num2str(multipl),...
        'Tag', 'edit1',...
        'CallBack', ('interfer(''Ch_omega2'')'));
```

The first line assigns to the control the handle `Hedit1`; it says that it is a `uicontrol` (user interface control), that it is the **child** of `H_fig`, and that its position

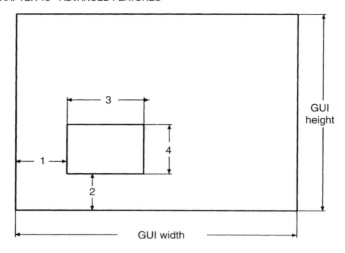

Figure 18.4   The order of elements in the 'Position' array.

and dimensions within the GUI are given in **normalized units**. By the latter term we mean that the position and dimensions of the box are measured as fractions of the figure width and height. In fact, the second line says that it refers to the propriety 'Position' whose value is defined in the vector that follows. As explained in Figure 18.4. the lower left corner of the box is situated at 0.05 GUI width from the lower left corner of the GUI, and 0.07 GUI height from the same corner. The width of the uicontrol is 0.15 the width of the GUI, and the height 0.05 the GUI height. The property Style gets the value Edit, that is the style of the uicontrol is an editable text box. The third line defines the character string that appears in the box, and the fourth line defines a **tag** with the value edit1. This tag univocally identifies the control and is known to all parts of the program. The last line is the **callback**, that is the action to be executed by the program after acting within the control. In this case, after changing the value displayed by String and pressing the Enter key, the GUI will call the segment identified as case Ch_omega.

The order of the lines in the uicontrol definition is not important, but the sequence *propriety-name, propriety-value* is compulsory. As seen, each line except the last one is terminated by the continuation device ', . . .', showing that the whole set of lines defines one control.

The second control, with handle Htext1, is a **text box**. It displays a string that cannot be changed. In our case, the string Frequency multiplier shows the meaning of the number in the adjacent editable box.

The third control is again an editable text box; the user can define in it the ratio of the second-wave phase to its period. Thus, writing 0.5 means that the second wave will be advanced half a period with respect to the first wave. After changing the value in the editable text box and pressing the Enter key, the control calls the program segment identified as case Ch_phase.

The fourth control is a text box that explains the meaning of the adjacent editable text box. The fifth control is a **push button**. Pressing this control calls the segment case 'Refresh'. The sum of the two waves is calculated and plotted in the lower window of the GUI. The second push button, H_button2, causes the program to return to its initial segment and restore the initial parameter values and display. The last two controls are text boxes that explain the meanings of the graphs in the adjacent windows. The line

```
Ha_up = axes('Position', [ 0.05 0.71 0.65 0.21 ]);
```

defines the window which will contain the plot produced by the next line. The position and the size of that window are again defined as fractions of the GUI width and height. The next two lines concern the lower window and the plot in it.

There then follows a block of statements that build a cell array and assign its cells the values of parameters that are passed between the different segments of the GUI. We use a cell array to store dissimilar data types, numeric values and character strings. The resulting cell array, Mydata, will be stored as UserData, a device used to pass data between the different parts of a recursive function. We have already used another device, namely the tag propriety. There is a third way of doing the same job, that is by declaring the parameters and the handles as **global**. This may be the simplest way, but it involves the chance of confusion with other global variables that inadvertently may have the same names. We prefer the other two possibilities as more 'hygienic' and we strongly recommend them.

An instance of the GUI screen is shown in Figure 18.5.

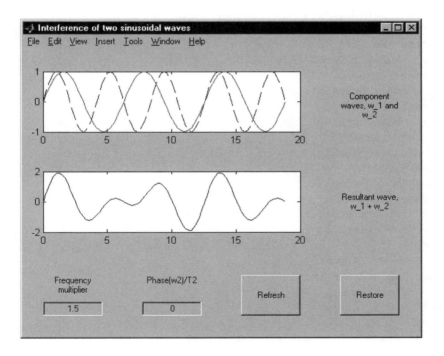

Figure 18.5   An instance of the interfer GUI screen.

18.6.3   A GUI for additive colour mixing

In Section 10.6 we explained the phenomenon of additive colour mixing. In this sub-section we describe a GUI that allows the user to change interactively the proportions of the three elementary colours and view the result. We again use the switchyard paradigm recommended in the previous susbsection, but this time in each 'case' the GUI function calls a subfunction that performs the required action. As explained in Section 5.10, subfunctions are written to the same file as the principal function that calls them and are known only to it. The listing of the GUI file is as follows:

```
% RGB GUI for demonstrating interactively additive colour mixing
         function [] = RGBcolr(cmd);

if nargin == 0,
   RGBcolr_init;
else
   h = get(gcf,'userdata');          % recover the handles
   switch cmd,
   case 'RedSlider',
    RGBcolr_RedSlider(h);
   case 'GreenSlider',
    RGBcolr_GreenSlider(h);
   case 'BlueSlider',
       RGBcolr_BlueSlider(h);
   case 'RedEdt',
       RGBcolr_RedEdt(h);
   case 'GreenEdt',
    RGBcolr_GreenEdt(h);
   case 'BlueEdt',
       RGBcolr_BlueEdt(h);
   case 'reset',
    RGBcolr_Reset(h);
   case 'quit',
       RGBcolr_quit(h);
   otherwise,
       error('RGBcolr called with unknown parameter');
   end; % switch
end; % if

function RGBcolr_init;
CurFig = figure;
Red  = 0.8; Green = 0.8; Blue = 0.8;    % initialize colours

sliderwidth = 0.2; sliderhight = 0.02;

txt = uicontrol('Parent', CurFig, 'style',  'text',...
```

```
                 'str', '  Playing with RGB colors ...',...
                 'Units', 'normalized',...
                 'pos', [0.375 0.85 0.25 0.05], 'call', '');

pb0 = uicontrol('Parent', CurFig, 'style', 'push',...
                 'str', '  quit  ', 'Units', 'normalized',...
                 'pos', [0.8 0.05 0.1 0.04],...
                 'call', 'RGBcolr(''quit'')');

pb1 = uicontrol('Parent', CurFig, 'style',  'push',...  % reset button
                 'str', '  Reset  ', 'Units',  'normalized',...
                 'pos', [0.3 0.4 0.4 0.4],...
                 'BackgroundColor', [ Red Green Blue],...
                 'call', 'RGBcolr(''reset'')');

sl1 = uicontrol('Parent', CurFig, 'style',  'slider',...   % slider red
                 'Units',  'normalized',...
                 'pos', [0.1 0.2 sliderwidth sliderhight],...
                 'value',  Red, 'call', 'RGBcolr(''RedSlider'')' );

sl2 = uicontrol('Parent', CurFig, 'style',  'slider',...
                 'Units',  'normalized',            ...
                 'pos', [0.5*(1-sliderwidth) .2 sliderwidth 0.02],...
                 'value',  Green, 'call', 'RGBcolr(''GreenSlider'')');

sl3 = uicontrol('Parent', CurFig, 'style',  'slider',...   % blue slider
                 'Units',  'normalized',...
                 'pos', [0.9-sliderwidth .2 sliderwidth 0.02],...
                 'value',  Blue, 'call', 'RGBcolr(''BlueSlider'')');

ed1 = uicontrol('Parent', CurFig, 'style',  'edit',...   % red edit box
                 'Units',  'normalized',...
                 'pos', [0.1 .25 sliderwidth 0.05],...
                 'string', num2str(Red), 'BackgroundColor', [ 1 0 0],...
                 'call', 'RGBcolr(''RedEdt'')');

ed2 = uicontrol('Parent', CurFig, 'style', 'edit',...  % green edit box
                 'Units',  'normalized',            ...
                 'pos', [0.5*(1-sliderwidth) .25 sliderwidth 0.05],...
                 'string', num2str(Green), 'BackgroundColor', [ 0 1 0],...
                 'call', 'RGBcolr(''GreenEdt'')');

ed3 = uicontrol('Parent', CurFig, 'style',  'edit',...  % blue edit box
                 'Units',  'normalized',...
                 'pos', [0.9-sliderwidth .25 sliderwidth 0.05],...
                 'string', num2str(Blue), 'BackgroundColor', [ 0 0 1],...
```

```
                    'call', 'RGBcolr(''BlueEdt'')')');

h = struct(        'CurFig', CurFig,... % collect all handles
                   'pb0',    pb0,   ...
                   'pb1',    pb1,   ...
                   'sl1',    sl1,   ...
                   'sl2',    sl2,   ...
                   'sl3',    sl3,   ...
                   'ed1',    ed1,   ...
                   'ed2',    ed2,   ...
                   'ed3',    ed3);
set(CurFig', 'UserData', h);            % save all handles

function RGBcolr_RedSlider(h);
Red = get(h.sl1, 'value');
set(h.ed1, 'string', num2str(Red));
Colors = get(h.pb1, 'BackgroundColor');
Colors(1) = Red;
set(h.pb1, 'BackgroundColor', Colors);

function RGBcolr_GreenSlider(h);
Green = get(h.sl2, 'value');
set(h.ed2, 'string', num2str(Green));
Colors = get(h.pb1, 'BackgroundColor');
Colors(2) = Green;
set(h.pb1, 'BackgroundColor', Colors);

function RGBcolr_BlueSlider(h);
Blue = get(h.sl3, 'value');
set(h.ed3, 'string', num2str(Blue));
Colors = get(h.pb1, 'BackgroundColor');
Colors(3) = Blue;
set(h.pb1, 'BackgroundColor', Colors);

function RGBcolr_RedEdt(h);
Red = eval(get(h.ed1, 'string'));
set(h.sl1, 'value', Red);
Colors = get(h.pb1, 'BackgroundColor');
Colors(1) = Red;
set(h.pb1, 'BackgroundColor', Colors);

function RGBcolr_GreenEdt(h);
Green = eval(get(h.ed2, 'string'));
set(h.sl2, 'value', Green);
Colors = get(h.pb1, 'BackgroundColor');
Colors(2) = Green;
```

```
set(h.pb1, 'BackgroundColor', Colors);

function RGBcolr_BlueEdt(h);
Blue = eval(get(h.ed3, 'string'));
set(h.sl3, 'value', Blue);
Colors = get(h.pb1, 'BackgroundColor');
Colors(3) = Blue;
set(h.pb1, 'BackgroundColor', Colors);

function RGBcolr_Reset(h);
Red      = 0.8; Green     = 0.8; Blue      = 0.8;
set(h.sl1, 'value', Red);
set(h.sl2, 'value', Green);
set(h.sl3, 'value', Blue);

set(h.ed1, 'string', num2str(Red));
set(h.ed2, 'string', num2str(Green));
set(h.ed3, 'string', num2str(Blue));

Colors = [Red Green Blue];
set(h.pb1, 'BackgroundColor', Colors);

function RGBcolr_quit(h);
delete(h.CurFig);
```

The resulting GUI is shown in Figure 18.6. As in the previous example, the GUI is defined as a recursive function; it is first called without input arguments. The function nargin identifies this situation and calls the subfunction RGBcolr_init that initializes the screen. The first action is to create a figure graphic object and allocate the handle CurFig (current figure) to it. The statements Red = 0.8, Green = 0.8 and Blue = 0.8 are used to initialize the *BackGround* property to a grey value. Remember: when all the elements of the RGB vector are equal we obtain a hue of grey. The vector [0 0 0] yields black, and the vector [1 1 1] white. A new uicontrol introduced in this example is the **slider**. The uicontrols of this style are called sl1, sl2 and sl3. A slider has the form of a rectangular box, with an **indicator** inside it. The indicator can be moved in the same way as the scrolling bars used in the Windows and Word screens. Thus, we can position the mouse over the indicator, drag it until we read in the edit box the colour value that interests us, and then free the mouse. Alternatively, we can click on the small buttons with arrows that limit the slider trough at the left and right.

In this second example of a GUI we abbreviated propriety names writing 'pos' for 'Position', and 'call' for 'CallBack'. This is possible as long as the abbreviations cannot be confused with other propriety names. The propriety 'BackgroundColor' refers to the colour that fills the rectangle of the respective uicontrol. Colours can be specified as here, by a vector of RGB values, or by the name of a MATLAB predefined colour, such as 'r' for red.

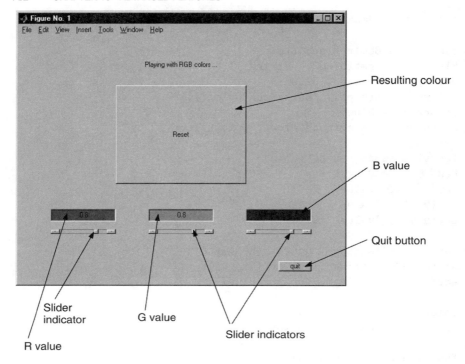

Figure 18.6   A GUI explaining additive colour mixing.

The handles of the various uicontrols are passed as arguments to the functions that implement the GUI. In this example the handles are organized in the structure called h. The various functions extract the handles with the aid of the function get and assign their values with the help of the function set.

18.7   A word on object-oriented programming

The newest versions of MATLAB are **object oriented**, in short **O-O**. In the last few years the term object oriented has become a frequently used 'buzz word'. Actually, the term covers an entire, relatively new way of thinking about various processes, software design being only one of them.

Weisfeld (2000) distinguishes between the older *procedural* and the newer *O-O* programming. In the former way, data were separated from procedures. Procedures could be considered black boxes requiring an input and producing an output. Data could be accessed by any procedures. In O-O programming the **objects** combine data and procedures, the latter now being called **methods**. In this way a certain data set can be accessed only by the appropriate methods. For instance, let us consider temperature data. It makes no sense to add or divide temperatures, but we are interested in temperature differences and in powers of temperatures. Then, a temperature

object should be packed together with the corresponding methods. While one given temperature constitutes an object, the paradigm for building that object is a temperature **class**. As stated, the paradigm should allow only those operations that make sense for objects in the class.

We mentioned at the beginning of this chapter that MATLAB has 14 built-in data types that are actually classes. Beyond this MATLAB allows the user to build additional classes. By doing so the user can benefit from a number of O-O facilities. For example, temperatures belong to a larger category that are, in fact, measures of potentials. Another measure of potential is the voltage for which more operations make sense; voltages can be added by connecting two voltage sources in series. Then, the user may think of a class of potentials, temperatures being a subclass, and voltages another one. The class of potentials would have a limited number of more general proprieties that are **inherited** by the subclasses *temperatures* and *voltages*, such as the 'difference method'. In addition to the inherited proprieties, the subclasses would have their own, specific proprieties, for example the class *voltages* will have a method for addition. In O-O terminology, the class *potentials* is the **parent** and the classes *temperature* and *voltage* are its **children**. MATLAB provides the instruments for constructing classes and propriety inheritance. These may be important subjects for software developers. For more details we refer the reader to the literature provided by The MathWorks and to the details that can be found in the help facilities.

To illustrate a few O-O ideas let us return to the examples of operations on unit-affected quantities presented in Section 17.4. This time we shall show how the MATLAB O-O facilities can improve performance. We build a new class *phquant*, an acronym for 'physical quantity'. To begin, we create a directory for this class and call it @*phquant*; that is, the name of the class preceded by the 'at' symbol, @. The new directory is not on the MATLAB path; it is a subdirectory of a user-created directory that is on the path. For example, if `mydirectory` is a private directory of the user, the files of the new class are written in the subdirectory `\mydirectory\@phquant`. However, the operations on physical quantities are carried on in `mydirectory`.

The subdirectory of the new class must contain at least two M-files: the **constructor** of the new class, and a file `display.m`. The constructor of the phquant class is as follows:

```
function p = phquant(v, u)

%PHQUANT Physical quantity class constructor

switch nargin
        case 0  % no input argument, create default object
            p.value = [ ];
            p.unit  = [ ];
            p = class(p, 'phquant');

        case 1 % insufficient data
            error('Only one argument supplied')
```

```
        case 2 % two input arguments supplied
            if isa(v, 'numeric')
                if isa(u, 'char')
                    p = struct('value', v, 'unit', u);
                    p = class(p, 'phquant');
                else
                    error('Second argument must be character string')
                end
            else
                error('First argument must be numeric')
            end
        otherwise % too many input arguments
            error('Too many input arguments')
end
```

If the function phquant is invoked without arguments, it will create a physical-quantity object with empty fields. If the function is called with two arguments, the first numeric and the second of the character-string type, it will produce an object with two fields, the first storing the numeric value of the quantity, and the second, the symbol of the unit.

The display function defines the way in which the physical quantity is displayed when an expression is entered without ending it with a semicolon, ;. The listing of the function proposed by us is

```
        function display(p)

%PHQUANT/DISPLAY Command window display of physical quantities

disp(' ')
disp([ num2str(p.value) ' ' p.unit ]);
disp(' ')
```

Other functions stored in the new-class directory are the methods that work on the objects of the class. We present here just one such method, the addition of two physical quantities. The function plus listed below **overloads** the plus operator, '+'. That is, for two quantities measured with the same unit, the function yields a physical quantity whose value is the sum of the values of the two operands, and the unit is the same as that of the operands.

```
        function s = plus(p, q)

%PHQUANT/PLUS Addition P + q for physical quantities

if strcmp(p.unit, q.unit) == 1  % identical units
        s.value = p.value + q.value;
        s.unit  = p.unit;
```

```
          s = phquant(s.value, s.unit);
else
          error('Input arguments are measured in different units')
end
```

Examples of operations with the physical quantities are

```
>> A = phquant(3, 'm')
3 m
>> B = phquant(5, 'm');
>> A + B
  8 m
```

Above, we defined the object A by calling the function phquant with two arguments of the proper types. As the call was not terminated with a semicolon, the resulting object is displayed by the function display. To add the objects A and B it was sufficient to write A + B, not uadd(A, B) as in Subsection 17.4.1. This simplification was possible because we overloaded the MATLAB built-in function plus that performs the binary addition of MATLAB arrays. Other functions can be overloaded, among them minus for subtraction, mtimes for multiplication and rdivide for right division. In the exercises we invite the reader to use them to extend the operations to physical quantities.

18.8   Example – querying a cell array

In Subsection 18.2.2 we built the structure persons, and in Subsection 18.4.3 we converted it into a cell array. We saw that the structure persons could be used as a small database and queried as such. So can the cell array cpersons. We can build our own query functions: for example, the following function persmean calculates the mean of the weights stored in the cell array:

```
%PERSMEAN Finds mean weight over cell array cpersons

[ m, n, lP ] = size(cpersons);

Wtotal = 0;                            % initialize sum
for k = 1: lP
   Wtotal = Wtotal + cpersons{2, 1, k}; % calculate sum
end
Mweight = Wtotal/lP                    % find mean
```

Another function, cweight, retrieves from a given cell array the weight of a person whose name is invoked. If the name is not stored, the function issues an error message.

```
%CWEIGHT finds weight for given firstname, in cell array DB

        function        w = cweight(DB, firstname)

found = 0;
[ m m l ] = size(DB);
found = 0;

k = 0;
while (found == 0) & (k < l)
        k = k + 1;
        if strcmp(DB{1, 1, k}, firstname)
                w = DB{2, 1, k};
                found = 1;              % firstname found in DB
        end
end
if found == 0
        error([ 'Name ' firstname ' not found' ])
end
```

Examples of applying the above two functions are

```
>> persmean
 Mweight =
 80
>> w_Charles = cweight(cpersons, 'Charles')
w_charles =
 75
>> w_John = cweight(cpersonsL, 'John')
???  Error using ==> cweight
Name John not found
```

In our examples we used the simplest strategy of searching over a given set, that is we scanned the database sequentially from the first element to the last one, or until we found a name that matched the required one. This method of searching is called **linear search** and in most cases it is not efficient. It is like searching for a name in the phone book by starting from the first name there and proceeding sequentially until a match is found. Linear search may be acceptable if the number of elements in the database is small. However, searching over larger data sets requires more sophisticated methods whose execution time does not grow quickly with the number of elements, for example **binary search**. The reader may find the theory of those procedures in specialized books.

18.9   Exercises

Solutions for Exercises 18.2, 18.4 and 18.9 appear at the back of the book.

■ **EXERCISE 18.1**   Query a structure

Write a function that queries the structure persons and retrieves the name and the weight of the heaviest person.

■ **EXERCISE 18.2**   Histogram over a structure

Write a function that plots the histogram of weights stored in the structure persons.

■ **EXERCISE 18.3**   Histogram over a structure

Write a function that plots the histogram of numerical values stored in a given field of a given structure. Try that function over the structure persons.

■ **EXERCISE 18.4**   Finding the index of a given person

Write a function that retrieves the index of a given person in the structure persons.

■ **EXERCISE 18.5**   Query a cell array

Write a function that queries the cell array cpersons and retrieves the name and the weight of the heaviest person.

■ **EXERCISE 18.6**   Histogram over a cell array

Write a function that plots the histogram of weights stored in the cell array cpersons.

■ **EXERCISE 18.7**   Structure to cell array conversion

Let us start with a three-dimensional structure array s of dimensions 3 by 4 by 5 containing two fields, f1 and f2:

```
for i=1:3
   for j=1:4
      for k=1:5
         s(i,j,k).f1 = rand;
         s(i,j,k).f2 = rand;
```

```
            s(i,j,k).f2 = rand;
        end
    end
end;
```

The reader is invited to verify that the cell array c, defined as:
c = struct2cell(s), is a four-dimensional cell array, of size 2 by 3 by 4 by 5, and that c(1, j, j, k) is equal to s(i, j, k).f1, while c(2, j, j, k) is equal to s(i, j, k).f2.

■ **EXERCISE 18.8**   Subtraction of physical quantities

Build a function that performs the subtraction of physical quantities. For this and the following exercises consult Section 17.4.

■ **EXERCISE 18.9**   Multiplication of physical quantities

Build a function that performs the multiplication of physical quantities.

■ **EXERCISE 18.10**   Division of physical quantities

Build a function that performs the division of physical quantities.

Appendix
Answers to selected exercises

Chapter 2

2.3
```
t = 0: pi/90: 20;
x1 = sin(2*pi*t); x2 = sin(2.2*pi*t);
x  = x1 + x2;
plot(t, x), grid
xlabel('Time, s'), ylabel('sin(2*pi*t) + sin(2.2*pi*t)')
```
2.4
```
M = 100: 100: 1000; % measured values
E = 30*100./M;      % Percent error
[ M' E' ]           % display
ans =
   1.0e+003 *
    0.1000    0.0300
    ...       ...
    1.0000    0.0030

M = 0: 10: 1000; E = 30*100./M;
Warning: Divide by zero
plot(M, E), grid
title('Errors of 3%, 1000 full-scale instrument')
xlabel('Measured value'), ylabel('Maximum error, %')
```
2.6
```
V = [ 0 0.9 ]; S = [ -1.5 0 ]; % velocities, km/h
T = V + S                      % true velocity, km/h
T = -1.5000    0.9000
true_speed = sqrt(T*T')
true_speed = 1.7493
deviation = (180/pi)*atan(1.5/0.9)
deviation = 59.0362
t = 1.1/0.9                    % time to swim across, h
t = 1.2222
BC = 1.5*t                     % km
BC = 1.8333
(180/pi)*atan(BC/1.1)          % check angle
ans = 59.0362
```
2.9 (1)
```
F = [ 2 2 2 ]; % force, N
P1 = [ 2 3 5 ]; % direct path, m
```

719

```
        W1 = F*P1'        % work along path P1, m
        W1 = 20
   (2)  O = [ 0 0 0 ]; A = [ 2 0 0 ]; B = [ 2 3 0 ]; P = [ 2 3 5 ];
        path1 = A - O
        path1 = 2      0      0
        path2 = B - A
        path2 = 0      3      0
        path3 = P - B
        path3 = 0      0      5
        path = path1 + path2 + path3
        path =  2      3      5
        W2 = F*path'
        W2 = 20
2.11    R(1) = [ 200 300 ]*[ 1050 - [ 350 750 ]]'/1050;
        R(2) = [ 200 300 ]*[ 350 750 ]'/1050
        R = 219.0476   280.9524
        sum(R) - sum(F)
        ans = 0
```

Chapter 3

```
3.3     F = 0: 50: 250; C = 5*(F - 32)/9;
        [ F' C' ]
        ans =
                    0   -17.7778
              50.0000    10.0000
             100.0000    37.7778
             150.0000    65.5556
             200.0000    93.3333
             250.0000   121.1111
3.7     L = [ 0 20 50 75 ];        % horizontal dimensions, mm
        sl = diff(L);              % section lengths, mm
        D  = [ 10 20 10 ];         % diameters, mm
        % calculate sectional masses, Kg
        M  = 7900*pi*((D/1000).^2).*(sl/1000)/4;
        a)
        Mtot = sum(M)              % shaft mass, kg
        Mtot = 0.1024
        b)
        Cg = (L(1:3) + L(2:4))/2;  % sectional centres, mm
        Scg = M*Cg'/Mtot           % shaft centre of mass, mm
        Scg = 36.1364
        c)
        I = sum(M.*D.^2)/8         % shaft moment of inertia, kg mm^2
        I = 4.0718
```

3.9   After forming the vector of weights, **weights2**, and the matrix of centres of gravity, **cg2**, we calculate the total weight by

```
        Fw2 = sum(weights2)
```

with the result 86.9000 kN. The centre of gravity is obtained from

```
CG2 = weights2*cg2/Fw2
CG2 = 0.0504    0.0545    2.4454
```

The factor of safety against overturning is given by

```
S2 = (Fw2*CG2(1))/(1.1*P*7)
S2 = 0.0387
```

The crane cannot be operated in this mode. We must change something and MATLAB allows us to do this easily. For instance, let us halve the radius of the load and at the same time use outriggers extending 1.7 m behind the rear wheels. As the jib is now closer to the truck, we change the x-coordinate of its centre of gravity by

```
cg2(3,1) = -1.8;
```

We use now the arrow keys to retrieve

```
CG2 = weights2*cg2/Fw2
```

We press Enter and we obtain

```
CG2 = 0.2616    0.0054    2.4454
```

Next we retrieve the expression for S2 and we edit it to become

```
S2 = (Fw2*(CG2(1) + 1.7))/(1.1*P*(3.5 - 1.7))
```

which yields S2 = 5.0641. This factor of safety is too large; the user should try other values until he reaches more reasonable results.

3.10
```
r = 100;                        % length of crank arm OA, mm
l = 240;                        % length of link AB, mm
alpha = 0: pi/90: 2*pi;         % angle of crank arm, rad
beta = acos(r*cos(alpha)/l);
s = r*sin(alpha) + l*sin(beta); % stroke, mm
subplot(2, 1, 1), plot(alpha, s), grid
ylabel('Stroke, s, mm')
dsdt = r*cos(alpha)*(1 + r*sin(alpha)/(l*sin(beta)));
                % stroke velocity, ds/dt, mm/s
subplot(2, 1, 2), plot(alpha, dsdt), grid
xlabel('Crank angle, alpha, rad')
ylabel('Crank velocity, ds/dt, mm/s')
```

3.13
```
I = [ 10 50 100 500 ];
R = 55./(I - 1)
R = 6.1111    1.1224    0.5556    0.1102
```

3.14
```
R = [ 6 1 0.5 0.1 ]; I = (55 + R)./R
I = 10.1667    56.0000   111.0000   551.0000
```

Chapter 4

4.5
```
alpha = 0: pi/90: 2*pi;
z     = -0.5 + 1.5*exp(i*alpha);
subplot(1, 2, 1), plot(real(z), imag(z))
```

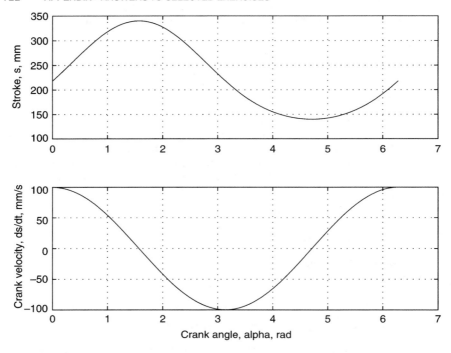

Figure A.1   Stroke and stroke velocity of compressor mechanism.

```
axis('equal'), grid, title('z plane')
xlabel('Real'), ylabel('Imaginary')
w       = (z + 1./z)/2;
subplot(1, 2, 2), plot(real(w), imag(w))
axis('equal'), grid
title('w plane, w = (z + 1/z)/2')
xlabel('Real'), ylabel('Imaginary')
```

The resulting 'aerofoil' is shown in Figure A.2. To move the circle in the z plane and obtain another aerofoil try, for example,

```
z1      = z + 0.5i;
subplot(1, 2, 1), plot(real(z1), imag(z1))
axis('equal'), grid, title('z plane')
xlabel('Real'), ylabel('Imaginary')
w       = (z1 + 1./z1)/2;
subplot(1, 2, 2), plot(real(w), imag(w))
axis('equal'), grid
title('w plane, w = (z + 1/z)/2')
xlabel('Real'), ylabel('Imaginary')
```

4.6   ```
V = 0.9*exp(i*pi/2); S = 1.5*exp(i*pi);
T = V + S
T = -1.5000 + 0.9000i
```
```

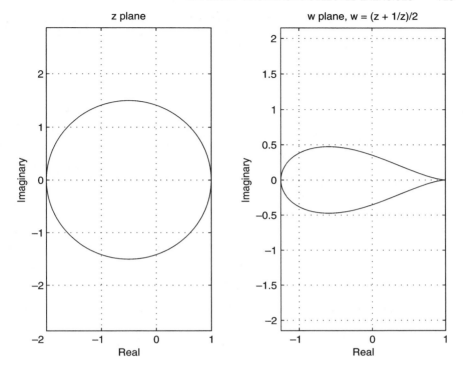

Figure A.2   Joukovski's transformation in Exercise 4.5.

```
       true_speed = abs(T)                % speed over bottom, km/h
       true_speed = 1.7493
       deviation = (180/pi)*angle(T)
       deviation = 149.0362
4.10 (a) f = 400;                          % frequency, Hz
       Z1 = 10000 - j/(2*pi*f*1*10^(-6))  % ohm
       Z1 = 1.0000e+004- 3.9789e+002i
       Z2 = 5000 + j*0.001*2*pi*f         % ohm
       Z2 = 5.0000e+003+ 2.5133e+000i
       R4 = 10000;                        % ohm
       R3 = Z1*R4/Z2
       R3 = 2.0000e+004- 8.0583e+002i\vspace*{-6pt}

   (b) f = 50;                            % frequency, Hz
       Z1 = 30000 - j/(2*pi*f*2*10^(-6))  % ohm
       Z1 = 3.0000e+004- 1.5915e+003i
       Z2 = 10000 + j*0.002*2*pi*f        % ohm
       Z2 = 1.0000e+004+ 6.2832e-001i
       R4 = 30000;                        % ohm
       R3 = Z1*R4/Z2
       R3 = 9.0000e+004- 4.7803e+003i
```

In both cases the calculated value of R_3 has a negative imaginary part. This means that the bridge cannot be balanced if R_3 is a pure resistance; there should be also a capacity.

Chapter 5

5.7
```
PO  = [ 0; 0; 1 ];                  % hinge centre
P1  = [ 0; -32.5; 1 ];              % rod end
rod = [ PO P1 ];
t   = pi/2: pi/60: (5/2)*pi;        % parameter of disk curve
diskx = 2.5*cos(t); disky = 2.5*sin(t);
disk = [ diskx; disky; ones(size(t)) ];
% translate disk to point -35
ndisk = trlate(0, -35)*disk;
pendul = [ rod ndisk ];
plot(pendul(1, :), pendul(2, :)), axis('equal')
hold on
% swing pendulum by 30 degrees
swinged = rtate(30)*pendul;
plot(swinged(1, :), swinged(2, :)), axis('equal')
```

Chapter 6

6.2
```
rats(pi)
ans = 355/113
rats(sin(pi*30/180))
ans = 1/2
rats(tan(pi*45/180))
ans = 1
rats(0.33333)
ans = 33333/100000
rats(sqrt(2))
ans = 1393/985
```

The number π is *transcendental* and cannot be represented as a rational fraction. The number $\sqrt{2}$ is *irrational* and cannot be represented by a rational fraction. A simple and elegant proof shows that the hypotenuse of a rectangular triangle with both sides equal to 1 is *incommensurable* with the sides. The rational representations of the other four numbers in this exercise are exact.

6.5
```
F = [ 100; 250; 250 ]; L = [ 200; 450; 900 ];
A = [ 1050 0; 0 1050 ]; B = [ F*[ 1050 - L ]'; F*L' ];
R = A \ B
R = 259.5238
    340.4762
```

6.6   Taking moments about the left-hand support we obtain

$$700F_1 + 1500F_2 = 2100R_2$$

The equilibrium of forces yields

$$F_1 + F_2 = R_1 + R_2$$

These two equations can be combined to give

$$\begin{bmatrix} 700 & 1500 \\ 1 & 1 \end{bmatrix} \begin{bmatrix} F_1 \\ F_2 \end{bmatrix} = \begin{bmatrix} 2100 \times 980 \\ 500 + 980 \end{bmatrix}$$

The calculations in MATLAB are

```
A = [ 700 1500; 1 1 ]; B = [ 2100*980; 500+980 ];
F = A\B

F =
   1.0e+003 *
      0.2025
      1.2775
```

We can check the results by calculating the moments about the right-hand support

```
[ 2100 - [ 700 1500 ]]*F - 500*2100
ans = 0
```

6.8   Let us write the equations for the mooring line ABC; those for the line DEF are symmetric. From the free-body diagram of point A we obtain

$$\sin 20° T_1 = B_f/2$$

The equations of equilibrium of point B are

$$\begin{aligned} -\cos 20° T_1 + \cos 10° T_2 &= 0 \\ \sin 20° T_1 - \sin 10° T_2 - W &= 0 \end{aligned}$$

Putting all equations together yields

$$\begin{bmatrix} \sin 20° & 0 & 0 \\ -\cos 20° & \cos 10° & 0 \\ \sin 20° & -\sin 10° & -1 \end{bmatrix} \begin{bmatrix} T_1 \\ T_2 \\ W \end{bmatrix} = \begin{bmatrix} B_f/2 \\ 0 \\ 0 \end{bmatrix}$$

The calculations in MATLAB are

```
Bf = 10;          % buoyancy force, kN
A = [sind(20) 0 0; -cosd(20) cosd(10) 0; sind(20) -sind(10) -1];
B = [Bf/2; 0; 0]; X = A\B
X =
    14.6190
    13.9493
     2.5777
```

The equilibrium of the external forces is verified with

```
Bf = Bf*[ cosd(90) sind(90) ];
W  = X(3)*[ cosd(-90) sind(-90) ];
T2right = X(2)*[ cosd(-10) sind(-10) ];
T2left  = X(2)*[ cosd(190) sind(190) ];
```

```
Bf + 2*W + T2right + T2left
ans =
   1.0e-014 *
      0.1776    -0.1776
```

This is practically zero, as expected.

6.9
```
A = [ cosd(20) cosd(10); sind(20) sind(10) ];
B = [ 8; 2 ]; L = A\B
L =
   3.3426
   4.9340
```

6.12
```
A = [ 499 -1 -1 -1; 99 99 -1 -1; 49 49 49 -1; 9 9 9 9 ];
B = 55*ones(4,1); R = A\B
R =
   0.1222
   0.4889
   0.6111
   4.8889
```

6.14   The mass of each end plate, in kg, equals

$$7850 \times \pi \frac{d^2}{4} t$$

with d and t measured in m. In the same units, the mass of the lateral plate is

$$7850 \times \pi(d + t)th = 7850 \times \pi(d + t)t \times 2d$$

and that of the concrete filling

$$2300 \times \pi \frac{d^2}{4} h = 2300 \times \pi \frac{d^2}{4} \times 2d$$

The design equation is obtained by summing the masses of the two end plates, of the lateral plate and of the concrete filling, equating the sum to the required mass and dividing all terms by π:

$$\frac{2300}{2} d^3 + 7850(\frac{1}{2} + 2)td^2 + 2 \times 7850t^2 d - \frac{M}{\pi} = 0$$

```
M   = 45;                  % specified mass, kg
t   = 0.005;               % plate thickness, m
c   = zeros(1, 4);         % initiate array of coefficients
c(1) = 2300/2; c(2) = 7850*t*2.5;
c(3) = 2*7850*t^2; c(4) = -M/pi;
roots(c)
ans =
   -0.1457 + 0.1980i
   -0.1457 - 0.1980i
    0.2061
```

Obviously, only the third root represents a feasible solution.

6.18
```
function       R = ayrton(range, amp, resist)
%AYRTON calculates resistances for an Ayrton multirange ammeter
%       Input:
%               range = array of ranges, mA, given in descending
```

```
%                           order and excluding the first range
%               amp     = movement rating, mA
%               resist  = ammeter resistance, ohm

n = length(range); A = -amp*ones(n);
for k = 1:n
        for l = 1:k
                A(k,l) = range(k) - amp;
        end
end
B = resist*ones(n, 1); R = A\B
```

Chapter 7

7.3
```
t = 0: 0.25: 90;
y1 = 15*ustep(t, 15);
y2 = uramp(t, 35);
y3 = -uramp(t, 50);
plot(t, y1+y2+y3), xlabel('t')
```

7.4   The function that calculates the sum is

```
function        S = powseq(n)
%POWSEQ(N, L)    sum from K = 1 to N of K^2.
%       Solves exercise 7.4.

K = 1:n;
S = sum(K.^2);
```

A script file that calls the above function is

```
%POWCOMP.M complexity of power sequences, solves Exercise 7.4.

flops(0)
for m = 1:10
        flops(0);
        powseq(m);
        f = flops;
        [ m f ]
end
```

7.9 (3) A function that solves this exercise is

```
function        V = tankv(M, V0, tol)
%TANKV(M, V0, tol) tank volume by iterative method
%       Input arguments: M total tank mass, t
%                        V0 initial guess
%                        tol stopping criterion, if omitted
```

```
%                              default value 0.0001 is used

if nargin == 2
        tol = 0.0001;
end
gf  = 0.83;         % diesel fuel density, t/m^3
gst = 7.85;         % steel density, t/m^3
c   = 6*gst*0.003; % coefficient of steel mass, t/m^2
V = (M - c*(V0^(1/3) + 0.003)^2)/gf
while abs(V - V0) > tol
        V0 = V;
        V = (M - c*(V0^(1/3) + 0.003)^2)/gf
end
```

(4) An experiment with this program is

```
tankv(0.05, 0.05)
V =
    0.0368
    ...
    0.0400
```

We can check the results with

```
Vc = ans;
a = Vc^(1/3)
a = 0.3420
Mfuel = 0.83*Vc
Mfuel = 0.0332
Mst = 6*7.85*(a + 0.003)^2*0.003
Mst = 0.0168
Mtotal = Mst + Mfuel
Mtotal = 0.0500
```

Chapter 8

8.2   A program that answers this exercise is

```
%CARFUEL1        Calculates litres fuel per 100 km

load carkm
km = input('Enter present km reading ')
l  = input('Enter litres of fuel bought ')
c  = num2str(100*l/(km - km0));
t  = ['Your car consumed ' c ' l per 100 km'];
disp(t)
delete carkm.mat
km0 = km;
save carkm km0
```

An example of program execution is

```
Enter present km reading 1046
km =
        1046
Enter litres of fuel bought 34
l =
      34
Your car consumed 10.46 l per 100 km
```

8.5   Prepare first the M-file kvisc.m as follows:

```
%KVISC  Fresh-water kinematic viscosity acc. to table 8.5.
%       Format: [ Temperature  Viscosity ]
%       Units;  deg C, m^2/s

kvisc = [
0       1.79
...
27      0.857
28      0.839 ];
```

The answers to the four questions are obtained as shown below.

(1)
```
kvisc
plot(kvisc(:, 1), kvisc(:, 2))
xlabel('Temperature, deg C'),
ylabel('Kinematic viscosity, m^2/s')
title('Fresh-water kinematic viscosity')
```

(2)
```
ti = 0.5: 27.5;
visci = table1(kvisc, ti)
visci =
    1.7600
      ...
    0.8480
plot(kvisc(:, 1), kvisc(:, 2), ti, visci, '*')
```

(3)
```
t = kvisc(:, 1);        % separate temperature
nu = kvisc(:, 2);       % separate viscosity
invertvisc = [ nu t ]; % inverted table
t09 =  table1(invertvisc, 0.9)
t09 =    24.8095
plot(kvisc(:, 1), kvisc(:, 2), t09, 0.9, '*')
```

(4)
```
nu30 = table1(kvisc, 30)
??? Error using ==> table1
x0 larger than all values in first column
```
The function table1 does not perform extrapolation.

Chapter 9

9.2   Writing

$$resid_2 = \begin{bmatrix} r_1 \\ r_2 \\ \cdot \\ \cdot \\ \cdot \\ r_n \end{bmatrix}$$

we easily see that

$$\begin{bmatrix} r_1 & r_2 & \cdots & r_n \end{bmatrix} \begin{bmatrix} r_1 \\ r_2 \\ \cdot \\ \cdot \\ \cdot \\ r_n \end{bmatrix} = r_1^2 + r_2^2 + \cdots + r_n^2$$

Try for yourself the numerical calculations.

9.5   We begin by

```
kvisc                % load data
t = kvisc(:, 1);  % separate temperatures
nu = kvisc(:, 2); % separate viscosities
```

To decide upon a suitable interpolation curve fit we first plot the data:

```
plot(t, nu)
```

Let us try a second-degree curve

```
c2 = polyfit(t, nu, 2) % polynomial coefficients
c2 = 0.0007    -0.0534     1.7738
ti = 0.5: 27.5;           % temperatures for interpolation
kvisci = polyval(c2, ti)
kvisci = Columns 1 through 7
 1.7473    1.6954    1.6449    1.5959    1.5483    1.5023    1.4576
...
plot(t, nu, ti, kvisci, '*')
xlabel('Temperature, deg C')
ylabel('Kinematic viscosity, m^2/s')
```

Let us also try a third-degree fit and compare it with the previous one:

```
nu2 = polyval(c2, t);
SSE2 = sum((nu - nu2).^2)
SSE2 = 0.0018
c3 = polyfit(t, nu, 3)
c3 = 0.0000    0.0014    -0.0605     1.7889
nu3 = polyval(c3, t);
SSE3 = sum((nu - nu3).^2)
SSE3 = 3.5356e-004
```

9.8

```
c = polyfit([32 212], [0 100], 1)
c = 0.5556  -17.7778
```
    To recognize immediately the proposed equation try

```
rats(c)
ans = 5/9        -160/9
```

The human-body temperature is obtained with

```
polyval(c, 96.8)
ans = 36
```

    The function polyval cannot be used with the rational approximations obtained
with rats. Try this for yourself.

9.11

```
U = [  12 18   25   30   35   40    45 ]; % measured voltage, V
I = [ 0.5   1 2.3 3.5 5.7 8.8 12.9 ]; % measured current, mA
plot(U, I), grid
xlabel('V'), ylabel('mA')
pause
c = polyfit(log(U), log(I), 1);
a = exp(c(2)), n = c(1);
y = a*U.^n;
plot(U, I, U, y, '*'), pause
% try now effect on alternating current, 48 V
f = 50;                                % frequency, Hz
T = 1/f;                               % period, s
t = 0: T/50: 2*T;                      % time scale, s
u = 48*sin(2*pi*50*t); i = sign(u)*a.*abs(u).^n;
plot(t, u, t, i), xlabel('s')
```

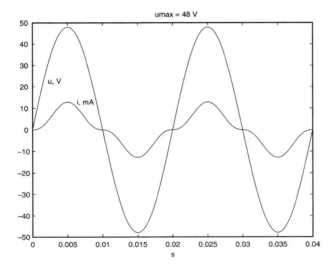

Figure A.3   Current distortion in a varistor circuit.

```
title('umax = 48 V')
text(t(5), u(5), 'u, V')
text(t(15), i(15), 'i, mA')
```
    The third plot is shown in Figure A.3.

Chapter 10

10.2
```
angle = (0: 5: 360)';
P = 900*[ cosd(angle) sind(angle) ]; % plane velocity in air
A = 105*[ cosd(135) sind(135) ];     % wind velocity over ground
n = length(angle);
T = P + ones(n, 1)*A;
speed = (T(:, 1).^2 + T(:, 2).^2).^(1/2);
polar(pi*angle/180, speed), grid
```
    The resulting plot is shown in Figure A.4.

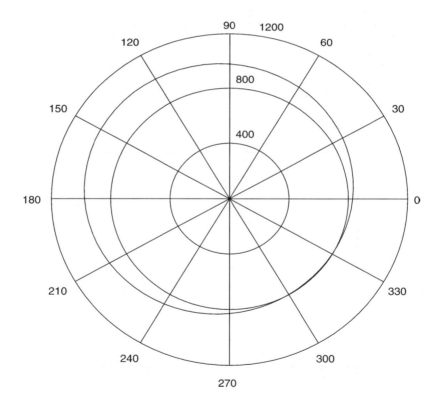

Figure A.4   Aeroplane speed over ground versus aeroplane course in air.

10.6   %WAVE ⟍ movie of water waves

```
% Generate a reference frame
L = 50;                    % wave length, m
k = 2*pi/L;                % wave number
h = 3;  % wave amplitude = half(crest-to-trough)
x = 0: L/50: 2*L;          % space axis
w = 2*pi*5;                % wave circular frequency, rad/s
t = 1;                     % time, s
z = h*cos(k*x - w*t);
plot(x, z)
axis([ 0 100 -3 3 ]), axis('equal')
pause
% generate movie
T = 1/5;                   % wave period, s
t = 0: T/10: T;
M = moviein(10);
for l = 1: 10;
        z = h*cos(k*x - w*t(l));
        plot(x, z)
        axis([ 0 100 -3 3 ]), axis('equal')
        M(:, l) = getframe;
end
```

10.9   %PENDUL1 animation of simple pendulum

```
P0  = [ 0; 0; 1 ];               % hinge centre
P1  = [ 0; -3.5; 1 ];            % rod end
rod = [ P0 P1 ];
t   = pi/2: pi/60: (5/2)*pi;  % parameter of disk curve
diskx = 2.5*cos(t); disky = 2.5*sin(t);
disk = [ diskx; disky; ones(size(t)) ];
% translate disk to point -35
ndisk = trlate(0, -35)*disk;
pendul = [ rod ndisk ];
% plot reference frame
plot(pendul(1, :), pendul(2, :))
axis([ -25 25 -40 10 ]), axis('equal')
% generate 12 frames
M = moviein(12);
angle = [ 0 5 10 15 10 5 0 -5 -10 -15 -10 -5 ];
for k = 1: 12
        swinged = rtate(angle(k))*pendul;
        plot(swinged(1, :), swinged(2, :))
        axis([ -25 25 -40 10 ]), axis('equal')
        M(:, k) = getframe;
end
```

10.11   %EXE10_11   Colombia's flag in Exercise 10.11

```
red   = [ 1; 1; 0; 1 ];
green = [ 1; 1; 0; 0 ];
```

```
blue  = [ 0; 0; 1; 0 ];
FLAG  = cat(3, red, green, blue);
image(FLAG), axis('off')
```

10.14   `%EXE10_14        Solves Exercise 10.14, RB plane of colour cube`

```
red   = zeros(11, 11);
green = zeros(11, 11);
blue  = zeros(11, 11);
for m = 1:11
        red(m, :)  = (11 - m)/10;
        blue(:, m) = (11 - m)/10;
end
RBplane = cat(3, red, green, blue);
image(RBplane)
```

Chapter 11

11.1
```
x = 0: 2;
numeric = trapz(x, x)
numeric = 2
```
   This is the exact answer and it should be so because the integrand is linear.

11.4
```
x = 0: 2/5: 2;
y = x.^3;
simpson2 = simp(x', y')
??? Error using ==> simp
Uneven number of intervals
```
   Above we tried to calculate the integral by using six ordinates. Let us now use Simpson's rule once over the first three ordinates, once over the last three ordinates, and compute the area between the third and the fourth ordinate by the trapezoidal rule.

```
s1 = y(1) + 4*y(2) + y(3);
s2 = y(4) + 4*y(5) + y(6);
s = 0.4*(s1 + s2)/3
s = 3.5840
missing = 0.4*(y(3) + y(4))/2
missing = 0.4480
s + missing
ans = 4.0320
```

   This value is larger than the exact result, 4. A plot of the curve $y = x^3$ can explain the reasons behind this error.

11.12   An M-file that solves this exercise is

```
%RM1    root-mean-square value of sinusoidal voltage

f   = 50;               % frequency, Hz
T   = 1/f;              % period, s
A   = 170;              % voltage amplitude, V
t   = 0: T/50: T;       % time base, s
U   = A*sin(2*pi*f*t);  % sinusoidal form, V
```

```
Ueff = sqrt(trapz(t, U.^2)/T)
```

```
% shift beginning and integrate again over one period
t0    = 0.15; t = t0: T/50: t0 + T;
U     = A*sin(2*pi*f*t);    % sinusoidal form, V
Ueff = sqrt(trapz(t, U.^2)/T)
```

A call of this file and the results are

```
rm1
Ueff = 120.2082
Ueff = 120.2082
(170/Ueff)^2
ans = 2.0000
```

11.13   An M-file that solves this exercise is

```
%rm2    rms value of current in first varistor example

U = [  12 18   25   30   35   40     45 ];  % measured voltage, V
I = [ 0.5   1 2.3 3.5 5.7 8.8 12.9 ];  % measured current, mA
```

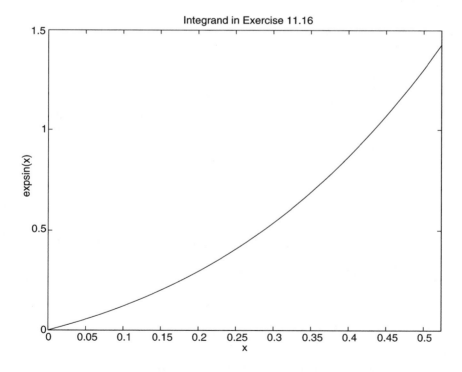

Integrand in Exercise 11.16

Figure A.5   Plot of the functions expsin

```
c = polyfit(log(U), log(I), 1);
a = exp(c(2)); n = c(1);
f = 50;                              % frequency, Hz
T = 1/f;                             % period, s
t = 0: T/50: 2*T;                    % time scale, s
u = 48*sin(2*pi*50*t); i = sign(u)*a.*abs(u).^n;
Imax = max(i)
Ieff = sqrt(trapz(t, i.^2)/T)        % rms value of current
```

A record of calculations is

```
rm2
Imax = 12.8203
Ieff = 10.6410
(Imax/Ieff)^2
ans =  1.4515
```

11.16 $\int_0^{pi/6} e^{2x} \sin x\,dx = \left| \frac{2e^{2x}(\sin x - \cos x)}{5} \right|_0^{pi/6} = 0.27635624634174$

The plot of the function expsin is shown in Figure A.5.

Chapter 12

12.2   `A = [ 0 1 0 0; 0 0 1 1; 0 0 0 1; 0 0 0 0 ]; A2 = A^2`
`A2 =`

```
        0       0       1       1
        0       0       0       1
        0       0       0       0
        0       0       0       0
```

The result shows, for example, that there is a path of length 2 from V_1 to V_3.

`A3 = A^3`
`A3 =`

```
        0       0       0       1
        0       0       0       0
        0       0       0       0
        0       0       0       0
```

We conclude that there is only one path of length 3, namely from V_1 to V_4.

`C = eye(size(A)) + A + A2 + A3`
`C =`

```
        1       1       1       2
        0       1       1       2
        0       0       1       1
        0       0       0       1
```

We see, for example, that there is no path from V_2 to V_1, while there are two from V_1 to V_4.

Chapter 13

13.1   We write the matrix of dimensions as

	P	ℓ	I	E	y
F	1	0	0	1	0
L	0	1	4	−2	1

We enter the matrix of dimensions and calculate its rank by

```
D = [ 1 0 0 1 0; 0 1 4 -2 1 ]
rank(D)
ans =
     2
```

We can write two independent equations and assign arbitrary exponents to three quantities. Therefore we continue by

```
A = D(:, 1:2); B = -D(:, 3:5)
```

Obviously, the deflection y must decrease with increasing I and E; therefore, we assign negative exponents to these two quantities:

```
C = [ -1 0 0; 0 -1 0; 0 0 1 ];
```

The solution is

```
X =rats(A\(B*C'))
X =
     0             1            0
     4            -2           -1
```

The resulting nondimensional groups are:

$$\pi_1 = \frac{\ell^4}{I} \; , \; \pi_2 = \frac{P}{\ell^2 E} \; , \; \pi_3 = \frac{y}{\ell}$$

Finally,

$$\pi_1 \pi_2 = \frac{P\ell^2}{EI}$$

Chapter 14

14.2 (1) Write the following function on a file derv2a.m:

```
function wd=derv2a(t,w);
% example of linear differential equation
% in the form required by ODE23 and ODE45

wd = - (1.2+sin(10*t))*w;
```

The solution is produced with the commands:

```
t0=0; tf=5; w0 = 1;
[t,w] = ode23('derv2a', t0, tf, w0); plot(t,w);
```

(2) Write the following function on a file derv2b.m:

```
function wd=derv2b(t,w);
% example of linear differential equation
% in the form required by ODE23 and ODE45

wd = (cos(t) - w/(1+t^2))/3;
```

and produce the solution with the commands:

```
t0=0; tf = 5; w0 = 1;
[t,w] = ode23('derv2b', t0, tf, w0); plot(t,w);
```

14.3 (1) Prepare the following M-file called derv3a.m

```
function wd=derv3a(t,w);
% example of linear differential equation
% in the form required by ODE23 and ODE45

[m,n] = size(w);
wd    = zeros(m,n);
wd(1) = w(2);
wd(2) = ( 2-2*t*w(2)-3*w(1) )/(1+t^2);
```

and obtain the solution with the commands:

```
t0=0; tf = 5; w0 =[0;1];
[t,w] = ode23('derv3a', t0, tf, w0); plot(t,w(:,1));
```

(2) Prepare the following M-file called derv3b.m:

```
function wd=derv3b(t,w);
% example of linear differential equation
% in the form required by ODE23 and ODE45.

[m,n]=size(w);
wd = zeros(m,n);
wd(1)=w(2);
wd(2)=w(3);
wd(3)= cos(t) ...
    -5*cos(2*t)/(t+1)^2*w(3)   ...
    -w(2)                      ...
    - w(1)/(3+sin(t));
```

and produce the solution with the commands:

```
t0=0; tf = 5; w0 = [1; 0; 2];
[t,w] = ode23('derv3b', t0, tf, w0); plot(t,w(:,1));
```

14.4 (1) Prepare the following M-file doga.m

```
function wd =doga(t,w);
% This function represents the model of the dog chasing problem,
% when the master walks on a straight line,
% in the form required by ODE23 and ODE45.
```

```
%
% The states are:
% w(1),w(2)               position of the dog

velD=10; velM=5;          % velocities of dog and master
[m,n] = size(w);
wd=zeros(m,n);            % make space to answer
xM = velM*t; yM=100;      % pos. of Master
xD = w(1);                yD = w(2);
dx = xM-xD;               dy = yM-yD;
d  = sqrt(dx*dx+dy*dy);
if (d>0),
  wd(1) = velD*dx/d;
  wd(2) = velD*dy/d;
end; % of if
```

and produce the solution with the commands

```
velD=10; velM=5;          % parameters
w0=[0;0];                 % initial conditions
t0=0; tf=10;              % initial and final time
% ---                     run simulation
[t,w]=ode23('doga',t0,tf,w0);
% ---                     build xD, yD, position of the dog
xD=w(:,1); yD=w(:,2);
% ---                     build xM, yM, position of the master
xM=velM*t;
[m,n]=size(t); yM=100*ones(m,n);
plot(xD,yD,'+',xM,yM,'o');
axis([0 100 0 100]);
axis('equal');
title('Dog chasing his master');
grid
```

(2) Prepare the following M-file called dogb.m

```
function wd =dog(t,w);
% This function represents the model of the dog chasing problem,
% when the master walks around the pond,
% in the form required by ODE23 and ODE45.
%
% The states are:
% w(1),w(2)               position of the dog

r=1; omM=1; velD=1;
[m,n] = size(w);
wd=zeros(m,n);            % make space to answer
al = omM*t;              % ang. pos. of Master
xM = r*cos(al);           yM = r*sin(al);
xD = w(1);                yD = w(2);
dx = xM-xD;               dy = yM-yD;
d  = sqrt(dx*dx+dy*dy);
```

```
if (d>0),
  wd(1) = velD*dx/d;
  wd(2) = velD*dy/d;
end; % of if
```

and produce the solution with the commands

```
r=1; omM=1; velD=1;     % parameters
w0=[0;0];               % initial conditions
tf=2.0;
% ---                    run simulation
[t,w]=ode23('dogb',0,tf,w0);
% ---                    build xD, yD, position of the dog
xD=w(:,1); yD=w(:,2);
% ---                    build xM, yM, position of the master
al=omM*t;
xM= r*cos(al);  yM= r*sin(al);
be=linspace(0,2*pi);
% ---                    build xB, yB, the bank
xB=r*cos(be);   yB=r*sin(be);
% ---                    plot
plot(xB,yB,xD,yD,'+',xM,yM,'o'), grid
axis([-1 1 -1 1]), axis('equal')
title('Dog chasing his master')
```

14.7   Prepare the following M-file called pend.m:

```
function wd = pend(t,w);
% This function describes the motion of a pendulum subject to
% gravity, in the form required by ODE23 and ODE45.
% The states are:
% w(1)                   the angle theta
% w(2)                   its derivative

l = 0.5;                % length of the pendulum
g = 9.81;               % gravity, m/s/s
[m,n]=size(w);
wd    =zeros(m,n);      % allocate space for wd
wd(1) = w(2);
wd(2) = -g*l*sin(w(1));
```

and produce the solution with the commands

```
t0=0; tf = 10;
w0 = [1;0];
[t,w]= ode23('pend',t0, tf,w0);
subplot(2,1,1), plot(t,w(:,1))
ylabel('th')
subplot(2,1,2), plot(t,w(:,2))
ylabel('th_dot');
```

14.10   Prepare the following M-file called `pliny.m`:

```
function hd = pliny(t,h);
% This function represents the model of the Pliny's intermittent
% fountain in the form required by ODE23 and ODE45

% --- define system parameters:

R      = 0.05;        % radius of the base
r      = 0.01;        % nozzle radius
hlo    = 0.025;       % orifice height
hhi    = 0.1;         % syphon height
C      = 0.6;         % discharge coefficient
inflow = 50e-6;       % one decilitre per second
g      = 9.81;        % gravity acceleration, m/s/s

% --- delete the following line if you are using a version of
% MATLAB prior to MATLAB 4.0
global syphon
% The global variable dry indicates whether the syphon is dry.
% If the level of water in the tank is below hlo,
% the syphon is empty.
% If the level of the water in the tank is above hhi,
% the syphon is full of water.
% If the level of the water in the tank is between hlo and hhi,
% the variable dry remains unchanged.

if h>=hhi,
   syphon=1;
end;
if h<=hlo,
   syphon=0;
end;

if syphon,
   v =C*sqrt(2*g*h);
   outflow = -pi*r^2*v;
else
   outflow = 0;
end;
hd =(inflow+outflow)/(pi*R^2);
```

The solution is obtained with the commands:

```
global syphon
syphon = 0;
t0=0; tf=100;
h0=0;
[t,h]=ode23('pliny', t0, tf,h0);
plot(t,h)
```

14.12   Prepare the following M-file called dcmot.m:

```
function omd = dcmot(t,om);
% this function represents the model of a DC motor

% --- Parameters of the motor:
Ra = 20;                    % armature resistance, ohm
Kt = 0.03;                  % torque sensitivity, volt/rad/s
Js = 1.0e-5;                % inertia (rotor + fly-wheel), kg*m^2

Ea = 15;                    % e.m.f., volt

Eb = Kt*om;                 % back e.m.f., volt
Ed = Ea-Eb;
Ia = Ed/Ra;                 % armature current, ampere
Tm = Kt*Ia;                 % torque, Nm
omd= Tm/Js;                 % angular acceleration, rad/s
```

The solution is produced with the commands:

```
t0  = 0; tf=2.0;           % initial and final time
om0 = 0.0;                 % initial condition
[t,om]=ode23('dcmot',t0,tf,om0);
plot(t,om), grid
title('Dynamics of DC motor')
```

Chapter 15

15.3
```
% define the gains
ngains = 20;                            % number of significant
                                        % gains
k=logspace(-2,2,ngains);                % array of gains
% define the transfer function

num = [0  0  0  10 ];                   % numerator of P
den = conv([1 1],conv([1 2],[1 4]));    % denominator of P

r = zeros (3, ngains);                  % allocate space for
                                        % the roots
for i=1:ngains,
    r(:,i)=roots(den+k(i)*num);         % closed-loop roots
end;
rr = real(r);                           % real part of the roots
ri = imag(r);                           % imaginary part of roots
plot(rr,ri,'r+');
grid
pause
hold on
for i=1:ngains,
  plot(rr(:,i), ri(:,i), 'bo');
  str =['Gain:', num2str(k(i)), '  For next value press Enter'];
```

```
            title(str);
            pause
          end;
          disp('A root with positive real part appears for the first    ');
          disp(' time for k approximately equal to 8.859                 ');
          disp('The value of k that leaves a gain margin of 4 is         ');
          disp(' k= 8.859/4');
          disp('                                                         ');
          disp(' For a more precise answer, assign to ngains a           ');
          disp(' larger value e.g. ngain =50 or 100.                     ');
```

15.5
```
          om        = logspace(-2,2);                % from 0.01 to 100 rad/s

          db        = zeros(size(om));
          magaxis   = [0.01 100 -20 20];            % extremes of mag. plot
          magticks  =-20:10:20;                     % ticks
          subplot(2,1,1);                           % upper subplot
          semilogx(om, db); grid;                   % draw upper subplot
          axis(magaxis);                            % define extremes
          set(gca,'Ytick',magticks);                % define ticks position

          pha       = zeros(size(om));
          phaaxis   = [0.01 100 -360 0];            % extremes of phase plot
          phaticks  =-360:90:0;                     % ticks
          subplot(2,1,2);                           % select lower subplot
          semilogx(om, pha); grid;                  % draw lower subplot
          axis(phaaxis);                            % define extremes
          set(gca,'Ytick',phaticks);                % define ticks position
```
15.7
```
          % --- USES UNWRAP, from Control Toolbox
          % --- USES some functions not available prior to MATLAB 4.
          %     Users of old versions are suggested to delete the
          %     lines that produce error messages. The result will be
          %     aesthetically less pleasant, but still correct.

          k   = 5;
          R   = 6;
          al  = 4;
          omn = 20;
          zi  = 0.6;

          num = k*conv([1/(R/al) 1],[0 0 0 omn^2]);
          den = conv([1/(R*al) 1],conv([1 0],[1 2*zi*omn omn^2]));

          om  = logspace(-1,3);
          s   = sqrt(-1)*om;
          ol  = polyval(num,s)./polyval(den,s);     % open-loop transfer function
          cl  = ol./(1+ol);                         % closed loop transfer
          function cldb = 20*log10(abs(cl));        % its magnitude, db
          cldeg= 180/pi*unwrap(angle(cl));          % its phase, degrees
          subplot(2,1,1);
          semilogx(om, cldb); grid                  % magnitude plot
```

```
        subplot(2,1,2);
        semilogx(om, cldeg); grid              % phase plot

        phaaxis   = [0.01 100 -270 0];         % extremes of phase plot
        phaticks  =-270:90:0;                  % ticks
        axis(phaaxis);                         % define extremes
        set(gca,'Ytick',phaticks);             % define ticks position
15.8    % --- prepare Bode grid
        mag = subplot(2,1,1);                  % handle to upper plot
        pha = subplot(2,1,2);                  % handle to lower plot
        noms = 50;                             % number of frequencies
        om  = logspace(-1,1,noms);             % array of significant
                                               % frequencies
        ommin = om(1); ommax=om(noms);         % margins frequencies
        magmin=-20;    magmax = 20;            % margins magnitude
        phamin= -360;  phamax = 0;             % margins phase
        magticks=linspace(magmin, magmax,5);
        phaticks=linspace(phamin, phamax,5);

        subplot(mag);
        magmargs = [ommin ommax magmin, magmax];

        semilogx(om, zeros(size(om)));
        axis(magmargs);
        set(gca,'YTick',magticks);
        grid on;
        hold on;

        subplot(pha);
        phamargs = [ommin ommax phamin, phamax];
        semilogx(om, zeros(size(om)));
        axis(phamargs);
        set(gca,'YTick',phaticks);
        grid on;
        hold on;

        % --- define P and plot its bode graph
        num = [0 0 0 2];
        den = conv([1 0],conv([1 1],[1/3 1]));
        s   = sqrt(-1)*om;
        p   = polyval(num,s)./polyval(den,s);
        pdb = 20*log10(abs(p));
        pdeg= 180/pi*unwrap(angle(p));

        subplot(mag);
        semilogx(om, pdb);

        subplot(pha);
        semilogx(om, pdeg);
        disp(' To determine gain margin, read db from the magnitude ');
```

```
        disp(' plot in correspondence of the frequency where the   ');
        disp(' phase is -180. The gain margin is then the opposite ');
        disp(' of the value you read for the magnitude              ');
        subplot(mag);
        [gom, gdb]=ginput(1);
        disp(['Gain margin: ', num2str(-gdb), ' db']);

        disp(' To determine phase margin, read deg from the phase   ');
        disp(' plot in correspondence of the frequency where the    ');
        disp(' magnitude is 0 decibel                               ');
        disp(' The phase margin is then the 180 degrees plus the    ');
        disp(' value you read for the phase                         ');
        subplot(pha);
        [pom, pdeg]=ginput(1);
        disp(['Phase margin: ', num2str(180+pdeg), ' deg']);
15.9    % --- prepare Bode grid
        mag = subplot(2,1,1);        % get handle to upper plot
        pha = subplot(2,1,2);        % get handle to lower plot
        noms = 50;                   % number of frequencies
        om  = logspace(-2,2,noms);   % significant frequencies
        ommin = om(1); ommax=om(noms); % margins frequencies
        magmin=-40;    magmax = 0;   % margins magnitude
        phamin= 0;     phamax = 90;  % margins phase
        magticks=linspace(magmin, magmax,5);
        phaticks=linspace(phamin, phamax,5);

        subplot(mag);
        magmargs = [ommin ommax magmin, magmax];

        semilogx(om, zeros(size(om)));
        axis(magmargs);
        set(gca,'YTick',magticks);
        grid on;
        hold on;

        subplot(pha);
        phamargs = [ommin ommax phamin, phamax];
        semilogx(om, zeros(size(om)));
        axis(phamargs);
        set(gca,'YTick',phaticks);
        grid on;
        hold on;

        % --- compute and plot lead compensators
        alphas = [sqrt(2) 2 2*sqrt(2) 4 4*sqrt(2)];
        s      = sqrt(-1)*om;
        for k=1:length(alphas),
            al = alphas(k);
            num = [1 1/al];
            den = [1 al];
```

```
        p   = polyval(num,s)./polyval(den,s);
        pdb = 20*log10(abs(p));
        pdeg= 180/pi*angle(p);

        subplot(mag);
        semilogx(om, pdb);

        subplot(pha);
        semilogx(om, pdeg);
      end; % for loop
```

15.11   ```
        % If you want to use this M-file regularly to draw Nichols Charts
        % it is advisable to make it into a function-type M-file.

        % --- Draw the Nichols grid
        xmin = -360; xmax = 0; ymin=-20; ymax=20;
        margins =[xmin xmax ymin ymax];
        ha=axis(margins);
        degs =xmin:5:xmax;
        dbs = ymin:0.5:ymax;
        [DEG, DB] = meshgrid(degs, dbs);
        ol   = 10.^(DB/20)   ...
                .*exp(sqrt(-1)*DEG*pi/180);   % open loop, num. val.
        cl   = ol./(1+ol);   % closed loop, numerical
        cldb = 20*log10(abs(cl));   % closed loop, decibel
        vals = [-12 -6 0 6 12];   % values to plot

        % --- plot the M-circles
        contour(DEG,DB,cldb,vals);
        % --- plot ticks and rectangular grid
        xticks=xmin:45:xmax;   % x-axis ticks
        yticks=ymin:5:ymax;   % y-axis ticks
        set(gca,'XTick',xticks);
        set(gca,'YTick',yticks);
        grid
```

15.14   ```
        % --- Draw the Nichols grid
        xmin = -360; xmax = 0; ymin=-20; ymax=20;
        margins =[xmin xmax ymin ymax];
        ha=axis(margins);
        degs =xmin:5:xmax;
        dbs  = ymin:0.5:ymax;
        [DEG, DB] = meshgrid(degs, dbs);
        ol    = 10.^(DB/20).*                  ...
                exp(sqrt(-1)*DEG*pi/180);      % open loop, num. val.
        cl    = ol./(1+ol);                    % closed loop
        cldb  = 20*log10(abs(cl));             % closed loop, decibel
        vals  = [-12 -6 0 6 12];               % values to plot
        % --- plot the M-circles
        contour(DEG,DB,cldb,vals);
        % --- plot ticks and rectangular grid
        xticks=xmin:45:xmax;                   % x-axis ticks
```

```
yticks=ymin:5:ymax;                     % y-axis ticks
set(gca,'XTick',xticks);
set(gca,'YTick',yticks);
grid on;
hold on;


% --- Draw the transfer function of the plant
pG      = 5.0;                          % plant gain
pP      = 10;                           % plant pole
pzi     = 0.7;                          % plant damping factor
pomn    = 15;                           % plant natural frequency
pnum    = [0 0 0 0 pG*pomn^2];
pden    = conv([1 0], conv([1/pP 1],  ...
                [1 2*pzi*pomn pomn^2]));


om      = logspace(-1, 2);
s       = sqrt(-1)*om;


P       = polyval(pnum,s) ./ polyval(pden,s);
magdb   = 20*log10(abs(P));
phadeg  = 180/pi*unwrap(angle(P));
plot(phadeg, magdb);

disp(' To determine gain margin, read the point where the  ');
disp(' graph intersects the vertical line of -180 degrees. ');
disp(' The gain margin is then the opposite of the value   ');
disp(' you read for the magnitude                          ');
disp('');
disp(' Press any key when ready ...                         ');
pause
[gpha, gdb]=ginput(1);
disp(['Gain margin: ', num2str(-gdb), ' db']);

disp(' To determine phase margin, read the point where the ');
disp(' graph intersects the horizontal line of 0 db.       ');
disp(' The phase margin is then 180 plus the value you      ');
disp(' read for the phase.      '); disp('');
disp(' Press any key when ready ...     '); pause

[pdeg, pdb]=ginput(1);
disp(['Phase margin: ', num2str(180+pdeg), ' deg']);

disp(' If you have access to the function MARGIN from the   ');
disp(' Control Toolbox, you can verify your answer against  ');
disp(' that computed by MATLAB, otherwise, you will get an  ');
disp(' error message.');
disp(' Press any key when ready ...                          ');
pause
[Gm, Pm, Wcg, Wcp]=margin(pnum, pden);
disp(['MATLAB reports   Gain margin:  ',num2str(20*log10(Gm))]);
```

```
            disp(['                    Phase margin: ',num2str(Pm)]);
```

15.16   To solve the exercise you must write the functions dervabk and invp; their listings
         are given after the listing of the script file that solves the exercise.

```
% The second part of this exercise requires the functions
% dervabk.m, and invp.m, listed separately.
%
% --- define parameters of the problem:
g = 9.81;                                 % gravity acceleration,
                                          % m/s^2
M =1;                                     % mass of the cart,
                                          % kg
m = 0.1;                                  % mass of the pendulum,
                                          % kg
l = 0.5;                                  % length of the pendulum,
                                          % m

% ---part a), method 1.
% --- The linearized equations are:
% (M+m)  * x_ddot + m*l *   th_ddot = u
% m*l    * x_ddot + m*l^2 * th_ddot = m*g*l * th
% The above system can be solved in closed form:
% x_ddot     = -m*g/M           * th + 1/M      * u
% th_ddot    = (M+m)/(M*l) * g * th - 1/(M*l) * u
% These two equations, together with the relations:
% w(1)'      = w(2)
% w(3)'      = w(4)
% provide a first solution to the linearization problem,
% the matrices A1 and B1

% --- solution by method 1.
A1= [0     1        0                  0;
     0     0        -m*g/M             0;
     0     0        0                  1;
     0     0        (M+m)*g/(M*l)      0];
B1= [0;
     1/M;
     0;
     -1/(M*l)];

% ---part a), method 2.
% Alternatively, we can let MATLAB do the work of solving the
% linear system numerically, providing the solutions A2 and B2:

% --- describe the system in the form:
%     E*w'= G*w + H*u

E = [ 0    (M+m)  0    m*l;
      0    m*l    0    m*l^2;
      1    0      0    0;
```

```
        0    0    1   0];
G = [ 0    0    0   0;
      0    0   m*g*l 0;
      0    1    0   0;
      0    0    0   1];
H = [ 1;
      0;
      0;
      0];

A2  =  E\G;
B2  =  E\H;
% You may check that, possibly up to numerical errors
% of the processor, A1 = A2 and B1 = B2. Let us choose
% one of the solutions and display it.
A   = A1
B   = B1
disp(' To produce K, press any key  ... ');
pause
% --- part b). Find the gain.
Q = eye(4,4);
R = 0.1;
K = lqr(A,B,Q,R);
% --- display K
K
disp(' To simulate the linearized system, press any key ... ')
pause

% --- part c). Simulate the linearized system
global A B K;
t0 = 0; tf=5;
w0 = [0.2;
      0.05;
      0.1;
      0.15];
[t_lin,w_lin] = ode23('dervabk',t0, tf, w0);
x_lin     = w_lin(:,1);
th_lin    = w_lin(:,3);

subplot(2,1,1);
plot(t_lin, x_lin); grid;
title('Linearized system');
ylabel('x_lin');
subplot(2,1,2);
plot(t_lin, th_lin); grid
ylabel('th_lin');


% --- part d). Simulate the non-linear system
disp(' To simulate the non-linear system, press any key ... ')
```

```
pause
[t,w] = ode23('invp',t0, tf, w0);
x     = w(:,1);
th    = w_lin(:,3);
clg
subplot(2,1,1);
plot(t,x); grid;
title('Non-linear system');
ylabel('x');
subplot(2,1,2);
plot(t,th); grid
ylabel('th');

% --- part e). Compare linearized and non-linear systems.

disp(' To compare the two systems, press any key ... ')
pause

clg
subplot(2,1,1);
plot(t_lin,w_lin(:,1), t, w(:,1));
ylabel(' Position of the cart'); grid;
title(' Comparison near the linearization point');
subplot(2,1,2);
plot(t_lin,w_lin(:,3), t, w(:,3));
ylabel(' Angle of the pendulum'); grid;

% --- part f). Show an appreciable difference between the two
% systems.
disp(' To compare the two systems around w=[0 0 0.5 0],     ')
disp(' press any key.')
pause;
w0 = [0.0; 0.0; 0.5; 0.0];
[t_lin,w_lin] = ode23('dervabk',t0, tf, w0);
[t,w] = ode23('invp',t0, tf, w0);

clg
subplot(2,1,1);
plot(t_lin,w_lin(:,1), t, w(:,1));
ylabel(' Position of the cart'); grid;
title(' Comparison away from the linearization point');
subplot(2,1,2);
plot(t_lin,w_lin(:,3), t, w(:,3));
ylabel(' Angle of the pendulum'); grid;
```

The function dervabk is written on the file dervabk.m that follows.

```
function xd = dervabk(t,x);
% this function returns the derivatives of the unit feedback
% system described by the equation:
% x'      =   A*x + B*u
```

```
% where u = -K*x
% the calling function must contain the definition of the
% matrices A B K and the statement
% global A B K;

% Delete next line, if you are using a MATLAB version prior to
% MATLAB 4.0.
global A B K;
u   = -K*x;
xd = A*x + B*u;
```

The function invp is written on the file invp.m that follows.

```
function wd=invp(t,w);
%INVP inverted pendulum on a cart.
% This function simulates the dynamics of an inverted pendulum
% on a cart.
% The states are:
% w(1)            position of the trolley,              x
% w(2)            its derivative,                        x_dot
% w(3)            angle of the pendulum from the vertical  th
% w(4)            its derivative                         th_dot
% The array K determines the external force u=-K*w applied to
% the cart and must be defined and declared global in the
% calling function
% The physical laws that define the system are:
%
% (M+m)        x_dd + ml cos(th) th_dd = ml  sin(th) (th_d)^2 + F
% ml cos(th) x_dd + m l^2        th_dd = mgl sin(th)

% --- define parameters of the system
g     = 9.81; % gravity acceleration, m/s^2
l     = 0.5;  % length of the pendulum, m
M     = 1.0;  % mass of the cart, Kg
m     = 0.1;  % mass of the pendulum
% --- compute external force
% if you are using a version of MATLAB prior to 4.0
% please delete next line

global  K;
F       =-K*w;

% --- compute second derivatives x_dd and th_dd
x     = w(1);
x_d   = w(2);
th    = w(3);
th_d  = w(4);
G     = [(M+m)                m*l*cos(th);
         m*l*cos(th)    m*(l^2)    ];
H     = [m*l*(sin(th))*(th_d)^2 + F  ;
         m*g*l*sin(th)             ];
```

```
Drv   = G\H;                      % [x_dd; th_dd]
[m,n] = size(w); wd=zeros(m,n);
wd(1) = w(2);
wd(2) = Drv(1);
wd(3) = w(4);
wd(4) = Drv(2);
```

Chapter 16

16.2 (1) This is the listing of the file deffiltm.m:

```
function [f0,M]=deffiltm();
% Define filter magnitude characteristics with the mouse.
%
% This function allows do define with the mouse the magnitude
% characteristics of a filter.
%
% Calling syntax:
% function [f0,M]=deffiltm();
% Call the function and indicate the points by clicking
% the LEFT button of the mouse as many times as required,
% and press the letter E (for Exit) when done.
% The function returns the vectors f0 of nondimensional
% frequencies and M of magnitudes, in the format required by
% yulewalk and remez.
% Note 1 : The first element of f0 is set to 0 and the last
% one to 1.
% Note 2 : A warning is issued if the frequencies are not in
% increasing order.

Nf     = input('Enter Nyquist frequency (Hz) ---> ');
MagMin = input('Enter minimum magnitude        ---> ');
MagMax = input('Enter maximum magnitude        ---> ');
disp('Use the mouse to define the points          ');
disp('Press any key (e.g. E for Exit) when done   ');
clg; axis([0 Nf MagMin MagMax]);
xlabel('Frequency (Hz)');
ylabel('Magnitude');
hold on; grid;
X=[]; Y=[];                       % initialize X and Y
[x,y,key ] = ginput(1);           % enter first point
while key <32,                    % point entered by clicking
                                  % the mouse
                                  % as opposite to key>=32,
                                  % that means:
                                  % A key was pressed on
                                  % the keyboard
    if X ==[], x=0; end           % first frequency must be 0
    if x < 0, x = 0; end;         % correct frequency within
                                  % bounds
```

```
if x > Nf x = Nf; end;
if y < MagMin, y = MagMin; end; % correct magnitude within
                                % bounds
if y > MagMax, y = MagMax; end;
if length(X)>0,                 % display segment
plot([x_old x],[y_old y]);
end % if
x_old = x;
y_old = y;
X = [X x];                      % add point to the list
Y = [Y y];
[x,y,key ] = ginput(1);         % enter new point and button
end % while

% --- Adjust last point and redraw the figure
l   =length(X);
X(l)=Nf;

clg; axis([0 Nf MagMin MagMax]);
xlabel('Frequency (Hz)');
ylabel('Magnitude');
hold on; grid;
plot(X,Y);

% --- issue a warning if frequencies not in increasing order
X0 = X; X0(1)=[];
X1 = X; X1(l)=[];
if any(X0<X1),
    disp('                                                ')
    disp(' WARNING: frequencies not in increasing order !');
    disp('                                                ')
end;
f0 = X/Nf; f0(1)=1;
M  = Y;
```

```
(2) disp('Write the file deffiltm.m of the function deffiltm, ');
    disp('(ffor DEFine FILter by Magnitude), that solves the ');
    disp('first part of the exercise                         ');
    disp('                                                   ');
    disp('Then click with the mouse the points:              ');
    disp('(0,1), (10,1), (20,0.5), (30,0.5), (40,1.0) (50,1.0) ');
    disp('and press E when done                              ');
    disp('                                                   ');
    disp('Press ENTER when ready ...                         ');
    pause
    [f0, M] = deffiltm;
    disp(' Array of normalized frequencies:');
    f0
    disp(' Array of magnitudes:');
    M
```

16.3

```
fHz0 = [0 100 150 180 200 240 300 400];
m0   = [0 0   2   2   0.5 0.5 1    1];
fs   = 800;
f0   =fHz0/(fs/2);
plot(fHz0,m0); grid; title('Desired Magnitude response')
pause
[bIIR6, aIIR6]   = yulewalk(6,  f0, m0);
[bIIR8, aIIR8]   = yulewalk(8,  f0, m0);
[bIIR10, aIIR10] = yulewalk(10, f0, m0);
fHz1       = linspace(0, 400, 50);
om1        = 2*pi*fHz1;
z          = exp(i*om1/fs);
m6         = abs( polyval(bIIR6,z)./polyval(aIIR6,z) );
m8         = abs( polyval(bIIR8,z)./polyval(aIIR8,z) );
m10        = abs( polyval(bIIR10,z)./polyval(aIIR10,z) );

plot(fHz0, m0, fHz1,m6);
    grid; title('Filter of order 6'); pause;
plot(fHz0, m0, fHz1,m8);
    grid; title('Filter of order 8'); pause;
plot(fHz0, m0, fHz1,m10);
    grid; title('Filter of order 10');
```

16.7

```
P=8; wn=20; Zi = 0.65;

num      = wn^2;
den      = conv([1/P 1],[1 2*Zi*wn wn^2]);

oms      = logspace(-1,2);
s        = sqrt(-1)*oms;

%--- compute magnitude and phase of the analog signal
H        = polyval(num,s)./polyval(den,s);
magHdb   = 10*log10(H.*conj(H));
phaHdeg  = 180/pi * unwrap(angle(H));

disp('                                            ');
disp(' Please enter sampling frequency fs,  ');
answer   = input('or 0 to exit ---> ');
while (answer ~= 0)
    fs = answer;

    %--- compute magnitude and phase of the digital equivalent
    [numd, dend]  = bilinear(num,den,fs);
    z             = exp(s/fs);
    Hd            = polyval(numd,z)./polyval(dend,z);
    magHddb       = 10*log10(Hd.*conj(Hd));
    phaHddeg      = 180/pi * unwrap(angle(Hd));

    %--- plot analog and digital-equivalent magnitude
    subplot(2,1,1);
```

```
              semilogx(oms, magHdb,   ...
                       oms, magHddb,'b:');    grid;
              str      = ['Sampling frequency: ',num2str(fs), ' Herz'];
              title(str);

              %--- plot analog and digital-equivalents phase
              subplot(2,1,2);
              semilogx(oms, phaHdeg,      ...
                       oms, phaHddeg,'b:');  grid

          disp('   ');
          disp(' Please enter sampling frequency fs, ');
          answer     = input('or 0 to exit ---> ');
          end; % of while loop

          disp('The variables fs, numd, dend contain the sampling ');
          disp(' frequency and the coefficients of the equivalent ');
          disp(' digital filter.                            ');
```

16.10
```
          T=0.5;                          % duration of the sampling
          fs = 256;                       % sampling frequency, Hz
          N=fs*T;                         % points sampled
          t=linspace(0,T, N+1); t=t(1:N); % sampling instants
          % --- part a
          x=zeros(1,N);
          Up = find(rem([1:N]-1,64)>=48); % samples when x=1
          x(Up) = ones(1,length(Up));     % define x
          plot(t,x); pause
          % --- part b
          X = fft(x);
          pwr = (X.*conj(X))/N;
          fr  = [0:(N-1)]/T;
          plot(fr, pwr); title('Power spectrum'); pause
          % --- part c
          [junk, Incr] = sort(pwr);       % Incr are bins in increasing
                                          % order
          Decr = Incr([N:-1:1]);          % Decr are bins in decreasing
                                          % order
          First5 = Decr([1:5]);           % Bins associated to the
                                          % first 5 frequencies that
                                          % contain most power
          % --- part d, complex exponential approximation
          Xappr5 = zeros(1,N);
          Xappr5(First5) = X(First5);
          xappr5 = ifft(Xappr5);
          plot(t,x,t,xappr5);
          title('Approximation by complex exponentials');
```

16.12
```
          [b,a]=butter(5, 0.5);

          Ts = 1/100; f=25; x=sin(2*pi*f*Ts*(1:500));
```

```
Zi=filteric(b, a, x, zeros(5,1));
y = filter(b,a,x, Zi);
plot(y(1:30));
```

Chapter 17

17.4   %EXER17_4 Movie of bending moment produced by a moving load.

```
F = 700;                    % travelling man's weight, N
l = 4;                      % bridge span, m
% Generate a reference frame
a = 1;                      % man's distance from left support, m
x = 0: 1/8: l;              %  axis along bridge, m
B = x.*(1 - a/l)*F;         % bending moment, Nm
for k = 1: length(x)
        if x(k) > a
                moment = B(k) - F*(x(k) - a);
                B(k) = moment;
        end
end
plot(x, B)
Mmax = F*l/4;   % Maximum-maximorum moment, Nm
axis([ 0 l  0 Mmax ])
pause
% generate movie
a = 0: 0.5: l;
M = moviein(length(a));
for m = 1: length(a)
        B = x.*(1 - a(m)/l)*F;       % bending moment, Nm
        for k = 1: length(x)
                if x(k) > a(m)
                        moment = B(k) - F*(x(k) - a(m));
                        B(k) = moment;
                end
        end
        plot(x, B), axis([ 0 l  0 Mmax ])
        M(:, m) = getframe;
end
```

         After writing this file, try for instance, movie(M, 3, 5).
         (*Note*: Maximum maximorum means the maximum of all maxima).

17.7   %UDIS   Displays units-affected quantities
         %   UDIS(X) displays the numerical value and the units of X

```
function      y = udis(x)
t = [ num2str(x.value) ' ' x.unit ];
disp(t)
```

17.15   First we must write a function that stores the value and the units of the quantity, the
         units being expressed as a vector of exponents:

```
%UDEFV   Assigns value and vector of exponents to a physical quantity
%        The order of exponents corresponds to the order of the units
%        [ kg m s ]. For example, to a speed im m/s corresponds the
%        vector [ 0 1 -1 ];

function        y = udefv(v, u)

y             = struct('value', 'exponents');
y.value       = v;
y.exponents   = u;
```

Next, we write a function that adds two quantitities whose units are defined
as a vectors of exponents:

```
%UADV    Adds physical quantities whose units are given as a vector
         of exponents. The order of the exponents is that of the
%        units [ kg m s ]. For example, to a speed in m/s corresponds
%        the vector of exponents [ 0 1 -1 ].

function        y = uadv(x1, x2)

if x1.exponents == x2.exponents
        y.value = x1.value + x2.value;
        y.exponents = x1.exponents;
else
        error('Quantities measured in different units')
end
```

Chapter 18

18.2   %WHIST PLOTS THE HISTOGRAMS OF WEIGHTS STORED IN STRUCTURE PERSONS

```
person       %load data stored on file 'person'

nb=[ 70 75 80 85 90 ]
[ n, x ]=hist([ persons.weight ], nb);
bar(x, n)
title('Histogram of weights in structure PERSONS')
xlabel('Weight, kg of force')
ylabel('Number of persons')
```

18.4   %NAMEINDEX SOLVES EXERCISE 18.4, FINDS ARRAY INDEX OF THE GIVEN PERSON

```
        function        nameindex = wupdate(firstname)

person                 % load data of structure 'persons'

lp    = length(persons);
k     = 0;
found = 0;
```

```
      while (found == 0) & (k < lp)
         k=k + 1;          % begin while construct
         if strcmp(persons(k).name, firstname)
            nameindex = k;
            found = 1
         end
      end                  % end while construct
      if found == 0
            error([' Name ' firstname ' not in database' ])
      end
18.9  function p = mtimes(r, s)

      %PHQUANT\MTIMES Multiplication p = r*s of electrical quantities

      % Example
      % a = phquant(3, 'V')
      % b = phquant(2, 'A')
      % c = a*b
      %  6 w

      p.value = r.value*s.value;

      %---------------- define vector of input units --------------------
      unit = cell(1, 5); % preallocate empty 1-by-3 cell array
      unit(1) = {'s'}; unit(2) = {'A'}; unit(3) = {'V'};
      unit(4) = {'ohm'}; unit(5) = {'S'};
      %---------------- define transition table  ----------------------
      mtable = cell(5, 5); % preallocate empty 5-by-5 cell array
      mtable(1, 2) = {'C'};
      mtable(2, 1) = {'C'}; mtable(2, 3) = {'w'}; mtable(2, 4) = {'V'};
      mtable(3, 2) = {'w'}; mtable(3, 5) = {'A'};
      mtable(4, 2) = {'V'}; mtable(5, 3) = {'A'};
      %---------------- choose row of transition table  ----------------
      i = find(strcmp(unit, r.unit == 1);
      if isempty(i)
         error('Unit of first input argument not defined')
      end
      %---------------- choose column transition table  ----------------
      j = find(strcmp(unit, s.unit == 1);
      if isempty(j)
         error('Unit of second input argument not defined')
      end
      %---------------- identify unit of product  ----------------------
      if isempty(mtable{i, j})
         error('Multiplication not defined')
         else
         p.unit = matable(i, j};
         p = phquant(p.value, p.unit);
      end
```

Bibliography

Akivis M. A. and Goldberg V. V. (1972). *An Introduction to Linear Algebra and Tensors* (translated and edited by Silverman, Richard A.). New York: Dover Publications

Alagič S. and Arbib M. A. (1978). *The Design of Well-Structured and Correct Programs.* New York: Springer-Verlag

Angel E. (1990). *Computer Graphics.* Reading, MA: Addison-Wesley Publishing Company

Angot A. (1961). *Compléments de mathématiques à l'usage des ingénieurs de l'électrotechnique et des télécommunications,* 4th edn. Paris: Éditions de la Revue d'Optique

Anon (1962). *Carene di pescherecci*, INSEAN (Vasca Navale), Roma, Quaderno n. 1, March

Arbenz K. and Wohlhauser A. (1986). *Advanced mathematics for practicing engineers.* Norwood, MA: Artech House. Translation of *Méthodes mathématiques pour l'ingénieur* (1982). Lausanne: Presses Polytechniques Romandes

Arnold V. (1984). *Mathematical methods of classical mechanics* (translated by Vogtman K. and Weinstein A.). New York: Springer. The Russian original is *Matematiceskie metody klassicheskoy mekhaniki,* 1974

Azzo, J. d' and Houpis C. H. (1988). *Linear control system analysis and design – Conventional and modern,* 3rd edn, New York: McGraw-Hill International Edition

Baase S. (1983). *Computer Algorithms: Introduction to Design and Analysis.* Reading, MA: Addison-Wesley Publishing Company

Baker, G. L., and Gollob, J. P. (1990), *Chaotic dynamics - an introduction*, Cambridge: Cambridge University Press.

Beaumont R. A. (1987). *Linear systems of equations.* In *McGraw-Hill Encyclopedia of Science & Technology*, 6th edn. New York: McGraw-Hill Book Company

Boor C. de (1990). *Spline Toolbox.* South Natick, MA: The MathWorks, Inc.

Bourke, P. (1993), *Logistic equation and bifurcation diagram,* http://astronomy.swin.edu.au/pbourke/fractals/logistic/

Brauer F. and Nohel J. A. (1967). *Ordinary Differential Equations – A First Course.* New York: W. A. Benjamin

Broch J. T. (1984). *Mechanical vibrations and shock measurements*, 2nd edn, 4th impression. Glostrup, Denmark: Brüel & Kjaer

Bronshtein I. N. and Semendyayev K. A. (1985). *Handbook of Mathematics*, 3rd edn. Frankfurt/Main: Verlag Harri Deutsch, and New York: Van Nostrand Reinhold

BSI (1973). *BS 4937 – International thermocouple reference tables – Part 1. Platinum – 10% rhodium/platinum thermocouples – Type S*. London: British Standards Institution

BSI (1982). *BS 6323: Seamless and welded steel tubes for automobile, mechanical and general engineering – Part. 1 – General requirement*, London: British Standards Institution

BSI (1984). *BS 1904 – Industrial platinum resistance thermometer*. London: British Standards Institution

Bu-qing S. and Ding-yuan L. (1989). *Computational Geometry – Curve and Surface Modeling*. Boston, MA: Academic Press, Inc.

Carlson A. B. and Gisser D. G. (1990). *Electrical Engineering – Concepts and Applications*, 2nd edn. Reading, MA: Addison-Wesley Publishing Company

Catchpole J. and Fulford G. D. (1987). *Dimensionless Groups*. New York: McGraw-Hill Encyclopedia of Science & Technology

Chapra S. C. and Canale R. P. (1989). *Numerical Methods for Engineers*, 2nd edn. New York: McGraw-Hill International Editions

Chertov, A.G. (1997), Units of physical measure, in Grigoriev, I.S, and Meilikhov, E.Z., editors, *Handbook of physical quantities*, Boca Raton: CRC Press.

Churchill R. V. and Brown J. W. (1990). *Complex Variables and Applications*, 5th edn. New York: McGraw-Hill Publishing Company

Collin R. E. (1985). *Antennas and Radiowave Propagation*. New York: McGraw-Hill Book Company

Cooley J. W. and Tukey J. W. (1965). An algorithm for the machine computation of complex Fourier series. *Mathematics of Computation*, **19**, April, 297–301

Corge C. (1975). *Éléments d'informatique – Informatique et démarche de l'esprit*. Paris: Librairie Larousse

Coulon F. de and Jufer M. (1978). *Introduction à l'électrotechnique*. St-Saphorin, Switzerland: Editions Giorgi

Coxeter H. S. M. (1980). *Introduction to Geometry*, 2nd edn. New York: John Wiley & Sons

Czichos H., ed. (1989). *HÜTTE – Die Grundlagen der Ingenieurwissenschaften,* 29th completely revised edn. Berlin: Springer-Verlag

De Facia B. (1992). *Beats*. McGraw-Hill Encyclopedia of Science and Technology, 7th edn, volume 2. New York: McGraw-Hill

Dierker P. F. and Voxman W. L. (1986). *Discrete Mathematics*. San Diego, CA: Harcourt Brace Jovanovich Publishers

Dietrich G. and Stahl H. (1965). *Grundzüge der Matrizenrechnung,* 3rd edn. Leipzig: VEB Fachbuchverlag Leipzig

Dieudonné J. (1992). *Mathematics – The Music of Reason*. Berlin: Springer-Verlag. French original (1987). *Pour l'honneur de l'esprit humain*. Paris: Hachette

Dimarogonas A. D. (1989). *Computer Aided Machine Design*. New York: Prentice-Hall

DIN (1985). *DIN 1072: Road and foot bridge – Design loads*. English translation of *DIN 1072: Straßen und Wegbrücken – Lastnahmen*. Berlin: Verlag Beuth

DIN (1097). *DIN 4710: Meteorologische Daten zur Berechnung des Energie- verbrauches von raumlufttechnischen Anlagen; Lufttemperatur-Luftfeuchte nach Monatsummen*. Berlin: Verlag Beuth

Dorf R. C. (1992). *Modern Control Systems*, 6th edn. Reading, MA: Addison-Wesley Publishing Company

Eckert E. R. G. and Drake R. M. Jr (1972). *Analysis of Heat and Mass Transfer*, International student edition. New York: McGraw-Hill Kōgakusha Ltd

Edwards H. W. (1964). *Analytic and Vector Mechanics*. New York: Dover Publications

Elgerd O. I. (1967). *Control Systems Theory*. New York: McGraw-Hill Book Com- pany, and Kōgakusha Company, Ltd.

Fahidy T. Z. and Quairashi M. S. (1986). Principles of dimensional analysis. In *Encyclopedia of Fluid Mechanics*, Vol. 1 (Cheremisinoff N.P., ed.). Houston: Gulf Publishing Company

Farin G. (1993). *Curves and Surfaces for Computer Aided Geometric Design – A Prac- tical Guide*, 3rd edn. Boston, MA: Academic Press, Inc.

Fehlberg E. (1970). Klassische Runge-Kutta Formeln vierter und niedriger Ordnung mit Schrittweiten-Kontrolle und ihre Anwendung auf Wärmeleitungsprobleme, *Computing*, **6**, 61–71

Fraleigh J. B. and Beauregard R. A. (1990). *Linear Algebra* (with historical notes by Katz V. J.), 2nd edn. Reading, MA: Addison-Wesley Publishing Company

Franklin G. F., Powell J. D. and Workman M. L. (1990). *Digital control of Dynamic Systems*, 2nd edn. Reading, MA: Addison-Wesley

Fuller G. and Tarwater D. (1992). *Analytic Geometry*. Reading, MA: Addison-Wesley Publishing Company

Gabel R. and Roberts R. (1973). *Signals and Linear Systems*. New York: Wiley

Gander, W. and Gautschi, W. (2000), *Adaptive quadrature* — Revisited, BIT. Vol. 40, N). 1, pp. 84–101.

Genta G. (1982). *Lezioni di meccanica dell'autoveicolo*. Torino: Libreria Editrice Universitaria Levrotto & Bella

Gerald C. F. and Wheatley P. O. (1994). *Applied Numerical Analysis*, 5th ed. Reading, MA: Addison-Wesley

Giardina B. (1970). *Introduzione ai metodi statistici*. Milano: Edizioni di Comunitá

Giedt W. H. (1987). Convection (heat). In *McGraw-Hill Encyclopedia of Science & Technology*, Vol. 4, 6th edn. New York: McGraw-Hill

Gillies R. B. (1993). *Instrumentation and Measurements for Electronic Technicians* 2nd edn. New York: Merrill

Giordano F. R. and Weir M. D. (1991). *Differential Equations – A Modeling Approach*. Reading, MA: Addison-Wesley

Goossens, M., Mittelbach, F. and Samarin, A. (1994), *The LATEX companion*, Reading, MA: Addison-Wesley Publishing Company.

Göldner H. *et al.* (1979). *Lehrbuch Höhere Festigkeitslehre*, Vol. 1. Weinheim: Physik Verlag

Gröber H., Erk S. and Grigull U. (1961). *Die Grundgesetze der Wärmeübertragung.* New edition prepared by Grigull Ulrich. Berlin: Springer-Verlag, English translation (1961). *Fundamentals of heat transfer.* New York: McGraw-Hill

Guggenheimer H. W. (1977). *Differential Geometry.* New York: Dover Publications

H & B (1961). *Elektrische und Wärmetechnische Messungen*, 10th edn. Frankfurt/Main: Hartmann & Braun AG

Hartley P. J. and Wynn-Evans A. (1979). *A Structured Introduction to Numerical Mathematics.* Cheltenham: Stanley Thomas

Hearn D. and Baker M. P. (1994). *Computer Graphics*, 2nd edn. Englewood Cliffs, NJ: Prentice-Hall International

Henrici, P. (1964). *Elements of Numerical Analysis.* New York: John Wiley.

Hill D. R. (1988). *Experiments in Computational Matrix Algebra.* New York: Random House

Hille E. (1959). *Analytic Function Theory*, Vol. 1. Waltham, MA: Blairdell Publishing Company

Holman J. P. and White P. R. S. (1992). *Heat Transfer*, 7th edn in SI units. New York: McGraw-Hill Book Company

Horowitz E. and Sahni S. (1983). *Fundamentals of Data Structures*, Rockville, Md: Computer Science Press

Hultquist P. F. (1988). *Numerical Methods for Engineers and Computer Scientists.* Menlo Park, CA: The Benjamin/Cummings Publishing Company

Institute of Electrical and Electronics Engineers (1985). *IEEE Standard for Binary Floating-Point Arithmetic* (ANSI/IEEE Std 754-1985). New York: IEEE

ISO (1988). ISO 286–1: 1988, *ISO system of limits and fits – Part 1, Bases of tolerances and fits.* Geneva: International Organization for Standardization

ISO (1988). ISO 286–2: 1988, *ISO system of limits and fits – Part 2, Tables of standard tolerance grades and limit deviations for holes and shafts.* Geneva: International Organization for Standardization

Janna W. S. (1986). *Engineering Heat Transfer.* Boston, MA: PWS Engineering

Jones A. (1987). Historical background, present status, and future perspectives of the aquaculture industry on a worldwide basis. In *Automation and Data Processing in Aquaculture* (Balchen J. G., ed.), Proceedings of the IFAC Symposium, Trondheim, Norway, 18–21 August 1986, 1–9

Johnson L. W., Riess R. D. and Arnold J. T. (1993). *Introduction to Linear Algebra*, 3rd edn. Reading, MA: Addison-Wesley Publishing Company

Kahaner D., Moler C. and Nash S. (1989). *Numerical Methods and Software.* Englewood Cliffs, NJ: Prentice-Hall

Kaplan W. (1991). *Advanced Calculus*, 4th edn. Redwood, CA: Addison-Wesley

Kerlow, I.V. and Rosebush, J. (1986), *Computer graphics for designers & artists*, New-York: Van Nostrand Reinhold Company.

Kronsjö L. (1987). *Algorithms – Their Complexity and Efficiency Analysis*, 2nd edn. Chichester: John Wiley & Sons

Lamport, L. (1985), *LaTeX — A document preparation system — User's Guide and Reference Manual*, Reading, MA: Addison-Wesley Publishing Company.

Leigh J. R. (1983). *Essentials of Nonlinear Control Theory*, London: Peter Peregrinus

Lipschitz S. (1965). *Probability*. Schaum's Outline Series in Mathematics, New York: McGraw-Hill Book Company

Lurçat, F. (1999), *Le chaos*, Que sais-je No. 3434, Paris: Presses Universitaires de France.

Markusevich A. I. (1961). *Complex Numbers and Conformal Mappings*. Delhi: Hindustan Publishing Corp. Translation of the Russian original *Kompleksnie čisla i konformnie otobraženia*, Fizmatghiz, 1960

Markusevich A. I. (no year indication). *Remarkable Curves*. Translated from the Russian original *Zametchatelnye krivye* by Zdorov Y. A. Moscow: MIR Publishers

Meirovitch L. (1970). *Methods of Analytical Dynamics*. New York: McGraw-Hill Book Company

Mendehall W. and Sincich T. (1988). *Statistics for the Engineering and Computer Sciences,* 2nd edn. San Francisco, CA: Dellen Publishing Company and Collier MacMilan Publishers

Mitschke M. (1972). *Dynamik der Kraftfahrzeuge*. Berlin: Springer-Verlag

Moody A. B. (1987). *Navigation*. In *McGraw-Hill Encyclopedia of Science & Technology*, Vol. 11, 6th edn. New York: McGraw-Hill

Munkres J. R. (1964). *Elementary Linear Algebra*. New York: Addison-Wesley

Niard J. (1971). *Électronique*. Paris: Masson et Cie

Nilsson J. W. (1993). *Electric Circuits*, 4th edn. Reading, MA: Addison-Wesley Publishing Company

Oppelt W. (1964). *Kleines Handbuch Technischer Regelvorgänge*. Weinheim: Verlag Chemie

Oppenheim A. V. and Shafer R. W. (1975). *Digital Signal Processing*. Englewood Cliffs, NJ: Prentice-Hall

Pedoe D. (1988). *Geometry – A Comprehensive Course*. New York: Dover Publications

Piskunov N. (1960). *Differential and Integral Calculus*. Moscow: Peace Publishers. Translated by Yankovski G. from the Russian original *Differentsialnoe i integralnoe ischislenya*

Poxton M. G. and Goldsworthy G. T. (1987). The remote estimation of weight and growth in turbot using image analysis. In *Automation and Data Processing in Aquaculture* (Balchen J.G., ed.), Proceedings of the IFAC Symposium, Trondheim, Norway, 18–21 August 1986, 163–70

Prather R. E. (1976). *Discrete Mathematical Structures for Computer Science*. Boston, MA: Houghton Mifflin Company

Rabiner L. and Gold B. (1975). *Theory and Application of Digital Processing*. Englewood Cliffs, NJ: Prentice-Hall

Ralston A. (1965). *A First Course in Numerical Analysis*. New York: McGraw-Hill Book Company, and Kōgakusha Company, Ltd.

Ramirez R. (1985). *The FFT, Fundamentals and Concepts*. Englewood Cliffs, NJ: Prentice-Hall

Rao S. S. (1990). *Mechanical Vibrations*, 2nd edn. Reading, MA: Addison-Wesley Publishing Company

Rice J. R. (1993). *Numerical Methods, Software, and Analysis*, 2nd edn. Boston, MA: Academic Press

Roberson J. A. and Crome C. T. (1985). *Engineering Fluid Mechanics*, 3rd edn. Boston, MA: Houghton Mifflin Company

Rosser J. B. (1967). A Runge-Kutta for all seasons. In *SIAM Review*, **9** (3), July, 417–52

Schumaker L. L. (1981). *Spline Functions: Basic Theory*. New York: John Wiley & Sons

Sears F. W. (1956). *Electricity and Magnetism*, Principles of Physics Series. Cambridge, MA: Addison-Wesley Publishing Company

Shigley J. E. and Mischke C. R. (1989). *Mechanical Engineering Design*, 5th edn. New York: McGraw-Hill Book Company

Spiegel M. R. (1968). *Mathematical Handbook of Formulas and Tables*, Schaum's Outline Series. New York: McGraw-Hill Book Company

Spiegel M. R. (1972). *Complex Variables,* Schaum's Outline Series. New York: McGraw-Hill Book Company

Spiegel M. R. (1974). *Vector Analysis – SI (metric) edition*. New York: McGraw-Hill Book Company

Spotts M. F. (1969). *Design of Machine Elements,* 3rd edn. New Delhi: Prentice-Hall of India Private

Stewart J. (1987). Dimensional analysis. In *McGraw-Hill Encyclopedia of Science Technology*. New York: McGraw-Hill

Taylor C. F. (1966). *The Internal Combustion Engine in Theory and Practice*, Vol. 1, 2nd edn. Cambridge, MA: M.I.T. Press

Thomas G. B. and Finney R. L. (1992). *Calculus and Analytic Geometry*, 8th edn. Reading, MA: Addison-Wesley

Traub J. F. (1964). *Iterative Methods for the Solution of Equations*. Englewood Cliffs, NJ: Prentice-Hall

Unholz K. (1988). Vibration testing machines. In *Shock and Vibration Handbook* (Harris C. M., ed.), 3rd edn. New York: McGraw-Hill Book Company

Weast R. C. and Selby S. M., eds (1970). *Handbook of Tables for Mathematics,* 4th edn. Cleveland, Ohio: The Chemical Rubber Co.

Webster (1988). *Websters Ninth New Collegiate Dictionary*. Springfield, MA: Merriam–Webster

Weil, J.F. (1997), Units of measurement, in *McGraw-Hill encyclopedia of science and technology,*

Weisfeld, M. (2000)., *The Object-Oriented thought process*, Indianapolis, Indiana: SAMS.

Wiesemann H. (1989). Netzwerke. In *Hütte – Die Grundlagen der Ingenieurwissenschaften* (Czichos H., ed.), 29th edn, pp. G1–G35. Berlin: Springer-Verlag

Wittenburg J., Zierep J. and Bühler K. (1989). Technische Mechanik. In *Hütte – Die Grundlagen der Ingenieur Wissenschaften* (Czichos H., ed.). Berlin: Springer-Verlag

Wylie C. R. and Barrett L. C. (1987). *Advanced Engineering Mathematics*, 5th edn, 4th printing. New York: McGraw-Hill Book Company

Zierep J. and Bühler K. (1989). *Strömungsmechanik*. In *Hütte – Die Grundlagen der Ingenieur Wissenschaften*, 29th, entirely revised edition. Berlin: Springer-Verlag

Zurmühl R. (1961). *Praktische Mathematik für Ingenieure und Physiker.* Berlin: Springer-Verlag

Index

MATLAB functions and commands appear in a program font, for example `abs`, `print`. The letter t indicates a reference to a table.

LIVERPOOL
JOHN MOORES UNIVERSITY
AVRIL ROBARTS LRC
TEL. 0151 231 4022